Green Parties and Political Change in Contemporary Europe

New Politics, Old Predicaments

MICHAEL O'NEILL

Ashgate

Aldershot • Brookfield USA • Singapore • Sydney

Published by
Ashgate Publishing Limited
Gower House
Croft Road
Aldershot
Hants GU11 3HR
England

Ashgate Publishing Company
Old Post Road
Brookfield
Vermont 05036
USA

British Library Cataloguing in Publication Data
O'Neill, Michael, 1946 Nov. 23-
   Green parties and political change in contemporary Europe :
   new politics, old predicaments
   1.Green movement - Europe 2.Political parties - Europe
   3.Europe - Politics and government - 1989-
   I.Title
   324.2'4'087

Library of Congress Cataloging-in-Publication Data
O'Neill, Michael.
      Green parties and political change in contemporary Europe : new
   politics, old predicaments / Michael O'Neill.
            p.   cm.
      ISBN 1-85521-786-4 (hc) 1-85521-790-2 (pc)
      1. Green movement–Europe. 2. Political parties–Europe.
   3. Europe–Politics and government–1945-   I. Title.
   JA75.8.064   1997
   324.2'187'094–dc21   97-25958
                                                                                CIP

ISBN 1 85521 786 4 (Hbk)
ISBN 1 85521 790 2 (Pbk)

Printed and bound by Athenaeum Press, Ltd.,
Gateshead, Tyne & Wear

Contents

Acknowledgements

To research and write a book is a solitary and self indulgent pursuit, and one that inevitably accumulates many debts of gratitude along the way. I am especially grateful to those colleagues in the Nottingham Trent University who have contributed in various ways to the finished product. John Stancer and George Thompson provided financial assistance at the outset that enabled me to travel to the great London libraries, to trawl the newspaper archives at Chatham House, and to talk with some of those people who have enabled me to formulate my opinions on the questions considered in this study. Christine Bellamy, the head of Politics in the University, kept my teaching within manageable bounds so that I could find those precious islands of time during the academic year 1995-96 in which to stiffen the intellectual sinews, confront blank pages and write the manuscript. Larry Wilde read a very early draft and was both encouraging and generous in his comments, even though he does not share by any means all of my views on these issues.

Sandra Odell made her usual steadfast contribution to the project by speedily turning round the various drafts, translating a mountain of hieroglyphs into legible text, and using her technical wizardry to shift about the material on disc. And she suffered my requests for successive revisions without any hint of the vexation she would have been entitled to show in the circumstances! Terry Hanstock in the University library likewise responded promptly and efficiently to my regular demands for obscure and far-flung material. Both of these contributions are very much appreciated.

I want to mention some longstanding intellectual debts: to A. H. Birch, whose unassuming brilliance at the lecterns of the University of Hull sparked my enthusiasm for academic politics. And likewise the contributions to my political education of Dennis Kavanagh and Robert Benewick in the tutorial rooms of that University, who between them showed what could be achieved by a well honed curiosity, measured scepticism, and sheer hard work.

I would also like to register my gratitude to the editor of the journal *Contemporary Politics* for permission to use part of the material published therein in an article by me (Volume 1, number 3, Autumn 1995) and included in revised form here in chapter one.

My final and major debt is to my wife Wendie, whose forbearance and support made all the difference between tentatively setting out into the foothills of this inquiry and eventually scrambling up its final peaks. This book is dedicated to her - small recompense indeed for her unstinting good humour.

Screveton, Nottinghamshire
1st January 1997

Part One: The Green phenomenon: roots and branches

"Great things are done when men and mountains meet;
This is not done by jostling in the street"

William Blake, **Notebooks**

1 The dynamics of Green party politics in contemporary western Europe

1. The rise of Europe's Green parties: mixed legacies and radical origins

The ecological movement in western Europe is undoubtedly a child of the cumulative post-industrial crisis which has settled on the continent over recent decades. This 'crisis' followed on from the political impact and economic repercussions of the oil price shocks of the seventies which disturbed the political landscape. The emergence of Green parties mirrored the growing disquiet within the political establishment itself and, beyond that, of publics increasingly concerned with both the negative consequences of three postwar decades of continuous economic growth, followed by the more recent threat of economic recession. The Club of Rome Report of 1972 - "The Limits to Growth"[1] - captured this newfound ambivalence about materialism. The Report's expression of unease marked a watershed. It questioned past nostrums of exponential growth and rejected the complacency associated with them. This concern was reinforced by a growing distaste in some quarters - on the political left and among the young particularly - with the West's increasing strategic reliance on nuclear weapons. A parallel concern was with the growing dependence on nuclear energy for peaceful industrial purposes.

These multiple anxieties fed into an initially inchoate radical protest movement throughout Europe. Originally rooted in localised and small-scale citizen action groups, these movements adopted various forms of direct action or protest. These included demonstrations, 'sit-ins', propaganda campaigns and lobbying the established 'system' parties.[2] Even in the early stages, and confronted by an unsympathetic and occasionally hostile response from the authorities, most of these 'alternative' movements emphasised their sense of political responsibility by discounting violence or ritualistic confrontation with authority for its own sake. Indeed, many of these movement activists - far from being anomic 'outsiders', social outcasts, misfits or otherwise marginalised individuals drawn from the social fringes - were more often than not well adjusted and, measured in terms of social or educational status, conventionally located members of society.[3] For the most part they were motivated neither by envy, malice or bitterness; nor were they committed to subverting the political order. Those activists who took up the case of ecologism emphasised their positive commitment to society. They were concerned above all to 'save' society from, as they saw it, an impending and serious ecological threat - an 'eco-disaster' waiting to happen.

This is not to suggest that the 'new politics' in any of its expressions is merely a factional off-shoot of established leftist politics. Or that ecologism is another, albeit more politically focused, expression of conventional middle class romanticism, channelled into fashionable or progressive issues such as nature conservancy or the defence of public health. On this first point, these new movements - whilst finding clear affinities with the issue agenda of the orthodox libertarian left - remained deeply disenchanted with what they regarded, by and large, as the 'old' left's complicity in and contribution to, the fundamental economic errors of industrialism.[4] The evidence on this count seemed damning. Socialist governments throughout western Europe had long been led by their redistributive agenda and unquestioning commitment to the industrialism paradigm to endorse the materialist culture of unlimited growth. More recently, during what the new left saw as the twin nuclear 'crises' of the early seventies, the orthodox left had even served in some of those governments which had taken 'heretical' decisions; both to install nuclear energy technology and to accommodate American strategic weapons.[5] Moreover, the problem seemed a systemic rather than merely a contingent one. European social democracy's close affiliation with the patron-client politics which sustains modern corporatism apparently precluded any fundamental revision of their policy priorities.[6] Of particular note here was the old left's enthusiastic commitment to the strategy of industrial expansion and economic growth, which had formed a central plank of its policy platform throughout this century.

Although the exigencies of politics have obliged radical ecologism to 'flirt' with social democracy within Europe's various national polities, there remains nevertheless a distinct ideological gulf between them. This clear rift of purpose and perception was further widened by abiding differences of political style and organisation. As far as social democrats were concerned, the new radicalism was both utopian and adventurist. Whereas the new ecologists, for their part perceived the old left as anti-libertarian, unimaginative, rigidly hierarchical, corruptible and authoritarian. In short, they dismissed it as an atrophied movement which discounted internal democracy and political self expression. Indeed, the conventional left seemed to its radical critics to be little more than a mirror image of the political establishment which had co-opted it and then distorted socialism's earlier progressivism. In direct contrast, the ecological movement shunned the velvet embrace of political conformity. It perceived itself to be an expression of an entirely new and radical politics. Within their own particular issue area, ecologists saw themselves as confronting the tacit environmentalism of the moderate conservation lobby.[7] The contrast here between ecologism and nature conservancy and its adjacent causes was more than one of emphasis.[8] What began to emerge out of the renaissance of Green political thought in the sixties was a wholly new cosmological paradigm - a *weltanschauung* in which technology, science, philosophy, ethics and politics were synthesised with the imperative to take political action in pursuit of 'real' change.[9] As one commentator has defined the radical thrust of the emergent Green movement: "Neither conservationist nor environmentalists believe that the Good Life is much different from the one we presently lead, but political ecologists most certainly do. It is in this sense that ecologism can properly take its place alongside other political ideologies.... Ecologism cannot be seen as simply embedded in other political ideologies, it is a political ideology in its own right".[10]

It was but a small step from such a damning critique of the status quo to launching an outright political challenge against establishment politics on its own ground, at the ballot box.[11] This challenge was, of course, an uneven one. The momentum for a Green party politics was fitful and dependent on local issues and other contingencies. Nevertheless, by the

1970s, a Green agenda was discernible across the western European political landscape. Green politics eventually took root at both the local and national levels and, subsequently, in the transnational arena of the European Parliament itself. One of the new movements' more insistent voices underscores the significance of this rebuttal of the old politics of confusion, duplicity and compromise, by recommending a wholly different agenda to that of the industrial polity; inasmuch as "the most radical (Green aim) seeks nothing less than a non violent revolution to overthrow our whole polluting, plundering and materialistic industrial society and, in its place, to create a new economic and social order which will allow human beings to live in harmony with the planet. In these terms, the Green Movement lays claim to being the most radical and important cultural force since the birth of socialism".[12]

The moral energy and political commitment which fuelled this critique was drawn disproportionately from the younger,[13] better educated[14] and more articulate strata of postwar European society. As a movement ecologism received its greatest political impetus from the disruptive aftermath of the major oil crisis of 1973-74. The 'oil shock' was a momentous event in postwar history. It can lay claim to many important legacies. Amongst its ramifications this catharsis helped to sustain the West's nuclear energy programme. It also raised up the issue agenda of even the conventional political parties concern about resource scarcity and material priorities. And by extension it presented the new radicalism with a major political opportunity. Likewise, the emergent Greens acquired further political momentum from NATO's dual track decision on its intermediate nuclear forces - followed in the early 1980's by the siting of Cruise and Pershing 2 missiles on European soil.[15] What had so far been localised and politically ineffectual factions, more concerned with 'parish' issues or giving vent to a disparate moral outrage, began to coalesce, albeit with variable success and speed, into a more cogent political movement on the ground.[16] They did so by regrouping under national and eventually European 'umbrella' Green party groups. No-one should underestimate here - and not least in movements that made a political virtue of libertarianism - the sheer variety of organisational patterns and policy priorities in the fabric of this new political ecologism. This was by no means the formula politics of the altogether more centralised and oligarchic 'catch-all' parties cast in the conventional mould. Nevertheless, the very imperatives of political organisation, and especially the dilemmas facing radical parties seeking in some way to locate themselves within the conventional political game, did tend to focus the internal debate within these new parties on some broadly comparable themes. In the course of their development divisions, both tactical and strategic, ensued. These conflicts were sharpened, as they always are in parties wedded to a pristine notion of ideology, by fundamentalist tendencies. Two of the critical fault lines which have given Green party politics its particular cachet occurred over the nature of political organisation per se - the anti-party debate - and indeed, over the elemental purpose of political activity itself - whether or to what extent ecologism represented a wholly novel agenda; or whether it was merely a radical accommodation with the established left. These debates certainly debilitated some of these movements. At the same time, they increased their political profile, if not always their electoral purchase. By the end of the seventies, the Greens could at least no longer be discounted as an entirely peripheral movement on Europe's political landscape.

2. The 'new politics': a model of institutionalised protest

Radical political movements operating on the margins of established polities and challenging their stewardship as resource managers and their legitimacy as guardians of the public interest are by no means a new phenomenon of western European politics. Anti-system - as opposed to extremist anti-regime - movements have been a permanent feature of the oppositional landscape of modern European politics. There are, however, distinct analytical and empirical differences between these earlier expressions of protest movement, and the current mode of 'alternative' politics. All forms of social movement radicalism are, by definition, primarily oppositional. Yet their intrinsic differences have encouraged students of comparative radicalism to treat them as entirely distinct entities. English Chartism, the food riots which accompanied the earliest phases of European industrialisation[17] or, indeed, the student protest movement of the nineteen sixties, remain quite distinct from the current phenomenon.[18] What distinguishes these earlier movements from the new social movements is their fluid and ephemeral nature. These protests were often reactive and occasionally the irrational expressions of marginalised or otherwise exploited social groups. They resonate with the sheer political frustration of 'victims' unable to control or influence those macro socio-economic changes or cyclical shifts of circumstance which periodically overwhelm the 'wretched of the earth'.[19] While the contemporary student movement in the sixties did reflect an ephemeral element in the social structure, given the relatively brief duration of the higher education process, it gave rise to more durable radicalisms, which were hardly marginalised in either the sociological or social psychological sense of that term. The new radicalism was also different in many other respects from the reactive mass movements which had littered Europe's historical landscape. Indeed, the student movement provides a useful analytical demarcation between what are clearly different social formations. To that extent it marked a clear boundary between the old and new politics of protest.[20] In so far as the subsequent Green movement drew on that source, for both personnel and ideas, it follows, too, that any caricature of ecologism as a merely romantic reaction to the imperatives of progress and socio-economic change is misplaced. While there are discernible elements of utopianism apparent on the broad ecological canvas, to misrepresent the Green movement as little more than a retrogressive or instinctive backlash against progress is to misunderstand both its relevance and unique contribution, both to contemporary political discourse and political organisation.

To make this particular claim is not to say that the new radical politics was merely a reprise of the successful translation, over the past century or so, of organised social protest and organised labour into effective modern mass parties. To take but one example of successful political inclusivism, the various European labour movements impinged on, and eventually acquired political space in, the continent's existing quasi-democratic regimes, precisely on the basis of their pre-existing industrial strength and organisation. In spite of deep ideological schisms and factional disputes within these broad movements, Europe's social democratic parties were, for the most part, soon reconciled to the parliamentary route, unfazed by the purpose of winning political power, and committed, whatever maverick dissidents might have suggested to the contrary, to using this political resource as the primary instrument for effecting socio-economic change. Europe's modern radical movements were, by no stretch of the imagination, even a pale shadow of these historical forerunners. On the one hand, student radicalism in Europe and elsewhere fitted the classical mold of a collective but essentially amorphous anti-system movement. To this extent, it coalesced a broad spectrum of leftist or libertarian tendencies.[21] These were little more than 'groupuscles' expressing a vague and selective neo-Marxian rhetoric; and rooted socially and somewhat uncertainly in a declassé and shifting clientele of youthful elements, passing briefly through higher education.[22] This historically distinct form of protest was, in part, a classic instance of

6

those periodic shifts in social expectation, which frequently occur between successive generations.[23] Such generational 'shifts' invariably have a political impact. They have accounted for many similar, if ill organised, political expressions of socio-economic disorientation. Such a 'zeitgeist' might be detected in, for instance, the shift to political militancy in many European democracies in the aftermath of the Great War, or in the enhanced popularity of collectivist or Keynesian 'solutions' to social welfare problems after 1945. The student challenge to the conventional morality of 'bourgeois' society throughout the 1960s was, likewise, an expression of distaste and even contempt for a 'failed' past; one that was expressed - indeed ostentatiously exhibited - in a lively if fluid counter-culture.[24]

This particular phenomenon was, however, more than a generational spasm or a mere iconoclastic protest. A longitudinal study by Whalen and Flacks[25] rejected the complacent view of the political establishment - either that these youthful rebels were only temporarily marginalized or that the lure of affluence and the responsibilities of careerism would soon reintegrate them into conventional society. The new left deposited instead alternative layers of meaning and ideas which laid the foundations, however irregularly, of a new radical politics that bore intermittent fruit thereafter. Over time, what began as an unstructured and reactive movement acquired its own gravitas as utopianism was replaced by expressions of radical realism.[26] The attempts of its enthusiasts, however spasmodic or spontaneous, to challenge what they saw as the structural and policy shortcomings of the contemporary social order, foreshadowed the elaborate critique enshrined in the 'new politics' which followed on from it.[27] The 'rationality' of this critique, with its awareness of the important linkage between political means and ends, was an important and discernible quality. This basic strategic sense, however naive or limited its content in some instances, demarcated these new radical movements from their merely reactive or spontaneous predecessors. Klaus Eder has appropriately identified this special characteristic as a form of collective learning. Collective learning does not depend on the mediation of ideas through centralised party machines with their elites, caucuses and oligarchies. Indeed, it is positively encouraged and stimulated in political organisations which are citizen based, where power is deconcentrated, and where ordinary members are encouraged to take ownership of policy and principles. Parties organised in pursuit of ethical concerns, rather than in defence of extant socio-economic interests, are especially amenable to this learning process. For, in Eder's view, "collective learning processes are concerned with particular interests but also with moral considerations. But as soon as moral questions arise, people have to talk with each other in order to be cooperative. The rationality of collective learning consists in the fact that in principle all questions can become the subject of argumentative debate .... the preconditions of the possibility of collective action are based on the ability of social actors to participate in argumentative debate. This is at the same time the point of departure for the autogenic development of this ability and for the construction and reconstruction of social reality".[28] The individualistic and libertarian world of the modern university as it emerged from the cloistered and conservative milieu of pre-war higher education was especially conducive to encouraging this 'autogenic' approach to political discourse and action. Without the experience of student radicalism, in which a new generation of articulate and self-confident radicals developed a persistent critique of the materialism of the status quo and served an important political apprenticeship, the more organised, 'new politics' of protest would not have emerged as quickly as it did, or with the same impact.[29]

For all of these reasons, student radicalism was an indispensable precursor of the new politics, of which the Greens were such a significant element. It left a pervasive legacy for its political successors in the new movements which followed on from it - a legacy they could build on. That legacy, in turn, shaped the new movements, moulded their issues and concerns and, not least, their political style and organisational dilemmas. Here was a model of protest politics that exhibited a vigorous, even abrasive, iconoclasm; an anti-elitist orientation, fashioned into an ultra democratic and participatory ethos.[30] Underlying the new movement politics was a common and shared agenda. One that rejected the endemic bureaucratisation of social life, opposed what it saw as the authoritarianism of modern organisations and its repressed social relations that instilled a narrow materialism rooted in a productionist ethic, and threatened both peace and the ecological balance.[31] It emphasised instead, direct action and grassroots participation in pursuit of non material goals, alternative cultural aspirations, public goods (defined in an altogether more radical sense than in the prevailing collectivist models) over private consumption, and a community rather than a narrow class based politics. The new radicalism owed more than an intellectual or inspirational debt to its student predecessor. The student movement also created a social base and a political clientele outside mainstream politics. The 'new left' was able to draw on a residue of recruits forged in the radical crucible of student militancy.[32] The postwar shift in the structure of welfare capitalism, to public sector employment and the development of service and educational 'industries', encouraged new, non instrumental, anti-utilitarian values. These structural changes and value shifts were mutually reinforcing. A gradually expanding pool of potential support for 'new age' issues was created as a direct consequence of this. Both from amongst individuals who had graduated into 'conventional' employment in the teaching profession, the expanding public sector (the welfare services and the 'caring' professions);[33] as well as from the relatively large numbers who had remained, as a response to their experience of higher education, permanently 'opted out' into alternative life styles.[34]

These recruits to the new politics had imbibed the potent cultural legacy of their youth. This resonated with political self confidence, reinforced by direct experience of clashes with authority in countless sit-ins, occupations and demonstrations. And it was sustained cognitively by high levels of education, particularly in the 'non dismal' social sciences which did so much to sharpen critical faculties and legitimise a radical alternative vision.[35] Moreover, these elements had acquired the essential organisational skills that accrued from these training and employment opportunities. All in all, these were invaluable resources for effective political organisation.[36] And they had a discernable political payoff. Regardless of their lack of political experience, the new radicals emerged across western Europe as an entirely new expression of direct action politics.[37] The new politics of the seventies, far from reflecting the transitory faddism, the reactive tilt at authority, or the ineffectual gesture politics of the socially marginalised,[38] was generally regarded by commentators as an attempt to address the rising concerns of key sections of public opinion in advanced industrial societies. Whereas the sixties student movement had been an unfocused, rootless and a largely self-indulgent phenomenon - a matter of style rather than substance - the new social movements that crystallised from out of these protests into the seventies, were an altogether more stable, cogent and goal oriented phenomenon. They were, in the nature of things, localised movements directed at particular targets - nuclear power installations, military bases, and 'imported' infrastructural projects that threatened the community, health and amenity values. This type of protest or discontent politics developed further in the eighties into a range of lifestyle or moral movements concerned with ecology, gender issues, racism and civil rights, and concerns with the third world and peace that juxtaposed local and global concerns. And all mobilised by a critical discourse which perceived the same 'social contradictions' (of class, bureaucratic, ecological, racial, patriarchal relations) visible in local communities and

8

simultaneously at work shaping power configurations at the global level.[39] In short, the new social movements came to political prominence precisely because they addressed a lacuna in contemporary political arrangements. For Carl Boggs they "expanded at a time when the growth of centralised power and the bureaucratisation of public life led to a narrowing of political discourse, to a gulf between the nation state apparatus and a more dynamic local sphere. In this context, an independent radicalism implied more than anything the struggle for empowerment, though a struggle confined primarily to civil society".[40] Boggs construed in these movements a real radical potential, even if this was somewhat blunted by their disparateness, specialisation and scope. To this extent, "if sixties radicalism was more turbulent and had more flair for the dramatic, new social movements carried forward a more sustained organisational presence, as well as a deeper oppositional theory and practice (thus) the complex and highly differentiated milieux of advanced industrial society has given rise to new modes of protest/revolt around plural forms of oppression, identities, and group interests; class forces no longer constitute a privileged agency of historical change. The era of new social movements is therefore also an emergent phase of post marxist radicalism. This momentous shift reflects a novel emphasis on the 'micro' sphere of everyday life - including personal and cultural politics - that was largely ignored by socialist parties, unions, and governments trapped in a world of hard politique".[41] At the same time, this struggle for identity against the conformity inducing tendencies imposed on society and culture by large scale organisations in both the private and politic domains, dissipates this radical potential by working "against the development of a genuine transformative politics".[42] The new movement politics was, in short, rational but not choate. The emergence of Green parties which have tried to assimilate the various, occasionally competing, strands of the new politics within a cogent party framework, has been the most serious attempt yet to address this problem.

Ronald Inglehart, amongst the many social scientists who have researched this issue, fashioned an explanation of the new protest phenomenon in precisely these rational terms. Inglehart identified what he chose to call a 'Silent Revolution', underway in the cultural and social fabric of advanced industrial societies. He based this dramatic conclusion, not so much on spasmodic or disparate instances of social disorientation rooted in the pathology of the uprooted or psychotic; on the contrary, he defined the universal phenomenon of protest politics as a symptom of a much deeper, structurally located unease with the fabric of modernisation. Moreover, this 'rational' if ethically motivated disenchantment with the prevailing materialism of post-industrialism by key social groups was by no means a modern cult or messianic impulse.[43] The rationality of post-materialism was evidenced by its political focus - the intrinsic belief that change could be engineered by harnessing moral protest into a political movement. Environmental issues and movements have played a key part in this 'new politics' phenomenon, although at its broadest extent, it has been far from exclusively concerned with ecologism. Indeed, these 'new movements' have embraced a spectrum of ethical concerns ranging from feminism[44] and racial discrimination, to peace and all manner of personal and civil liberties.[45] To some extent this diffuseness was unavoidable. The politics of libertarianism and virtuous individualism will follow the contours of ethical preference wherever they lead. The flowering of a multifarious issue agenda was a sign of the times and reflected the sheer ferment of grass roots politics in Europe as the complacency of the fifties gave way to new issues and moral concerns. This, in turn, gave rise to a new age of radical dissent. The environment issue was particularly important here inasmuch as it coalesced several politically adjacent themes into a viable if fluid movement. As such, it provided a focal point for what grew, by degrees, into distinct and relatively coherent political organisations.

This new form of movement politics gained both political impetus and a degree of salience denied to many of the more organisationally dispersed or culturally peripheral fractions of the 'infantile' new left. This was due in part to organisational and other contingent factors. We should not lose sight here of the cultural resonance of Green ideology with the long-established European radical tradition. Without in any way discounting the hiatus between ecologism and Europe's mainstream ideologies across the political spectrum, the Green parties were able to call upon progressive instincts already deeply rooted in European political culture. The Greens represented the concerns of a long-established radical discourse, a 'great tradition' of liberationist thought and reformist impulses, refined and constantly updated in the post Enlightenment discourse during the long haul of modernisation. This, however, is a general assessment which needs to be qualified by more detailed reference to the actual political experience of the various European Green parties. Two key issues provide a critical lens through which to view Green politics in Europe. The degree of accommodations to the supposedly 'failed ' politics of the status quo links them and makes for a useful matrix for mapping the European Greens. The critical issue for any progressive movement - of how it orientates itself to the organisational conventions and procedures of the established political order - is a clear test of commitment, principle and intent; the very criteria by which political scientists have long assessed putative forms of radicalism.[46] The history of every European Green party shows a remarkable degree of similarity of response to this dilemma, as between a movement and party orientation. Almost without exception, their legacies from the ideology and sub culture of alternativism, protest, activism and direct democracy, were carried over to the new parties. The conflict between community and participation, versus organisation and order - the classical Rousseauian theorem - has pervaded Green party politics over the duration.

An equally critical issue, as far as the Green parties were concerned, was their response to adjacent political forces, particularly on the 'radical' left. There are both practical and philosophical reasons why this issue is salient for new and radical movement parties. These are by no means mass parties with entrenched electorates. They therefore require tangible signs of success, if they are to make their mark and win converts to their cause. This is a matter of political expediency. Some commentators have suggested that the ephemeral nature of protest politics is likely to consign such 'flash' or milieu parties to oblivion anyway.[47] For the most part, their local roots in a wide range of lobbies and protest movements have disposed them to the art of political networking - even with conventional political groups and interests. Clearly, some ecologists - both pure Greens and the eco-anarchists or far left - have resisted what they see as selling out their radical credentials. Ecologism as a philosophy and as a movement has long debated the extent to which 'nature', with its own esoteric interests, might coexist with man and his preternatural materialism. Translated into conventional political discourse, Europe's Greens have therefore engaged in a deeply divisive debate over whether a pure green strategy, disowning any alliances with the 'old' left, is preferable to a red-green or coalition approach, rooted in the search for progressive common denominators and inevitable compromises.[48]

These two issues have been the meat of Green party politics over recent years. Locating where individual Green parties, or, indeed, different factions of the same national party, stand on these issues should enable us to better understand the movement, and its political momentum and direction vis a vis other actors in the universe of national and European politics. The rise of the Greens, in short, enables us to comprehend the broader patterns of change underway on the landscape of politics. This mapping exercise suggests a key to understanding the movements' generic or transnational quality through its shared outlook and common affinity to the radical ecological cause that sustains ecologism and gives it political dynamism. At the same time, this exercise also illustrates those important differences over strategy and principle which have reduced the movement's political impact, at a time when the cultural climate might have suggested an altogether better electoral performance in the new and increasingly fluid politics of post industrial society.

3. The dynamics of a modern radicalism

Green parties reflecting a spectrum of ideological persuasions from individual libertarianism to a form of radical reformism bordering on socialism have undoubtedly made an impact on the recent electoral politics of western Europe. The first Green deputy to win a seat in a national parliament anywhere in the world under his own colours, did so in Switzerland (at Lausanne), in October 1979. By 1993, after a decade or more of unprecedented postwar electoral volatility which rocked the confidence of political establishments across Europe,[49] Green parties had secured representation in almost every democratic national legislature in Europe. There have been, at some time or other throughout the recent past, Green parliamentarians in Germany (pre and post unification), France, Belgium, the Netherlands, Austria, Luxembourg, Switzerland, Sweden, Finland, Italy, Greece, Ireland, Portugal and Malta. The most notable absence from this impressive list is the British Parliament, where a combination of political culture and unfavourable 'opportunity structures',[50] most notably the plurality electoral system,[51] have conspired to keep the British Greens out of Westminster. Since the European elections of 1984 there has also been an active bloc of Green and associated MEP's in the European Parliament.[52]

There are remarkable similarities between these Euro-Greens.[53] This is apparent whether we focus on the demographic profile of their membership and support base in their respective national settings. Or whether we examine the programmatic content of their manifestos. By the same token, Europe's Green parties reflect much the same internal fault lines, identified above, that provide ecological politics with its procedural dynamism and ideological raison d'être. Whether we concentrate on their intrinsic similarities or their internal divisions, the Green parties represent a distinctive phenomenon in contemporary European politics. At the same time, we must be wary of glib over generalisation. It by no means undermines the importance and necessity of the comparative task which confronts the political scientist, to admit to the singular quality of every national political culture. Indeed, the dialectic between uniqueness and correlation - the particular and the general - is what makes for the intellectual stimulus and the endless fascination of political science. It is certainly the case that the precise configuration of circumstances, contingencies and the sort of issues which galvanised grassroots ecological protest movements into becoming organised parties, have differed - sometimes markedly - from one country to another. There is a clear sense in which each of the national case studies of Green party politics in Europe tells a unique story - one that reveals much about the generic process of political change under the unique circumstances of advanced or post industrial societies, as well as the interaction of these broad themes and those cultural configurations and institutional or procedural constraints which shape every country's politics into distinctive national patterns. These particular patterns indicate as much about the particularities of the response to the common structural circumstances which constrain all modernised societies, and of the adaptation of individual parties to the exigencies of social change underway in each European country, as they do

11

about the universalities of that process of change per se.

We must certainly not lose sight of these particularities in our search for those meaningful, cross cultural comparisons that illustrate the shifting ground and emergent contours of post industrial politics. We need to keep a weather eye on the sui generis quality of each polity. To pursue theoretical abstraction at the expense of descriptive clarity, is to substitute categorical generalisation for its own sake, for real insight into the way politics actually works on the ground. At the same time, a surrender to detail and the avoidance of hypothesising and model building as an aid to understanding and explaining this reality, is also an abdication of intellectual responsibility. The excessive subjectivity of ethno-methodology - that we can only 'know' social reality by depending on the cognitive assessment of the reasoning behind social behaviour by the primary actors concerned - is patently absurd. We must indeed take proper cognisance of the subjective interpretation of their situation by those actors involved in social action. Not to do so would be to compound the ethno-methodological error. What is required, however, by the way of viable explanation of social action, is an appropriate synthesis of both the actor's subjective and the broader structural frame of reference, within which and from which those individual choices and actions derive both social significance and acquire meaning for the individuals involved. This, then, is the primary task of the model builder; as Kitschelt sees it, to "give meaning to a sequence of exchange". For as Kitschelt observes, "social and political processes (do) bring about intended consequences that cannot be reconstructed from the actors perspective alone, but require a structural and behavioural analysis".[54] It is necessary, then, for the methodology of comparative politics to combine the subjective dimension - what actors themselves choose to see as significant or important - with an account of the objective or structural framework in which they interact. Model building, in short, should discern social patterns from individual behaviour. The procedure begins with the formulation of testable hypotheses. It then processes hypotheses into models, theorems and even full blown theories. All of which stand or fall by the usual scientific criteria, of testing for verification or refutation against the accumulated empirical evidence.

The contribution of this study to this rigorous process is a modest one. It discerns two patterns or indices of political behaviour at work across the spectrum of Green (or for that matter, any other expression of) party politics in western Europe. The success of Green parties in building a base in national politics across the continent has been impressive but it raises more questions than it resolves. Most notably, a debate over whether the Greens are, as some critics have suggested, merely 'flash' parties representing a temporary discontent or 'fad', buoyed up by a recent and uncharacteristic cycle of electoral volatility across a continent confronted by national anxieties and compounded by global insecurities. Yet for all that, a protest doomed - and sooner rather than later - to political oblivion because it was incapable of resolving the dilemmas and addressing the hard choices that confront all serious contenders for political office. Opponents of this sceptical outlook maintain that the Greens, on the contrary, are here to stay; that they will consolidate around a new social cleavage and thereby become a force for change capable of consolidating their position on the continent's political landscape. These are important questions. We will return to this issue of the permanence or obsolescence of a 'new' politics in the concluding chapters. We can only begin to address these questions by undertaking a detailed examination of the dynamics of Green party politics. Two critical issues hold the key to this task. The first of these issues - the radical dilemma - mirrors the persistent dilemma of all progressive movements that aspire to change the world by persuasion rather than by violence. The other issue - the ideological dilemma - reflects the particular strategic dilemma of how to respond to other conventional parties with whom they might strike bargains for mutual political benefit. For under contemporary circumstances in western Europe the Greens can hardly expect to transform the political scene, let alone the social economic situation, on their own. To exert even a modicum of influence over policy outcomes requires that they strike alliances with other progressively minded parties. These two issues are distinct but, as we shall see, closely connected. Both of them confront Europe's Green parties with deep and disruptive predicaments. How they respond to these issues will do much to determine their impact and, indeed, their chances of political survival. These patterns of party behaviour certainly do have their subjective roots in what the political actors themselves define as being both ideologically significant to their definition of ecologism as a political theory, and as a movement for social change. At one level these are subjective preferences. However, these individuated preferences do occur with regularity across a number of national Green parties. They are part of the structure of radical politics in contemporary European societies. To that extent, they acquire an objective significance and are socially or structurally meaningful. This makes them amenable to comparison between one polity and another. As such, they require a more reliable explanation than that suggested by the merely subjective or ethno-methodological approach. In so far as it is possible, the subjective and the structural imperatives of 'good' social theory must be accommodated within a composite model of party politics. One way of achieving this synthesis is to acknowledge the ambivalent quality of the individuals who make up the membership of all political movements and parties. At the same time these mixed motives are reflected at the level of collective behaviour in the factional tensions over preferences and goals that divide all political parties, in some measure against themselves.

Politics is both a micro pursuit and a macro activity. Individual actors bring to their political roles immensely complex and invariably ambiguous patterns of ideals, values, attitudes, prejudices and expectations. Behaviouralists employ sophisticated techniques for capturing these heterogeneous cognitive profiles. At the same time, individuals who gravitate towards, and invest their political energies in, movements find it necessary to correlate or orientate their individual preferences around much broader or macro configurations which give them a sense of belonging or political identity, and thus connects them with likeminded activists. These are hardly neat, composite arrangements but they do tend in actual political movements, to be expressed as ideological factions or tendencies. The imperative to seek out ideological soul mates is both an intellectual or cognitive impulse, and an organisational or behavioural necessity; a normal part of the 'logics' of party politics. These factions are defined in reference to one another, along various continua. The notion of a left or right orientation has been the dominant response to this imperative and in some degree has been incorporated into the ideological morphology of every political movement, in order to give expression to these affective and organisational imperatives.[55] Issues or principles are grouped according to these identity clusters, albeit in ways that reflect each party's ideological roots and the political sociology of the societies which give rise to and nurture them. To this extent, the terms 'left' and 'right', although drawing upon a general historical legacy that reflects to an extent a common European experience of modernity, industrialism and democratisation, are also movable feasts that equally reflect different and distinctive national experiences.

To complicate matters further, individuals, being the perverse and complicated creatures that they are, and disposed to a degree of volition that permits all sorts of apparent inconsistencies or ambivalences to inhabit the same personality, may identify with both a radical and conservative cause simultaneously. It is not unusual to find conservatives who favour retributive punishment as the basis of the criminal justice system (a conventional right wing issue), but who also prefer an interventionist state and welfare as an antidote to crime. Individuals are not programmed and are likely to exhibit all manner of eccentric political propensities. This is no less true of radical politics, where the exclusion from power and its necessary compromises tend if anything, to reinforce an individual's ideological resolution. In principle, any number of permutations of value preferences is possible. In fact, individual activists do tend to at least correlate their value and ideological preferences. That is, they organise them into manageable and easily defensible clusters. Much of what passes for ideologism, and some of what purports to be contributions to critical scholarly discourse, has been generated by a perceived need (whether emotional, intellectual, or for the purposes of practical politics and public consumption) to reconcile the apparent incongruities between thought and action. The search for consistency is a pervasive impulse in all variants of party politics. There is no simple formula at work here. But most political parties are universes populated by broad constellations or loosely associated galaxies, rather than by infinite varieties of unconnected nebula. The Greens are no exception to this 'logic' of party development and organisation. To this extent Green politics is a manageable rather than an unfathomable universe to explore. More so than many of the established 'catch-all' parties, whose ideological core has shrunk or diminished in significance, or the sharpness of its focus blurred as the political exigencies of winning or holding onto power have tamed them, or otherwise persuaded them to adapt to a political market dominated more now by instrumentalism than by primordial beliefs. This is by no means to discount the importance of ideology for the conventional parties of modern liberal democracy, but merely to underline the fact that, in comparison with radical outsider parties on the political margins, other more immediate factors loom larger in the expectations of their supporters and the aspirations of their activists.

The mapping exercise is further complicated by all manner of subtle ideological shifts within and between the broad pragmatist-fundamentalist categories which encapsulate the two axes of the model used here. The time dimension, for instance, adds further complications. Green politics, as with all forms of radicalism, is a far from static phenomenon. Changes continue to occur within the Green movement that reflect ongoing intra party debates, local turbulence caused by current issues, personality clashes, as well as electoral considerations and other contingent factors. It is not unheard of anywhere in the volatile world of movement politics for erstwhile conservatives to be radicalised and vice versa. Green politics, conducted as it is in parties with small memberships, with a high proportion of well-educated activists who place a higher premium on direct participation, and in many cases experiencing for the first time tangible political success by winning representation and even governmental office at every level of European politics from local communes to Strasbourg, have been amenable to tactical shifts and ideological revisionism, in both directions along the ideological-organisational axes highlighted here. What has been particularly noticeable as a trend amongst Europe's Greens, has been a propensity - in both predominantly pure Green parties such as those of Britain, France or Italy, as well as in the mainly radical ecosocialist movements such as Germany's Die Grunen - for some activists who began their political lives as 'fundis', yet impelled by the experience of party office or electoral success, to move towards a more moderate or 'realist' stance. In other words, the map of political ecologism in Europe is further complicated by a group of Greens who, in varying degrees, occupy both an eco-socialist, a red-green (rather than a purist) approach, and yet who choose to pursue these ideological objectives by pragmatic means on the moderate, accommodationist or 'realo' side

14

of the organisational axis. Such shifts within factions need to be tracked and recorded if we are to chart a subtle rather than a crude map of the European Greens. This temporal or diachronic momentum is evident from the movements within many Green parties on the two critical dimensions of party identity indicated in Table Two. These movements reveal not only the precise configurations at any given moment, but also the momentum of contemporary ecological politics. For these patterns of conflict - ideological as well as factional - have been one of the critical dynamics of European Green politics. These shifts are important, too, for what they tell us about the political momentum of these parties and, indeed, of the likelihood or not of a significant degree of change in the party systems in which they operate. In other words, the map of Green politics is constantly shifting, but perhaps less so in random fashion than in response to an unexpected degree of success by Green parties in playing the alien game of 'normal' politics.

This broad observation does not in itself invalidate the unavoidable caveat that must accompany any study of real politics; that every national case study of political ecologism will, in significant degrees, be different from others and thus be unique.[56] At the same time, however, the use of such broad reference points, rooted as these are in the empirical minutiae of national Green politics, does facilitate comparative analysis. The approach may be far from perfect, it is certainly flawed, but it offers a start - a way into the maze of detail across the spectrum of Europe's Green parties. The two comparative themes used here provide useful insights into, or indicators of, what we might call 'the meaning of Greening' in contemporary European party politics. Used in conjunction, they provide us with a reasonably accurate map or template against which to examine and assess the dynamics of each individual national Green party. At the same time, they offer a way into the more daunting comparative task. And one which surprisingly few students of Europe's Green parties have been prepared to undertake.

4. Mapping the Greens: the 'grid references' of political ecologism

Regardless of the caveats discussed above, Green party politics can be mapped transnationally, according to a matrix which consists of comparative qualities or related themes. By employing this technique we deepen our understanding, not only of the Greens per se, but also of the broad processes of change underway in the politics of Europe's advanced industrial societies. Alongside the undeniable differences and cultural distinctiveness that make Europe's national political traditions rich in their diversity, are those common responses to the pervasive systemic problems which socio-economic change invariably brings in its wake. The prospect of inexorable change in itself is one which every party of whatever ideological orientation has been obliged to confront over recent decades. Accordingly, the notion of an esoteric and wholly 'local' politics, impervious to those cumulative and ever more insistent transnational influences which are reshaping the political economies of all advanced societies, is fanciful. It has been undermined by a rising awareness amongst political activists and political scientists alike, of the centripetal impact of the global forces which now impinge on all modern polities. In the circumstances of what Keohane defines as 'complex interdependence',[57] comparative politics has increasingly come into its own. Carole Webb has discerned in this cumulative process of interactions, "the growing economic and technological interdependence of the world, and the rapidly increasing opportunities for global communication, transportation, movement of finance and persons .... (with a) chain reaction, leading from this heightened sensitivity of societies to one another, to the loosening of governmental control over contracts between societies".[58]

Structural change, such as that which is undoubtedly underway in the very fabric of European advanced societies, is also causing clear shifts in values and expectations. These, in turn, are certain to trigger further social and political shifts.[59] The relatively sudden rise of Green politics over the past decade or so is a manifestation of this process of change.[60] At the same time, we should never oversimplify what is an immensely complex process - or lose sight of its variable pace. These issues are sufficiently important to require some further elaboration. We shall therefore return to the problematics of political change in the conclusion. The political expressions of change, whatever outward political form they may take - from ecological protest to much less seemly forms of ethnic or regional protest politics - are a far from uniform phenomenon. They must always be filtered through the particular prism of 'local' circumstances and contingencies. This explanatory requirement demands then, both proper cognisance of the uniqueness of each set of national circumstances; as well as due recognition of the similarities of those structural imperatives and transnational circumstances to be found in adjacent social systems. This precise formula certainly captures the essence of the problem confronting comparative analysts of the Greens - or for that matter, of any other European political movement. It is essential, therefore, to acknowledge this juxtaposition between what are common transnational trends and national specificity, in any account of political ecologism. The accommodation of diversity and convergence in a common framework is indispensable if we are to deepen our understanding of the contemporary European political process. And to understand the role therein both of the dynamic forces for progressive change, such as the Greens, as well as those political forces resistant to such change. Radicalism and reaction are present in the same political milieu at one and the same time, and the dialectic or tension between these conflicting impulses is present in every political movement.

In order to map the complex patterns that these competing motives give rise to, in so far as they apply to Green politics, we need to bear in mind that ecological politics does revolve around some broadly cognate axioms of commitment and principle. These encapsulate what it is to be 'Green' in the contemporary discourse and practice of European politics. Nevertheless, the superimposition of one of these thematic axes over the other indicates a multidimensional map of political preferences and dispositions, rather than a uniform model in which the key reference points of political identity are mutually reinforcing. The two axes under review here may well be cognate, inasmuch as they are descendent from a common radical instinct and intellectual ancestry. But they are not at all identical, as the evidence of intense factional disputes throughout Europe's Green parties over recent years indicates. The application of this grid to Europe's Green parties reveals a complex map. One in which markedly different Green orientations compete and contest the real meaning, the very 'soul', of ecologism. It offers, too, a useful gauge of the diversity and intensity of contemporary ecological politics, along its two principal trajectories of political identity and ideological meaning. We will now examine in turn these measures of political identity.

(a) **The radical dilemma**

The first of these significant themes - the vertical axis in Tables One and Two - concerns the critical distinction frequently identified by observers of all political movements; the tension between 'extremism' and 'moderation'. These are by no means unproblematical terms and must be cautiously employed. For one thing, they are highly subjective concepts which are as much

Table 1: Mapping European Green Parties - The Formative Phase 1973 - 1989

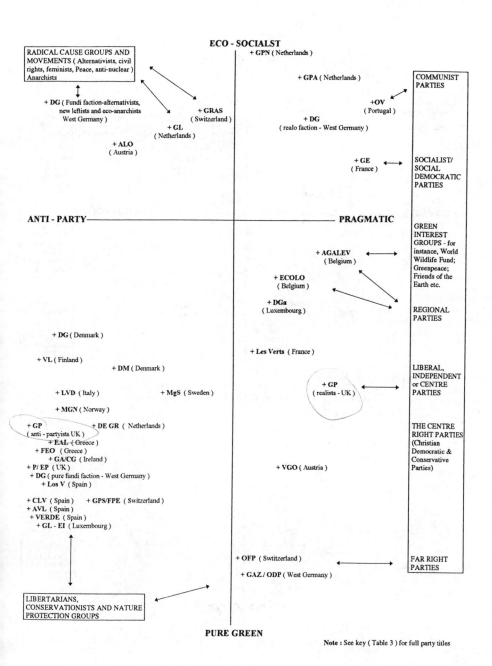

ECO - SOCIALST

+ GPN (Netherlands)

RADICAL CAUSE GROUPS AND
MOVEMENTS (Alternativists, civil
rights, feminists, Peace, anti-nuclear)
Anarchists

+ GPA (Netherlands)

COMMUNIST
PARTIES

+ DG (Fundi faction-alternativists,
new leftists and eco-anarchists
West Germany)

+OV
(Portugal)

+ GRAS
(Switzerland)

+ DG
(realo faction - West Germany)

+ GL
(Netherlands)

+ ALO
(Austria)

+ GE
(France)

SOCIALIST/
SOCIAL
DEMOCRATIC
PARTIES

ANTI - PARTY ———————————————————— **PRAGMATIC**

GREEN
INTEREST
GROUPS - for
instance, World
Wildlife Fund;
Greenpeace;
Friends of the
Earth etc.

+ AGALEV
(Belgium)

+ ECOLO
(Belgium)

+ DGa
(Luxembourg)

REGIONAL
PARTIES

+ DG (Denmark)

+ Les Verts (France)

+ VL (Finland)

+ DM (Denmark)

LIBERAL,
INDEPENDENT
or CENTRE
PARTIES

+ GP
(realists - UK)

+ LVD (Italy)   + MgS (Sweden)

+ MGN (Norway)

+ GP   + DE GR (Netherlands)
(anti - partyists UK)
+ EAL (Greece)
+ FEO (Greece)
+ GA/CG (Ireland)
+ P/ EP (UK)
+ DG (pure fundi faction - West Germany)
+ Los V (Spain)

THE CENTRE
RIGHT PARTIES
(Christian
Democratic &
Conservative
Parties)

+ VGO (Austria)

+ CLV (Spain)   + GPS/FPE (Switzerland)
+ AVL (Spain)
+ VERDE (Spain)
+ GL - EI (Luxembourg)

+ OFP (Swtitzerland)

FAR RIGHT
PARTIES

+ GAZ / ODP (West Germany)

LIBERTARIANS,
CONSERVATIONISTS AND NATURE
PROTECTION GROUPS

PURE GREEN

Note : See key (Table 3) for full party titles

17

Table 2 : Mapping Green Parties in Contemporary Western Europe

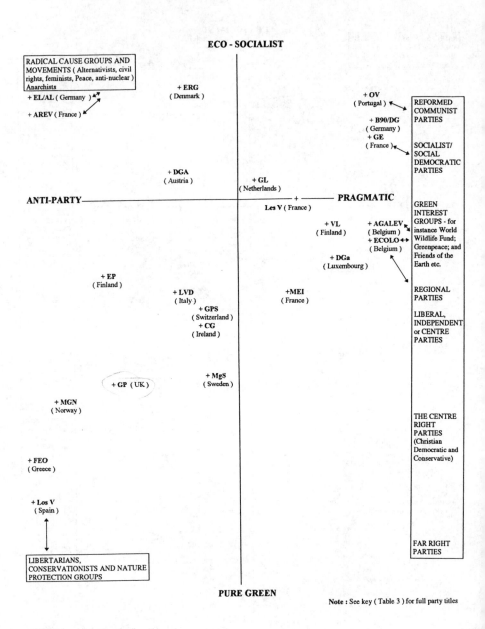

ECO - SOCIALIST

RADICAL CAUSE GROUPS AND
MOVEMENTS (Alternativists, civil
rights, feminists, Peace, anti-nuclear)
Anarchists

+ EL/AL (Germany)

+ AREV (France)

+ ERG
(Denmark)

+ OV
(Portugal)

+ B90/DG
(Germany)
+ GE
(France)

REFORMED
COMMUNIST
PARTIES

SOCIALIST/
SOCIAL
DEMOCRATIC
PARTIES

+ DGA
(Austria)

+ GL
(Netherlands)

ANTI-PARTY———————————— + ———— **PRAGMATIC**
Les V (France)

+ VL
(Finland)

+ AGALEV
(Belgium)
+ ECOLO
(Belgium)

+ DGa
(Luxembourg)

GREEN
INTEREST
GROUPS - for
instance World
Wildlife Fund;
Greenpeace; and
Friends of the
Earth etc.

+ EP
(Finland)

+ LVD
(Italy)
+ GPS
(Switzerland)
+ CG
(Ireland)

+MEI
(France)

REGIONAL
PARTIES

LIBERAL,
INDEPENDENT
or CENTRE
PARTIES

+ MgS
(Sweden)

+ GP (UK)

+ MGN
(Norway)

THE CENTRE
RIGHT
PARTIES
(Christian
Democratic and
Conservative)

+ FEO
(Greece)

+ Los V
(Spain)

FAR RIGHT
PARTIES

LIBERTARIANS,
CONSERVATIONISTS AND NATURE
PROTECTION GROUPS

PURE GREEN

Note : See key (Table 3) for full party titles

18

Table 3: Western Europe's Principal Green Parties, 1973-1997

AGALEV	Wallonian Green Party (Belgium)
ALO	Alternative Liste Osterreich (Alternative List, Austria)
AREV	Alternative rouge et verte (Red-Green Alternative, France)
AVL	Alternative Verde List (Spain)
B9O/DG	Bundnis 90/Die Grunen (Germany)
C.G	Comhaontas Glas (Green Party, Ireland)
CLV	Confederacion de los Verdes (Spain)
DM	Danemarks Miljopartiet (Denmark)
DE/GR	De Groenen (The Netherlands)
DG	Die Grunen (The Greens, West Germany)
DGa	Die Greng Alternativ (Luxembourg)
DGA	Die Grune Alternative (Green Alternative Party, Austria)
DGe	De Gronne (Denmark)
ECOLO	Flemish Green Party (Belgium)
ERG	Enhedaliste de Rod Gronne (Green-Left Unity List, Denmark)
EP	Ecology Party (Finland)
EAL	Ecologists Alternatives List (Greece)
EL/AL	Ecological Left (Germany)
FEO	The Federation of Ecological Associations (Greece)
GAZ	Grune Aktion Zukunft (Green Action Future, West Germany)
GE	Generation Ecologie (France)
GL	Groen Links (Green Left, The Netherlands)
GPA	Groen Progressiff Akkord (The Netherlands)
GPN	Groen Partij Nederlands (The Netherlands)
GL-E I	Greng Lesch-Ekologesch Initiativ (Pure Ecology Party, Luxembourg)
GPS/FPE	Federation der Grunen Parteiten der Schweiz (Switzerland)
GP	Green Party (UK)
Les V	Les Verts (France)
LVD	Liste Verdi: La Federazione Della Liste Verdi (Federation of Green Lists, Italy)
Los V	Los Verdes (Spain)
MEI	Mouvement ecologiste independant (Independent Ecologist Movement, France)
MGN	Miljopartiet De Gronne (The Green Party of Norway)
MgS	Miljopartiet de grona (The Green Party of Sweden)
ODP	Democratic Ecology Party (West Germany)
OV	Os Verdes (Portugal)
PE	Parti Ecologiste (Switzerland)
P/EP	Peoples/Ecology Party (UK)
VERDE	Vertice Espanol Revivindicacion de Desarrollo Ecologia (The Spanish Vertex for the Reclaiming of Ecological Development)
VGO	Vereinte Grune Osterreich (United Greens, Austria)
VL	Vihrea Litto (Green Association, Finland)

part of the demonology as they are of either the sociology or philosophy of political analysis. Above all, they are difficult to quantify with any degree of precision. This is so, even where they are used judiciously by commentators more concerned with accurate analysis than with awarding perjoratives or plaudits. As it is employed here, this operational continuum is intended to have a descriptive purpose rather than either a prescriptive or philosophical one. It is used as a measure of political disposition; of how and in what ways, individual actors or groups of actors (factions) orientate themselves to the political process. 'Militancy' here, or its antithesis, 'moderation' - or indeed any operational measure of political commitment in between these extremes - is translated as discernible attitudes towards political organisation. These dispositions are measurable in behavioural terms in a way that is empirically verifiable from the accumulated practice of Green party politics throughout contemporary Europe. It deals with the relatively straightforward tactical and strategic issues of how the Green case is actually prosecuted within the available processes and procedures of the established political order. This particular axis has a cognitive (attitudinal) as well as a behavioural quotient. All that is suggested here is the prospect of measuring moderation or 'militancy' in terms of a discernible orientation for or against the normal, established procedures of liberal democratic politics. This axis is amenable to empirical research over time, as the movements in various party positions charted as between Tables One and Two well illustrates. And to this extent, it provides a useful indicator of change - in both its behavioural and value-attitudinal dimensions.

The operational variable is principally concerned to distinguish degrees of conventional, moderate or pro-system behaviour from their opposite, militant or anti-system expressions. Of course, in politics as in life things are not always what they seem. Accordingly, these basic conditions need some additional qualification. It does not necessarily mean, for instance, that actors who take up an extreme posture, or otherwise show a disinclination to compromise their fundamental political principles, preclude themselves from participating in such routine or conventional political activities as electoral politics, courting public opinion or lobbying the authorities. What this axis does illustrate is the dialectic within radical parties who take their ideological debates seriously, between deeply divisive conflicts over principles and the incentives to play the conventional political game. This is a familiar dilemma to every student of non-revolutionary radical politics. Radical politics presents difficult choices and is full of ambivalence for those actors who must face them. Revolution is an uncompromising political strategy; reformism is altogether more conditional. Choosing to work within the political system in order to fundamentally change it, presents radicals with a real predicament. The traps and seductions of the 'sordid' game challenge the radical's sensibilities and exercise his conscience. This is by no means a new phenomenon. The risks of accommodating the system have been the meat of radical discourse over decades. Those radicals who become reconciled to the imperatives of compromise may themselves be captured by the beast they would tame - and thus become 'corrupted' in the process.

The alternative prospect is no less problematical. Radicals who adhere rigidly to moral absolutism and refuse to grasp the unpleasant nettle of compromise, usually find themselves marginalised and faced with political impotence. Moral naval gazing is no substitute for tangible achievement, however modest, for those in a hurry to change the world. This choice between integrity and trimming is the essence of the radical dilemma. Michels identified this predicament in his classic text on radical parties.[61] It principally takes the form of a conflict between two distinct philosophies of party organisation. On one side are those activists who choose to put principle before pragmatism. The merits - indeed the moral imperatives - of democratic participation are infinitely more preferable to the imposed didactism of party oligarchies. The virtue of pursuing incorruptible principle soars above tendentious compromise. On the other side of the debate to these 'fundamentalists', are those radical realists who counsel the necessity of strong party organisations, the requirement of effective leadership skills, and firm discipline in pursuit of political influence. This disruptive - and frequently painful - dilemma has visited every radical movement that has opted to pursue political change through the ballot box. The Greens are no exception here. In Europe's Green parties this dilemma crystallised into a protracted debate over organisational disposition and political style. Conflict has ensued between those Greens who preferred an ultra democratic party under grassroots direction, and those who opted instead for participating in an orderly, and in their terms, effective electoral politics. This animus has been a constant source of tension in Europe's Green parties. It is easy to see why this is so. The Greens' early roots in alternativism and in local, single issue movement and direct action politics predisposed many Green activists to retain an abiding suspicion of conventional party politics. This approach placed a premium on spontaneity and participation, rather than the conformity to rigid discipline, hierarchy and leadership preferred in the conventional party model. The stark choice between these competing types of party organisation provided visible and contentious criteria against which the respective factions might, and often have, fought for the soul of many of these parties. This catalogue of dispositions amounts to a ready reckoner of radical intent - a test both of trust and of motives, and a gauge against which to measure and thence to dispute, the meaning of radical commitment. The disputes over organisational questions became a persistent source of friction within Europe's Green parties. As between those fundamentalists hostile to compromise, and pragmatists prepared to entertain procedural and other adjustments to party style and structure, in order to broaden the party's appeal - both with the electorate and with the governing establishments who determine access to the policy process.

An energetic debate has broken out in most Green parties about whether, or how far, they should compromise their radical credentials and conform to a conventional party model. We must illustrate the febrile quality of this debate and its centrality to Green politics before we can gauge its strategic significance, assess its political costs, and estimate its likely impact on the future of an effective Green politics in western Europe's post-industrial states. These schisms over an appropriate style of political organisation have provided the Greens with their most disruptive fault line. This dispute reflects the origins of these parties in social movements, where community based campaigns, assertive localism, the sovereignty of the grass roots, and fierce libertarian instincts held sway over mere organisational exigencies. There are countless instances of Green discord and even civil war over this critical issue. There is not a single Green party in western Europe over the past decade that has avoided conflict over these dilemmas in some measure. The European Green movement resounds with ambiguities. They have confronted even those activists otherwise persuaded of the pragmatic requirements for, or strategic benefits which accrue from, accommodation within conventional parliamentary procedures. All Green activists, wherever they stand on this particular issue, entertain genuine doubts about the traps set for the unwary, by the 'tainted' bourgeois system.[62] Worse even than corrosive self doubt over this issue for the Greens have been its political consequences for party unity. There has been at times a spectacular and debilitating stand off between these 'reluctant' pragmatists and their uncompromising fundamentalist opponents. Most 'extremists' in this context are by no means revolutionaries manqué. They are, however, serious and principled activists for whom militancy, anti-partyism, anti-elitism

21

or some other demonstrable expression of radical commitment remains infinitely preferable to 'sordid' compromise or accommodation with the 'failed' political establishment. These are elements for whom 'normal' political behaviour is at best suspect for what it represents; or at its worst, is corrupting, in so far as it might seduce the purist or blunt the radical cutting edge.[63]

Almost every European Green party has experienced, at some time or other - but with very different outcomes - challenges from those fundamentalists who see it as their task to be the keepers of the movement's political soul; against those, often in leadership positions, who would compromise these pure principles by engaging in conventional politics. This is a perennial problem which has, sooner or later, faced all forms of radical movement as they become involved in the established polity and take part in its political procedures and institutions. The 'old' left parties faced the same dilemmas of inclusivism a century previously, when they sought to shift the issue agenda and direction of the bourgeois state. The problems of 'outsiders' playing within 'the system' are always traumatic. Ideals come up against political exigencies. This conflict between the preferred and the possible invariably creates deep tensions within any radical movements committed to real and far reaching change. The Greens are no exception to these strictures. On the one side of this divide are those cadres, frequently but not exclusively at the leadership and parliamentary level, who are persuaded of the need to follow the conventional logic of party and electoral organisation, in order to exert policy leverage and maximise their political impact - not least because modern governance is a complex, rational-technocratic and hierarchical process. These realists are also aware of the constraints imposed on uncompromising radical politics by a predominantly staid and cautious public opinion which is either deeply conservative, or otherwise aligned to pre-existing patterns of political partisanship whose primary focus lies beyond the new ecological issue area. On the other side of this political equation are those Green activists who prefer to inhabit an uncompromising fundamentalist and utopian universe. Translated into the politics of Europe's national Green movements, this had to be seen as a tendency rather than a uniform or permanent condition. One which has attracted different groups in varying degrees of rigidity at different times, and over different issues. In some Green parties it has spilled over into virtual civil war, with electorally damaging consequences. Elsewhere, it has amounted to a relatively benign and resolvable issue. Again, the rich variety of detail of actual situations within European Green politics requires that we enter the usual caveat here. These are broad behavioural trends. Any map is only a two dimensional approximation of a three dimensional landscape. There are, then, in the 'real world', infinite gradations of response to this critical issue of political accommodation to the conventions and procedures of bourgeois politics.

The available evidence from the recent history of western European Green parties suggests that the more radically inclined ecologists, whether of a pure Green or red-green disposition, are less disposed to place any trust in conventional political procedures. As such, they cultivate, by and large, a principled detachment from what they maintain are the temptations and seductions of a system which fundamentalist ecologists hold responsible for exploiting mankind and nature alike; and, above all, for ravaging the biosphere on which life itself depends. Mere moderation is condemned as plain hypocrisy by those who practise it in the name of ecologism.[64] Withdrawal or aloofness from conventional political channels, taking refuge in some esoteric expression of eco-anarchism, and venting opposition to the party's pragmatists as much as against the bourgeois political world at large, is a far more typical response of eco-fundamentalists than the politics of violence. Where direct action, protest politics or confrontations with the 'authorities' - for instance, over hunting or animal liberation - are the preferred tactics, these are expressions of anarchistic protest with staunchly libertarian overtones, rather than an exercise in revolutionary politics. To this extent, they are as much a statement of an alternative and principled form of 'political refusal', a denial of state authority, as they are an outright challenge to it. This oppositionalism in the Green's case usually takes the form of peaceful demonstrations, energetic campaigns on ecological themes, and other tepid forms of the politics of refusal. This radical legacy was imported by its practitioners into Green party politics, along with the liberationist credo of the post 1968 new left movements.

By the same token, those who inhabit the 'moderate' tendency in Green politics may be more inclined to cultivate the conventional tactics of political insiders who wish to use the leverage available from the normal routines of the political system. But they do so, for the most part, with ambivalence rather than enthusiasm. And do so, too, for what they continue to regard as principled and radical purposes.[65] At the individual cognitive level these pragmatists may be no less happy about making such 'necessary' compromise with their radical principles than those Greens of a more extremist disposition. They are merely more convinced of the political advantages for furthering the ecological cause, and of the utility of such measured moderation.[66] These utilities are defined here as those tactical advantages which are assumed to accrue from organising what would otherwise be disparate and thereby politically ineffectual movements, into a fully fledged party; of establishing an organisation capable of extending its electoral appeal beyond its immediate activists. And by this means, of exercising a degree of political influence. The procedures for exerting such influence are the routine ones - the occupation of political office, seeking a role in coalitional politics, lobbying government, and so on.[67] The rationale behind this strategy is to extend influence into a degree of political power. This does not mean, however, that Green pragmatists will necessarily gravitate towards an alliance or working arrangement with other broadly progressive forces, such as the socialist or social democratic parties; although this might be - and has been - one option available to them. For analytical purposes, these two axes are distinct rather than complementary. Any number of strategic choices may be, and have been, exercised in the universe of Green politics. Some red-green parties or factions therein have gravitated towards the conventional left, as an expression of ideological affinity; others will treat the established left as cautiously as any other 'bourgeois' political group. Others, again, continue to define 'left' in narrow terms drawn not from the labourist or Marxian tradition, but from its alternativist, new left and utopian or libertarian roots. Likewise, some pure Green parties or factions who share the pragmatist disposition, have been inclined to strike tactical bargains with the old left. Whereas others remain aloof from such 'coalitions' of interest for reasons that are a complex mix of ideological resistance and strategic calculation.

These critical strategic questions are by no means automatically a matter of contention between Greens of different ideological disposition within the same party. There are, for instance, some generally moderate Green parties which have struck, or attempted to strike, alliances with more radical Greens, by negotiating suboptimal compromises over a range of strategic, organisational and ideological issues - if only to sustain the movement as a serious force in national politics. This equivocation over political means is reflected in the behaviour of the pragmatic wing of the movement. Many of the ecological groups that have embraced full party status, and all of the compromises that go with it, have by no means precluded miltant expressions of protest politics from their political armoury. They continue to see themselves as a radical and progressive force for change. Their intellectual roots, and the reasons they entered politics in the first place, continue to influence their outlook and shape their political perceptions. If this was not the case, we would indeed be confronted with a remarkable case study of the 'end of ideology' thesis. Many of these groups began their political life, alongside more radical colleagues, as local, grassroots movements, organised to challenge official policies in, for instance, the controversial nuclear sector. Adaptation to political exigencies for tactical reasons has nowhere transformed even the most moderate Green party into a clone of the political establishment. Or at least not yet! At the same time, it does present a variable and complex picture of political responses. This unpredictability is one of the reasons why Green politics, in comparison to the politics of the reinvented and 'safe' left, is so fascinating.

The variable responses of the Greens to the important tactical and strategic choices which confront all political activists are apparent on the ground of European politics. They provide a useful organisational indicator or measure which helps to distinguish between different types of Green party; or indeed to illustrate in more detail the texture of those intra party factional conflicts which have afflicted many national parties, and in some instances have blunted their political effectiveness. These distinctions between and within Green parties over tactical and strategic issues alike, are important in as much as they reflect the variety of responses amongst current ecological opinion to the 'great game' of politics. This is an issue of critical importance in defining the 'meaning of Greening'. As such, this organisational issue suggests a key coordinate or reference point in the exercise in ideological mapping, which is central to the argument here. Some examples will put substantive flesh on the conceptual bones of this framework for analysis.

The long and debilitating animus amongst the French Greens over the organisational issue serves to illustrate its significance in the Green experience of party politics. Clear positional differences over the appropriate orientation to the French polity marked out the consensus politics of the moderate. French ecological party, Generation Ecologie (GE), from the more fundamentalist approach of Les Verts. The French Greens had their origins in the alternativist movements spawned by the 1968 'revolution'. The movement retained an abiding suspicion of the 5th Republic and its political structures. This was reflected in a staunchly decentralised organised model based on regional groups that retained considerable autonomy from the centre. At the same time, the degree of autonomism in the party's procedures has recently been under challenge from pragmatists, especially in the wake of its poor electoral showing after the brief surge in support at the 1989 European elections. Les Verts has certainly moved in a north-easterly direction within their quadrant, as between Tables One and Two. This momentum precisely illustrates the flexibility of this mapping exercise. It provides a useful template against which to chart the impact on the party's organisational orientation to this internal debate. It reflects, too, the rationale behind Les Verts eventual if grudging accommodation with their more moderate rivals in GE. To this extent, this mapping exercise offers useful insights into the changing electoral strategy which has altered the political orientation and prospects of both of France's Green parties, after they had assimilated the implications for the Green constituency of their continued antagonism, revealed by their poor showing in the 1992 French regional elections. Their respective performances at these polls, and the data on voter attitudes collected from electoral surveys, obliged Les Verts to soften their hostility to Generation Ecologie's attempts to find a place for ecologism within the established political order.

This shift of emphasis has had important implications for the strategies of both parties, but more especially for the militants in Les Verts. The available electoral data indicated not only that both parties were in danger of nullifying the genuine if modest potential for building a Green constituency in contemporary France, by each retreating into their respective provincial strongholds. It also suggested that a stubborn refusal to cooperate with one another, or indeed with other progressive political elements on the left, had alienated many potential Green voters. This had significant consequences for the strategies of both parties, but particularly for the militants in Les Verts. The eventual assimilation of these facts, in the form of an electoral pact between the two parties, indicates the rational potential of even radical movements, regardless of their ambivalence about playing the electoral game. It also posts a warning to the student of political parties and movements, by indicating the extent to which apparently explicit terms such as 'moderate' and 'extreme', are temporally specific and potentially misleading. These are always conditional terms which must be employed cautiously and translated into a precise political cultural context, rather than given some fixed and universal meaning. More recently, the very same issue has contributed to the consolidation of the divisions within Les Verts, into two antagonistic (pragmatic and fundamentalist) factions. The organisational axis will, in these circumstances of flux, continue to shed useful light on the dynamics of French political ecologism.

These caveats must also be applied to similar fault lines over organisational dispositions reflected in the internal squabbles and factional rifts which have visited and similarly debilitated many other Green parties. Admittedly, in a way that reflects different national opportunity structures or historical legacies. Parties as diverse in their ideological orientation, political salience and strategic orientation as West Germany's Die Grunen or the British Green Party, have exhibited deep rifts over this particular issue. A division over party tactics appears, albeit in a much less overt or electorally damaging way, to add a further complication to the unique division of Belgium's Green politics into two entirely separate parties, reflecting that country's linguistic divisions. The Belgian Greens in this instance proved incapable of surmounting the dominant cleavage of the national political culture and indeed accommodated to it. The dispositional differences here, between the anti partyist tendencies and the pragmatists complemented rather than compounded the communal differences between ECOLO, Belgium's more moderate French speaking Green party, and the initially more overtly radical, Flanders based AGALEV, with its origins in alternativism. AGALEV overcame initial misgivings amongst its rank and file and established an executive committee (Uitroerend Comité) of full-time employees wielding considerable authority within the party organisation. ECOLO, on the other hand, with its roots in more alternative soil, adopted a more decentralised party structure.[68] Neither party, however, has been militantly opposed to playing the conventional political game. Moreover, they share a progressive consociational outlook on the critical issue of recent times, that of Belgian statehood.[69] Both, too, are amenable to participating in the complex coalitional politics required by the country's bifurcated politics.[70] The Belgian case illustrates precisely the interaction of contextual and common variables in accounting for a given pattern of party political behaviour.

The unique combination of national history, political culture and what are, in the terms of the dispositional or organisational axis, in effect differences of strategic temperament, helps to account for the variations within European Green party politics. The organisational dimension is not, then, the independent variable which, on its own, explains the dynamics of ecologism. The only claim made here is that this is one important element in a complex equation. The second, and equally significant, theme in this matrix is discussed below. Neither of these variables can be separated out from the political culture in which they find expression. The differences between 'extreme' or 'moderate' dispositions to political organisation are situational and relative rather than universal and absolute. They acquire their precise meaning and significance only within a particular political context. And especially within the framework of the party system, with its own distinctive values, norms and rules of engagement. The particular expressions of what it is to be 'moderate' or 'extreme' relate in part to local political culture as much as they do to universal absolutes. Nevertheless, national systems do not exist in isolation. The increasing interdependence of modernised social systems has ironed out many of the local or anthropological particularities of politics. Political discourse and practice, certainly within the western European region, has become more uniform if not yet convergent. Modern politics operates according to similar rules, procedures and expectations that facilitate comparison along a set of broadly common principles and shared assumptions. The use of the dispositional variable as a frame of reference for comparing radical movement parties such as the Greens is by no means misplaced. The internal politics of these parties suggests that they can be located on a comparative transnational map. Regardless of their national particularities, Green parties have addressed during their relatively brief existence the same critical issue of their accommodation to a form of politics they originally emerged both to challenge in moral terms and to confront politically.

The differences of orientation to the political order within Die Grunen, the German Green party, illustrates the deep seated tension within the movement over the organisational issue. The fault line here has covered both the question of intra-party democracy as well as the party's general orientation to the Federal Republic's political system. From the party's inception in 1980 its congresses, workshops, local party meetings, and subsequently the meetings of its elected caucuses at city, Laender, and Bundestag level, agonized over an appropriate response to the 'bourgeois' polity. These battles are well documented.[71] The very fact of them - and their negative impact on Die Grunen's electoral prospects - provides graphic evidence for the centrality of this theme in identifying the meaning of political ecologism per se. It precisely reflects the real dilemmas facing new, radical parties which operate within, whilst trying to change, established and conservative polities. This battle has been fought out in many other Green parties. But it was joined early and was particularly hard fought in the West German movement. Libertarian and anti-authoritarian elements, with their origins in citizen action and grass roots initiatives (*Burgerinitiativen*) contested from the offset what they regarded as Die Grunen's unduly hierarchical party system. The tensions between pragmatists and fundamentalists over this issue were palpable at numerous party congresses throughout the eighties. The issue was debated vigorously but without resolution. An uneasy stand off on the issue was followed by periodic outbreaks of internecine warfare. The conflict intensified after 1983 when Die Grunen won parliamentary representation in the Bundestag. The dilemma of a radical party playing 'normal politics' came to a head with this breakthrough into the very heart of the liberal democratic system.

The party's pragmatists responded by seeking changes that would maximise the Green impact on parliamentary politics. The anti-partyists, meanwhile, resisted what they saw as dangerously elitist attempts to accommodate the party to the professional political milieu. Compromises, or more accurately truces, between the 'fundis' and 'realos' were periodically declared on this issue. The deep division over an appropriate organisational structure, for what was after all a self-proclaimed radical party, dominated Die Grunen's internal affairs throughout its first decade.[72] These tensions, however, even at this stage, when ideology drove the party and pragmatic considerations were secondary, were more a matter of degree than an unbridgeable chasm between two wholly irreconcilable factions. Had that been so it would, paradoxically, have been easier to manage if not to resolve. For in spite of their growing differences there were also ideological affinities and emotional bonds between the pro-party and anti-party factions. These cross-cutting ties ensured that there were both pure Greens and red-greens on both sides of the dispositional and organisational question. At the same time this drew them into coalitions or networks over policy content and the ideological orientation issues that were by no means a straightforward schism between two discrete and entrenched factions. Nevertheless, the dispositional rift widened as the party became established in national politics.

In spite of shared interests and concerns that spanned Die Grunen's party/anti-partyist divide, an emergent Green parliamentary establishment, encouraged by steady electoral success throughout the eighties,[73] eventually brought this dispositional issue to a head. The outcome of the 1990 unification election, when the West German Greens failed to make it back into the Bundestag, [74] merely accentuated the party's internal ferment over the organisational issue. The 'realos' had gained a degree of ascendency in the party during the preceding decade. They seized the initiative at the Neumunster party congress (1991), and proposed a programme of procedural changes. These included an end to the arrangement, whose roots were in the anti-party culture of alternativism, whereby parliamentary delegates were periodically rotated in order to retain contact with grass roots opinion. Neumunster went some way to consolidating the notion of a functioning party, by legitimising the role of the parliamentary cadre. The intention of these reforms was clear; to rescue the party from the prospect of electoral decline. Ludger Volmer, an executive spokesman elected at this congress, summarised this instinct for political survival when he observed that, "we hope to consolidate the party in order ... to have a realistic chance of making a comeback in parliament in four years".[75] Another moderate, Christine Weische, who secured election under the new reform arrangements as one of the two national spokespersons, also recommended an imaginative but above all a practical approach to the country's immense structural problems. She personified the 'realos' position on this issue when she reminded delegates that, "on the ground at local and state level, we need practical politics not theorising".[76] In similar vein, Udo Knapp saw the task ahead as that of supplanting the FDP as Germany's natural 'half' party. [77] This required a change in electoral perceptions, especially amongst those middle-class professionals who had become Germany's principal opinion leaders. [78] The decision of a joint party congress in Hanover in 1993 to amalgamate Die Grunen and Bundnis 90 (the Green Party of the former DDR) into a single party (Bundnis 90/Die Grunen) confirmed this tendency towards organisational realism. The 'new' Greens have used this solid foundation to re-establish their credentials with the electorate. As a consequence, they not only returned to the national parliament in the 1994 elections; they also moved ahead of the FDP as Germany's third largest party measured by electoral performance.

Similar factional disputes over this dispositional issue have appeared, with variable consequences for political effectiveness and electoral appeal, in many other European Green parties. In Britain, for instance, a rift between anti-party elements drawn from the eco-socialist or eco-utopian fringe, and 'electoralists' who opted for a more pragmatic approach which included cooperation with the Liberal Party, and a parliamentary rather than a local and alternativist strategy, has shadowed the Green Party from its earliest days.[79] The party began life as did so many other Green parties, as a loose amalgam of local cells, fiercely jealous of their democratic prerogatives. The constraints imposed by the opportunity costs for small parties of Britain's electoral system, with its particularly discriminatory electoral rules, encouraged the pragmatists to push for a more conventional party format. It was felt that this would be more likely to convince a notably conservative electorate to put their trust in the party. As a consequence, increasingly divisive battles were fought over the party's organisational format throughout the 1980s.[80] This animus eventually came to a head in the aftermath of the party's failure at the 1992 general election to capitalise on a remarkably good showing (14.9 per cent and 2.25 million votes) in the 1989 European elections. The shock of defeat reopened wounds that have not fully healed. With the party falling in the polls and membership plummeting, pragmatists confronted what one of them called the 'fantasists' over the need to face the realities of a highly conservative political culture with its entrenched tradition of two party politics, and to reorganise the party and repackage the Green message. The reformists had already begun to raise these issues for debate before the 1992 débâcle. The scale of this defeat merely reinforced their sense of urgency. The electoralists evolved a strategy for making the party electable on a pure green platform. This required moving the party away from the self-indulgent eco-anarchism which appealed to many of the party's grass roots. The need for change became urgent once the established British parties began to address Green issues within their own policy agencies, in a deliberate attempt to marginalise the Greens.[81] In the process the reformists faced resistance from the anti-party faction in a guerilla war which sapped the party's energies and brought its electoral momentum to a halt. The British Greens were overwhelmed by intense factionalism, and particularly by the determined opposition of the 'anti-party' faction. A small, inchoate but determined group of militants, libertarian anarchists and assorted mystics, formed a pure Green alliance. This 'faction' eventually turned the party back - 'rescued' it as they saw it - from a brief and unsavoury flirtation with realism, in the aftermath of a disappointing outcome to its campaign in the 1992 General Election. Something akin to civil war broke out in the party. Unlike the German case, where the very real prospect of electoral success in an entirely different opportunity structure galvanised the pragmatists, the British 'realos' for the most part quit the party.[82] They redirected their energies instead towards the altogether more influential green lobby.

Disagreement over the dispositional issue has likewise visited most of Europe's Green parties. On balance, there were more cases in the early stages of party development where anti-partyism was the prevailing response, than those where Green parties remained comfortable with the conventions and procedures of hierarchical and centralised party politics. Yet, where these debates did occur, they were by no means divisive or debilitating to the same degree. Moreover, as we will see in the case studies that follow, even where Green parties were once deeply divided over these issues, a combination of electoral success and cumulative experience of governance at first or second hand gradually shifted the balance of power within most of these parties in favour of an accommodation with the rules of the political game. Some Green parties were more easily reconciled to these adjustments than others. In the Netherlands' movement pragmatic idealism, encouraged by a consociational political culture, did much to ameliorate the effect of the philosophical differences over both the party issue, and the second of the major issues which characterise Green party politics - the prospects of links with the broad left. The movement here had its origins in disparate alternativist, anti-nuclear and ecological protest.[83] On the face of it, the cachet enjoyed by radicalism should have opened a political space for the Greens. At the same time, an enlightened political culture combined with a positive government response to the ecological agenda, and the opportunity structure (particularly an electoral system) favourable to small-scale parties, disposed the Greens to eventually set aside fears of playing the political game. Circumstances, however, conspired against them. A combination of internal squabbling and competition from other progressive but better organised political parties on the left, reduced the Greens ' scope for seizing the available radical space in Dutch politics. This issue was, however, never entirely resolved. An active anti-partyist tendency and debilitating quarrels over party policy continued to plague both De Groenen and the more eco-socialist Groen Links parties, even after their nominal merger in 1989.

Anti-partyism has also characterised Luxembourg's Die Greng Party. The party was founded from an extensive network of local ecology and citizen action groups and electoral lists. Concern to ensure full intra party and grass roots democracy initially encouraged a strong anti-partyist tradition. The party's Statutes authorised the rotation of delegates in the party's structures. Nevertheless, the party did avoid those damaging factional rifts over this issue which were apparent elsewhere. The party's structures and especially its national Coordinating Council - the organisational hub of the party - reflect Luxembourg's conservative political culture and encourages conciliation amongst its factions and the building of consensus over policy, rather than the constant civil war that would almost certainly ensure electoral oblivion. The party, by confronting this potentially disruptive issue and by putting common sense before ideology, has managed to consolidate a small but useful niche on the Duchy's political landscape.

The two Swiss Green parties who initially pursued the ecology issue also reflected the impact of a conservative political culture on a potentially progressive movement. Both were coalitions of disparate political groups. The GPS/FPE was a federation of mainly middle class environmentalists more reconciled to normal politics and amenable to a conventional electoralist strategy. Whereas the more radical GRAS/GBS drew support from a rainbow of radical activists and alternativists committed to broadly 'fundi' issues. [84] GRAS's local and participatory ethos was hardly a severe handicap in the decentralised Swiss polity. The emphasis on referenda as a decisional device sat easily with both parties' active role in campaigning politics vis a vis the eco-threat, even if this democratic procedure has worked, in practice, rather less in favour of green causes than it might have done.[85] Nevertheless, pragmatism as much as principle has been evident in the development of the Swiss Greens. So much so that the two parties have by and large overcome their differences, both over procedures and political principles, and now operate as a single party (Grüne Partei Schweiz). This pattern was mirrored in the Austrian green movement. A pure United Green party (VGO) co-existed with an alternativist list (ALO). Differences over ideology did not, however, prevent them from cooperating in order to maximise their electoral pay off, and the access this gave to Austria's generous state funding for political parties. Both parties displayed a pragmatic orientation to the Austrian polity, without surrendering either their natural caution about such accommodations, or their commitment to grass roots politics.[86] The level of cooperation was such that they submerged their differences and in 1987 formed a united Green Alternative Party.

The Mediterranean Greens have displayed similar internal tensions over their approach to the established political order. The issue here was compounded by the special circumstances confronting post-materialist politics in what were, by and large, economically under-developed societies. In Greece, Portugal and Spain, the experience of democratic politics had been truncated by long years of fascist dictatorship. Even in Italy, an altogether more promising scenario for radicalism, politics had been dominated by strongly entrenched traditional cleavages; clericalism countered by an influential secularist Communist or Socialist tradition. New left and alternativist politics tended to address the issue agenda of the post fascist state, rather than the new politics per se. A motley of local eco-groups did negotiate the foundation of a national Green party. The Liste Verdi was convened primarily as a decentralised umbrella organisation for national electoral purposes - a way of maximising the electoral prospects of local ecology groups in an electoral system which, even with its unreformed proportionality arrangements, penalised poorly organised parties. The Green Federation was not intended to be a party in any formal sense. Anti-party tendencies have remained endemic in the Liste Verdi. The recent corruption scandals have merely confirmed the movement's contempt for a failed system. At the same time, the imperative for political organisation induced by the new electoral rules and for inter-party cooperation in order to maximise electoral leverage has encouraged the Federation's pragmatists to position the party with the other democratic and progressive forces opposed to the new Italian right. Playing within the system is now seen not as a matter of political conviction, but rather as a necessary evil.[87] But with a peaceful political revolution under way and with so much to play for, the Italian Greens have become reconciled, by and large, to a pragmatic strategy.

Ecologism in Spain has echoed this experience. It grew from an amalgam of quite moderate nature conservationists and radical anti-nuclear, but non-socialist, pure ecology groups. Although these elements did eventually coalesce into a national party organisation (Los Verdes) in 1984, they did so out of necessity rather than conviction; and primarily in order to meet the legal requirement of being registered as a party proper under Spanish electoral law. This tactical decision did not resolve the deep residual differences, either over policy or the party's disposition to the political system per se. Alternative ecological lists resisted even this limited coherence, in defence of local autonomy. A unification congress was held in 1993, with the Euro-elections in prospect - but without resolving this perplexing dilemma. Los Verdes remains, then, a disparate organisation and Green politics enjoys its greatest salience in a succession of localized, single issue campaigns. In Greece and Portugal, too, Green party politics are minimalist, localised and divided between purists and more radical groups. In Portugal the Greens emerged under the tutelage of conventional parties who played a role in confronting the Salazar dictatorship. The pure ecologists have invested more energy in green pressure groups (Amiga de Terra and the Liga Parca Posteacco de Natureza) than in conventional party politics, whereas the progressive faction of Os Verdes has been subsumed under what is a thinly veiled Communist Party front organisation. Green party development in Greece is an altogether more discrete affair, but one which is no more effective. Not because of any continuing tensions between various factions over the party's status - which were largely submerged in order to maximise its electoral prospects in altogether unpropitious circumstances for a post materialist party - but precisely because of an electoral milieu that remains largely unreceptive to its message, compounded by political inexperience and a certain organisational crassness.

Ireland's Greens were organised as a national party from the outset. This arrangement brought together a spectrum of utopians, peace movement activists (for instance, CND), ecologists in Earth Watch, and the lobbyists of the Friends of the Earth. A central committee coordinated a network of local and for the most party urban-based branches. In spite of adopting a national programme the party remained insular, preferring to build on its regional and community base rather than adopt a national strategy working for a realignment of the nascent radical forces in Irish politics.[88] The party's constitution emphasises autonomy from the central organisation and puts local above national party prerogatives. The change of name in 1983 to 'Green Alliance', in order to better reflect this preference for localism, speaks for itself here. This approach is, however, quite compatible with electoralism, under a plurality electoral system as the Greens' recent commendable showing in the 1994 Euro-elections indicates.[89] The Irish Greens were always more concerned with practical politics in an indifferent yet fluid political milieu. And while they have engaged the same arguments as other Green parties about appropriate procedures for a radical party, they have resolved them for the most part in a practical rather than a utopian direction.

Green parties in Scandinavia were likewise reluctant at the outset to embrace the procedures of conventional party politics. There is only a nascent Green party in Norway with a modest local presence but no national profile as such. In Denmark, a wrangle between a local Green party formed in Jutland (the Danemarks Miljopartiet) and a national movement (De Gronne) allowed other radical parties (The Socialist People's Party and the Left Socialists) to occupy the Greens' natural electoral territory. [90] De Gronne remained dominated by anti-partyists and adopted a highly devolved decision making system, as well as displaying an extreme libertarian disposition. This combination of factors has contributed to the paradox of Danish ecologism - the marginalisation of Green politics[91] in a country whose population is as susceptible to the issues raised by the environment debate as any in Europe.[92] Green parties have fared rather better in both Finland and Sweden. In both countries, local roots in both nature conservancy and the more radical anti-nuclear causes initially reinforced the strong anti-party tendency in the Finnish Vihrea Litto (Green Association) and the Swedish Miljopartiet de grona.[93] In Finland, an electoral system favourable to loosely organised parties served to delay the Association's emergence (in 1987), compared with the earlier establishment of Green parties elsewhere in Europe. The Finnish Greens' reluctance to become involved in national politics was emphasised in 1989 by their parliamentary representatives' refusal to play any constructive part in resolving the country's deep political impasse. The Green Association has learned to reconcile these doubts about its role in 'normal' politics. Indeed, its parliamentary delegation has been sufficiently disciplined to support the latest coalition government, and to endorse the participation of one of its number in the cabinet. Sweden's Greens, while displaying at the outset a similar strong anti-partyism and a negative disposition towards the political order, did cash in its leverage in the Riksdag, to secure important concessions on nuclear policy from the minority coalition government led by the Social Democrats. In both of these Scandinavian cases there was a discernible tension between the party's local roots, preferences for local control over party hierarchies, and an acknowledgement that political influence requires both compromises and a degree of party discipline. The recognition by some of the pragmatists in these parties' national organisations of the advantages that accrue from electoral leverage has also moved these parties closer to the idea of party organisation, albeit in pursuit of radical post-materialist values.[94]

The contentious and protracted debate within all of these Green parties, over the meaning of party status, was and remains, a critical axis of debate, disagreement and division. The origins of these parties as radical political outsiders, and the intellectual and emotional baggage that activists brought with them into these new parties, meant that it could hardly have been otherwise. The 'map' of party dispositions on this issue (Table One), and the degree of change over time as they assimilated the demands of parliamentary politics (Table Two), illustrates how far from a notional 'break even' point on this axis these Green parties - or indeed, factions of national parties - are. Some Green parties have fared better than others in this regard. While not entirely of one mind, nor conformist vis a vis the political establishment, they opted from the outset for a more pragmatic if cautious orientation to their political environment. The precise political and cultural milieu in which they found themselves, their local and national opportunity structures, the degree of political and particularly electoral success, were the key determinants of their disposition on this matter.[95] The detailed evidence across the Green party universe also points to a trend in these parties, rather than any inexorable political law, towards a gradual accommodation to a realist rather than a fundamentalist position on this critical issue. Although this is entirely a matter of degree, and reflects those unique circumstances which shape the destiny of every particular member of any party family. The calculation of organisational shift here is, of course, a qualitative rather than a quantitative one. It involves interpretation as much as precise measurement. It is, nevertheless, an evaluation based on observable issues and themes which do lend themselves to measurable comparisons, rather than hunches or mere guesswork. Charting the development of Green party politics goes beyond intuitive leaps. The task of mapping the evolving response of these parties to their political environments' calls on the evidence from a number of recurrent issues which have prominently figured in the ongoing intra party debates over the place of the Greens in contemporary politics. For instance, the degree of centralisation or hierarchy in the party structure; the nature and extent of the parliamentary accountability of Green MPs; the relationship between party organisers and professionals, and the grassroots; or between the centre and local parties over the virtues of parliamentary politics, as opposed to direct action through various forms of community or local politics. The mapping exercise on this range of related issues is notional but by no means arbitrary. A qualitative assessment of each of these issues, in sequence, suggests the likely location of a particular Green party or faction along this horizontal axis. The closer a party or group is to either side of the continuum, the more militant it is assumed to be, as measured by its response to these issues. Moreover, if these responses are viewed sequentially over time, we are better able to chart these parties' trajectories of development, and thereby to gain some insight into the dynamics of political change at various levels - within individual parties, for a genre of related members of a party family, and even for the state of European party politics per se. The same principles of measurement operate in the mapping exercise along the vertical or left-pure ecology axis.

(b)   Cucumbers and watermelons:the pure Green-socialist axis

The second critical issue that has exercised Europe's Green parties and shaped their response to the political system concerns their ideological bearings, and in particular the movement's response to adjacent parties on Europe's left-right spectrum. The caveats discussed above also apply to this major division between and within Europe's Green parties. The vertical axis on the map of political orientations demarcates the Green movement into ideological propensities, rooted in the intellectual history of ecologism. At both the individual or cognitive, and at the collective or factional levels, these differences reflect a response or reaction to the culture of industrialism - the capitalist/modernisation syndrome - which has defined much of Europe's culture, economy, sociology and politics over the past two centuries. This particular axis not only maps how individuals or groups respond to these important ideological issues. It also implies a more precise behavioural response, which has a bearing on political action. This dimension, too, is 'mappable'. It charts the principal reference points in the ideological morphology of political ecology. These ideological coordinates have implications for social action, as well as for framing a subjective political identity at the level of individual cognition. Competing ideological preferences have encouraged internecine quarrels over strategy and the appropriate orientation of these radical parties to the national political milieu - a debate that has occupied Green parties everywhere over the past decade or so. What we are essentially concerned with here is political strategy rather than ideological hubris per se; the self perceived relationship of Green parties to the

32

political firmament in which they find themselves. The movement's responses to pre-existing political forces - from conservatism in its various guises, through to the complex spectrum of leftist politics, including mainstream social democracy and Marxism, to anarchism - also provides important clues to the meaning of Green politics, as we will see in more detail in the national profiles in Part Two. The main concern here is with the Greens' positioning vis a vis the conventional left - or what we might call the red-green issue. This is less straightforward than it might seem, either for the Greens or those who try to map their politics. The left is by no means a cohesive force in European politics. It is as broad a political church as it has ever been. Socialists have certainly addressed ecologism in recent years. The combination of a palpable environment crisis, a rising awareness of ecology in the public at large, and an emergent Green electorate in most European democracies, has focused the left's attention on this issue. This has further complicated the radical prospectus. There is no singular or coherent leftist outlook on the ecology issue, but instead a myriad of positions. 'Eco-socialism' is a generic term which covers a wide ideological spectrum from post-Keynesian social democracy to the further reaches of militant eco-anarchism or bioregionalism.[96] The diffuseness of the eco-left is an important consideration when trying to chart the position of Green parties or factions along this particular ideological coordinate. All manner of alliances are possible, both in the mind and on the ground. Even the pure Greens, who perceive ecologism as a unique commitment to nature, and who reject the 'artificial' political divisions of left and right as irrelevancies and distortions of the *Gaia* imposed by a materialistic industrial culture, sometimes echo the polemics of the left. They do so inasmuch as they share the autonomist and iconoclastic forms of eco-socialism otherwise located at some distance on the conventional ideological spectrum from their own preference for pure ecologism.

The hard strategic choices facing Europe's Green parties are bound to engage them with other political forces. Indeed, the issue of ideological positioning is a direct outcome of the Green movement's attempt to find its strategic bearings in an inclement political climate. The 'pure' Greens on one side regard ecologism as a unique political paradigm, above class politics, and for that matter remote from any other narrow social or exclusive ideological base. The pure Green tendency covers a wide spectrum of ideas about the threats posed by mankind's ill judged stewardship over nature, as well as exhibiting markedly different political temperaments about how best to organise a Green response to them. It includes activists of both a realist and fundamentalist disposition. In other words, pure Greens harbour an unrelenting hostility to the procedures and routines of liberal democratic politics. The realists, on the other hand, acknowledge the need to make bargains - to connect with potential allies within the system, in order to exert some influence over policy outputs. On the other side of the pure green-red green spectrum are those ecological activists who have more in common with socialist ideas and leftist agendas. Again, these red-greens are far from being a coherent faction. They cover the entire gamut of the leftist persuasion; from green social democrats to militant eco-socialists and anarchists. And these ideological divisions are further complicated by the dispositional divisions discussed above - that is, between pink 'realists' who are prepared to reach accommodations with the moderate left, and a fundamentalist or dark red tendency who prefer direct action and militant tactics. These 'fundis' resist strategic alliances with the mainstream left. At the same time their anti-party disposition draws them emotionally, if not always ideologically, towards the far left, with whom they share the same distaste for the routines and entrapments of the conventional political game.

In essence, some Green activists, whether of a pure or red-green persuasion, are altogether more comfortable with, and even prepared to engage, the 'old' politics than others.

This ideological and temperamental flux has had two broad consequences for Europe's Green parties, as we will see in the profiles of the various national parties in Part Two. In some Green parties a strong anti-party tendency has combined with fundamentalism, of either a pure or red-green ideological temperament, to make for a chaotic politics. Elsewhere, the particular blend of ideological and organisational dispositions, combined with the particularities of national political culture and the exigencies of the political opportunity structures, has caused much less damage to Green electoral prospects. In some national situations, the precise blend of ideological temperament and organisational disposition has been debilitating. Whereas in others it has been, if not conducive to overt success, at least more politically benign. The issue of ideological positioning has been as critical for defining an effective Green strategy as that of party organisation. In contemporary circumstances the most likely source of Green party influence over policy agendas will come from their linkages with the mainstream parties. They can expect, at best, modest influence rather than any real power. And the Greens' best opportunity here lies with the left for all sorts of reasons. The libertarian right has flirted with ecology, but this issue means little more to them than a notional genuflection to the fickle logic of the market. The abiding notion of a 'global commons' shared by both pure and 'red' Greens, reflects more surely the collectivist thread that runs through all forms of socialist thought. If the Green parties do resolve the radical dilemmas that have preoccupied them, and seek to build alliances to further the cause of ecologism, the left beckons them more assuredly than the right. The Greens' libertarian and new left roots do predispose them to look left rather than right for political allies. Moreover, there are some grounds for modest optimism here. Europe's left is likely to be more receptive to such overtures, faced as most socialists parties are with deepseated dilemmas of their own about the direction of progressive politics in a post Communist, free-market era. There are the makings here of a common issue agenda between these two progressive movements. The left, too, has begun to address the trade-off between environmental damage and human health. The onset of structural unemployment has also opened up a debate about alternative economic strategies. And the Left too remains instinctively wary about nuclear energy in all of its applications.

Accommodation here may be politically expedient, but is nevertheless fraught with difficulties. Cooperation and compromise do not come easily to radical activists engaged, as they see it, in virtuous and novel projects for 'real' change. Radicals are instinctively adversarial. Controversy, however, is often the best way to test the strengths of, and explore the potential for, new political bargains. The Greens do still prefer to emphasise their unique prospectus and remain endemically suspicious of a left which embraced industrialism and, for the most part, still does. Misgivings about the left's motives also play their part. The left everywhere in Europe over recent decades has had to deal with defeat, and even to confront the prospect of political decline. The response here has been some of the most creative political thinking of the century, amounting to a virtual reinvention of the left. However, not every prospective ally has been convinced by this spectacle of renewal. The development of new left agendas that embrace ecologism as part of the project of political renaissance seems to many Greens to be an opportunistic as much as a serious conversion to the cause. Even if this shift is taken at face value, it remains suspect because it is only a partial or selective embrace. The prospects for radical networking are further complicated by the possible ideological permutations. Left wing politics is no more viscous than political ecologism; it is just as fluid and unpredictable. All sorts of alliances are possible here - between, for instance, pure green realists and social democrats, which many Green fundamentalists would reject out of hand as a contract with the devil. Or between red-greens of both moderate and even fundamentalist persuasions over single issue campaigns; for instance, to rethink energy or roads policy, or to address national and regional defence priorities in the aftermath of the Cold War. There have indeed been other curious juxtapositions between ecologism and mainstream politics. One of the most unlikely combinations was the synthesis of an extremist orientation with a pure green preference, which led to the emergence of a few right wing Green parties or factions. These hybrids had an affinity with an established European tradition of political authoritarianism. Herbert Gruhl, a disenchanted German Christian Democrat, who had initially flirted with Die Grunen in its formative period, before it embraced an unmistakeable radical ethos, quit in order to found the German Ecological Democratic Party (ODP), with right-wing credentials close to those of its equally reactionary predecessor, the German Action Future (GAZ) also launched by Gruhl in 1978. The Austrian ALO and the Swiss GPS both exhibited a similar right of centre ethos in their early days.[97]

These are interesting but typical examples of political ecologism in action. They do illustrate, however, that concern for 'mother earth' is by no means confined to one side of the political spectrum.[98] On the contrary, it has evoked an intensely emotional and philosophical appeal, capable of spanning the ideological spectrum. While 'nature' conservation appeals as readily to the romantic conservative right as it does to the utopian ecocentric left, ecologism sits more easily with progressive than with reactionary ideas. The empirical evidence speaks for itself on this. Although this fact, in itself, by no means resolves the practical dilemma confronting radical Green parties; of whether or not to pursue an independent political line, or instead to develop links with the non-eco left. This dilemma has been a persistent and prominent theme in Green party politics. It suggests another comparative axis to set alongside the dispositional one. A line of inquiry that encompasses elements of both discourse and action, and along which we might expect to collect and collate data on Green political orientations. This, in turn, should help to further elucidate the 'meaning' of political ecology - and especially to demarcate more clearly the 'watermelon' or red-green tendency from the 'cucumber' or pure Green variant of ecologism. This is not to suggest a simplistic calculus of ideological preferences. The same reservations expressed above also apply here. It offers a useful line of inquiry, and one which must be treated with caution if its methodological pitfalls are to be avoided.

The selection of appropriate data to illustrate this particular axis is, nevertheless, relatively straightforward. As committed activists with a sense of political mission, Europe's Greens have been voluble in support of their agendas. The material which reveals where they stand on their key issue areas is drawn from policy or programmatic statements, election manifestos, interviews, speeches by Green members of parliament and councillors, as well as the material produced at party congress and in party workshops. A cursory analysis of this material indicates that Europe's Green parties have been exercised as much by this ideological axis as they have been by the organisational coordinate - and frequently to the point of immobilism and to the detriment of their electoral prospects. The political liabilities for Green parties of a civil war over the movement's ideological orientations compounds the costs of divisions over the party status issue. In some cases, these two fault lines have been complementary and mutually reinforcing. In others, they cut across one another. In the debate over the political identity of Germany's Die Grunen, for example, the 'realo' faction included pure Greens, as well as those radicals who were amenable to forging closer links with the SPD at the local and national levels, and for ideological as much as for electoral reasons. In the British case, the pragmatist or electoralist wing of the Green Party was led by individuals such as Porritt and Parkin who were pure Green in orientation, but who saw a political alliance with either the Liberal Party or with sympathetic Labour Party members as the only feasible route to a radical realignment of British politics.

The degree of animus between those 'watermelon' Greens disposed to an eco-socialist strategy, and the purist or cucumber tendency, is dictated by several factors. Amongst the most significant are the movements' origins. Whether, for instance, a particular national movement has its roots in the libertarian or new left. Or in those alternative, anti-nuclear and citizen action movements with close ideological affinities to radical leftist politics. This was the case in a number of European Green parties, where a leftist orientation was incorporated into the party's identity from the start. Not all of these parties embraced a red-green ethos with the same degree of alacrity. Indeed, in almost every case, deep tensions and a persistant ambivalence about 'the left', and its complicity with industrialism, has ensured a lively discourse on this issue. Nevertheless, those Green parties which do harbour a leftist inclination in whatever degree have invariably been influenced here by their particular origins. Other factors, too, have helped to shape the Greens' response to the party political universe. National political culture clearly plays a part here. An important influence on how Green parties orientate themselves to the existing political scene, are cultural arrangements and the procedures which stem from them - a regime's stability quotient; the rules of the electoral game; party funding arrangements; broadcasting regulations and so on. The impact of 'mere' regulations and procedures on the fortunes of new parties should not be underestimated for they frame political opportunities. No-one can say with any degree of certainty whether the British Greens, for instance, would alter their uncompromising approach to the conventions of liberal democracy if they stood the same chance of winning a share of political influence that the German electoral system has accorded Die Grunen. It is, however, a reasonable assumption that the prospect of political success does harbour the potential to alter political behaviour. There are no hard and fast rules here. Even those Green parties with indisputably radical and leftist credentials are just as likely to regard an electoral alliance or coalition with left-wing parties as bad politics. And, on the other hand, to have their own overtures for some kind of cohabitation spurned by their prospective allies on the left - who are, after all, competing for the same progressive constituency. The prospect in Germany before the 1994 national elections, of an SPD-Green cohabitation in the event of a 'hung' Bundestag, is a good case in point. The Greens saw this as their best hope of the breakthrough the 'realos' had worked for. But they were under no illusions that this held as many dangers for them as it did opportunities. Scharping's SPD, on the other hand, avoided coalitional talks with a party it saw as an unreliable and even a politically dangerous ally. Neither side of this prospective political coalition openly welcomed the prospect. Yet both the SPD and the Greens were sufficiently pragmatic to see it as a possible option should political circumstances require it.

The refusal of Waechter's Green's in France to respond to Rocard's overtures[99] for a realignment of the left likewise illustrates the abiding tension between the old left and the new radical politics. In this case, the issue was resolved differently because Les Verts was a party of the 'cucumber' not the 'watermelon' variety. Rocard's gambit merely confirmed the Green purists' belief that the politics of industrialism was in terminal decline. This assumption was sustained by the collapse of the Socialist vote during the latter years of the 1980s. Why compromise then when the future promises so much?[100] Waechter remained insistent that Les Verts should not be the "Green salad between pink and red tomatoes".[101] The German case illustrates that even Green parties with extensive ideological roots and personal links with the new left prefer at most to consider an affair of convenience rather than a complete marriage with the parties of the established left. Cooperation was confined to local politics. The resultant pacts and cooperation agreements put together in several Laender reflect Green pragmatism rather than unalloyed political realignment. This tentative rapprochement between the left and the Greens in Germany and, after Waechter's passing, in France too, has been echoed in other European polities, especially where native Green movements drew on a radical leftist tradition. This does not mean that those Green parties which displayed a distinct leftist orientation were unequivocally socialist. Europe's Green parties are all complex coalitions. Most of them, given the movement's emphasis on participation, libertarianism and anti-elitism, contain a lively ferment of radical ideas. Many of these parties, too, have experienced a situation akin to ideological civil war. Table One charts where Green parties or their principal factions initially stood in their formative years on the key issues here. There are, of course, temporal limits to any such mapping exercise. A map of the ideological territory drawn up some years later (Table Two), or indeed any future projection, shows a rather different configuration. Nevertheless, the value of the two variables chosen for measurement is precisely their durability over time in the new politics of ecologism. When these two themes cease to provide the crucial grid references of the political content of ecologism, the Green parties will either be defunct, or they will indeed inhabit an entirely different political landscape - a situation that is unlikely for the foreseeable future.

The flux of ideological tendencies illustrated by the second coordinate reflects, then, the intense debates within the Green movement over its appropriate response to 'the left'. This theme embraces more than the strategic question of political cohabitation. It covers, too, complementary ideological and policy issues. Some of these issues will be touched on in the national party profiles that follow in Part Two. We raise for consideration here some of the more notable examples where ideological conflict between these 'cucumber' and 'watermelon' tendencies has shaped the content of Green politics and influenced each movement's strategic orientations within its national political environment. The German case is again significant; in part because the German Greens have been by far Europe's most politically successful example of political ecologism. This degree of electoral success launched Die Grunen, not only into a protracted debate about its disposition towards the political system per se; it has also encouraged a parallel debate on the prospects for a German political realignment. In a polity where no government is likely under present arrangements to govern without a formal coalitional arrangement, the issue of the likely role of an electorally successful Green party in any future government coalition led by the SPD was bound to figure in the party's deliberations. This sparked a lively debate between purists and leftists, and between the left-pragmatists and the party's more libertarian left membership. Die Grunen was a rainbow coalition from the outset. Tension between pure Greens and assorted leftists was further complicated by the flux of leftist opinion within its ranks - from neo-Marxists and Leninists at one extreme, to alternativists and autonomists on the other. These factions saw the Green party as the best vehicle for advancing their particular radical prospectuses. Electoral success, especially at the local level where the Laender Greens (most notably in Berlin, Hamburg, North-Rhine Westphalia, Hesse and Bremen) have worked in government with the SPD, has only sharpened this debate over an appropriate radical strategy. There was no question of even the Green leftists endorsing the reformist SPD. However, the pragmatists saw a political advantage in consolidating a working relationship with the 'old' left. This strategic issue became the focus of a protracted debate that enveloped Die Grunen from the mid 1980s. The battle lines here were no more clearly drawn than those over the organisational issue. These intra party divisions were not a straightforward ideological cleavage between pure ecologists and socialists. The 'realo' wing attracted both purists and leftists, who shared at least a pragmatic commitment to consolidating the Greens on the electoral landscape. They were opposed by fundis of both a far left and pure Green outlook, who were entirely hostile to normal politics. The 'fundi' view on coalitional politics was clearly expressed by Jutta Ditfurth, who argued that, "Reformism, in its Green-Social democratic form, starts out from the assumption that there will be no radical break in our society. The time for revolution is past so the illogical conclusion is drawn that reform is the only option. This is pretty sloppy political thinking. For any serious analysis must take into account the fact that every variant of reformism has proven itself historically bankrupt".[102] The pragmatists on the other side of the issue were equally convinced that ecologism needed to build bridges to non-conservative politics. They drew historical parallels from the heavy price inflicted on democracy in Germany by the insularity of the Weimar left. Otto Schily warned in precisely these terms that "some sections of the Greens underestimate the dangers of a shift to the right, as is clear from their formula of a conservative foreign and security policy. We must take into consideration what effect our rejection of a realistic left coalition perspective would have on the right and how this would clear the terrain for rightist policies".[103]

These statements neatly encapsulate what was at stake in this argument over political alignments. While it has about it a peculiar German ring it has, too, more general application. For similar strategic considerations surfaced in the strategic debate over this issue of political alignments in other Green parties. They were apparent, for instance, in France, in the rift between Generation Ecologie and the purist Greens of Les Verts. They resurfaced more recently in the challenge and overthrow of Antoine Waechter in Les Verts' 'palace coup' in 1993.[104] Similar tensions between pure Green and eco-socialist tendencies, and over prospective accommodations with conventional leftist forces on the national political landscape, have afflicted many other European Green parties. Again, as with the dispositional issue, the intensity of this conflict and especially its negative electoral consequences depends on local circumstances. In Ireland, national politics is still dominated, despite recent signs of change, by clerical and nationalist issues left over from the civil war in the 1920s. The Greens have found a marginal post materialist constituency, but new politics in Eire such as it is has largely gravitated around the Labour party and other conventional party groupings. The Irish Greens concentrated on building local bases on specific issues. A brief challenge to this strategy by a red-green faction in 1986 failed either to undermine the pure Green ascendance in the Green Alliance, or to refocus the party's policy away from ecological issues and towards a class based politics. The party did embrace protest politics as a matter of course. But there was no sense here of a party in the grip of a fundamental ideological ferment, and a degree of electoral success in recent years has seen the party engage in an intense but as yet non divisive debate over its role in the prospective realignment of Irish politics.[105]

Even in those movements where tension does exist between purists and eco-socialists - over electoral or political strategy, or over policy and programmatic issues - the outcomes are variable rather than predictable. In Belgium, the differences between AGALEV's more leftist and alternativist approach and the pure ecologism of ECOLO, has not prevented the two parties from cooperating with one another in parliament, where their representatives sponsor joint initiatives and swear the parliamentary oath in one another's languages as a gesture of inter communal conciliation in that fractured polity. In the Netherlands, on the other hand, factional splits between activists of both a pure Green and red-green propensity caused the national movement to divide into two competing entities. This ideological split was consolidated into two separate parties - a Groen Links, amenable to socialist ideas; and the 'cucumber' party, De Groenen. The Greens' poor electoral record suggests a measure of their failure to impact on a polity whose opportunity structures favour both new and small parties. Luxembourg's Greens, on the other hand, have concentrated on pure-Green issues (deforestation, water pollution, noise and so on) As such, they have managed to avoid such ideological tensions and to steer clear of the debilitating factionalism that wracked other parties.

The Austrian Greens did divide at the outset along the ideological axis into two parties. The VGO campaigned on a 'cucumber' programme, whereas the ALO adopted a more militant and class based politics. However, neither these differences nor their formal separation prevented them from working together towards agreed goals. Subsequently, tensions arose over their respective red-green and purist preferences. These gained added salience and threatened to diminish the apparently excellent prospects for ecologism in the national issue agenda, especially as EU membership and related issues of traffic congestion, air pollution and other environmental damage from infrastructure development, struck chords with a conservative but otherwise conservation-minded electorate. Both sides of this ideological discourse over the meaning of Greening have apparently assimilated these dangers and opportunities, and now work together within the new unified Green Alternative Party.

Similar tensions are apparent in Mediterranean Green politics. In Italy, a nascent Green movement was weakened in the early days by an absence of red-green and pure green consensus. The recent political crisis has injected a degree of purpose into Green party politics which has brought the Greens into the anti-right coalition, but as much from necessity as conviction. This alliance with the left has brought some limited electoral success, notably the mayoralty of Rome and the guarantee of a modest haul of parliamentary seats under the umbrella of the 'Olive Tree' coalition that recently formed a progressive government. Green pragmatists have begun to draw their own conclusions from these developments, about the best way to secure a measure of influence over national policy outcomes. Green parties elsewhere in the Mediterranean region are either disparate or too new to impact much on national politics. The intense factionalism of Spain's Los Verdes and between it and other local groups (the Catalonian Alte Verde list for example and the conservative VERDE Group) has revolved primarily around personality and regional differences rather than ideological schisms. Portugal's Os Verdes has manifested a clear socialist orientation which reflects the party's dependence on the Communist Party and its successor. However, Os Verdes' role in the United Democratic Coalition (CDU) said more about the agenda of the Communist Party than it did about the prospects for an independent Green party politics. In the Greek case, multiple fractionalism and personality conflicts, rather than ideological factionalism per se, have plagued a Green movement which has found great difficulty in orientating itself to a politics where economic growth rather than post materialism is the principal objective of the mainstream parties. The disparate Green movement has resorted to an extra parliamentary strategy. The Greens' aversion to developing links with the political mainstream was clearly illustrated by the refusal of the Alternative Ecological List to prop up Papandreou's Socialist coalition when it lost is parliamentary majority in 1989. The potential for ideological disputes between the purists and more radical elements have so far been contained. Should ecologism here become as politically viable as it has elsewhere in Europe, the sheer diffuseness of the movement, faced with the prospect of developing a national strategy, could well encourage disputes between the pure Greens and more radical elements that have been familiar elsewhere.

The situation in Scandinavia remains a mixed one on this particular theme. In Denmark the Greens vacated political space to other more overtly leftist parties vis a vis the ecological and adjacent issues. The most protracted debate within the Danish Green movement has been over policy issues rather than political strategy. These have embraced both pure Green conservationism and more radical agendas, and indicate the movement's affinities with new left and libertarian issues (direct democracy, anti-bureaucracy and so on). Likewise in Finland, where a disparate amalgam of regional groups covering the full red-green spectrum of concerns has engaged in wrangling over leftist or social issues - social equality and child care provision for instance. The pure greens, meanwhile, continue to favour conservationist issues. This positioning has not, however, split asunder the Green movement. A strong anti-partyist tendency united both factions, and the reluctance to enforce a definitive party line enables the Green party to function. Vihrea Litto's response to the national crisis of 1989, when it remained aloof from the business of coalition making, indicated its ambivalence about the political establishment. More recently, however, the party has grasped the nettle of practical politics and joined the latest coalition government. It has been moved to do so by recognising that only by working with other parties, can it hope to influence the national policy agenda. Ambivalence was apparent, too, in the Swedish case. Some of Miljopartiet de grona's most prominent figures - including its pragmatic leader Per Gahrton - tried in the late 1980s to persuade the party to adopt an unequivocal red-green stance. They did so with a view to securing support amongst the progressive and post-materialist constituency that was apparent in this civilised and highly developed democracy. Although the issue was addressed at the Karlskroga Congress in 1988, it was by no means resolved. The Swedish Greens remain divided without being politically debilitated by this issue, and the party has so far avoided changing direction from a 'cucumber' to a 'watermelon' party.

(5)   From Green politics to the greening of politics?

This discussion of the dynamics of Green politics enables us to mark out its distinctive territory and to see more clearly where it fits on the map of contemporary radicalism. The outcome of these dilemmas is the core of Green political dynamics, and provide it, for good or ill, with its principal momentum. The issues raised by these Green dilemmas are symptomatic, too, of the intrinsic challenges and opportunities that confront the 'new politics' per se, as changes in public values impact on social change and alter the rules of political engagement. A mood of change is discernible in the European body politic, even if it is so far an inchoate one. The old politics is far from obsolete, yet there remain, too, prospects for a new radicalism, if the political groups and movements that compose it make a shrewd calculus of their options and steer their course by careful strategic rather than narrow ideological lights.   The route taken by the German Greens rather than that chosen by their British counterparts represents the most fruitful option. We might well recall here Blake's precept that "great things" indeed may "be done when men and mountains meet" but that this feat "is not done by jostling in the street".   The point is, that the conditions conducive to radical change are more likely to be brought about by properly conceived and carefully managed strategies, than they are by misguided militancy or mere wishful thinking.   Of course, the future remains an open prospect. Whether the new politics movement, of which the Greens are the most consistent expression, can capitalise on their cultural opportunities and secure a sufficient and durable electoral support to make them the political force to be reckoned across the continent that they have become in Germany remains to be seen.   They are on the verge of a breakthrough of sorts in several countries. But if they are to consolidate their position and defy the predictions of those who see in them merely a 'flash' or transient phenomenon in inherently fluid societies, they must confront and resolve the critical dilemmas discussed in this chapter. The prospect for a new politics is one of the fascinating questions for students of European politics as the new century approaches. The picture so far is a mixed one. And Europe's Green parties do represent the acid test here of the new politics, for some quite obvious reasons. The Greens, in one sense, are the least ephemeral expression of the new politics. Over the past decade or more they have been the most persistent, visible and indeed successful challengers to the old political order. Europe's Green party politics provides a crucible for the persistent tension between pragmatism and principle in the politics of contemporary mass democracy. Europe's Green parties incorporate those critical dilemmas that have defined the politics of advanced industrial democracies throughout its development, since the twin revolutions of the eighteenth century. As we have seen in these brief glimpses of Green parties, the politics of realism and moderation confronts utopianism with some obvious consequences. If the Greens cannot resolve these dilemmas, they will almost certainly fail to harness the deepseated concerns of the post-materialist, post-industrial and post-modern constituencies who are their most likely source of support. The current evidence here is less than reassuring. But these are relatively early days and the case of the German Greens shows what can be achieved if a radical party confronts the unavoidable predicaments of playing within political rules it has little empathy with or commitment to.

This is by no means an inquest on the Greens. If it was the verdict would at this stage be an open one. There is as yet no corpse to ponder over. Yet the Green body politic is much healthier in some places than others. An interim judgement, on the basis of the available facts, must be that the current outcome of the divisive civil wars that have wrecked these parties has damaged, and at the very least delayed, the opportunity of the Greens to help address the contemporary crisis of liberal capitalist societies. Let alone to bring about the radical realignment all Green activists covet, regardless of their ideological preferences. This is, of course, a prescriptive judgement which follows only if we accept the premises on which liberal democratic politics is based. It can, nevertheless, be justified by the electoral data. Those Green parties most obsessed by internecine wrangling and arcane sectarian squabbles have tended to dissipate the electoral support identified in countless opinion polls in favour of a positive ecological agenda. Of course, there is no simple equation between 'realism', defined as a conventional party status or accommodations with the mainstream parties, and electoral success. Even the most pragmatic and accommodating Greens have failed to make any startling electoral breakthrough. This is hardly surprising. All 'new' parties require time to adjust to, and indeed to be adjusted to in turn by, the political establishment. As harbingers of an alternative politics bearing an unpalatable ascetic message for the citizenry of hedonistic societies, they would have an electoral mountain to climb even in the most propitious circumstances. The tendency to shoot the messenger if the tidings are bad is as true in politics as ever it was!

Nevertheless, the Greens are not merely victims of cultural entropy. In some measure they have continued to bring about or add to their own difficulties, and have thereby played into the hands of their opponents along the way. The much publicised spectacle of unseemly and often bitterly contested factional disputes, principally waged around the issues outlined here, has undoubtedly dissipated much political energy and alienated many prospective Green voters, as the polling evidence from several countries confirms. Some of these quarrels have also been accurately perceived by critical electorates to be self indulgent and out of all due

41

proportion to the degree of ideological and strategic differences involved. The continuing tension within the movement between principle and pragmatism is not seen by those large numbers of well-informed citizens with a genuine concern with environmental matters, in quite the same light as those Green activists engaged in this febrile conflict. What many of these activists regard as the defence of sacrosanct principle, more discerning electorates translate as rank indiscipline - a modern outbreak of the 'infantile disorder' that periodically afflicts progressive politics. The credibility gap between the Greens and their latent constituency continues to be at the root of the radical dilemma.

Some Green activists have avoided rather than resolved this dilemma by turning their backs on the electoral route altogether and concentrating their energies instead on single issue politics prosecuted by the well-organised Green lobby. The apparent advantages of Green lobbying seem incontestable, even in societies less susceptible to Green parties. Britain is the most obvious case in point here. In stark contrast to the Greens' continuing electoral irrelevance, some 5 million Britons are members of a spectrum of ecological cause groups and subscribe millions of pounds annually into their coffers - from Greenpeace and Friends of the Earth, down to the heritage groups and the animal rights lobby. But these groups are just as active in polities where Green parties are a more visible presence than in Britain. The case for these transnational pressure groups is self evident, given the insidiousness of pollution, the global reach of its multinational industrial agents and the universal quality of the nature they threaten with their excesses. In short, the two strategies - lobbying and electoralism - are complementary rather than mutually exclusive. Single issue politics is an essential element of agenda change in any democracy, but consolidating change requires durable political influence. And this is more surely guaranteed by a bedrock presence in the councils of government at every level. It is this logic that took Green parties, against their basic instincts in most cases, into the political arena in the first place.

The Green fundamentalists, for reasons which illustrate the nature of their dilemma, would refute much of this criticism. They would do so on the same grounds that have inspired serious radicals since Robespierre's well attested preference for a 'seagreen incorruptibility' of pure principle over 'sordid trimming'. This kind of absolutist faith will hardly serve well today's radicals. There is too much at stake in this issue to retreat into an ethical ghetto. Chernobyl, Three Mile Island, Bhopal and an untold number of eco disasters waiting to happen, illustrate how much is at stake here. Nor, from the Greens' point of view, can the issue be safely left to other parties. After all, it was the governments formed by these establishment parties who presided over the industrialism that is responsible for much of this environmental blight. And the political debts of these parties to both sides of industry raises serious doubts about their trustworthiness and reliability. If the governing parties are to chart a new course, for reasons of electoral convenience if nothing else, they need to be kept to it. Green parties have a distinctive role to play here in their self-appointed role as the conscience and guardians of a new political economy that balances present utility with the concern for 'futures'. This stewardship function requires that they consolidate their place on the political landscape. If they do not do so, other parties will steal the opportunity and close down the available space - but without getting to the core of the problem. If the Greens fail to face their predicament and resolve their dilemmas, they will indeed be little more than 'flash' parties. The progressive left everywhere is engaged on a crusade of revisionism, to catch up with and re-connect with fast changing public sentiments. As the new right runs out of steam and the market fails to live up to the blind faith of its recent apostles, conservatism, too, may be more susceptible to a new collectivism in tune with public fears and popular aspirations. The political space currently available to the Greens is a territory whose freehold will almost certainly be expropriated by less serious ecologists, unless its parties can establish a proper title to it.

The Green parties of western Europe are new in several ways. They represent the aspirations and concerns of new social groups. They challenge the materialism and wastefulness on which the current economic order is built. They offer new political solutions to address these ills. The Greens, on all sides, are the vehicle for a distinctive and radical agenda. The cachet of their novel message can only gain in political salience as an increasingly sophisticated, better informed and restless electorate is faced with a rising catalogue of ecological crises; from oil spillages to public health scares; from declining air quality and climatic changes to the immense problems of disposing of toxic waste, without irreparably damaging the finite quality of the global commons. The recent Brent Spar campaign underlined the potential for harnessing public concern and consumer sovereignty, to shift even the most powerful multinational corporations and the most entrenched governments. But this issue, too, was orchestrated by Greenpeace - a globally organised pressure group - not by any particular Green political party. Greenpeace faced an altogether more intransigent opponent in its campaign to halt the French government's nuclear tests on Mururoa atoll. Even so, these 'rainbow warriors', backed up by the consummate professionalism of an organisation well in tune with international sensibilities, through the communications wizardry of cyberspace, put Paris on the moral defensive on this issue for the second time in a decade.

The Green parties have much to live up to when their modest policy achievements are compared with these lobbyists. The threat to the biosphere is, *in extremis*, a challenge to the global commons. The Green parties, preoccupied with esoteric agendas and narrow ideological tribalism, seemed for the most part, curiously unprepared to meet it with the full force of their moral convictions. If the Green parties cannot resolve these strategic and ideological dilemmas, they can hardly expect to be in a position to develop an effective national, let alone a global, strategy. In these circumstances, the loud protestations of concern for mother earth that emit from Green propaganda have about them a hollow ring. They suggest a sham in which the mere articulation of a radical and shocking message amounts to little more than a sort of ideological fetish - a verbal totem that means more in itself than the practical political accommodations needed to realise it. As we will see in the case studies that follow, some of western Europe's Green parties have addressed these critical issues - the litmus test of political relevance - with greater purpose than others. The stakes are high and there is much to play for. There are by no means any guaranteed outcomes as the Green parties continue to face the dilemmas that have visited every radical movement that seeks to use democratic politics to bring about far-reaching socio-economic change. The course of politics is guided not by teleology but by contingency. Chance prevails over certainty. But there are, nevertheless, some structural imperatives - a situational logic at best not a positivist one - that narrow down the likely options, without closing off any particular outcome.

Political ecologism is a live issue. It is likely to remain so and even to gather momentum. Whether the Greens can respond positively to this opportunity is less certain. There are, however, some encouraging signs as the following studies indicate. The Greens are in with more than a reasonable chance of playing their part in the radical politics of the coming century. The extent of their influence and the scale of their impact is impossible to forecast with any accuracy. Suffice to say that they have a chance to put their imprint on future agendas in a world where there are few certainties and much doubt and insecurity. The Green party activists may be fickle and disorientated, but they have come a long way in a short while. All of these parties seem aware of their situational dilemmas and many of them have embarked on resolving the predicaments raised by them. A start has clearly been made here in most of Europe's Green parties. The potential for a change of direction in the political economy of Europe's advanced post-industrial societies by no means obscures the problematics facing the Greens, or for that matter any other radical movement. Nor does it guarantee that these radical activists will resolve their predicaments in time to steal a march on their rivals in the established catch-all parties. Understanding these fascinating dilemmas and their significance for the future of progressive politics goes some way to deepening our understanding of the dynamics of contemporary European politics. In order to see more clearly how these predicaments have been played out in, and affected the political future of, Europe's various Green parties, there follows a catalogue of case studies which incorporates these broad comparative themes.

Notes

1.   "The Limits to Growth", Club of Rome (Earth Island, 1972).
2.   P. Lowe, J. Clifford and S. Buchanan, "The Mass Movement of the Decade" Vol.1 (1980), at pp.26-28.
3.   Frank Parkin, "Middle Class Radicalism: The Social Bases of the British Campaign for Nuclear Disarmament" (Manchester, 1968).
4.   Social theorists have endorsed this critical instinct by pointing out the structural complicity between established elements of the inherently conservative corporatist network which lead to clientist trade offs and insular bargains. See for instance, R Harrison, "Pluralism and Corporatism: The Political Evolution of Modern Democracies" (London, 1980) and S. H. Beer, "Britain Against Herself: The Political Contradictions of Collectivism" (New York, 1982).
5.   T. Rochan, "Mobilising for Peace: Anti-nuclear Movements in Western Europe" (Princeton, 1989).
6.   G. Smith, "Politics in Western Europe" (Aldershot, 1990) at p.37.
7.   J. Porritt, "Seeing Green" (Oxford), at p.5
8.   For a comparative analysis of modest resource conservationist or environmentalist movements and more radical ecologist expressions, see P.R. Hay and M.G.Hayward, "Comparative Green Politics: Beyond the European Context?" Political Studies 36 (1988) at pp.433-48.
9.   This transition was by no means a rapid one. Much of the early 'path finding' work was a far from radical kind of ethical theory. The transformation (and incipient radicalisation) of ecologism began with the work of theorists such as Rachel Carson, "Silent Spring" (Boston, 1962); Barry Commoner, "Science and Survival", (New York, 1966) and ibid, "The Closing Circle" (New York, 1972). And Edward Goldsmith, "A Blueprint for Survival" (Harmondsworth, 1972). D. Dickson, "Alternative Technology and the Politics of Technical Change" (Glasgow, 1974). The scientific reappraisal that accompanied the rise of ecological awareness also fed into and sustained that movement itself. In the process, it helped to legitimise it with a wider audience. In this dialectical way, there emerged an ecological lifestyle (or 'culture') and a new scientific paradigm which complemented and sustained it. See S Toulmin, "The Return to Cosmology: Postmodern Science and the Theology of Nature" (Berkeley, 1982).

10.   A. Dobson, "Green Political Thought" (London, 1990) at p.13.
11.   J. Ridgeway, "The Politics of Ecology" (New York, 1970)
12.   J. Porritt and N. Winner, "The Coming of the Greens" (London 1988) at p.9.
13.   See the survey findings on the age factor in the German Greens' support base in "The Social Background of the Green Voters", chapter two of Gerd Langguth, "The Green Factor in German Politics" (London, 1986), at pp.23-43. The preponderance of youthful support has been repeated across the spectrum of Europe's Green parties.
14.   For evidence of the positive correlation between higher than average levels of educational attainment and a propensity to vote Green, see W. Herenberg's survey in R. Mettke (ed), "Die Grunen; Regierungspartner von morgen?" (Hamburg, 1982); for comparative evidence from Belgium, see K. Deschouwer and P. Stouthuysen, "The Electorate of AGALEV" (Centre for Research in Socio-Political Information, Brussels, 1984); and for Denmark and Italy see S. Schuttemeyer, "Denmark: De Gronne" and Mario Diani, "Italy: The Liste Verdi", in F. Muller-Rommel (ed), "New Politics in Western Europe" (London, 1989) at pp.57-58 and pp.117-119 respectively.
15.   See F.H. Buttel, "The environmental movement: historical roots and current trends", in C.R. Humphrey and F.H. Buttel (eds), "Environment, Energy and Society" (Belmont, Calif. 1980)
16.   See P. Byrne, "The Campaign for Nuclear Disarmament" (London,1988) for a discussion of the linkages between the peace movement in Britain and the Greens; D. Nelkin and M. Pollak, "The Atom Beseiged: Extra Parliamentary dissent in France and Germany" (Cambridge, Mass, 1981); and T.Rochon, "Mobilizing for Peace: Anti-nuclear Movements in Western Europe" (Princeton, 1989).
17.   Charles Tilly, "European Violence and Collective Action Since 1700", Social Research 52 1985 at pp. 714-47.
18.   G. DiPalma, "Antipathy and Participation: Mass Politics in Western Societies" (New York, 1970)
19.   See the discussion in Harold Perkin, "The Origins of Modern English Society 1780-1880" (London, 1972), at pp.32-33.
20.   For a review of the debate of the 'newness' of the 'new politics', see C. Offe, "New Social Movements: Challenging Boundaries of the Political" Social Research 52 1985, at pp.817-68; ibid, "Challenging the Boundaries of Institutional Politics: Social Movements Since the Sixties" in C.S. Maier (ed), "Changing Boundaries of the Political" (Cambridge, 1987); Karl Werner Brand, "Cyclical Aspects of New Social Movements: Waves of Cultural Criticism and Mobilization Cycles of New Middle class Radicalism", in R. J. Dalton and M. Kuechler, "Challenging the Political Order" (Cambridge, 1990) at pp.23-42.
21.   For a comparative review of this phenomenon see O. Klinberg, M. Zavalloni, C. Louis-Guerin and J. Ben-Brika, "Students, Values and Politics: A Cross Cultural Comparison" (New York, 1979).
22.   See C. Rootes, "Student radicalism:politics of moral protest and legitimation problems of the modern capitalist state", Theory and Society 9 (3) 1980; and ibid, "Student radicalism in France: 1968 and after", in P. Cerny (ed), "Social Movements and Protest in France" (London, 1982).
23.   For a discussion of the role of the young and the generational factor in political change, see R. Flacks, "The revolt of the young intelligentsia: revolutionary class consciousness in post-scarcity America", in R. Aya and N. Miller (eds), "The New

American Revolution" (London, 1971); and R.G. Braungart, "Family status, socialisation and student politics: a multivariate analysis", American Journal of Sociology 77 1971 at pp. 197-202.

24. See for instance, George Melly, "Revolt into Style" (Harmondsworth, 1975)

25. J. Whalen and R. Flacks "After the Barricades: The New Left Grows Up" (Philadelphia 1989).

26. See G. Katsiaficas "The Imagination of the New Left: A Global Analysis of 1968" (Boston, Mass. 1987).

27. The debates at the leading centres of student radicalism - the London School of Economics, the Sorbonne, the Berkeley campus of the University of California, and on the campuses of Berlin - addressed not only educational reform, but the wider issues of Third World exploitation, militarism, industrial relations and the cultural 'poverty' of 'advanced' societies.

28. Klaus Eder, "The 'New Social Movements':Moral Crusades, Political Pressure Groups or Social Movements?" Social Research Vol.52 Part 4 at pages 886-87.

29. H. Kitschelt, "New Social Movements and the Decline of Party Organisation", in R.J. Dalton and M. Kuechler, "Challenging for Political Order: New Social and Political Movement in Western Democracies" (Cambridge, 1990) at p.190.

30. J. Mushaben, "The Struggle Within" in B. Klandermans (ed), "Organizing for Change" (Greenwich,1989).

31. C. Boggs, "Social Movements and Political Power" (Philadelphia, 1986), at Chapter two.

32. W. Rudig, "Peace and ecology movements in Western Europe", West European Politics 11 1988.

33. See S. Cotgrove and A. Duff, "Environmentalism, Middle Class Radicalism and Politics", Sociological Review 2 1990 at pp.333-52.

34. A point illustrated by H. Kitschelt, "The Logics of Party Formation: Ecological Politics in Belgium and West Germany" (Ithaca, New York, 1989).

35. T. Poguntke, "New Politics and Party Systems: The Emergence of a New Type of Party?" West European Politics 10 1987 at pp.76-88; see also S. Barnes and M. Kaase (et al), "Political Action" (Beverley Hills 1979).

36. H. Kitschelt, "Left Libertarian Parties: Explaining Innovation in Competitive Systems", World Politics 40 1988, at pp.194-234; and R. J. Dalton, "Cognitive Mobilisation and Partisan Dealignment in Advanced Industrial Democracies", Journal of Politics 46 1984, at pp.264-84.

37. Alberto Melucci, "The New Social Movements: A Theoretical Approach", Social Science Information 18 1980, at pp.199-226.

38. W.M. Chandler and A. Siaroff, "Post Industrial Politics in Germany and the Origins of the Greens", Comparative Politics 18 1986, at pp.303-325.

39. C. Boggs, "The Socialist Tradition: from Crisis to Decline" (New York 1995) at p.208.

40. C. Boggs, ibid, at p.208.

41. C. Boggs, ibid (1995) at pp.211-212.

42. Ibid at p.212.

43. Ronald Inglehart, "The Silent Revolution in Europe:Intergenerational Change in Post Industrial Societies", American Political Science Review 65 1971, at pp.991-1017.

44. P. Byrne and J. Lovenduski, "Two New Protest Groups:The Peace and Women's Movement" in H. Drucker et al (eds), "Developments in British Politics" (London, 1983).

45. J. Freeman, "A Model for Analysing the Strategic Options of Social Movement Organisations" in J. Freeman (ed), "Social Movements of the Sixties and Seventies" (New York, 1975); also M. Bookchin, "Post Scarcity Anarchism" (San Francisco, 1971).

46. R. Michels launched this line of iniquity in 1911 in his "Political Parties" (see the London 1962 edition).

47. Wilhelm Burklin, "Governing Left Parties Frustrating the Radical Non-Establishment Left: The Rise and Inevitable Decline of the Greens", European Sociological Review 2 No.2 (September 1987) at pp. 109-126.

48. R. Eckersley, "Environmentalism and Political Theory: Towards an Ecocentric Approach" (London,1992).

49. For a summary of the significance of these events, see S.B. Wolinetz, "Parties and Party Systems in Liberal Democracies" (London, 1988); H. Daalder and P. Mair (eds), "Western European Party Systems: Continuity and Change" (London, 1983); and I. Crewe and D. Denver (eds), "Electoral Change in Western Democracies:Patterns and Sources of Electoral Volatility" (London,1985).

50. See H. Kitschelt's discussion of this critical independent variable in "Political Opportunity Structures and Political Protest", British Journal of Political Science 16 1986.

51. For a discussion of the impact of the electoral system on the chances of small parties, see Arend Lijphart and R. W. Gibbard, "Thresholds and Payoffs in List Systems of Proportional Representation", European Journal of Political Research 5(3) 1977 at pp.219-44.

52. W. Rudig. "The Greens in Europe:Ecological Parties and the European Elections of 1984", Parliamentary Affairs 38 1985.

53. There is an immense and growing literature on Europe's national Green parties. A useful selection includes the following studies: W. Hulsberg, "The West German Greens" (London,1987); E. Gene Frankland and D. Schoonmaker, "Between Protest and Power: The Green Party in Germany" (Boulder, Col. 1992); H.Kitschelt, "The Medium is the Message: Democracy and Oligarchy in Belgian Ecology Parties" in W. Rudig (ed), "Green Politics One" (Edinburgh, 1990), at pp.82-114; ibid, "Organisation and Strategy in Belgian and West German Ecology Parties", Comparative Politics 20 1988 at pp.127-54; H. Kitschelt and S. Hellemans, "Beyond the European Left:Ideology and Political Action in the Belgian Ecology Parties" (Durham N.C., 1990); D. Nelkin and M. Pollak, "The Politics of Participation and the Nuclear Debate in Sweden, The Netherlands and Austria", Public Policy XXV (1977) at pp.333-57; T. Chafer, "The Anti-Nuclear Movement and the Rise of Political Ecology" in P. Cerny (ed), "Social Movements and Protest in Contemporary France" (London,1982); B. Prendiville, "France: Les Verts", in F. Muller-Rommel op.cit 1989; John McCormick, "Environmental Politics" in P. Dunleavy, A. Gamble, I. Holliday and G. Peele, "Developments in British Politics 4" (Basingstoke, 1993).

54. H. Kitschelt, op.cit (1990), at p.85.

55. G. Smith, "Stages of European Development: Electoral Change and System Adaptation", in D. Urwin and W. Paterson, "Politics in Western Europe" (Harlow,

1990) at pp.251-69.

56. F. Muller-Rommel, "The Greens in Western Europe, Similar but Different", International Political Science Review, November 1985.

57. R. O. Keohane and J. S. Nye (eds), "Transnational Relations and World Politics" (Cambridge, Mass, 1972)

58. Carole Webb, in the Introduction to H. Wallace, W. Wallace and Carole Webb, "Policy Making in the European Communities" (London 1977) at p.22.

59. See J. Gibbons (ed), "Contemporary Political Culture:Politics in a Post-Modern Age" (London,1989)

60. The German Green party (Die Grunen) was founded in 1980 from an alliance of radical social movements and alternative groups. A motley of radical Christians and alternativists in Flanders coalesced into a political party (AGALEV) in 1982 following the Wallonian or French speaking Belgians who had formed a regional based Green party to contest the 1974 elections. The prospect of the 1984 European elections led to Green party lists in the Netherlands - the Groen Progressiff Akkord (GPA). A youth ecology movement (Jeunes at Environment) emerged in Luxembourg on the back of the anti-nuclear campaign at the end of the 1970s. This movement subsequently firmed up in 1983 to form Die Greng Alternativ party. Local campaigns also launched two Austrian Green parties (Vereinte Grune Osterreich - VGO and Alternative Liste Osterreich - ALO) in 1982, which coalesced into Die Grune Alternative in 1987. Swiss environmentalists and rather more radical groups formed the GPE party in 1979 alongside several localised or cantonal Green parties. The first national 'Ecology List' anywhere in Europe was formed in France prior to the 1974 Presidential elections. After factional in-fighting a unified Green party, Les Verts confederation-ecologiste-parti-ecologiste, was established in 1984. Italian Green politics remained dispersed and localised during the late seventies and early eighties but formed an unstable Green federation in 1986 (Liste Verdi) in order to coordinate their forces for the 1987 elections. The Greek Greens, to date, have followed a similar route, although these disparate groups (over ninety in all) did coalesce into a loosely organised party, the Alternative Ecologist movement. Spanish and Portuguese Green politics were delayed by the experience of dictatorships which prevented the natural emergence of libertarian and new left politics. Even when democracy was restored, radical or anti-system politics were heavily discounted. Nevertheless, the ecological banner is carried in Spain by Los Verdes, formed in 1984. And in Portugal, ecological politics was subsumed under the flag of the PPM, an anti-dictatorship party and the MDP, a neo Marxist party although a semi-independent party, Os Verdes, did emerge in 1987. Britain boasts the oldest ecological party - the People's Party (1973). This has metamorphosed several times and became the Green Party in 1986. The Ecology Party of Ireland (EPI) was established in 1981, changed its name to the Green Alliance (Comhaontas Glas) in 1983, and to the Green Party in 1989. The Finnish Greens began to show in local elections as early as 1976, formed a national list in 1983 and eventually established a Green Association (Vihrea Litto) in 1987. Denmark's regional Green party, the Danmark's Miljopartiet, was formed in Jutland in 1984. A national Green party, De Gronne preceded it in 1983. The Swedish Greens, Miljopartiet de grona, was founded in 1981. The Norwegian Greens (Miljopartiet De Gronne) only adopted national party status in 1989.

61. R. Michels, op.cit (1962 edition), "Final Considerations", at pp.364-71.

62. W. P. Burklin, "The German Greens: The Post Industrial Non Established and the Party System", International Political Science Review 6 1985 at pp.463-81.

63. ibid, "The Split between the Established and Non Established Left in Germany", European Journal of Political Research 13 1985 at pp.283-93.

64. J. Mushaben, "The Struggle Within", in B. Klandermans (ed), "Organising for Change: Social Movement Organisation Across Cultures" (Greenwich, 1989).

65. H. Kitschelt, "New Social Movements and the Decline of Party Organisation", in R. J. Dalton and M. Kuechler, "Challenging the Political Order: New Social and Political Movements in Western Democracies" (Oxford,1990), at pp.179-208.

66. H. Kitschelt, "The Logics of Party Formation: Structure and Strategy of Belgian and West German Ecology Parties" (Ithaca,1989).

67. D. Foss and R. Larkin, "Beyond Revolution: A New Theory of Social Movements" (South Hadley,1986).

68. H. Kitschelt, "Democracy and Oligarchy in Belgian Ecology Parties", in W. Rudig (ed), "Green Politics One" (Edinburgh, 1990) at pp.82-114.

69. See J. Fitzmaurice, "The Politics of Belgium: A Unique Federalism" (London 2nd edition,1996), at p.217.

70. H. Kitschelt, op.cit (1988) at pp.127-54; see also H. Kitschelt and S. Hellemans, op.cit (1990).

71. There is a veritable avalanche of material on Die Grunen's internal battleground. Amongst the best of this literature is E.Gene Frankland and Donald Schoonmaker, "Between Protest and Power" (Boulder, Col. 1992); E. Kolinksy, "The Greens in West Germany:Organisation and Policy Making" (Oxford,1984); G. Langguth, "The Green Factor in German Politics" (Boulder, Col,1984) and T. Scharf, "The German Greens" (Oxford,1994).

72. Some of these issues are discussed in E. Gene Frankland, "The Role of the Greens in West German Parliamentary Politics", Review of Politics 50 (1) 1988 at pp.99-122.

73. See the discussion in W. Paterson and D. Southern, "Governing Germany" (New York, 1991) especially at p.121.

74. The East German ecologists Bundnis 90 Grune (DDA) capitalised on their reputation as a citizen based oppositionalist group in the former DDR to win seats in the enlarged Parliament.

75. The Guardian, 29.4.91.

76. ibid, 29.4.91.

77. See F. Pappi, "The West German System", West European Politics 7 (4) October 1984 at pp.1-27.

78. Financial Times, 12.5.89.

79. W. Rudig and P. Lowe, "The Withered 'Greening' of British Politics: A Study of the Ecology Party", Political Studies 34 (1986) at pp.262-284.; H. Berrington, "New Parties in Britain: Why Some Live and Most Die", International Political Science Review 6 1985 at pp.441-61.

80. P. Lowe and A. Flynn, "Environmental Politics and Policy in the 1980s", in J. Mohan (ed), "The Political Geography of Contemporary Britain" (London,1989).

81. B. Clark and T. Dickson, "Towards a Green Consensus", Financial Times, 12 April 1989.

82. The Observer 6.9.92.

83.   D. Nelkin and M. Pollak, "The Politics of Participation and the Nuclear Debate in Sweden, the Netherlands and Austria", Public Policy XXV (1977) at pp.333-57.

84.   L. Rebeaud, "Di Grunen in der Schweiz" (Bern,1987).

85.   Financial Times, 17.2.94.

86.   The European, 25 February - 3 March 1994.

87.   Financial Times, 23.11.93; ibid, 6.1.2.93.

88.   R. K. Carty, "Ireland: From Predominance to Competition", Chapter 10 of S. Wolinetz (ed), "Parties and Party Systems in Liberal Democracies" (London, 1988) at pp.222-245.

89.   Financial Times, 13.6.94.

90.   F. Muller-Rommel, "New Social Movements and Smaller Parties: A Comparative Analysis", West European Politics 8 1985, at p.41.

91.   W. Rudig, "Green Party Politics", Environment, Vol.33 (8) (1991) at p.26; see also M. Pedersen, "The Birth and Life and the Death of Small Parties in Danish Politics", in F. Muller-Rommel and G. Pridham (eds), "Small Parties in Western Europe" (London, 1989).

92.   O. Knutsen, "Materialist and Post Materialist Values and Social Structure in the Nordic Countries", Comparative Politics 23 1990, at pp.85-101.

93.   See E. Bedung, "The Environmentalist Party and the Swedish Five Party Syndrome", in K. Lawson and P. Merkl, "Why Parties Fail" (Princeton, 1988).

94.   O. Knutsen, op.cit (1990).

95.   T. Poguntke, "New Politics and Party Systems: The Emergence of a New Type of Party System?" Western European Politics, 10/1 January 1987.

96.   For a flavour of some of the extensive literature on this most radical dimension of ecologism, see Murray Bookchin's classic testament, "The Ecology of Freedom: The Emergence and Dissolution of Hierarchy" (Palo Alto, California); Kirkpatrick Sale, "Dwellers in the Land: The Bioregional Vision" (San Francisco, 1985); R. Bahro, "Building the Green Movement" (London, 1986); T. Roszak, "Person/Planet: The Creative Disintegration of Industrial Society" (1981); E.Goldsmith, "The Great U-Turn: De-industrialising Society" (Hartland, UK, 1988). And for a critique of this position, see R.Paehlke, "Bucolic Myths: Towards More Urbanist Environmentalism" (Toronto, Centre for Urban and Community Studies, 1986).

97.   T. Poguntke, op.cit (1987).

98.   For a discussion of the postmaterialist right, see James Savage, "Postmaterialism of the Left and Right. Political conflict in Post Industrial Society", Comparative Political Studies 17(4) 1985, especially at pp.441-47.

99.   The Guardian, 12.2.93.

100.   Reuters New Service Report, 16.2.93.

101.   ibid, 24.2.93.

102.   J. Ditfurth quoted from "Skizzeneiner radikalo ologischen position" in T. Kluge (ed), "Grune Politik".

103.   O. Schily, "Socialismus" 11 1984.

104.   Reuters, op.cit., 26.9.93; Guardian 31.8.93; ibid 15.11.93

105.   Irish Times, 24.5.93.

Part Two: Green parties and Europe's changing political order

"The road of excess leads to the palace of wisdom"

William Blake, **Proverbs of Hell**

2 Die Grunen in Germany

(i)   Green roots

Die Grunen in the Federal Republic of Germany has undoubtedly been Europe's most politically successful and conspicuous Green party. Although it was launched along the lines of a radical anti-party, on the momentum created by Europe's most persistent alternative movement - a fact which itself has much to do with West Germany's postwar political culture - Die Grunen's early success as both a protest movement and as a more conventional electoral force, helped to establish a firm electoral base. This has sustained the party throughout the eighties - a decade during which it became a force to be reckoned with in domestic politics as well as an inspiration to Green parties elsewhere in Europe. In spite of providing such a spur the German Greens benefitted from more favourable structural conditions, and indeed events, than Green parties elsewhere - a situation that does much to explain the party's successes as well as its remarkable durability as an electoral force.

The Greens' rise in Germany has not, however, been one of unmitigated success. The party has suffered setbacks - a combination of internal strife and electoral rebuffs as the focus of German politics shifted dramatically, and the country was obliged to come to terms with the socio-economic fallout of unification that followed the unexpected fall of the Berlin Wall in November 1989. Doubts about a revival of German nationalism, the return of inflation, internal mass immigration from the east, and the immense fiscal burden of merging two structurally unbalanced economies and divergent social systems, downgraded those ecological issues and libertarian concerns central to Die Grunen's appeal on the new Germany's political agenda. Nevertheless, the Greens have weathered this turbulence. There are signs that the political fortunes of the new East-West German Green alliance (Bundnis 90/Die Grunen), set in motion in 1992 and implemented in 1993 after a joint congress followed by separate membership ballots, have begun to revive. A modest but firm electoral core of Green voters remains the basis of an effective role for the party in national politics, and even more surely, in regional (Laender) and local/city politics.

Die Grunen was founded in 1980 from an alliance of radical social movements and alternative groups many of which represented a distinctive sub-culture of collectives opted out of the politics, as they saw it, of the 'bourgeois mainstream'. Although by no means were all of them committed to a clearly defined, let alone a coherent, radical agenda. Instead, a culture of ideological eclecticism prevailed in the movement. One activist subsequently wrote, that "we are neither left nor right, we are in front... In the end, however, most of us were and are convinced that a Green party has to amalgamate ecological and new left thinking".[1] These extensive local and national networks provided the new party with a base for organisation as well as a degree of electoral purchase at the various levels of the West German polity. Moreover, the liberal rules governing the practice of politics in the West German state, established by the Basic Law of 1949 - for instance, a federal constitution with dispersed powers at local or state (Laender) levels; public funding for political parties which secure a minimum 0.5% of the votes in Laender or in federal elections;[2] an electoral system that incorporates a degree of plurality for electing half of the Bundestag seats by way of single member constituencies alongside the proportional system based on national party lists - all provided an opportunity structure conducive to an effective role for minority parties. Political culture has also played its part here. An electorate already sensitive to the costs and humiliations of war, with quite recent memories of dictatorship, military defeat and occupation - and touched with a latent sense of guilt about the issue of civil liberties and minority rights after the tyranny of the Third Reich - was particularly receptive to the emotive message canvassed by the pervasive anti-war and libertarian movements which prefaced the rise of Green politics. This painful history has certainly helped to shape Germany's postwar politics, and the values and preferences that inform it. One commentator has maintained that, "generational conflict was more acute in West Germany than in other industrialised democracies. New left students, in coming to terms with the heavy burdens of Germany's history, were confronting the silence and complacency of their elders. In contrast to other student radicals, young West Germans felt a crisis of identity as well as a crisis of authority. In effect, the new left was engaged in a dual protest against the present Bonn Republic and the past Third Reich.[3] This endemic ambivalence explains much that is unique about radical politics in West Germany since the war. In such circumstances, ecologism in Germany had a particular resonance that was less apparent elsewhere on the continent. The movement had a particular appeal for the first postwar generation to come to political maturity in Germany.

While we should not exaggerate the novelty of the German situation it was, nevertheless, the case that public opinion there was particularly receptive to the notion of environmental damage and the consequences of generations of rampant industrialisation. This legacy had been accentuated by the new production processes and technologies stimulated by the frenetic push for growth[4] that had sustained West Germany's 'wirtschaftswunder' - the postwar economic miracle.[5] Ecologism impacted disproportionately on the sensibilities of the educated middle class.[6] During the 1970s concerns about the direction of public policy across a spectrum of issues - from the merits of the work ethic and the meaning of intellectual freedom, to the costs of contemporary social organisation, and the media domination of 'authoritarian' press barons - coalesced into a broad anti-system protest spearheaded by a 'new' postwar generation mobilised against supposed social oppression. The political experience of refusal, reinforced by direct action and confrontation with what was seen on the new left as a 'repressive' state, centred on a number of critical issues. The experience, overall, radicalised this generation in a way that their elders - concerned to rebuild their shattered lives after the traumas of defeat - could hardly begin to comprehend let alone to sympathise with.[7] This 'politics of refusal', of course, appeared as a recurrent theme at this juncture within the new left and libertarian movements in every advanced industrial societies.[8]

In West Germany this inchoate issue-oriented movement fomented, as it did elsewhere, a novel form of grass roots politics committed to open confrontation with the authorities. Direct action here took the form of university strikes, 'sit ins', and demonstrations; against American policy in Vietnam, as a forceful anti-nuclear energy movement, as well as in associated protests and campaigns against everything from NATO bases in Germany, educational 'authoritarianism' and what was deemed the 'new nazism' of the German capitalist establishment, symbolised in one notable campaign against Axel Springer's influential newspaper group.[9] This iconoclastic mood spilled over into the campuses, communes, collectives and feminist 'sororities'[10] which became the communal expression of an expansive radical network. Protest politics here took a step towards political consolidation when many of these alternative groups found their way into the extra-parliamentary and citizen action groups, and even on to electoral lists drawn up to give formal political expression to these organic communities by confronting the 'bourgeois polity' on its own ground at the ballot box.[11] The Greens were the direct outcome of this extensive Extra-parliamentary Opposition (APO) and eventually became its 'institutional embodiment'.[12]

Amongst the most prominent of these alternative groups was the Hamburg Bunte Liste (BL), an assorted alliance of 200 or more local grass roots organisations. Another local example was the Green list for Environmental Protection, the Grune Liste Unweltschutz (GLU), which emerged in lower Saxony as a coalition of ecology groups, and whose activities did much to encourage a national Green party, influencing similar local Green lists in Hamburg, Hesse, North-Rhine Westphalia, the Rhineland Palatinate and Baden Wurtemberg in the same direction. The latter was more committed to reformist and to parliamentary politics than the BL and was also more strongly supportive of pure ecologism than of a leftist or libertarian agenda.[13] Both groups, however, had an input into organisations which helped to launch the German ecologists on the road to electoral politics. On the 'right hand' side of this 'rainbow' mixture, the Action Committee of Independent Germans (AUD) synthesised those traditional themes of the ecological universe which are predisposed to bucolic romanticism and a folklore attuned to the mysticism of soil and forests[14] into a blend of populistic conservatism.

These various *'Burgerinitiativen'* were so successful on the ground as a direct focus of grass roots discontent, that their membership actually matched that of the established 'mass' parties.[15] They even attracted some of the more disillusioned members of these parties into their ranks - especially emigrés from the conventional left, where the shift of the SPD away from its radical roots and its transformation, after the adoption of the Bad Godesberg programme in 1959, into a 'catch-all' electoral machine, discounted ideology and emphasised instead 'safe', centrist, and vote maximising issues.[16] This replacement of radical substance with mere electoralism, was followed in 1966 by an 'unholy' Grand CDU/CSU-SPD coalition, and latterly by the SPD government's conventional, even conservative, strategy in office, including an endorsement of nuclear power and the standing of NATO's middle range nuclear hardware on West German soil.[17] These developments appeared to many radicals to close down the political space available to the conventional 'left' in German politics.[18] At the same time, they opened up the prospect for an alternative vehicle for radical opposition. This initially took the form of an Extra Parliamentary Opposition (APO).[19] The momentum, fuelled by a discernible disenchantment, particularly amongst the young and well educated, eventually encouraged the launch of a new type of alternative party at local and Laender level.[20] By 1977, beginning in Lower Saxony, anti-nuclear and assorted citizen and environmentalist groups were compiling an alternative list to fight the local elections.[21] Ideological intensity, personal rivalries and an outlook which shunned pragmatism or compromise, determined that competing radical lists frequently cancelled out one another. Not surprisingly, by the late seventies these alternative groups had won only a handful of local council seats. At this stage, the only real tactical gain was a steady media interest which kept alive public curiosity. In part, the stimulus for common action came from radicals concerned that the right wing Greens under Gruhl's aegis might make the running. The initial efforts to synthesise these various left-right factions bore little fruit. However, the prospect of the first direct elections to the European Parliament in 1979 - to be held under a fully proportional electoral system which was bound to enhance the chances of minor parties - galvanised a group of ecologists to organise a heterogeneous alliance of these existing Green lists, minor parties (for instance, the GAZ, the GLU and the Grune Liste Schleswig-Holstein (GLSH) and alternative and

Burgerinitiativen groups. The outcome was the Sonstige Politische Vereinigung "Die Grunen" (Alternative Political Alliance).

Although the SVP enjoyed only modest success - with 3.2 per cent of the national vote and thereby failing under the 5 per cent threshold to gain any seats - the impact of an organised national campaign increased the participants' determination to cement this loose coalition into a permanent Green party in order to contest the 1980 federal elections. This ambition was further encouraged by the first notable electoral success in October 1979, when the Bremen Green List passed the 5 per cent threshold and won seats in the city-state parliament. The significance of this electoral threshold as an incentive for disparate green groups to coalesce into a movement should not be underestimated. The absence, too, of election deposits - and thus of the cost to depleted party funds of losing them - also encouraged the Greens to embark on some form of institutionalised participation. The fact that successful parties (with over 0.5 per cent of votes) have had their election expenses defrayed from the public purse meant that in the 1979 Euro elections, the SVP national Green list received DM 4.5 million on the basis of its vote share. This accelerated the formation of the Green party. It has to be said, too, that the German electoral system - with each voter receiving two votes - has helped rather than hindered the Greens. Some erstwhile SPD voters have split their ticket and given their second vote to the Greens, particularly where the SPD seems likely to come off second best to the CDU, as it has now for over a decade.

(ii)   Party formation

Die Grunen was launched as a national party on the back of this modest local success in January 1980. However, the fragile unity of such a mixed, radical coalition was apparent from the start. By no means did all of West Germany's disparate ecological or alternative groups throw in their lot with the new party. Some groups staunchly resisted what they saw as the 'trap' of playing bourgeois politics. The absence of groups such as the Hamburg Bunte Liste: Wehrt Euch! Initativen fur Demokratie und Umweltschnutz (BLW-Multicoloured List: Resist! Initiative for Democracy and Environmental Protection) and the Alternative Liste fur Demokratie und Umweltschutz from Berlin, which had close links with the Communists, illustrates the almost infinite variety of the German rainbow left at this time. The problems of organising these groups into an effective national movement with an agreed programme and strategy, were manifestly obvious from the outset. There were also intense and divisive debates provoked both within and by those groups who remained formally outside, if ideologically compatible with, the new party organisation, over the definition of party membership and party loyalty. Some pure green elements in the new party were content to sustain this new-found but tentative unity, by seeking to refine the idea of party discipline, so as to exclude 'rogue' infiltrators and entryists from the far left parties. In part this was a pragmatic response - the exclusion of those whose 'extremism' might undermine the party's broader electoral appeal. In ideological terms, it represented an attempt to consolidate the party's ecological credentials. Either way, it signalled the sort of factional divisions which would confront the new party over the medium term. The libertarian and anti-party elements predictably regarded such prescriptions as a narrow-minded authoritarianism more in keeping with the hierarchical mass parties they were organising to confront. A compromise was eventually reached at the Offenbach congress which typified the pure Green and anti-party radical dynamic, in this as in many other Green parties in their formative stages. It was left to the constituent parties operating on the ground at Laender level to formulate their own membership rules, appropriate to local preferences and conditions.

Similar and equally intense conflicts broke out at this congress over the party's ideological and programmatic content. Because these issues went to the heart of what the Greens saw as their radical mission within the bourgeois polity, they have proved troublesome and difficult to resolve. The pure green faction wanted to concentrate exclusively on ecological or closely related issues. The rainbow leftists, on the other hand, with their roots in the broader alternative networks, continued to canvass a more eclectic domestic and international programme. Some of these leftists imported into the Greens a mixture of far left ideological predispositions, from neo-Marxism to anarchism and eco-libertarianism. The Marxists among them were particularly committed to the Leninist notion of an activist party, dedicated to raising class consciousness.[22] Although active in the new party, these leftists reduced their impact by fomenting divisive sectarian quarrels over 'appropriate' tactics. Nevertheless, some semblance of organisational common sense did eventually prevail. Drawing on the negotiating and coalitional skills honed in the campaigning milieu of radical movement politics,[23] a party constitution was eventually agreed at a party Congress held in Karlsruhe in January 1980. This was followed, in March 1980, by the adoption of a national programme. Not surprisingly, the protracted confrontations that prefaced this outcome displayed an eclectic catalogue of ecological, social and libertarian commitments, which reflected the party's diverse rainbow origins. It was, at the same time, a clearcut radical programme based on the so-called 'four pillars' - of ecologism, grass roots democracy, social responsibility and non-violence.[24] The ultra-conservative eco-purists, led by Herbert Gruhl, were marginalised and drew their own conclusions. Many of them followed him out of Die Grunen and into a rival, conservative environmentalist fringe party, the ODP.

The new Green coalition had only a minimal electoral impact and was dismissed by many commentators as a passing fad amounting to a wasted vote. Although it polled a mere 1.5 per cent of the total national vote in the 1980 federal elections, it did make steady progress at the Laender level. This, in turn, sustained the growing impression that Die Grunen was an emergent political force. Moreover, this limited success was clearly not hampered by - and may indeed have reflected - the party's decentralised nature with its strong roots in local politics. In March 1980, for instance, it won 6 seats in the Landtag (state parliament) of Baden-Wurtemburg. Between 1981 and 1983 the Greens built on these local successes and took seats in another four Landtage; in Berlin, where the Alternative List won 9 seats (May 1981); Lower Saxony, 11 seats (March 1982); Hesse, 9 seats (September 1982);and Hamburg, 8 seats (December 1982).

This steady progress at local level provided the party with a solid base for a successful federal election campaign in March 1983. For the first time the party breached (with a 5.6 per cent national vote) the 5 per cent electoral threshold and gained 27 seats in the federal Bundestag. This outcome made 1983 a landmark election in the erstwhile cautious postwar politics of the Bonn Republic. The Greens thus became the first party in a generation - a significant term here, given the youthful and new middle class profile of much of its electoral support - to challenge the national ascendancy of the established parties;[25] and with that, to confront the country's passive civic culture sustained by a materialistic consumer ethos. Radical ecology provided the movement's driving force here. But it was driven, too, by a broader social agenda, that incorporated other radical concerns from anti-nuclearism to gender politics, anti-racism and a host of other alternative and new social movement issues.[26]

Sceptics who dismissed this achievement as a mere fluke were obliged to reassess the situation after Die Grunen polled a commendable 8.2 per cent in the admittedly 'second order'

European election of 1984 - a success which brought the party 7 Euro seats and launched it on the supranational stage. By the time of the 1987 federal elections, the Greens - polling by now a steady 8.3 per cent of the total vote (which yielded 44 Bundestag seats) - achieved their best national result so far. Yet in spite of undoubted electoral success at every level, which made Die Grunen thereafter a significant factor in Germany's shifting coalitional politics, the party continues to perform consistently better at state and local level. The Greens have regularly polled around the 10 per cent mark in the radical enclaves of Berlin (1985), Hamburg (1986) and Bremen (1987). While the party's vote elsewhere has fluctuated according to local and prevailing national circumstances, it has managed to clear the 5 per cent hurdle necessary for translating votes into seats in the majority of Laender elections held, not only during the halcyon years of the eighties, but also in the more difficult times for progressive let alone ecological politics into the nineties. The party's best successes have occurred in those areas where local ecological events gained political salience. Or else in those demographically favourable constituencies such as university cities, where a higher than average percentage of the radical youth vote is concentrated.[27] Overall, the party managed to win election to the majority of the Federal Republic's local councils during its successful first decade. Political success, of course, tends to breed further success. Electoral victories and the attendant publicity that accrues from them was reflected in the rise in party membership. In 1980, with barely 13,000 members, Die Grunen had a smaller support base than even the Communist Party (KPD). By the end of the decade, this had virtually quadrupled to some 45,000 - still less than the liberal FDP, but sufficient to accord it the status of a national political force.

If anything, this figure understated the political base on which the party could draw for electioneering, campaigning and other purposes. For by no means are all Green activists full party members. Moreover, the party has never embraced the mass membership strategy favoured by the mainstream 'catch-all' or *staatsparteien* (official parties synonymous with the state per se), preferring instead to adopt the status of a people's party or *volksparteien*. The Greens also tend to have fewer non-activist members than these mass parties. This proportionately high level of activism - which is reflected in a higher ratio of voters to members than that enjoyed by the mainstream parties[28] - is an invaluable organisational resource. The party was committed from the outset to an anti-elitist, non-hierarchical new party politics model based on its preference for grass roots democracy, local autonomy, accountability and transparency. On the down side, such activism, with its strong participatory ethos,[29] has nourished a discordant climate in the conduct of party affairs, in which personality clashes and intense factionalism have been rife. These squabbles dissipated much of the party's abundant energy, and in turn squandered its political opportunities, by diverting some of its political vigor into internecine squabbles.

Introversion thus, has presented difficulties for most new radical parties across the European political landscape. Die Grunen has proved to be no exception to the 'law' of diminishing political returns, whereby there is usually an inverse ratio between the extent of internal disunity and any positive political pay off. The party was deeply divided between those fundamentalists who disavowed any hint of compromise with first ideological principles; and those more pragmatic elements, or 'realists' as they came to be regarded, who increasingly averred that the route to electoral success and maximising political impact lay precisely through accommodations with that system.[30] Such 'realism' took many forms; from displaying sensitivity to polling data in framing party programmes, to a willingness to negotiate and cooperate with other parties, notably the SPD, at every level, even to the point of giving serious consideration to a national red-green coalition. This strategic option has remained on the 'realos' agenda from the moment the Greens broke through and won representation in state legislatures. It has generated, as we saw in Chapter One, an animated debate on the prospects for a red-green consensus at the heart of a major realignment in German politics. While this has exercised the other parties less than it has Die Grunen, it has, over time, impinged on the national debate about German political futures.

The fundamentalists or 'fundis' for their part rejected out of hand anything that smacked of incremental bargaining and the trade offs, or otherwise implied a sell-out of everything the Greens stood for by way of a genuinely radical agenda. They argued instead for a strategy in which the Greens remained aloof from the 'corrupt' politics of the status quo, and preferred instead to maintain a cordon sanitaire between their 'principled politics' and the 'squalid' short termism of conventional party politics.[31] Jutta Ditfurth, a leading fundi throughout this period, wrote disparagingly about the limitations of such moderation. She argued thus that: "Reformism, in its Green-social democratic form, starts out from the assumption that there will be no radical break in our society. The time for revolution is past, so the illogical conclusion is drawn that reformism is the only option. This is pretty sloppy political thinking. For any serious analysis must take into account the fact that every variant of reformism has proven itself historically bankrupt".[32]

The pragmatists - who eventually gained the ascendancy in this debate, and in so doing, established an agenda with the potential for producing a unique model for a progressive post-industrial politics in such advanced societies[33] - invariably took a broader outlook on the German democratic landscape. They drew on what they saw as the salutary lessons of the recent past, and in particular the heavy costs of the insular leftist politics that prevailed during the Weimar years, which had allowed a minority Nazi party first to seize power and then to subvert a liberal state. Seen in this light, the case for a political accommodation with other progressive forces - a red-green bargain - seemed indisputable. It was frequently canvassed by various realists in party fora in precisely these term. Otto Schily, for instance, writing at a time when this tactical debate was at its most febrile, warned the party that, "some sections of the Greens underestimate the dangers of a shift to the right, as is clear from their formula of the lesser evil, and they underestimate the dangers of a conservative foreign and security policy. We must take into consideration what effect our rejection of a realistic left coalition perspective would have on the right and how this would clear the terrain for rightist policies".[34]

The realists have, in the interim, won this particular argument and have come to dominate the party's structures and to shape its policy agenda. One outcome of this has been coalitional agreements with the SPD, both at Laender and local level across the Federal Republic. In Berlin the city's radical Alternative Lists, after initially refusing in 1981 to lend its support to a minority SPD government, eventually did so in 1989. Similarly, in the aftermath of the 1982 elections in Hamburg, the Green Alternative List (GAL) attempted to strike a 'toleration agreement' with the local SPD, although at this time the gap between the parties proved unbridgeable and an agreement failed to materialise. At this early stage, the tension between the 'fundi' and 'realo' tendencies was rife. Nevertheless, the urge of some local parties to experiment with coalitions strengthened the appeal of such a pragmatic outlook. This success was increasingly measured, from the mid eighties onwards, by the prospects of cashing in a sizeable Green vote in order to strike workable local deals with the Social Democrats. The first signs of a positive breakthrough in these terms came in Hesse. Between 1983 and 1987 the Greens in the Landtag there struck an informal and subsequently a formal arrangement with the minority SPD government. This produced an SPD-led government and the first taste of ministerial responsibility for German Green politicians when the state's environment ministry and two state secretarial posts were allocated to Die Grunen members. In almost every case where coalitions were formed, the Greens' preferred allies were the SPD. Only in Stuttgart did the local Greens, influenced by a group of conservative inclined eco-liberationists (*Okolibertaten*) contemplate a similar toleration agreement with the CDU.

These developments impacted, in turn, on the internal debate within Die Grunen as the party's initial red versus green axis of conflict was supplemented and largely supplanted by an even deeper split between 'realos' and 'fundis' over political strategies. The fundis, however, did not yield easily or without a staunch rearguard resistance. For a time this impasse left the party stranded between a 'realo' parliamentary wing and a 'fundi' dominated party organisation. Nor has the gradual tactical success of the pragmatists entirely resolved, even for many 'realos', their abiding and deep suspicions about the ecological commitments and political reliability of those Social Democrats who, whether at local or federal level, have courted them as coalition partners. These doubts have been sustained by the political experience of actual coalition arrangements in several Laender or city states. In short, Green-SPD relations continue to be fraught with tension on both sides. This outcome has continued to impact on Green politics. The value or otherwise of such alliances, on the grounds of the credibility and influence they afforded the Greens, continued to be fiercely contested in party congresses throughout the eighties. This conflict far from reflected a straightforward horizontal division between party elites and the party faithful. It has divided the party along the vertical plane at every level. Nevertheless, the pragmatists began to win the argument, and they were increasingly sustained in their campaign to accommodate the Greens within the existing political framework by the evidence of polling data which conclusively showed the preference of Green voters for Red-Green coalitions rather than for a continued self exclusion from governance.

The split in the Hesse party which accompanied a local coalitional arrangement with the SPD was, in effect, a dress rehearsal for the deep ambiguities that overshadowed the party's steady electoral success throughout the decade. For cumulative success at the polls contributed to widening the split in the party's ranks. The more often electoral success placed the Greens in a position of coalitional kingmaker, the more intense was the feuding over this issue. The outcome in Hesse showed the way out of this impasse, even if it did not assuage the wrath of the 'fundis'. The 'realos' began to win over many sceptics, without actually securing control of the local party organisation. But they did confirm the straight choice between these two irreconcilable and increasingly unavoidable options. Above all, this approach demonstrated the irresistable appeal of cooperation to those Greens who preferred to weigh in the party's growing electoral appeal. And it reinforced the view that any radical party that seriously seeks to influence policy outcomes and thereby to sustain public credibility simply cannot afford to retreat into a principled wilderness, once the electorate has delivered them opportunities to exert such leverage.[35] The Greens in Hesse, in what became known as 'the experiment' - as well as elsewhere, where similar arrangements eventually operated - initially agreed to endorse SPD budgets in exchange for securing additional resources for a range of environmental and social programmes. These included everything from computer data protection and energy policy to waste disposal projects. Although the Hesse coalition eventually fell apart in a dispute over the demand for the closure of a plutonium processing plant, it did provide an indicative model for what could be achieved by tactical bargaining in the political market place. This modest but tangible success undoubtedly helped to solidify the Green vote at both the national and local levels, by reinforcing the pragmatists' case within party councils in favour of pursuing this 'toleration' tactic. This outcome was tentative rather than conclusive. The 'fundis' were outmanoeuvred everywhere. Events in the Saarland, where in 1984 the Greens refused a coalitional arrangement offered by the future national SPD leader Oskar Lafontaine, and in North-Rhine Westphalia, where in 1985 only a tentative toleration accord was struck, provided evidence that this debate over political strategy was far from resolved. In Hamburg meanwhile, where the process of inter party bargaining followed the 1986 elections, the GAL blew simultaneously hot and cold over this issue, using its position of holding the balance of political power to both endorse and oppose particular legislative measures proposed by the minority SPD government as it saw fit.

The issue of a suitable radical party political strategy highlighted by such local deals was critical to Die Grunen's very raison d'être in national politics. Especially so as the strategy of consolidating a parliamentary base after the party's success at the 1983 elections was apparently holding steady, according to the evidence of national opinion polls as the 1987 federal elections approached. The issue eventually came to a head in 1986. As Die Grunen's federal assembly debated the issue, all of the fault lines which had opened up in the party at Laender level were displayed on the national stage. These deeply disruptive conflicts spilled over into 1987. For a time, the party seemed to be openly at war with itself. Ideological divisions between leftists and pure ecologists were overlaid - though by no means displaced - by a new 'realo'-'fundi' fault line over dispositions to the political system. This cleavage, which was already simmering at the local level, had been accentuated by the party's participation in national parliamentary politics. In spite of clinging to its radical ethos of a 'movement party' - a bottom up model in which activists remained the principal source of authority, and hierarchical notions of leadership were discounted as merely an organisational convenience in order to accommodate the necessary party functions - the onset of a parliamentary wing of 'professional' politicians, was bound to cause tensions amongst the rank and file. The party was pulled in two directions. The 'realos' - whether of the 'watermelon' or 'cucumber' variety - preferred a moderate strategy of compromise, even to the point of cooperating with other progressive politicians in line with the coalitional relations already experienced in some Laender governments. This was not merely a clash of political styles but an unbridgeable chasm between two entirely different philosophies of politics.

The pragmatists continued to recommend accommodation with the 'real world' of politics; whereas some fundis publicly empathised with the militancy of the Autonomen group, whose members had been involved in acts of violence that led to the deaths of two policemen at Frankfurt airport. The issue rumbled on into 1988 when a non decision making national conference was called in Bonn to try to resolve it. Eventually, the 'realos', or 'super realos' as both critics and supporters now saw them, prevailed. A policy was endorsed which sanctioned the notion of a red-green coalition, depending on prevailing circumstances and the concessions wrung from the SPD. With this compact, Die Grunen was now as surely launched as any radical party ever could be on a pragmatic trajectory. This paid, in turn, the electoral dividends that it was intended to deliver - at least until the turbulent politics of unification temporarily derailed the Greens. This victory for what seemed to most German voters to be political common sense, did much to distract public attention away from the continuing bizarre reminders of Green extremism. For instance, such politically embarrassing incidents when local Greens in North Rhine-Westphalia included in their manifesto a resolution to legalise sexual relations between adults and children - and the occasion when

61

two Bundestag Greens, by no means extremists, corresponded with two convicted Baader Meinhof terrorists who had gone on hunger strike.

The tension between these extreme positions was more than simply a stand-off between two entrenched party factions. If this had been the case, it would undoubtedly have been easier either to manage or resolve. The root of this discord was a difference of emphasis between those elements prepared to operate within the conventional political universe, and those for whom any kind of co-operation with 'the system' was a fundamental denial of their commitment to an alternative politics. For both sides of this less than clear cut dispute, being 'Green' was regarded as a principled position; one which reflected the basic philosophical predispositions and emotional preferences of conscionable radicals operating inside an alien, conservative and broadly hostile political environment. Seen in these terms, as emotional propensities and ideological perspectives grouped around shared radical commitments and a common self image of committed radicalism,[36] it is clear that the distinction between the 'realos' and 'fundis' has been too starkly drawn in some commentaries. These differences of emphasis were, nevertheless, apparent and continued to preoccupy the party throughout its formative years. The essence of this conflict was two competing visions of radical politics; one was essentially utopian, the other rooted in the present. The utopians defined ecologism as something more far-reaching than a challenge to the current socio-economic and political order. It represented instead a revolutionary rupture with a failed past. The realists, on the other hand, shared an equally radical vision, albeit one committed to participating in current politics. The rift between these factions widened further as Die Grunen tasted electoral success. What was at stake here, apart from the usual personality clashes which accompany political factionalism everywhere, were deepseated if by no means always clear cut differences over the most appropriate strategy for a new movement committed to open up a distinctive political space for itself within the political order. The pragmatists preferred a 'new politics' that was defined less by gestures or polemics than by concrete action and an appeal to potential support in the electoral milieu. This course of action implied necessary compromises and accommodations rather than ideological rhetoric. Whereas the fundamentalists saw the polemics and the substance of politics as two sides of the same coin. To compromise one was to dilute or deny the other.

In spite of these significant differences, there were also ideological affinities and emotional bonds which drew these various factions together and, initially, kept them in the same party. These ties enabled both sides to work together, after a fashion, during those election campaigns whose outcomes, ironically, became the focus of so much of their strife. Certainly, adherents of both factions did share some commonly held assumptions. Not least, a mutual distaste for the 'iniquities'of industrial capitalism.[37] Most of the German Greens shared, too, at the very minimum, the radical outsider's wariness of compromise, although the 'realos' were convinced that in order to be politically effective, ecologists had to play the political game. Both sides were equally cognisant of what Michels in his classical account[38] had identified as the oligarchic and anti-democratic tendencies of modern party politics, with its strategy of vote maximisation and short term electoralism.[39] Where they did divide, however, was over the extent of their optimism about how such authoritarian tendencies might be overcome. This schism caught the new party, in these early stages, on the horns of a dilemma it seemed quite unable to resolve. Jurgens Maier, a member of the party's Federal Executive Committee, reflected this predicament when he observed, that " the party seems to develop a tendency to lose the advantages of a grass roots democratic organisation without really gaining at the same time the advantages of a professional organisation structure".[40]

This deepseated conflict over the style and disposition of Green party politics remained its main source of internal tension throughout its first decade or so. Nevertheless, casual observers, especially in the media, who were unsympathetic or hostile to those they saw as pompous, or otherwise saw the Greens as gesture politicians, tended to over-simplify this factional divide. To insist on using such a narrow, one-dimensional focus - for instance between pragmatism and fundamentalist idealism - is to ignore what the Greens shared, regardless of their differences over strategy. A deep emotional pull, and an insistence that only dramatic changes in public policy and private expectations could change society for the better and improve its chances of survival, demarcated all Greens from other, even radical, political movements. These mutual principles kept all of these groups under a common political umbrella throughout this turbulent period. The less than clear demarcation between these factions was underlined, too, by shifts in support between the two 'camps', depending on the issue.

Die Grunen's evolving and eclectic programme illustrated precisely the extent of these shared values and, at the same time, the festering discord amongst the rank and file members. From the time that the party began to put considered programmes before its potential electors, its choice of policy options reflected its diverse 'rainbow' roots. Die Grunen from the start rejected the Keynesian preoccupations with economic growth, productionism and consumerism as the driving forces of 'appropriate' economic activity. They focused instead on the cost to 'real' human liberation of the profligate resource wastage and ecological damage which they claimed were the direct consequences of such materialistic obsessions. The Alternative Movement's roots in the 1968 generation, with its attendant iconoclasm and anti-elitism, was also reflected in a host of policy statements which emphasised the value of individual or self actualisation, self discipline and self determination as the roots of social order. Society in this outlook was disaggregated into meaningful face to face communities or networks - the locality, the family, educational establishments at every level, and the workplace. Individuals were exhorted to take back control of their own lives from the 'system' which had 'alienated' humanity from itself. It followed from this that political participation was defined in active rather than the passive terms - a clear rejection of the hegemony of the politics of mass democracy imposed on 'citizens' by the dominant volksparteien model utilised as a form of social contract by the conventional parties of both left and right.[41] Another broad policy theme here was a commitment to social justice, especially of the redistributive kind - from gender discrimination right up to the global level itself. Third World exploitation was regarded as symptomatic of the deep structural inequities at the heart of the capitalist system. All sides of the party were vehemently opposed to the nuclear stance of NATO because it represented the very antithesis of a civilised and citizen based approach to defence and security issues.[42]

These policies came under closer scrutiny as the party became established as an electoral force. In order to preempt the familiar charges of utopianism, inconsistency and extremism which accompanied critical attention from the media, the realists sought to clarify, explain and inject this radical programme with a greater sense of coherence. This merely sharpened the factional tensions between the party's factions. As early as 1983, with a federal election looming and the polls predicting a degree of success for the Greens, the federal party assembly sanctioned an action programme (the Sofort programme) consisting of medium and short term measures to address what were defined as the worst problems of industrial decay and social injustice. It included proposals for a legislative programme on work sharing, overtime restrictions, ecological investments in the energy and transport sectors, inducements for industry to abandon ecologically damaging projects, and for industrial retraining programmes. Many of these policies held particular appeal, on both ethical grounds and out of self interest, to the new middle class elements who were disproportionately represented in Die Grunen's electorate.[43] At the same time, this was a critical and discerning electorate with a tendency to whimsy and volatility. The first warning here was delivered in the 1985 Laender elections in North Rhine Westphalia, where a 9 per cent vote achieved in local elections late in 1984 melted almost immediately to 4.6 per cent the following spring. The 'realos' took their cue from such events and became more insistent on both policies and political conduct designed to consolidate such capricious support rather than alienating it.

In 1986, Die Grunen went even further down the pragmatic road. A move to further refine or sanitise party policy with the ballot box in mind, saw the adoption of the *Umbau* or Reconstruction programme consisting of feasible, properly costed measures rather than utopian visions.[44] This merely confirmed the 'fundis' suspicions that the 'realos' were more concerned to convince the wider public of their political maturity and reassure their potential electorate of the feasibility of this programme within current German economic conditions, than they were to pursue a full blooded and confrontationist alternative programme. The *Umbau* programme included practical 'trade-offs' between pollution controls, public ownership and Green taxes. These were not to be imposed immediately but more feasibly over a four or five year period. The adoption of this programme confirmed the 'realos' growing ascendancy in the party's national fora. The 'realos' drew further encouragement for their incremental and policy specific approach from the fact that the political and industrial establishment[45] had now begun to take the environment seriously, and to address ecological issues head on. All of the major parties proposed models of eco-auditing and eco-management which owed much to Die Grunen's imaginative and innovative programme. The most notable testament to the impact of this ecological osmosis on the political establishment came in April 1989. The federal Chancellor, Helmut Kohl, proposed in a speech in the Bundestag, the enshrining of environmental protection in the Federal Constitution. As the 'realos' saw it, sensible politics had begun to pay dividends. The 'old' parties had been obliged to respond to their initiatives. Kohl's attempt to syphon off growing electoral support from the Greens by setting up a Federal Environment Ministry in the aftermath of Chernobyl was a good case in point here. Further measures were also announced to increase the safeguards against chemical and nuclear accidents, encouraging the use of lead free petrol for new motor cars, as well as a pro-active approach by Germany in the EC's Council of Ministers to encourage the moves towards a new (5th) Action programme. As well as the EC wide installation of pollution reducing converters on all EC manufactured cars by the mid nineties. As the national issue agenda began to incorporate a Green dimension, however, the tensions within Die Grunen over the party's response to these concessions came to a head.

Some elements on both sides of Die Grunen's ideological divide took comfort from the fact that creative tension over policy and strategy was precisely what demarcated the party from its conventional rivals. This accommodation was facilitated, too, by an implicit acknowledgement on every side of their opponents' commitment to an entirely new politics. In spite of the 'realo's' acceptance of a parliamentary role, their Bundestag members continued to show ambivalence towards 'normal' politics. On the one hand, the Bundestag was regarded positively as a visible platform in which to advertise the virtues of alternative politics. Green parliamentarians proved as adept at using parliamentary procedures for tactical purposes as the members of other parties.[46] At the same time, there were residual doubts about the 'traps' of bourgeois politics. The Greens tried to square this awkward circle by implementing safeguards drawn from the *Basisdemokratie* principle, designed to ensure that the party remained open and democratic at every level. For instance, its leaders were obliged to regularly submit to a gauntlet of party boards and congresses. This bottom-up model of conducting party decision making continued to provide the 'fundis' with a firm political platform, even while they were in a minority in the party. These arrangements ensured that the new cadre of parliamentary 'leaders' from whichever faction did not lose sight of their dependence on the membership's will, freely expressed in the party's openly democratic assemblies. They likewise reinforced the prevailing ethos that political office was always a conditional appointment - one held in trust as a mandate from the rank and file. And that decision-makers, not least parliamentary representatives and party office holders at whatever level, should always be held accountable, and could indeed be recalled from office under the equally radical principle of rotation. These ideas about the exercise of power in the party and the purpose of holding political office at whatever level as a form of trusteeship and not as a matter of personal property were, at least in these formative stages of party development, the prevailing mood of the party per se across all of its factions. This radical bent initially provided the new party with the ideological glue to counter its centripetal tendencies to fall out over programmatic and other matters. From the outset, all sides of the party stood by a broad commitment to implement a new style of party democracy. They saw this as a critical yardstick demarcating the Greens as a radical movement-party from the 'ossified' establishment parties. Even the most pragmatic members of the 'realo' faction remained amenable at this stage to this principled argument. For the time being at least, the professionalisation of party politics was to be kept at bay.[47] But events were to put this consensus under increasing strain.

(iii) **Political developments**

The combination of a broad ecological commitment, continuing wariness of the seductions of conventional politics, and an abiding preference for democratic structures that maximised accountability by office holders to party members, permitted the ideological divisions within the party to at least be accommodated within a coherent party framework, if not actually reconciled. At the same time, as the party consolidated its organisation, these democratic national structures provided the very arenas in which such ideological confrontations could be played out, made visible and gain in intensity. At best, a kind of uneasy truce prevailed based on an awareness of the deep differences between the new and old politics. For the time being, this enabled the party to close ranks to a degree when national or European elections had to be fought. Moreover, the relative success of these campaigns, in turn, enabled Die Grunen over a relatively brief duration, to open up a discernible political space for ecological politics in Germany. At the same time, the full impact of this new political movement was reduced by the party's failure to seriously address the questions of political self discipline and even of political orientation that were beginning to widen the factional rifts in the party's organisational and ideological fabric. Sara Parkin, a pragmatic British Green whose sympathies were clearly with the 'realos' identified, as she observed these developments during 1987-88, the deep animus that confronted all Green parties. She noted the same flaw in the radical model of party democracy that the German 'realos' - indeed, Green pragmatists everywhere, who had begun to enjoy even a modest degree of political success - had started to heed. As Parkin saw this quandary, "many of the difficulties encountered by the German Green party have been impossible to resolve because the structures and the framework for handling conflict are missing. Not all conflict can necessarily be channelled constructively, but most organisations require at least a few damage limitation mechanisms to survive serious differences of opinion or abuses of power within them.... Until they do face up to their organisational problems it is not likely that Die Grunen will be able to resolve their present political predicament".[48]

The events that surrounded the unexpected and rapid reunification of Germany between 1989 and 1990, and threatened Die Grunen's existence as a major force in national politics, forced the Green party to face up to these organisational constraints. In the process of making these adjustments, the prevailing if uneasy intra party consensus came under severe strain. Impelled by their electoral achievements, the Greens had begun to move, however tentatively, away from their deep distrust of 'normal' politics and along a realist trajectory. Or rather, the party's parliamentary wing became more favourable to such an approach. The real breaking point here came as electoral success at every level forced the party to confront some unpalatable choices. A combination of relatively successful local coalitions and a slump in the fortunes of the CDU/FDP government in the national opinion polls tested the marriage of convenience between 'realos' and 'fundis' to what turned out to be breaking point.

The 'realos', who largely dominated the Green parliamentary groups at both the Bundestag and Laender levels, became frustrated by the constant need to refer even relatively trivial decisions to the grass roots via the multiple channels of *Basisdemokratie*. Many Green parliamentarians quite simply were impatient with what they came to regard as an obsession with accountability - not to improve the quality of decisions but simply for its own sake. The 'fundis', with their power base in the local and regional party executives, for their part insisted on such a mandate. As such, opposition became obscurantist. It assumed an obligatory status as an end in itself. The outcome in policy terms was more often than not chaotic and merely harmed the party's public image. Petra Kelly, a Green whose radical credentials were beyond reproach, captured the growing weariness of those party members for whom Green politics was primarily a vehicle for effective politics and genuine change, rather than merely a ritualistic oppositionalism, when she condemned those Greens who declared war within their own party and worse, who "sometimes .... create an artificial struggle that does not even exist".[49]

Anxious to capitalise on an opportunity to increase the Greens' impact on national policy making, the pragmatists became convinced of the parallel requirement of reassuring the SPD - the only likely coalition partner for the Greens - that they could do business with Die Grunen rather than their erstwhile coalition partners, the Free Democrats (FDP).[50] Vogel, the current SPD leader, had already gone on record as portraying the Greens as an awkward and unreliable coalitional prospect in national government.[51] The 'realos' faction in Die Grunen's leadership met this objection by toning down the level of their policy demands. While they continued to insist on large defence cutbacks as a condition for partnership, they also made it clear that they would compromise their unrealistic demand for West Germany's withdrawal from NATO.[52] What is clear from this emergent strategy is that the Green party's pragmatists had become convinced that Die Grunen could supplant the FDP as the natural 'half' party in the German party system.[53] In order to fulfil this ambition the 'realos' became convinced that they had to consolidate, and if possible to widen, their electoral base, by altering the electorate's perceptions of the Greens. Knapp and those who shared this ambition, believed that the Greens particularly needed to win a far greater share of the young, conscionable middle class professional vote which had become the fount of leading political opinion in German society.[54] In these circumstances, battle was now firmly joined for the soul of the new party.

The rising conflict between the two factions eventually spilled over in March 1989 at the party's Duisberg congress. The background to this watershed congress was a period of debilitating and much publicised infighting amongst prominent figures from both factions, which led to an exodus of members. The spectacle of civil war touched the public mind and undoubtedly damaged the party. The moderates pressed on regardless by calling for the party to choose a clear path. The 'realos' prevailed inasmuch as they obliged the party at Duisberg to at least face the need to confront the endemic divisions within the party over its political orientation. They persuaded the party to face up to what had become a slowly unfolding and festering débâcle. The 'fundis', who had by and large retained control of the party machine, were heavily censured here by their 'realo' critics, and chose to resign in ideological high dudgeon. They subsequently failed to win back any seats in the new executive elections. The balance of power in the party began to move here perceptibly if not yet conclusively towards the 'realos'. At the same time, Duisberg was a setback for the 'fundis' rather than a complete rout. This congress marked out the battle lines for the final confrontation that was to come, but for which neither side yet seemed quite ready. The party delegates papered over clearly discernible ideological fissures, settling instead for a tolerance of factional differences even as the 'realos' parliamentary leaders moved into the ascendancy in party affairs. This marked but by no means decisive shift towards the 'realos' was further reinforced by events on the ground. After protracted negotiations, the SPD and the Green Alternative List in Berlin agreed a 21 point coalition programme. In exchange for their support, the GAL secured 3 of the 13 cabinet posts in the city's government. A similar arrangement was negotiated in Frankfurt. On the national level, however, it seemed as if the Greens' reluctance to settle their festering differences would cost them dear. Not least because the country's issue agenda was changing in a direction that the Greens, with their endemic radicalism, seemed unable to address.

The dramatic events that unfolded in post unification Germany, and the heavy losses incurred by the Greens in the first all German elections in 1990 proved to be the final straw for this uneasy truce. Many 'fundis' quit the party in the tense aftermath of the reunification process. This exodus from leading positions in the party came too late to save the Greens from an electoral rout in those post unification elections. The demise of the Greens in the Bundestag was quite unexpected. In the 1987 Federal elections the party had polled a respectable 8.3 per cent of the national vote, which again dented SPD support in what it had come to regard as its 'natural' constituency amongst the young, better educated and new middle class. They had followed up this modest success with a steady 8.4 per cent in the 1989 European poll (securing 8 Euro seats). By 1990 the Greens had some 7,000 elected representatives at every level of German government from the Bundestag to 11 of the Landtage - the highest proportion of representatives to members of any current German political party. The party seemed well set to replace the FDP as the third force in German politics and, with that, to establish itself as the country's national coalition broker. In the event, a combination of factional strife and the seachange in German politics that followed the collapse of the DDR regime in the eastern part of Germany, conspired to halt this electoral upturn in its tracks.[55]

The party's new moderate image was further damaged by a series of events which damaged the Greens as the national mood moved discernibly to the right. The sudden collapse of the SPD-GAL coalition in Berlin in November 1990, when the local Greens withdrew after the forced eviction of militant squatters from tenements led to 3 days of much publicised violence, and the use of Molotov cocktails by militant activists associated in the public mind with the Greens. It took some 4,000 policemen to keep public order and this notwithstanding, led to some of the worst scenes of street violence seen in Germany for over a decade. As if to confront the public mood rather than to mollify it, the fundis expressed a preference for cooperating with the discredited if reformed former East German Communist Party. A similar lack of political tact amounting, as the 'realos' saw it, to a political death wish, surrounded the militant Greens' extravagant gesture of printing and distributing leaflets calling on Allied troops to desert rather than fight in the Gulf War. This act put the party before the German courts. Whatever the moral probity of such a position, it was clearly out of step with the public mood and was hardly conducive to the sensible strategy of winning support from those voters necessary to push the party over the electoral threshold, in circumstances already stacked against a party with such a radical persona.

Not all of the blame for the 1991 defeat can be laid at the door of the 'fundis'. The times were out of joint for the party in another, more damning, sense. The party's refusal to endorse the nationalistic mood that surrounded Unification counted heavily against it. The Greens' staid and cautious approach here stood in marked contrast to the euphoria of other parties on this, the most critical issue of these elections. The receding tide of Green electoral fortunes was already becoming clear from results in Laender elections. In Saarland, for instance, in January 1990, the Greens had polled a mere 2.7 per cent - admittedly not one of their most promising regions (they had only polled 2.5 per cent in 1985, winning no seats on either occasion). In the Lower Saxony poll of May of 1990 - supposedly a much better prospect - the Green vote fell markedly, from 7.1 per cent in 1986 to 5.5 per cent, with a corresponding drop in its Landtag seats from 11 to 8. Only in North Rhine Westphalia did the Green vote rise fractionally, from 4.6 per cent in 1985 to 5 per cent, a performance which actually increased their seats tally to 12. These were hardly signs, in the run up to the country's most important postwar elections, of the Greens holding their own, let alone of the electoral breakthrough they had hoped for.[56] The situation of Die Grunen's East German sister party stood in marked contrast to this demise. Bundnis, after a poor showing in the preliminary parliamentary elections held in East Germany in March 1990, actually took a promising 6.9 per cent in the state elections to the new Laender there later in that year and seemed on course to make a showing in the first all German elections.

The costs of unification for Die Grunen's forward momentum were such that they require some explanation. Although the 'realos' did eventually manage to swing the party conditionally behind the reunification project, on the radical grounds that it at least offered the prospect of negotiating a much more democratic Constitution than the 1949 Basic Law, few neutral observers were really convinced of the party's genuine enthusiasm for the "all-German" project. Die Grunen's initial preference was for a confederation of two independent German states and its initial condemnation of reunification as an 'Anschluss' won little support in a country carried away on a tide of national fervour. Instead, the unification dilemma merely opened up the festering wounds of the 'realo-fundi' schism and threatened to alienate some of the party's pragmatists. Ralph Foeks, a prominent 'realo' activist, in an open letter to the party's leaders, accused them of fostering a fatal current of "anti-nationalism" - a stance which preferred to perpetuate the artificial division of the country in order to unfairly saddle a new German generation with an undeserved guilt about the Nazi era.[57] He saw this situation as a lost opportunity; the failure to use an unprecedented and historic opportunity to positively encourage radical change in the national constitutional compact, away from the oligarchical 'old' politics, and towards something altogether more progressive. The unification issue thus

68

overlaid older, deeper divisions and finally brought to a head the animus over the party's dispositions to the political system that had been working through the party since its formation as a national political party.

When the newly united Germany went to the polls, in December 1990, the political portents for the Greens were far from encouraging. The signs had been there since the fall of the Berlin wall, that a mix of internal and external factors had sapped the party's political vitality and stemmed its electoral momentum. The party's electoral campaign itself, not least its determination to campaign primarily on ecological issues, was lacklustre and clearly out of touch with the prevailing national mood.[58] Nevertheless, not even the pundits, and still fewer activists, were prepared for the scale of the Greens' defeat. In the Western part of the new country the Greens were swept aside. Polling some 4.8 per cent of the total national vote they failed, for the first time in a national election since 1983, to win any Bundestag seats. It was indicative of the overall national swing to the right, that the Greens lost some 600,000 of their former voters to the SPD - especially amongst the vitally important constituency of young and student voters in the University towns. Whereas the SPD for its part ceded a critical part of its usual blue collar support to parties even further to the right.[59] The Greens were further depleted by the loss of their more fluid 'protest' support to other new parties such as the reformed ex communist PDS and the militant senior citizens movement, the 'Grey Panthers'. At the same time, the much smaller and far less coordinated eastern Greens - a motley of civil rights, citizens movements, ecologist and assorted radical groups, of which a prominent East German activist, Jens Reich, had disarmingly observed, "actually, we don't really fit together at all" - did markedly better with their list.[60] Regardless of their lack of ideological cohesion, Bundnis did benefit from a degree of organisational focus developed during its opposition to the authoritarian Communist state. Bundnis was also able to draw on an underlying opposition to the hugely damaged environmental legacy of the Communists' industrial policy.[61] Trading on their courageous opposition to the deposed dictatorship, 'Bundnis 90', with the support of an independent women's movement (UFV), passed the electoral threshold, and with 6.1 per cent of the eastern vote won 8 seats in the enlarged 662 seat Bundestag.[62] The decision of Die Grunen to permit Bundnis to stand on its own rather than as a minor element in a larger, unified Green party dominated by its western elements, at least for this critical election, cost the Greens their place in the Bundestag. The figures speak for themselves here. A combined all German Green ticket would have passed the electoral threshold and yielded 26 Bundestag seats.

Die Grunen's response to their defeat was a mix of serious reappraisal and mutual recrimination between its factions. At one level, the party used the revival of German nationalism as a convenient scapegoat for their defeat. One apologist in this vein typified the party's remarkable complacency over the cause of its defeat. Lippelt sought to shift the blame onto mere circumstances, arguing that "it was not our issue, Die Grunen is an internationally minded party, a party of the twentieth century, and its members are largely anti-nationalists. We thought the unification of Europe as important as the unity of Germany and that Europe would be better off with two democratic Germanies, than with one unified one. We therefore went into the election campaign with the slogan: 'They all are speaking about the nation, we are speaking about the weather', and we spoke about the depletion of the ozone layer. We clearly misjudged the issue badly".[63] Even the 'realos' seemed disposed to complacency, ignoring the fact that any radical party wishing to consolidate its place in national politics cannot wilfully ignore the present needs and concerns of the electorate. 'Realos' and 'fundis' alike indulged this complacency by attributing defeat to circumstances beyond the party's control. Christian Stroebele, a leading pragmatist, typified this approach by proclaiming that "we fell under the wheels of German unification, of 'Deutschland euphoria'". The 'fundis', for their part, used the defeat to pay off some old political scores, blaming the 'realos' for showing weakness in the face of rampant nationalism rather than resisting the unification juggernaut more firmly.

The party seemed ill equipped in the face of these internal divisions to cope with such a severe electoral reverse. The official press conference called to 'explain' the defeat descended into farce when no fewer than four spokespersons offered conflicting assessments of the outcome, spiced with mutual recriminations. The factionalism that had been, to a degree, held in check during the party's steady electoral momentum before 1990, now spilled over into bitter conflict. The prominent Hessen 'realo', Joschka Fischer, who subsequently emerged as the party's national leader, accused the 'fundis' of ignoring the "laws of political physics". Fischer attributed the defeat to "a home made débâcle" and used this claim to mount a campaign to put an end to the rotation principle.[64] The vagaries associated with the radical model of party democracy were held responsible, in this critique, for depriving the party of the indispensable electoral requirement of stable, and effective leadership. The 'realos', in short, called for a model party organisation not dissimilar, in its essential principles, from that employed by the conventional parties, albeit with some continuing safeguards for grass roots party democracy. They wanted, above all, a more disciplined party framework with proper leadership based on visible personalities; leaders who could speak unequivocally for the party and with whom the electorate could identify. The rotation principle was held to be responsible for a degree of turbulence that had deprived the party of some of its ablest and best respected national leaders, such as Petra Kelly and Antje Vollmer. Both had been obliged to vacate their parliamentary seats in mid-term just when the electorate and the mass media had become used to them. The prospect of half-time mandates had also, according to this account, both prevented the recruitment of good calibre individuals, and driven many excellent activists - Otto Schily for instance - out of the party.

The 1990 election result was held up by these 'realo' critics as an object lesson, handed out by an electorate confronted by the concerns associated with unification and all that this entailed for German futures. A critical public was wholly unimpressed by the incessant posturing, squabbling and the spectacle of political dilettantism that characterised Green politics, and which ensured that Die Grunen lacked the minimal organisational coherence of even the minor radical parties on the European Left.[65] In the 'realo' prospectus, the principal cause of the defeat - and the reason why the Greens remained so far out of touch with the popular mood - lay close to home. As Lippelt later acknowledged, "the problem (was) our tarnished image. We had to acknowledge that our concept of an alternative party had not stood the test. We had been aiming for a party without flexible power structures so as to offer all its members and all those engaging themselves even without formal membership, to participate in formulating and executing our policies - therefore the insistence on the principle of rotation, on the separation of party functions and parliamentary mandate. Prevented from undergoing the process of democratic selection they felt themselves obliged almost to establish secret headquarters where their leadership was never questioned. We had been aiming for a party that included society into its deliberations - open proceedings had been the slogan. And we had opened the doors of even the highest executive committees and of our parliamentary groups to the public. But we had to realise that we were no longer living in a democracy of the early Greek model. In our case, with all these high ambitions of building a party in accordance with the ideas of the second half of the twentieth century, party reform also meant to strike a balance between those ideas and the need for good performance".[66] This appraisal of where the Greens had gone wrong up to the 1990 defeat precisely captures the new realism, and the commitment to reform. It required not so much an abandonment of the new party model the Greens everywhere claimed as their novel contribution to the practice of modern politics, but rather its rationalisation. In essence, to accommodate the radical impetus with the requirements of practical politics - "not to .... fall in line with the structures of the old parties, but to find out exactly where we went wrong."[67]

The internal backlash which followed this critical election crystallised the tension and unease at the heart of the party.[68] The 'realos' seized the initiative and pressed for major organisational reforms. They were strengthened here by the success of the prominent Hesse 'realos' in the Laender election in January 1991 with 8.8 per cent of the poll, double its recent tally of 4 per cent in the general election. The Hessen pragmatists chose deliberately to fight this campaign - held soon after their national discomfiture - as an object lesson of what discipline and organisation could achieve. This was a gauntlet deliberately thrown down as a challenge to the anti-party zealots in Die Grunen's ranks. This success was followed in April by another good Laender result (6.4 per cent, up from the 5.9 per cent in the national elections) for the moderate Greens of the Rhineland-Palatinate. Significantly, the polling data here suggested that SPD supporters were again reverting to their former habit of ticket splitting to ensure local power sharing with the Greens. The final reckoning between the two factions that had riven the Green party from the outset was not long in coming. At the Neumunster national party Congress held in April 1991 - and designated by many neutral commentators and activists alike as a 'make or break' affair in this protracted confrontation - the 660 delegates were faced with an uncompromising demand from the 'realos' for major organisational changes that would better fit to the party to the tasks associated with the practices of 'normal' politics and government. The case for change was strengthened by the fact that some Laender parties where the 'realos' held sway had already reformed their party organisations along these lines. Many of these critics also let it be known that they were actively considering withdrawal, should their proposals be defeated. The campaign was led by pragmatists such as Antje Vollmer, representing 'the Awakening Group' - who had predicted the party's demise should it fail to make such changes - and by Hubert Kleinert.

The Neumunster conference was asked to consider a set of proposals, already endorsed by the party's executive which, if carried, would considerably alter the party's format into a professional, structured and even, by degrees, into a hierarchic organisation cast in the conventional party mold.[69] The central concern of the reformers was with the organisational changes necessary to improve all round efficiency and thereby to enhance the party's electability. There were a number of serious shortcomings here; two will suffice by way of illustration. The bi-annual rotation principle was discredited because it simply did not 'fit' a four year parliamentary term and inflicted immense disruption on the Green representatives in the Bundestag when the mid-term handover occurred. This two year mandate also undermined - as it was designed to do - the professionalisation of the party's political leadership. The disbursement of election and other party funding under Germany's generous party regime, further increased the tensions between the parliamentary group and grass roots party members. For these funds tended to ensconce the parliamentary group in its capacity as professional politicians much more than it helped the party organisation per se to pursue its radical, anti-party preferences. During election campaigns the use of this funding tended to confirm the control of the party's head office over the party machine - in the face of an endemic anti-party culture amongst many rank and file members. These militant dispositions were far less apparent in the ranks of the parliamentary party. And it is this group that tended to benefit most from state funding, using it to finance their electoral campaigns and to subsidise their parliamentary work. This dependence on state funding had not only drawn the parliamentary 'professionals' further away from the grass roots. It has also compromised the party's founding principle of *Basisdemokratie*. Poguntke has claimed that a marked degree of organisational 'drift' was underway here. He notes that "in 1988, the Green (parliamentary) faction could spend more money for its parliamentary work than the national (party) leadership could use for both running the party machine and supporting extra-parliamentary activities - and the latter had, after all, been envisaged to be the pivot on which the Green political game turned".[70]

The widening gap between the principle and practice of party politics under the conditions of advanced democracy - in essence, a tension between two competing styles of radical politics - finally forced the endemic conflict at the heart of Green politics to come to a head at Neumunster. The 'realo' driven programme at Neumunster proposed an end to the rotation principle and the imposition of time limits for party office holders and elected representatives alike. A new *Landerrat* (States Council) was instituted as the party's main decision making forum in between party congresses, to replace the unwieldy federal steering committee, and thereby to facilitate a more efficient organisation - especially at the federal executive level - as well as ensuring greater coherence between the party's distinct federal and Laender levels. The new procedures reduced the size of the executive (to 9 from 13 members) to better facilitate internal coordination; with the number of national spokesperson's similarly reduced from 3 to 2. These changes were recommended as an attempt to improve intra party democracy, even though the new Council was also accorded the prerogative of excluding the public from its internal deliberations. This unprecedented move sat uneasily with the party's much vaunted claim to democratic transparency, but it was eventually sanctioned on the grounds that such open access also permitted a generally hostile media the opportunity to distort deliberations; and equally, that publicity merely encouraged internal posturing. The Neumunster reforms thus institutionalised the de facto separation of the specific parliamentary and wider party functions, and went much further towards the conventional party model than Die Grunen had previously contemplated.

The objective behind such changes was a revision of the radical party model in the light of experience, rather than complete surrender to the dictates of the old politics model. In effect, the reform of failed procedures had a radical as much as a pragmatic impetus; the better to adapt to electoral and organisational exigencies, and thereby to maintain a radical presence at the centre of German national politics.[71] The revisionists did not see their proposals, in any sense, as the abandonment of a radical project with far reaching consequences for German futures. On the contrary, the 'realos' defined their task as one of principled pragmatism - the setting up of what Raschke has called a "professional framework party" - a disciplined, coherent yet flexible set of procedures, in order to provide a viable framework for the effective participation and interaction of those diverse social movements attracted to the Greens as the only vehicle for radical change in German politics.[72] The 'realos' faced some resistance to their reforms. The grass roots still preferred to disperse power rather than to concentrate it in the hands of a narrow party oligarchy. A proposal to allow simultaneous party office and a parliamentary mandate was narrowly defeated. Even so, many 'realo' dominated Laender parties had already taken steps to abolish this demarcation at state level. Above all, the aim here was to rescue the party from its present decline and reinstate it as an effective force in German electoral politics. One of its two spokespersons, Ludger

Volmer, elected at this Congress, said that, "we hope to consolidate the party in order .... to have a realistic chance of making a comeback in parliament in four years".[73]

These reforms were endorsed, in the main, by the Green's East German sister party. Although the Bundnis (Alliance) were already represented in the Bundestag, the party's influence there was modest and its impact on policy nominal. In order to consolidate a Green presence in the fluid post-unification political climate, to put pressure on government to clean up the heavily polluted east, as well as to strengthen parliamentary support for the state funded social programme, both Green parties approved the changes.[74] Bundnis were convinced of the need for a Green presence in the western Laender. Die Grunen's 'realos' rose to meet this challenge. Antje Vollmer canvassed an ecologically sound response to Germany's current problems, by proposing the establishment of a nationwide party dedicated to ecological civil rights, which she believed would smooth the awkward path of integration between the two Germanies. Not by indulging in the hubris of the mainstream parties, but instead by tackling head on the major structural problems involved in the project.[75] Another moderate, Christine Weische, who secured election under the new reform arrangements as one of the two national spokespersons, likewise recommended an imaginative but above all a practical approach to the immense difficulties confronting the newly united nation. Above all, Weische claimed, "on the ground at local and state level, we need practical politics not theorising".[76]

The first stage in the task of building a moderate Green party capable of bridging the divide between the two Germanies, was to carry the reform agenda in Die Grunen, the senior partner of the proposed Green coalition. Neumunster saw the successful launch of this project. The delegates there carried almost all of the proposed changes by the requisite two thirds majority - no mean political achievement in light of the party's deep divisions. Although the changes agreed at Neumunster were undoubtedly a significant turning point in the development of Die Grunen, it hardly amounted to a complete reversal of the party's radical commitment. An abiding suspicion, even on the pragmatic wing, of the dangers of unfettered leadership and elitist propensities was revealed by the defeat at Neumunster of proposed changes which would have ended the prohibition on national MPs concurrently holding office on the party's national executive. Moreover the executive elections here were by no means dominated by the 'realo' slate. Some leftist candidates also polled well and secured representation. Nevertheless, it is undoubtedly the case that Neumunster did amount to a major shift in the party's balance of power. The outcome of the Newmunster congress crystallised the 'realo-fundi' schism. After two days and more of intense and often bitter debate, Die Grunen embraced what amounted to a clear break with the past. Manon Tuckfield, a committed 'fundi' and member of the party's executive, attacked the ascendant reformers as elitist, pro-capitalist elements determined to hijack the party and transform it into its very antithesis - a technocratic, bourgeois party. Jutta Ditfurth, who had recently published an uncompromising pure Green tract, "Live Wild and Dangerously" hostile to any "cosy compromises" with the 'repressive' German state and social system, likewise warned of the threat posed by reformers determined to transform the Greens, as she saw it, into a shadow liberal party. Ditfurth advocated instead a view of politics as a permanent resistance - the continuing fight for what she called "concrete utopias".[77] She translated these utopian aspirations into campaigns, for example, against poverty and in favour of carfree cities.[78] In spite of such spirited resistance, Ditfurth and her supporters were obliged to acknowledge defeat once the controversial reform programme had been passed. She and her supporters quit the party for other parties more to their militant tastes, to the cry of "it's all over, it's no longer our party". Some joined the reformed Communist party (PDS). A core of some 200, led by Ditfurth, tried to reclaim ecologism for the 'fundis' by reviving the spontaneous anti-party model of a decade previously. They emerged as an extra-parliamentary opposition - the Ecological Left/ Alternative List - an anti-party outfit, but one whose members would at least be permitted to take part in parliamentary politics. The extent to which these exiled radicals were out of touch with events was revealed in the first Land election after Neumunster, in Hamburg in June 1991. An alternative list stood here against Hamburg's Greens (GAL) purged of their troublesome 'fundi' minority and polled barely 0.5 per cent against the official Greens' 7.2 per cent.

These changes, and the subsequent consolidation of a moderate and pragmatist approach as the core of German Green politics, has done much to revive the party's political fortunes. In the Land elections in Bremen (September 1991) the Greens took 11.4 per cent - enough to put them into coalition with the SPD and FDP. Likewise in Baden-Wurttemburg (April 1992), in an election where racism was on the agenda in the shape of the Republikaner Party, the Greens polled their best local vote to date of 9.5 per cent. This result provided a further testament of the Greens' new-found respectability. The CDU proposed preliminary coalition talks with the Greens, who in the end settled for its preferred option of negotiating a joint government with the SPD. The same pattern of modest progress and progressive moderation continued elsewhere. The Greens (also in April 1991) took 4.97 per cent in Schleswig-Holstein, double their 1988 result although insufficient in this unfavourable territory to yield any Landtag seats. In the Berlin elections of May 1992, on the other hand, the Greens surpassed all expectations and polled a commendable 13.3 per cent. This vote must, however, be put into its proper perspective. Much of this represented a protest against the established parties (the CDU vote fell sharply to 27.5 per cent) rather than a positive endorsement of the Greens in what soon became the less than euphoric aftermath of unification, with its immense economic costs to western Germans, and the equally disappointing decline in expectations amongst eastern voters.[79] Nevertheless, the Greens were much readier to seize their chances now than they would have been before the party's twin lurch towards pragmatism and moderation. By the end of 1992 the Greens had at least consolidated their electoral position at the local level, forming part of the governing coalitions in 4 of the 16 Laender - Lower Saxony, Hesse, Bremen and Brandenberg. The September 1993 Hamburg poll which yielded the Greens 13.5 per cent was clearly a reward for a party now firmly in the grip of 'realos' such as Krista Sager. The party was now deemed sufficiently 'safe' to attract large numbers of former SPD supporters, disgruntled both with that party's poor Bundestag performance and its weak leadership. This judgement was merely confirmed by the decision of the local SPD to ignore the expressed preferences of many of their own voters for a red-green government. It chose instead to govern with a faction of the CDU.

The principal outcome of this rapid comeback was to increase the speculation about a realignment of the German left, with a Green-SPD coalition as one possible outcome of the next national elections scheduled for 1994. The Greens gave this prospect serious consideration in the light of the SPD's failure, as the costs of reunification and recession continued to mount, to capitalise on the unpopularity of the conservative government. The omens at this stage seemed promising. While the Green's spokesperson, Ludger Volmer, continued to canvass what he saw as "a credible political line",[80] the SPD leader, Bjorn Engholm, writing in *Der Spiegel*, seemed ready to abandon his party's previous caution about dealing with the Greens. He floated the prospect of a multi party, SPD-FDP-DG coalition as the best available radical alternative to the government. The Greens, for their part, responded to the situation by addressing their organisational shortcomings. The decision of a joint party congress in Hanover in January 1993 to amalgamate the west and east German Greens into a single party was a natural consequence of the 1990 débâcle. The decision was overwhelmingly approved by delegates from both parties, although Bundnis 90 still had its own 'fundis' (the New Forum group), who continued to express reservations about surrendering a free wheeling movement for a rigid party structure. A joint commission representing both parties began its deliberations during 1992. The Bundnis minority (3,000 members compared to Die Grunen's 37,000) resisted any loss of their identity in a takeover and the new name - Bundnis 90/Die Grunen - was a testament to both their determination as well as to the tolerance of their western German colleagues. The inter-party commission accorded special recognition to the Bundnis identity in the new party charter. The easterners, for instance, may establish their own *Bürgerbeweging* (citizens movement) within the new party. As such, the new Greens could lay claim to be, as Joschka Fischer has put it, "the first truly pan German party". Moreover, these events were welcomed by the SPD's national manager, Karlheinz Blessing, as making a positive contribution to the realignment of the moderate German left and, thereby, of improving the prospects for "replacing the Kohl government".[81] A poll of all Green party members conducted in April 1993 ratified the decision to amalgamate by large majorities - 91.8 per cent of Die Grunen's and 85.7 per cent of Bundnis 90's membership voted in favour.[82] At a unity congress in Leipzig - the symbolic centre of the 1989 pro-democracy uprising in the DDR - delegates dedicated the new party to a "willingness to assume responsibility" and to "say yes to power".[83] This might have been a slogan but, in the light of Die Grunen's longstanding ambivalence about its place in normal party politics, it was a revealing one. It was noticeable, too, that this overt commitment to political pragmatism was broadly accepted without any of the drama or acrimony previously associated with strategic intra-party deliberations. Delegates displayed a similar restraint, and what many commentators applauded as a new "political maturity", when it came to electing its two co-chairpersons and postponing a potentially divisive debate on military intervention in Bosnia. The new Greens clearly relished their new moderate image. One of the party's new co-chairs, Ludger Volmer, recounted with some satisfaction and a barely disguised irony, that "some people are saying that this party congress has been rather dull. But I think we will also be able to overcome this crisis!"[84] The new Greens seemed to be safely launched on a moderate trajectory with the same clear goal, according to Marienne Birthler - an Alliance 90 member and one of the new party's leaders - that had exercised Die Grunen's 'realos' faction; that of replacing the FDP as Germany's third largest parliamentary force.[85]

These secure organisational foundations and a continuing preference for pragmatism have served the new party well. There have been promising signs of a Green revival, with some good electoral performances at Laender level. In Hesse, for instance, in March 1993, the Greens polled 11 per cent (compared to 9.1 per cent in 1989). This success needs to be qualified, even in an area which has always been relatively promising territory for the Greens. One cause of the Greens' success here - and for that of other 'minor' parties on both the extreme right and on the left - was a significant slump in the electoral support for the two main parties. Political commentators referred to this exodus of voters from the main parties as *parteienverdrossenheit* or 'party weariness'.[86] The Emnid political research Institute concluded from its polling data, that barely 1 in 11 of west Germans and 1 in 20 easterners remained "convinced voters".[87] The SPD vote - the most likely source of Green converts - fell dramatically from 44.8 per cent to 36.4 per cent, with the CDU (which lost votes to the far right Republican party) down to only 32 per cent. The Hesse result in 1993 reflected the widespread disorientation and disillusionment with the ability of the established parties to provide clear answers to the severe economic and social problems facing the new Germany, and for redefining its role in post Cold War Europe. A similar outcome was apparent in the mid term elections held in Hamburg, occasioned by a constitutional challenge because of electoral irregularities uncovered in 1991. The main parties again lost support to the political fringe. The CDU haemorrhaged over 10 per cent of its 1991 vote, and both it and the SPD recorded their worst postwar result in the city-state, with the FDP falling below the 5 per cent threshold. The Green list, on the other hand, recorded 14 per cent and took 19 seats. But the two ultra-right parties also totalled 8 per cent and an eclectic 'Instead Party' - formed only two months previously - took 6 per centre.[88] This mood of electoral disengagement was hardly ameliorated by revelations about corruption scandals in the mainstream parties. None of this necessarily amounted to an incipient seachange in German party politics. Electoral volatility on this scale in what are, after all, second order elections, could easily be discounted as a transient phenomenon.[89]

We should certainly be wary of drawing any far-reaching conclusions about the prospects for political realignment from the current electoral flux.[90] It is far from clear whether, or how far, the current mood of instability might assist the Greens to achieve their goal of exerting a significant leverage on future coalition making. Not least because their preferred partners, the SPD, seem unable to overcome their own identity crisis, let alone to fully capitalise on voter's doubts about the CDU. National opinion surveys conducted in the early part of 1993, indicated that some 40 per cent of those polled preferred neither Kohl nor Engholm as Chancellor.[91] Moreover, the beneficiaries of this medium term electoral discontent with the main parties are by no means progressive parties such as the Greens. The rise of the ultra nationalists and the far right is testament to an altogether more negative mood. The prospects for a realigned left including the Greens are far from promising in these circumstances. The prevailing cynicism, as well as an equally widespread concern to protect the hard won, individual material benefits associated with postwar prosperity, was a notable feature of recent electoral discontents and could just as easily provoke a political backlash against progressive politics as to encourage it. These rising anxieties might undermine the level of tolerance for post material and ecological concerns that has been such a feature of recent German political culture. The ramifications of this for the Greens are by no means entirely encouraging. The Green vote may not in these circumstances be readily consolidated into new patterns of electoral partisanship. Instead of breaking the mould of 'normal' politics the party may have to settle for an altogether more modest status; that of a temporary or occasional vehicle for residual protest. The current electoral climate of volatility hardly provides the most secure foundation for the pursuit of a radical programme, let alone of third party status.

The Greens are aware of these constraints, and they have responded positively to them. In line with their pragmatic approach to party strategy, the reformed party has treated electoral fluidity as an opportunity rather than as a threat. And with good reason. For they are as likely, taking the broader view, to be as much its beneficiaries over the duration as any other party. Joschka Fischer was quick to seize on the Hesse result in 1993, not only as a vindication of the Greens' cautious line on unification, but also a portent of a more popular discontent to come, which the party could draw on. The Greens now feel equipped to respond to these widespread concerns and channel them into building a wider support base. There was certainly a debate within the Green party about the significance of these developments and the long term prospects for political change. Optimists amongst the party's strategists remained convinced of the opportunity for a far-reaching shift in German politics and even beyond. They saw in the rising discontents of publics across Europe, the possibility of confirming the place of ecologism at the issue-centre of post Cold War European politics. It was precisely with these ambitions in mind that Ralf Foeks, the Green party's environment minister in Bremen claimed that: "We experience in Europe, from Germany to Italy and France, tremors in the political system that are much greater than any previous ups and downs. We have the historic chance of filling the resulting political vacuum with a thorough redefinition of policies in all areas".[92]

The Greens' strategic response to what its current leadership regards as a genuine opportunity opening up in the German polity after reunification, has been to leave all of its options open. Not least, in the light of the FDP's collapse in the Hamburg city state elections in September 1993 - a result which not only provoked debate within the CDU that the FDP was a 'spent force', but caused some conservative strategists to voice the once 'unthinkable' post 1994 electoral option of a CDU-Green alliance. Results elsewhere reinforced this tendency to anticipate a new politics. The outcome of the state elections in Brandenburg in December 1993 saw the combination of a poor CDU result and a Green vote of 6.3 per cent (ahead of the FDP on 5.4 per cent).[93] The Greens also polled well in Schleswig-Holstein in March 1994, increasing their vote by 4.3 per cent to 10.3 per cent overall. And in the eastern state of Saxony-Anhalt, the SPD leader Reinhard Höppner opted to form a coalition with the Greens rather than with either the CDU or the reformed Communists (PDS).[94] On the back of these results, the Greens co-spokesman, Ludger Volmer, remained convinced that the Greens were laying the electoral foundations for a red-green coalition with the SPD.[95] The Greens certainly continued to regard the SPD as the more congenial partner. The outcome of the March 1994 Land elections in Lower Saxony, which saw the re-election of an SPD administration there, sent out a mixed message on that score. Although the SPD's options remained limited, they remained coy about the coalitional prospect. The then leader of the SPD, Rudolf Scharping, was reluctant to admit to his party's endemic minority status and preferred instead to talk up its place in the mainstream of German politics rather than surrendering to the idea of the SPD as merely the keystone of a coalition of minority interests. As he put it, "rainbows are very pretty but rainbow coalitions simply cannot take the strain. Only a party with a strong centre has the strength and independence to face new questions and new developments, to protect small groups and minorities and take up their ideas".[96]

This reticence was born out by events on the ground. In spite of an increase in the Green vote in Saxony from 5.5 per cent in 1990 to 7.3 per cent, the fall in the CDU vote to 36 per cent - its worst result in the state for thirty five years[97] - caused the local SPD to break away from its Green coalitional partners.[98] The claim by the state premier, that "a majority is always better than a coalition",[99] underlined the SPD's preference to govern alone, at whatever level. Although this has become much less of an option after the slump in SPD support during the 1994 elections at every level, and over the years since then, there are few positive signs that there is any widespread support in SPD ranks for a permanent realignment on the radical side of German politics. Events do however have their own way of shaping political outcomes. The less than steady support for the CDU before the 1994 federal election, and the collapse in the FDP's vote, does suggest that the mood of volatility that overshadows German politics is here to stay, at least for the foreseeable future. The Greens have been the main beneficiaries of the current electoral unpredictability. A combination of a collapse in confidence in the liberal FDP and a steady increase in Green support has confirmed their position as Germany's third party. A crisis of political identity within the SPD, and amongst some of its erstwhile electorate, in common with most other democratic socialist parties in western Europe, makes the outcome even more difficult to predict. These developments have opened up German party politics to at least the prospect of far-reaching changes. This situation may, at some future juncture, provide the Greens with an opportunity to play the role enjoyed to date by the FDP, and replace it as the coalitional broker of German politics. This has yet to happen, but the recent shift means that the Greens have at least built this goal into their strategic armoury.[100]

The strategy meeting held in Leipzig in 1993 confirmed the party's pragmatic orientation. The delegates decided that tactical flexibility would best equip the party to maximise its prospective influence, and thus enable it to negotiate from strength, should the erosion of support for the principal parties further change the electoral calculus and open up the coalition prospect. The message conveyed there by Fischer, now the de facto party leader, underlined a central plank in the Greens' current strategy; that "Germany is changing and we must become the decisive factor in this change". At the same time, ambition here may just as easily outreach concrete achievements. For the Greens are no more surely in control of these events than any other political party. They, too, continue to be faced with some awkward dilemmas and difficult choices. The 'fundis' may have quit the party in a fit of ideological pique but a persistent debate over strategy continues to present the party with a quandary familiar to every radical party. The need both to change in order to accommodate present realities, and at the same time to retain its radical credentials with the post-materialist constituency that continues to provide the party with its bedrock support remains a persistent dilemma. The Greens may have embarked on a pragmatic strategy, concerned to maximise electoral support so as to increase its leverage on governance. But this does not, per se, make the party ideologically rudderless or simply opportunistic. Nor has the exodus of hardline fundamentalists, which undoubtedly eased the resistance to compromise and increased the taste for accommodation with other parties, transformed the Greens into a carbon copy of the 'unprincipled' vote maximising parties the Greens came into being to oppose. Political maturity and tactical shrewdness should not be equated here with the embrace of unprincipled politics. The party has tried hard to convince both the electorate at large and the SPD, its potential coalition partners, that it has changed. At the same time it has also retained its self image and its appeal to its bedrock support, as a real force for radical social and ecological change. The debate over the 'meaning of greening' continues, albeit in more disciplined tones, in a party whose grass roots remains alert and mobilised, and whose leadership remains committed to finding a proper balance between sound ecological principles and the pursuit of practical politics. There have been several examples of friction over precisely this issue in recent years. In July 1993, the Greens withdrew from all party talks on the one symbolic issue which is still capable of tapping into the movement's most radical inclinations - the future of Germany's nuclear energy programme. The Greens, for all of their policy shifts and accommodations, refuse to compromise on this bedrock principle - whilst they justified their non cooperation here on the altogether pragmatic grounds of resisting what they saw as the extremism and, in the post Cold War world, the out-datedness of their opponents' views on the related issue of nuclear weapons. Although the Greens remain committed to the closure of all nuclear plants, they exited these discussions less in a fit of ideological pique, than on the grounds that the pro nuclear parties and the powerful nuclear lobby were simply not prepared to compromise with them. The issue continues to reverberate in German politics, permitting the Greens to mobilise widespread opposition to the production of energy and related questions such as the disposal of nuclear waste.[101]

The Greens face another persistent dilemma as between the politics of principle or pragmatism over militarism, related as this is to the equally daunting questions of German national identity and regional purpose in post Cold War Europe. The party has continued to canvass in their election manifestos and policy statements, the abolition of the *Bundeswehr* (armed forces), as well as Germany's withdrawal from, and the winding up of, the NATO arrangements and their replacement by a vague proposal for a pan European security arrangement. The party's *Landerrat* endorsed, in October 1993, a peacekeeping role for German troops in the former Yugoslavia, with the eastern Greens instrumental in ensuring the vote in favour - only to face a grass roots revolt and a specially convened party congress that overwhelmingly restored the anti-military position.[102] This continuing commitment to a radical option that puts considerable distance between the party and its most likely partners amongst the mainstream parties places real obstacles in the way of the Green's participation in any national coalition or governing arrangement with the SPD for the foreseeable future[103] - although not necessarily an insuperable one.[104] Careful political management here by the leadership has seen movement and a degree of compromise, even on this issue. Fischer issued a policy discussion paper in 1995 which recommended that the party abandon its blanket opposition to military intervention, to enable the Greens to support Germany's participation in peacekeeping in Bosnia.[105] The statement addressed head on the underlying issue of the party's credibility, both with the electorate and with their political allies in the SPD. It noted that the party was facing an "elementary conflict of fundamental values" that must be resolved "if it is not to come to pieces at its very heart".[106] This policy shift was recommended to the party as being entirely consistent with the party's commitment to higher moral endeavours. It argued that the former stance of unmitigated pacifism and anti-militarism was a relic of the Cold War; that altogether new responses were now required to deal with new dangers - not least the entirely novel regional problem of policing the continent against the threat from the new Nazis who cared nothing for international rules, human rights or the non-violent mediation of territorial disputes. An endorsement by the Greens of a German role in regional, and indeed 'out of area' peacekeeping, has been steadily canvassed by the leadership - with some tangible success - as an element of genuine 'Europeanism' indispensable in the post Cold War milieu. More cynical commentators have detected in these recent shifts much less evidence of a seachange in ideas amounting to a new version of pacifism, than of Fischer's tactical wish to placate continuing SPD doubts about its involvement with such a radical partner. Tactical considerations were certainly one element in this equation. The Green MP, Albert Schmidt, saw in these moves an attempt "to shape policies which he (Fischer) can live with were he to become a future foreign minister in a coalition government".[107] But these overtures did not mean that the Greens' leadership had abandoned any attempt to reconcile principles with pragmatism. Neither Fischer nor his supporters saw these goals as mutually incompatible.

Not that this has made the issue any easier to deal with. So far, the Green party has showed signs of movement on this issue, without altogether resolving the conflicting positions of the various factions over the issue. The Greens are hardly more exercised by this matter than other German parties. The government's decision to contribute forces to the allies' Rapid Reaction Force[108] raised old spectres and confronted postwar sensibilities in other parties too, not least the SPD, about playing the sort of military role in international security commensurate with the country's economic weight. Uncertainties continue to abound over this issue,[109] but especially for the Greens, with their particular ideological roots in pacifism. As such, the issue retains its potential to divide the movement. So much so that a special congress had to be called in Bremen to unite the party around a common position. The pacifists eventually won the argument here, against the advice of the parliamentary leadership. Even on this issue, there were encouraging signs of the party's new-found political maturity. For one thing, the debate in Bremen was business like and orderly rather than chaotic. And the party vote there at least marked a clear movement towards the official position - 38 per cent of delegates supported the motion for deployment compared to less than 10 per cent when the issue was first broached in 1993 - which suggests that the issue may be far from closed. Moreover, although a subsidiary motion demanded that the parliamentary party oppose the government's offer to send 4,000 troops to join the UN peacekeeping mission in Bosnia, the fact that a number of Green MPs approved this deployment provided yet more concrete evidence of the closing of the gap between the Greens and the other parties on this critical issue. The moderation theme was underlined at the party's 1994 annual congress in Munich, where the delegates obligingly endorsed, with a minumum of fuss, a reform package proposed by the leadership. Alongside a continued proposal to wind up NATO and to replace it with a non military security system, there were the usual proposals for various energy taxes - which included an immediate 20 per cent rise in fuel duty to reduce road congestion. The delegates displayed unprecedented realism, however, by approving a statement by Reinhard Butikofer, a party budget expert, that neither public expenditure nor the level of the public sector deficit were limitless.[110]

(iv)   Prospects for political change

The political moderation practised by the Greens certainly has not led yet to any significant realignment in German party politics, even if it has contributed to the process of dealignment that must precede it. The present political setup is, nevertheless, some way removed from the altogether more stable situation that prevailed in the early years of the Federal Republic, when the two main parties - the so-called 'Modell-Deutschland' - enjoyed a virtual monopoly of the electorate. The evidence of the two major elections held in 1994 for the European and Federal Parliaments, and of recent Landtage elections, suggests that a more fluid situation prevails in the balance of party political forces than at any time since 1945. There has been an acceleration of those trends already apparent in the 1990 election and its aftermath; of a persistent identity crisis and rather more mundane problems over leadership qualities and policy in the SPD; and of a general disillusionment with mainstream party politics once the shortlived euphoria of unification became overshadowed by immense and costly structural complications. The revival in support for the Greens and the parallel decline in the FDP vote alongside the presence in an increasingly complex electoral jigsaw of the PDS - a regional party based in the east (an eastern equivalent of the Bavarian CSU) and drawing on the residual electorate of the former SED (Communist Party) but capable of gathering a significant protest vote which limited the electoral prospects there of every other national party from the CDU to the Greens - underlines the flux of contemporary party politics in Germany.

This trend was crystallised in the European poll of 1994 and confirmed in the federal elections held later that year. A further slump in the vote of both the SPD (at 32.2 per cent, down from 37.3 per cent in 1989) and the FDP (who fell below the 5 per cent threshold and lost their Strasbourg seats) was matched by only a modest increase for the CDU/CSU partnership, which had been saddled since the euphoria of 1990 with a twin electoral liability; the imposition of significantly higher taxation on the western Germans to cover the costs of transfer payments for structural modernisation in the east and currency equivalence; and an equally damaging image amongst voters in the east of failing to meet their exaggerated expectations of achieving a quick and painless prosperity.[111] The Greens (at 10.1 per cent and with 8 Euro-seats), were the only party to show any degree of success in these elections. This owed much less to the appeal of ecologism than it did, at a time of considerable post-Maastricht uncertainty over economic integration and the threat to the D-mark from prospective monetary union, to their call for a shift away from the prevailing pattern of economic integration and greater efforts to bring about political integration, in order to counter the rise of atavistic nationalism in Germany and elsewhere. The success of the PDS in these elections in the eastern constituencies was largely a matter of its negative impact on the SPD. In spite of being marginalised in the eastern Laender the PDS took enough votes from the SPD to hurt them there. The emergence of the PDS - even as a regional party of relatively minor significance - impacted indirectly on the Greens by increasing their prospects for leverage in national politics. The PDS's presence further complicated an already complex electoral equation. One commentator graphically described them as "a huge boulder on the chessboard of possible ruling coalitions" in Bonn, around which the contenders for office had to negotiate.[112]

The European elections in Germany were a precursor of trends that were repeated in the federal elections later that year. Confident of re-entering the Bundestag, the Greens drew comfort from the electoral flux apparent in the European poll. They played up their new image as a moderate party aiming to replace the FDP as Germany's power broker. To this end they put forward a measured programme designed to appeal as much to the SPD in the event of a 'hung' Parliament as to any militant agenda. This included a call for industrial restructuring; changes in transport policy; the imposition of Green taxes (in place of rather than in addition to conventional income tax) to better reflect the ecological costs of production; measures and new technologies to encourage energy and other resource conservation; an increase in the price of energy, fuel and waste disposal; the now familiar radical achilles heel of army disbandment and withdrawal from NATO, to be replaced by a vaguely conceived pan European security system. At the same time, Fischer and his colleagues minimised dogma and reiterated that the programme's only non-negotiable elements were the demand for an end to nuclear energy, the introduction of speed limits on the overcrowded autobahns, and the elemental principle of eco-taxation.

This election, too, produced clear losers rather than obvious winners. The CDU won the largest vote of any single party, although this was two per cent down on its 1990 turnout. The SPD, already showing signs of the turmoil that would follow yet another defeat apparently snatched from the jaws of victory, hardly fared better and saw only a modest increase in its 1990 vote - itself a rock bottom performance even by that party's recent standards. And this after the most turbulent period in postwar German politics should, under the normal rules of adversarial party competition, have helped the Opposition to turn out a far from popular government. The FDP, who had begun to lose their radical vitality by participating as a junior coalition partner of both major parties,[113] also reaped its share of the electorate's disillusionment. They barely managed to limp across the 5 per cent electoral threshold. Moreover, they only managed this modest achievement by adopting a negative rather than positive strategy which included both an attack on the Greens and an attempt to expropriate some of their ecological credentials.[114] Once again, the principal beneficiaries were the Greens (7.3 per cent and 49 seats) - except in the east, where the PDS (4.4 per cent nationally, 19.8 per cent in its eastern heartland) gained 4 seats on their own account which entitled them to a further 26 seats on the 3 outright constituency wins or 5 per cent of the national vote threshold rule.[115]

There was some evidence in this outcome of at least a degree of flux, if not yet outright dealignment underway in the fabric of German politics.[116] Matthias Jung, head of the Forschungsgruppe Wahlen (The Mannheim Political Research Institute) detected a structural problem here rather than a merely tactical one, especially for the SPD, as the underlying electoral shifts of recent years indicated a weakening of both the ideological and confessional loyalties that have provided the main electoral cement of Germany's major parties. On the evidence so far the CDU, assisted to some extent by its role in government and the powerful incentive to realism this tends to induce, has coped rather better than the SPD with this sociological challenge to the patterning of cleavages that has sustained postwar German party politics.[117] The dominance of the mainstream parties has begun to unravel and small parties have increased their foothold. Should this trend continue, this is bound to have important repercussions for parliamentary tactics and the logic of coalitional formation alike. As things currently stand, the Greens are bound to figure in this new political equation. While they are yet to be involved in government negotiations at federal level, reaching this landmark, too, might only be a matter of time - a question of when rather than if. The Greens have benefited electorally as much from protracted SPD divisions accentuated by that party's ideological and leadership squabbles, and sharpened in turn by the tensions engendered by successive defeats in federal elections, as from any more positive perception of what they stand for. This may turn out to be a shallow foundation for more durable success. The Greens continue to provide a residual home for voters with very different preferences. Alongside an entrenched post-material constituency there are many disconcerted socialists, disillusioned liberals and the generally discontented, looking for a protest vehicle. This is in itself not the stuff of political realignment. Nevertheless, it may amount, if the mood continues, to the beginning of dealignment. The Greens have staked their claim to a place in national politics during less than propitious times for a radical party with their particular agenda. Indeed, Fischer's popularity ratings have frequently been higher than those even of Helmut Kohl. And although the Greens' own core vote is ageing - and is now middle aged and mostly prosperous - the fact that a new generation of German voters no longer shares the militancy and idealism of the previous generation, and exhibits many of the instrumental concerns with employment and the national identity issue of earlier generations, has helped the 'realos' to cement their control of the party. At the same time as offering a sufficiently progressive stance on many of the issues that exercise the present discontents of voters. As Renate Koecher, of the Allensbach polling institute sees the situation, "the Greens have changed because society has changed. The idea of a protest party is not as popular now as it was in the 1970s because people now favour harmony over conflict".[118]

None of these short term changes ensure that a seachange in politics is imminent. There are enough uncertainties here to leave in doubt the precise balance of any future left of centre coalition. The SPD would certainly provide such a government with its parliamentary anchor. Depending on the relative strength of the minor parties further to its left, and indeed that of the centre-right parties, the Greens are likely to be cast at best as a junior partner. Although, and depending on circumstances, no one could rule out the PDS - currently an outside player in the Bonn game in every sense - joining such a coalition, this is a less likely outcome than a Green presence in cabinet and would only be acceptable to the SPD, even under the radical leadership of Lafontaine, if the political equation demanded it. And only then if the PDS - with their roots in the barely reconstructed Marxism of the former DDR's

Communist Party (the SED) and their deep suspicion of the 'bourgeois' and 'imperialist' state that is, in their view, the unified Germany - were to show signs of the same sort of accommodation to 'normal' politics undertaken by the Greens over the past decade; a metamorphosis they have so far resisted. A measure of the PDS's distance, even from the present radical locus of German politics, is their condemnation of the Greens as merely another establishment party.[119] At the same time, we cannot discount the pull of electoral logic over ideology. Opportunity structures are a major influence on voters' perceptions of how they exercise their choices.[120] The second vote system employed in Germany encourages such a calculus, especially as partisan patterns weaken and voters take on a more instrumental, or at least a short term, view on exercising their democratic choice. The German system certainly suggests ways of imposing citizen preferences on the politicians. The second vote is important - and the potential determinant of outcomes in the conditions of increasing electoral volatility - because of its impact on the composition of the Bundestag. It becomes more important, too, in relation to the number of voters who realise the impact of tactical switches on the electoral outcome. The FDP used to be the main beneficiary of this tactical awareness, although this was minimised by the reservoirs of consistent partisan support for the two main class-based parties. More recently, however, the alternative and 'new' left parties have been the principal recipients - the Greens in the western part of Germany and the PDS in the east. There may even be the makings here of a future tactical voting strategy that belies the current mutual hostility between these two radical parties - a liaison that would have dramatic consequences for German politics. For these 'alternative' parties have as much in common as divides them - not least a rejection of NATO and deep unease at the prospect of German militarism; as well as sharing progressive social ideas on gender equality for instance. All of which might well serve as the foundations of a future common accord between them. Whatever their own deep reservations about political cooperation, they may find their own electorates reducing their resistance to such a radical cohabitation. There is already evidence on the ground amongst the eastern electorate - a tendency if not yet a consistent trend - for some voters to make either the PDS or the Greens their first choice, and to exercise their second vote tactically for the 'other' radical option. Even the SPD may be drawn into this voter-led calculus. In the last general election, for instance, some 25 per cent of Green 'first choice' voters and 18 per cent of SPD voters opted for the PDS in their second ballot. The PDS continues to represent a clear sense of discontent amongst eastern voters, that national unification was a 'takeover' by the west, and one carried out on disadvantageous terms.[121] They have nurtured this resentment and created on the back of it a viable electoral constituency. They speak to an electorate with a strong sense of disillusionment with their marginalisation and apparent exploitation; and who harbour a deep irritation over glib promises made but, as they see it, renaged upon by the Bonn establishment.[122] The Greens share many of the same reservations with establishment politics. They, too, have been obliged by recent events to look hard at their own political options. This may not be a marriage made in heaven, but it might conceivably be a convenient liaison for both sides, if future political circumstances change sufficiently to put them both within touching distance of exercising some real political power at the centre.

The more immediate question for the Greens, however, during the recent election, and indeed since then, has been whether to position themselves as potential coalition partners for the SPD; or instead to continue their role in opposition, perhaps cooperating with the other minor parties - such as the PDS - who have sprung up on the political landscape. This predicament was mirrored by a debate in the SPD itself; on the one side as between Rudolf

Scharping and his allies, who saw the party's future as firmly rooted in the middle ground of politics as a modern social democratic party, combining a social market orientation, fiscal discipline and greater labour efficiency with progressive welfare policies to reassure its trade union constituency. Against this conservative tendency were those critics (led by Gerhard Schröder) who advocated a profusion of alternative strategies - from pro-business to a 'keep left' approach that encompassed a red-green alliance.[123] These tensions are far from resolved in spite of some successful local experiments in red-green coalition making in the western Laender, and more recently with PDS endorsement in the east.[124] Oskar Lafontaine's coup in winning back the party leadership at the 1995 party congress does, however, suggest that the SPD leadership, after years of hostility,[125] may be finally moving towards a genuine rapprochement with the Greens. If this were to be translated into a formula for government, it would indeed represent a major shift in the political landscape and the most significant acknowledgement so far of the Greens' contribution to political change.

The run of electoral success enjoyed by the Greens at every level since the defeat of 1990 confirms that the party has consolidated its position in German politics. It has begun to move beyond its customary role as the temporary residuum of the protest vote. In the process it has replaced the FDP as the intermediate or balancing force in the national political equation. While it is premature to make any confident predictions either way, the evidence of recent polls suggests that the Greens have begun to draw on support beyond their main post-material constituency - never much more than the 5 per cent or so that helped it across the electoral threshold from its early years onwards. The Greens have now begun to make some inroads into a much broader and even less choate liberal electorate exercised by civil liberties and related citizenship and asylum question - and one disaffected too, by the FDP's apparent cynicism in switching its coalitional favours to the conservative CDU/CSU.[126] Ursula Feist of the Infas polling institute in Bonn has observed that the Greens' core vote has now outstripped that for the FDP. At the very least, the Greens have become "an accepted element of the German party system",[127] and are, in fact, more integrated into the national political fabric than at any previous moment in their brief history. Some commentators have gone beyond such modest or interim judgements and claimed more; that the Greens have contributed to the substantial modification underway in the German party system, by adding an entirely new politics cleavage to the old party and largely class based cleavage system that previously characterised party competition in Germany.[128] It is too soon to make any bold predictions for far reaching political change, although there are signs, as we have seen, of an incipient shift. At the moment, the evidence points to only a gradual - and perhaps temporary - dealignment, rather than to any inexorable realignment.[129] The Greens certainly nurture the ambition to realise something more than this by becoming Germany's permanent third party because, as Heidi Ruehle their campaign coordinator in 1994 said, this "is the only way to make yourself heard". In the meantime, there is scant evidence to endorse this aspiration let alone to confirm the sweeping claim behind this tangible shift in the respective electoral fortunes of the main parties on the centre-left, that the new Green vote represents something firmer than a protest by supporters of other parties disaffected by their policy agendas or performance.[130] Or, indeed, that it will stick with the Greens if political circumstances change.[131] The critical question for the Greens for now, is an altogether more modest one. Whether they can build on this foundation , cash in their new found influence to good effect, and thereby to at least consolidate their recent levels of support and sustain any incipient trend towards further dealignment.[132]

There are as many indications of the impermanence of these recent changes as there are of their durability. The elections of the 1990s have revealed both good and bad portents for the Greens. The 1990 election reminded the party of the fickleness of their own electorate. Poguntke has identified amongst this cohort, 'cognitively mobilised' voters, detached from any narrow tribal or ideological allegiance, who exercise a "high level of political skills" in order to fulfil their value preferences and thus "tend not to rely on symbolic cues or feelings of psychological attachment when they make their voting decision. Instead, they are capable of forming their opinion quite independently from political parties"and tend "to be loyal to political goals, not to political parties".[133] In other words, the Greens cannot take anything for granted and will have to work at least as hard as other parties to keep their newly won support. There are many current Green voters who remain outside the ideological community of the cognitively committed eco-left. This is a whimsical and instrumental electorate whose political preferences are driven by issues and by events. They remain vulnerable to allegiance shifts if any party fails to match their particular aspirations. The electoral threat to the Greens is as discernible here as it is to the FDP, the SPD or any other party unable to respond to the discontents of an increasingly volatile electorate. And nowhere more so than when new discourses emerge to fashion policy debates and frame issue agendas. The rising debate about Germany's national identity, its appropriate role in world affairs due to its size and resources, the immense social costs of reunification, and the impact on all of these issues of the question of regional integration in Europe, is a significant case in point here. These are all issues that have in some measure inflicted damage on almost every German political party. All of these new discourses, too, have diminished the salience of the ecological issue in domestic politics. The extent to which the Greens have managed to survive this handicap and even, to a degree, to prosper electorally, is some indication of the interplay here of two parallel sets of circumstances - the damage wrought by current changes on other parties; and the extent to which the Greens have widened their appeal, enabling them to over-ride such handicaps.

They may not be able to count on such fortuitous circumstances in future. At the same time, the Greens have seized their opportunities and adapted to the conditions they have found themselves in - a prelude to survival for any political party that aspires to consolidation. The Greens are hardly yet - nor do they aspire to be - a 'catch-all' party in the conventional sense. They have, however, managed to develop an appeal to a broad constituency beyond the ecological left. And they have been successful enough here to persuade even the CDU, especially after the far from decisive outcome of the 1994 election, to modify their previous hostility. There may have been more panic than conciliation about Kohl's reference to the prospect of some future, if unspecified 'cooperation'between the CDU and the Greens. But in light of the usual currency of German politics this was indeed new territory.[134] There were more overt signs here, too, as when the parliamentary CDU supported the candidature for the Bundestag praesidium and the post of deputy speaker of the Greens' spokesperson, Antje Vollmer. The logic of this accommodation had tangible advantages to recommend it to both parties. From the CDU's perspective, it drove a convenient wedge between the Greens and the SPD. Whereas for the Greens, it enhanced their national credibility and raised their parliamentary profile as a force separate from the SPD with alternative options. Vollmer herself commented on the political symbolism of her elevation, in as much as it freed us from the somewhat slavish relationship that has existed between the Greens and the Social Democrats. The SPD never ceased to treat us as their own youth branch which had to bear the interests of the mother party in mind".[135]

The CDU/CSU parliamentary leader, Wolfgang Schauble, made tentative overtures to the Greens immediately after the 1994 election, offering them the long denied inclusion on the Bundestag's parliamentary committees. Whether this was calculated as a reward for their new-found moderation, or was merely a bribe for their anticipated support over some policy issues to alleviate pressure in a tighter than usual parliamentary arithmetic, is open to debate. Schauble's comment, that "if the Greens change as much in the next ten years as they have done over the last ten years, we can talk about cooperation", suggests that the former interpretation held greater sway. If so, it was a tacit acknowledgement of the Green party's adaptation to the rules of parliamentary politics, and in particular a reference to how far they had moved in the eyes of their greatest opponents, from its wilder days. In 1983, at the height of the crisis over the installation of medium range missiles, the Greens had threatened not to abide by the secrecy rules that applied to these parliamentary committees. By 1994 the party had drastically altered their views on 'the system', to the point where the CDU felt able to endorse their claim even to sit on sensitive parliamentary committees supervising the secret services, and those monitoring mail interception and police eavesdropping operations.[136] Fischer, who played a leading role in these delicate negotiations, was now able to maintain, that "for us it is utterly normal that the Greens should play a part in the control of the executive". This recent 'respectability' in no sense suggests a wholesale abandonment of a radical outlook. When the tactical question of cooperation with the CDU was broached at the national congress in Potsdam in December 1994, even moderate delegates led by Fischer dismissed any notion of cohabitation with the centre-right parties as a direct threat to the party's radical credentials.

The Greens are, for the moment at least, camped on ground once occupied by other radical parties. The party's success has, nevertheless, brought with it problems as well as opportunities. For one thing, the party's success in raising ecologism up the national issue agenda has invited retaliation - in the form of outright competition - from other parties (especially the SPD). Any party with serious aspirations to participate in German governance must now, in varying degrees, exhibit some form of green credentials of its own with what is unquestionably the most environmentally aware electorate in Europe.[137] Recently, there have, too, been even more pressing problems facing the Greens. The current national agenda, as we saw with the military issue, is bound to confront the party with hard choices that threaten it with renewed internal political disruption. The party's defence of the rights of immigrants, and its demands for a more open asylum policy are cases in point here. While this outlook continues to appeal to the Greens' core electorate, as well as to a number of the enlightened middle class won over from the FDP, deep uncertainty about Germany's new role in the world, fewer inhibitions about asserting nationhood, a strong continuing commitment across the spectrum of mainstream parties to the social market system and its conventional model of economic growth,[138] and the pressures provoked by unification, all conspire to cap the potential for widespread support for the Greens on these critical issues. Meanwhile, the ecological issue itself stands discounted. This is not to say that ecologism has peaked or that it lacks political potential. But rather that in the present climate it has lost much of the prominence and electoral appeal it enjoyed in the altogether more prosperous and politically less complicated 1980s. Not least, with some 4 million unemployed Germans and with the rate rising to 14 per cent in the east of the country. Concern with fostering employment and economic growth alike are bound to take priority now over sensibilities about pollution.[139]

Some commentators, however, remain guardedly optimistic even on this score, arguing that "once the politics of unification and economic crisis are overcome there might be a strong potential for an increasingly important ecological discourse".[140] In the meantime, the Greens are as likely to suffer the same electoral squeeze as other parties, with liberal instincts confronted with new public concerns that encourage a conservative reaction and draw on defensive instincts. The Greens' interim strategy here must, of necessity, be one of biding their time and waiting for more favourable circumstances to ply their distinctive political message. At the very least, they need to avoid alienating their own core vote; and to consolidate as much as possible of the protest or discontent vote attracted from other parties, whilst at the same time avoiding any commitments that smack either of extremism or outlandish utopianism. This is the minimum requirement if they are to consolidate sufficient support to keep them in the game as feasible partners in any future radical coalition with the SPD. For in spite of occasional overtures from the CDU this narrow option is likely to be the Greens' only feasible route into the federal government. Even then, it remains fraught with traps, difficulties and dangers that go to the heart of the Greens' mission as a radical party in pursuit of a genuinely new politics. For one thing, they will remain junior partners in any such realignment, and as such are dependent on the responses of their prospective partners rather than fully in control of their own political destiny. The recent emergence of Oskar Lafontaine as SPD leader illustrated the Greens' continuing dilemma here. This leadership change represents a shift to the left in the SPD, which on the face of it makes the same degree of radical realignment a more likely prospect, given the former leader Rudolf Scharping's reluctance to embrace any radical manoeuvre that compromised what he saw as the SPD's twin imperatives - to challenge the CDU for the electoral middle ground and to avoid alienating its productionist vote amongst the working class preoccupied as this constituency is with job security and concerned that ecologism might threaten employment by imposing eco taxes and driving up labour costs. Lafontaine, on the other hand, is a shrewd politician committed as much to the electoral revival of the SPD as the reinvention of the German left per se. As such, his entire strategy will be conducted with that aim in mind. While he may well be more receptive to change he is, at the same time, more likely to try to reclaim the radical space to the left of the SPD abandoned to the Greens and others during the tenures of Scharping and Engholm.

None of these calculations rule out some future realignment, even if they do suggest that it will continue to be driven by SPD priorities rather than by some inexorable shift hastened by more radical political forces. A left-libertarian strategy by the SPD - in conjunction with the Greens and possibly even with the PDS (who supported a minority SPD-Green government in Saxony-Anhalt, but otherwise continues to sap SPD votes in the east) - is more likely to favour the Greens than it is to damage them electorally.[141] Yet the situation on the left remains fluid and there are no certainties to reassure the Greens' strategists. The recent crisis in the SPD-Green coalition in the most populous German state of North Rhine Westphalia well illustrates the delicate balance - between the need to accommodate their political partners in the mainstream, and the costs thereof of appeasing the ecological conscience that provides the party with its bedrock support.

The Greens had continued to build on their success in the 1994 national and Euro elections by polling well in Laender elections. In Bremen and in North Rhine Westphalia - also Germany's most industrialised state - the Greens won a commendable 13 per cent and 10 per cent respectively, more than the FDP with the aid of a low turnout and some defections from that party's former voters.[142] The tight parliamentary arithmetic in North Rhine Westphalia brought about an SPD-Green coalition, in spite of Scharping's instinctive opposition to what he saw as the symbolic capitulation of a once great national party by sharing power with the Greens in what had been the SPD's historic industrial heartland. This coalition was, however, rather more easily concocted than it was maintained. The tensions between the two 'governing' parties from the start - underlined by the fact that it took over four weeks of negotiations to even agree a basis for power sharing - were illustrative of the doubts and dilemmas each party continued to bring with them into any red-green alliance. The Greens nevertheless exhibited a degree of moderation and restraint here that would have been unthinkable in similar circumstances a decade earlier. But there were limits even to this new found realism. In particular, they could not allow compromise on key ecological issues. Whereas the SPD, with its strong emphasis on economic growth and its dependence on its industrial and trades unions constituency for party finance and mass support, likewise felt unable to dilute its abiding commitment to the productionist ethic. These endemic differences were overlaid and further highlighted by local issues. There were deep divisions from the start over the Greens' support for local residents opposed to the planned extension of the Gazweiler brown coalfield - the largest opencast site in Europe and the cornerstone of the state's future power generation plan. The SPD's special congress was lobbied by 4,000 angry members of the IG Berzbar miners union, worried about job losses if environmental concerns took priority.

The situation deteriorated and the coalition government was soon in trouble. In spite of tangible concessions to the Greens - for instance a reduction in budgetary expenditure on the state's trunk roads and cuts in traffic at Dusseldorf airport, including a ban on a proposed runway extension[143] - the incipient tensions between a policy of growth and one of ecological retrenchment soon came to a head. This time over the planned expansion of Dortmund airport. Restrictions on night flying at the region's main airport in Cologne, brought about by Green party pressure, had already persuaded the international courier company, TNT Express, to switch its base for operations to Belgium, with the loss of over 500 local jobs. The Dortmund issue revived similar concerns. After crisis talks the Green members of the Landtag did defuse the row and voted narrowly (13 to 11) to approve a growth oriented budget formulated by the SPD, and to cease opposition to the proposed airport extension. A special Green party congress to review this crisis and its outcome agreed (by almost 2 to 1) to persevere with this red-green alliance as the only possible way of removing the stranglehold of the centre-right parties on national politics. A minor disruption of the proceedings by militants indicates the residual tensions that continue to surround this strategy, even for a party purged of its 'fundis'. The Greens were clearly torn here, as they still are at every level of the party, not between a militant and moderate prospectus; but rather, over residual differences about how best to operationalise a feasible realism that would deliver effective rather than token influence over policy, without surrendering the partys genuinely radical instincts. The crisis in North-Rhine Westphalia crystallised this dilemma precisely. And it will certainly revisit the party with compound interest should it ever find itself involved with the SPD as junior partners in a national coalition. The insult thrown by the FDP, that "the Greens have lost their innocence, that in the end they put simply clinging to power above their own principles",[144] certainly touched a raw nerve here amongst even many otherwise committed 'realists in the party. They continue to judge this strategy of accommodation by how far it ensures genuine concessions to the Green agenda as an outcome of power sharing, rather than the thin veil of ideological rectitude that enables party leaders to keep their consciences while enjoying the fruits of political office.

The German Greens continue to walk this uncomfortable tightrope. The party does have at least one critical resource to help them negotiate these turbulent waters. Recent organisational changes have ensured a greater degree of party discipline, more cogent, better structured, and even tempered debates, especially on controversial issues such as the issue of a German military role in Bosnia. The emergence of a recognised party leadership and of a professional parliamentary cadre with its own prerogatives, has improved the competence as well as the image of a radical party now able to confront problematical issues without raising the sort of rancour exhibited by the fundis' before 1992. This successful adaptation to serious parliamentary politics has been achieved precisely because internal democracy is now balanced by professionalism at the top and by realism throughout the party's ranks. The Greens have not in the process ceased to be a radical party. They have merely adapted, to become a party for whom protest is now a means to the end of progressive politics, rather than the end per se. The party at large has come to accept, albeit with varying degrees of reluctance, that any party that remains detached, in splendid ideological isolation from its surroundings, can do little to change them; that it can only influence events by compromising and becoming part of a broader coalition.[145] This critical shift of emphasis has been the principal change in Green party politics during the current decade. As such, it has built on and consolidated the foundations laid by the party's 'realo' faction throughout the 1980s.

Movement politics has not been entirely replaced in this formula, but instead has been accommodated to more conventional organisational procedures. Poguntke sees these changes as a finely balanced trade off between the old and new politics, rather than the exclusive victory of one over the other; for "since they have retained most essentials of *Basisdemokratie*, they should still be capable of keeping in touch with movement politics without being almost entirely dependent on movement mobilisation".[146] This is indeed a fine compromise between the radical movement impetus that originally brought the Green party to life and gave it political energy, and the organisational requirements that have so far entrenched it and increased its political leverage.[147] Nevertheless it appears to work. Anna Nilger, a Green party spokesperson has voiced this new realism at the centre of the party's strategic thinking: "We started on the grass roots level, as an environmentalist party committed to green issues and civil rights and opposed to nuclear power. We believed that it was time to translate these issues into the federal level in a coherent way. I think our voters expected us to move forward, otherwise we risked becoming irrelevant or at best, remaining a fringe party".[148] This may yet be the Greens' destiny, although it looks a less likely outcome as things currently stand. Of course, the fate of the Greens in this matter is by no means entirely in their own hands. Nevertheless, political fortune does tend to favour those parties who at least help themselves by accommodating to the world as it is rather than as they would prefer it to be - that is, by developing relevant not fanciful strategies, and by improving their image and the way they conduct party business, and refining their receptiveness in a shifting political landscape to other parties.

With another general election due in 1998, the Greens have continued to hold their own in recent Laender elections and for reasons - not least the continued poor performances of the FDP (who have failed more often than not to clear the 5 per cent hurdle) and the SPD - that reinforce the view that a realignment of the left might be the only way of turning out the right. The SPD's vote of 30.4 per cent in the Berlin city election of October 1995 on the back of internal party turmoil, and with defections to both the Greens (whose vote rose from 9.3 per cent in 1990 to 13.3 per cent) and the PDS (who took 26 per cent in east Berlin and 14.7 per cent in the city as a whole) strengthened the mood for a radical shift inside the SPD and undoubtedly helped to bring about the election of Oskar Lafontaine as the party leader most likely to bring about a major shift in political direction.[149] The most recent state elections have confirmed the Greens' consolidated strength vis a vis the SPD's continuing electoral crisis.

The Greens' gains in Baden-Wurtenberg, Rhineland-Palatinate and Schleswig Holstein (where they have won Landtag seats for the first time) were admittedly more modest than they might have been had the FDP not staged a modest revival.[150] The Greens, too, clearly retain the potential to damage the SPD, whose vote share in these polls fell between some 4 and 6 per cent, even on its poor showing in the polls before the leadership change at the end of 1995.[151]

The outlook for the Greens looks promising then, without being exceptional. There are, after all, still some difficult hurdles to negotiate and as many traps and quandaries for the political unwary as ever there were. The critical dilemmas that the party managed to successfully negotiate in North-Rhine Westphalia awaits the party on all manner of policy issues should it eventually take its place in any national government. And these may well be even more difficult to resolve, precisely because there will be much more at stake. The continuing dilemma at the heart of the Green party politics is easy to project into this unknown future. Adopting the pragmatic mode in order to build bridges to other parties, risks alienating the radical idealists - both as activists and voters - who continue to put their faith in the Greens as a new politics party embarked on a genuinely radical alternative prospectus. At the same time, much of the Greens' recent political success has stemmed from a general perception on the left, amounting in some cases to utter frustration, of the endemic weakness of the SPD. These favourable circumstances may well not last. Lafontaine should prove to be a more formidable and certainly a more charismatic leader than his immediate predecessors. He may yet increase his party's scope for cutting away the radical ground from the Greens - or at least to shrink their vote back to more modest proportions as his and the SPD's own electoral stock rises. If Schröder, the popular Laender politician, leads the party into the next federal elections, his organisational talents and his wide appeal to 'middle Germany' will make him an equally formidable focus of discontent with the CDU amongst mainstream voters. The Greens' leader, Joschka Fischer, for his part, remains optimistic about the his party's long term prospects. As he sees the situation, the Greens have already broken the traditional mould of German political competition. But teven if this is so, it remains an ambiguous prospect.

The adoption of Green policies by every other German party represents another threat as much as it indicates how effective the Greens have been at changing the policy agenda over a relatively short timespan. Imitation may indeed be the most sincere form of flattery, but it might just as easily lead to political marginality as to consolidation. Fischer is well aware of the dangers for the Greens in this situation. He has warned that the greening of politics "can cut both ways. The parties can chisel away at our agenda and adopt some of our policies which means we have been successful in making them change. Look at how many jobs the recycling industry has created. On the other hand, it also shows that we have to keep up the pressure, that there is support for our policies, and that *our* voters expect us to keep pushing them higher up on the agenda and act as a forceful opposition".[152] This is a timely reminder of the Greens' vulnerability in the current German political equation. It should serve as a clarion call for a party whose best chance of remaining a significant actor might lead it to avoid the lure and compromises of office; to avoid the seductive cooption held out by the predatory mainstream parties in exchange for what will be at most a modicum of real influence. And to retain instead its own independence as a force for principled opposition within the system. On the other hand, the choice of 'seagreen incorruptibility' is also a recipe over the longer run, for political impotence. Whichever option the Greens choose will present it with real and enduring problems that will present a stern test of its new-found maturity. That test may come soon enough. The German Greens stand on the threshold of a new political era, even if they have as yet failed to usher it in. If they do succeed in negotiating a place in a future governing coalition it will be, whatever its eventual outcome, a reward for their persistence, a measure of their ideological and organisational transformation, and a testament to the success of their adaptation to the rules of conventional politics - all of them changes that have refashioned a party of protest into one potentially of government. Above all it will represent a remarkable conclusion to a decade that has witnessed some deep-seated shifts in the political landscape of Germany, of which the Greens have been one of the principal agents and beneficiaries.

Notes

1.   Helmut Lippelt, "Green Politics in Progress: Germany", in M.P. Garcia-Guadilla and J. Blauert (eds), "Environmental Social Movements in Latin America and Europe", International Journal of Sociology and Social Policy (12) 1992, at p.191.
2.   This subsidy has been of vital importance to Die Grunen over the duration. With a higher proportion of its membership drawn from the youthful, the less well off, from housewives and the unemployed, or the simply economically 'opted out', compared with the activists of the established parties, it is hardly surprising that less than ten per cent of Die Grunen's total revenue comes from membership dues. This is less than one third of the amount for the dominant parties, the CDU or SPD. By far the lion's share of the Green party's income (over half) comes from public subsidies, calculated on a sliding scale which reflects, and thereby rewards, votes won at both state and federal elections. In addition, the Greens' Parliamentary Fraktionen is also in receipt of extra resources to cover its administrative expenses.
3.   E. Gene-Frankland, "Germany: The rise, fall and recovery of Die Grunen", chapter 2 of D. Richardson and C.A. Rootes (eds), op.cit (1995), at p.25.
4.   Lewis Edinger, "West German Politics", (New York, 1986) at pp.32-70; see also D. Jahn, "Nuclear Power, Energy, Policy and New Politics in Sweden and Germany", Environmental Politics Vol.1(3) 1992, at pp.383-417.
5.   R. Dahrendorf, "Society and Democracy in Germany" (New York, 1967).
6.   R. Eckersley, "Green Politics and the New Class: Selfishness or Virtue?" Political Studies 37(2) 1989, pp.205-223.
7.   For an appraisal of the conventional idea of Germany rejected by the alternativists, see W. Paterson and G. Smith (eds), "The West German Model: Perspectives on a Stable State" (London, 1981).
8.   For a comparative review of the early rise of European Green movements, see W Rudig, "The Greens in Europe: Ecological Parties and the European Elections of 1984", Parliamentary Affairs 38 No.1 (winter 1984-85) at pp.56-72.
9.   D. Nelkin and M. Pollak, "The Atom Beseiged: Extra Parliamentary Dissent in France and West Germany" (1983).
10.   Eva Kolinsky is, however, less than convinced of Die Grunen's sincere commitment to the feminist cause as judged against its actions. See E. Kolinsky, "Women in the Green Party", in E. Kolinsky (ed), "The Greens in West Germany: A Social and Political Profile" (London, 1988).
11.   D. Murphy and R. Roth, "In Many Directions at the Same Time? The Greens - An Artifact of the 5 Per Cent Clause?" in R. Roth and D. Rucht (eds), Neue Soziale Bewegungen in der Bundersrepublik Deutschland (1st ed Frankfurt, 1987).

12. E. Gene Frankland op.cit (1995) in D. Richardson and C.A. Rootes (eds), op.cit (1995), at p.25.
13. W. Hulsberg, "The West German Greens" (London, 1987) at p.82.
14. See "Confronting Modernity: The Greens and the German Historical Legacy", Chapter Two of E. Gene-Frankland and D. Schoonmaker, "Between Protest and Power: The Green Party in Germany" (Boulder, Col. 1992) at pp.15-40.
15. J. H. Helm, "Citizen Lobbies in West Germany" in P. H. Merkl (ed), "Western European Party Systems" (New York, 1980).
16. Russell Dalton, "The West German Party System Between Two Ages", in "Electoral Change in Advanced Industrial Democracies" (Princeton, 1984), at pp.104-133; see also, C. Hauss and D. Rayside, "The Development of New Parties in Western Democracies Since 1945", in L. Maisel and J. Cooper (eds), "Political Parties: Development and Decay" (London, 1978) at pp.31-58.
17. G. Braunthal, "The West German Social Democrats: 1969-1982, Profile of a Party in Power" (Boulder, Col, 1983).
18. For a comprehensive account of the developments in West German party politics, see T. Poguntke, with B. Bull, "Germany", in R. Katz and P. Mair (eds), "Party Organizations: A Data Handbook" (London, 1992), pp.317-88.
19. Jutta Helm, "Citizen Lobbies in West Germany", in P.H. Merkl (ed), "West European Party Systems" (New York, 1980), at pp.383-97.
20. W. Kaltfleiter, "A Legitimacy Crisis of the German Party System?", in P. H. Merkl op.cit (1980).
21. W. Rudig, "The Greening of Germany", The Ecologist 13, 1983 at pp.35-39.
22. W. Hulsberg, "The Greens at the Crossroads", New Left Review 152 July/August 1985.
23. F. Capra and C. Spretnak, "Green Politics" (London, 1985), at p.21.
24. ibid (1985) at p.36.
25. David Conradt and Russel Dalton, "The West German Electorate and the Party System: Continuity and Change in the 1980's", Review of Politics 50 No.1 (Winter 1988), at pp.3-29.
26. A.S. Markovits and P.S. Gorski, "The German Left: Red, Green and Beyond" (Oxford, 1993).
27. For an analysis of the German Greens which emphasises particularly this local dimension, see Elim Papadakis, "The Green Movement in West Germany" (London, 1984).
28. Langguth calculated this in 1984 at 87:1 and used this high ratio to categorise the Greens as a 'cadre party'. See G. Langguth, "The Green Factor in German Politics" (Boulder, Col. 1986) at p.47.
29. Peter H. Merkl, "Conclusion: Were the Angry Old Men Wrong?", in P.H. Merkl (ed), "The Federal Republic of Germany at Forty" (New York, 1989).
30. Eva Kolinsky, "The Green Party: A New Factor in the West German Political Landscape", in E. Kolinsky (ed), "Parties, Opposition and Society in West Germany" (New York, 1984) at pp.297-300.
31. Michael Hoexter, "It's Not Easy Being Green", New Politics 2 No.1 (Summer 1988) at pp.110-112.
32. Jutta Ditfurth, quoted from "Skizzeneiner radikalokologischen Position", in T. Kluge (ed), "Grune Politik" and cited in Sara Parkin, "Green Parties: An International Guide"

(London, 1989) at pp.124-25.

33. For a discussion of the problems of "intermediation" facing radical alternative movements and the political establishment, including the mass parties, see B. Nedelmann, "New political movements and changes in processes of intermediation", "Social Science Information" Volume 23 1984 Part 6, at pp.1029-1048.

34. Otto Schily, in "Socialismus" 11 1984.

35. See K. von Beyme, "The Role of Deputies in West Germany", in E. Suleiman (ed), "Parliaments and Parliamentarians in Democratic Politics" (New York, 1986) at p.156, for a discussion of the impetus on German parliamentarians towards professionalisation.

36. Hans-Joachim Veen, "The Greens as a Milieu Party", in E. Kolinsky (ed), "The Greens of West Germany" (Oxford, 1989).

37. E. Gene Frankland, "Green Politics and Alternative Economics", German Studies Review 11 No.1 (January, 1988) at pp.111-132.

38. That message was even more poignant, given that Robert Michels had formulated his oligarchic model on the basis of a German radical party of a previous epoch. The SPD had begun life as an ideologically committed outsider and finished up, as far as many of the refugees from it who had fled to the Greens see it, as a party short on principle and long on cynicism. See R Michels, "Political Parties" (1962 edition).

39. Elim Papadakis, "The Green Party in Contemporary West German Politics", Political Quarterly 54 No.3 (July, 1983).

40. Jurgen Maier, "The Green Parties in Western Europe", Die Grunen: Monatszeitung (Bonn, Die Grunen, 1990).

41. Gordon Smith, "The German Volkspartei and the Career of the Catch-All Concept" in H. Doring and G. Smith (eds), "Party Government and Political Culture in West Germany" (New York, 1982).

42. Hans-Georg Betz, "Strange Love? How the Greens Began to Love NATO", German Studies Review, 12 No.3 (October, 1989), at pp.487-505.

43. See Gerhard Loewenberg, "The Remaking of the German Party System", in K. Cerny (ed), "Germany at the Polls: The Bundestag Elections of 1976" (Washington DC, American Enterprise Institute, 1978) at p.20.

44. Die Grunen "Umbau der Industriegesellschaft", (Programme officially approved at the national conference, 26-28 September 1986, Die Grunen, Bonn).

45. On the industrial front, the impact of the Greens on the economic/industrial debate can be seen from the massive increase in company expenditure on pollution control. For instance, the industrial giants such as Bayer AG spent 1.78 billion marks on environmental protection during the 1980s; BASF spent 1.60 billion marks over the same period; and Hoechst AG had spent 15.2 per cent of its total investment on similar measures. These major enterprises were also at the forefront, after unification, of the drive to clean up the heavily polluted industrial sector of the former GDR.

46. E. Gene Frankland, "The Role of the Greens in West German Parliamentary Politics", Review of Politics 50 No.1 (1988) at pp.92-122; the same impetus has also been visible in local government. See Thomas Scharf, "Red-Green Coalitions at Local Level in Hesse", in E. Kolinsky (ed) (1989) op.cit, at p.173.

47. Peter Katzenstein, "Policy and Politics in West Germany: The Growth of the semi-sovereign State" (Philadelphia, 1987), at pp.356-59.

48. Sara Parkin, op.cit (1989).

49.   Petra Kelly, quoted in F. Capra and C. Spretnak, "Green Politics" (London, 1985) at p.148.
50.   The Independent, 29.7.89.
51.   Financial Times, 9.3.89.
52.   The Independent, 6.11.90.
53.   See F. Pappi, "The West German System", West European Politics 7(4) October 1984, at pp.7-27.
54.   Financial Times, 12.5.89.
55.   E. Kolinsky, "Introduction" in E. Kolinsky (ed), "The Greens in West Germany: Organization and Policy Making" (Oxford, 1989), p.8.
56.   For a detailed analysis of these results, see Mannheim, Forschungsgruppe Wahlen e V (1990), "Bundestagswahl 1990: Eine Analyse der ersten Gesamtdentschen Bundestagswahl am 2" Dec 1990, Berechte No.61 (Mannheim).
57.   R. Foeks, "Okologie und Burgerrechte: Pladoyer Fur eine neue Allianz", in R. Foeks (ed), "Sind die Grunen noch zu retten?" (Reinbeck, 1991), pp.33-43.
58.   See Die Grunen, "Das Programm zur 1 gesamtdeutschen Wahl 1990" (Bonn, Die Grunen, 1990).
59.   For an overview of the 1990 Federal election, see P. Pulzer, "The German Federal Election of 1990", Electoral Studies 10(2) August 1991, at pp.145-54; K. von Beyme, "Electoral Unification: The First German Elections in December 1990", Government and Opposition, 26(2) Spring 1991, at pp.167-84; and B. Boll and T. Poguntke, "The 1990 All-German Election Campaign", in D. Farrell and S. Bowler (eds), "Electoral Strategies and Political Marketing" (London, 1992), pp.121-43.
60.   T. Poguntke and R. Schmitt-Beck, "Still the Same with a New Name? Bundnis 90/Die Grunen after Fusion" German Politics Vol.3(1), pp.91-113.
61.   H-J. Veen and J. Hoffmann, "Die Grunen zu Beginn der neunzinger Jahre" (Bonn, 1992), at pp.144-146.
62.   Daniel Hamilton, "After the Revolution: The New Political Landscape in East Germany" (Washington DC: American Institute for Contemporary German Studies, 1990).
63.   H. Lippelt in M.P. Gracia-Guadilla and J. Blauert (eds), op.cit (1992), p.194.
64.   The Independent, 29.9.94.
65.   The Times, 4.12.90.
66.   H. Lippelt, op.cit (1992), at p.194.
67.   Ibid, p.194.
68.   See T. Poguntke, "Goodbye to Movement Politics? Organisational Adaptation of the German Green Party", Environmental Politics, 2(3) 1993 pp.370-404.
69.   We should not underestimate here the 'taming' impact on these 'realos' of their participation within the parliamentary process. See the discussion in W. Paterson and D. Southern, "Governing Germany" (New York, 1991) especially at p.121.
70.   T. Poguntke, op.cit at p.389.
71.   See A. Panebianco, "Political Parties: Organisation and Power" (Cambridge, 1988), at p.11.
72.   J. Raschke, "Krise der Grunen, Bilanz und Neubegin" (Marburg, 1991).
73.   The Guardian, 29.4.91.
74.   The Guardian, 24.4.91.

75. Antje Vollmer, Wolfgang Templin & Werner Schulz, "Grune und Bundnis 90", Aus Politik und Zeitgeschichte B5/92 (1992).
76. The Guardian, 29.4.91.
77. See J. Ditfurth, "Lebe wild und gefährlich. Radikalökologische Perspecktiven" (Cologne, 1991).
78. The Guardian, 26.4.91.
79. The right wing and racist Republican party polled 8.3 per cent in Berlin; the PDS (the former Communists) won 11.3 per cent.
80. The Independent, 10.6.91.
81. Reuters News Service Report, 17.1.93.
82. See the account in J. Raschke, "Die Grunen: wie sie wurden was sie sind" (Cologne, 1993).
83. Reuters News Service Report, 19.4.93.
84. Reuters News Service Report, 19.4.93.
85. Reuters News Service Report, 15.3.93; by the spring of 1994 the Greens seemed to be well on target to pass that important political milestone. See the report of the Lower Saxony Laender elections, The Guardian 15.3.94.
86. Tony Paterson, "Germans turn their backs on politics", The European 14-20 January 1994.
87. Ibid.
88. The Guardian, 26.9.93.
89. Reuters News Service, ibid, 8.3.93.
90. See Scott, C., Flanagan and R.J. Dalton, "Parties under Stress: Realignment or Dealignment in Advanced Industrial Societies" West European Politics Vol.7(1) 1984, pp.7-23.
91. Reuters News Service Report, 8.3.93.
92. Reuters, ibid, 17.5.93.
93. The Guardian, 6.12.93.
94. Financial Times, 4.7.94.
95. T. Paterson, "Rise of Greens shakes rivals", The European 25/31 March 1994.
96. Q. Peel, "Earnest about important allies", Financial Times, 11.4.94.
97. D. Gow, "In the ashes of the Kohl age", The Guardian, 15.3.94.
98. The Guardian, 16.3.94.
99. The Guardian, 14.3.94.
100. M. Lindemann, "Greens' leading light goes for broke", Financial Times, 11.10.94.
101. Q. Peel, "Germany's nuclear fallout", Financial Times, 23.8.94.
102. The Times, 12.10.94.
103. Financial Times, 30.6.95.
104. David Gow, "In the ashes of the Kohl age", The Guardian, 15.3.94.
105. Financial Times, 2.8.95.
106. Ibid, 2.8.95.
107. Financial Times, 4.12.95.
108. I. Traynor, "Tomorrow belongs to Germany", The Guardian, 1.1.96.
109. Peter Norman, "Germany: Giant cloaked in Uncertainty", Financial Times, 23.10.95.
110. The Guardian, 19.9.94.
111. Financial Times, 4.1.96; see also P. Norman, "Sweet and sour experience", Financial Times, 3.10.95.

112. Herbert Prantl, "The Losers", Suddeutschezeitung, 16.6.94.
113. J. Demsey, "The Centre May Not Hold", Financial Times, 23.10.95; ibid, "FDP closes ranks around Kinkel", Financial Times, 13.12.94.
114. Financial Times, 9.9.94.
115. The Guardian, 18.10.94.
116. Q. Peel, "Battle to hold the middle line", Financial Times, 18.10.94.
117. Peter Norman, "Ideologies on the Wane", Financial Times, 23.10.95.
118. Quoted in The Observer, 21.5.95.
119. The Guardian, 15.3.94.
120. See D. Jahn, "Changing Political Opportunities in Germany: The Prospects of the German Greens in a Unified Germany", Current Politics and Economics of Europe Vol.14(4) 1994, pp.209-225.
121. Financial Times, 28.9.94; see also, "Restructuring of Eastern Germany", Financial Times Survey, 4.5.94.
122. J. Demsey, "Where Socialism is down but not out", Financial Times, 23.10.95.
123. Peter Norman, "Lunch time in Mannheim", Financial Times, 14.11.95; ibid, 2.10.95.
124. Financial Times, 16.7.94.
125. J. Delware, "Post materialism and Politics: The 'Schmidt SPD' and the Greening of Germany", German Politics Vol.21 pp.243-269.
126. W. Rudig and M.N. Franklin, "Green prospects: The future of Green parties in Britain, France and Germany", in W. Rudig (ed), "Green Politics Two" (Edinburgh, 1992), at pp.37-58.
127. T. Poguntke, "Goodbye to Movement Politics? Organisational Adaptation of the German Green Party", Environmental Politics Vol.2 1993, at p.399.
128. D. Jahn, "The rise and decline of new politics and the Greens in Sweden and Germany", European Journal of Political Research Vol.24 (1993), at pp.177-194.
129. F. Muller-Rommel, "The Greens in the 1980s: Short term cyclical protest or indicator of transformation?" Political Studies 37(1) 1989, at p.21.
130. F. Muller-Rommel and T. Poguntke, "Die Grunen", in Alf Mintzel and Heinrich Oberreuter (eds), "Parteien in der Bundesrepublik" (Munich, 1992), at p.352; see also T. Poguntke, "Alternative Politics: The Green Party" (Edinburgh, 1993).
131. T. Poguntke, "Goodbye to Movement Politics? Organisational Adaptation of the German Green Party", Environmental Politics Vol.2 (1993), at p.385.
132. E. Gene Frankland and D. Schoonmaker, "Between Protest and Power: The Green Party in Germany" (Boulder, Col, 1992).
133. T. Poguntke, "Goodbye to Movement Politics", op.cit (1993), at p.386.
134. The Guardian, 21.11.94.
135. Ibid, 21.11.94.
136. Ibid, 21.11.94.
137. J. Raschke, "Krise der Grunen: Bilanz und Neubeginn" (Marburg, 1991).
138. David Goodhart, "There's still life in the old model", Financial Times, 12.4.94; see also ibid, "The reshaping of the German Social Market" (Institute for Public Policy Research, London, 1994).
139. Financial Times, 4.1.96.
140. D. Jahn, "Ecological Discourse in Decline? The Political Agenda in Sweden and Germany between the 1970s and 1990s", unpublished paper presented to the Green Politics in the New Europe Workshop, 24th Joint Session of Workshops of the ECPR,

Oslo, 29 March/3 April 1996, at p.12.

141. H. Kitschelt, "The Green Phenomenon in Western Party Systems", in S. Kamieniecki (ed), "Environmental Politics in the International Arena" (Albany, New York), pp.93-112.

142. Financial Times, 12.5.95.

143. Financial Times, 3.7.95.

144. Reuters News Service Report, 17.3.96.

145. H. Lippelt, op.cit (1992), at p.197.

146. T. Poguntke, "Goodbye to Movement Politics", op.cit (1993) at p.401

147. See the argument in E. Gene Frankland, "The Greens' Comeback in 1994: The Third Party in Germany" in R.J. Dalton (ed), "Germans Divided" (Oxford, 1996) at pp.85-108.

148. Quoted in the Financial Times, 23.10.95.

149. Financial Times, 21-22/10/95.

150. Financial Times, 26.3.96.

151. Financial Times, 25.3.96.

152. Financial Times, 23.10.95.

3 Green parties in Benelux

1. Belgium

The electoral politics of Belgium is complicated by the country's linguistic divisions into French and Flemish speaking components, with a small German speaking population in the south of the country. This separation into two major linguistic communities is further complicated by a less geographically precise religious-secular cleavage.[1] All of these communal divisions are superimposed on the more usual social class and economic divisions which pervade every industrial society. This degree of social diversity, in a country with a population density of only 10 millions contained in scarcely 30 thousand square kilometres - less than half the size of the Irish Republic - has produced a map of electoral variations and party political allegiances which reflects a richly diverse politics.[2] The emergence of an ecological dimension corresponding to a broad generational shift towards post-material values and alternative lifestyles has added even more diversity to the overall pattern. At the same time, the replication of the existing communal cleavage within Belgium's new movement politics, with predominantly French and Flemish speaking Green parties existing side by side, serves to illustrate one of the abiding facts of Belgium's political culture. It is unique amongst western Europe's advanced industrial countries inasmuch as it has no national parties. Instead, its political dynamics revolve around and are conducted within, a motley of regionally based parties.

The Belgian Greens were obliged to conform to this prevailing ethnic model of politics. On the other hand, with no fundamental ideological differences between them, both linguistic wings of the Green movement in Belgium have managed to surmount the suspicions and prejudices imposed on the conventional camps of the 'left' and 'right' parties by the country's political sociology. Not only do the two Belgian Green parties cooperate amicably; they also regard one another as sister parties, pursuing a common cause, along similar although by no means identical organisational and programmatic lines.

Both parties have from the start campaigned jointly in local and national election campaigns. After winning representation in the House of Representatives (the lower house of the national parliament) and the Senate, the two parties formed a single parliamentary group. As a symbolic gesture of solidarity, MPs from both parties have sworn the Parliamentary oath in each other's language, as well as in their own. The parties also conduct regular joint meetings and have a 'coordination bureau' which works to maximise cooperation. By such means, the Greens became the only interlinguistic party operating at the Parliamentary level and they co-jointly sign all legislative proposals, as well as co-sponsoring common legislative initiatives. This amity notwithstanding, the experience of cultural separation which has increasingly pervaded postwar Belgian politics, has left its mark on both parties. Each one of them has inevitably been shaped by particular local events or communal circumstances. As a consequence, the Flemish party, AGALEV, is regarded as somewhat more radical and rather less disposed to pure ecologism, than the Wallonian or French speaking ECOLO.

(a)   AGALEV

(i)   Green roots

The first development in Green politics in Belgium began in Flanders in 1970. A revival group or *herlevingsgroep* of radical Christians based in Antwerp and dedicated to 'self improvement', 'contemplation' and 'counter-values' (solidarity, sobriety and silence), broke away from the Catholic Peoples Party. By 1982 they had expanded an alternative movement electoral committee into a fully fledged party. This group initially concentrated on local protest politics, including a campaign against environmental degradation. As the movement gained momentum through the successes of its numerous action groups - and on that basis increased its public profile - one constituent group organised the Anders gaan leven (AGL) 'to go and live differently'. This transformed what had begun as local campaigning politics (for instance, opposition to a canal building project near Antwerp in cooperation with other community environmental groups) into a conventional party format. Within a year they had won 2 seats in the national House of Representatives. This transition to party status was not taken lightly in a movement grounded in direct action and alternative politics. There was reluctance, even resistance in some quarters, to compromising the movement's anti-hierarchial roots.[3] An organisational compromise was initially reached when the AGL decided that winning political influence was the surest way of effecting real change.

Instead of participating directly in electoral politics on its own merits, the AGL endorsed (in the 1974 national and 1976 local elections) 'green lists' of approved, ecologically sound candidates from other parties and local campaigning movements (*aktiegroepen*), which had developed their radical political instincts on a range of issues - Green cyclists, and the anti-canal campaign for instance. This turned out to be a less than satisfactory outcome when, after securing election under AGL's approval, these individuals reverted to type and continued to behave as conventional members of their parties of origin. In short, AGL operated less as a conventional party than a focal point for a medley of diffuse groups. The internal diversity of the movement was further widened in 1974. Local sections or reflection groups were set up which developed a broader global perspective on ecologism. The Greens were therefore caught on the horns of a dilemma, familiar to all social movements which try and act through political surrogates in order to retain their principles and avoid compromising their integrity. Although AGL did not want to become a permanent party organisation - and continued to reflect the abiding anti-party suspicions of similar radical social movements across Europe - it found itself drawn increasingly into the formal political arena. Not least, because its abiding principles were all about implementing tangible changes in government policy which the mainstream parties were reluctant to consider or loath to deliver.

(ii)   Party formation

Accordingly, for the 1977 elections in Antwerp, AGL's national council (*Landelijk Beraad*) forwarded its own Green list (AGALEV). Its initial impact merely confirmed an abiding ambivalence amongst activists about the electoral process, and reinforced the assumption of many movement orientated members that its party status was only a temporary arrangement.

The emphasis on grassroots democracy rather than hierarchism was underlined by the movement's insistence that the 'politicians' must seek permission to stand for election from the *Landelijk Beraad*. Nor were its initial results especially encouraging. AGALEV secured a fractional 0.3 per cent of the Flemish vote in 1977. It did only marginally better (with 0.7 per cent) when it stood in the 1978 national elections. The decision in 1978 to establish a political working group - *Agalev Weskgroep* - was an acknowledgement within the party of a need to better organise its political operations. Even a modest improvement (with 2.3 per cent of the vote in Flanders) in the 1979 European election, hardly seemed to amount to a significant breakthrough in what many pundits discounted anyway as a second order election. However, this result, in conjunction with an even better performance by the Wallonian Greens (ECOLO), became the platform for a modest 'take off' for Green politics in Belgium. For one thing, it increased national publicity, as well as attracting additional recruits, both from other parties and from alternative movement activists who had previously shunned all forms of party involvement.

The increased momentum which followed improved organisation after 1979 showed up in AGALEV's performances in successive local and national elections. In 1981, the party secured its first representation in the Belgian Parliament on the back of 4 per cent of the Flemish vote, which translated into 2 seats in the lower House, 1 in the Senate and seven provincial seats. This modest success increased the impetus to organise the party's parliamentary role more effectively. The movement and the party remained formally separated. Although the latter's reliance on the former was acknowledged in extensive exchanges of personnel and a continuing dialogue between them. It became accepted that the newly elected national representatives required a more reliable means of finance, professional support and a coherent programme to put before the electorate. After an animated and occasionally divisive internal debate, the AGL movement separated from this nascent party organisation in February 1982.

The 1982 municipal elections saw the Green momentum continue with a 5.6 per cent poll for the AGALEV lists. In spite of consolidating its transition to full party status in the eyes of the electorate, modest electoral success inevitably provoked intensive debate over strategy in what was still an alternative movement party. Nevertheless, success tends to produce its own balms and, regardless of some misgivings amongst the rank and file, the formal professionalisation of the party was consolidated in 1986 with the installation of an executive committee (*Uitvoerend Comité*) composed of full time party employees. The UC members gained additional authority within the party's structures to match their organisational responsibilities.

(b)   ECOLO

(i)   Green Roots

Although the Wallonian Greens in many ways mirror the experience and pattern of alternative or new social movement politics throughout Europe's advanced industrial societies, there were also factors behind their emergence and mobilisation which were unique to the regional politics of French speaking Belgium. For one thing, ECOLO's political roots were more diffuse than those of its Flemish counterpart. It drew support from a wider 'coalition' of ecological, regionalist and radical groups including the Young Christian Labour Movement (JOC) and the Christian Peace Movement. Moreover, its response to party status and electoral politics was somewhat more muted. Not least because it began its political life inside rather than outside the established political arena, in response to an intra-party quarrel within the Namur section of the Wallonian regionalist party, Rassemblement Wallon (RW), over the candidature for a local Presidency nomination in the aftermath of the 1971 regional elections.

The displaced candidate and his supporters created their own 'action and reflection' movement (Democratie Nouvelle). This movement had clear 'alternative aspirations'. Apart from ecologism and radical economic ideas, it emphasised the non-hierarchical, anti-oligarchic virtues of direct democracy; as well as integrated federalism, with its emphasis on consociational reconciliation and cooperation, rather than the less flexible model favoured by Belgium's traditional linguistic parties, with its propensity for institutionalising ethnicity in a way that consolidated the growing separation between the two halves of the country. In other words, the Wallonian Greens enshrined a progressive concept of Belgian statehood which clearly distinguished the 'creative' political community from the persistently divisive, reactionary and potentially racist notions of the 'volk'. This radical prospectus was completed by a commitment to reduce the legendary patronage system over civil service appointments, operated by the traditional parties for their own advantage; the employment of referenda to more accurately gauge public opinion; and party structures that would better ensure grassroots control over party elites.

(ii)   **Party formation**

For all of these radical proposals, ECOLO remained a party more at ease with organisational professionalism than with the movement idealism familiar to other Green parties in the earliest stages of their development. ECOLO's conventional origins favoured those activists who wanted to create a formal party structure, albeit one under strict democratic control. The outcome of this compromise was a decentralised model which paralleled Green party structures throughout Europe; one which allowed considerable autonomy to local sections, and a national decision making process (centred on a national *Assemblée*) that provided considerable scope for direct membership participation and, when 'crises' arose, for conciliation (by means of the *Comité d' Arbitrage*).[4]

ECOLO presented an alternative list at the 1974 national elections, and secured a modest 2.4 per cent in its heartland - the Namur constituency. The party persisted and presented another joint list (Combat pour l' Ecologie et l'Autogestion) at the 1976 local elections in Namur. Securing only 1.9 per cent of the vote and no seats, this coalition melted away. But not before the case of the Democratie Nouvelle - which had founded the Belgian branch of the transnational Friends of the Earth lobby (Les Amis de la Terre) - had networked with ecologists (for instance, the members of an association for ornithological studies) to formulate a political programme whose twin aims were enhanced democratic opportunities for citizens and ecological reforms. The fruits of this networking crystallised in the 1977 legislative elections[5] with assorted Green lists - some of which were explicitly radical -being fielded in Brussels as ECOLOG. As well as a handful of Wallonian constituencies as Wallonie-Ecologie. The initiators of these local lists eventually became the founders of ECOLO.

The electoral outcome of these efforts, yielding a total vote of between 0.3 and 2.3 per cent, was hardly a success measured against conventional yardsticks, even in such a politically fragmented polity. Of more permanent significance, however, was the fact that in 1978, Wallonie-Ecologie emerged from its transitory status into that of a permanent organisation. This positive development undoubtedly helped to stabilise Green politics in the region. The WE adopted a programme which drew heavily on Les Amis de la Terre's environmentalism. On the other hand, the Wallonian Greens were afflicted with the problem, common to all radical movements; that of responding effectively to the exigencies and demands of the conventional political system. Ideological disputes over strategy - the familiar party/anti-party divide - fractured the movement and blunted its political impact on the ground. In 1978, for example, the Belgian Friends of the Earth divided into opposing factions with the minority group - who created the Reseau libre des Amis de la Terre - insisting on retaining total political autonomy for each local section. The immediate consequence was a reduction in electoral effectiveness, which permitted the WE to stand in only six arrondissements, with two minor Green lists putting up in Brussels (Ecolog and Ecopol). Even a modest increase in support here failed to yield any seats. These squabbles were intense and stylised by the usual radical chic, although by no means irresolvable. Pragmatic considerations also played their part and the obvious weakness of such self-imposed divisions impelled rival factions, faced with unfavourable electoral rules and thresholds, to unite as a common list (Europe-Ecologie), in order in 1979 to contest the first direct elections to the European Parliament.

These 'second order' elections, where protest is safe and little is at stake, delivered - as they did for AGALEV - a solid electoral return in response to this outbreak of common sense.[6] The common Green list secured a respectable 5.1 per cent of the Wallonian vote, without winning any seats. AGALEV, meanwhile, won 2.3 per cent where it stood. Neither Belgian Green party secured any representation at Strasbourg, regardless of the fact that this combined vote produced the best result for any Green party in these elections across the EC's then 9 states. A more lasting legacy was the organisational payoff from this achievement. For this electoral success helped, in turn, to resolve the intra-party tensions over the structural question and reinforced the mood in favour of adopting full party status.

As a result of these developments, ECOLO emerged in March 1980 as a party in its own right after two *assemblées générales constitutives* adopted formal statutes creating a federalist, self governing organisation. While this was undoubtedly a positive step towards consolidating regional Green politics, as such it did not finally resolve the ideological and interpersonal clashes within the movement about direction and structures which reflected the party's diverse movement origins in Democratie Nouvelle, Combat pour l'Ecologie et l'Autogestion, Les Amis de la Terre and Wallonie-Ecologie and Europe-Ecologie. The ideological dilemma between remaining a more fluid movement, or adopting a more hierarchial party status continued to affect ECOLO, as it did other Green parties caught between a similar radical-moderate predicament. In the 1981 elections, for instance, the dissident radicals chose to present their own list (ECOLOS). In the Brussels constituencies - a capital city whose politics are a microcosm of the ethnically fractured national polity - numerous Green lists were raised across the linguistic and right-left spectrums. These were soon acknowledged by those concerned, however, for the vain gestures that they were. Drawing parallel lessons from AGALEV's integrationist role in Flanders, ECOLO, from this time forward, began to function as the aggregative focus of Wallonian Green politics. ECOLO was the only Green list to appear on the ballot in every Wallonian constituency. As such, it won 5.9 per cent of the Wallonian vote and 3.1 per cent in Brussels, which secured the party 2 seats in the Chamber and 3 in the Senate.

This election was a defining moment for Green politics across Belgium because both ECOLO and AGALEV, which had also gained 2 seats, entered the national Parliament at the same juncture, thereby cementing the ties between them at national level - a full two years before Die Grunen reached the national political stage in West Germany. Both parties had secured 4.8 per cent of the national vote. By 1982 they occupied 120 local council seats and in 1984 each of them won a Belgian seat in the European Parliament with an impressive regional vote of 7.1 per cent (AGALEV) and 9.4 per cent (ECOLO) respectively.

(iii) Political developments

The history of both parties from that moment of significant national recognition, has been one of modest but steady success, in both local and national politics. Both parties, too, have consolidated themselves at the provincial and national levels, and regionally competed in and secured representation at elections from their earliest days. The figures largely speak for themselves here. Each party has consistently managed an impressive minimum vote of 5 per cent. This sound electoral foundation was largely a reflection of the parties' moderation - a willingness to forego the wilder reaches of ideologism, but without abandoning ecological priorities; and an aptitude to at least adjust their policies and institutional performance, at whichever level, to the actual events and agendas that exercised an electorate concerned with the constitutional changes peculiar to this divided country. In some measure, too, the Greens cornered a steady share of the social discontent vote which was mobilised here, as much as anywhere, by new insecurities fostered by the unpredictable and disconcerting impact of globalism on a delicate social compact - a prospect which threatened a generous welfare system that, to date, has enabled this fragmented country to manage its linguistic diversity, as well as those other socio-cultural tensions recently compounded by the pressures of deindustrialisation that have fallen unevenly on the Francophone part of the country. The Greens have undoubtedly been assisted in this modest political breakthrough, too, by precisely the fractured and frequently crisis ridden politics familiar to this much divided state. The rising ethnic-linguistic intensity of Belgian politics, the resultant flux and instability of its heterogeneous minority governing coalitions, which has encouraged frequent changes in the political balance of the governing coalition has furnished the ideal conditions in which these two minor yet cooperative transcommunal parties have been able to exert some joint if modest leverage on policy outcomes. Albeit, not yet on the actual composition of governments. These pragmatic tactics have been encouraged by a form of proportionality employed in the Belgian electoral system which does not discriminate against minor parties which enjoy a concentrated 'cultural' support base. The d'Hondt system, which employs lists based on local arrondissements for national elections, and lists divided along linguistic lines for other elections, provides a fairly accurate mirror of voter preferences. The system likewise allocates extra seats by aggregating 'surplus' votes across a number of districts within each province. Clearly the stimulus towards greater party coordination inherent in this, as in most electoral systems, has impelled Belgium's Green lists towards a more concerted and cooperative approach to their electoral arrangements. These opportunity structures were made even more favourable to minor parties in 1993, when a new law provided financial support for parties, as long as a party wins representation in both national chambers - a formula which combines fixed fiscal amounts with a proportionate funding element based on votes secured.

The political payoff for the Greens' adjustments to these favourable circumstances can be seen in successive electoral performances. In the 1985 national elections, AGALEV polled 3.7 per cent of the national vote (4 seats) and ECOLO 2.5 per cent (5 seats); in the 1987 national poll, AGALEV won 4.5 per cent of the national vote (7.3 per cent in Flanders and

6 seats), whereas ECOLO polled 2.6 per cent (6.4 per cent in Wallonia for 3 seats). This excellent result was sustained in 1989 with AGALEV winning 7.6 per cent in its regional heartland and ECOLO 6.2 per cent in its own territory. However, the benefits afforded to small parties by this type of proportionate electoral system yielded an impressive 9 seats each for both of them. Similarly, in the 1989 Euro-elections, AGALEV significantly increased its national vote to 7.6 per cent (1 seat), with ECOLO clocking up an equally notable regional vote of 6.3 per cent (2 seats). This result was secured mainly at the expense of established parties such as the Flemish Socialists (SP) and the French speaking Liberal party (PRL).

There were even better results to come. In the national elections in 1991, the Green parties together received a commendable 10 per cent of the national vote. In communal terms, AGALEV won 7.8 per cent of the Flemish vote, which gave it 7 seats in the House, 5 in the Senate, and 24 provincial seats. ECOLO doubled its previous (1987) turnout and won 13.75 per cent (10 House seats, 6 in the Senate and 41 in the provincial legislatures). This was a remarkable outcome in both national and comparative terms. In West Germany, for instance, Die Grunen have never won more than 8.3 per cent of the total vote in any national election. Moreover, in the same year (1991) in Germany, an uncertain political climate not dissimilar from Belgium's, and dominated by related questions of statehood and national integration, saw ecological issues and the Green party, however temporarily, cast aside as voters wrestled with questions of apparently greater moment. This comparison suggests a degree of cohesion in the Belgian Green movement as favourable to the party's future development and prospects as anywhere on the continent. Closer analysis of the Belgian Greens' electoral performance reveals something of both Green parties respective strengths and limitations. They have both performed better in second order European elections than in national elections. This is a general rather than a national trend and suggests the ephemeral and conditional nature of a proportion of the Green vote everywhere; that where 'real' power is at stake and the election of governments with what electors perceive to be the clout to accommodate individual interests and shape national destinies, the inclination to merely participate or protest is replaced by a willingness to make difficult choices. The apparent ceiling on the Greens' performance in national elections after 1981 - before the upsurge (rather than breakthrough) of 1987 - can be explained primarily in terms of their core electorate's mixed verdict on their performance as a 'serious' political party. This ambiguous response, too, was a reflection of their own difficulties in coming to terms with the discipline and organisational requirements that confront every party that stands in national elections and seeks to weigh in its influence in the policy process. Both ECOLO and AGALEV faced the same real difficulties on this count as every other Green party in Europe. ECOLO, for instance, was tardy about setting up an effective and extensive local party (rather than a movement) network.[7] The continuation of internal factionalism also inflicted damaged on the party's image as a responsible and united force for change. The familiar and well-publicised division between a moderate reformist tendency and the radical leftist-libertarian wing, caused defections within the party's ranks which did little to induce the electorate's confidence.[8] The fact, too, that the two Socialist parties (the Flemish SP and the Francophone PS) were in opposition to a centre-right coalition between 1981 and 1987, drew away a proportion of the radical vote which, while it is less inclined to vote for the left when these two parties are in government with the centre Christian Democrat parties, the Flemish Christian People's Party (CVP) and the Francophone Social Christian Party (PSC), tends to be more amenable when they are in opposition. Being in opposition at this juncture did enable the socialists to tap into and harness a proportion of the new politics constituency. Events played their part in this outcome. The prominence of the peace movement across western Europe in the wake of the American led NATO decision to station primed nuclear weapons on the continent helped the conventional left here to galvanise the protest vote.

The 1991 national election reflected as much as it provoked the most intense political crisis in Belgium for over two decades. A mixture of recession, the general mood of anti-establishment politics sweeping western Europe, and intensified communalism - represented in the steep rise in support for neo-fascist and xenophobic parties such as the Vlaams Blok (VLB) in Flanders, which won 12 deputies seats and took almost 20 per cent of the poll (and quadrupled its vote) in some of the regions and industrial cities, especially in Antwerp - rocked the Belgian political establishment. This was as much a backlash - a protest against rising economic and social crises, and an accompanying mood of disillusionment with the perceived failures of the established political order - as it was a positive vote for ecologism. To some extent Green politics is the politics of such residual protest all over Europe, but by no means exclusively so. Green politics in Belgium is also a reflection of the underlying political scene as it is anywhere else. The combination here of a system of compulsory voting and a rising disillusionment with the way the mainstream parties had handled the nation's affairs raised the potential for a protest vote. Belgian politics is more familiar than most of western Europe's advanced democracies with a simmering crisis at the heart of the state. And although the degree of discontent has increased over recent years, with the additional complications of deindustrialisation and the revival of an irredentism that was temporarily stilled during the boom years of the 1950s and beyond, the predictions in some quarters of an impending political disaster have yet to be realised.

Even in these unpropitious circumstances, the scope for realising an altogether 'new politics', detached from the deep-rooted tensions that have accompanied the country's political development, is perhaps less than it might be. Some of the Green vote amounts to little more than a negative comment on the perceived failures of the 'old' politics to heal these persistent divisions. The Greens, of course, have preferred to put a more positive gloss on this electoral arithmetic. Party spokespersons saw in the 1991 upturn, signs not merely of protest or discontent with the established parties, but also an indicator of a more deep-seated electoral shift. Jacky Morael, an ECOLO MP maintained, somewhat optimistically, that "we were carried to power by the will for change" and on the back of a primary concern with the environment - for "we are interested in all ecological matters, our position is well known, and when the people voted for us it was a conscious vote for the ecologists".[9] This optimum account was only accurate to a degree. But there was then, and there remains, a distinctive bedrock post-materialist constituency in Belgium, amidst the prevailing mood of communal atavism - a constituency for whom the Green parties do continue to represent an attractive ideological and programmatic option. In this they are similar to Green parties everywhere, whose electorates disproportionately reflect the same demographic profile of positive support from the young, better educated voter. Those who are disenchanted with the status quo, who exhibit the same broad mixture of post-materialist values and reflect the concerns of economically marginalised or devalued groups that have suffered, either from rapid, technologically induced change or from unemployment caused by the deindustrialisation of their communities.[10] Many of these Green voters, too, in the particular Belgian context were instrumental or rational ecologists, attracted either by the non ethnic appeal of the Greens, or by the prominent demand in their manifesto for large public expenditure to clean up Belgium's 'rust belt', provide education and retraining, improve housing, health care and public transport, clean up its river network and the polluted North Sea coast, as well as measures for reducing the national dependence on nuclear power and pollution.

Although this programme flew directly in the face of the established parties' urgent drive to massively reduce public expenditure, in order to control what was already the EC's largest national debt (as a percentage of GNP) and to meet the convergence criteria agreed at Maastricht for EMU participation, the national political impasse in Brussels led to a realistic possibility that the Greens, with a significant block of 17 seats across the communal divide in the then 212 seat House - the strongest Green representation in a national parliament in Europe - might be invited to join a coalition government. There was even some speculation at one stage that the late King Baudouin might appoint an ECOLO member to be the *formateur* or 'honest broker', whose task as official interlocuter in this cluttered parliamentary landscape, is to facilitate negotiations between the potential coalition partners. There was speculation, too, fuelled by the Finance Minister, that the Greens might be induced to join a rainbow coalition, as they already had at the regional level. This prospect was enhanced before the election results were declared, by the widely predicted losses for the mainstream parties and the requirement of a two thirds majority for the passage of the major constitutional reform - in the direction of enhanced federalism - that these parties considered to be vital in order to keep the Belgian state intact. The Greens endorsed the Accord de la St Michel (September 1992) which brought about the de facto federalisation of the Belgian state. Both Green parties kept their political heads at a time when the rift between the governing parties and some of the opposition parties threatened serious constitutional impasse. They made clear the price of such cooperation and adopted a joint programme that called on the governing parties to take much more stringent measures for combating the heavy pollution of the North Sea coast and the country's rivers, measures to prevent further damage to the ozone layer, and a massive reduction in national dependence on nuclear energy sources. The Greens also demanded environmental improvements in the transport and agricultural sectors, as well as action on a range of social measures - on housing, public health, education and social security provision - all of which involved increased expenditure, at a time when the major parties were committed to making inroads into Belgium's large national debt.

Perhaps the best indicator of the lack of seriousness of the Greens' intent to strike a bargain with the centre-left came from their politically unrealistic demand for the dismantlement of the country's seven nuclear power stations. Certainly, no activist on either side of the Green movement would have been able, had this ambitious programme become the subject of any serious bargaining with the mainstream coalition parties, to level any accusation of a sell out. The official ECOLO spokesperson set out his party's stall here by observing that "if we participate in power, it is not just to be a green cherry on the top of the cake".[11] In the event, the Greens refused to join the coalition-making negotiations, let alone any government that might have resulted from them. They took this stance, not so much because they shunned pragmatic politics per se, or because they had collectively lost their faith in the conventional political process. They insisted instead that in the frenetic, crisis ridden conditions that currently prevailed in the country, ecological issues, as the various bargaining positions taken up by the prospective coalitional partners indicated, were bound to be heavily discounted. The Greens were, however, encouraged by their longer term prospects, and rather than damage them preferred to bide their time. The Green parties' ability to attract over 1 in 10 Belgian voters even at this election, with up to a quarter of this vote in ECOLO's case, switching from the Wallonian Socialist party, amounted to a remarkable breakthrough by any yardstick. The 1991 election thus marked a significant development in the consolidation of Green politics in Belgium. It also represented a landmark in the movement's evolution - from its original localised, peripheral, and single issue status, into a political movement quite capable in time, not only of spanning the deep and dangerously destabilising linguistic divide that permeates Belgian politics. But also, secure on that foundation, of maximising its political leverage on the governmental establishment and, thereby, of playing a constructive rule within the fragile national political equation.

This bridging role is likely to be increased rather than diminished over the foreseeable future, given the structural constraints that the Belgian electoral system imposes on any decisive outcome. The peculiarities of Belgium's electoral system have served merely to enhance the critical importance of regionally based and relatively minor parties in the elaborate calculus that surrounds government formation here. The electoral arithmetic of the d'Hondt system precludes any party securing a majority of parliamentary seats. All Belgian governments must therefore be coalitions of both Wallonian and Flemish parties. The same constraints of proportionality and party fragmentation also prevail at local level. After the 1985 elections in Wallonia, the regional Liberal party (PRL) and the Christian Democrats (PSC) only managed to secure 52 of the 103 seats in the regional Assembly. This ensured that ECOLO's 3 seats had considerable purchase and increased its bargaining power over the new administration's legislative programme. The new government eventually decided to reject the Green's offer of ad hoc support on particular measures, but it lost some electoral credibility for so doing.

The communal crisis which has pervaded Belgian politics has also played a part in boosting the Greens' political credibility. While the politics of mutual accommodation and realism seem to have eluded the major party actors over the years, with regionalist parties replacing classical, integrative 'national' parties ranged along a stable left-right cleavage, once the politics of industrialism began to unravel in the 1960s,[12] the Greens, have moved markedly and visibly in the opposite direction. Although they retain their respective communal identities, in accordance with their origins and the esoteric rules of Belgium's electoral politics, they continue to liaise and cooperate across the communal divide. They are also amenable to ideological linkages, particularly with left of centre parties. This openness has borne fruit at the local level. In Liège, between 1983 and 1985, ECOLO held 3 of 11 seats on the city's governing committee, as a result of its power sharing arrangement with the local Socialists. Such local deals have produced a variety of pacts - from outright coalition to medium agreements to support legislative programmes, or particular policy measures in exchange for due consideration depending on local political arrangements. None of these accommodations have occurred without the same predicaments that have visited other European Green parties. These local deals, as much as any prospective national coalitional arrangement between the Greens and the establishment parties - which has been in the offing but has yet to materialise - provoked the very same unease and misgivings amongst Belgium's 'reasonable' and moderate Greens, given their ideological and emotional roots in alternative, 'new' and movement politics, as they did in Green parties elsewhere. However, even the prospect of a national cohabitation with the 'failed' establishment parties in 1991, did not produce the incipient crisis in Belgian Green politics that a similar red-green prospectus induced in the German party.

This outcome largely reflects the very different origins of these two Green movements. Fundamentalism has provided only a minor strand of Belgian ecological politics, on both sides of the movement.[13] According to the comparative classification developed in Chapter One, both Belgian Green parties are positioned on the pure-green/moderate axis. Both, too, are certainly wary of engaging in any undue flirtation with eco-socialism, even though many Greens share some of the moderate reformist inclinations of mainstream social democracy, as well as some of the libertarian and alternativist concerns favoured by the idealistic new left. But both parties continue to place a much higher premium on ecologism than they do on more radical social issues, although these are by no means regarded as mutually exclusive issue areas. This moderate Green propensity is reflected in their electoral support profiles. The data collected by Eurobarometer indicates that Belgium's Green voters are markedly less inclined to identify with issues associated with the left of the political spectrum than are Green voters in either France or Germany, even if party activists run ahead of their electorate here and are found to have significantly more radical inclinations. A study of activists conducted by Kitschelt and Hellemans[14] indicated that well over two thirds of them 'self identified' with the centre-left and signalled a mixture of ecological, left-libertarian preferences which identifies the Green activist in Belgium as very much the same sort of post-materialist who, under different national circumstances, has mobilised behind moderate Green politics elsewhere in Europe. But variation in the degree or the intensity of support for these issues makes all the difference here as to the political significance of such ideological positioning.

The unreliable or volatile electoral support base of the Belgian Green parties must also be accounted for. The vulnerability of the discontent quotient or protest factor to those more central issues (productionist and constitutional, rather than post-materialist and non-instrumental) which dominate Belgium's complex political equation, and pattern its increasingly precarious coalitional outcomes, has clearly played a part in limiting the Greens' impact on national politics. For this reason in particular, the Greens reached a quite modest electoral plateau, even at a time when ecologism enjoyed a higher salience with the wider population than it presently enjoys. The deepening impact of the country's communal cleavages and the particular policy issues these gave rise to has tended to diminish the appeal of a new post-materialist politics. This over-riding political fact has been reflected in the performance of both Green parties during recent elections. These contests have been dominated by two sorts of issues. The first of these is the preoccupation with finding constitutional solutions that allow for a better political management of cultural diversity in this fragmented society. A parallel concern has been with the very same social and redistributive issues - above all the balance of social costs, the burden of welfare spending (with 7 per cent of GDP spent on health provision and 5 per cent on pensions), and the large budget deficit which is a consequence of this - that have preoccupied political elites in every advanced European nation state. Most particularly, those endeavouring to meet the commitment undertaken in the European Treaty of Union (the Maastricht Treaty) to adopt an appropriate fiscal discipline - not least, to cut the budget deficit to 3 per cent of GDP by 1996, and to reduce debt as a percentage of GDP over the same timespan, in order to facilitate a system of European Monetary Union by 1999. And all at a time when, in the Belgian case, national unemployment had risen steeply - to 14.2 per cent by 1994.

(iv)   Prospects for politial change

An essentially materialist agenda has undoubtedly dominated Belgian politics since 1991. Both the material and constitutional elements of the 'old' politics continue to interface with each other. The rediscovery of communalism has been sharpened by growing disparities in the economic fortunes of the two linguistic communities. The sense that the linguistic fault line that divides the country reflects an uneven pattern of socio-economic deprivation has, in turn, heightened these communal tensions. The rising dangers of social disintegration have put constitutional politics back at the centre of the national agenda. Wallonia, once the economic engine of Belgian industrialisation, now suffers disproportionately, along with many other regions of primary industrialisation, from the legacies of its pioneering role. The discontent engendered in Wallonia by economic decline has considerably contributed to political uncertainties there. The Socialist Party suffered an erosion of its natural support base. In part due to widespread apathy and a more modest exodus to the far right Front National and other minor racist parties, prepared to use local anxieties to pursue their vendetta against ethnic minorities. Flanders, in contrast, benefited from its late development, as well as from the dynamic impact of Brussels on its regional economy. The city's status as the diplomatic 'centre' of the European Union, has fostered growth in its tertiary and service functions. It acts, too, as a magnet of inward investment and development capital. This success has persuaded many Flemish voters, particularly encouraged by the region's neo-liberal PVV (Partij voor Vrijheid en Vooruitgang), to endorse a separatism based on this prosperity - similar in some ways to the insular regionalism that has given rise to the Northern League in Italy. Resentment by the comparatively prosperous at the idea of subsidising, through taxation and other social costs, a welfare state which disproportionately benefits members of the other language community, has done little for national integration and much to weaken the social cement that holds this state together.

These issues have come to dominate Belgian politics during the 1990s. They have decided the outcome of the last two national, and the accompanying regional, elections. 'New' politics has been much discounted in the process. The decline in the salience of the ecological issue saw support for the Greens in the 1995 election dip for the first time since they made their national breakthrough in 1979. Even the Green parties' increase in support in the 1991 poll has to be put in context. On the face of it, their performance suggested a real breakthrough. In fact, the Greens benefited as much from a large protest vote as from any incipient sense that Belgium was ready for a 'new' politics. In the prevailing circumstances 'new' took on an inverse meaning from that conventionally employed by its radical theorists. It was, in other words, a 'new' politics whose rationale was negative not positive, pessimistic not optimistic, more authoritarian than participatory, didactic rather than progressive. Above all, it was a politics rooted in widespread disillusionment with the established parties, and not a little fear about the country's prospects in an ever more demanding competitive environment; rather than one that anticipated the end of 'normal' politics and their replacement by more democratic procedures. The Greens did benefit from this discontent, but largely as a vehicle for protest than as the harbingers of a positive seachange. The figures are revealing in this respect. The remarkable success enjoyed by ECOLO in 1991 was largely at the expense of the Socialists - who dropped from 24.2 per cent in 1987 to 19.6 per cent in 1991 and yielded 80,000 votes to the Greens.[15] In contrast, the Flemish Greens did less well. Not because of any deficiency in their organisation, but rather because the regional circumstances in Flanders were less favourable to them. The electorate there were no less well disposed to protest against what it saw as ineptitude, indifference or corruption at the political centre. They found, however, another party vehicle for their anti-system protests; one that was more in tune with the prevailing mood. In this region, too, the dominant party - the CVP - suffered a major electoral setback, dipping to 26.9 per cent (falling below 30 per cent for the first time). The main beneficiary of electoral volatility here was not the Greens but the Vlaams Blok party, regarded by many conservatively inclined Flemings as the most fitting vehicle for their disillusionment with the mainstream parties. Vlaams Blok was shrewd enough to maximise this protest vote. It kept the worst excesses of its racist ideology under sufficient wraps to enable decent citizens to square a vote for it with their consciences. But their overt ethnic symbolism tapped deep instincts for separatism amongst many working class voters looking for easy scapegoats for their plight.[16]

The research conducted into the Vlaams Blok constituency reveals much the same blend of motives that recur in the dynamics of extreme right populist parties across the continent. A mixture of virulent racism and a bewilderment, confusion or a sense of betrayal amongst the young, the unemployed and those blue collar and lower middle class - and disproportionately male and poorly educated-section of society, who feel displaced or peripheral in the current pattern of social change. Even Jean Marie Le Pen, hardly an objective witness of a phenomenon he has both encouraged and ridden to electoral success, reflected something of the social anomie of the marginalised and dispossessed that has been crystallised in the support for these movements, with his observation - after Vlaams Blok's signal success in the early 1990s - that its voters were reacting against global forces for change beyond their control and comprehension; in short, "against the dangers of cosmopolitanism and world wide policies".[17] Vlaams Blok (with 10 per cent of the regional vote) outpolled in 1991 both the moderate regionalist party (Volksunie), as well as the more obvious vehicles of regional protest - the anti-political and libertarian Rossem list (which still managed 5 per cent) and AGALEV itself. AGALEV's close identification with the plight of the immigrant community was unlikely to inflict much direct damage on the party. The social profile and preferences of far right voters hardly corresponded with that of potential Green voters. Indeed, the efforts by some AGALEV members in Antwerp, who set up a grassroots 'club' -*Vreemd Maar Vriend* (Foreign but a Friend) - in the city's Moroccan dominated suburb of Borgerhout, may have attracted support from some of the naturalised Afro-Arab electorate. The club's founder member, Sebbahi Mohammed, who later stood unsuccessfully for the Greens in the 1994 communal elections, certainly used his influence to ensure that immigrant voters were less favourably disposed to the mainstream parties. He campaigned on the message that "the Socialists and Christian Democrats have had a monopoly for more than 70 years and they have misused their mandate".[18]

The extent to which this apparent success disguised peculiarly local circumstances, was revealed by the outcome of the 1995 national election. The interim period saw little to alleviate the pressures that had been building in the Belgian polity and society. Communal tensions, aggravated by recession and an accelerating budgetary crisis, had increased the disillusionment with the main parties. This, in turn, had raised the pitch of communal unrest. In response, the mainstream parties sharpened their resolve to alleviate some of these inter-communal pressures in this unitary state, and to push on with the third stage in the incremental federalising of the Belgian polity. The plan was to implement direct elections to four regional and community assemblies each empowered to exercise autonomy over an impressive range of policy areas. The Green parties' ambivalent response to the federalisation process reveals their limitations in an electoral climate gripped by rising linguistic tensions. They were favourable in principle to any measure that deconcentrated political power, as they were to measures that eased social pressures. On the ground, the Flemish Greens worked in their regional assembly with the three mainstream regional parties to contain the extremists. This, in turn, enhanced their reputation for moderation. At the same time their primary concern with ecological issues caused them to have doubts about reform measures that, as they saw it, weakened the chances of a common national response to environmental pollution. Although some of Belgium's most serious environmental problems are regionally or locally specific - for instance chemical emissions which impact on the fisheries, wildlife and habitat on the Flemish coast - both Green parties regarded the country's ecological balance as a national issue that required concerted solutions. All of Belgium's cities and regions shared similar problems of river borne pollution. The Schelde and the Meuse had badly polluted eco-systems. Likewise, industrial smog, the impact of the car culture (with some 4 million cars in a population of barely 10 million), excessive urban congestion (with 300 people per square kilometre), and a high concentration of nuclear power stations, were all seen by the Greens as essentially matters that demanded a national rather than a regional solution. Yet on this issue, as in so many others, the incremental federalising of Belgian public policy threatened to undermine what the Greens regarded as the best policy approach.

Federalism required the devolution of responsibility for the environment issue from the centre, which made effective national coordination difficult to achieve. The national Environment Ministry did retain overall responsibility for both the nuclear energy sector and for those issues - North Sea matters for example - where Belgium needed to negotiate agreements with other sovereign governments. But on many other environmental matters - such as recycling, waste incineration and disposal - responsibility passed to the newly empowered regions, and responsibility for the management of rivers that crossed political boundaries remained confused. There were other problems, too, with the new arrangements. In spite of the Environment Ministry's claims that the bifurcated approach worked well, with effective national policy action in key areas - including the outlawing of dumping at sea (agreed in 1989), banning incineration at sea and the prohibition of aerosols (both passed in 1990), financial incentives for cars purchased with catalytic converters, as well as a national annual environment budget of some 5 billion francs, and regular consultations and joint deliberations conducted under the new administrative framework with the regional authorities - the Greens saw in these measures more problems than solutions. The Greens were equally sceptical about the government's motives for holding on to the receipts from the introduction - in June 1994 - of a joint agreement with neighbouring governments of a motorway toll for trucks. These actions seemed to be both a recipe for administrative confusion and a convenient alibi for the avoidance of a properly managed and adequately resourced strategy for national environmental management. This problem was compounded by the increasing role of the EU in these matters. Devolution has undoubtedly increased the sources of friction between the centre and the regions, and has in the process made the enforcement of EU directives that much more difficult.

The resolution of these uncertainties was hindered by the shift in national priorities that separated the Greens even from those parties with whom they shared a broad commitment to the virtues of a continuing national polity. The electoral signals for the Greens remained confused as they tried to consolidate their impressive 1991 vote. They opted to underline their continuing preference for new politics issues by fashioning a distinctive critique of the government's neglect of the environment. In one sense, the times were out of joint for them as the national political agenda remained dominated by the 'old' politics of distributive and communal interests. Ecologism was at least as discounted in Belgium as anywhere else, given the onset of another deep global recession, with the accompanying budgetary pressures. The fall in the Green vote that eventually followed at the 1994 Euro and commune elections was in part the culmination of this broad agenda shift, compounded by the Greens' determination to push for unpopular eco-taxes. The cabinet had wrestled with this contentious issue since it was first broached in 1993. After intensive lobbying from those industries most affected, they eventually settled for a modest measure that diluted the original proposals. The law that was eventually approved in December 1994 covered five products, from pesticides to non-recyclable bottles. The government claimed this as a victory for environmental protection, when in fact one of the principal reasons for their adoption of this measure had less to do with any full conversion to ecologism than with its appeal as a short term fiscal solution to make up for some of the projected shortfall in the social security budget. The Greens' criticised the measures as a sellout and demanded far more sweeping proposals. Nevertheless, the economic impact of these measures won them few friends amongst the main 'social partners' and widened the gulf between both Green parties and those mainstream parties - particularly on the left - who were their best prospects as political partners. The downturn in the salience of this issue was reflected in the electoral arithmetic. In the 1994 Europoll ECOLO's vote share in Wallonia dropped from 16.5 per cent (1989) to 13 per cent, which cost it one seat (down to one); AGALEV also lost ground but managed to retain its single Strasbourg seat. Vlaams Blok captured 2 seats with 12.8 per cent of the Flemish vote (up from its previous best of 6.6 per cent and largely at the expense of the CVP, down 7 per cent to 27.4 per cent of the regional vote). In Wallonia, where a burgeoning scandal surrounding leading Socialist politicians severely dented the vote of the leading provincial party (the PS vote fell 9 per cent to barely 30 per cent), the neo-fascist Front National was the principal beneficiary, rising to 7.9 per cent (1 seat) from a negligible base in 1989. These broad trends were repeated in the 1994 commune elections. The rise in support for extremism was most notably signalled in Antwerp where Vlaams Blok polled 28 per cent, doubled its tally of seats and overtook the Socialists on the city council.

These electoral trends, repeated in the 1995 national elections, and significant in themselves, contained evidence of a degree of tactical voting that had implications for both Green parties. They confirmed, too, the endemic volatility of the Belgian Green electorate.[19] At the same time, these electoral shifts suggest more than an ephemeral protest quota in the Green electorate, but rather a bedrock of radical commitment amongst those who remained loyal to the two parties. This commitment is expressed as consistent support for political ecologism, whichever variant of the centre-right (up to 1987) or centre-left coalition that is the axis of normal politics here finds itself in government. This does not ensure, however, that the Green vote per se remains solid. It has been as amenable to fluctuation as the vote of any other modern Belgian party. The recent decline in the Green vote has to be understood in the context of the wider, emergent pattern of electoral politics; and in particular, of the rise of the far right parties and the threat they pose to the politics of moderation, civility and decency. The conversion of the mainstream opposition Liberals - especially the Flemish PVV - to harsh neo-liberal 'remedies' for Belgium's budgetary problems has also played its part in determining the electoral tactics of the country's radical constituency. With the prospect of a new centre-right coalition being seriously mooted as a potential electoral outcome, many progressively inclined voters simply swallowed their deep ideological reservations about supporting the Socialists. They preferred to see them back in government, if only as the most effective guarantor of a degree of social justice that was unlikely to ensue if the right returned to power. This calculus was a particularly appealing one in Wallonia, which had more to lose from a rightwards shift in the balance of the governing coalition.

These arguments were particularly potent in the context of the 1995 national elections. There was much more at stake in elections to determine the shape of the national government and the economic balance of power that would follow this, than in either of the second order elections of 1994. A tactical calculus similar to that used in these previous elections helped to shore up the Socialist vote - in spite of the damage caused by recent corruption revelations. The progressive constituency was persuaded not to abandon them, whether for the Greens or other radical parties or, at least, not to the extent that some pundits had forecast. The fact that Belgium has a system of compulsory voting also played its part in determining the eventual outcome. Regardless of unprecedented levels of disillusionment with politicians,[20] Belgium's electors felt obliged to make a straight political choice or risk a fine. In the circumstances, and with issues of great import at stake for every elector, large numbers of them resisted the temptation to indulge in an empty protest and, as many saw it, 'waste' their votes - whether on one of the record number of outlandish alternative or anti-parties on offer, or for more cogent radical parties. The Greens in these unpropitious circumstances were invariably squeezed. The prospect of a fall in Green support was apparent from the pre-election opinion polls. This shortfall had little to do with the demonology peddled in the press or by rival parties - a misplaced image of an extreme or utopian organisation wholly out of touch with the concerns of moderate opinion. On the contrary, the Belgian Greens had largely exorcised these demons and were more in tune with widespread public disquiet with the inefficiency and remoteness of the political establishment than the mainstream parties.[21] They underpinned their own reputation for moderation by standing foursquare behind these established parties - in line with the majority of public opinion - in their staunch opposition to what they saw as the dangerous populism of the far right and the threat this posed to an already fragile communal compact. Ironically, it was the very credibility of this extremism and the threat it conjured of a national abyss - which the Greens gave credence to amongst their own potential support - that persuaded so many of them to exercise a tactical option in favour of those parties regarded as the most effective bulwark against it.

Both Green parties were voluble in their opposition to anything that confirmed what they saw as a destabilising xenophobia, from whatever source. They criticised in particular the government's move to appease Flemish militancy by its opposition to any increase in foreign residency in Brussels and its environs - a development that some extremist politicians had provocatively called an "oil stain" - by securing a derogation from the European Union treaty to restrict foreign nationals' voting rights in local elections.[22] The Greens condemned the government for "giving our country a negative image",[23] and opposed this reneging on international responsibilities as an unseemly intolerance. Worse than that, they saw it as blatant hypocrisy for a country that not only housed the core EU institutions, but also laid claim to being one of the mainstays of European integration. By launching this criticism the Greens emphasised their commitment to a far more supranational vision of European integration than that represented by current European *acquis*. They detected, too, in this outcome, an institutional legitimisation of the insular nationalism that had nurtured the overt racial discrimination of Belgium's extremist parties, against people much less able to defend themselves than foreign diplomats, journalists and the like. By taking this radical stance, the Greens confirmed their continuing commitment to a progressive politics ethos drawn from a new social movement agenda. This was further emphasised by the Greens involvement in the anti-racist 'Objectiv 497,917' - a movement whose name included the size of the vote for the extreme right when it made its national breakthrough in the 1991 elections. 'Objectiv' was active in extra-parliamentary politics. It collected over one million signatures (more than one in ten of the populace) on a petition that called for better rights for immigrants - including automatic citizenship after five years residence. It was also instrumental in organising in March 1995, a major anti-racist demonstration in Brussels. By their support for these campaigns, the Greens cemented their links with street politics. They were also associated with the Belgian contribution to the remarkable upsurge in grassroots concern for animal welfare which was launched by a mixture of ecocentrist alternativists and public opinion over the live export of animals in the EU. A 'Gaia' animal rights group collected over half a million signatures in March 1995 on a petition that called for restrictions on the sale of domestic pets and horse racing.

Opposition to all forms of intolerance and racial injustice have been a prominent theme in Green politics during the nineties. AGALEV objected to the provocative decision of the provincial government in Flanders to curtail budgetary provision for the French language and culture. Both Green parties likewise opposed the Flemish Liberal party's equally divisive proposal to appease its own constituency, even at the cost of further antagonising Wallonian opinion, by federalising the social security system and the national debt - at 49 billion francs (1.6 billion US dollars), the highest in terms of GDP in the EU. These proposals were designed to further shift the burdens of structural deindustrialisation in the region onto a Wallonian population much less equipped to cope with them. The PVV were playing sectarian politics here, and had the Social Christian Party (CVP), the region's dominant party, firmly in their sights. Outflanking their rivals on the social policy question amounted to the PVV's principal electoral strategy. Fostering communal mistrust and resentment at 'propping up' the 'other' community, persuaded the Liberals to adopt a series of policies influenced by the Gingrich model of new Republicanism in the USA. These included a proposed drastic cut of ten per cent in social charges, extensive privatisation of public utilities, and the de rigueur use of private pensions to reduce the pressure on taxpayer and employers of Belgium's generous state provision. This strategy, in turn, impacted on the Greens as much as it did on its principal political target.

The reaction to the new right agenda affected the outcome of the 1995 election campaign - not least the Green vote - as much as the menace from the far right extremists. The Liberals' overt challenge to generous welfare state provision, at a time of deep recession and widespread economic insecurity, helped to reinforce the sense of an impending communal breakdown. The threats posed by the extremist parties did much to convince a wary electorate that even an ineffectual status quo was preferable to unleashing the dramatic changes posed by the two, albeit competing, forces of the 'new' and far right. The outcome was a squeeze on the peripheral parties. A protest vote now seemed to be a luxury the country could ill afford. The major traditional parties in their respective communal homelands were the main beneficiaries of this prevailing mood of 'rational' caution. The Liberals' threat to a properly funded and equitable welfare system damaged, as a result of the electoral osmosis that affects Belgium's electoral outcomes, the PVV's liberal sister party (PRL-FDF) in Wallonia. This, in turn, helped to stem the tide of Socialist defections there to the available radical alternatives, and especially to ECOLO, even though the corruption scandal was diligently uncovered by public prosecutors throughout the election campaign. In Flanders, too, moderate voters shied away from experimentation, with either the neo-liberal or far right, and gave the CVP the benefit of what the opinion polls suggested was a considerable doubt. In short, radical parties across the country - not least the Greens - were caught out by a last minute rush to embrace caution. The inclination to unduly weaken the governing parties was tempered by the acknowledgement that a protest vote might be an expensive luxury with unpalatable consequences if it provided a route back into government for the Liberals - an outcome that would almost certainly ensure an altogether harsher centre-right government, and just possibly an entreé for the far right as the country's power brokers.

The Greens were squeezed, then, by circumstances rather than by any perception of their own failures. In an election campaign dominated by the cross-fertilisation of two issues of momentous import for the country - communalism and budgetary retrenchment - ecologism was bound to be relegated to the sidelines as a secondary issue. The two Green parties were perceived to be peripheral actors, and in these unpropitious circumstances they settled on a joint programme which threw any caution to the wind and addressed these prevailing issues from a radical perspective. Outflanked in their radicalism by seriously extreme parties (and in the case of the PVV, by an establishment party determined to bid for the discontented vote in its region even at the risk of further fracturing this already fragile state), the Greens found themselves in something of an electoral cleft stick. On the one hand their preference for the continuation of the existing state as the lesser of evils left them at a distinct disadvantage vis a vis the moderate parties of the centre-left. They were equally outbid for the votes of those electors disconcerted by the conventions and shortcomings of bourgeois politics, by more overtly populist parties on the right. The Greens made their electoral pitch in these difficult circumstances, by standing on a radical programme built around staunch opposition to the austerity programmes broached by most of their rivals on every side of the ideological spectrum. The Greens opposed any drastic reduction in the budget deficit, on the grounds that fiscal retrenchment would both diminish social justice and further erode national unity. They also condemned the recent drift to regionalism which, far from managing social diversity, had merely, as they saw it, institutionalised and entrenched communalism.[24] The proposal of the PVV's leading politician and president of the Flanders's region, Luc Van den Brande, just prior to the elections, for a confederal state of four quasi-autonomous regions, had already galvanized Green opposition on this critical issue. It provoked an official Green spokeswoman, Mieke Vogel, to liken him to Berlusconi, and to argue that the majority of Flemish voters were realists not xenophobes who "know that Flanders is not an island".[25]

At the same time, the Greens mixed the pro-state moderation with which they had been accustomed with an alternativist agenda designed to minimise any loss of their hard core and post-materialist support base to other parties, persuaded as many of this constituency clearly were by the desire to neutralise the impact of the radical right. In a distinctive three part programme, the Greens suggested a radical fiscal 'solution' for transforming the public debt into public loans; the promotion of inter-communal 'fiscal justice', and an endorsement of the traditional leftist collectivist model of the state - including opposition to the privatisation of both welfare provision and the public management of utilities. The Greens' solution to the shortfall between the state's revenues and its welfare commitments was to simply clamp down on tax evasion and fraud - an unconvincing 'solution' to cutting back a large public deficit to 1.2 per cent by the year 2000, without any loss of social benefits or increases in taxation. In similar vein, the Greens proposed a social security system that discriminated in favour of the weakest. They continued to resist, on grounds of national equity, the federalisation of this elemental 'national' responsibility. On pensions provision too - another critical theme in the 1995 campaign - the Greens advocated generous basic state provision for all, with extra variable provision financed out of additional individual contributions. On the law and order issue - another issue manipulated to great effect by the far right - the Greens found it more difficult to offer convincing solutions that conformed to their radical propensities at the same time as they played to public sensibilities. For although their consistently radical preference for legalising soft drugs and prostitution were designed to court the youth and alternativist libertarian constituencies, these proposals proved altogether too radical to appeal to most mainstream voters.

The looming political issue of reformulating Belgian statehood determined the outcome, both of the 1995 election and, for the foreseeable future, has limited the prospects of the Belgian Green parties making any significant advances in this uniquely divided political landscape. The electorate has other priorities to contend with than quality of life issues. The collective political mind was thus concentrated, and its electoral choices galvanised, by an altogether different set of issues than those raised by the new politics. Nothing less than the future stability of the Belgian state was at stake in this election. The electorate was confronted in these circumstances by a stark choice; between extremism on the one side and two variants of 'normal' coalitional politics on the other, one of which - a new centre-right coalition giving vent to the PVV's vision of a novel form of social contract between the individual and the state, and between the linguistic communities themselves - implied a social revolution almost as disruptive in its long term consequences as anything threatened by the extreme parties of the far right.

The eventual outcome of this conflict of visions was the re-election of the outgoing centre-left government. This election was as much a political tale of two regions as it was a single national contest. The Greens were squeezed in both regions as prospective radicals voted tactically, and in a way calculated to reduce the chances of political disruption and social dislocation. The damage inflicted on the Socialists in Wallonia - although the PS lost some support to the far right Front National (FN up from 1 per cent in 1991 to 2.1 per cent)[26] - was less evident than the projections of the opinion polls. The PS vote in Wallonia fell from 13.5 per cent (1991) to 12 per cent. The Francophone Liberal party (PRL-FDF) was clearly damaged by its association with its sister party's unmitigated neo-liberalism, and failed to capitalise on the severe discontent with the centre-left parties. In short, the electoral mood here suggested a reluctance to translate discontent into something worse by switching support to either of the parties of the right. The radical vote played its part in minimising the electoral slippage from the regional status quo, either by refusing to abandon the Socialists to the extent the polls had predicted; or by resisting a large vote for ECOLO in order to block the advance of the right in Wallonia as in the country as a whole. ECOLO polled a modest 4.1 per cent and although it took seats, suffered a drop of 1 per cent on its 1991 poll with the loss of one parliamentary seat.

In Flanders, a somewhat different but parallel alignment of regional political forces resulted in a similar outcome. Both for the local Green party and in terms of contributing to the overall national outcome. In this region, too, the main political dynamic was a dual onslaught on the dominant CVP by its main rival, the PVV. A secondary electoral contest, albeit an important one for its effect on the national outcome, was the impact of the far right on all of the mainstream parties. The figures tell a similar story overall to the Wallonian situation. The CVP vote actually increased (from 16.9 per cent to 17.1 per cent) largely on the back of Prime Minister Jean Luc Dehaene's image as a conciliator and political fixer, and the promise he held out in contrast to the Liberal's more disruptive image, of presiding over peaceful change and communal harmony. The Liberal PVV only increased its vote in 1991 by barely one percent (from 12 per cent to 13.1 per cent) The electorate - especially in the more prosperous rural and suburban parts of Flanders, resisted the divisive appeal of Vlaams Blok. The party failed to make any breakthrough and only marginally increased its 1991 vote (up to 7.8 per cent from 6.6 per cent). Remarkably enough, the Socialist Party (SP), regardless of the taint of corruption that spread from its sister party, actually increased its vote share on 1991 (from 12 per cent to 12.6 per cent). A similar pattern here - of resistance to the available radical alternatives and a consolidation of support for the centre-left, regardless of widespread discontents and reservations - also saw the radical protest (and potential Green vote) limited to its modest bedrock post-material constituency, built up in previous national elections. AGALEV saw its 1991 regional vote (4.9 per cent) drop slightly (to 4.1 per cent), which yielded the party the same number of seats (5).

A clear trend was discernible in the 1995 election. Policy issues wedded firmly to the materialist or redistributive concerns of the 'old' politics crowded the agenda and shaped both voters' perceptions and, in the end, the electoral outcome itself. Albeit in quite distinct and by no means in identical ways, in both linguistic communities. New politics issues came off badly in a contest dominated by recession, external (global or regional) pressures for fiscal reform and greater austerity, and the likely impact of these factors on the country's delicate communal balance. The Belgian Greens are certainly down but by no means entirely out of the political game. A small but - as the 1995 poll indicated - persistent ecological constituency still exists there. Whether this peripheral aspect of Belgian politics can ever become a more central element in the national equation is debatable as things currently stand. Nevertheless, to suggest that this electoral niche is likely to be eroded or entirely overwhelmed by the mainstream ideological forces currently at work in Belgium, is to ignore not only the deep ethical roots of ecologism in Belgium, but also its continuing appeal to a discernible and, arguably, a growing post-materialist clientele. The very structure of Belgium's bifurcated polity has, paradoxically, helped to consolidate this Green vote and to ensure that it is not absorbed into more powerful, resourceful and better organised political parties. But these same circumstances have ensured that the Green vote remains smaller than its potential constituency might suggest. Belgium continues - in spite of recent social changes - to be divided into distinct sub-cultures or 'pillars' (*zuilen*). These communities cut across both class and ideology, and continue to shape its pattern of party politics into a unique arrangement of split or linguistically based parties. This 'pillarisation' process (*verzuiling*) touches almost every aspect of political and social organisation, for as Rihoux observed, "the pillars consist of tightly built inter-organisational networks of interest groups, social service organisations and political parties. This is why Belgium has often been defined as a 'partyocracy'; the major political parties, linked to their respective strongly structured and hierarchical pillars, play a dominant role in the policy-making process. Radically new demands are not easily assimilated by pillars, and this is an important factor not only in the emergence but the durability of the Greens".[27]

In other words, the Greens are able, in this otherwise tightly structured society, to represent those universal and 'new' politics issues that do not easily fit into this conventional arrangement. Nor are they likely to find their agenda readily assimilated by mainstream parties that are otherwise engaged by their own narrow concerns with communalism. At the same time, as long as the state is confronted by the serious identity crisis that pervades both polity and society, those mainstream parties better equipped to hold the civil fabric together are likely to stem the flow of support from even progressively minded or radical Belgians to the Greens. The Socialists, who remain the Greens' main rivals for a youth vote less attached to the social vested interests of the existing pillars, and for the radical vote per se that is less enamoured of any appeal to tradition, remain pillarised in two distinct if cooperating parties rooted in distinct communal constituencies. And while the Socialists, during their period in opposition between 1981 and 1987, did move onto the Greens' natural alternativist territory, by opposing the standing of nuclear weapons by NATO on western European soil, this rivalry was modulated by the peripheral importance of this issue in Belgian radical politics. Unlike many neighbouring countries where this issue became a real bone of contention in the battle for the hearts and minds of the old and new left alike, the anti-nuclear movement here had little political salience even on the political left. This was a remarkable fact given the sheer size of the nuclear energy sector, with 7 reactors for a country of only 11,780 square miles. The Greens were therefore able to appropriate this issue for themselves.

Of course, this issue yielded little by way of political potential. Its value was limited by the national predominance of other materialist issues that consolidated the traditional cultural cleavages and reduced the political appeal of the new politics agenda. The impact of the recent constitutional reforms that have transformed Belgium from a unitary into a federal state, and that have consolidated communalism, even if it has softened the worst atavistic instincts across the linguistic divide, continues to ensure that truly national issues, let alone the post-material ones associated with post-modern politics, are much less likely to find a proper outlet or win a fair hearing from an electorate whose preferences are shaped by a much narrower frame of political reference. At the same time, the sheer fragility of pillarisation, and the prospect here for political disintegration if communal divisions are taken to the extremes promised (or threatened) by the two right wing Flemish parties, and to a lesser extent, Wallonia's FN party, has helped to concentrate more moderate minds within the political establishment on the need to soften these communal boundaries. And thereby to find those joint issues and common agendas that will keep the sense of Belgian nationhood alive and a viable state intact. The Greens have undoubtedly contributed to this process - and in a way that has helped to bring them in from the cold and to establish them as supporters of a moderate, consociational national politics in which communal rights and the overarching national interest are reconciled within a coherent, viable polity based on a carefully managed diversity. The Greens' reputation for political responsibility and moderation has grown in relation to their contribution to making the national polity work. The Green parties' contribution to honest brokering across the linguistic fault line offers a positive contrast to the frequently insular, ideologically self indulgent and socially divisive, approach to critical policy issues of all of the mainstream parties, at least some of the time. They have yet to practice these skills in a national coalition government, but there is every sign that should that opportunity arise, the Belgian Greens would have both the aptitude and the commitment to face that challenge and carry it off. Where they have held office at local level - and especially in the governance of some of the major cities - (ECOLO in Liège between 1982 and 1988 and in Brussels (1988) for instance) - the Greens, like their German counterparts, have only enhanced their reputation for moderation and diligence.

There are, however, severe constraints imposed on Green politics and its longer term potential by opting to play the game of 'normal' politics to this extent. The commitment to cementing the existing Belgian polity as the lesser of the available evils, has cost the Greens votes amongst their own potential radical constituency, as much as it has improved their reputation amongst the electorate at large. By endorsing the idea of an impending threat to national stability, the Greens have encouraged many otherwise radical voters to 'lend' their votes to those centre-left parties better able to keep that threat at bay. The Belgian Greens have certainly confronted, if not entirely resolved, some of the critical dilemmas confronting Green parties everywhere. Even in the most unpropitious political circumstances that have prevailed in Belgium during the first half of the recent decade, they have managed to hang on to a distinctive if modest electoral niche. Whether they can enlarge that support base depends as much for the forseeable future on the circumstances that prevail in national and even international politics as it does on their own actions.

2. The Netherlands

(i) Green roots

Green politics in the shape of an independent party came relatively late to the Netherlands' already complicated political equation.[28] And compared to political ecologism's steady progress elsewhere in continental Europe, it has made only a marginal impact on the political scene. In some ways this is surprising in a country which is both densely populated and suffers from the considerable pollution which has built up in the Rhine estuary. A more pointed 'paradox' is the sheer incongruity between a receptive social foundation for effective Green party politics in the Netherlands' flourishing new social movements from the 1970s onwards, and the ineffectual response of local Green politicians to these otherwise promising circumstances.[29] There was an extensive presence of these new movements as the traditional 'pillarised' (*verzuillen*) social system - rooted here in a religious rather than a linguistic cleavage - softened under the impact of modernisation.[30] These movements were especially appealing to the emergent 'new' middle class, but their failure to coalesce into an effective national Green party stands in marked contrast to similar developments elsewhere on the continent.[31] Numerous reasons can be given for this state of affairs, not least a marked tendency to cautious conservatism amongst Dutch voters when it comes to embracing political experimentation.[32] Another reason for this slow start was the fact that the ecological issue predated the Green movement and was therefore colonised early by other progressive parties. A motley of small radical and pacifist splinter parties from the mainstream Catholic and Labour parties, with a direct appeal to the Netherlands' alternative movements, had to some extent already closed off this particular electoral option.[33] The PSP (Pacifistische-Socialistische Partij) attracted much of the new left vote, whereas the PPR (Politieke Partij Radikalen) made much of the early running on ecological issues.

The delayed arrival of a Dutch Green party was preceded by many examples of successful environmental campaigning. For instance, there was a notable campaign to halt the offshore dumping of nuclear waste. Successive governments, aware of the country's lack of fossil fuels and a rapid shrinkage in its supplies of natural gas, had embarked on a nuclear energy policy. This, in turn, prompted the rise of a well supported peace and anti-nuclear protest movement. This particular campaign was boosted by a widespread hostility to the nuclear option, epitomised by the protests against the construction of the Kalkar fast breeder reactor in Germany, the enlargement of a uranium plant in the Netherlands, and the support given to neighbouring Belgium's flagging anti-nuclear movement - a mood that was subsequently reinforced by the intensive publicity which followed the Chernobyl disaster. The energy issue was coupled, in what is broadly a progressive political culture, with rising opposition to the political establishment's decision to install American Cruise missiles in the Netherlands. Three million signatures were collected on a petition out of a population of barely 15 millions. The political credibility of Dutch environmental campaigning was further enhanced by its widespread reputation for diligent research and the factual accuracy, rather than the merely negative 'doom saying' or rhetorical idealism of its pronouncements. This impact has been reflected, in turn, by the seriousness with which the political establishment responds to ecological issues.[34] Governments here have tended to treat 'green' matters earnesty and have incorporated environmental planning into their macro economic strategies.[35]

The positive governmental response to ecological issues mirrors in no small measure the structural constraints imposed on all parties by the Dutch political system.[36] Of particular relevance here is the degree of proportionality in an electoral system that makes the outcomes of elections especially sensitive to quite small shifts in public opinion.[37] This has obliged the conventional parties, from whose parliamentary ranks governing coalitions are eventually formed, to respond positively and promptly to salient public issues. The rising concern of public opinion with ecological issues over the past two decades has figured increasingly on the map of national politics. The progressive Catholic party, the Politieke Partij Radikalen (PPR) for example, incorporated green ideas as the issue gained in political salience. While the direct outcome was little more than an uneasy cooperation with likeminded groups elsewhere, the PPR was active in the negotiations which established the rainbow group of radical and Green parties in the European Parliament in 1979 after the first direct elections to that chamber.[38] In the opinion of the Director of the Documentation Centre on Dutch Political Parties, Gerrit Voerman, the greening of the PPR was a significant factor in reducing the impact of an independent Green party;[39] that "the rapprochement between Radicals, Pacifists and Communists, which assumed greener colours in the course of time, then delivered the final blow to the pure green experiment".[40] Ecology was only one amongst several of the PPR's ideological concerns. The Radicals and Pacifists advocated more direct and grassroots democracy, although the former were more favourably disposed to conventional forms of political organisation and had already cooperated with the PvdA (Labour party) in a coalition cabinet (1973-77).

The PSP, on the other hand, was closely involved in the wider peace and extra-parliamentary movements and also shared the Pacifists' abhorrence of nuclear weapons and militarism per se. The political consequences of these manoeuvres led to the outflanking of the nascent pure Green party as its political space became occupied (almost overcrowded) by a more broadly based coalition of alternativist and new left groups. The result of these developments was a political paradox; that in spite of electorate's amenability to enlightened ideas and radical causes, including ecologism, an independent Green party has struggled to break free of those politically adjacent movements which expropriated the idea. This, in turn, greatly complicated the direct expression of a pure Green message from one party political source. These three parties shared a broad radical programme that incorporated peace, ecology, antipathy to nuclear power, gender politics and a commitment to sustainable economic development.[41] In the circumstances this not only delayed, but undoubtedly helped to discount, the impact of the independent Green party which did eventually emerge in 1983. And this, in spite of the fact that a national opinion poll indicated that some 30 per cent of the electorate were favourably disposed to the idea of such a party. For once a public opinion with a sophisticated grasp of the relevant issues, and well enough aware of the impact of 'negative externalities' and the costs of environmental damage, was actually ahead of the ecologists. Moreover, it remained largely unconvinced by the new party's attempts to promote the Green cause in isolation from those complementary social movements in which the green idea in this country was already firmly rooted.

(ii)   Party formation

In spite of these unpropitious political circumstances, an independent Green party was eventually formed in the Netherlands. But this development was shaped by special political exigencies. It was inspired as much by external events as by any inclination to fill an ideological lacuna in Dutch politics.[42] Concern in some radical quarters that the PPR, the standard bearer of progressive ideas, might fail to make the 4 per cent threshold required to win seats in the 1984 elections to the European Parliament - a marked rise from the mere 0.7 per cent required under electoral law for national representation - activated a debate inside that party about the tactical benefits of appropriating the popular 'Green' label, in order to pre-empt a similar move by extreme right groups. It was felt that this would give the party a distinctive title with electoral appeal. It was on this opportunistic basis that two leading PPR members as required by law, registered a new party, the Groen Partij Nederland (GPN) with the country's Electoral Council. This was more of a 'party' in name than substance. It was little more than a diffuse constellation of radical groups to the left of the Labour party. This outcome was but one aspect of a complex electoral and coalitional strategy which is peculiar to Dutch politics. The move was therefore motivated, in part only, by a genuine concern with prosecuting ecological issues. The PPR was already active as part of a broad green platform, consisting of groups focusing on a range of environmental issues. But short term electoral considerations also played their part here, not least the desire to muster enough votes to secure a seat in the Strasbourg Parliament. The Dutch ecologists were also influenced in their decision by representations from the German Greens, who were actively canvassing the idea of a pan-European front of radical and alternative parties to fight the 1984 Euro-elections on a common front.

The PPR President responded to these events by negotiating a joint Green list drawn from like-minded Dutch partners. This Groen Progressiff Akkord - GPA, consisted of the PPR (ranked 2nd on the list), the Pacifist Socialist Party - PSP (ranked first), the Communistische Partij van Nederland - CPN (ranked third), the Evangelical People's Party - Evangelische Volkspartij - EVP (ranked fourth), and the Groen Platform (ranked fifth). It was also agreed to implement a rotation system for any members who were elected, and to withhold any discussion of collaboration with other parties until after the election. The PPR efforts to tilt the Akkord's programme for the 1984 Euro elections more firmly in favour of ecologism was thwarted by factional wrangling with the other members. The GPA programme amounted to little more than an ephemeral wish list in which environmentalism ranked lower than social issues (especially unemployment) and international peace.[43] Not surprisingly, the Green Platform activists showed considerable reluctance to join such a pragmatic Akkord which might compromise their pure Green principles. They met at Utrecht in December 1983, and created instead their own party - De Groenen. Even this dedicated Green party reflected a narrow agenda. It was born out of a negative resistance to rival factions competing for ecological credibility, rather than any positive attempt to build a viable Green coalition. As such, it brought together moderate, non leftist ecologists - left liberals and progressive Christian Democrats were much in evidence - alarmed that the Green label should be appropriated by a list that even included a non-Stalinist Communist party.[44]

After unseemly legal wrangling over the question of the entitlement to authoritatively use the 'Green' label, the courts did allow the Utrecht Greens to officially register its name. Standing on its own merits, and unencumbered by any hint of electoral opportunism with which the earlier deal making had saddled the Akkord, De Groenen failed to commend itself to the electorate. De Groenen polled a meagre 1.3 per cent. Meanwhile, the coalition of conventional but ecologically sympathetic parties which had contested De Groenen's right to stand as Greens, carried out their plan to contest the Euro elections under a Green banner. They gained some credibility here, by winning the endorsement of the successful German Greens. Although the Akkord did much better than their Green rivals, polling 5.6 per cent (which translated into 2 Euro-seats, 1 each for the PSP and the PPR) this was a comparatively disappointing result in terms of the national outcome. For it amounted to less than the total votes which had accrued to these 'coalition' partners when they stood separately at the 1982 national elections. The sense of disappointment was magnified, given that a pre election opinion poll had predicted a Green vote of approximately 13 per cent. The new Green party made an unsteady start. For one thing it was prone, as untried and radical parties tend to be, to making serious tactical mistakes. Not the least of these was its curious decision not to participate in local elections, universally regarded by Green parties across Europe as 'softer' electoral targets and, therefore, offering a sound platform on which to hone organisational skills, to win the confidence of citizens, and build upwards from the grassroots. This abdication of a role in local community politics further distanced this small party from those enthusiastic groups and lobbies who are the key source of membership, political energy and salient issues in most radical political movements. In short, by this act of political self denial they cut themselves off from the resources necessary to mobilise any marginal political movement - certainly one that has serious aspirations to open up a suitable political space at the national level. This serious miscalculation took its toll on the new party's electoral fortunes. The combination of tactical blunders and the electoral failures they contributed to actually caused some members to quit the party, further reducing its political impact. The cycle of impotence was tightened when these tribulations encouraged further fragmentation that led to the emergence of even smaller, more disparate splinter groups - most of them committed to a form of pure Green ecologism preoccupied with decentralisation, small scale enterprise, direct democracy and an economic self sufficiency that facilitated their preferences for self directed politics, but did little to overcome their intense factionalism. For example, a radical ecologist group nominated their own independent candidate on a "Green Federation" List for the 1986 national elections, winning a mere 0.2 per cent. The Amsterdam Greens - a city with a well established anarchist tradition - also focused on local issues.

The federated Greens did succeed in 1988 in merging with the Amsterdam Greens and recycled the De Groenen label for their own purposes. But again, this was more a matter of ideological positioning within a diffuse radical hinterland, than it was a symbol of reconciliation between rival sects. The outcome of this unsteady attempt at party development was a notable paradox; a rich legacy of radical ideas in which ecologism figured as a major theme, alongside the failure to build on this foundation an organisationally coherent or politically effective national Green party in order to give it effective expression. Much of the energy, enthusiasm and political initiative which was channelled elsewhere in western Europe into at least nationally organised, if not always cohesive, Green parties, was dissipated here in disjointed, peripheral and frequently utopian activities. A significant measure of this relative failure to make any real impact on the national political scene was the stark contrast between the Greens' poor electoral performance and the opportunity structures of a polity which positively favours both new and small parties. In spite of one of the most proportionate electoral laws in Europe - the d'Hondt highest average method, with the lowest threshold, as a share of the total national vote anywhere in western Europe, requiring only 0.67 per cent to secure representation in the Lower House - the Green party has been less successful here than the country's progressive political culture indicated that it ought to be. Failure at the polls had compounded the problem. It persuaded Green politicians to conserve their meagre finances, and to avoid risking the financial penalties of electoral failure. Parties unable to meet the threshold forfeit their deposit of one thousand guilders - although there is in effect only one such electoral district for the entire country. A cycle of political reticence operated here in which factionalism, enhanced by poor organisation, increased the prospects of defeat in an otherwise open electoral system. This, in turn, sustained a reluctance amongst Green politicians about risking scarce resources, which ensured that the Green message was less vigorously canvassed than it might have been.

(iii)   Political developments

The more favourable circumstances for ecologism that surrounded the 1989 European elections - a potent mix of post-Chernobyl anxieties and a deep current of electoral volatility brought on by widespread discontent across Europe with established politics - markedly improved the prospects for a 'Green' space in Dutch politics. The Dutch Green Akkord, which stood on this occasion under the 'Rainbow' logo and drew support from the local networks of its constituent parties, managed to capture a reasonable share of the protest vote, albeit in a second order election with little at stake. The Greens won 7 per cent and secured 2 European seats. This success was not followed up at the 1989 national elections. With considerably more at stake than mere protest, the Green party only managed to poll 4.1 per cent; a modest rise on the 1986 Green vote of 3.3 per cent. The rival De Groenen list managed only 0.4 per cent, although this produced 6 seats in the 150 seat legislature - double the number previously held by the new parties' constituent parts, and with some notable gains from the Labour party. This result was nevertheless a disappointment for the Greens, given a climate that was more than ever condusive to new politics issues. The 1989 poll in the Netherlands was the first one anywhere in Europe to be precipitated by an ecological crisis. The coalition government had collapsed over the particular issue of environmental clean-up costs. The fact that this issue acquired the status of a 'coalition breaker' emphasised the prominence of green issues in European national politics at this time. The coalition had proved unable to agree on the costings of a plan to cut pollution to 70 per cent of current levels by the year 2010. The Christian Democrat Premier, Ruud Lubbers, proposed a range of 'Green taxes' - for instance, raising fuel taxes and abolishing tax breaks for car commuters. Whereas his Liberal coalition partners in the national assembly, the Binnenhof, predictably objected on the grounds that the country was already over taxed. The crisis here elevated those acutely difficult environmental choices that face all advanced societies, to the top of the national political agenda.

On the face of it, this seemed to promise a better future for Green politics. This expectation has, however, remained largely unfulfilled. In part, this reflects the Greens' failure to insulate the ecological issue from the political mainstream, whose parties were able to steal a march on the Greens on this issue and incorporate it into their agendas rather than surrendering this territory to them. In part, too, the Greens' failure here is also an indication of their abiding inability to overcome their intrinsic factionalism. This liability continued to dissipate their political energies and to saddle them with an image amongst progressive voters, otherwise receptive to their message on this issue, of a party unable through lack of internal discipline, to turn support into political purchase where it mattered. Rather than throwing in their lot with De Groenen, the disparate red-green parties who had uneasily cohabited in the electoral Akkord, chose to perpetuate these divisions and underline their political weakness, by forming their own Green party - the Green Left (Groen Links) in November 1990. Not that this new arrangement was easily achieved between parties with such variable ideological roots and policy preferences. Although an 'open letter' was published early in 1989, in which activists from the gender and ecology movements and the trades unions endorsed the idea of a 'strong left-Green formation',[45] negotiations became stalled. It was only the imminence of the 1989 elections that resolved the issue.

124

The new party improved on its disappointing national performance in the 1991 provincial elections (5.2 per cent) in line with the trend for second order elections almost everywhere in Europe - with a mere 0.6 per cent for the pure Greens. In the most recent national elections (May 1995) even this figure has been trimmed back to a modest 3.5 per cent. These figures hardly represent a promising electoral return for a party which boasts an extensive and active membership. With a combined membership of some eighteen thousand, GL became the second largest Green party in western Europe after the German Greens, yet its political promise has hardly been fulfilled. Again, some of the blame for this shortfall lies with the party's own approach to politics, rather than with unpropitious circumstances entirely beyond its control. Much of the political energy that might have been mobilised to better effect in a more united party, has been used in the pursuit of the factional differences which are barely contained within this radical 'pastische' party. The party continues to be caught on the horns of a familiar ideological dilemma. To date, the party has tried to compromise between what Voerman has aptly called "the red Scylla and the green Charybdis" that fight for its political soul.[46] One side of this ecological dialectic advocates the ideal of social equality and more equal income distribution; whereas the other gives priority to ecological sustainability and prefers punitive taxation on pollutants.[47] The tension within the new party between its red and green elements must not, however, be exaggerated. Accommodations have been reached over time. The conflict has been ameliorated if not entirely resolved.[48]

The GL's second party congress (December 1991) agreed that ecologism should provide the principal focus for all policy matters, whilst building into their preference for fiscal correctives to bad eco practice (green taxes), a clear element of redistributive social justice. The party also undertook to accept a clear ecological line in its economic policy; in particular, that the market economy could and ought to be reconciled with proper ecological management. More recently, in 1993, the party's parliamentary group endorsed the priority given by the wider party membership, to put ecology before traditional leftist preoccupations with employment and economic justice - as long as these two objectives were reconciled as far as was possible.[49] We can put these developments into broader perspective. To an extent, they represent a mixed legacy. While the Green Left has begun to show a degree of realism in its recent internal compromises, the perpetuation of a major rift in the Netherlands' ecological politics between a distinctive red and pure green politics, underlines the continuing weakness of the ecological cause in a polity otherwise culturally receptive to its message. By emerging on the national stage as a party in its own right, the Green Left institutionalised and even perpetuated this rift between red-greens and the purists[50] which, in some other national contexts (most notably in West Germany), was contained, albeit with 'creative' tensions, within an umbrella organisation that gave ecologism a distinctive national focus - and for electoral purposes offered the electorate a clear Green choice. If this choice in Dutch politics has recently become somewhat clearer, this has more to do with a wearisome acceptance across the Green spectrum of the continuing folly of internecine squabbling, than it has with the rational pursuit of any national Green strategy. The pure Greens, divided over strategy and committed to a decentralised style of politics wholly unsuited to holding together a viable coalition of ideologically diffuse groups ill-adjusted to the routines, disciplines and compromises of practical politics, have slowly faded away. They have preferred instead to mobilise in the local community around specific issues. De Groenen continues to exist, if more in name than political substance. But it is hardly more now than a nominal electoral force. A succession of splits have hardly helped the cause of consolidating pure Green politics here and in 1992, after a particularly fraught and divisive party congress, the party seemed about to formally disband.

The public perception of these divisions between pure and red Greens - whether between the two distinctive parties, or just as damaging, the continuing tensions over direction and policy within Groen Links itself, where the socialist elements have responded to the recent surge in support for ecologism by forming its own 'Left network' - have hardly assisted the Green party cause in the Netherlands. Moreover, the perception of a movement divided against itself, in a country where other parties have seized on the political opportunities offered by ecologism, does much to explain the continuing paradox of one of Europe's most progressive societies failing so far to provide more than modest support to an independent Green party. This situation has continued, even though the ecological issue has enjoyed greater political profile since 1986. A mixture of local political culture and the Greens' own failure to overcome their factional differences and monopolise the ecology cause for themselves, instead of sharing it with other radical parties, suggests that the future looks less propitious for Green party politics here than it should be. There are some moderately encouraging signs to set against this pessimistic outlook. The Green Left have at least been moved to address the question of party discipline and organisation within their own ranks. Following a less than satisfactory showing in the 1989 poll - after opinion polls had predicted a much better outcome, yielding up to 10 parliamentary seats - the party responded by establishing (in October 1989) Vereniging Groen Links - VGL (the Association of Green Left). This organisation was designed to hold the party together and to focus its collective mind on the usual requirements that any serious party must address; those of coherent policy making, sound administration, effective electioneering and, not least, sufficient resources. The belated attempt to instil some organisational coherence was taken further in the reforms agreed in 1990. Affiliated organisations, party representatives and research bureaux were combined within a single coherent structure. The four constituent parties were disbanded in November 1990 and their individual members finally merged into one new party.

It may well be that these changes came too late to rescue the party from its past, or to restore an image for disciplined radical politics that might persuade enough members that there is an extensive progressive constituency which might switch its allegiance from those other parties that currently challenge the Greens for the alternative vote. None of these adjustments to the demands of 'normal politics have achieved much more than a marginal improvement in the Green party's capacity to take part in the national political game. As much as in most other advanced European polities, events continue to conspire against a Green breakthrough, even though the dominant groups in the Green movement have finally begun to assimilate the costs of resisting pragmatic compromises between themselves, as well as the advantages of adopting an organisational strategy better suited to wider public concerns. The problem is that the recent disposition to realism has come precisely at a time when the key issues of public debate have certainly increased the prospects of a major political shift in the Netherlands. Nevertheless, one that still revolves almost exclusively around the old productionist concerns rather than those of the new post-materialist politics.

(iv)   Prospects for political change

The impact of the Netherlands' current issue agenda on national political alignments was well illustrated by the outcome of the 1994 national elections. The CDA/PvdA coalition government had faced the very same combination of fiscal and demographic pressures as those that have exercised other governments throughout western Europe. Increasing global competitiveness and the impact of a prolonged recession obliged the government to review the burden of social costs on economic efficiency, as well as its implications for public expenditure. The CDA had already offended some of their own natural constituency, particularly amongst the elderly or middle aged, by pursing concerted fiscal retrenchment. The budget deficit was cut from 10.1 per cent of net national income to 3.8 per cent during the course of Ruud Lubbers' tenure as Prime Minister, whilst the absolute level of public debt had continued to rise. The 'grey' vote was particularly disaffected by government proposals to freeze state pensions, in order to switch funding to job creation schemes - seen as a way of simultaneously increasing the tax base, cutting back social costs on state and employers alike, and thereby facilitating the Netherlands' entry into EMU by accommodating the country to the convergence criteria agreed in the Maastricht negotiations. Political and business elites remained, by and large, as convinced as their predecessors that the national interest could best be served by staying on course for deeper European integration. Those groups who were asked to pay the price of this scheme were, however, more equivocal about this option. The impact of these deliberations on the country's stable politics was apparent from the marked rise of discontent and special interest parties (some 26 parties stood in the 1994 election), many of which rivalled and even surpassed the Greens as a suitable vehicle for electoral protest. The fastest growing of these parties - the Algemeen Oudersen Verbond (General League of the Elderly) - reflected this rising mood of uncertainty and won 7 seats in the 1994 elections. Even an overtly racist party - the Centrum Democrats - came from nowhere in this usually tolerant country and, following the familiar pattern of the populist right elsewhere on the continent, massaged public anxieties about crime and job insecurity into a strident campaign against migrants and the country's liberal laws on asylum and nationality - which yielded them 3 parliamentary seats.[51]

The most effective populist threat to the official Green party vis a vis its progressive constituency came, however, from a relatively new party that straddled the traditional ideological boundaries of left and right, but also managed to incorporate an ecological theme into its eclectic appeal. The Demokratien '66 party, which had its origins in a breakaway from the conservative VVD, offered a home for electors looking for a party that combined fresh ideas, a real commitment to democratic change, and a rejection of the 'complacency' of mainstream parties, alongside some familiar radical themes. D66's capture of 12 seats in 1994 on a progressive but far from militant platform, precisely illustrates the problems that face the Greens in a polity where their natural political territory remains, by and large, colonised by a party with far fewer reservations about playing the game of 'normal' politics, and enjoys a greater potential for capturing the new middle class vote necessary to bring about these changes.

The Greens were also confronted by other obstacles that have closed off, for the foreseeable future, any real prospect of a far reaching radical breakthrough. Political change may well be in the air here as it is elsewhere in the continent, but not in a direction that favours the Greens. If the Greens are to influence outcomes to any degree, they must expect to accommodate current exigencies rather than to resist them. Although all three of the Netherlands' mainstream parties came - in variable degrees - to accept the need for an overhaul of the country's generous welfare system, the inter-party and ideological tensions generated by this new agenda have impacted on the balance of political forces in a way that has encouraged a significant degree of political dealignment. The outgoing coalition partners in 1994, the CDA and the PvdA, both lost seats - an outcome that reflected a number of factors, not least a widespread mood of disillusionment with an insular, corporatist politics whose favoured 'insiders' had lost touch with public concerns. A poll conducted just prior to the 1994 elections revealed the extent of the problem. It showed deep cynicism amongst voters concerning the political establishment; 91 per cent of respondents believed politicians to be duplicitous and 37 per cent regarded Ministers as self interested. The same opinion poll found evidence of the electoral volatility that was exhibited in the election proper. An unprecedented number - 41 per cent, compared to merely 27 per cent in 1989 - remained undecided as to their voting intentions just prior to polling day.[52] These figures do not suggest that there was a problem here with political apathy. On the contrary, an 80 per cent turnout in the 1994 election underlined real discontent with traditional political arrangements, and a clear desire - expressed in political choices that saw a fall in support for the conventional parties of both right and left, and a rise in support for new and progressive formations - for political change. The Greens on 3.5 per cent (down from 4.1 per cent) and with 3 seats (down from 6) performed badly at a time when the mood in favour of change was both alert to new agendas and yet, paradoxically, showed a degree of resistance by large sections of the electorate to the perceived threats to their material self interest. This was more than an electoral quirk. The extent of the Greens' problem was underlined in the result of the European elections which followed the national poll. The Greens usually do better in second order elections where there is little at stake and voters can safely indulge in a protest vote. Nevertheless, the trend in the national elections was repeated in this poll. The two main parties either lost support (as did the PvdA), or maintained an already reduced support base (in the CDA's case). The main winners of the Strasbourg poll were protest parties, but not the Greens. The VVD and D66 both increased their support from 1989; whereas the Green vote slumped from 7 per cent (1989) to 3.8 per cent, very much in line with the national election result.

The most tangible sign of the realignment reflected in the 1994 national elections was the slump in the CDA's fortunes. The Netherlands' dominant political party - which had been in government more or less permanently in its various guises since 1918 - lost half of its former support and a record number of seats in the Binnenhof. The social democrats also lost votes and twenty per cent of its 1989 tally of seats, largely because its bedrock blue collar supporters felt betrayed by the party's involvement with Lubber's earlier attempts to cut back welfare expenditure. The popularity of its leader, Wim Kok, prevented even greater losses and the PvdA emerged as the single largest party - a position from which it was enjoined to negotiate a workable if unlikely coalition with the ascendant VVD and - given the parliamentary balance of power - a third party. The obvious coalition candidate here was D66. The Greens were not even considered as a remote prospect for a role in the coalition, unlike Green parties elsewhere, where a similarly tight electoral arithmetic has also resulted in multi party arrangements - for instance, in Belgium, Finland, Greece and Italy. There are several reasons for this exclusion, some of which reflect the status of the Greens per se, and others that are a direct consequence of the changing national political configuration. Dutch governments are invariably coalitions of two or at most three parties. As the 1994 coalition equation indicated, with its unique outcome of a left-right-progressive (or 'purple') coalition, the country is ripe for political experimentation. But only within the limits prescribed by the sort of ideological complementarity and political consensus with which the electorate here is familiar. If ecologism is to move closer to the mainstream of national politics, it may have to depend on parties other than the official Greens. One prospective route may come via D66. Demokratien '66 are a progressive party with some ideological roots in mainstream liberalism and a radical outlook that appeals to some elements in the PvdA. In so far as ecologism has any cachet in this environmentally conscious country, D66 has been able to incorporate its agenda into a new progressive consensus. The appeal of the Green Left so far has been altogether too narrow to win over even the majority of the post-materialist vote. The party's paltry showing, lack of seats, and even its perceived extremism, have continued to exclude it from any part in the recent novel coalition pact. The Liberals, whose increased support gave them considerable leverage over both the shape of the new coalition and its agreed policy programme, found it difficult enough brokering a deal with social democrats and the progressives of D66. The prospect of including left-ecologists in the equation was deemed to be wholly unacceptable. Moreover, an alternative minority coalition of the left-PvdA, D66 and including GL, would have failed to reflect the general drift of public opinion and was simply a non starter during these protracted negotiations. Even if GL had been able to build on its ideological affinities with D66, that party's narrow preoccupations - both its views on ecology but especially its approach to the dominant issue of welfare reform, put too much ideological distance between them. Certainly enough to ensure that the Greens excluded themselves from the informal wheeling and formal brokering that always precedes coalition making in the Netherlands. The Greens remained on a different political wavelength - a remoteness encouraged to a great extent by a political culture of factionalism and by a splendid isolation that was the principal legacy of their fractious past. In short, the Greens were neither ideologically amenable nor temperamentally suited to the sort of structural reforms - based as these must be on carefully stage managed and suboptimal trade offs between entrenched socio-economic interests - that the mainstream parties (and even D66), for all of their differences of emphasis and ideological preferences, now regard as unavoidable in pursuit of national economic efficiency and international commercial competitiveness.

It was these issues that have preoccupied political elites and electors alike in the Netherlands and have been the stuff of party politics there for most of the present decade. There has been little in this unpalatable agenda for the Greens to capitalise on, or to use as a bridge to the other parties in the political market place. The new government's attempt to balance the preferences for social justice of its progressive wing with those for fiscal probity, reduced social costs, and all round privatisation urged by its liberals, has made for a volatile politics whose outcomes are far from predictable. The push to achieve economic efficiency has been tempered by modest concessions to D66, on whose votes the government depends for its survival. A system of referenda has been utilised as a way of including all citizens in major policy issues. The reform of the country's already liberal drugs regime was mooted and then withdrawn after domestic protest and international pressure from the Netherlands' prospective partners in the EU's Schengen accord. Ecological issues remain some way down the government's list of priorities and Groen Links is in no position, either in terms of the size of its support base or of its available parliamentary leverage, to do anything much to alter this situation. The party remains a victim of its own squandered opportunities, compounded by a major shift against post-material issues in the national and indeed the international political agenda. The most the Greens can do in this situation is to respond to, rather than to activate, those ecological initiatives favoured by green pressure groups, local campaigns and, most gallingly for a party that claims to be the authentic Green voice in national politics, a rival party (D66) that has certainly stolen some of its ideological clothes.

The most recent instances of public policy acquiring an ecological dimension have been those essentially single issue campaigns that have little consequence for the major structural shifts underway in the country's political economy. Or at least, only inasmuch as these issues reflect concern with economism rather than ecologism as their principal driving force. The new government has, for instance, addressed transport policy as part of its commitment to take advantage of the trade opportunities available in the Single European Market. The environment issue has been both a winner and loser here. On the positive side, the government has proposed stricter noise limits on night flights into Schiphol, the country's main international airport, and resisted business pressure to build a new airport at Rotterdam. The Government, with a mind to keeping D66 on board in an already fragile coalition, has also brought forward proposals for encouraging cleaner industrial production, by reducing VAT on environmentally friendly manufacturing methods. The Minister for Public Works, Transport and Inland Waterways has likewise called for a new feasibility study - in the face of considerable protest from local residents and environmental groups, working as much, and perhaps with more direct effect, through D66 than the Green Left - of the proposed cargo-rail link between Rotterdam, (already the largest port in the world) and the industrial heartland of northern Germany, and with links beyond that to the new markets opening up in east and central Europe. The "Beteweljin" project has, however, been revisited not so much on environmental as on economic grounds. The new study will be more a costs-benefits than an environmental impact assessment. The pressure of concerned local authorities to attract inward investment, the desire of the country's leading industrial and employers federations for more infrastructural development to build on the Netherlands' strengths in the service and entrepôt trade, and the government's singular concern with creating employment (with a target of 350,000 new jobs by 1998) as the best way of reducing an immensely heavy welfare burden (with some 30 per cent of GDP, when adjusted for purchasing power spent on social protection - twice the EU average and 9 people receiving some form of benefit for every 10 in work), rather than any ecological considerations per se, stand behind this project.

Little has changed over the course of recent events to improve the prospects for the Greens, either in policy terms or for any decisive shift in their electoral fortunes. The most recent set of elections, the Provincial elections held in 1995, confirmed the tendency revealed in the 1994 national election - that the Dutch electorate remains disconcerted yet ambiguous as to the challenges facing the country in a rapidly changing world. Indeed, the extent to which the present national mood remains preoccupied with immediate rather than post-material concerns, was underlined in these national elections with the unexpected downturn in D66's vote - down from 15.9 per cent in the 1989 poll to 9.2 per cent. The party was penalised because of its reservations - couched in terms of environmental protection - about the 'delta plan' proposals for improving flood control by a major dike building project in the aftermath of the heavy floods of February 1995, which caused over a quarter of a million citizens to be evacuated. The fact that Groen Links actually increased its vote in this poll - and took 8 of the 150 seats compared with 3 in 1989 - actually confirms the party's limited political influence, rather than holding out any real hope of an improvement in its fortunes.[53] The electorate continued to see D66 as the main voice of an otherwise 'naive' ecologism on this highly visible and contentious national issue. The Greens, for their part, had much less of the peripheral protest or discontent vote to lose, and were even able to attract back some of D66's genuinely radical voters patently disillusioned with that party's 'unseemly' compromises in government on ecological as on wider social issues. The Greens' continuing modest electoral performance confirms that the paradox at the heart of ecological politics remains largely unresolved. That whatever realistic opportunity might exist in a more favourable post-material climate to cash in on the salience on the ecology issue was largely squandered - initially by factional divisions within the Green movement that helped other radically inclined parties to colonise this electoral space for themselves. The prospective realignment, if indeed it is underway in Dutch politics, may yet yield a political space for the Greens. But the odds remain as heavily stacked against them as ever. For one thing, D66 continues to compete for the same electoral territory. Whereas, the national agenda seems to have moved on from the more favourable climate of the eighties. The party now seems to have absorbed some of the unpalatable lessons learned earlier, and with better effect, by Green parties elsewhere. Even so, the window of opportunity may have closed, at least for the time being, as the country wrestles with an altogether different agenda.

Without translating issue salience into votes and thence into seats, the Green party in the Netherlands is unlikely to raise itself above its marginal place in the increasingly complex electoral equation. Moreover, the pragmatic use of ecological and related issues by the mainstream parties - and particularly D66 and to a lesser extent the PdvA - is likely to ensure the continued marginalisation of the Greens for the foreseeable future. The evidence so far available suggests that any realignment which might be taking place amongst the electorate here is largely confined to shifts in the power balance between the mainstream parties, rather than between these practitioners of 'normal' politics and altogether more radical parties pursuing an entirely new politics agenda.[54] If the Greens are to weigh in their influence in these circumstances, they will need to settle for a strategy of cooperation with the left parties in this conventional equation - in much the same way as Green parties facing this awkward dilemma elsewhere in the continent's changing politics. This is a formula for realism that the Netherlands' Greens have much less experience of, although on recent evidence an increasing aptitude to embrace.

3.   Luxembourg

(i)   Green roots

With a population counted in tens of thousands rather than in millions Luxembourg, even in the 1970s, had boasted a well supported, if conservatively inclined, environmental protection lobby of ornithologists and assorted nature preservationists. Although alternative and radical ecologist movements began to flourish even in this unlikely milieu, as they did elsewhere in Europe at this time, they made little political impact. Success was largely confined to issue-based campaigns. There were isolated successes for the anti-nuclear movement. In 1975 for instance, it campaigned successfully against plans to build a nuclear power station. This movement also had some success with a campaign to focus public attention on the secondary health hazard from the French reactor across the border at Cattenom.

By the end of the seventies, a youth ecology movement (Jeunes et Environnement) had established the non-party campaigning Mouvement Ecologie. A more radical source of support for ecologism were those supporters of the Socialist Party disillusioned with its coalitional cohabitation with other establishment parties,[55] as were radical Marxists impatient with the Communist Party's unimaginative, and formal 'party-line' hostility to new politics issues. A direct outcome of this dissidence on the left was a small 'Alternative List' - Alternative Lescht-Wiert lech (AL-WL) wedded, as its sub title of 'Defend Yourself' suggests, to direct action or citizen based politics; but one which nevertheless included an electoral strategy. The AL-WL List stood in all four regional electoral districts in the 1979 national elections for the Chamber of Deputies, polled a meagre 0.9 per cent, and was immediately disbanded. Throughout the eighties - a more favourable decade for Green issues across Europe - public opinion in Luxembourg as elsewhere became more receptive to the ecologists' message about cumulative environmental damage. Apart from the increasingly visible impact on local forests from toxic emissions, Luxembourgers' green concerns were also rasied by plans to put this small Duchy at the centre of plans to extend the trans European motorway network.[56] The direct economic benefits from what would be mostly transit traffic seemed marginal, especially when weighed against the likely environmental costs.

(ii)   Party formation

These events stirred an intense debate, encouraged in part by the object lesson of Belgium, another small, neighbouring EC state, where Green politics had already begun in 1981 to make its mark on similar matters of local community concern. The outcome was an agreement in June 1983 by a host of eco-protest groups - from former members of the AL-WL to assorted ecologists, feminists and the peace and anti-nuclear movements - to establish another Green list (Die Greng Alternativ) to attract the disparate green and related protest vote at the impending and concurrent 1984 European and national elections. This first foray into national politics, by a new, and essentially anti-party movement of barely more than 120 paid up members[57] promising to follow the usual radical formula of rotation and anti-hierarchical grassroots principles familiar to radical ecologism elsewhere, was remarkably successful. The List polled a commendable 6.1 per cent in two of the country's four electoral districts. The party was assisted by a favourable and 'fair' proportional voting system. In Luxembourg, electors may cast as many votes as there are seats available. In this particular election, for instance, electors each had 23 votes and 25 votes respectively to deploy in the populous and more heavily urbanised Central and Northern districts where the Greens made their mark. The larger the number of seats available, the lower the percentage needed to win representation. As a direct consequence of this electoral formula, the Green List took 2 seats in the 64 member Chamber - an achievement that at least equalled that of the more established and better organised Communist party which had, after all, been contesting these elections for over half a century.

(iii)   Political developments

The Greens in Luxembourg were not readily enticed into the ways of 'normal ' politics by this early success. They proved incapable of reconciling their internal differences in 1983 and factional strife - as much a matter of personality clashes as ideology - continued to plague the party. These differences were institutionalised as competing electoral lists - a political luxury that has proved to be costly in a small and focused electorate of less than half a million people. A particularly divisive split before the 1989 national and European elections - which are held simultaneously - was especially damaging. A group of pure ecologists, seeking to take advantage of a favourable climate for political ecologism, broke away from the main party and established their own list - Greng Lesch-ekologesch Initiativ. Although the three major parties did lose some ground in the face of a rising mood of popular discontent, with the two Green Lists taking four seats between them, the latter failed under the proportionality rules to do as well as they should have done if they had remained united. The split almost certainly cost the Greens one of Luxembourg's six seats in the European Parliament - an important and influential political prize in the EC's smallest polity. In fact, the principal political beneficiary of the anti-government mood was a citizen based initiative (the ADR list), campaigning for a radical variant of 'old' materialist politics - improved pension rights for private sector employees.

These internal divisions - and not least their negative political consequences for the movement - were not easily healed. But the party was helped by the lack of any unbridgeable ideological edge to these quarrels. Cooperation and close networking amongst Luxembourg's Greens eventually ensured that common sense prevailed. Confronted by what most activists recognized as an altogether tougher electoral climate leading up to the 1994 elections, the two parties negotiated a joint list. The electoral pay off here - at a time when the Greens in many other European countries were struggling to maintain their political profile, let alone hold onto the unprecedented 'breakthrough' achieved in the 1989 Euro elections - saw the party returned in both the national and European parliaments.

(iv)   **Prospects for political change**

The Luxembourg Greens remain a paradox. On the one hand, they have courted the predictable electoral consequences of flouting their divisions before a small and critical electorate focused on a narrow range of national and, for the most part, 'old politics' issues. At the same time, these divisions have never been deep enough to preclude working together at the local and parliamentary levels, and more recently in European election campaigns. Pragmatism has been more in evidence on the ground than any schism fomented by ideology. The Green Alternative party tried to hold its various factions together from the start by adopting party statutes that encouraged factional conciliation rather than fragmentation. This initially helped to reinforce a positive image of political responsibility rather than one of disharmony. A Coordinating Council presided over what was still a vigorous system of local control and participatory democracy. The Council provided the party with its administrative and organisational core. It tried to ensure party cohesion if not consensus, by channelling all potentially disruptive factional disputes through a mechanism capable of resolving them. This was not entirely successful and the centripetal tendencies that afflict all Green parties in some measure overcame this organisational pragmatism, leading to the party split of 1989. More recently, electoral considerations have begun to heal this breach.

The abiding sense of realism here has been complemented by the avoidance of ideological extremism in Die Greng's policy and electoral programmes. A reservoir of shared ideals has strengthened the glue that holds the Greens together. Common aspirations overcame narrow jealousies and eventually helped the divided Greens to reconcile their differences and reunite in 1994 under a common banner. The party remains, by and large, a pure green or 'cucumber' party, concerned primarily with environmental protection. All of its factions have campaigned energetically on issues such as deforestation, better planning procedures to avoid urban sprawl, alternative energy production, as well as against air, water and noise pollution caused by irresponsible industrialism. Rather than rejecting the industrial system per se, the party has called, in moderate rather than utopian terms, for an environmentally responsible industrial sector, and for diversification away from polluting heavy industry and towards new, cleaner sectors. Social issues are not entirely excluded from this 'cucumber' agenda, but they are not amongst the party's central priorities. The party has campaigned on overtly radical communal issues, and civil liberties. It recently supported the government's attempts to use the law to stamp out an incipient racism in a country where half the working population are immigrants. Women's rights are also on the agenda - the rules for the Green Alternative party list and the conduct of party meetings requires equal representation of the sexes. The party has, nevertheless, placed far less emphasis on these controversial social politics that have split Green parties elsewhere, and improved its political cohesion as a consequence.

Above all, the Greens have opted for pragmatism and built on the success of an issue-led rather than on an ideologically driven approach to politics. This notwithstanding, the Greens at the outset did become caught up in a general mood of protest against the entrenched power of the almost feudal corporations who control Luxembourg's economy. But they chose issues that did not isolate them from a much more broadly based campaign on this issue. They capitalised, for example, on a deep crisis in the local steel industry - a sector vital to employment prospects in such a small country, and critical for the competitiveness of Luxembourg's vulnerable economy.[58] Although this was not natural political territory for this essentially pure Green party, they harnessed the rising potential for discontent that accrues when the conventional Keynsian compact begins to break down. In Luxembourg the steel crisis reflected what happens to normal political alignments when this arrangement - whereby a disciplined labour force that had exchanged cooperation for the usual economic pay offs and welfare benefits - comes under competitive strain. The impact of an international recession, compounded by deindustrialisation, in a mainstay industry - a situation accentuated by EC policy decisions - began to bite hard. Unemployment rose and with it the level of economic anxiety. The Greens tapped into the new uncertainty and gained politically from it. In a country as dependent on a single industry as Luxembourg is on steel, the only viable solution to these structural changes was economic diversification. The government used fiscal measures - tax concessions, loans and infrastructural developments such as new highways and office buildings - to attract inward investment and create new sources of employment. Many of these schemes invaded prime farmland or greenbelt and threatened residential areas. This, in turn, exacerbated community unrest and provided a source of support to be tapped by the Green movement. The newly unified Green List has capitalised on public concerns rooted in both the 'old' and the 'new' politics as Luxembourg, faced by its own past standards, a rising sense of economic uncertainty, unprecedented levels of unemployment, inflation, bankruptcies, and many of the other consequences of the new globalism.[59]

These uncertainties were manifested in the 1994 campaigns for both the national and European elections. General dissatisfaction with the centre-left coalition - the Social Christian Party (CSV) in coalition with the Socialists (POSL) - did not find an expression in rising support for the opposition Democratic party, which threatened even greater retrenchment in the shape of a neo-liberal programme of reforms. The Greens instead, provided one of a number of vehicles for political protest. They won a healthy 10.9 per cent of the vote, along with various other discontent parties. Nor was this sizeable protest vote for the Greens an entirely negative (anti-government) vote. The Greens, whose leading candidate, Jup Weber, was a distinguished expert on forestry policy, positively appealed to a small but mobilised ecological constituency. The Greens' record of effective campaigning against the opening of an industrial waste plant on the border with Belgium, and the extensive construction of motorways across this small, quite densely populated country, helped considerably their cause, yielded 5 national parliamentary seats and, more remarkably still, the capture of a Strasbourg seat from the CSV. At the same time, this outcome should be put into due perspective. The Luxembourg Greens have recovered, on the evidence of the 1994 polls, from the self inflicted damage of earlier divisions. Whether this is a reliable base for consolidating Green politics is much less easy to confirm. For there may still be an irreconcilable gap between the Greens' pursuit of post-material goals and the more pressing and mundane concerns of the electorate at large, as global pressures impact on the structure of the local economy, and demand in turn new forms of employment to meet the population's expectation of high living standards. This continuing tension between the 'old' and 'new' politics could prove to be an unreliable foundation for consolidating the Greens' place in national politics. Any future downturn in support might well place the new found Green consensus under stress. The movement's tendency to quarrel over relatively trivial matters -symptomatic perhaps of such a small party - has been a drawback and might be so again. What the Greens have managed to achieve so far is to move the ecological issue up the political agenda and to raise its electoral profile. For the time being, the Greens look better placed than they have so far been in the national political firmament. With some effective leadership and a clearer sense of political purpose than they managed to muster between 1989 and 1991, the signs are set for a more sustained impact on national politics. In many ways, Luxembourg's Greens are less a reflection of the Belgian ecologists they initially looked to for inspiration, than of the situation in Ireland - another small EU country also confronting the disconcerting consequences of economic change. And another country, too, whose politics are dominated by a largely retrospective electoral cleavage that limits the capacity of the Greens to play a more effective role in national politics, without excluding them altogether.

Notes

1. Keith Hill, "Political Change in a Segmented Society", in R. Rose (ed), "Electoral Behaviour: A Comparative Handbook" (New York, 1974).

2. See J. Fitzmaurice, "The Politics of Belgium: A Unique Federalism" (London, 2nd edition, 1996).

3. This tension between organisational 'logic' and anti-partyism was also evident in ECOLO. See H. Kitschelt, "Democracy and Oligarchy in Belgian Ecology Parties", in W. Rudig (ed), "Green Politics One" (Edinburgh, 1990), at pp.82-114.

4. See H. Kitschelt, "Organisation and Strategy in Belgian and West German Ecology Parties", Comparative Politics 20 1988 at pp.127-54.

5. Wallonia consists of thirteen electoral arrondissements, divided into cantons and, beneath that level, into communes.

6. The safety valve of the 'safe' protest vote in 'second order' elections is a recurrent theme in the electoral record of Green parties across the continent. For an overview of the significance and implications of these elections, see K. Reif and H. Schmitt, "Nine Second Order National Elections: A Conceptual Framework for the Analysis of European Election Results", European Journal of Political Research 8(1) 1980; and K. Reif, "National Electoral Cycles and European Elections 1979 and 1984", Electoral Studies 3(3) 1984.

7. B. Rihoux, "Belgium: Greens in a divided society", in D. Richardson and C. Rootes, op.cit (1995), at p.101.

8. Ibid, p.101.

9. Reuters News Service Report, 6 December 1991.

10. H. Kitschelt and S. Hellemans, "Beyond the European Left: Ideology and Political Action in the Belgian Ecology Parties" (Durham N.C., 1990) at pp.54-55 and pp.91-92.

11. Reuters News Service Report, 6 December 1991.

12. See Xavier Mabille and Val R. Lorwin, "Belgium" in S. Henig, "Political Parties in the European Community" (London, 1979).

13. K. Deschouwer, "Belgium: The "Ecologists" and "AGALEV"", in F. Muller-Rommel (ed) "New Politics in Western Europe: The Rise and Success of Green Parties and Alternative Lists" (Boulder, Col. 1989).

14. H. Kitschelt and S. Hellemans, op.cit (1990).

15. See A-P. Frognier, "Le vote ecologiste et d'extrême - droit en Wallonie", (Louvain la-Neuve, 1992).

16. J. Fitzmaurice, "The Extreme Right in Belgium: Recent Developments", Parliamentary Affairs Summer 1992.

17. Reuters News Service Report, 11 October 1994.

18. Reuters News Service Report, 20 October 1994.

19. See B. Rihoux, op.cit, (1995), at p.102.

20. See the account of the national mood in Reuters Textline, 18 May 1995.

21. Reuters News Service Report, 17 May 1995.

22. Reuters News Service Report, 17 January 1995.

23. Reuters News Service Report, 18 January 1995.

24. The most recent changes effected by law in 1988 and 1993, had enlarged powers and policy prerogatives for both communes and provincial governments - to include, amongst their policy competencies, education, public works, science policy, oversight of lower forms of governance within the provinces and increased fiscal autonomy. See Els Witte, "Belgian Federalism: Towards Complexity and Asymmetry", West European Politics, Vol.15(4) 1992, pp.95-117.

25. Le Soir (Brussels), 14.12.94.

26. All of these figures are the regional vote for each of these parties, calculated as a percentage of the total national turnout.

27. B. Rihoux, op.cit (1995), pp.103-104.

28. Galen A. Irwin, "The Netherlands", in P.H. Merkl (ed), "Western European Party Systems" (London, 1980); see also Arendt Lijphart, "The Politics of Accommodation: Pluralism and Democracy in the Netherlands" (2nd edition, Berkeley, 1975).

29. G. Voerman, "The Netherlands' Green Paradoxes", Capitalism, Nature, Socialism. A Journal of Socialist Ecology 3(3) 1992, pp.17-27.

30. Adriana Pappalardo, "The Conditions for Consociational Democracy: A Logical and Empirical Critique", European Journal of Political Research 9 (1971), pp.365-390.

31. See H. Kriesi, "New Social Movements and the New Class in the Netherlands", American Journal of Sociology 94 1989, pp.1078-1116.

32. Hans Daalder "Opposition in a Segmented Society", in R. A. Dahl, (ed) "Political Oppositions in Western Democracies" (Yale 1966); for an updated perspective on Dutch politics, see K. Gladdish, "Opposition in the Netherlands" in E. Kolinsky (ed) "Opposition in Western Europe" (London 1987)

33. G. Irwin and K. Dittrich, "And the Walls came Tumbling Down: Party Realignment in the Netherlands" in R. J. Dalton, S. C. Flanagan and P. A. Beck (eds), "Electoral change in Advanced Industrial Democracies; Realignment or Dealignment" (Princeton 1984), argue that noticeable voter movement began to occur after 1967, and especially amongst younger voters. Even so, the greatest impact of this rising political volatility remains confined to shifts between the established, status quo parties which opened up new coalitional possibilities between them. And this, regardless of evidence for the emergence of post-materialist values amongst the younger cohort, after the cultural impact of the sixties - which was as apparent in the Netherlands as

it was in every other advanced European Society. See especially at pp. 291-96.

34.   D. Nelkin and M. Pollak, "The Politics of Participation and the Nuclear Debate in Sweden, the Netherlands and Austria", Public Policy XXV (1977), at pp.333-57.

35.   Marijke de Jong, "Dutch gas drillers fuel Green debate", The European, 5-11 November 1993.

36.   Hans Daalder, "The Netherlands", in S. Henig (ed), op.cit (1979); see also Arend Lijphard, "The Netherlands: Continuity and Change in Voting Behaviour", in R. Rose (ed), "Electoral Behaviour: A Comparative Handbook" (New York, 1974).

37.   Hans Daalder, "Extreme Proportional Representation: The Dutch Experience", in S.E. Finer (ed), "Adversary Politics and Electoral Reform" (London, 1975); and Arend Lijphart, "The Dutch Electoral System in Comparative Perspective", Netherlands Journal of Sociology" 1978.

38.   A.P. Lucardie, "The New Left in the Netherlands 1960-1977; A Critical Study of New Political Ideas and Groups on the Left in the Netherlands with Comparative References to France and Germany" (Kingston, Ontario, 1980).

39.   G. Voerman, "The Netherlands' Green Paradoxes", Capital, Nature, Socialism, Vol.3 Part 3 1992, p.21.

40.   Ibid, p.21.

41.   G. Voerman, ibid (1992) at p.23.

42.   Although there was some scope for realignment, given the significant decline in religious voting during the 1970s. See R. Inglehart, "Changing Paradigms in Comparative Political Behaviour", in A. Finifter, (ed), "Political Science: The State of the Discipline" (Washington, American Political Science Association, 1983), at p.443.

43.   G. Voerman, "The Netherlands: Losing colours, turning green", in D. Richardson & C. Rootes (eds), op.cit (1995), at p.113.

44.   G. Voerman, "Premature Perestroika: The Dutch Communist Party and Gorbachev", in D. Bell (ed), "Western European Communists and the Collapse of Communism" (Oxford, 1993), pp.157-71. From 1977, the CPN had adopted its own variant of Euro-Communism and rejected much of its Marxist-Leninish dogma, including the idea that the class struggle was the main dynamic of progressive political change - a form of revisionism that made it much more amenable to the ecological gender and new politics issues of its 'partners'. See G. Voerman, "A Drama in Three Acts: Communism and Social Democracy in the Netherlands since 1945", in M. Waller, S. Courtois and M. Lazar (eds), "Comrades and Brothers. Communism and Trade Unions in Europe" (London, 1991), pp.102-123.

45.   Cited in G. Voerman, op.cit (1995), at p.117.

46.   G. Voerman in D. Richardson and C. Rootes, op.cit (1995), at p.118.

47.   G. Voerman, op.cit (1995), at p.118.

48.   Paul Lucardie, Jelle Van der Knoop, Wijbrandt Van Schuur and Gerrit Voerman, "Greening the Reds or Redding the Greens?: The Case of the Green Left in The Netherlands", in W. Rudig (ed), "Green Politics Three" (Edinburgh, 1996), especially at pp.105-109.

49.   G. Voerman, ibid p.118.

50.   E. Gene Frankland and D. Schoonmaker, "Between Protest and Power: The Green Party in Germany" (Boulder, Col. 1992) at p.213, cite a private attitude survey conducted in Holland by P. Lucardie, in which the majority of activists in this new

party defined themselves as either 'left' or even 'far left'; whereas Muller-Rommel's mid eighties survey of De Groenen categorised them, in issue terms, as "an alternative Green" party. See F. Muller-Rommel, "The Greens in Western Europe: Similar but Different", International Political Science Review 6, No.4 (1985) at pp.483-99.

51.   D. Suchard, "Dutch Far Right Flex their muscles", The European, 18/24 February 1994.

52.   The poll findings were published in Financieele Dagblad, 17.9.94.

53.   These provincial seats are translated by means of indirect election, into the allocation of the 75 seats in the Senate; the Green Left were awarded four, unchanged from 1989.

54.   K. Gladdish, op.cit (1987), at p.230.

55.   Dick Leonard, "Benelux", in V. Bogdanor and D. Butler (ed), op.cit (1983), at p.159.

56.   N. Buckley, "Leading role at the centre of the EU", Luxembourg: Financial Times Survey, 30.9.96.

57.   W. Rudig, "The Greens in Europe: Ecological Parties and the European elections of 1984", Parliamentary Affairs 38 1985 at p.61.

58.   M. Hirsch, "The 1984 Luxembourg Election" West European Politics 8 1985, at pp. 116-18

59.   N. Buckley, "Drive for jobs, investment", Luxembourg: Financial Times Survey, 30.5.96.

4 Alternativists and alternatives: Green party politics in Alpine Europe

1. Austria

(i) Green roots

Green politics in Austria has been influenced by developments in Germany. At the same time, it has taken on more of a pure Green demeanour than it did there. The primary focus on ecological rather than on social issues reflected the absence in Austria of a strong tradition of radical alternative politics originating, as it did in Germany, from the militant student and new left movements of the sixties. In so far as the Austrian Greens pursued political issues per se, they did so in a way that reflected the country's special international status. The Greens endorsed Austria's enforced postwar neutrality as between the cold war superpowers. Not in any radical sense that put them beyond the pale of political respectability, but in accordance with the prevailing view held across the political spectrum, that it was in the country's abiding national interest to stay out of this dangerous quarrel. Even the Greens' bolder contribution to the anti-nuclear power movement which effectively launched Green politics in Austria was sanitised by local circumstances and reflected an entrenched, even conservative, mood of cultural romanticism rather than unalloyed radicalism.

Green politics originated with the campaign to reverse the decision to commission a nuclear power station. It mirrored the movement's eclectic ideological roots and attracted campaigners of every political persuasion.[1] The effectiveness of this movement in reflecting widespread public concerns can be gauged by the government's decision in 1978 to hold the first national referendum since the end of the war; over half of the electorate refused to endorse the proposal. Another broadly based movement successfully campaigned, demonstrated and even employed direct action tactics - culminating in an impressive street demonstration in Vienna in December 1984 - against the installation of a hydro-electricity dam scheduled to be built on the Danube at Hainburg. Although it failed to prevent this project, the site was effectively exported, along with Austrian technical expertise and investment capital, across the border into neighbouring Czechoslovakia and Hungary, where it provoked a similar outcry.[2] There was further success in mobilising public opinion on this issue, with the campaign against the already completed nuclear power installation at Zwentendorf.

(ii) Party formation

These campaigning successes, not least the organisational experience they afforded local ecologists and their positive impact on public opinion, contributed significantly to raising ecological awareness in Austria. More directly, they provided in 1982 the launching pad for two Austrian Green parties, each one committed to campaigning for parliamentary representation in the Nationalrat in the 1983 national elections. The particular origins of Austria's Green parties in a successful national election campaign, ensured that they emerged at the outset as dedicated national parties. These origins are in stark contrast to the altogether looser federations of local lists and groups that gave rise to Green party politics in neighbouring Switzerland. Of course, the similarity of their origins and, to an extent, of their political purpose, by no means ensured a uniform political style. One close observer of these events noted that "the various local Green parties (in Austria) are often distinctly different creatures which can include maverick rightists or serve as a catch-all party of a disenchanted middle class, as so-called *Burgerlisten*".[3] Moreover, at this early stage, these local variations were compounded by quite pronounced ideological differences as between the two parties, which precluded a joint manifesto or an electoral pact that would have ensured the Greens crossing Austria's electoral threshold and winning representation in the national parliament. The Austrian Constitution is quite favourably disposed to the proliferation of small, issue based parties. Few restrictions are placed on the formation of a party. All that is required is that the party statutes are lodged with the Interior Ministry and published, with a nominal number of signatures, to endorse the prospective electoral list of any party not already represented, either in the 183 seat parliament or in the Provisional Council which elects the upper house of parliament or Senate.

The United Greens (Vereinte Grune Osterreich - VGO) consisted of pure green moderates politicised by the impact and experience of the anti-nuclear protest movement and committed to a reformist programme. This group was just preceded into the party lists by a more militant group. The alternative list (Alternative Liste Osterreich - ALO) had also been galvanised by the nuclear issue, but in a way that orientated them towards a more radical prospectus. This twin launch hardly amounted to a seismic shift in Austrian party politics. The Greens, nevertheless, had every incentive to try to maximise their electoral potential in 1983. Austrian elections are conducted under a variant of the d'Hondt system and, despite a four per cent or one constituency seat threshold to overcome, this uses the largest remainders version of this system for allocating constituency seats and a higher tier seat allocation formula calculated to encourage one of the highest degrees of proportionality anywhere in Europe. These arrangements offer a real inducement to small parties as long as they remain internally cohesive. The cost of party divisions within the Green 'family' were patently obvious from the early results. The VGO took a disappointing 1.9 per cent of the vote and the ALO merely 1.4 per cent. If the two parties had pooled their efforts, under the d'Hondt formula even their modest 3.3 per cent total would have yielded in at least 5 Nationalrat seats, with perhaps even an additional 'bonus' vote as a reward for their pragmatism and tactical common sense. However, the Green impact cannot be entirely discounted in what political scientists had previously regarded as western Europe's most stable party system.[4] The marginal shift to the Greens underlined a real prospect for political change, as a degree of realignment took place in Austrian politics after a long period of Socialist party dominance from 1970-1983 under Chancellor Kreisky.

At the same time, this realignment was due at least as much to shifts within the political establishment as it was a significant opportunity to launch an effective campaign based on post-materialist politics. The prevailing mood in Austrian politics - as in many other European democracies - was rising uncertainty, rather than any receptiveness to a radical shift in the pattern of party politics. Plasser cites evidence to suggest that throughout the 1980s up to 20 per cent of the Austrian electorate were prospective Green voters, and that a 'core' electorate emerged of some 4 to 6 per cent over the same period.[5] The Greens benefited from the usual protest quota, but this was an unreliable foundation for any new party. The ephemeral quality of this support was underlined by both the ALO's and VGO's minimal vote (a total of a mere 1.6 per cent between them) in the regional elections in lower Austria later the same year; albeit balanced by a significantly improved performance in local elections. In these local contests an alternative Burgerliste achieved a remarkable 17.7 per cent (and 7 local council seats) in the Salzburg poll. This gave the Greens their first direct influence on 'governance' by way of the executive post of municipal councillor for urban planning and the environment. Success here was followed by a 7 per cent poll for the ALG local list in Graz (and 7 council seats).[6] These modest achievements prompted the two movements to overcome their initial reticence about electoral cooperation. Not least because of the twin financial and political benefits accruing from maximising votes. Apart from any prospective gain in seats, Austria's generous state funding arrangements for political parties awarded resources to those parties with a minimum of 5 parliamentary seats, as well as a proportionate cash sum per vote to any party which managed a minimum 1 per cent of the poll.

(iii)   Political developments

In 1984 the electoral success of the tenuous VGO/ALO alliance indicated that there might indeed be an electoral space available for a moderate Green strategy. In the regional assembly elections at Vorarlberg, the joint list took a very respectable 13 per cent and 4 seats. Indeed, this outcome strengthened the pragmatic tendency in both parties, although neither party had an easy ride here. The grassroots 'alternativists' and the pure green fundamentalists in the two movements continued to resist what they saw as undue compromises in pursuit of short-term electoralism. For a while things began to unravel on the ground. The 1985 regional elections in upper Austria were contested by three separate Green Lists - the VGO, ALO and a marginal group known as Die Grunen Ostereichs - thereby splitting the vote and ensuring defeat. The penalty of pursuing principle at all costs was eventually assimilated. This spurred the establishment, in September 1986, of a unified Green party - Die Grune Alternative. Not that such a major adjustment and the difficult compromises it entailed, came any more easily to groups of activists holding often diametrically opposed views about the role and purpose of the Greens in 'normal' politics, than it did anywhere else. In order to see how these differences kept the Austrian Greens divided and imported tensions into the united party when it did form, we need to examine these ideological fault lines more closely.

The pure Green 'cucumber' VGO party adopted typical ecological, non-leftist programmes. This placed considerable emphasis on the primacy of the individual, the family and the community and avoided the abstract ideologism, with its holistic frame of reference, preferred by red-green radicals. The party's economic policy was a conservative mix that favoured deregulation and privatisation to collectivism. It pursued a strategy for environmental reform built on self restraint rather than on state regulation or outright interventionism. This cautious approach was mirrored by a moderate political strategy that precluded extremism and was carried out within the rule of law. It mirrored a support base drawn largely from older, less educated, more conventionally middle class and disgruntled supporters of the established parties.

The ALO - and through its pre-eminence in the eventual newly merged party, the Green Alternative (ALO-GA) - advocated a rather different programme of radical economic, social and political change in line with its appeal to a younger, more radical cohort of voters. From the outset, this party took a clear line on 'injustice and life-threatening aggressions' and called for income redistribution.[7] But even in this radical prospectus, the emphasis was placed less on a collectivist outlook rooted in a class-based ideology, than on a progressive ethos in which liberated citizens would have genuine choices and enjoy real opportunities for self expression in order to reshape their own lives.[8] These goals were not, however, to be achieved through the medium of traditional relationships as defined in the more cautious VGO prospectus, but rather through meaningful participation by non-alienated citizens in the social milieux, structures and networks - in local communities, the family, schools, universities and the workplace - through which, as they saw it, only real change can be brought about. In effect this is a sociological perspective on political change which accords much more closely with the anarchist or eco - libertarian tradition than it does with either pure Green reformism; or indeed, with the eco-socialist or eco-Marxist legacy. The ALO-GA programme did manage to touch base with conventional leftist and eco-socialist thinking, over its emphasis on more direct, economic controls, a degree of public sector involvement in economic management - for instance, its preference for an increased role for public transport and some redistribution of economic resources. This programme also revealed its radicalism in other ways. The emphasis on anti-militarism and pacifism was hardly exceptional and accorded with the broad national consensus on doing nothing to undermine Austria's sensitive international status. The party's call, however, for an end to arms production - an industry which had grown into a major export sector in Austria - went beyond this consensus, and its anti-productivist ethos represented a distinctively radical strand of ecologism.

The existence of this ideological fault line within the Austrian Green movement clearly affected the prospects for Green representation in the national Parliament. Negotiations between the respective factions failed to resolve their deep policy differences, or to quell the mutual suspicions engendered by them. This impasse encouraged further divisions. A group of prominent Greens - the so called 'promis' with national reputations as anti-nuclear campaigners or elected Green representatives and who remained above narrow factionalism - took the initiative. Led by Frau Meissner-Blau, a Presidential candidate in 1986, whose 5.5 per cent vote had forced a run-off ballot between the two main contenders - the 'promis' ostentatiously formed a third group, with the intention of contesting the forthcoming national elections on the basis of this modest success in the Presidential contest. The movement's respective grass roots factions continued, however, to squabble over the questions of policy substance and strategy. The aptly named Bürgerinitiative für das Parlament - Citizens Initiative Parliament - invited the entrenched 'factional' groups in the two parties to reconsider their ideological differences and to opt instead for a joint List to fight the 1986 national elections. The gesture worked to the extent that this ad hoc electoral pact, Die Grune Alternativ List Freda Meissner-Blau, did win 4.8 per cent of the vote and took 8 parliamentary seats. But the new Green coalition was a largely one sided affair. The ALO dominated the new alliance, and held the bulk (7) of its parliamentary seats; whereas the VGO deputy - solitary in more than just the numerical sense - opted to sit as an independent. This was, however, the first step in a more protracted process of political reconciliation. Standing for the first time under its new unified title - in the local elections in Styria in 1986 - DGA polled a modest 3.7 per cent, but enough to give it 2 seats and encourage those who saw this joint approach as the only way forward.

After a turbulent sequence of splits and reconciliations, not unknown to Green parties elsewhere, these two factions in 1987 consolidated their relationship as a Green Alternative

Party (Die Grune Alternative). The new party is a federal arrangement. The federal congress (*Bundeskongress*) draws its legitimacy from delegates elected by the nine autonomous provincial party groups. Professional party politics is abjured, although a semblance of organisational coherence does come from a federal executive (elected by the *Bundeskongress*) and a loose style of guidance and collective leadership, rather than oligarchism, from two salaried federal party managers. The party's emphasis on activism ensures that continuing ideological differences are openly expressed in the party's councils. The party drafts its policies in the open fora of federal working groups (*Bundesarbeitzgemeinschaften*) which include parliamentary, federal committee and provincial activists. It sounds out policy ideas in party working group (*Arbeitskreise*). These arrangements ensure that the policy mill grinds slowly and is not without the usual factional tensions associated with transparent and directly democratic structures. The party has managed these tensions well enough, but in spite of its pragmatic response to the political situation it has to live with, activists from both tendencies have continued to harbour doubts about their coalition. This ambivalence has prevailed in the party - and remains a hindrance in a difficult electoral milieu. The party has continued to be preoccupied with these frictions even if it refuses to be overwhelmed by them. Pure green fundamentalists confront those, particularly on the former ALO wing, who remain convinced of the imperative, under Austrian conditions, to maintain Green unity at all costs, whilst maintaining a commitment to a genuinely progressive programme. A persistent tension continues to haunt the party and the tensions generated by it have undoubtedly damaged the Greens' public image, its reputation for competent politics and, ultimately, its electoral fortunes. Not least, because this wrangling gets in the way of framing a coherent and politically appealing party programme. And this in spite of the fact that the amalgamated party secured the support of the majority of VGO members.[9] These continuing divisions took their toll in the 1990 elections. The Green vote was divided; the DGA wing took 4.8 per cent and 10 seats (a gain of 2) with VGO candidates taking 2 per cent and no seats.[10] The electoral momentum continued at the local level with 9.1 per cent (57 seats) in the city-state parliament. In the 1992 presidential campaign Robert Jungk, the official Green candidate, secured 5.7 per cent.

The Green deputies in the early days did little to improve their image with the electorate at large. They engaged in posture politics almost for the sake of it. Many were exhibitionists; some flaunted their eccentric sartorial styles in an otherwise conservative assembly; a few of the female Greens even insisted on publicly breast feeding their infants during the parliament's crowded plenary sessions. This flamboyant political behaviour damaged the party and caused it to lose considerable support in a round of local and provincial elections.[11] Events came to a head as the party faced similar choices about style and direction that were exercising many other Green parties at about the same time. After an internal party crisis that almost destroyed the party, the remnants of the radical ALO leadership were voted out of office and a new, capable leader, Madelaine Petrovic, moved to refashion the party along pragmatic lines. Not least to make it more responsive to the electorate's broader electoral concerns. Petrovic's philosophy of politics brought together a sincere commitment to practical ecological measures with strategic awareness; and in particular, an acute eye for what the public will tolerate in this distinctly conservative polity. She reminded her party, for instance, that it was unrealistic to try "to reach out to people by dogmatically presenting basically correct principles." The party's recent tactics have reflected this shift towards pragmatism. They continue, as radical parties must, to give vent to their own progressive instincts, by engaging the usual set piece protests, if only to maximise publicity. For instance, they undertook a 42-hour long parliamentary filibuster to protest against the rescinding of a law on the identification of tropical hardwoods. But the party is known, too, for its steady and increasingly effective participation in the 'normal' procedures of parliamentary debates and committee work. Petrovic's message to the electorate could not have been clearer on this score; that "we have really become a party working within parliamentarianism".[12] The Greens' parliamentary experience has reconciled them to, rather than alienated them from, conventional politics. Frankland concludes that "as a general rule, (Austria's)Green activists were not ideologically opposed to parliamentary democracy; they sought a strengthening of the parliament's decision-making role in response to the decades of private corporatist arrangements that had reduced the parliament to a ratifying body. Thus, Green parliamentarians settled into the role of constructive opposition rather than fundamentalist opposition".[13]

There are, nevertheless, clear limits to this achievement. Moderation has not, of itself, guaranteed the Greens a role at the centre of Austrian national politics that compares with that enjoyed by their German sister party. The Austrian political environment, for one thing, is by no means receptive even to a new politics party now wedded to a cautiously selective radicalism. Green issues have clearly enjoyed a similar if modest salience amongst Austria's younger, better educated and post-materialist voters, as they have elsewhere in western Europe. But there has been more uncertainty behind the persistent Green vote in recent Austrian elections than any obvious sign of a shift from 'old' to 'new' politics. The signals here remain altogether more confused. Political change may well be in the air, but this phenomena is driven by many, and by no means consistent, causes. The vote for alternative parties including the Greens, reflects the imperatives of a much deeper structural change underway in the fabric of Austrian politics on the back of a significant degree of electoral dealignment. After 1986 the Austrian party system evolved from its customary configuration as a stable two and a half party system, into an altogether more volatile four party system.[14] The conventional class based parties are ranged along the customary left-right class spectrum. The Socialists (SPO) and the conservative People's party (OVP) suffered a marginal, but in electoral terms a significant, seepage from their partisan support bases. This, in turn, released some voters to the smaller or newer parties ranged across a wide ideological spectrum. The political establishment was obliged to share its increasingly volatile electorates with two 'protest' parties - the Freedom party (FPO), a neo-liberal right wing party, and the new Green Alternative.[15]

The steady dealignment in the traditional pattern of Austrian political allegiances has undoubtedly provided the Greens with a potential political base, even if it has not ensured it a constant or reliable following. Indeed, its potential electorate is larger than the support that has actually accrued to the party as a steady unravelling of once durable electoral allegiances has continued since the early 1980s. The Greens - especially since they ended their internal civil war - have had some notable success in attracting a proportion of the principled as well as the protest vote that characterises the better educated and progressively inclined middle class constituency. They have certainly won over some disillusioned middle class social democrats, disaffected with the squalid and occasionally corrupt machinations of Austria's 'cosy' corporatist system. But this straight switch from red to green is a far from cumulative electoral phenomenon and by no means reflects the entire picture. The Greens have drawn, too, on a broader constituency. For as the size of the Green vote has grown, the proportion within it of Socialist 'switchers' diminishes. This would seem, as one commentator suggests, "to indicate that the Greens are capable of mobilising substantial segments other than those of disenchanted Social Democrats".[16] The potential to attract liberally minded voters with a strong sense of civic virtue is not, in itself however, an expression of a large latent constituency for ecologism. It reflects just as much the widespread disdain with the closed or 'back stairs' operation of the Austrian polity as it does on the positive appeal of a Green agenda per se.

In the special circumstances that shape political expectations in Austria, the Greens fulfil the same expressive or protest function as any other new discontent party. This, paradoxically, is as much a measure of their limitations as it is of their potential. What is seen as an opportunity to change the political agenda in favourable circumstances, can just as easily evaporate when the public mood changes. Kreuzer's study of these recent voting patterns suggests that a combination of the political circumstances that gave rise to the Green party and raised the concerns of its support base up the political agenda, have had more direct effect on the party's electoral performance than the ethical appeal of the ideological preferences of its activists. In other words, the fortunes of the Greens remain in the hands of others. They are carried along with, rather than directly shaping, the tide of change that has started to run in Austria's erstwhile staid politics. The Greens remain essentially a peripheral element on the broader political canvas. As Kreuzer sees it, "in Austria, therefore, the oppositional stance of the Greens takes the form of protest. Such opposition, by its very nature, is usually heterogenous in ideological content and populist in style".[17] The Greens are, then, a much less critical factor in the current momentum for change in the Austrian context than the generalized account of the new politics anticipates. Of course, the picture is a complex one that precludes any simplistic conclusions, but the broad trend, illustrated by recent elections, seems irrefutable. The potential for dealignment in Austrian politics indicated by the significant reduction in the hold of the two main parties over their contemporary electorates suggests a much less favourable prognosis for Green politics. In spite of a social profile that indicates that the Green party has attracted a preponderance of centrist and even some far right support, not least on the basis of a rising disenchantment with the big traditional party of the right (the OVP), this modest gain of conscionable bourgeois support almost pales into insignificance alongside the startling success of Joerg Haider's new ultra nationalist party. The far right and populist Freedom party, launched on a wave of materialist discontents, xenophobia and sheer intolerance, has proved much more capable of winning over support from both the old left and right parties, and from across the social classes, than the altogether more politically benign and - compared with many other ecological parties - far from militant Austrian Greens.

A number of conclusions can be drawn from these bald facts. Kreuzer has identified two that are specific to the Austrian situation. In the first instance, the political salience of post-materialism in this broadly conservative political culture is limited to - or at least channelled through - practical matters, rather than motivated by ethereal or utopians ideals; that is, it is activated by "objective necessities" instead of normative concerns.[18] The fact that even the unified Greens, with a more radical than pure Green image due to the ALO faction's dominance in the party, have attracted as much support 'from disillusioned and former conservative party voters as from socialists is as much a cause for concern as for self congratulation. It says much about the ideological flux and unreliability of this anti-establishment protest vote over the longer term.[19] It might well find a political home, however temporary, in support for parties other than the Greens. The OVP's failure to stem the tide running to the far right may keep some of those latent conservatives with a civic conscience in the Green camp. But this is by no means a guaranteed outcome in the current climate of electoral volatility. The more recent breakaway of a moderate neo-liberal faction - the Liberal Forum - from Haider's nationalists is also unpromising, as far as consolidating the Green vote is concerned. For it closes off an additional Green support base on the conventional right, and offers conscionable conservatives a new political home in a party that is both anti-system yet comfortably conservative. Nor is there any greater comfort for the Greens when we consider its more natural social base amongst the post-materialist constituency. A combination of political culture and 'events' - and how the Greens have responded to both - offers some explanation of the relative lack of politicisation of post-material values in Austria. These values remain, by and large, a matter of private rather than public concern. What has mobilised Austrian public opinion over the period since the Greens emerged has been a series of issues connected to the workings of the Austrian state; disillusionment with the foibles and follies of politicians - civic incompetence or worse - the relative costs, burdens and beneficiaries of what was one of Europe's most generous welfare systems, and the rigid and insular nature of the country's corporatist structures.[20] These are all issues capable of generating radical protest. Moreover, that mood of discontent had now become sufficiently mobilised to show up in a changing pattern of party politics. Unfortunately for the Greens, the radical instinct can find many outlets These issues are just as useful to a new party peddling simplistic populist slogans, offering the easy scapegoats of ethnic minorities and immigrants, and seeking to turn rising anxieties over the socio-economic changes that are impinging on every advanced society to their electoral advantage, as they are to more principled parties such as the Greens.

Nevertheless, the survey evidence on political attitudes in Austria suggests that the potential does exist for consolidating a modest Green electoral presence. Kreuzer's analysis of the data reveals that the Austrian Green parties have consistently failed in their various guises to attract a majority of those who are identified as post-materialist voters - some 15 per cent of the electorate (a figure comparable with Germany, where Die Grunen do much better at translating these concerns into votes).[21] In Austria a relatively high proportion of post-materialist voters opt to support the mainstream parties - of both left and right. This lacuna in Green support suggests, in part, a tactical failure by the Greens - although there are undoubtedly other important cultural, structural and political elements to explain this shortfall, which are considered below. The tactical difficulties that have contributed to this failure to consolidate the post-material constituency are more easily identified. In so far as the two Green parties and their unified successor were obliged to draw up programmes for the electorate, these have too often been hastily concocted and inconsistent affairs - the result of political convenience rather than conviction. Considerable political energy, too, was diverted into bickering over candidate lists and the like, none of which was conducive to maximising the party's electoral appeal. Another handicap here was that throughout the late eighties, the purist VGO remnants resisted complete absorption into the unified party. The ALO on the other hand, with its ascendancy in the new party, has willingly embraced the pragmatic unification approach as a preface to effective electoral politics. As such, it has pursued a radical but by no means an extremist or irresponsible strategy - which consists of a mixture of ecological and left libertarian issues. The potential for galvanising this latent electoral potential around issues that are central to the Green agenda, rather than dancing uncomfortably to tunes borrowed from the ideological repertoire of other parties, was revealed by the recent, successful referendum campaign in neighbouring Switzerland to ban heavy lorries from crossing the Alps. This issue likewise raised the tempo of the debate on environmental damage amongst Austrian public opinion.[22] This may, however, be a case of too little pragmatism utilised too late. Especially in a political system whose rules and norms are stacked against progressive movements pursuing radical change.

The willingness of these factions to submerge their ideological differences in response to the opportunities to challenge the 'old' politics in Austria's changing political landscape has by no means guaranteed a secure place for the Greens on the electoral map. An inchoate support base and the volatile nature of the protest against the unwieldy corporatist (*sozialpartnerschaft*) structure and insider (*proportz*) system that has dominated the country's political and policy processes since the war,[23] suggests that the Greens have yet to move much beyond their present status as a convenient home for the residual protest vote. The old political culture and the rules of the political game it gave rise to were undoubtedly a major handicap for the Greens and indeed, a disincentive to compromise. The exclusivism of the corporatist system confirmed radical outsiders in their unconventional and often immoderate sentiments. The country's non-participatory political culture - in stark contrast to nearby Switzerland - merely reinforced the political status quo.[24] The current survey data confirms this absence of a secure electoral niche for the Greens alongside the prevalence of an unreliable support base. Only a small proportion of current Green party voters unequivocally identify themselves as 'positive' supporters, in the sense that they share an emotional or intellectual attachment to ecologism and are ideologically in tune with the party's programme. The impact on this situation, of an effective and articulate party leader with an abiding sense of political realism has only marginally - and perhaps temporarily - improved the Greens' electoral prospects. Nevertheless, the Greens have at least responded positively to what they regard as a notable shift in the established political order. Social change has, over the past decade, finally caught up with and begun to challenge these now dated political structures. Austria's long standing 'civil tranquillity'[25] has recently been overtaken by a rising electoral volatility and incipient party dealignment, reflecting a widespread 'embourgeoisement' of politics that has begun to loosen traditional tribal loyalties across the continent.

The Austrian Greens have responded well to this electoral shift, as they have to the emergence of new social groups and value cleavages on the back of this new political agenda. After an impressive round of television interviews and debates by Madelaine Petrovic during the course of the 1994 election campaign, the polls indicated a doubling of the potential Green vote to 15 per cent, with young and first time voters especially impressed by her virtuoso performances.[26] We may surmise here that the party's electoral prospects might have fared better if the moderate pure Green VGO faction, rather than the more radical ALO, had succeeded in capturing the party. This would almost certainly have made little difference to the Greens' prospects over the medium or long term. But the fact is, that 'the Greens' are now perceived by media and public alike to be, in effect, the Green Alternative Party and the VGO is merely a minor irritant - albeit one with potential to attract enough votes in some instances to prevent the main Green party from crossing the electoral threshold, and thereby costing it both provincial seats and a degree of influence. A move to pre-empt some of this damage, by re-naming the party 'the Greens', not only rekindled an old battle with the VGO rump - who claimed legal title to that name by dint of precedence - but also raised objections within the DGA itself from local groups and alternativists who shelter under the party's umbrella, but remain opposed to any hegemonic nomenclature.[27] Although the VGO's cautious and temperate approach to Green issues would at that stage have been more in tune with the broadly conservative tenor of Austria's political culture, the fate of Green party politics here has almost certainly had much more to do with the structure and culture of the Austrian polity than it has with ideological demeanour, let alone with the choice of a party name. The Green party has acknowledged this singular fact by its own behaviour. The party, under Petrovic's leadership, did manage to respond to the need to be 'sensible', and transformed itself into a competent and responsible party. Indeed, one that was capable of a cohesive political strategy, despite its residual ideological tensions. It was able, at the same time, to cope with these abiding political differences in its ranks without falling apart.

As one leading Austrian political analyst saw these developments, "the upswing of the Greens is continuous and has three reasons: the symbolic figure of Petrovic, the altered image and the shift towards an all embracing political programme".[28] The party managed this feat only by setting aside its earlier prediliction for putting ideology before practical politics. And by undertaking a delicate balancing act between those middle class discontents, who regard it as a suitable vehicle for protest, and the more ideologically constrained ecologists who provide the core of its activists. By taking their dispositional cues from the abiding constraints on radical options in this conservative state, the unified Green party has tried hard to swim with the political tide - to accommodate to the political situation as it is, not as they might prefer it to be. This is by no means to suggest that the Greens - or any other radical new politics party - can expect an easy ride. The old system may well be unravelling but it nevertheless retains a degree of stubborn persistence. Old political loyalties die hard, especially when these are reinforced by clienteles who benefit from them. The impact of globalism and the drive for international competitiveness that drew Austria into the European Union will almost certainly take its toll of these inherited structures designed to manage deep diversities and to reintegrate a 'nation' savaged by the schisms that pervaded prewar Austrian society. The primary objective of the postwar state, of depoliticising critical policy issues and producing technical, non-zero sum solutions in the key redistributive issue areas, worked well in its time. Nevertheless, social change and new policy demands subsequently revealed those arrangements to be outmoded. The costs of this corporatist system were a degree of social exclusivism and economic inefficiency that no modern economy could afford to carry in an increasingly competitive global economy. This traditional system has begun to unravel, and with that change have come altogether new values, expectations and indeed political identities.

(iv)   **Prospects for political change**

There is a sense in which these social and political changes may favour political outsiders. It is certainly the case that the political system is no longer dominated by the rigid bi-partisan corporatism of the *sozialpartnerschaft*, with its exclusive 'carve up' of political patronage and public goods between the established elites of the dominant class-party cleavage. Likewise, recent political volatility, amounting at least to a degree of electoral dealignment, has opened up at least the prospect of party realignment on both sides of the mainstream national ideological spectrum. Both of these developments have long term significance for the pattern of politics. Each, in its own way, offers real opportunities to any party that can capitalise on this mood for change by articulating current discontents. Identifying a prospect is not enough, of course, to bring it about. The Greens are certainly not well placed here to reflect, and even less to shape, this current mood of national unease than some other 'new' parties - not least the FPO, whose leader Haider exudes an easy populism that appeals to deep rooted public prejudices, rather than to the principled and long term sacrifices that figure on the ecological agenda. The Greens face other difficulties that also limit their scope for retaining the levels of electoral support they already enjoy, let alone for consolidating this into a secure support base or a new political cleavage. For the Austrian Green electorate contains a smaller element of those classical post-materialists who prevail as a distinct cultural cleavage in many other European societies. Paradoxically, the Austrian Green party's current role as a vehicle for diffuse middle class protest may well reveal an underlying weakness. At the moment it benefits from a share of a residual anti-establishment, as much as a decidedly Green, vote. Circumstances change of course, and this electorate may just as easily shift and become more permanently aligned to other parties. Moreover, the party disproportionately attracts young voters, and while these, too, may be 'won' over to the party in the long term, their political loyalty is by no means automatic. As voters age instrumentalism tends to displace idealism and their policy priorities likewise alter to reflect this. These facts do not, however, confirm Burklin's scepticism that all Green parties, dependent as they are on such youthful voters, are 'flash' parties destined for certain obsolescence. What is indisputable is that there are severe problems, here as well as elsewhere, with political identity formation and concern about contemporary issue agendas, that need to be sensibly addressed by all Green parties. The Austrian Greens are, then, a party in flux, rather than one that is consolidating a 'safe' post-materialist constituency. Whether they flourish or flounder depends not on the fates, but rather on how they respond to the volatile circumstances which surround them.

There are clearly major obstacles in the way of the Greens tapping into this widespread discontent and converting it into a radical mass movement. However, these difficulties notwithstanding, the political situation in Austria remains fluid. Moreover, this flux by no means excludes the prospect of a radical shift in the political fabric, whereby a well-organised, ideologically coherent and moderate Green party might play its part, and thereby consolidate its place, in the realignment of political forces that is clearly underway. There are clear signs that the party leadership has assimilated the facts - both the constraints and the prospects - of their situation, and are accordingly pursuing an appropriately realistic strategy. The current strategy is a continuation of the moderate response to those issues that presently confront Austria, that have been followed by the party leadership since the merger. The Green Alternative Party illustrated this urge to moderation, for instance, in its response to the national referendum in June 1994 on Austria's proposed entry into the European Union. Concern about the dilution of Austria's stringent environmental regulations, and the usual preoccupations of Europe's Green parties with the EU's growth oriented and autarchic commercial and agricultural policies, persuaded the party to oppose Austria's accession to the Union. Confronted by an overwhelming referendum vote in favour of entry (by a margin of some 2 to 1), and a pro-EU consensus amongst the country's social partners and the media,[29] the party's executive board immediately committed its parliamentary delegation to endorse the accession treaty as "a sign to respect the clear decision of the people".[30] Building patiently and diligently on their secure roots in local politics, and using whatever protest and campaigning issues have come to hand to preach a clear progressive message, the Green party has, nevertheless, continued to come up against electoral resistance. The party has enjoyed modest rather than unbounded success. In the 1990 national elections, for example, they repeated their 1986 vote (4.8 per cent) which yielded, under the usual complicated electoral arithmetic, 2 additional seats - one each gained from the two main parties - to take their total to 10 in the 183 seat Parliament. After this modest consolidation, the Greens experienced the same electoral slippage that afflicted other Green movements during the current decade. They performed poorly in the round of provincial elections between June and October 1991, gaining no seats in Burgenland or Upper Austria and losing their two extant seats in the Styrian assembly. In the elections in Vienna, meanwhile, an altogether more focused and better organised campaign around concrete issues at least pointed the way to a shift from inchoate movement politics to a more professional approach to politics. In the recent national elections - which were staged against the most turbulent backcloth of any postwar election, and with the critical issues of national political identity at the heart of the campaigns - the Greens added no more than a modest two per cent to their tally. This is hardly the stuff of a radical breakthrough. The efforts after 1990 to improve internal party procedures does denote at least a determined attempt to address the lessons learned during the party's early development; in short, that slogans and passion are no substitute for practical policies targeted at particular electoral constituencies. The party congress held at Gmunden in May 1992 took a signal step forward in this regard. The party's federal structure was revamped - with better management of party business, improved coordination between the various provincial, federal and parliamentary (*Klub*) elements - but without surrendering the abiding commitment to internal party democracy. In Frankland's estimation, "the thrust of (these) changes is to move from a loosely integrated, competitive pattern to a more integrated, cooperative pattern of intra-party politics".[31]

There is, then, in these circumstances, more uncertainty than comfort for Austria's Greens. The situation is, by and large, out of their hands, regardless of their pragmatic strategy. There have been signs of the party leadership adopting a tactical rather than strategic outlook, to respond to the national mood, rather than to follow its own ideological instincts regardless. In the circumstances, this is probably the approach that will yield the best electoral pay off, even if it is the one most calculated to open up old ideological wounds between the pragmatists and ideologues in the party's ranks. The best chance for the party, at least in electoral terms, seems to lie with avoiding any action that might alienate those protest votes it has attracted from the mainstream parties - especially those from the conservative OVP - whilst continuing, wherever possible, to keep on board its core ecological support. There are, however, distinct difficulties in walking this ideological tightrope. The tenuous nature of the party's support base is threatened, paradoxically, by the parallel development of other discontent parties - a direct expression of the seismic shift in the Austrian body politic over the past decade. The figures on electoral support almost speak for themselves here. In the 1945 general election, the OVP and the SPO held 85 and 76 seats respectively, with no other party winning representation. The FPO had made a modest appearance in Parliament with 8 seats as late as 1962. By 1986, the parliamentary balance between the OVP (down to 77 seats), SPO (80), FPO (up to 18) and the Greens (8), indicated the clear arrival of multi-party politics, albeit at a stage somewhere short of conclusive mould breaking. In 1990, the Liberal Forum entered the lists with 5 seats. By 1995, the mold was, if not yet quite broken, certainly badly cracked with the total support for the once dominant parties down from 90 per cent to 63 per cent in barely a decade. The statistics for this latest election tell a remarkable story of discontent and even of incipient dealignment. The SPO with 35.2 per cent (down 7 per cent) held 66 seats (a drop from 80 in 1990); the OVP fell below 30 per cent for the first time (down to 27.9 per cent from 32.7 per cent with 52 seats, a loss of 8); whereas the FPO went above the psychological barrier of 20 per cent for the first time (22.6 per cent and 42 seats - a remarkable rise of 12 seats). The Greens, meanwhile, with 7 per cent of the vote won 13 seats (up from 10); and the Liberal Forum, on 5.7 per cent, took 10 seats (up from 5).

Although the two 'grand coalition' parties still secured a majority of the Parliamentary seats (118 from 183), they did lose 22 seats to alternative parties. Equally disruptive of Austria's much vaunted political stability, was a significant drop in turnout - down from 86 per cent in 1990 to 78 per cent (the lowest since 1945) - and this in a country where voting is a ritual that once symbolised the country's pervasive sense of civic duty. The far right Freedom party (FPO), after a modest start to its political life, doubled the parliamentary representation it had won in the 1990 election. It managed this feat by pursuing an altogether uncompromising brand of nationalism - one that held immigrants to be directly responsible for increases in crime, and called for strict limits to be imposed on what were once amongst the most liberal laws on immigration and political asylum anywhere in western Europe. The Green party has been as wrong footed by this far right populism as have the mainstream parties. It has consistently found itself, for the best of motives, on the opposite side on this potent issue, as it has too, in spite of its moderation, on many other sensitive issues. As a party with a genuinely radical disposition, the Greens have imposed some limits on their aptitude for compromise and political realism. The constraints of principle here have disadvantaged them vis a vis other new parties with fewer ethical inhibitions. The FPO, for instance, has been better placed in current circumstances to project itself as the voice of the 'little' man and the best vehicle for radical change, because it occupies a narrowly xenophobic ideological niche that the Green party - or for that matter, the new centre-right Liberal Forum - simply do not wish to contest. Even on those issues where the Greens have found themselves on the same side as the FPO - for instance over the corruptions of the corporatist state, the inequities of the proposed welfare cuts to meet the budget deficit problem, and the democratic deficit of corporatism - the ultra nationalist's simplistic solutions and easy scapegoating have always enjoyed greater popular resonance, and given them a distinct electoral edge, over the Greens. The Greens, for their part, have been obliged by the constraints of a progressive ideology in a largely conservative political culture, to offer explanations and 'solutions' which fail, by and large, to square the circle of the electorate's deep disillusionment with the established political order, and its desire for solutions that confirm their prejudices and promise facile, short term solutions.[32]

A notable case in point here was the stark contrast between the Greens' preferences for a decentralised, transparent and directly democratic decision making system to replace the opacity of corporatism; and the same political language employed by Haider to recommend a new Republic based, in spite of his nominal abjuration of the '*fuhrerprinzip*' favoured by most ultra right and neo-fascist movements, on a caesarist model of plebiscites and referenda. The Greens recommended a genuine system of pluralism in tune with their democratic instincts - a system in which the suboptimal trade offs and the bargaining between multifarious interests determines political outputs. The FPO, on the other hand, threatened to replace the conventional liberal democratic model with a direct, unmediated, simplistic and, in essence, manipulatable liaison between an autocratic political leadership and the people.[33] The FPO appears to have caught the mood of public anxieties more surely than their radical rivals. By massaging popular anxieties and summoning up the worst atavistic instincts of a troubled people, the FPO has come closer by far than any of Austria's new parties to breaking the political mould. The Green party remains in the process, as much disadvantaged by the configurations of Austria's evolving political equation as it is was by the old corporatist politics it emerged to challenge.

In these difficult electoral circumstances, the Greens have been obliged to tread warily and avoid undue flamboyance or even the boldness which is the raison d'être of radical parties. In the process they have acquired a political caution that keeps them in the electoral game, even if on some issues the party has been an outspoken critic of public policy on grounds of principle, which might have cost it some of its more tentative electoral support. In altogether different political circumstances than those which currently pertain here, where the Green vote was both more homogenous and radical, even a leadership exercised by this degree of cautious pragmatism might have considered making a pact or some other type of informal parliamentary arrangement with the conventional left. The accommodation reached early in the amalgamated party's life between factions led by Peter Pilz - who preferred a pure green party capable of attracting support from discontented conservatives and social democrats alike, and 'ordinary' voters rather than dedicated alternativists and post-materialists - and Johannes Voggenhuber, a radical who was more amenable to a red-green strategy, illustrates that while the party's strategic differences over these matters are not easily resolved, they are by no means now a major cause of turbulence. Voggenhuber advocated a party that, while not disengaged from the system, places more store in radical movement politics. Pilz, on the other hand, emphasised issue orientated and project based politics - a model of politics that looked more nervously at Haider's populism than it did favourably upon a link up with the SPO. These divisions remain, but neither side of this argument has pressed its respective claims as vigorously as their predecessors. Indeed, Voggenhuber successfully backed Pilz for the important position of federal speaker at the 1992 congress at Gleichenberg, against a candidate - Franz Fluss - who was perceived by both factions to be merely a party manager. Sooner or later, however, the party will have to confront this strategic question, and its chosen direction will determine the party's future status in national and provincial politics alike.

The realignment that is underway in Austrian politics, with the steady drop in support over successive elections for the Socialist party, might seem, other things being equal, to offer a way forward for Austria's Greens. After all, political cohabitation with the left has been a route chosen by many other pragmatic Green parties elsewhere, as a means of securing a degree of influence over policy outcomes, and even of gaining a modest share of power. The exigencies of the political situation in Austria, however, make this option a more difficult one for the Greens to embrace. The best chance for the Austrian party to at least consolidate its tenuous hold over its electorate requires the avoidance of any such daring initiatives that might alienate any part of the Green coalition. This has made the party leadership reluctant to entertain any direct alliance with the SPO or the Liberal Forum, although the idea of a party realignment on the left - to counter what many pundits and activists alike predict will be a reformulation of forces on the right with an OVP-FPO arrangement - has been regularly mooted, as the old political order continues to undergo the strains of dealignment. Haider, the FPO leader, has drawn on similar experiences of right wing populism elsewhere as the inspiration for this strategy. He mooted a 'Forza Austria' movement modelled on the precedent of Berlusconi's populist front in Italy. In this project he has constantly referred to a Gingrich style 'contract with Austria' built on citizen based, anti-statist initiatives. When the idea was raised in the early 1990s, of a similar left oriented front to counter this sinister threat, the Greens' leader Petrovic neatly sidestepped the issue as the minefield it threatened to be. She turned what, in the circumstances, was an electoral necessity into an apparent virtue, with her claim that the Greens were too inexperienced in the arts of governance to join any centre-left cabinet. She underlined the dangers here of being drawn into coalitional arrangements that threatened to dilute the party's radical identity. Her real concern, however, was to avoid being swallowed up by a political alliance dominated by other parties - and, thus, to avoid opening up latent schisms in her own party over this controversial proposal.

This may well only be a postponement of an unavoidable if uncomfortable issue that the Greens - along with the other progressive forces in Austrian politics - will have to confront sooner or later, if support for the centre parties continues to unravel and that for the far right gathers greater momentum. The urgency of this matter has been downplayed by those parties - including the Greens - with the most to lose from political change of this magnitude. An understandable reaction, perhaps, but a dangerous one in the long term if the threat from the right is not addressed in time, as it has been in Italy for example. It has to be said that while Austrian politics are in a cycle of change, they are by no means in a state of flux, let alone anything like melt down. Despite the almost constant climate of crisis that has surrounded this most turbulent period in postwar Austrian politics, when the governing coalition was, after the outcome of the recent (1995) election, for the first time denied the two thirds majority of Parliamentary seats necessary for the passage of important constitutional measures, the dominant coalition party - the SPO - continued to assume that recent events were no more than a mere blip on a familiar political landscape. It did little more than allude to the fact that the government would have to call on the support of minor parties (other than the FPO) such as the Greens, to secure the passage of legislation. This is a degree of complacency that may yet prove to be the undoing of the conventional left. There is more evidence to suggest that important structural changes are afoot in Austrian politics than there is for the view that its broad patterns remain largely unaltered by recent developments. If the Greens can assimilate these changes and respond to the political opportunities they present, and in the process convince the mainstream left that they share a common cause - at least on political essentials - their prospects will be enhanced accordingly. In the circumstances of the new multi partyism, the Austrian Parliament will cease to be the rubber stamp it was under the old two party hegemony, and will acquire an altogether more prominent status. In the event, the new parties will enjoy - whether formally in office or not - real opportunities to strike political bargains and shape legislation. State President Klestil emphasised the impact of recent changes on the procedures of government, when he referred to "a far reaching restructuring, with completely new opportunities and challenges for political life in Austria".[34] Chancellor Franz Vranitzky's offer to negotiate with other political groups as a way out of the parliamentary impasse that followed the 1995 elections was a tacit acknowledgement of this new bargaining power accruing to minor parties, including the Greens. And while the Chancellor's implicit agreement to go outside the old corporatism and coopt new politics forces was hardly a political seachange, it was a breakthrough. In the light of the insular political arrangements that have prevailed throughout the 'quiet' years of postwar Austria, this development did point to a critical shift - one that has opened up for the Greens, if they are bold enough to take it, at least the prospect of a place in the political sun.

The most recent electoral evidence merely confirms this opportunity. The steady rather than remorseless trend to the nationalist right continued apace and indeed gathered some momentum, in the elections for Austria's allocation of 21 seats in the European Parliament in October 1996, and in the Vienna city elections held on the same day. An electorate disillusioned with their early experience of EU membership and exercised by a medley of narrowly nationalistic concerns (from open borders, especially to the east, and the loss of fiscal sovereignty) had these fears massaged by the glib populism of the far right. They turned out in large numbers for a European poll (a 67.21 per cent turnout) to inflict the heaviest defeat on the SPO in postwar history. The Socialists (29.1 per cent and 6 Euro seats, down from the 38 per cent it won in the Parliamentary poll) lost its accustomed position as the 'first' party to the Peoples Party (OVP) - slightly up to 29.6 per cent from 28 per cent in 1995 and with 6 seats. The real winners, however, were the Freedom Party, whose vote rose from 22 per cent to 27.6 per cent (and with a clear lead over all parties in three of Austria's 9 provinces) - albeit in what was a second order election with its classical protest opportunity, and conducted essentially on a single issue wholly unfavourable to the governing parties. This political configuration was repeated in the provincial poll with the SPO losing even more ground in its traditional heartland (down from 48 per cent at the previous state election to a post 1945 nadir of 39.1 per cent; and with the FPO in second place - 28 per cent, up from 22.5). The Greens, who likewise benefited from their consistent opposition to the Maastricht Treaty's version of European integration, took 6.8 per cent in the Europoll (up from 5 per cent in 1995), gained one Strasbourg seat and beat the Liberal Party into fourth place.[35] The loss of the SPO's majority in the Vienna city council for the first time since 1918 will impel it to work with other parties prepared to keep the FPO at bay. If this trend is more persistent than the 'mid term blues' identified by the former Chancellor Vranitzky, and continues beyond the next Parliamentary elections, the cosy establishment consensus may well reconfigure Austrian coalitional politics and provide the Greens with a modest opportunity to influence, if not to participate in, government at both the state and national levels. The Greens are certainly somewhat more in control of their own political destiny than they were at the outset. The united Green party's transition into a moderate and politically disciplined Green party makes it better able to take advantage of these far-reaching changes than it was when Green politics first emerged in Austria.

2.   Switzerland

(i)   Green roots

Green politics in Switzerland at both the cantonal and federal levels had its roots in moderate, issue based campaigning politics - for instance, in the 'forests crisis'. This placed it in the broad tradition of pure environmental protectionism, rather than in the more radical ecological camp.[36] There had already been, earlier in the present century, the development of environmental conservation groups similar to those elsewhere on the continent. The Schweizerische Vereinigung für Hematschutz (1905) and the Schweizer Bund für Naturschutz (1909) were the precursors of the usual nature preservation and protection groups - bringing together diverse groups, from ornithologists to noise abatement campaigners. By the mid 1980s these had expanded to include some 70 separate organisations. These groups utilised both direct action-demonstrations, mass protests - as well as the conventional political channels for contributing to political debate and influencing public policy. By employing such moderate methods, environmentalists made a positive contribution to the drafting of the 1983 law on environmental protection. Alternative politics in this small, conservative and prosperous country were thus confined to the margins, in the form of the radical Progressive Organisations of Switzerland (POCH) - a party whose roots were in the 1968 student movement, which did not entirely bypass Switzerland.[37]

Environmental campaigning per se can be traced as far back as the opposition of peasant movements in Uri and Graubunden, to protect their pastures from the power companies. It was rekindled in the early 1970s in the French speaking region of Neuchatel, with a failed attempt by petitioners to halt the building of a motorway extension in a place of outstanding natural beauty.[38] The campaigners opted to oppose this measure from within the political system. A convention was thereby established, much as it was elsewhere, of using direct action to pursue specific issues, each with its own particular clientele. The success of this campaigning strategy was reflected in the regular use of *votations*. These popular votes - by no means always full scale referenda - are a particular attribute of Switzerland's unique system of democracy. They enable single issue movements to bypass the routine party route and to directly influence the public issue agenda. The green movement took full advantage of the opportunity here to contribute to the incorporation of environment protection legislation, both into the federal constitution and onto the statute book. This campaign also developed an electoral dimension. The Mouvement populaire pour l'environnement (MPE) stood and won 8 seats in the 1982 communal elections, and emerged as the third largest party behind the mainstream Free Democrats (FDP) and the Social Democrats (SPS). It drew support from all sides of the conventional political spectrum and was consequently able to exert enough leverage to have the decision rescinded on the contentious road project.

(ii)   **Party formation**

A similar, pragmatic 'issues focused' campaigning movement, encouraged by the success of the motorway protest, emerged in 1975 in the French speaking canton of Vaud. Other events, too, contributed to raising the profile of the environment issue; not least, a proposal for a nuclear power station in Kaiseraugu and the Seveso spillage. Members of the Ecole polytechnique federale (Lausanne) set up the Groupement pour la protection de l'environnement (GPE). By 1979, the GPE made its electoral mark by becoming the first European party to secure representation in a national legislature, as well as extending its electoral base in the 1982 cantonal elections. It was hardly a coincidence that this year also saw the passage through the Nationalrat of a law implementing the 'polluter pays' principle. A like minded protectionist lobby grew into a fully fledged but localised party status in German speaking Switzerland in 1978. The Grune Partei des Kantons Zurich (GPZ) emerged as a self consciously centrist but Green initiative, as did the Bern Frei Liste, to pre-empt an extreme right wing group which sought to draw on the popularity that accrued to environmental campaigning, by putting up a list of 'Green' candidates for the forthcoming national elections. In 1982 an Association pour la Creation du Parti Ecologiste and the Parti Ecologiste Genevoise (PEG) added to this diversity; and in 1983, environmentalists secured election to the cantonal parliament in Zurich.

As ecological issues gained in significance on the Swiss political agenda, and eco-political activity increased, the development of local Green parties followed the haphazard pattern apparent in other countries. The route of community politics chosen here, reflected the Swiss aptitude for decentralisation. This outcome illustrates, too, the extent to which the actual expressions of Green politics have everywhere been shaped by the prevailing local circumstances. Green 'groups' and 'parties' reflecting a range of particular issues sprang up almost spontaneously in many cantons. Groups committed to alternative, safer and renewable energy sources took up a broadly leftist stance on ecology alongside 'pure' green organisations. All of these groups, however, tended to share a broad commitment to a political strategy that combined local campaigning with more conventional parliamentary politics.

This rich profusion of groups reflected both the strength and weakness of the Green movement in Switzerland. The sheer number of parties certainly spoke of a vibrant grassroots activism. On the other hand, these essentially localised and geographically dispersed movements did prove resistant - with national elections imminent in 1983 - to attempts by some national activists, to capitalise on ecologism's growing political salience, and to regroup under a single Green party umbrella.[39] The initial attempt here was led by the Demokratische Alternative-Bern (DA-Bern). It was unsuccessful precisely because it reflected rather than

155

ignored this endemic factionalism. This initiative brought ideological tensions to the surface, by seeking to retain the local movement's pure green credentials and excluding from the negotiations what the purists saw as the ideologically 'tainted' radical parties of both the left (for instance, the POCH and the Socialist Workers Party - SAP) and the far right. The latter was represented by the National Action (NA) party, coming out of an entirely different *'heimat'* tradition that dwelt on the spirit of locality and nationhood. This movement, too, divided against itself when, in 1986, a breakaway Libertarian Ecology Party (OFP) emerged, similar in essence to Gruhl's right-wing ecology party (ODP) in Germany, and the fore-runner of those subsequent new right movements that have opposed radical (or 'red') ecologism in defence of what they see as some elemental 'nature force'. The political mainstay of Swiss ecologism remained, however, those radical ecologists of both the alternativist and dark Green varieties. Continuing tensions between these two variants of ecologism prevented at this stage the development of a uniform Green party. With so much at stake politically, and with local sensibilities compounded by competing ideological preferences, the deep divisions within the Swiss Green movement were bound to show through. Although a loose federal arrangement of sorts was negotiated, as much out of political necessity as from any conviction of the need to reconcile these differences, this arrangement was far from being at this juncture a unified let alone an effective national party. What actually emerged from these circumstances in Switzerland - as in Austria and the Netherlands under comparable circumstances - were two loosely organised ideological groupings, as antagonistic to one another as they were to their conventional party opponents.

The reformist and 'pure' Greens coalesced around the Federation der Grunen Parteiten der Schweiz (GPS/FPE), which cast itself as a moderate 'system party', operating in the conventional sense within the Swiss polity. In spite of its ideological novelty, and the usual Green party propensity for factionalism, the GPS/FPE followed the organisational model that typified Swiss party politics. Established as a federal party, it was neither the kind of 'catchall' party familiar to students of electoral politics elsewhere in western Europe. Nor was it an ideologically coherent, politically disciplined party cast in the radical leftist mould. It was, instead, a loose arrangement of factions and groups throughout the French and German speaking cantons, all broadly sympathetic to the radical, post-materialist variant of ecologism, yet committed, for all that, to a moderate political strategy. Nevertheless, residual tensions over political strategy remained. There were - and there have remained - those in the party who continued to harbour doubts about the extent of the party's complicity in a cosy bourgeois system. The more radical activists were, at the very least, ambivalent about conforming to the logic of electoral politics, in so far as this put compromise before campaigning. This faction continues to argue for activism rather than 'institutionalised hypocrisies' as the core of political strategy. Although this issue has not been as divisive as it was in some other Green parties - most demonstrably in Germany's Die Grunen - the party has remained, at best, uneasy rather than confident with its compromises here. While the party organisation over time has accommodated differences over strategy, and whereas a degree of political successes - not least as influence over policy outputs at every level - has quietened these doubts, they are by no means entirely resolved. Compromise continues to be regarded here as a necessary price to be paid for playing a moderately effective role in the Swiss polity. The party is typical of many other Green parties on this score. While it exercises a degree of political discipline at every level, plays the political game as far as its resources allow, campaigns on the usual range of Green issues and, wherever possible, is open to making alliances or cooperating with other progressive forces, both in the conduct of parliamentary business and in the frequent *votation* campaigns, and even assumes office in cantonal coalitions, ambivalence remains its watchword in all of these activities. As Church has observed, "while some (party) elements are willing and able to take office in cantonal governments, with the *Frei Liste* campaigning under the slogan 'competent and Green', there are fears of getting sucked into unpleasant compromises because of coalition government. So when some ecologists do accept office they can make a determined effort to break with the normal secrecy and consensus of collegial administration.... such attitudes can produce an unpopular *frondeur* spirit, which betrays a certain opposition-mindedness".[40]

Nevertheless, regardless of these misgivings, the party did adjust to the conventional political milieu. It drew together within its ambit a host of local groups and campaigning organisations; for instance the GPE; the MPE - later renamed Ecologie et Liberté; the PEG; the Grune Partei des Kantons Zurich; the Grune Partei Nordwest Schweiz (GPN) Basel; the Grune Partei des Kantons Thurgau; Frei Liste, Bern; and the Parti Ecologiste Fribourgeois - with a number of 'observers' from other Green associations. As it consolidated its place in national politics, the party also developed conventional procedures and organisational arrangements - for instance, a party secretariat - to facilitate its role in party politics. By utilising its resources and developing contacts with other parties it became, almost in spite of its radical persona, a reasonably effective player in the parliamentary game. The party was, nevertheless, more than merely a clone of the conventional party model. For one thing its membership profile was as markedly different from that of the mainstream Swiss parties as it was from more radical Green parties - including its Swiss rival, the GRAS. It reflected a broader demographic appeal and attracted disproportionate support from women (rather than 'feminists'), the middle class - although less so amongst middle aged property owners with something to 'conserve' - and from the professional classes. Many of this latter group - the archetypal 'new middle class' - worked as engineers, architects or planners. Their concern for ecologism was less an ideological or emotional response and much more an 'informed', scientific or objective one born out of their career experience or concern with instrumental 'quality of life' issues. The moderate Swiss Green vote also seemed, on the evidence of contemporary survey data, to appeal more to German speakers,[41] perhaps reflecting the parallel impact of the German Greens at this time through easy access to German news and media coverage. The linguistic-cultural spatial cleavage which still shapes Swiss politics has impacted on Green party politics in another, though less than clearcut way. While the German speakers have been more prominent in the environmental movement and amongst its electorate, this is far from confirming, on the evidence, that this somehow denotes a fundamental cultural cleavage between the two communities, let alone any greater inclination by the German Swiss to make sacrifices for a better environment.[42]

The Green party's internal divisions are not a matter of ethnicity but are rather about those issues and ideological preferences that have shaped Green politics everywhere. Of course, issues play differently in the regions, depending on local circumstances. Differences over the European issue which has recently dominated national politics likewise reflected distinctive preferences between these two linguistic communities, with the German speakers more hostile to what they saw as a threat to uniquely 'Swiss values'. Whereas the Francophone community generally expressed more support for ratifying the European Economic Area (EEA) proposal. But again this was by no means an exclusive division of opinion along ethnic lines. Those commentators who have translated this disproportionate preference for ecologism into a rooted schism between German speaking 'fundis' and Francophone 'realos', simply misconstrue the complex cross-ethnic patterns of opinion on the environment as against other issues. A much more plausible fault line - apparent, too, in the other momentous national and foreign policy issues that have prevailed in inter and intra-party debate here during the past few years - is the one between modernisers and traditionalists. The political sociology of Switzerland, and its unique cultural legacies, have merely overlaid and complicated complementary divisions over the new issue agendas that confront every advanced European society in a rapidly changing world. To this extent, the Swiss Greens have faced similar problems to those of their sister parties elsewhere in Europe. And they have confronted broadly the same difficult choices and predicaments. These dilemmas reflect a political cleavage in which ethnicity is no more than an incidental factor in the political equation. The political costs of supporting stringent environmental controls in societies committed to the productionist ethic, and the constraints therein on radically shifting the national issue agenda by building a political platform for that purpose on the secure foundation of a steady electoral base, remains the principal obstacle facing every Green party in the context of contemporary European politics.

Those radical ecologists who rejected the compromises required by this moderate strategy and who felt excluded from the GPS/FPE coalition, formed their own party, the Grune Alternative der Schweiz (GRAS). This organisation remained committed to a programme of fundamental social change. It recruited a wide 'rainbow' of activists and sympathisers from the usual 'fundi' or new social movement networks of feminists, anti-nuclear and peace groups, 'third worlders', and pacifists. These activists were by no means all radicals. The party also attracted a motley of 'progressives' and 'quality of life' campaigners, alongside the usual radical ballast, motivated by a range of reformist or humanist principles and other strands of political liberalism.[43] Radical and new left ideas were, however, the predominant theme in this party's programme. GRAS represented a typical rainbow blend that rejected nuclear energy policy, embraced liberationist issues, recommended improved social policy and better working conditions, and urged open borders and solidarity with 'oppressed peoples' everywhere.[44]

The endemic tension between the two Green movements and the fact that they were, after all, competing for a narrow political constituency, was mirrored in their weak electoral performances. Neither party capitalised on the widespread support for green issues generated by earlier, often successful, local campaigns. All new parties require time to adjust to the rigours of the electoral game. But there was more to this shortfall than mere organisational inexperience. Instead, election campaigns showed up their persistent divisions and presented their prospective constituency with an image of exaggerated ideologism and even petulance. The early results were disappointing. In the 1983 elections to the Nationalrat (the Federal Assembly), conducted under the d'Hondt system of proportionality - which favours small parties, because it operates no percentage threshold for seat qualification, permits cross list voting and even allows for 'write-in' candidates - the GPS polled only 1.7 per cent (2 seats) and the GRAS a minuscule 0.8 per cent (no seats). Factional divisions undoubtedly helped to undermine the environmentalists cause, too, in the anti-nuclear referenda campaigns. Although the Greens' show was on the road, and while they did succeed in winning seats during 1984-85 at both the municipal and cantonal levels, the impact of both parties on the political scene was weakened and their respective resources squandered by their mutual antagonism.

(iii)   Political developments

These continuing divisions prevented the Greens from reaping the full benefit of a more promising climate for environmentalism in the latter years of the 1980s. There was only a modest improvement in support for Green candidates at the 1987 elections; and this at a time - especially after Chernobyl and the escape of toxic chemicals over Basle - when ecologism was at the forefront of the Swiss political agenda. The main blame for this disparity between ecological awareness and its political payoff cannot be laid at the door of the local Green groups who continued to organise and campaign around particular issues. On the contrary, many of these had enhanced their reputation for serious, even effective, politics in the communities in which they lived and campaigned. These issue based groups had confronted environmental hazards on several fronts; for instance, in the major conurbations of Geneva, Zurich and Bern where an informed population in tune with these progressive agendas were prepared to support issue based campaigns. These enlightened elements tended to be less tolerant, however, of the narrow and arcane ideological squabbles within and between the two main Green parties. Despite the fact that the dominance of the GPS in this family squabble suggested that a national Green party of sorts had by now emerged, the slow, reluctant assimilation of these competing factions into a coherent movement to secure the limited Green vote sapped its political energies and alienated many amongst an otherwise receptive Green constituency. As in so many comparable situations elsewhere in western Europe throughout the eighties, where these factional disputes continued to distract new Green parties from putting forward a coherent front against the mainstream parties and their productionist agendas, the actual electoral performance of the Swiss Greens failed to match their promise as indicated by the opinion polls.

There were other reasons for this short-fall in the Green vote in Switzerland. The structure of party competition in Switzerland which, on the face of it, might seem to enhance the prospects for small parties in a polity fragmented by multiple regional, linguistic, ideological and economic cleavages, played its part in actually confounding the Greens. The party system here in effect confronts genuinely radical 'outsider' parties with severe difficulties which they must overcome if they are to consolidate on the national political landscape. Swiss political culture is notable for its endemic apathy. Turnout figures for federal elections are astonishingly low and reflect in part, the provincial insularity of this small, neutral, and federated polity with a distinctive history that has kept it apart from much of the continental mainstream that surrounds it.[45] This singularity is reinforced by the disproportionate number of Swiss voters who are middle aged, bourgeois and male. Such a narrow clientele hardly amounts to a progressive constituency, let alone one likely to be well disposed to the new and radical movement that is the Greens.[46] Supporting a local issue based campaign in pursuit of a precise objective is one thing; endorsing a national Green party with a mandate that threatens to disrupt a comfortable life style is quite another matter. The electoral system has operated to limit Green success in another sense too. The majority of Nationalrat seats are allocated to the most populous and urbanised cantons. These are precisely the places where the well established traditional parties are likely to enjoy the benefit of efficient organisation on the ground. New and small parties, less well resourced and with an ephemeral membership to match an unpredictable electorate, are bound to find it much harder to compete on anything approaching equal terms. GPS membership, for example, never rose much above 4500, even when ecologism was at its height.

The difficulties confronting new parties of recent lineage were repeated in elections to the 'upper' house or Standerat (46 members, elected by the cantons, for the most part on the plurality principle) to which each canton sends two councillors - in effect, state senators - and each half canton one councillor. Established parties are altogether better placed to maximise their chances in these contests. As they are, too, in the unique pattern of political bargaining that produces national governments. The Federal Assembly of 246 members (the 200 Nationalrat and 46 member Standerat combined) elects a 'government' of 7 Bundesrat (Federal) Councillors, who serve a 4 year term, dispense government portfolios and manage the federal administrative departments. The limited opportunity for breaking into this inner circle - the *Konkordanzsystem*, a cosy multi-party arrangement designed precisely to stabilise Swiss politics - denied the Greens the incentive to settle their internal differences that was afforded the Green parties in other polities, where the exercise of real influence, if not in some cases a degree of actual power, was a less remote prospect. By the conventions of this all party alliance, the Federal government is managed by a left-right coalition whose party component's electoral share hardly used to fluctuate between successive elections. Such a hegemony of power precluded even the modest leverage exerted over government by smaller parties, where electoral volatility tends to ensure a degree of flux in coalitional arrangements. A final structural constraint on the Swiss Green parties came from the less generous state funding arrangements for parties than exists in some other European democracies - except in the canton of Geneva. This makes parties without a secure electoral base rather more cautious about contesting the available seats. It explains why, for instance, some while after the two Green parties had become established, they only contested 18 out of the 26 cantons between them in the 1987 elections. This reticence was bound to depress the Green vote, and both parties did less well than most pundits had expected.

The Swiss Greens carried other liabilities into their role in national party politics. They have suffered as much as   Green parties elsewhere from their legacy as successful local, campaigning, and often spontaneous issue based groups, rooted in the specific politics of the community. These resources are indeed useful in mobilising support in local or even regional politics.   They are less appropriate, however, for the more exacting task of organising a disciplined national party capable of running an effective national campaign - let alone for sustaining a challenge to better resourced rival parties with an established support base and much experience of playing the political game to good effect. Altogether different political skills and resources are required for competing effectively in the national arena. The demanding game of 'normal' politics is a marathon rather than a sprint. It favours the hierarchical organised mass parties, battle hardened by many electoral contests, over the iconoclasm, inexperience and ill-focused enthusiasm of movement politics. These liabilities were demonstrably apparent in the early electoral failures of the Swiss Green parties. Both Green parties here expended scarce energy and resources pursuing recondite and debilitating squabbles over competing ideological visions. The least ideological of the two parties, the GPS, even found itself hampered by its own moderation. Unable to call upon the committed support of those radical activists drawn to the GBS (the direct heirs of the GRAS), they found themselves competing for enlightened but essentially moderate voters - precisely the same electoral market that formed the constituency of the established centre-left parties. This was hardly likely to yield these moderate ecologists a stable support base. Indeed, the GPS had to rely on a large number of floating voters; a notoriously unreliable clientele, who are just as likely to 'float' away from them in successive elections, as the issue salience shifts and the political agenda accordingly changes course. The GBS, for its part, experienced different problems. It had only a very limited radical constituency to draw on, because its radical ethos

160

precluded its appeal to the mainstream electorate. This situation reflects an electoral dilemma the Swiss Greens have in common with both fundamentalist and moderate Green parties throughout Europe. It is a dilemma that neither wing was disposed to resolve in the early days of Green politics in Switzerland. The situation was allowed to drift, and in the course of these events, both parties squandered whatever modest opportunities existed, particularly among younger voters, to consolidate the Greens on the electoral landscape.

The gap between these factions widened rather than narrowed as they faced the usual pressures of electoral politics. The moderate Greens dropped the federal tag from their title and laid claim to being *the* Swiss Green Party - the Grune Partei der Schweiz (GPS) The progressive Greens - GRAS - continued, meanwhile, to emphasise their radical preferences and opened their ranks to all manner of rainbow and alternativist groups who had no obvious 'home' in Swiss politics. GRAS campaigned as something more than a discrete Green party, preferring a broader image as an Alliance of radicals. The decision to change the party's name reflected this ambition. As the Grunes Bundnis Schweiz (GBS), the radical Greens embraced all manner of progressive causes as far removed from deep Green ecology or middle of the road environmentalism as it was possible to be. The main ecological ground was ceded to the GPS. Yet even this rift between the two parties was less of a clean break than it might have been. The Bundnis consisted of ten different parties - from Zug, Schaffhausen, St Gallen, Vaud, and three local parties from Fribourg and Zurich. These local parties covered a wide range of policy preferences, albeit under a common radical umbrella. This federation existed as little more than a loose, ideologically fragile and fractious coalition. It was hardly surprising that when the groups' symposium was held in Lucerne in 1988, it found great difficulty in adopting a common programme.

The GPS, at least, saw an opportunity in these circumstances, to carve out a Green niche on the Swiss political landscape. It set its sights on securing a place in the political mainstream, and with 5.1 per cent (and 9 Nationalrat seats) in the 1987 Federal elections, it worked hard to establish the political foothold it had been distracted - by the intense factionalism within the Green movement - from pursuing from the outset. A modicum of electoral success followed with some significant gains during 1986-87 in the important cantonal elections in Berne, Lucerne and Zurich. GBS, too, enjoyed a modest upturn in its support, polling 4.3 per cent in 1987 (and gaining 5 seats). These events confirmed an impression amongst commentators that the Green movement, after defining its albeit competing identities, and consolidating them into the distinct party formats, had finally arrived on the national stage. This fact was eventually underlined by the parties' apparent success in consolidating their respective local strongholds, and securing almost one hundred cantonal seats between them, across the country. The conventional parties began to take notice, and not only to take the Greens more seriously - the Social Democrats lost 6 seats in 1987 with some of their usual electorate switching to the Greens - but also to fight back. Using the flexible rules of the electoral system, the mainstream parties began, for instance, to adopt more eco-conscious candidates onto their party lists, both to tempt the Green electorate as well as to keep hold of their own voters.

By 1987, Swiss ecologism had made a breakthrough of sorts.[47] In spite of the constraints on Green politics in Switzerland, whether self inflicted or imposed either by circumstance or political culture, the Greens had undoubtedly confirmed their place on the national scene. They have, since then, held their admittedly modest ground. The Greens and the issues they represent are now taken seriously by the other parties. In part, this is due to a sympathetic media, but it is also because public opinion had gradually become educated by the successful campaigns waged by the Greens themselves at local level. For all of these reasons, the environment issue remains high on the national political agenda. The Greens have capitalised on this continuing issue salience and have managed to exert a degree of influence at every level of Swiss governance. They have had their greatest impact at the municipal and cantonal levels - by no means peripheral levels of decision making in this decentralised polity. There are, at the same time, considerable limits to this influence. This is most apparent at the federal level. The 'magic formula' that apportions national power amongst the members of a multi-party coalition of left and right parties excludes the Greens from any significant role in 'high' politics. The Greens remain, at best, a peripheral force in resolving these major policy issues. They depend for exerting any influence on public policy, on the support they can muster from the mainstream parties themselves, once these began to take an interest in the environment issue from the mid 1980s. Similar constraints are also evident at the local level.

Not all of the blame for this relative impotence can be laid at the door of an unsympathetic political system. The Greens, here as elsewhere, must take some responsibility for blunting their own political appeal. The Greens' reluctance to embrace political responsibility, and thus to enhance their own credibility, by taking on both formal legislative and executive positions, confirmed their self image as political 'outsiders'. Of course, the scope for an effective role for the Greens in any bourgeois polity is bound to be limited. But there was a greater capacity for the Greens to play a more effective role in Swiss politics than these parties were initially prepared to countenance. This is a familiar story across the Green landscape. By and large, the Swiss Greens have not matched their emergence as a national party with the resolution to act like one. The Greens have undoubtedly been hindered by their reluctance to embrace a model of party politics and governance which they tend to identify with what they see as a corrupt and failed system. Representation in the Nationalrat has enabled them to participate in the election of the Federal Council, but by preferring to adopt an oppositional stance they have not used even this modicum of influence to its best effect. In December 1991, for instance, they tried unsuccessfully to delay the Council's election until Parliament had agreed a legislative programme for the coming term. There was no apparent benefit to the Greens from this stance, other than political self indulgence. On the contrary, it was largely an empty gesture that merely served to emphasise their own political isolation. It amounted to little more than an object lesson in the weakness of Swiss parliamentarians in the face of the *Konkordanzsystem*, which confirmed some Greens in their anti-system prejudices. It certainly did little to help the Greens build effective bridges to potential allies (the SPS in particular) in the legislature.

However, this is only one aspect of the question. Apart from occasional gestures, the Greens have begun to be reconciled to parliamentary politics. The Greens learned these lessons first, in those cantonal parliaments where they made a good early showing - in Bern, for instance, where they won two seats on the cantonal executive and where they did much to shape local policy on higher education and policing. So much so, that the mainstream parties (in this case, the SVP and the LDU) resorted to reducing the size of the executive in order to weaken the Greens' exercise of power. The Greens now, for the most part, even across the pure-alternativist divide, tend to take a realistic view of Parliament, as a major channel of influence over policy outputs. They participate in the parliamentary process at every level, in the usual ways. Individual members propose motions and table questions. As a party group in the Nationalrat the Greens have made good use of their role on its standing committees. The party - now in its unified form - has been represented on the influential conference of 'Presidents of Groups', which determines the parliamentary timetable, and on the Nationalrat's important emergency committees, where it has eventually come to be regarded by the other parties as a full member. While it has yet to play its part in the central committees, the procedural committee or on parliamentary delegations, the Greens have done much, and in a relatively short period of 'insider status', to belie their early image as an anti-system party.[48] The GPS has some considerable achievements to its credit for its role in the parliamentary system. It helped, for instance, to bring about a review of the Kopp affair by effectively participating in the relevant parliamentary committee; it was successful in its support of a widespread call for an official inquiry into the impact of European integration on Switzerland; it contributed more effectively than many other conventional political groups to the campaign in 1989 to put pressure on the government to abandon the Kaiseraugst nuclear power station project and on energy policy in general.[49] And it has campaigned equally effectively in favour of rail transport, and for the maintenance of reduced speed limits and other environmental restrictions on motorways.

The decentralised Swiss polity has done much to facilitate this rising influence. The Swiss federal system, with its emphasis on semi-autonomous localism, the institutionalisation of regular referenda and open public meetings in some of the smaller cantons, maximises the political impact of even small, weakly organised parties who emphasise spontaneity and participation by 'part-time' enthusiasts - as long as these parties are prepared to play the political game and make some minimal organisational concessions to the normal imperatives of party politics. Moreover, the proportional electoral system here, which is largely 'threshold free' - apart from variable thresholds in the French speaking cantons of between 5 and 10 per cent of the vote - is more encouraging, especially in cantonal elections, to small 'fraction' parties.[50] The Greens, not surprisingly, have performed much better at the local and cantonal level. Since 1983 the moderate Greens (GPS) have gained and held onto dozens of seats in a number of the more urbanised cantons - with their best performances in the German speaking and urban cantons of Zurich and Basel, where they have, on occasions, won up to 10 per cent of the vote. All manner of Green factions and local 'parties' have found their way into the cantonal parliaments. The ideological moderation, organisation, resources and the relative effectiveness of the GPS in the political game have given it the political edge over its alternativist rival in the contest for electoral advantage in this confined political space. The message here - of the need to put political success before ideology - began to tell on both sides. In 1988, for instance, alternativist sympathisers in Aargau decided to put pragmatism before polemics, and threw in their lot with the GPS. The GBS was further weakened by divisions over strategy. At its 1989 meeting a stand off between supporters of a distinct red-green strategy, and pragmatists prepared to join the GPS to ensure an effective Green presence in Swiss politics, dealt a body blow to the idea that this small country could sustain two separate Green parties. The GBS yielded the ground as a serious party, avoided adopting a comprehensive 'party' programme, and settled instead for factional or pressure group status based on an issue-based strategy within the broader party on issues such as women's rights, anti-militarism and social issues. With many of its constituent party groups opting for observer status within the GPS, the GBS decided at its 1990 convention to merge with its former rival.

From its own side of this political 'bargain', the GPS helped to guarantee the success of this reconciliation by extending a commendable degree of tolerance to the incomers. It resisted ideological triumphalism, and regarded the coming together of these disparate factions much less as a takeover and more as a merger. This certainly amounted to a change of heart. For as recently as 1990, GPS activists had indicated that the political differences between these two entities were too wide to be bridged. In effect, a gradual shift has occurred in the gravity of Green politics; from an intense alternativist-pure green stand off, to a reconciliation under the aegis of the new GPS. This should not disguise the real shift in the balance of ideological power represented by the merger. But the GPS was well enough aware, both of the electoral advantages of the merger and of the latent potential for internecine warfare in its own expanded ranks, to soft pedal here. It has avoided any attempt to try to impose ideological conformity on the party, other than the insistence - a prerequisite of effective party politics per se - that a coherent policy position be adhered to by all members. Further evidence of this tolerance of diversity occurred in the 1991 national election, when the newly unified party allowed joint lists with more radical alternativists in Zurich and Vaud. The outcome of this tolerance was the further consolidation of the party. For the alternativists performed less successfully than the 'official' Greens, and by 1992 it was accepted beyond dispute on every wing of the movement, that the Greens' only chance of electoral consolidation under Swiss conditions was as a single national party. The merger has kept the Greens in the national political game. It has not yet, however, elevated the party beyond its peripheral status, let alone ensured it that of a major national party.

(iv)   **Prospects for political change**

The prospects for Green politics in Switzerland remains, as they do elsewhere, highly problematical. The evidence of recent years suggests a more conditional verdict on the prospects for the Swiss Green party than seemed likely only a few years ago, when some commentators were boldly predicting that it was not only firmly ensconced but fairly well placed to expand its influence in the Swiss polity.[51] The current signs are moderately encouraging rather than entirely promising. The party has faced many difficulties; some of its own making that stem from the nature and political style of ecological parties per se, and some that follow from the special circumstances pertaining to party competition in Switzerland. The exigencies of political fashion and the shifting issue agenda also figure in this Green calculus. Ideological schisms, even in the unified Green party - and similar to those which complicate Green politics across Europe -continue to weaken the party's appeal to the country's progressive constituency, more concerned with concrete issues than ideological hubris. At a time when the electoral volatility apparent throughout the advanced industrial democracies has touched Swiss politics too, this failure to capitalise on those voters prepared to shift allegiance, holds serious consequences for the viability of Green politics. For one thing, it precludes a significant electoral shift to ecological parties by those dealigned voters amenable to more radical alternatives. Some elements of the Green agenda have certainly struck a chord with Swiss voters. It is easy to see how ecologism might hold an instrumental rather than a utopian appeal for a wider constituency in a country that depends for its prosperity on protecting its habitat - its scenery, rivers and lakes - because of their direct economic value for tourism, winter sports and so on. Switzerland is especially vulnerable to environmental ravages and ecological disasters. The large scale changes in continental transportation networks promised by the recent acceleration of the Single European Market and future European integration is a good case in point here. These were the very threats which activated local Green politics in the first place and, significantly, attracted many ordinary citizens to back these campaigns, alongside the ideologically committed ecological activists who dominated its movements and parties. Any future neglect by the Authorities of their responsibilities in these sensitive areas - now under the scrutiny of an environmentally receptive populace - might well benefit the Greens and add to their political clout. But this is by no means a foregone conclusion. On the other side of this equation, some negative factors cloud these prospects. Perhaps the most important factor here is the Green party's failure to make any deep inroads amongst those voters who share the sociological profile of the 'typical' Green supporter - especially new voters and the highly educated and new middle class cohorts. This shortfall is underlined by the party's failure to capture the support of an extensive interest group clientele mobilised around ecological issues that is much larger than the Green's electorate per se. This is by no means a problem that is unique to Switzerland, even if it is one that causes the Green party here at least as much mystification as it does elsewhere.

There are already some encouraging signs that a well-organised and focused Green party could tap into the current mood of disaffection that is as rife here as it is in any advanced European democracy. Ecological issues gained in salience in Switzerland throughout the 1980s as they did elsewhere - in part, as a direct consequence of economic growth, with its usual by-products of urban development, rising emissions levels and the other pollutants of land, water and atmosphere. The catastrophe at Chernobyl and a local disaster at Schweizerhalle raised the tempo here. A poll conducted in 1988 indicated that 75 per cent of the population regarded the environment as *the* major national problem.[52] Referenda results in favour of improving the rail network and protecting natural habitats against military usage have reinforced this mood. Switzerland's place as a transit centre in Europe's emerging transcontinental transportation network, along with high levels of automobile ownership, continue to threaten a once pristine alpine scenery.[53] The reticence of the mainstream party elites to confront the productionist or materialist preferences of most of their electorates by acknowledging these dangers, let alone by doing anything to ameliorate them, did at least allow the Greens to lay claim to a distinctive ecological agenda. The party, as we have seen, did not take full advantage of these opportunities. It wasted valuable time by putting arcane ideologism before practical politics. As the public mood shifted in favour of these issues, Green prevarication allowed the political establishment to move onto the same territory and even to expropriate it; to incorporate the issue into their own agendas, albeit in a qualified form that tamed it, and reconciled merely cosmetic reforms with their continued commitment to economic growth. The Christian Democrats (CVP), for instance, have adopted modest measures for environmental management, including eco-taxation and the 'polluter must pay' principle. The SPS, too, has endorsed conventional fiscal measures for discouraging pollution and fostering eco-friendly production, even though it has been prepared to work with the GPS and even more radical green groups at the cantonal and municipal levels. Even the conventional right wing and the far right parties have added ecological insult to injury by challenging the Greens' claim to be the sole representatives of this issue. The Radicals (FDP), the Liberals (LPS), and the agrarian based Peoples Party (SVP) have all claimed that Switzerland already enjoyed the highest environmental standards in Europe; and that to maintain this merely requires stricter enforcement rather than the further intrusions into personal liberty and the rights of business prescribed by the Greens.[54] These parties, too, have recently hitched this issue to the anti-Europe campaign that has boosted their electoral fortunes, and in a way that has further loosened the direct connections between the Greens and the environment issue. This issue remains crucial for the future of the Greens. Its consequences for the party's prospects are further discussed below.

The rising salience of the ecology issue in Swiss politics is by no means the same thing as claiming that the Greens per se have a promising future in the country's shifting politics.

The once confident predictions of a Green breakthrough - the triumph of a new post-modern paradigm in Swiss politics - has long since evaporated. It has been replaced by an altogether more sober account of the Green party's prospects. The impact of the recent recession and the new crisis of national identity which was, to an extent, a response to the global economic changes that are penetrating every modern economy, has relegated the ecological issue some considerable way down the national issue agenda. The Greens, in circumstances that have threatened to overwhelm them, have had to settle for a relatively modest role in contemporary politics. The potential may well be there to expand on this, but by no means in isolation from other political forces in the national equation. Whatever strategy the Greens employ here must, if it is to yield any degree of real influence, be largely dictated by circumstances. The Greens, for one thing, have been challenged by varying degrees of success on the ecological issue - and by better established parties, more favourably placed to exploit their limited concern for the environment. The nature of the Swiss political system merely compounds these difficulties. It is a system that operates according to a strict separation of powers, enjoys a considerable degree of electoral stability (in spite of some recent dealignment), and is based on a corporatist formula that discriminates, as we saw above, against new parties - or at the very least minimises their impact and reduces their value as coalition partners.[55] The rules of Swiss consociationalism ensure that new cleavages are difficult to generate and even harder to consolidate. And while this is far from being a closed or static system, the established and broadly accepted rules of the political game are more likely to ensure that any new social cleavages are absorbed or incorporated into the concordat of existing parties, rather than retain any potential to effectively challenge that political order let alone to subvert it.[56] In these circumstances, the Greens' options are limited rather than open ended. They are much more likely to survive if they can strike a balance, or work out a suitable modus operandi, with a partner in the political mainstream. The centre left (SPS/PSS) are their most probable, but by no means the only possible, allies in a polity where striking coalitional bargains on particular issues is an endemic feature to the national political culture.

The country's novel arrangement for facilitating direct democracy (*votations*) reinforces the logic of this strategy of political bargaining. The unique Swiss system of conducting popular votes enables opposition groups and parties to challenge official policy, or to propose an alternative if they can secure sufficient signatures to legitimise the challenge - fifty thousand signatures for a direct challenge and one hundred thousand signatures if a group prefers to put its own alternative constitutional amendment before the electorate.[57] The considerable pressure here on financial and organisational resources counts against smaller parties and the GPS, in spite of its ideological preference for direct democracy and citizen initiatives, has been less adept at using *votations* than the better resourced mainstream parties and interest groups. The attempt by the GPS, for instance, to block the alpine rail tunnel proposal - which was particularly popular in the French speaking cantons - underlined the political and resource costs of taking the lead over radical issues lacking in widespread public support. The Greens were embarrassed, too, by their unwanted dependence during this campaign on the automobile lobby. As a direct consequence of this, the GPS has appeared to draw back from the very aspect of the routine political game that conformed most to its ideological preferences for grassroots political action, over more hierarchical or 'top down' forms. To some extent, this reticence about engaging in activities that expose the party to public criticism and weaken its electoral appeal illustrates a sensible caution in a country where ecologism is by no means firmly or unequivocally ensconced on the national agenda. The fact that the political right has proved far more adept at employing this democratic procedure to block progressive ecological measures, and even to propose anti-environment measures, has contributed much to the Greens' continuing political education and has, in the process, reinforced their embrace of a pragmatic political outlook. The environment issue retains much of its ambivalent quality in this economically prosperous country. Concern with landscape and other amenity issues has to be set alongside the possessive individualism and the entrenched neo-liberal temperament of this wealthy country.[58] The single minded pursuit of material success equates more surely, amongst key elements of the electorate on both left and right, with an insistence against 'unnatural intrusions' on individual liberty, as represented by more radical eco-management measures. It was this singular mood that inspired the rise of the Auto and the Automobile parties as determined opponents of Green interventionism. The Auto partei was able to build a solid cantonal base on the strength of unashamed hedonism, and even to take seats from the Greens. Their success encouraged those larger right wing parties - the SVP and FDP in particular - which had been pressed into supporting stricter environmental controls in the Federal Council, to return to their basic instincts and resist further strict control measures such as a proposed energy tax.

The Green party's reluctance to use *votations* to push for more stringent measures is more than a reaction to such determined opposition. The party has also had to come to terms with the ideological conflicts that still reside in a party that emerged from an uneasy synthesis of two competing Green traditions. Both the alternativists and the pure green factions shared a libertarian legacy that showed a marked aversion to using the democratic process in order to impose didactic policy solutions which compromised individual sovereignty. Apart from taking the lead on a proposal to implement quotas for women in public office, the GPS has preferred to follow a policy agenda largely fashioned by other parties. It tends to give support where it sees fit to proposals originating elsewhere. It has, for instance, lent support on measures to limit traffic in the Alps; on the alpine initiative; in opposition to the airforce purchase of F1A18 fighters; on anti-motorway challenges; and over initiatives to improve the coordination of national transport. The party has also weighed in its support for the challenge to Swiss IMF membership, the proposal for a ten year moratorium on new nuclear installations, and in favour of a new energy act. By these somewhat circuitous means, the Greens have helped to maintain the place of the environment issue in the political arena, without in any sense establishing it as the primary national political issue.[59]

The prospects for political dealignment in such a conservative, stable and prosperous polity are discernible without being excessive. If the parties who make up the present inter-party coalition fail to signally respond to rising public discontents - as a similarly constituted governing concordat in neighbouring Austria has failed so to do - the scope for a new politics cleavage in which the Greens might figure could well raise the party's political profile. On the current evidence, this seems a remote prospect. The signs so far are discouraging. Issues - to do with national identity and economic prospects - that favour other parties continue to dominate the agenda. Although the Greens have responded pragmatically enough to the current opportunities for political change, and have even tried to give these issues an ecological slant, they remain for all that a largely peripheral force in Swiss politics. The situation may, of course, swing back in their favour just as it has recently moved against them. Environmental concerns do, certainly, retain a degree of political potency here, although less so than they did when the Swiss electorate were more exercised by the damage to forests and the threat of motorways and the like and less than they appear to be just now as the country confronts monumental decisions about its place in the expansive global market place. But even these materialist issues, as the Greens realise, retain a latent ecological potential. The political trick is to uncover it and cash it in electorally - a feat that has so far confounded Green parties, albeit in varying degrees, across the continent.

This potential remains, however, and may yet be realised, or at least gather salience, if circumstances change. If future governments fail, for instance, to respond appropriately to the very real ecological challenges that confront Switzerland, as they do every industrial society, the young - that particularly large residue of generally politically apathetic citizens - may well become as successfully mobilised around such ecological issues nationally as they have occasionally become at the local level. The recent referendum vote to ban heavy lorries from crossing the Swiss Alps underlined this latent potential.[60] The GPS are the likely electoral beneficiary of such a change. The prospect is far from certain however. The potential for promoting Green politics on the national stage was also confirmed by the outcome of recent national elections. In the 1991 poll, for example, both factions of the united Green party consolidated their position at the federal level, winning a total of 14 seats in the Nationalrat and polling a respectable 6.2 per cent of the national vote. The breakdown of this overall vote highlighted the complexity of Swiss electoral sociology rather than revealing any clear cut national pattern. The GPS both won and lost seats to its nominal allies on the social democratic and far left, but also to the new populist right in the shape of the anti-ecological Auto-Partei (AP). This confusing electoral pattern suggests an increasing propensity for protest politics, and perhaps even for real dealignment, if the mood of discontent discernible in recent electoral shifts takes hold as the country faces the same destabilising influences on its economic and social order that have encouraged a similar trend of volatility elsewhere on the continent. The Greens may profit from their role as a vehicle for an entirely new post-modern agenda from such widespread discontent and even widen their electoral base in the process.[61] But this is by no means a foregone conclusion.

On the available evidence, the Swiss Green party is more likely to maintain its appeal as a minority party with a modicum of influence over those issues which are central to its political raison d'etre, than it is to make anything that remotely amounts to a political breakthrough. And even this modest achievement, if it should occur, would fall some considerable way short of those extravagant claims and expectations held out for the party by members and pundits alike, that were currency in the late 1980s. The progress of the Swiss Greens thus far - after the high hopes that accompanied, in 1979, the election of the first Green national representative anywhere in Europe - underlines the modest impact of the new politics cleavage on this insular polity. The picture is by no means, however, entirely bleak. At the same time, the prominence of this issue did help the GPS in 1991 to become the country's fifth largest party, albeit with a popular vote some way behind that for the major parties of right and left.[62] This modest national success was confirmed at the municipal and cantonal levels, where the party had secured 154 seats in cantonal parliament by 1991 (an increase of 35 on the 1987 result), with its best performance of eleven seats in the Basel Landschaft. In spite of a massive shift in the issue agenda against ecologism between the elections of 1991 and 1995, the Greens have managed to maintain that position.[63] In short, the GPS appears to the electorate - and to its potential allies amongst the other parties - as a disciplined party with a coherent programme - a party that is now seen as both safe to vote for and reliable enough to be considered as a prospective coalition partner. This represents real progress in contrast to the party's shaky reputation on both of these counts at the outset. The party has contributed to its own success in two distinct ways. It has adopted a realistic strategic overview of the current state of Swiss politics, and it has played itself into the system without giving even a quite conservative, or at least cautious, Green electorate any good reason to abandon it. This moderation has, in turn, facilitated the party's cooperation with other party groups and social movements, without which any party in this complex democracy will remain isolated and be politically ineffective. The GPS has also developed suitably pragmatic organisational arrangements to facilitate its by now customary role in the conventional game of party politics. It now appears, both to the electorate and to its potential political allies, to be part of the political order, rather than merely outside and against the system. This remains the case even though the national issue agenda has moved against it, with a political climate that is now much more favourable to the right and far right parties, whose blatant atavism highlights those deep and unresolved national anxieties that have continued to colour Swiss politics over recent years.

A brief word about the new agenda will put the Greens' current dilemma into a balanced perspective. From the beginning of the present decade the Swiss polity has had to address the same critical issues that confront every modern state in an increasingly interdependent global political economy. In Switzerland these attendant problems were accentuated by the country's long tradition - and shared mind set - of 'splendid isolation' from international entanglements. One Swiss political scientist, Hans Hirter, has identified this mood as a leitmotif of national political culture. He notes that "the Swiss are taught from the day they first enter school that throughout history Switzerland has always done well by avoiding foreign alliances". Accordingly, "the Swiss react very sensitively to any threat to traditional Swiss values of neutrality and independence".[64] The problem facing modern Switzerland is that this option, of remaining aloof from such entanglement, no longer seems to be as straightforward as it once was. The remorseless onset of global trends have impacted in turn on this national psyche and propelled the country into a crisis of national identity.[65] This is encapsulated in a series of major - and very divisive - policy decisions, about whether or not to join various international and regional regimes - the European Economic Area, the EU and, in the wake of the Bosnian embroglio, whether to participate in a Nato peacekeeping role.[66] This new agenda has relegated ecologism to a second order issue, without altogether burying it.[67] Concern to maintain a clean environment is a matter of national pride rather than one of radical political commitment. Complacency rather than militancy is the usual order of the day, even when environmental issues acquire salience on the national agenda. A feeling amongst the population at large that Switzerland already enjoys higher environmental standards than most other countries coexists with a widespread reluctance to take on ever more stringent measures - for example, on the use of the automobile, positive eco-taxes, or to encourage resource conservation - especially where such sanctions would infringe possessive individualism or diminish a generally high level of material comforts.

The Greens, in these circumstances, face an uphill struggle. They have had to adopt a more cautious stance than more militant Greens might prefer, or risk squandering their hard won place in national politics. They have tried to harness the critical issues that currently dominate Swiss politics to their own agenda, by teasing out a series of ambivalent responses on racism and xenophobia, that has pervaded recent national debates. A good example of this attempt to find relevance for an ecological perspective on this agenda has been the Greens' proposal for a 'genuine' internationalism as an alternative to the 'false' internationalism that, as they see it, is the current 'European' project, driven as this is by a narrow productionist logic whose eventual goal is an economic and cultural fortress. The European Union has been rejected by the majority of Swiss public opinion, and on far more atavistic grounds than those recommended by this argument. This issue encapsulates the Greens' dilemma. Ecologism has much to say on local matters that touch the lives of communities on specific issues. But it has failed so far to connect with the national psyche, and continues to find difficulty in persuading an insular and increasingly nervous electorate to identify with the unique brand of universalism that underlies political ecologism. In these circumstances, a suitable political motto of the Swiss Greens might well be, 'so far, but not far enough'.

The extent to which the Greens have failed to address these prevailing concerns has been underlined by the emergence of the populist right as the harbingers of a new right agenda that combines radicalism (as an anti-establishment stance on the European and related questions) and reaction (a shrill and mean spirited xenophobia) in equal measure. The emerging battle lines of Swiss politics have been drawn up, and ecologism only figures on this new political landscape as a secondary or at best a subsidiary issue. The political establishment - or most of it - took the view that a combination of events - a deep international recession, the end of the Cold War and the new regional uncertainties unleashed by that event, the extension of the European Single Market project as a direct response to increased global competitiveness, along with the EU's imminent enlargement into Efta and the former Comecon blocs - all required an urgent reorientation of Swiss foreign policy. In the ensuing debate, it became apparent that the nation was deeply divided, although by no means as deeply as some commentators have maintained - with preposterous claims about an emergent schism as deep as anything that has visited this normally well integrated polity since the civil war of 1848.[68] A bare majority, led by a business community concerned less about Euro idealism than about the costs of disengagement from this powerful regional economic bloc, and convinced of the need for 'Euro compatibility' over a range of issues (business practice, company merger and competition law, work practice, technical standards, customs and excise policy and so on), was seemingly persuaded of the need to respond to these external events. Yet, as events have showed over recent years, Switzerland's population have not yet been prepared to make the actual commitments necessary to embrace a positive pro-European strategy. A notable populist politician, and prominant industrialist, Christophe Blocher, touched on a deep vein of national chauvinism when he argued for resistance to the assimilation of common Euro-practices and standards. The facile dismissal of the idea of using regulations to level the commercial playing field was, for Blocher and his supporters, an affirmation of national purpose. Regional integration was nothing less in this xenophobic prospectus than an admission of failure, a convenient alibi for incompetence. The widespread appeal of this view says much about the national mood and illustrates the emotional and ideological distance between ecologism as a radical creed rooted in universal values and aspirations, and the current climate of Swiss public opinion. Even the government, which led the pro Europe campaign, was caught out by its own abiding ambivalence over these issues. While its representatives continued to negotiate the amelioration of the most debilitating aspects of exclusion from 'Europe', Switzerland's wouldbe partners in the project stalled the talks as a direct response to Berne's refusal to make fully reciprocal arrangements - for the entry and rights of EU nationals into the country as well as over the protracted disagreement about through traffic and the axle weights of transit vehicles.

New right wing forces have risen to political prominence on the back of these issues. A cluster of parties and groups - the Swiss Democrats, the Confederate Democratic Union, the Lega dei Ticinesi, and most effectively, the Association for a Neutral and Independent Switzerland led by Blocher - made the running in a number of *votations* on the Europe-national identity theme during the first half of the 1990s. These new groups have fastened onto an endemic mood of caution, and helped to fashion it into a militant and highly effective anti-Europeanism, and occasionally into an ugly and xenophobic nationalism. Throughout the

1990s there has been a succession of divisive *votations* on this issue - on EEA membership in 1992; on responses to EU traffic that saw the banning of alpine transit traffic after present arrangements run out in 2004, with alternative rail transit arrangements (1994);[69] over the nationality issue (1994); asylum regulations (1994); racism (1994); property rights for foreigners (1995); and over an appropriate Swiss contribution to keeping the regional peace (1994).

None of these setpiece confrontations, between a 'national' position with the unpalatable compromises such a consensus demands, and the outward looking pro-European perspective, has helped the Greens to consolidate their agenda, or to firm up their political position and build on their earlier modest breakthrough into national politics. The GPS has tried hard to put a green spin on these issues, but given the insular tenor of these debates this universal outlook was difficult to sustain. This concern with futures was by no means easily apparent or well received by an electorate caught up in a much more primordial debate about the meaning of 'Swissness' in a rapidly changing world. The recent *votation* on the proposal to ban Swiss arms exports (June 1997) led by the Greens, the Swiss Democratic Party and some 80 local campaign groups, well illustrates this dilemma. On the one hand, there was support for this moral gesture amongst younger voters, particularly in the French cantons where far fewer jobs depended on the trade. Whereas older voters, agitated by what they regarded as the unfair portrayal, especially in the foreign media, of the role of Swiss banks in the Second World War concerning the deposit of Jewish reserves, took the opportunity in this referendum to resist this 'attack' on a traditional industry. They cast their votes in defence of what they took to be the 'national honour' by endorsing the arms trade. In the event, hostility to radical gesture politics competed with indifference and the proposition was heavily rejected by 77.3 per cent on a very low turnout. This *votation* encapsulated two distinct political outlooks and competing visions of the national purpose - a juxtaposition that is hardly encouraging for ecologism's preference for a universalist ideal.

To this extent, events have hardly favoured the greening of Swiss politics. The Greens have not found the task of consolidating a post-materialist, post-nationalist politics easy. The requirement of shaping the materialist and national issues that dominate the Swiss agenda to their own ideological last, has hardly been to their liking. The most that can be said so far is that they have persevered and do remain in the political game. It is not entirely impossible to put an ecological gloss on the current issues of commerce, trade, technical standards, and their international consequences, even if the majority of the electorate continue to see such issues in straightforward productionist and materialist terms. This is not, of course, a problem confined to the Swiss Greens. The GPS have drawn on the experience of Greens across European, confronted by similar problems of political relevance in the face of a rapidly changing issue agenda. The Green parties represented in the European Parliament for instance have become adept at making 'Europe' and its consequence an issue with strong ecological overtones. However, neither the Swiss electorate nor the GPS have much experience in connecting these issues, and the sudden emergence of the European fault-line in Swiss politics did wrongfoot the GPS in contrast to their populist rivals on the right. Of course, the Swiss Greens did try to make an ecological case against the current institutional project for European integration - much in line with that made by their sister parties across the EU. The usual arguments that condemned a productionist, autarchic fortress economy primarily concerned with crass materialism and growth, at the expense of resource conservation, environmental protection or any moral concern for the world's less developed economies, have been raised by the GPS in the context of the Swiss debate on EU entry. The Greens continue to make the point that both the pro-Europe Swiss establishment and their xenophobic opponents on the right, offer the country a false choice between two essentially insular and selfish models of political economy - and that, in contrast, only an outward looking, non-bureaucratic or 'people's Europe', genuinely open to the world, can solve mankind's welfare, security and ecological needs. But to little avail. For an electorate less concerned with these neat sophistries tends to see in the GPS a party that lacks ideological consistency; one that preaches globalism and universal values, only to find itself on the same side as its diametric opponents from the far right when it comes to crunch, in many of the key referenda on these issues. This is less a hypocritcal stance than an ambiguous one, but none the easier to explain away or sell to a sceptical electorate for all that. The task of making a distinctive 'Green' case in the current context of Swiss politics has certainly proved harder to achieve than once seemed likely.

The GPS faces, as it did at the outset, some unpalatable political facts that continue to limit its political options. The conditions of party competition in Switzerland determine that any small, outsider party must construct working arrangements with other parties if it is to operate effectively in the political system as it is currently constituted. The dispersal of political power, both from the centre and between parties and institutions at the federal level, ensures that any party that realistically seeks to influence policy outcomes has to avoid isolation. Regardless of its ideological preferences, it has to operate as what Kerr calls a 'responsible, pro system opposition'.[70] Although the complexity of the party system (with some 15 parties represented in the national parliament alone), and the deconcentration of power in the formal confederal arrangements means, as we have already seen, that any number of political permutations, especially on *votations*, may be possible, a coherent Green strategy suggests, as it does elsewhere, that the left parties present the only real option for partnership. The left offers the GPS its best chance of forging political alliances on those issues - for instance, social reform or gender issues - with which they share a common ideological interest. But this is by no means true of every issue. Consequently, the Greens may need to cast their net even wider if they are to exert any influence on the entire range of their policy preferences. The nature of the Swiss multiparty and governmental systems[71] requires an altogether more flexible and variable response to coalition making at every level of the polity, than that which operates in more adversarial systems.[72] The recent experience of pluralist coalitions in Finland, Italy, France and the Netherlands may serve to remind the Swiss Greens of how much can be achieved - as well as the sacrifices required - by keeping an open mind on potential allies. The style of consociationalism that operates in Switzerland remains unique. But some of the rules that have facilitated effective 'rainbow' coalitions elsewhere may be easily learned and absorbed into a political and party system premised on the very notion of power sharing and inter-party alliances. Church has summarised the very requirements of effective bargaining under these fragmented and pluralistic conditions thus: "With increasing dealignment, issue-voting and the breaking down of religious and social cleavages, no (Swiss) party can afford to compete simply with one other force; each party has to fight on as many fronts as possible in order to win votes and cannot always afford too much differentiation. Hence parties can be rightist on some issues, leftist on others. Apparently odd alliances, usually of a very transient kind, are thus quite common".[73]

All of this points to the need for the Greens to develop a flexible strategy, rather than embrace the straight jacket of a formal alliance with the SPS. The positive response so far of the GPS to these system constraints are a measure of the party's assimilation into the national political culture and their acceptance of its rules of engagement. Both the reconciliation of competing ecological factions into a single party, and the willingness of this new party - however difficult that task for any organization with a clear radical purpose - to balance its strong ideological preferences with the need to build workable alliances with other party groups across the political spectrum are a testament to the prevailing realism of the Swiss Green party. The times are presently out of joint as far as its ecological preferences are concerned. Yet the GPS has managed, as the outcome of the recent (1995) general election showed, to confirm its modest presence in national politics. This is a real achievement in the less than favourable climate that prevails. There are few signs of real advance, but no indication either that the Swiss Greens are a radical chimera in a static and conservative society. The most that can be said for them at the present time is that they continue to exist, and await more fortuitous circumstances in which to pursue the greening of Switzerland.

Notes

1. D. Nelkin and M. Pollak, "The Politics of Participation and the Nuclear Debate in Sweden, the Netherlands and Austria", Public Policy XXV (1977), at pp.333-57.

2. A. Pelinka, "The Nuclear Power Referendum in Austria", Electoral Studies 2 1983, at pp. 253-61.

3. Markus Kreuzer, "New Politics: Just Post-Materialist" The Case of the Austrian and Swiss Greens", West European Politics 13(1) (1990), at p.13.

4. See the comments on the Austrian polity in S. Bartolini and P. Mair, "The bias towards stability", Chapter 3 of S. Bartolini and P. Mair, "Identity, Competition and electoral availability" (Cambridge 1990) at pp. 68-95.

5. F. Plasser, F. Sommers and P. Ulram, "Eine Kanzler-und Protestwahl, Wahlerhalten und Wahlmotive bei der Nationalratswahl 1990", in A. Khol, G. Ofner and A. Stirnemann (eds), "Osterreichisches Jahrbuch für Politik 1990" (Vienna: Verlag für Politik), cited in E. Gene Frankland, "The Austrian Greens: From Electoral Alliance to Political Party", in W. Rudig (ed), "Green Politics Three" (Edinburgh, 1996), at pp.197-198.

6. H. Dachs, "Citizen Lists and Green-Alternative Parties in Austria", in A. Pelinka and F. Plasser (eds), "The Austrian Party System" (Boulder, Col, 1989).

7. C. Reinhold & P. Ulram, "Gruen Alternative Parteien in oesterreichischen Gemeinden", in A. Khol et al (eds), "Oesterreichisches Jahrbuch fuer Politik, 1984" (Vienna, 1988), at p.513.

8. C. Haerpfer, "Austria: The 'United Greens' and the 'Alternative List/Green Alternative' ", in F. Muller-Rommel (ed), "New Politics in Western Europe" (Boulder, Col, 1989).

9. J. Fitzmaurice, "Austrian Politics and Society Today" (London, 1991), at p.112.

10. D. Meth-Cohn and W. Müller, "Leaders Count: The Austrian election of October 1990", West European Politics 14 (1991), pp.183-88.

11. See M.A. Sully, "A Contemporary History of Austria" (London, 1990).

12. Reuters News Service Report, 7.10.94.

13. E. Gene Frankland, op.cit (1996), at pp.203-4, notes that this small party representing about 4 per cent of parliament's membership, was responsible for some 23 per cent of resolutions and bills and 24 per cent of written inquiries during the 1986-90 session.

14. A. Scott, "The Austrian General Election of 1986", Electoral Studies Vol.6 (2) August 1987.

15. S. Bartolini and P. Mair, "Ideology, competition and electoral availability; The stabilisation of European electorates 1885 - 1985" (Cambridge 1990) at pp. 301-2.

16. M. Kreuzer, op.cit (1990), p.17.

17. Ibid, p.26.

18. Ibid, p.22.

19. A. Scott, op.cit (1987), p.158.

20. K.R. Luther, "Austria's Future and Waldheim's Past: The Significance of the 1986 Elections", West European Politics 10 1987.

21. M. Kreuzer, op.cit (1990), at pp.14-15.

22. The European, 25 February - 3 March 1994.

23. See B. Marin, "Austria - The Paradigm Case of Liberal Corporatism?" in W. Grant (ed), "The Political Economy of Corporatism" (London, 1985); and ibid, "From Consociationalism to Technocorporatism: The Austrian Case as a Model-Generator?" in I. Scholten (ed), "Political Stability and Neo-Corporatism: Corporatist Integration and Societal Cleavages in Western Europe" (London, 1987).

24. P. Gerlich, E. Grande and W.C. Müller, "Corporatism in crisis: stability and change of social partnership in Austria", Political Studies 36 1988 pp.209-23.

25. M. Kreuzer, op.cit (1990), at p.27.

26. Reuters News Service Report, 7.10.94.

27. E. Gene Frankland, op.cit (1996), at p.209.

28. Reuters News Service Report, 7.10.94.

29. I. Rodger, "Austrians see no joke in EU membership", Financial Times, 6.7.95.

30. Reuters News Service Report, 21.6.94.

31. E. Gene Frankland, op.cit (1996), at p.208.

32. For a discussion of the roots of political discont in the contemporary Austrian electorate see K.R. Luther, op.cit (1987).

33. The Times, 7.10.94.

34. Reuters News Service Report, 10.10.94.

35. Eric Frey, "Austria swings to right in European poll", Financial Times, 14.10.96.

36. For an account of the multifarious origins of green politics in Switzerland, see M. Laver and N. Schofield, "Multi party Government" (Oxford, 1990); A. Ladner, "Switzerland", in F. Muller-Rommel (ed), "New Politics in Western Europe: The Rise and Success of Green Parties and Alternative Lists" (Boulder, Col, 1989), pp.159-175; F. Walter, "Les Suisses et l'environment" (Geneva, 1990); J. Rohr, La Democratie en Suisse" (Paris, 1987), pp.412-418.

37. C.H. Church, "Swiss History and Politics since 1945", in "Western Europe: A Handbook" (London, 1988).

38. L. Rebeaud, "La Suisse Verte" (Lausanne, 1987).

39. For an account of this development, see L. Rebeaud, ibid (1987).

40. C.H. Church, "Behind the Consociational Screen: Politics in Contemporary Switzerland", West European Politics 12 (1989).

41. C. Longchamp, "Analyse der Nationalratwahlen 1983" (1984).

42. C.H. Church, op.cit (1989), at p.49.

43. L. Rebeaud, op.cit (1987).

44. The 1987 party programme was published as 'Gruner Bundis' (Lucerne, 1987).
45. See Christopher Hughes, "Cantonalism: Federation and Confederacy in the Golden Epoch of Switzerland" in Michael Burgess and Alain-G. Gagnon, "Comparative Federalism and Federation" (London, 1993).
46. See O. Sigg, "Switzerland's Political Institutions" (Zurich, 1987).
47. Y. Papadopoulos, "The Swiss election of 1987: A 'silent revolution' behind stability", West European Politics 11(3) 1988, pp.146-49.
48. C.H. Church, "Switzerland: Greens in a confederal polity", in D. Richardson and C. Rootes, op.cit (1995), at pp.154-155.
49. C.H. Church, ibid (1995), at p.155.
50. I. Rodger, "A Nation based on will", Switzerland: Financial Times Survey, 15.4.96.
51. J. Steiner, "European Democracies" (2nd edition, 1991), at p.62.
52. ISOPOP poll, Bulletin-Credit Suisse Banking Magazine, IV 87, pp.4-5.
53. F. Williams, "Looking for the right way in", Switzerland: Financial Times Survey, 15.4.96.
54. D. Seiler, "Postscript" to H. Kerr op.cit , "The Swiss Party System", in H. Daalder, (ed) "Party Systems in Denmark, Austria, Switzerland, the Netherlands and Belgium" (London, 1987), at pp.185-86.
55. Y. Papadopoulos, "Quel role pour les petits partis dans la democratique direct", Schweizerisches Jahrbuch fur Politische Wissenschaft 31 1991, pp.131-50.
56. See M. Finger and P. Sciarini, "Integrating New Politics into Old Politics", West European Politics, 14 (1) 1991, pp.98-112.
57. See W. Linder, "La décision politique en Suisse" (Lausanne, 1987).
58. See R. Segalman, "The Swiss Way of Welfare", (Ithaca, 1985) and T. Hueglin, "Yet the Age of Anarchism", Publius Vol.15 (2) 1985, pp.101-112.
59. M. Kreuzer, op.cit (1990) , p.25.
60. The European, 25 February - 3 March 1994; Financial Times, 17.2.94.
61. M. Kreuzer, op.cit (1990), p.17 and p.20.
62. C.H. Church, "The Swiss Election of 1991", West European Politics 15 (4) 1992, pp.184-88.
63. "Guide to the West European Left", New Statesman, 5.1.96, p.28.
64. Reuters News Service Report, ;31.7.94.
65. See Daniel Thurer, "Switzerland: The Model in Need of Adaptation?", in J. J. Hesse and V. Wright (eds), "Federalizing Europe?" (Oxford, 1996), at pp.224-29.
66. I. Rodger, "A rare paralysis grips", Switzerland: Financial Times Survey, 15.4.96.
67. See Longchamp's 'index of concern' cited in C.H. Church, op.cit (1995), at p.159.
68. See D. Sidjanski, "The Swiss and their Politics", Government and Opposition, Vol.11 (3) 1976, pp.294-321.
69. The European, 25 February - 3 March 1994.
70. H. Kerr, "The Swiss Party System", in H. Daalder (ed), "Party Systems in Denmark, Austria, Switzerland, the Netherlands and Belgium" (London, 1987), at p.115.
71. S. Hug and M. Finger, "Green Politics in Switzerland", European Journal of Political Research,21(3) 1992, pp.298-99.
72. C.H. Church, op.cit (1989), at pp.39-41.
73. C.H. Church, op.cit. (1995), p.163.

5 Les Verts in France

(i)　Green roots

The origins of French alternative politics lie in the eruption of new left radicalism in 1968. This 'cultural revolution' released a diffuse stream of protest movements and radical groups into a political tradition which, although rich in revolutionary mythology,[1] was at the same time structured around a bipolarised and disciplined party system, and contained by a highly centralised state.[2] To this extent these radical movements were regarded, by their participants and opponents alike, as a challenge to the legitimacy of the political and institutional status quo. The classical revolutionary tradition in France had largely been absorbed into, and eventually tamed by, the political routines and rituals of the liberal democratic state. The liberationist ethos of the '68 eruption - a revolution *manqué* - sought to reinvent what had by now become a largely rhetorical legacy. And even to fashion it into a genuinely confrontational and anti-establishment politics. More than that, it attempted to invent an entirely new form of radicalism - a mix of anti-statism and iconoclasm inspired, to a degree, by the anarchist credo. As such, it was motivated by a principled libertarian opposition to what these critics regarded as inflexible, hierarchical and authoritarian institutions imposed by the French polity on society at large.[3]

This reincarnation of a 'lost' tradition of leftist oppositionalism saw the revival of a bewildering range of 'old left' and principally neo-Marxist ideas - the cult of Maoism or Trotskyism for instance. Together with exotic notions of an entirely 'new left' rooted in the autonomist concepts of self development, inspired by the Frankfurt school of critical theory and its intellectual heirs in the radical social sciences. These alternativist ideas emphasised the normative virtues, the therapeutic value, and the practical application of participation, activism, refusal and direct democracy for their own sake. This widespread mood of dissent recommended the construction of a wholly alternative existence. Many radical activists, drawn into this broad movement but ultimately disappointed by the rapid collapse of the 1968 protest in the face of determined establishment opposition, opted out of formal politics altogether. They joined all manner of communes, adopted unconventional non-materialistic lifestyles, and undertook novel and utopian experiments. Many of these new radicals retreated as far as possible from the ethical predicaments and moral dilemmas imposed on them by an involvement with conventional radical politics. They embarked instead on what they saw as 'internal journeys' of self discovery; by 'returning to nature', merging literally into remote rural landscapes in Provence or Brittany for instance; or by defending dying local languages and culture as far away, as they saw it, from the repressive metropolitan artifact that was the modern centralised state.

Other radicals rejected this route to 'self awareness' as merely a self indulgent expression of rural romanticism - and one that amounted to little more than an inherently conservative retreat from political and social reality. Those radicals who preferred political engagement to withdrawal, and harboured a desire to change the world and improve the human condition, regrouped on the political fringes and opted for various expressions of radical activism and protest politics. One important strand of what became a new 'politics of refusal', in France as elsewhere in Europe, formed around the peace and anti-nuclear movement.[4] There was ample stimulus for this form of protest politics in France, not least the decision by President Giscard d'Estaing to increase France's dependence on nuclear energy.[5] This decision became the crucible, throughout the seventies, of numerous libertarian, new left and ecological groups. They were able to form on the basis of this opposition, a distinctive if, given their variable ideological dispositions, a far from cohesive movement.[6] This broad progressive movement also contributed to a rising ecological awareness on the 'outside left' of French politics. Nevertheless, France's self imposed distance from NATO, following President de Gaulle's unilateral withdrawal from that organization's integrated military command structure in 1966 - and the absence of American bases and missile emplacements on French territory - ensured that this issue lost something of the political cutting edge the superpower dimension gave to alternative social movement, and eventually to Green politics, in West Germany, the Netherlands and Britain.[7]

Ecologism in France had its particular origins as a distinctive sub group that grew out of this '68 inspired movement. It shared with the inchoate elements of this diffuse movement an abiding iconoclasm and - at both the level of political discourse and practice - a preference for far more radical ways of addressing what they saw as the deepseated problems confronting every advanced industrial society. In the ideological eclecticism unleashed by the post '68 radical movement, there was no singular or ideologically coherent source of French ecologism. Movements sprang up simultaneously in several places.[8] Green groups began to contest local elections in their own right from 1973, with mixed results. By the time of the 1976 cantonal elections some of these groups began to make their mark and achieved reasonable results. This encouraged other groups to put up candidates for the local elections of March 1977. The Greens won some 30 seats and amassed 270,000 votes, winning between 5 and 13 per cent of the vote in the seats they contested. They managed, notably, to secure an average vote of 10 per cent in Paris on the back of local concerns about urban congestion and associated problems. The still dispersed and localised Greens built steadily on these promising local and regional foundations, eventually using this base as a launching pad for a national campaign. With the 1978 parliamentary elections in prospect, 3 local groups managed to amalgamate into a Collectif Ecologie '78, whilst distancing themselves in the process from the established polity and its 'tainted' structures. For these 1978 elections, the Greens nominated candidates in 201 of the 478 constituencies in metropolitan France. Despite another promising vote in Paris, where some Green candidates again took up to 10 per cent of the vote, and noticeably in those regions where a well organised opposition existed against nuclear power stations, the overall electoral pay off was disappointing. Ecologie '78 candidates polled a mere 2.8 per cent. A similar umbrella list for the first European elections - Europe Ecologie - likewise took only a marginally improved 4.4 per cent (890,000 votes), missing the 5 per cent threshold by a mere 0.6 per cent.[9]

The movement's deepest roots were in those local communities where environmental problems were most visible and where, to a degree, the population could be mobilised for remedial action. Not surprisingly, local campaigns took precedence over a national strategy. If Green politics had any vitality at this time, it came from this strong attachment to grassroots campaigning. These early ecological activists remained suspicious of involvement in larger scale, more structured forms of politics. They regarded the 'real' or local as opposed to the imagined or national community as the optimal level at which to practise democratic politics. This assiduous concern to consolidate a viable 'home base' was reinforced, precisely because it paid political dividends. By the time of the 1983 elections, albeit with a smaller share of the vote (some 147,884 votes) - but facilitated by the measure of proportionality introduced into the local electoral process by the Mitterrand government - 757 ecological candidates won election to municipal councils. The Greens, similarly, won 3 seats in 1986 on the new elected regional councils. By 1989, on the basis of these modest but incremental local successes, they were successfully launched as a national political party. Green candidates by now occupied an impressive tally of 1,369 seats at the municipal government level. The Greens continued to achieve their best results in the smaller towns and medium sized cities. They did particularly well in those districts or towns where ecological issues were of paramount local interest; for instance, in the towns that ringed the Cap de la Hague reprocessing plant, or the Flamanville nuclear plant near Cherbourg, or in Alsace. The importance of local roots was not lost on the emergent Green movement. Even in the early stages of this slow if steady emergence from a disparate social movement to full party status, the Greens knew their political limitations in this less than favourable political culture. They sensibly opted for what Prendiville has identified as a 'stable minority' status.[10] Even those amongst them who were impatient to build a national Green profile, realised that solid local foundations remained indispensable in the French political context.[11]

National ambitions continued to accompany these local successes, rather than merely following on from them as they did elsewhere in Europe. The first national 'Ecology List' anywhere in Europe was formed in France prior to the 1974 Presidential elections. A group of ecologists nominated the eminent development economist, René Dumont, as their presidential candidate. Dumont polled a minuscule 1.7 per cent (337,800 votes), but at least the nascent Greens had signalled their presence on the stage of national politics. It is arguable whether this national move was premature or even appropriate. What it did do was provide an excuse for blood letting in a movement built from diverse, loosely connected and competing ideological factions. Rather than providing the focus for the successful national launch of Green politics, the Presidential gambit merely provoked dissent within the ranks, led by those elements who remained firmly wedded to the conviction that social movements could never compete with established parties on their own terms - and that as such they merely left themselves open to defeat, ridicule and demoralisation. From this point of view grassroots alternativism and local autonomy were the Greens' real strengths and were abandoned only at great political cost to the movement. This staunchly autonomist faction rejected any involvement in the established political institutions. 'Normal' politics for them was merely a betrayal of the spirit of pure ecologism. For this reason, this tendency stayed aloof from supporting the Green candidature in the 1974 Presidential campaign.[12] At the same time, the movement's territorial roots enabled Green candidates to poll better in local elections, including the commendable 10 per cent poll in the municipal elections in Paris in 1978.

Fault lines developed within the movement on the back of this febrile debate on political strategy. Resistance to any involvement in conventional politics was essentially couched in ideological rather than in tactical terms. These intense philosophical debates, which reflected the national appetite for serious political discourse, were brought into focus by events on the ground. Not least, by the impact on the Green movement of the occasional but violent clashes between the anti-nuclear lobby and the state authorities at the site of the reactor at Creys-Malville near Lille. In the mutual recriminations which followed, the pure ecologists charged the leftists with political manipulation - with cynically hitching their ideologically motivated, anti bourgeois bandwagon to the rising star of ecologism.[13] This particular confrontation sowed the seeds of a residual mistrust which flowered later on in the deep divisions within the French Green movement as between its pure green and red-green tendencies.[14] There were already discernible tensions here, for instance, between the staunch eco-regionalists of Brittany, the dark Greens in the Alsace movement and the Parisian Greens more attracted to eco-socialist and new left ideas.[15] Even at this early stage, the confrontation over fundamental political objectives - not least as to their timing and appropriate tactics - was made more complicated by parallel ideological divisions over the movement's links with adjacent political organisations and social movements; whether with conventional forces on the left, or with all manner of feminists, libertarians and other radical activists who make up the outside left in this expansive ideological spectrum. These early tensions drove deep wedges between the various strands of the movement. A direct consequence of these rising strains was the prevention, for almost a decade, of a fusion between two of the movement's prominent groups, the Confederation Ecologiste and the Verts - Parti - Ecologiste. It was only in 1984 that a unified Green party was eventually created out of a merger between these entrenched rival factions. Even then, the legacy of residual mistrust born of these early quarrels, as much as the significance of these philosophical differences per se, permeated the new party and complicated its politics.

In the meantime, deprived of a national umbrella organisation, the movement faced real difficulties in its attempts to mount effective nationwide campaigns in defence of particular environmental issues. The Greens were obliged to improvise - as in 1980 when a movement of Political Ecology (MPE) was formed, precisely to provide a durable political structure to compensate for this legacy of fragmentation. The lack of any coherent national centre also counted against the Greens in the electoral stakes. This electoral weakness was revealed at the polls; for example, the poor showing of a tentative Green List, Aujourdhui Ecologie, which polled no more than a nominal 1.1 per cent in the 1981 parliamentary elections. The existence of a structured political organisation can, of course, be as much a source of conflict as a focus for ideological coherence. Especially so in an organisation which lacks a strong tradition of party discipline, or the incentive to unity provided by a realistic expectation of political office. But in a political system as centralised and highly structured as the 5th Republic, the virtues of a formal party arrangement almost certainly outweigh its attendant vices. The Greens have been handicapped throughout by this reluctance to embrace formal structures. Even after the movement did acquire a national presence as a party of protest, it remained electorally disadvantaged by its persistent image as a single issue party - with the status of being little more than a pressure group that fielded local candidates.[16]

If the Greens were handicapped by their internal factionalism, they were not particularly helped either by the prevailing political opportunity structure. Or for that matter, by a political culture[17] dominated by class politics, rife with a tradition of left-wing adversarialism, and all conducted within a polity as highly centralised as anywhere in western Europe.[18] The Greens were essentially sidelined by an entrenched 'old' politics. As one recent précis has identified these constraints: "the Fifth Republic had not yet managed to achieve an alternation in power; aspirations for social change (including ecological change) rested firmly upon the mainstream left-wing parties, especially the Socialist Party. The ecological constituency was thus imperfectly represented by existing political parties.... or else by effective pressure groups".[19] Even the rapid decline in support for the Communist Party (PCF) and the equally sudden emergence of the populist right wing National Front (FN) thereafter dinted rather than cracked the conventional mould of French party politics, leaving the Greens - in spite of a surge in support after 1989 - squeezed between a reinvented left and an expansive right. The renaissance of the old left in the 1970s represented a major repositioning of those traditional political forces that had dominated French politics throughout the decades since the Great War. The continuing 'revolution' on the French left since the Mitterrand 'coup', has provided a magnet which attracts as much as it repels the new radicalism and social movement activists.[20] The Greens have had to address these 'old' politics forces, even if it would still prefer to avoid any contact with them. This debate, too, has been an abiding and disruptive theme in French Green politics.

In the earliest stages of Green party politics, these frictions were redolent. The difficulty the Greens faced as they tried to select a candidate for the 1981 Presidential elections revealed the depth of these ideological differences. Brice Lalonde, a maverick with an ecclectic ideological pedigree, won 3.37 per cent on a Green ticket. The legacy of the campaign, however, was the emergent frictions over everything from ideology to tactics between Lalonde and his main rival in the movement, the dark green Antoine Waechter.[21] These divisions - the explosive mix of ideology compounded by a personality clash - were carried forward to the 1983 parliamentary elections. They ensured that the internal rift remained open and that Green candidates would continue to stand under various factional labels. Tensions within the movement reflected, and were accentuated by, quarrels over policy as much as they were by differences over an appropriate radical strategy. The election, in May 1981, of a Socialist government for the first time in the 5th Republic's existence opened up a new element in this debate within the Green movement - the beginning of a fault line between those Greens who preferred a broad left cohabitation and those who counselled determined political independence. Although neither the pure ecologists nor the alternative leftists entertained high hopes for environmentalism from the new government, the advent of the Mitterrand regime did witness a noticeable softening in the outright hostility to the political system from many radical groups on its margins. Some Greens shared this general, if short lived, expectation of real change.

After almost a quarter century of centre-right dominance, the prospect of at least a modest degree of social change was in the air, as anyone who witnessed the expectancy on the streets of Paris on election night in 1981 will confirm. This mood of anticipation persuaded some 'alternativists' to reconsider their outright antipathy to playing any role in institutional politics. The Greens who took this line believed that the Socialists would be more amenable than the right had been to at least a shift in French nuclear policy. In this brief honeymoon period, the new government gave out some positive signals - not least, the decision to shut the military installation at Larzac and to close the nuclear plant at Plogoff. The appointments of Michel Crepeau, the leader of the small Left Radical Party (MRG) and Huguette Bourchardeau, the 1981 Presidential candidate of the small Unified Socialist Party (PSU) - both respected politicians with impeccable radical credentials - as the joint spokespersons responsible for conducting Ministerial briefings on environmental policy, gave the Greens further signs for hope. This brief flowering of trust between the assorted radical anti-nuclear and Green lobby and the new Government soon evaporated. In the event, it did more harm than good. The only legacy here was a negative one. The experience managed to drive an even deeper wedge between the various factions of the Green movement. Between, for instance, those committed to building an effective party organisation out of grassroots social movements, and those who preferred to avoid such formalism and regarded ecology as merely an agenda - a political space to be occupied, not by rigid structures but grassroots campaigners as political circumstances required. There were bound to be many sources of potential conflict over these issues in such a diffuse movement.

When the Socialist Government eventually reverted, in what their radical critics saw as typical opportunistic fashion, to a pro-nuclear policy option, and allocated only minuscule budgetary resources to environmental issues, the radical Greens had their worst suspicions confirmed. Any prospect of a tentative cohabitation disappeared - at least as far as the mainstream pure Greens were concerned. The movement's response was mixed, even confused. One instinctive reaction was to reassert their abiding suspicion of the traps and corruptions of 'normal' politics. At the same time, however, this experience of 'betrayal', also strengthened the determination of many activists to become involved in national politics on their own terms, if ecologism was to make any impact on the policy process. These pragmatists drew much the same conclusions as Green realists everywhere: that effective politics requires involvement in, rather than aloofness from, the political game. The most appropriate route to political influence in this pragmatist credo was through electoral politics, and the indispensable means for even modest success here was a political vehicle capable of getting the Green message across - in short, a unified, coordinated national movement capable of maximising the Green impact on national institutions and of influencing public opinion at large. The introduction of a modest degree of electoral proportionality in 1985, which usually favours small parties, also encouraged the pragmatists in their campaign to coalesce these diverse eco-groups into a coherent Green party.[22]

(ii)   **Party formation**

The pressure began to yield dividends. A direct outcome of this momentum for organisational coherence was a five point communiqué, agreed by various ecological groups in October 1982. Although this reiterated the virtues of sustaining Green political autonomy from existing movements inside and outside the political establishment, it also acknowledged the advantages of establishing a distinctive Green organisation to compete electorally in order to occupy a discrete political space for Green ideas and policies. The main objective here was much the same as that which has attracted all manner of radical movements to launch a formal party; to work for the 'greening' of the political system from the inside. The communiqué also confirmed that an independent Green party would conform to the usual strictures of the party concept - not least, a degree of 'necessary' party discipline. Dual membership of the Green and other parties was prohibited; in part as an affirmation of a distinctive Green political identity but also as a defence against subversion by, or any temptation to compromise with, other parties in the political establishment. The communiqué went further in confirming this pattern of party politics by implementing structured decision making arrangements, based on majorities, but with respect for minority positions. Although these provisions avoided the oligarchic traps of cadre parties formed around a distinct leadership group, and established the individual as the unit of membership, it did acknowledge the value of localism and recommended proper recognition within party structures for the existing regional movements. These decisions laid the foundations of a national party, even if the tensions over the meaning of party status that have affected Green parties everywhere, were far from resolved.

A further exploratory meeting was held in Besancon in May 1983, but the proposed national convention necessary to sanction these organisational arrangements and launch the party proper behind the five point charter, in time for the forthcoming 1983 municipal elections, proved impossible to organise. The breakthrough eventually came in January 1984 at a meeting held in Clichy. A national Green party was established along the lines agreed in Besancon. It was, of necessity, a compromise between the competing traditions of alternativism and realism, and pure Green and more radical interests. In the circumstances the new party was bound to be a loose arrangement that drew on the divergent dispositions about party organisation, the purpose of party politics and the variable ideological tendencies that had been active in the French Green movement for a decade or more. The main components of the new party were Les Verts-parti-ecologiste (formerly the MEP with its strong electoralist but pure Green inclination) and les Verts - confederation-ecologiste, a loose organisation as its title suggests, which emerged in the early eighties as a consortium of Green splinter groups and campaigning grassroots activists from various lobby groups (for instance, the Friends of the Earth). This latter 'organisation' was, by and large, more favourably disposed towards an autonomist or freewheeling approach to the political process. A further pointer to future discord came with the refusal of the leading spokesman of Les Verts: parti ecologiste, Brice Lalonde, to join the newly 'unified' Green Party.

The full and unwieldy title of the new party, Les Verts confederation-ecologiste-parti-ecologiste, conveys precisely its intrinsic tensions. These were further sharpened by the constraints of working within a single party structure whose procedures provided ample opportunity for factional strife. The new party was less a meeting of minds than it was a marriage of political convenience. The organisation represented an uneasy and far from stable compromise between competing ideas about how to play politics, as well as between the competing ideological propensities that are French ecologism. The tentative nature of this compromise was clearly visible in the new party's structures. These differences were contained by a system of local party cells on which this national edifice was raised, and were reflected, too, in the preference for non-hierarchical and decentralised community politics. The principal forum for national Green politics was a General Assembly, to which any party member could present proposals for change (including in the party's rules), so long as they secured the minimum support of ten per cent of the membership spread across one third of the regions. These arrangements institutionalised the deep suspicion of political leadership on both sides of the pure Green-radical divide. The practice of direct democracy turned the party assembly into a forum of intense factionalism, usually over trivial matters, which damaged the new party's reputation with those electors who might otherwise have been persuaded to vote Green for reasons of policy rather than ideology.[23] Far from being a liability, many Greens regarded their isolation from 'normal' politics as a vindication of their role as an entirely new type of party. The rising political star of the Green movement and its most dominant influence, Antoine Waechter, took immense satisfaction from the party's distance from the established parties.

The widespread preference amongst party members to create and practise an entirely new concept of party politics was also apparent in the party's internal operations. A grassroots system of representation permeated the party's decision making arrangements. The National Inter-regional Council, the party's 'parliament', depended for its mandate on ordinary members. The principle and practice of strong accountability downwards was enshrined in party procedures from the outset. One quarter of the Council's 60 or so members were elected at the regular party Assemblies which any ordinary member could attend. The right to elect the remainder was reserved specifically to the regional activists. This arrangement dispersed power in the party and made coordinated decision-making difficult and effective leadership elusive. The notion of executive leadership was subject to similar constraints. The Inter-regional Council was authorised to annually elect the party's Executive College (20 or so members), which elected, in turn, the party's national 'spokespersons'. But these were party leaders more in name than practice, and the perjorative concept of 'leadership' was deliberately avoided.

(iii)   Political developments

An anti-party ethos was incorporated into these arrangements and shaped the new party's internal politics from the start.   An abiding tension between what were assumed to be incompatible notions of organisational hierarchy associated with mass parties and normal politics, and real democracy as direct participation and control of party affairs by ordinary members, was built into the fabric of the party.   There were bound to be tensions between this normative theory and those 'necessary' accommodations to the usual requirements of effective party politics as the party developed.   The Green party was not entirely successful at maintaining this anti-elitist preference.   At the same time, the anti-party ethos enjoyed widespread support and the Green party continued, for the most part over the intervening decade, to work hard to convince both itself and its electorate, as well as its traditional opponents wedded to the usual practices of party politics, that Les Verts represented a unique experiment in democratic politics.   The party's increasing political prominence, following on from a degree of electoral success, obliged Les Verts to at least   make some significant concessions to the conventions of electioneering.   The most controversial of these was the greater emphasis given to the hierarchical leadership function - in part an accommodation to the mass media and the electorate's insistence on a figure to speak for and embody the party's message.   The requirement of the French system of Presidential elections for a single party candidate merely added to these pressures.

The reason for these changes was, in part, a response to the exigencies of the French polity.   The 5th Republic confronts minor, let alone new, parties with formidable obstacles. General de Gaulle had deliberately framed the Constitution to avoid what he regarded as the shortcomings of the previous 3rd and 4th Republics, wherein the National Assembly had been dominated to the point of immobilism by a plethora of small parties.   The current electoral system - a second round or run off between the front runners in first round contests - was designed principally to set up a stark political choice between those ideological traditions that had dominated French politics throughout its political modernisation from the late nineteenth century.   First round elections are largely symbolic primaries to clear the ground for the decisive contest to come.   While these primaries provide an opportunity for small parties to publicise their ideas or let off steam without destabilising the Republic, they tend to be squeezed by their mainstream rivals of the right and the left in the second round.   This classic adversarial system provides only a minimal role for minor parties such as the Greens.   This might, in turn, easily encourage cynicism or exhibitionism and it frequently does.   At the same time it instils, even in radical politicians with little chance of winning through on their own account, a recognition of the logic of accommodation; that even a modest degree of support on the first ballot might be traded for some subsequent influence over policy, with other parties looking to build winning coalitions in the second round.   To engage in this brokerage at all requires the capability of delivering a substantial bloc of support.   And this, in turn, demands a degree of party organisation.   The Greens have remained divided over the virtues of playing this particular game.   A good showing by the party in the first round of the 1981 elections strengthened the Greens' hand in negotiating with the Socialists for the cancellation of the proposed nuclear plant at Plogoff.   While good first round preferences kept the party in the political limelight during the frenetic bargaining that often occurred between election rounds throughout the eighties, the party remained divided over both the practice and purpose of such trade offs.   The pragmatists certainly accepted the responsibilities - and opportunities - that went with full party status. Whereas many other Green activists were at least ambivalent about, or even opposed in principle to, formally recommending to their first round electors to switch their votes to another 'tainted' party.[24]

In some measure this situation reflected the alienation from the conventional ideological spectrum, of predominantly 'pure' Greens who saw themselves as neither 'left' or 'right' - but rather as 'outsiders' who continued to feel unsure of their place in the established polity. There were, however, more practical considerations at work here. The Greens had ideological divisions of their own to contend with which complicated their preference as between the other parties. Some Green party voters were leftists who switched to the Greens as a political 'home' after what they saw as the policy 'betrayals' of Mitterrand and the Socialist Government. Another group consisted of voters with a centre-right orientation. Although the French Green vote has tended, overall, to be a more centre-left than a right wing phenomenon - drawn disproportionately from the socially marginal elements who form the new middle class[25] - this preference is by no means clear cut. In the 1988 Presidential election, for instance, whilst the largest single bloc of the Greens' 3.8 per cent first round vote switched in the decisive second round to Mitterrand, 24 per cent actually moved behind Giscard, with another 26 per cent abstaining altogether. The nature of the political compromise that led to the foundation of Les Verts, has ensured that the red-green preference is far from decisive in the party. These divisions complicated the idea of a singular Green preference as between the other parties. Either stark choice threatened Les Verts fragile unity by alienating one or other of these different electoral constituencies.

Ambivalence about how far to accommodate the procedures of 'normal' party competition has pervaded both the practice and the discourse of Green party politics from the start. The party's emergence as a national force, and its modest but notable advance in one of Europe's established party systems, which yielded a degree of electoral success at every level, owes much to Waechter's decisiveness and political professionalism during these critical early years. His sheer determination to impose a degree of national cohesion on the party in order to hold together an otherwise diffuse movement inclined to factionalism undoubtedly helped to establish the movement as a viable national force in French politics. Waechter's political skill and energy also helped to minimise the tendency in the party to 'infantile disorder'. There were limits, however, even to Waechter's prowess as a conciliator. For there were forces at work in the new party which preferred to move it in an entirely different direction. The deepseated tension between these competing concepts of party politics has provided Les Verts with its principal fault line ever since. Moreover, the party's open arrangements encouraged these tensions to be played out in full and in public. The party's fora became channels, not merely for genuine accountability and democratic decision making but, more negatively, for intense factionalism, embittered personal attacks, power struggles, and an almost obsessive tactical manoeuvring. The apparent dialectic here between competing notions of utopianism and realism were nowhere more apparent than in Waechter's own political career. This is by no means a dilemma confined to Les Verts - it constantly surfaces, in some degree or other, in the conduct of Green party politics everywhere. That the party under Waechter's leadership was brought to face these unpalatable choices, and sooner rather than later, is at least a testament to the element of realism in the party and the desire to become an effective vehicle for alternative ideas. This pragmatism was rewarded, too, by a steady if unspectacular increase in its electoral support.

This compromise with fundamental principles brought the party as many problems as it resolved. Combined with a party structure strongly imbued with the very opposite notions of 'bottom-up' democracy, the leadership role has been a constant focus of damaging division.

Nevertheless, once the Greens decided to embrace party status, they were obliged to accommodate some of its conventions and procedures. The rise in the Green vote which followed these changes may be purely coincidental, but it did serve to reinforce the views of leading party figures that such accommodations, however regrettable, were unavoidable. Waechter emerged during the eighties as Les Verts' dominant personality.[26] Unfortunately the pre-eminence of such an outspoken figure merely served to personalise the residual ideological divisions in the Green movement and contributed in the end to a clash between Waechter and his main rival, Brice Lalonde, that split the movement into two separate parties and seriously damaged the Greens' political credibility. Without Waechter's prominent role in Les Verts, however, and his development of a proper leadership capacity, it is doubtful whether the Greens would have had quite the impact they did on national politics - or as quickly.

But even this degree of success failed to quell the deep divisions that were incorporated into the new party from the start. The 1984 decision to opt for national political status was by no means a reflection of any consensus on either ideological or strategic matters. It represented instead, both a compromise between internal party factions and an attempt to maximise the limited electoral potential for ecologism in an otherwise inhospitable political environment. The Greens did manage to at least contain their potentially disruptive divisions within a fairly coherent party framework. In spite of the political obstacles faced here by any fringe party, this strategy did prove to be reasonably successful. They succeeded, by and large, in translating a broad range of concerns - and even markedly different political preferences - into a distinct constituency. The Greens achieved this feat on the basis of a radical agenda for environmental, social and political reform whose expressed aim was to protect the natural environment from the ravages of unrestrained materialism and economic growth. The Greens offered instead a distinctive ecological approach which shared much in common with Green manifestoes elsewhere. It included proposals to tackle the social evils of unemployment by job sharing and reductions in the working week. The party also proposed to confront racism by encouraging multiculturalism. According to this canon these reforms would, in turn, increase social solidarity and free up time for individuals to take back control of their own lives from the bureaucracies that currently dominated them, thereby enabling them to run their own communities. The Greens proposed nothing less than a social revolution; to open up a genuinely radical political space that was neither left nor right. They proposed to deconcentrate power away from existing centres and replace the current hegemony with individual self determination and community self management (or 'eco-gestion'). The objective here was to 'resensitise society' to the elemental values of non-violence, anti-nuclearism, and non-nationalism - by replacing the existing state system as the primary fount of political identity and legitimacy, with a supranational Europe of semi-autonomous regions.[27] This radical *weltanschauung* also included an expression of global solidarity, especially with the 'exploited' third world.

We can draw some useful comparisons here with the situation facing the Greens in West Germany. In spite of the immense differences of political context - in as much as France and Germany offer markedly different institutional structures and cultural milieux for playing radical politics - the Green parties in both countries confronted essentially the same fundamental dilemma. Both parties had to make difficult choices and compromises over their organisational arrangements and ideological preferences, as they tried to reconcile their party status with a radical disposition. They differed less over the extent of these dilemmas, or even over the way they were finally resolved - in favour of realism tempered by idealism - than they did over their ideological positioning as to the meaning of greening. These ideological preferences said much more about the historical roots of Green politics in each country than about fundamental disagreements over the choices faced by radical parties seeking to maximise their potential in essentially conservative polities. In many ways, the philosophical and cognitive roots of Green politics are remarkably similar throughout Europe. What do differ from place to place - and in ways that shape the style and operation of each national Green party - are those configurations of events, and the precise ideological, cultural and historical variables, which shape political outcomes in each national situation. When these variables are accounted, it is much easier to understand why Green politics differ from one place to another. The preference of Les Verts for a pure green rather than the red-green approach of Die Grunen reflects how this unique configuration of historical and cultural circumstances has shaped these respective national movements.[28]

In either case, the internal strains imposed by competing visions of Green party politics found their expression rather than their resolution in the formal party structures that were created to accommodate them. The agreement in 1984 by France's ecologists to organise into a single party, far from settling the abiding differences over ideology and tactics, provided a national arena in which to pursue them with even greater vigour. This factional strife was apparent from the outset. The pure Greens who have tended to dominate the party argued for disengagement from existing party alignments. The radical tendency grouped around Brice Lalonde, whose supporters drew political inspiration from the May 1968 tradition, were more amenable to cohabitation with the left. Lalonde, for instance, saw ecologism as merely one strand in a much broader radical network - whereas Waechter preferred to see it as a unique and distinctive movement in its own right. The radical Greens were further divided into militants (eco-Marxists and eco-anarchists) and exponents of a more moderate eco-socialism who, eventually, under Lalonde's leadership, broke away from the nascent Green party in pursuit of a political rapprochement with the governing Socialist Party. Lalonde, who subsequently served as a Minister of State in the Socialist Administration in these early stages, remained suspicious of even the modest compromises implicit in the new party's organisational format, and preferred instead a loose, federated alliance of groups. Yet another faction, led by Yves Cochet, bridged the divide between Waechter's pure Green realists and Lalonde's left radicals, and supported a more disciplined party model which drew on the legacy of the old left. These divisions over strategy were further complicated by a further split between the dominant pure green faction,[29] and leftists of whatever persuasion who preferred to ally with sections of the Alternative left in order to create a Rainbow Alliance.

These debates over the meaning of greening, as might be expected in a political culture that takes ideology seriously, were far from incidental. The tensions here were clearly displayed in the new party's inability to present a single Green list of agreed candidates for the 1984 European elections. The Greens carried their ideological differences to damaging extremes by running two lists. La Liste des Verts/Europe Ecologie, headed by the leftist inclined pure ecologists such as Didier Anger, Yves Cochet and Solange Fernex, polled 3.4 per cent (667,826 votes). La Liste entente radicale ecologiste (ERE) européenne, led by the leftist maverick, Brice Lalonde, in a nominal pact with the left radical party, the MRG, and some moderate centrist support, polled 3.31 per cent (664,403 votes). This outcome pointed to the costs of carrying factionalism to the point of outright electoral competition. A unified list would have put the Greens comfortably across the 5 per cent threshold and secured them seats in the Strasbourg Parliament. Pragmatists on both sides of the pure green/red-green divide drew similar conclusions and pushed even harder for reconciliation. What happened instead was a coup rather than a compact. Events came to a head in November 1986 when Waechter and the pure green tendency with its roots in Alsace movement won control of the party from a divided opposition. Lalonde and many of those with leftist views quit Les Verts. Lalonde eventually formed his own alternative Green party with a distinct red-green orientation. Under Waechter's moderate but resolute leadership - and rescued for the time being from the disruptive factionalism that had distracted and debilitated it - Les Verts rallied around his pure-green ideals. Les Verts now launched itself firmly on the road to electoral politics. Mitterrand's introduction of proportionality rules for elections to the new Regional Councils ensured that the party enjoyed some modest success when these elections were held in 1986.[30] Proportionality by no means ensures the success of minor parties, but it undoubtedly helps. Not least because it provides an incentive to engage in the system rather than - as in the case of the British Greens - standing aloof from it at the risk of alienating potential support. The modest Green performance in the 1986 regional elections (1.2 per cent overall and 2.4 per cent where Green lists stood) helped to consolidate Les Verts regional bases especially in Normandy and Alsace.[31] The polling evidence also suggests that the Greens tended to reap a discontent premium amongst disillusioned PS and other leftist voters.

Les Verts failed, nevertheless, to take full advantage of even this modest opportunity. The party was still suffering the aftershock of its recent factional strife and was unable to capitalise, either on the profound impact on public opinion of the Chernobyl disaster, or the illegal sinking in Auckland harbour of the Greenpeace ship 'Rainbow Warrior'. The party soon reverted to a culture of internecine wrangling that had not been uprooted, but merely channelled into other issues and personality clashes, by the victory of the pure green faction. Waechter was obliged to devote much of his political energy to thwarting an attempt by his radical opponents, Didier Anger and Yves Cochet, to deny him the party's Presidential nomination for the 1988 election. Waechter successfully resisted this challenge but the squabble opened up old wounds and reminded the party's potential electorate that all was still not well in the recently purged party. Waechter did at least manage in the 1988 poll to consolidate the Greens' 1981 performance, winning a 3.8 per cent share with 1 million votes. This result was respectable rather than spectacular, but it did confirm Waechter's ascendency in the party and consolidated the pure Greens' hold on Les Verts at the expense of the red-green minority. Progress on the electoral front was at best, steady. In the 1989 municipal elections the Greens polled only 1.47 per cent (and took 0.27 per cent of France's municipal council seats) even though the new organisational arrangements enabled the party to field twice the number of candidates compared with 1983. This outcome could hardly be counted as even a qualified success. The party's local performance was markedly better - with over 1300 local councillors, albeit some way below Waechter's ambitious target of 3000, but above their 1983 yield,[32] and more at this stage in their respective developments than the National Front, France's other rising political force. These 1989 Municipal elections at least represented a landmark in the strategic sense. With votes of over 10 per cent on the first round in many constituencies, Les Verts was able to enter the run off ballot in their own right. In the event, the Greens went on to compete in all but the 5 most unwinnable constituencies of the 50 larger municipalities where they had exceeded 10 per cent in the first round. The results were mixed. They won no outright control anywhere, yet confirmed the party's continuing electoral momentum. The party was left in a strong enough position to influence the post-election bargaining in several major cities and in every region of the country - from Dunkirk in the north to Strasbourg, Mulhouse and Colmer in the east; through Limoges and Poitiers in central France, to Quimper, Lorient and Saint-Brienc in the west, as well as Aix and Avignon in the south. As in the 1989 European elections, which followed the municipal poll, Les Verts achieved their best results in districts where environmental issues were already prominent on the local political agenda. They scored, for instance, a remarkable 19.5 per cent and 15.8 per cent in two adjacent municipalities to the east of Paris where Euro-Disney was under construction.[33]

The Greens' strong if selective showing on the first round produced more tangible signs of Les Verts arrival on the political scene. It obliged the Socialists to acknowledge their existence. If pale imitation is a form of flattery, the fact that the Socialists tried to claim their own Green credentials represents a victory of sorts for Les Verts - a sign that they could no longer be merely discounted as political outsiders. President Mitterrand hastily added environmental issues to the agenda of the upcoming G7 Conference. Prime Minister Rocard also reiterated the government's commitment to ecologism and emphasised its role in organising the 24 nation environmental protection summit at the Hague. In addition, the government produced an inventive if modest plan to make companies responsible for the recycling of materials used to package their products.[34] Not to be outdone on the Green front, the opposition RPR announced a proposal to create a new government post for environment affairs and Jacques Chirac, the right's eventual Presidential candidate in 1988, began his cautious courtship of the Greens. Whatever the sincerity of his 'conversion', Chirac did eventually inform an RPR Congress in 1991 that it was time to consider "laying the foundations of an agreement with those ecologists who share our beliefs" - a clear appeal to the 'green-greens' and a further confirmation that the party was by no means beyond the political pale, even if it was still on the margins of French politics. The degree of realpolitik in these belated conversions to the ecological cause, was confirmed by the patently absurd attempt by Le Pen, the far right leader, to claim that his Front National were the only genuine Green party in France!

Beneath the surface of their recent enthusiasm for ecologism, the establishment parties undoubtedly had in mind an altogether short term consideration - both to shore up their own support and to secure an endorsement by the Greens for their candidates where Les Verts had stood down in the second round. The Greens refused to play this game with any enthusiasm, although Waechter did try to use this situation to exert some leverage on the mainstream parties. As Waechter put it, "we are not the fifth wheel on any car.... whether it's a left or a right model. We are nobody's subsidiary".[35] Instead, he drew up a list of demands which included more proportional representation, constitutional changes to increase parliament's power over the executive, an effective Environment Ministry and a halt to the French nuclear energy programme. The persistent if calculated overtures from the major parties, on top of some creditable if patchy local performances did much to increase the Greens' political self confidence. As well as to reinforce the conviction of the party's pragmatists that there was more to be gained from participating in the system than turning their backs on it altogether. The 1989 municipal poll also confirmed in the minds of many electors who may have harboured doubts about it after the previous bouts of factionalism, that a Green vote was by no means a wasted one. This poll, however modest, did register the Greens as a force to be reckoned with, at least in sub-national politics. It was a breakthrough that was to pay real dividends in the European elections later the same year. The European elections provided another opportunity for Les Verts to demonstrate just how far they had travelled towards political maturity.[36] A number of factors conspired to make these elections - in which they polled 10.59 per cent and 1.9 million votes (winning 9 Euro seats)[37] - the most successful by far in the party's brief history. The full proportional system which operated in these elections maximised the impact of the party's regionally dispersed vote. They were assisted by an electoral law which provides for the reimbursement of campaign funds to parties achieving 5 per cent of the total vote. Public funding is especially useful for any party without corporate support or reliable income from membership subscriptions. Green party membership in France tended to hover around the 1000 to 1300 mark, rising to only 3000 in April 1989, and to no more than 5000 when environmental awareness peaked after Les Verts success in the European elections.

The 1989 Euro success was also, paradoxically, a reflection of the relative insignificance in voters' minds, of the Euro-poll. The Greens benefitted from the abiding sense that little was at stake - for this was a second order and a mid-term election that provided an opportunity for harmless protest against the mainstream parties. This protest phenomenon was quite apparent in these elections. The governing Socialist party, as well as the traditional opposition parties, were hit by the same groundswell of public discontent heaped on establishment parties across the European Community. Even on the most positive reading of this outcome, the European poll broke less new ground than it confirmed the party's steady advance as a national political force, with some consistent but by no means spectacular support across the country, including a few regional pockets of exceptional electoral strength. Les Verts polled over 5 per cent in each of France's 95 departments and over 10 per cent in half of them, again blunting the impact of the National Front (which totalled 11.7 per cent). The party did particularly well in the eastern and western regions (in Alsace, Brittany, and Basse-Normandie) with areas of significant secondary support in the heavily polluted Rhône Valley, the Isle de France, where Parisian overspill threatened to swallow up greenbelt, and in Nord-Pas-de-Calais, which was undergoing deindustrialisation.[38] The weakest areas for support were in those traditional bastions of the right, in southern and central France.

It was clear from these results - confirmed both by previous and subsequent elections - that the Greens polled better in those areas directly threatened by some form of pollution or environmental degradation. The Green vote was notably high in constituencies adjacent to the Loire Dam project; in Strasbourg, where the new metro scheme threatened the conservation of this ancient Rhineland city; in Alsace, where acid rain had become an important issue; in Brittany, facing coastal pollution and proposed new port developments and nuclear power installation; in Limoges, where uranium mining was high on the local agenda; and in Marne La-Vallée (the site of the Euro-Disney project). In many of these areas post-material and quality of life issues, encouraged by the direct experience or the imminent threat of pollution or environmental degradation, had won the party some electoral purchase by enabling the local Greens to concentrate their campaign on environmental issues. The breakdown of the Green vote illustrated, too, that the party could, in the right circumstances - and not least where there was already a radical tradition - harness a discernible post-materialist constituency. Les Verts polled disproportionately well amongst the younger 18-34 cohort of voters, as well as with the various components of the so-called 'new middle classes' - teachers, professionals, white collar and public sector workers; and disproportionately amongst women.

On the face of it, the Euro-poll represents the French Greens' most comprehensive political achievement to date. But it proved difficult to sustain this momentum. At the time it seemed, as it did across the EC, as if ecologism had come of age; and that the Greens everywhere had been swept along on a rising tide of Green awareness amongst the public at large. If this was true, it proved to be a fickle phenomenon. In many ways, too, the 1989 successes represented a vindication of Waechter's maturity as a politician able to control of his party, and quite capable of realism in pursuit of his ambition to make Les Verts the third major political force in France. These achievements need, however, to be put into a balanced perspective. This unprecedented level of success created those very conditions under which the residual ideological divisions within the party were sure to resurface; and in a way that undermined the party's recent successes. The logic of French electoral politics encourages all parties - not least minor ones - to build alliances of mutual convenience. Les Verts were obliged by the circumstances of their recent success to play this game. In doing so, the party opened up a damaging rift over strategy that distracted the attention of the party activists from the task of building on their achievements, and eventually alienated many of those voters recently won over to the Green cause.

The disruption began with a tactical manoeuvre by the ruling Socialist Party - concerned by the FN's erosion of its working class constituency, and confronted by an electoral pincer movement from the centre-right and radical parties such as the Greens, which threatened to push them well below the forty per cent needed to remain in contention to form the next government.[39] Socialist strategists made a bold bid for Green support. The bait was a purposeful appeal to unite in order to defeat the racist FN. The proposal was especially attractive to the party's red-green minority, led by Cochet, who raised the issue at the 1990 AGM in Strasbourg. Cochet argued that Green party candidates should stand down in second round elections if it looked likely they would split the anti-FN vote, thereby ensuring the election of racists. Waechter, however, refuted this political logic. He saw this tactic as merely playing into the Socialist Party's hands and his opposition on this point carried the vote. The pure Greens retained both their identity and their control of Les Verts, even at the price of losing some potential support alienated by their apparent lack of political vision[40] - and perhaps, too, of passing up the chance of setting in motion a fundamental political realignment in French politics. Les Verts themselves cannot be held entirely responsible for this outbreak of Green factionalism. The Socialist Government had already mapped out a strategy of encouraging divisions within the Green movement for their own political ends before this qualified offer of cohabitation was made. In 1988 the Socialists had appointed Lalonde, Waechter's main opponent, as the Minister of State for the Environment.[41] Although an ideological maverick, Lalonde had always favoured a red-green rapprochement of sorts. Waechter regarded this appointment as both opportunistic and, indeed, as a calculated insult. This move - or stunt as he saw it - merely confirmed his worst suspicions of left ecologists and of the shallowness of the Socialist Party's recent conversion to serious ecologism. Waechter's rejection of Lalonde's extravagant claim that the Socialists were capable of a progressive environment policy only served, however, to deepen existing fault lines in the movement. Lalonde's launch of a new Green party, Génération Ecologie (GE) in May 1990, based on the idea of a progressive coalition on the left of French politics, and including Greens, turned what had been a simmering quarrel into a virtual declaration of civil war.[42]

Lalonde's move was by no means entirely opportunistic. His commitment to leftist politics went back to his involvement in the '68 movement, and his new party formation has to be seen in this light, as a deliberate response to moves that were unfolding on the centre-left, in favour of a realignment of the socialist coalition put together by Mitterrand and formally constituted at the Epinay Congress in 1971. Lalonde believed that the best opportunity for exerting a Green influence would be as part of a broad radical coalition. The strategy he employed was a rare synthesis of political realism and eco-socialist ideas. Accordingly, he made a determined effort to trade what he saw as feasible policy options with which the left could reasonably identify, in exchange for substantive concessions from the

Socialist Government on environment policy. This was to be no supine surrender of principle, let alone an ex parte deal to fulfil Lalonde's ambitions for political preferment, but rather a genuine if clumsy attempt to accelerate political change. He was prepared, for instance, to accept a continuation of France's nuclear capacity for the time being, in return for a freeze on atomic energy production at current levels. He also demanded more stringent regulations on the storage of nuclear waste. Even this modest shopping list proved too much for the moderates under Mitterrand's aegis, who retained control of the Socialist Party's central councils. The combination of Lalonde's assertive leadership style, his hard bargaining and perhaps, in the end, a recognition by the arch strategist Mitterrand that Lalonde could not deliver a sufficiently large Green vote to make any real difference to the Socialists, given the resilient independence of even the moderate green vote, eventually cooled Mitterrand's courtship of ecologism. Other parts of old left, as we shall see, approached the matter of realignment with altogether more open minds. All that this early attempt at red-green reconciliation managed to achieve, therefore, was a deepening of the ideological rifts within the Green movement.

The prospect of a major realignment on the centre-left drew down Lalonde's fire on Les Verts and especially on Waechter. Lalonde criticised the party's reluctance to dealing with the government, as a policy fashioned by ' infantile fundamentalists'. Lalonde believed that to be effective, radical politics had to be practical politics; a matter of exerting leverage within the political system rather than merely engaging in principled posturing. "Ecology", he said, "must not become a handful of hardliners who think only of preserving their identity and are obsessed with denouncing those closest to them. We think of ecology as a force for reform. My leftist past left me with a desire to change the world".[43] Lalonde presented a clear alternative strategy to what he regarded as a party whose leaders were out of touch with events - an updated technocratic ecologism, quite compatible with the other progressive forces at work reshaping French society. At the same time, the conduct of his politics - and his didactic leadership style - was hardly calculated to win over even those realists in Les Verts who shared a similar impatience with Waechter's purist stance. Génération Ecologie was a hierarchical structure with little internal democracy. The lines of internal command flowed down from a highly personalised leadership style based in Paris, rather than upwards from a mobilised grassroots membership. Yet at the outset, Lalonde seemed to have tapped a vein of realism in the Green movement at large. Lalonde's critique of Waechter's preference for pure Green isolationism was echoed elsewhere in the European ecology movement. On the basis of transnational Green cooperation in the European Parliament, Die Grunen backed Les Verts against GE. Nevertheless, several prominent 'realos' in the German party were less than impressed by Waechter's refusal to work with other progressive forces in the French ecology movement, and were openly critical of what seemed to be a lost opportunity to reshape the French left. Daniel Cohn-Bendit, a comrade of Lalonde's in the Sorbonne occupation of 1968, and now the Greens' deputy mayor of Frankfurt, publicly endorsed Lalonde's pragmatism as the best way forward for political ecology. Cohn-Bendit actively canvassed for Lalonde's candidates in the 1992 elections (who included his own brother), and critically observed that "the present leadership of the French Greens has achieved something which even the German fundamentalists never managed; a takeover by intolerant people of a movement which is supposed to be open and really democratic".[44] Waechter's response to this attack was predictable. He reaffirmed his faith in a pure Green strategy and rounded on Lalonde as an opportunist, and on Génération Ecologie as socialist dupes and "accomplices of the nuclear state". Waechter dismissed them as a party of thinly disguised materialists who "share the same road which destroys the soul and beauty of our regions". Les Verts, under his leadership, remained wedded to an uncompromising vision of ecologism across its policy agenda; from scrapping both nuclear weapons and nuclear energy facilities, to abating 'needless' road building. None of these policies were available for compromise or dilution but were recommended instead as part of a holistic "global vision .... not just a way of minimising the effects of the system".[45]

The split between the two Green parties received considerable media attention and, as subsequent developments suggest, undoubtedly damaged the cause of ecologism. For one thing it opened up old wounds as well as providing a new focus for the deep personal animus that tends to be generated by internecine ideological feuds. This fresh outbreak of civil war could not have come at a less propitious time. It occurred at precisely the moment when some elements in France's progressive electorate seemed prepared to accept that Green politics was worthy of serious consideration. The onset of civil war presented a major distraction, at a time when the Green party should have been consolidating its recent electoral successes and exploiting the degree of leverage with the increasingly nervous alliances on the left, in order to influence the national policy agenda. Lalonde, at least, seems to have acknowledged these dangers, by offering a reconciliation to his principal opponent. Waechter, however, refused any notion of compromise, and the damage increased when the two faction were reduced to trading insults. The real costs of this quarrel soon became apparent during the 1992 local elections. These elections were a case of, so far but by no means far enough, for a party that had recently seemed on the verge of a modest but under French conditions, a significant electoral breakthrough. The 1992 election results showed a mixed picture of the current health of the Green movement in France. For the first time since the emergence of a unified Green party in 1984, Les Verts managed to field candidates in all 95 mainland departments. At the same time, Waechter's intransigence ensured that they also faced rival GE candidates - and the prospect of a split vote - in 85 departments, including many of their most favoured districts. Génération Ecologie were aided here by party rules that permitted them to recruit members of other parties to join - a procedure that conveniently allowed many dissatisfied local PS activists, many of them with considerable influence, to put their local campaign networks at Lalonde's disposal,[46] to campaign under a new political banner, and escape being tainted by that party's current unpopularity. In spite of strong residual support for Green politics, the existence of two distinct ecology lists cancelled out what would otherwise have been an impressive performance. No doubt, too, the unwarranted luxury of two competing Green parties alienated some voters impatient with a movement that promised a social revolution but proved unable or unwilling to agree on how best to bring it about. The political costs of this fallout were apparent from the results. The total poll for ecologism per se, reached almost fifteen per cent of the total vote - half as much again as the Greens had polled in the European elections. Nevertheless, the sheer incomprehension of many Green voters during the campaign turned to disenchantment or worse when the results were declared. The Green vote divided into two almost equal blocs - Les Verts won 7.55 per cent and GE 7.13 per cent. It seemed apparent to many progressive voters that a real opportunity to take advantage of widespread discontent with the mainstream parties had been squandered. And perhaps, too, the chance to contribute to a degree of dealignment in France's established party system. The Greens, in fact, were the only party group to register significant electoral gains across the country. The Socialists dropped to a mere 17.87 per cent (down from 23.61 per cent in the 1989 European poll). Even the opposition centre-right and conservative candidates, at precisely a moment in the electoral and economic cycles which should have favoured them, only managed 33.06 per cent of the total vote - a reduction of some 4.5 per cent since 1989, much of which was lost to the extreme right. The National Front won 13.9 per cent, an increase of 2 per cent on 1989.

These results confirmed a sense of a lost opportunity amongst many voters who had lent their votes to the Greens in anticipation of a real prospect of change. Of course, the pattern of results reflected other motives, too, not least a mid-term protest by many Socialists who merely wanted to register their disapproval of the Government. But there was more at stake here than a mid-term blip. Green intransigence in these circumstances had deflected any opportunity for real political change. It is easy to exaggerate the prospect for far-reaching change on the basis of a sequence of election results over the short term. There was, however, during this period a sense that the pattern of French party politics was indeed beginning to shift. Socialism has been in crisis everywhere in western Europe as socio-economic change and policy agendas have eroded its traditional *ouvrièrist* foundations.[47] The left has begun to undergo the process of reinvention necessary to adapt it to a new post-industrial politics.[48] The particular crisis of French socialism during the late eighties was merely one aspect of this broader train of events. There was much more to the dramatic shifts in French electoral behaviour during these years than a momentary disillusionment with the Socialist Party or its leader. There was instead a growing sense that Mitterrand's leftist coalition was beginning to unravel - and also that a new political space might conceivably be opening up in French politics for those progressive elements prepared to rethink radical options and take advantage of the opportunity. The Green impasse certainly alienated many voters, but when the electoral costs were assimilated, members of both Green parties began to soften their mutual hostility. Lalonde's reasoned appeal to Les Verts, to open itself to a broader vision of ecologism in order to consolidate their place in the changing political landscape, began to gain wider acceptance within Les Verts.

There was more at stake here than mere wishful thinking. The Socialists were showing signs of regenerating their movement by accommodating the new politics agenda. The Greens figured in these plans, not as convenient dupes to help restore Socialist electoral fortunes, but as a key element in a new radical coalition. During the year that followed their 1992 poll débâcle radical socialists, led by Michel Rocard, assiduously courted the Greens. Rocard raised the prospect of forging a new progressive alliance to keep the resurgent right - and far right - at bay. The Socialist Minister, Jacques Lang, proposed a form of political cohabitation with Les Verts on the basis of pacts to govern the four regions where there had been no decisive electoral outcome in 1992. As Lang saw it, this was about something more than short term political advantage. The strategic consequences of such arrangements were paramount; these "new majorities(and) progressive coalitions with a desire for positive change, modernisation and taking more account of the environment .... will replace the conservative minorities which they control".[49] Lang was well enough aware of the Greens' strong roots in local politics. Both GE and Les Verts had at this juncture, at least as much clout in the regions as the Socialists, who had been reduced to controlling only one of France's 22 regions. The shift in the local balance of power was particularly well illustrated in the Nord-Pas-de-Calais region - a traditional bastion of socialism that had already undergone chronic de-industrialisation, and now faced another onslaught on its environment and amenity value from the impact of the Channel Tunnel project. A sensible power sharing arrangement by pragmatists from both Green parties showed what mutual tolerance and common sense could achieve. A Green candidate was able to muster enough leftist support to win the regional Presidency. This was indeed a significant political milestone - the first occupancy by a Green of a post in regional government. This outcome began to soften resistance in Les Verts to the new politics of progressive cooperation. It signalled, too, another period of factionalism in that party, as pragmatists and Green fundamentalists battled it out for the soul of the party.

These events, meanwhile, encouraged Lalonde in his belief that a Green reconciliation was now possible. He reopened his overtures to Waechter. As a sign of good faith, he quit his Ministerial post. When the new Socialist Prime Minister Beregevoy solicited Les Verts to replace him, the party declined his offer. There were mixed signals here; a combination of the party's instinctive isolationism still encouraged by Waechter's pure Green faction; and an attempt, too, to play up to the party's rising importance in national politics as a preface to a vibrant new politics. Les Verts issued a list of demands as a minimum condition of partnership, confident that the government would be unable to meet them. These included a moratorium on nuclear arms tests on Mururoa atoll; an end to motorway building and the dismantling of the 12000 megawatt Superphenix fast breeder nuclear reactor at Creys-Malville (an emotive and longstanding Green cause); a prohibition on any new nuclear plants - itself not too far removed from the Government's own prospectus, but in addition the closure of all existing nuclear plants within 15 years; new,[50] ecologically sound, social measures to halt unemployment; and a significant extension of proportional representation in time for the 1993 parliamentary elections.[51]

Lalonde may have suspected that Waechter was engaged here in his familiar tactic of impossibilism, in an attempt to keep the red-green option at bay. In the event, Waechter found, in the government's bad faith, a convenient excuse for avoiding any entanglements with the left. A decision to reverse a regional agreement on the prohibition of new motorway building in the Nord-Pas-de-Calais region was seized on as a typical example of establishment duplicity. It was enough to provide the Green isolationists with an excuse to turn their back on the overtures from the left. Lalonde was not so easily thwarted. He was more firmly convinced than ever of the need for a green rapprochement. After burning his bridges with the Socialists - at least for the time being - Lalonde persisted in his overtures to Les Verts. A protracted and difficult series of negotiations ensued and Waechter, who could no longer ignore the ferment in his party in favour of reconciliation, was moved to describe Lalonde as 'mon frère ennemi'. The two Green parties did eventually agree to at least hold a joint meeting in November 1992, in order to present a 'united front' at the 1993 Parliamentary elections. This was an achievement in view of the bad blood between the two parties, but it was by no means an ideological reconciliation, let alone a political merger. And it was something less than a stepping stone to any wider *rélance* of the progressive forces in French politics. In effect it was a damage limitation exercise - a limited agreement to form an *Éntente Ecologie*, or 'electoral non aggression pact' as Lalonde called it, which involved settling for the modest goal of avoiding the duplication of candidates. Both parties undertook to test the market for their respective brands of ecologism. Accordingly, each party agreed to put up their own candidate in the first ballot, but to run only one candidate in the second round where the Greens received the requisite total of the 12.5 per cent, and to withhold endorsement from any other party candidate wherever the Greens had failed at this hurdle. This latter condition confirmed the impression that Lalonde, putting Green cooperation before his broader ambition to encourage a radical realignment, had conceded more ground that Waechter. At the same time, Waechter's agreement to treat with GE was itself a testament to the growing influence of those realists in the ranks of Les Verts, who were increasingly impatient with Waechter's isolationism. Even so, this tentative reconciliation was far from smooth or untroubled. The long legacy of residual mistrust between the two parties made cooperation difficult - not least over the critical issue of the precise allocation of constituencies.

The mood in favour of overcoming residual problems counted as a measure of success of sorts. By the beginning of 1993 these differences were, for the most part, resolved. A testament to this achievement was the relative ease with which local territorial squabbles over party primacy and candidate selection were settled, in stark contrast to the continuing tensions between the conservative parties over the very same issue. The RPR and the UDF were still engaged in these 'turf wars' in over 100 constituencies only a few months before the 1993 elections. This electoral pact cemented the relationship between the Green parties in other, equally significant ways. The two parties set out an agreed list of common aims, and minimised those other issues on which they remained divided. This mutual 'manifesto' concentrated on pointing up, as far as possible, common aims. It included a call for major constitutional changes - such as proportionality in national elections - favourable to small parties; and changes in working arrangements to boost employment without incurring environmental costs. Even more significant, given the deep differences between them over the issue in the recent past, they agreed to call for the 'eventual' phasing out of the national nuclear energy programme and to endorse as well, 'world wide' nuclear disarmament. The ability of the Greens to coalesce around both an electoral pact and a shared if generalised programme, signalled both alarm and hope to the Socialist Party. Socialist Party tacticians saw in the Green *éntente* a clear threat - an alternative home for the post-materialist and new social movement element amongst the volatile PS electorate. Socialist strategists with a longer vision, however, saw in the Green *rélance* a more positive prospect for the radical realignment mooted by Rocard. Both groups, for very different reasons, saw political mileage in courting the Greens. These tactical and strategic imperatives came together in the offer by the party's First Secretary, Laurent Fabius, of a clear run to Green candidates in some 30 constituencies (out of the total of 577).

The Government moved to appease the Greens on other fronts too. It had already hastily established a multi-party Commission in 1992 to review electoral reform. The continuing ambivalence in the PS over whether the Greens were friends or foes, was reflected in the outcome of this proposal. Although this Commission did eventually recommend increased proportionality, Prime Minister Beregevoy's refusal - on political grounds - to countenance any such changes before the 1993 elections,[52] alongside the Greens' own estimation that they had only been offered unwinnable seats, ensured that they rejected such overtures. These limited offers of reform were refused, then, but not this time as a token of Green isolationism. On the contrary, the Greens on all sides were beginning to accommodate to the idea that they might hold out for more radical measures. Even Waechter was coming round to this view. What was notable about his current rebuttal of the Socialists' overtures, was not his objection that they were made at all, but that they did not go far enough. Waechter dismissed the proposals on electoral reform as no more than "a bit of patching up, whereas real reform was needed".[53] On the radical wing of Les Verts, activists such as Yves Cochet, who also made it clear that their appetite was fully whetted for weighing in the Greens on the side of a fundamental political realignment, responded to the lame offer of uncontested seats by claiming that "we are not selling out for a few constituencies.... Our main aim is to unite all catalysts to redesign France's political scene around this ecologist pole". In the event, the Greens opted to stand alone but united in the 1993 elections. They did enter into a few tactical arrangements with the left at local level, but only in order to ensure the defeat of the National Front.

The 1993 Parliamentary elections were a disappointment rather than a disaster for the new Green *éntente*. With some pre-election polls predicting a 19 per cent Green vote, which would have yielded a good haul of seats - and larger than some polls had forecast for the Socialists - the Green surge actually failed to materialise. The ecological vote fell dramatically from its potential 'take off' point in the regional poll. The combined Green list in the first round secured only 7.6 per cent - 4.05 per cent for Les Verts and 3.65 per cent for GE, and neither Green party won any seats as the tide of French politics, with the help of the electoral system, again drifted rightwards. Only two Green candidates - one from each party - made it through to the second round. And neither Voynet's second stage candidature for Les Verts in Jura, nor Barthnet's for GE in Haut-Rhin, were successful in spite of an improved performance in this run-off round. Any number of reasons may be given for this shortfall. The electoral mood was hardly receptive to radical politics of any colour. The country had been plunged into another recession. A post-Maastricht crisis had opened up new doubts and uncertainties over what many commentators now regarded as a less secure or settled outlook on national identity. If the omens were bad for the Socialists, they were hardly much better for the Green parties, intent on raising idealistic issues that many electors regarded as political luxuries in a country threatened by rising unemployment and all manner of imminent crises. The Greens themselves must shoulder some of the responsibility for their electoral débâcle. The Green bubble may have finally burst, as France finally came to terms with a major recession and a currency crisis. But there was undoubtedly in these results an element of backlash against the Greens' previous self indulgence and squabbling. None of these conclusions offers, in itself, a satisfactory or complete answer to the Greens' poorer than expected performance in 1993. After all the Greens, ironically, had showed a greater willingness to deal with both their own internal difficulties, as well as to address the general 'crisis' of confidence in party politics, than at any previous time in their history. The most likely explanation of the poorer than anticipated performance, was that the times were quite simply out of joint for any form of progressive politics. This shortfall in Green support underlined the broad malaise which had settled over French politics as the Socialist era and the Mitterrand Presidency gave off the unmistakeable odour of terminal decline. In these circumstances, with the perception of governmental failure uppermost in the mind of the electorate at large, and with electoral rules in place that confirmed political bi-polarity, an organised, well funded opposition able to draw on the deep well springs of conservatism was simply bound to profit from the Socialists' demise as the electoral pendulum swung against the radical side of the political spectrum. And that prevailing mood change harmed the Greens in relative terms, as much as it did the PS. Not that this election was a trimph for the right, but rather it gave them rather a victory by default. The high abstention rate of 30.8 per cent in this highly politicised country, with an abiding sense of civic responsibility, says much about the sceptical mood of the electorate.

Defeat did not demoralise the Greens or immediately send them back to the ideological bunkers from whence they had ventured. The prevailing mood was one of conciliation, orchestrated by realists on both sides concerned that the benefits of the *éntente* should not be squandered; and alert, too, to the enhanced prospects of exerting even more leverage on the battered and demoralised Socialist Party. These revisionists were encouraged by parallel moves on the left to reinvent itself in ways that were compatible with a genuine radical realignment. From this perspective, 1993 represented much less a climactic defeat for the Greens than a periodic disappointment. Rocard had already canvassed energetically, even before the elections, for what he called a 'political big bang'[54] - a major review of radical options. Moreover, his progressive credentials for leading such a crusade seemed genuine enough. He was something of an iconoclast, even an outsider, in his own party. Above all, he had a reputation for innovative thinking and for responding creatively to political events. He was fully convinced that the Socialist Party's electoral demise reflected an altogether deeper malaise with the body politic, given that "everywhere throughout Europe, traditional parties are being put into question".[55] Rocard already had good political connections with Les Verts, which made him better placed than any other Socialist politician to cement a red-green alliance. Many of Les Verts more radical activists had found their way into the party from Rocard's own previous party - the Parti Socialiste Unifié (PSU). What Rocard envisaged was a new progressive coalition of centrists, socialists, reformed Communists, libertarians, human rights activists, anti-racists and Greens, who together offered the prospect of a 'political renaissance' that would confront what Rocard identified as a dangerous xenophobia on the far right. This would be a new progressive movement capable of coming to terms with the problems of late twentieth century industrialism.[56] Rocard's new politics vision was buoyed up by polling data which suggested that many of the electorate already saw the left and the Greens[57] - in spite of Les Verts attempts to fashion for itself a pure green image and programme - as part and parcel of a new radical force for change. The Greens for their part remained as ambivalent as ever about this prospect. Waechter's instincts were to distance his party from any such radical osmosis. He was concerned lest the Socialists - sure to be by far the dominant force in any realigned radical movement, regardless of their recent difficulties - colonise or swallow the Greens, thereby neutralising their political influence.

Waechter was quite aware of Rocard's ambitions to secure the Socialist Party's Presidential nomination in 1995, and he was determined to resist becoming what he called the "Green salad between pink meat and red tomatoes".[58] Waechter and his supporters maintained their autonomist line, which held that socialism simply could not be made compatible with ecologism, unless it underwent a fundamental 'cultural revolution'. According to this pure green outlook, it was "the ecologists not the socialists (who) are the alternative to the right", now that "the Right-Left divide which has shaped political life for the last two centuries does not exist any more. We have to be realistic and see new political thinking. Ecology is this new political thinking".[59] While it is easy to see why the pure greens would argue this case, the evidence on the ground was altogether less convincing. The Greens had certainly raised their profile, and the collapse in electoral support for the Socialists had improved their bargaining position. Otherwise, the portents were less than favourable. For one thing the Greens, as a minor party, still had to face the immense obstacle of the unfavourable political structures and constitutional arrangements of the 5th Republic. In the circumstances, Waechter's ambition for the Greens on their own to break the mold of French politics amounted to little more than wishful thinking. In his desire to pursue a strategy that conformed to his abiding political precept of remaining aloof from 'dangerous' entanglements with 'unscrupulous' allies, he lost sight of the constraints on minor parties under the current regime. The informed judgement of more objective commentators was that the Greens had emerged as an element in the national political equation, but were far from being a major force for political change; that "support for the Greens represents something more than single issue environmentalism and something less than the ecological conversion spoken of by Waechter. The Green politics are seen by supporters and others alike as a source of pressure on the political system, and without some results, that pressure will seem ineffectual".[60] 'Results' in the form of a consistent electoral performance, even in second order elections, required large enough support to put pressure on the Socialists - both to make significant policy concessions, and above all to deliver the degree of electoral reform that would ensure Green representation. Measured against this practical yardstick, the Greens had failed to deliver. The assimilation of this failure began to rekindle unease and eventually opposition in the party's ranks that amounted to a civil war - this time within Les Verts' ranks.

The disappointment that followed the 1993 election impacted just as much on the Greens as it did on the Socialist party. Rocard persisted in his attempt to court Les Verts. A group of progressive ecologists - Verts et pluriels - led by Dominique Voynet, was already in existence (formed in 1991). This group had been prepared from the time of Lalonde's overtures to at least review party strategy. Above all, they were united in their opposition to Waechter's determined isolationism. There was little surprise, either inside the party or without, at the revival of intense factionalism; or that it should be focused on the strategic question of whether to pursue a pure green or red-green orientation. After all, this had been the principal fault line in French ecologism from the outset. Aside from the Waechter-Lalonde antagonism which provided the principal animus in Green politics per se, Les Verts itself was also exercised by intra-party troubles. The party had always been a coalition of rival factions held together by a collective leadership under Waechter's not always steady hand. This combination was quite capable at any time of breaking out into conflict over the full range of strategic and ideological divisions that are resonant in every Green party. Les Verts are, after all, an archetypal Green party, in which, as two of its historians observe, "there is no unified leadership.... (and) instead, fluid factions representing different sides in internal conflicts have risen and fallen according to the level of support received from activists".[61]

Not the least cause of the squabbles that afflicted the French party was the strategic question - of how they should position themselves vis a vis the mainstream parties, in order to better foment the realignment of French party politics. The Green pluralists pursued this issue from the moment it became apparent - under Lalonde's prompting. As they saw it, the Greens could hardly expect to exert any influence on this centralised and adversarial polity, without resolving their own internal differences and building bridges to other progressive, reform minded groups. There were initial rumblings at the 1991 Assembly, where Waechter managed to hold the line. Again at the party Assembly in Chambery in 1992, Waechter survived only by a compromise that saw his harshest critics - Cochet and Voynet - taken into a collective leadership as joint spokespersons.[62] This was probably the turning point of the revisionist campaign. Thereafter, Waechter was obliged to retreat by degrees in the face of his critics. The real measure of this seepage of Waechter's influence was his failure to secure the nominal leadership position of National Secretary in the CNIR meeting of November 1992. These internal splits deepened further over Waechter's qualified support for the Maastricht treaty at the 1993 party congress in Paris. Dominique Voynet emerged as the focus of an anti-Waechter faction. The battle lines here were by no means clearly drawn by this stage. They were more a matter of finesse or political management than they were about intractable divisions over ideology. Both sides remained committed to a pure ecology programme. Waechter and Voynet were both realists, to the extent that they endorsed a model of party politics based on discipline and the usual procedures of structured decision making. Voynet's realism, however, went further and encouraged her in the view that pure ecology had little practical future in the current political circumstances of the 5th Republic - other than that as an isolated sect - unless it was prepared to engage in serious dialogue with a wider progressive conspectus.

At the same time, as Voynet's influence grew in the party's counsels, she was insistent on dispelling any suggestion that a radical rapprochement with other groups meant the wholesale abandonment of a distinctive ecological outlook. Voynet worked hard to convince the rank and file that she was just as hostile to any surrender to the old left - the covert subplot which Waechter's supporters believed they had identified in Rocard's agenda. As an articulate voice of 'green reason' Voynet won many converts within the party for a novel strategy that involved building an anti-right and progressive *éntente*, rather than submerging the Greens within the broad ranks of the left. She had in mind here the greening of socialism rather than any abject surrender to it. The appeal of this approach grew in the party's ranks as a majority of members came to accept that Waechter's isolationism had simply failed to deliver any sustainable political breakthrough. The resurgence of the right - and not least the insidious threat from the far right - only served to reinforce the appeal of this pragmatic approach. This was particularly apparent in the behaviour of local Green parties confronted with difficult choices on the ground. The terms of the 1992 electoral pact - to withhold support in the second round of elections from any other candidate, even if no Green candidate stood - had always been modified in practice, almost as soon as the ink had dried on this green *éntente*, where local circumstances suggested that such abstentions would merely help the right. Local Green parties in some constituencies did endorse PS candidates in the second round in 1992. The left reciprocated by recommending support for Voynet in the Jura. Voynet had absorbed this tactical lesson; that cooperation between progressives was indispensable as a bulwark against reactionary forces. "We have", she said "to risk opening up, but this does not mean renouncing the independence we have always favoured".[63]

It is a measure of the Greens' growing political maturity that these potentially destructive debates were actually handled with a commendable degree of aplomb. The 1993 Conference, held in the aftermath of the national election, showed a greater appetite to bind up the party's wounds rather than allow them to fester. As a gesture of reconciliation if not of unity per se, the party's factions postponed the difficult choice of the 1995 Presidential candidate - always a focal point of factional fighting on previous occasions. As the trauma of the election defeat receded, however, these factions lost some of this cohesion experienced in adversity. The concern of Waechter's critics, to see that the party faced its predicament rather than retreating from it ensured that the factional strife was rekindled. Waechter and his allies became increasingly marginalised in a party that had grown more convinced that political networking was their only real choice in a changing political landscape. Waechter put himself at the head of a minority determined to resist overtures from the left at any price.[64] As this faction grew more isolated, they threatened to split the party by forming, what amounted to a party within the party. 'The Coordination for the independence of ecology', went as far as to stand against Les Verts' candidates in the 1994 European elections. What had initially been contained as a factional dispute between two essentially pure green groups, neither of which shared a particularly fundamentalist or anti-party outlook had escalated, by degrees, into a full blown civil war. The scene was finally set for precisely the sort of confrontation over an appropriate strategy for political ecology in a non-radical landscape which has broken out and characterised the politics of Green parties elsewhere in western Europe.

The destructive potential of this animus was, in this instance, remarkably short lived. To some extent, the delay in the outbreak of serious conflict over these issues ensured that the pragmatists on both sides of the argument had already accumulated considerable experience of how damaging these quarrels can be to Green credibility. Another factor here was that the disruptive and debilitating influence of an anti-party or 'fundi' faction in Les Verts was very limited. This debate was largely conducted between groups who shared at least the baseline commitment to a coherent party structure as a vehicle for their respective political ends. Waechter made his bid to retain control over the party. He was not motivated by any desire to undermine it or turn it into a permanent revolution of grassroots ferment against the formal party structures. Once it was clear that he had lost the battle for the party's political mind he, along with some of his supporters, quit the scene and tried to build a rival party that embodied the pure green preferences he had endorsed during his time at the helm of Les Verts. Voynet, on the other hand, after leading a successful coup against the party leadership - which ironically mirrored Waechter's own success in capturing control of Les Verts in 1986 - pursued a strategy of political cohabitation with the left rather than cooption by it. She was determined to strike a balance here between independence and interdependence that Waechter, in his tenure as leader, had been equally determined to avoid. As she put it, "we will do no favours to any ally but we don't want to sink into sectarian autonomy that condemns us to impotence".[65]

(iv)   Prospects for political change

In some ways the events of 1993-94 brought Green politics in France full circle. The renewed divisions within Green party ranks over its strategic orientation, as well as a continuing debate over ideology opened up by Rocard's overtures, have continued to plague Les Verts. Recent events indicate that the party is again revisiting the same dilemmas over its place in a political system notoriously unfavourable to minor parties that have plagued it over the duration. Its response to these predicaments continue to suggest that, regardless of the victory of Voynet's brand of realism, it is no better placed to resolve them now than it has been at any stage over the past decade or so. The party's failure to build on its remarkable performance in 1989, and become a constant if not yet a pervasive force in a political landscape whose patterns of partisanship are suffering the same tendency to a modicum of dealignment apparent across the continent, in spite of the corset of an electoral system whose combination of vote thresholds, limited proportionality and second ballots have encouraged a greater degree of party persistence than in many other polities, is a reflection of the Green party's continuing factionalism. The unhelpful political opportunity structure for minor parties that is the 5th Republic, provides only a partial alibi for the party's poor performance. There is in every political environment a sense in which the fates help those parties that help themselves. Or rather, they punish parties that squander their political opportunities by pursuing narrow ideological obsessions. The clear if limited opportunity that social change offers the Greens to respond to the anxieties that exist in all post-industrial societies, has not yet been taken up with the alacrity that is required if the tempo of political change is to be accelerated. The French Greens are by no means alone in their reticence to seize their opportunities. Of course, no Green party enjoys any automatic advantage from current circumstances. What is on offer everywhere is an opportunity, however limited, to present discontented electorates, unsettled by rapid economic change and undergoing shifts in their social identities that open up some prospect of political dealignment, with altogether new political choices. There are multiple options available here. Social dislocation clearly encourages some respondents to reinvent narrow cultural identities, or to resist change by resorting to reactionary palliatives. Movements that preach narrow xenophobia, economic protectionism or some other form of social exclusivism are one political response to this predicament. There is, on the other side, the potential for a radical and cosmopolitan response to these contemporary dilemmas. Ecologism is part of this radical prospectus and Green pragmatists everywhere have been moved to consider how they might improve their political profile by negotiating a new agenda together with other progressive groups. The recent tensions within Les Verts can be best understood in the context of this strategic discourse.

The outcome here has so far been modest; a shift from the obduracy of Waechter's tenure - and epitomised by the stand off between Waechter and GE on one side, and Les Verts and the PS on the other - and the realism Voynet brought to Green politics during her time as party leader. The French Greens were in a good position after 1990 to build on a notable electoral breakthrough whatever the unusual circumstances that facilitated it. Nothing succeeds in changing rigid stances, altering outlooks, enhancing expectations, and diluting ideology in politics quite like electoral success, and the prospect of more to follow. Even under Waechter's tenure, the party did begin, if tentatively, to travel down the road to realism in the pursuit of such objectives. This in turn provoked an important debate - an awareness of the need to respond imaginatively to events that were unfolding in the wider political milieu. The Greens finally appeared to have quit the political wilderness they had confined themselves to when the party adopted a pure green preference, following Waechter's dominance of party counsels after 1986. The 1989 breakthrough, coupled with the apparent demise of the old left PS, suggested that Les Verts were on the threshold of playing an effective and an increasingly prominent role in an impending political realignment. The fact that the Greens were so assiduously courted by the Socialist Party, was both a measure of their impact on French politics over a brief timespan; and a pointer to the admittedly difficult route they must take if they were to consolidate this narrow electoral base and cash it in as real influence. By retreating back into internecine squabbling, they squandered that brief opportunity. The events of 1994-1995 underline the real cost to the Greens of such political self indulgence. An internal crisis of confidence, tinged with intense disappointment at the 1993 election failure, eventually imploded into a familiar infighting. While a degree of forbearance was practised - and this quarrel was by no means as destructive as it might have been - the preoccupation with internal affairs and the reluctance to look outward and embrace a fortuitous but genuine opportunity to help refashion French progressive politics has, by and large, ensured that the party remains confined to its customary role on the margins of French politics.

The facts almost speak for themselves here. They tell the story of a party and a movement still divided against itself over elemental strategic issues - a situation that is bound to ensure political impotence for any party ruptured thus, under the restrictive political rules that pertain in the 5th Republic. These problems have a long pedigree in French Green politics, as they do in other ecology parties. They have continued to overshadow the party and thereby to weaken it. In the 1994 European elections, for instance, the party's various factions failed to agree a common strategy. Waechter, ironically, found himself canvassing a revival of the 1992 electoral pact. He argued for a joint list with Lalonde's GE. Lalonde's grip on his party, too, was less sure than it had been, and he faced an unprecedented revolt in the ranks over his tentative support for the Gaullist RPR Prime Minister, Edouard Balladur. In the event, both the GE and Les Verts stood as separate lists, with predictably results. Both Green parties were in a ferment, with factions in each organisation canvassing a range of political alignments in the run-up to the forthcoming 1995 Presidential elections. Lalonde's maverick nature and his apparent opportunism presented the main obstacle here to a Green alliance. Les Verts demanded Lalonde's replacement as the price of a joint list. Waechter weakened his own already discredited position, by endorsing links with Lalonde, in spite of the latter's apparent courting of the right. His reward was the humiliation of being placed in a low position in Les Verts candidate list.[66] Waechter had already made his decisive break with the party when he lost the leadership. The 1994 rift merely presented him with an opportunity to quit the party over a matter of principle, and to inflict as much damage to the party's electoral credibility as he could muster. He formed the breakaway Mouvement écologiste indépendant (MEI), and even threatened to stand in the Presidential election against the official Green Party candidate. Lalonde, who furnished the excuse for these machinations, but at this stage was by no means the principal cause of Green discord, dismissed them as 'suicidal', but did not make any positive overtures of his own.

The impact of these events on the sizeable Green constituency was predictable enough. According to polling data, well over half of Green voters were alarmed by the rise of the right and expressed a clear preference for the Greens to strike an 'understanding' of sorts with Rocard's Socialists.[67] There was at the same time little coherence to this outlook, or momentum behind it, other than a discernible fear of the impact of a right wing government committed to renewed nuclear te?:ng, unlimited economic growth and a weaker commitment to anti-racist or libertarian issues. Moreover, the realignment of the left was still an option at this stage, in spite of the abiding suspicions of many radicals, including some Greens, that Rocard's timely repeat of his 1993 offer to forge a 'new alliance of the left', was little more than a belated attempt to salvage a political career damaged beyond repair by internal factionism within the ruling Socialist Party. Other progressives were less cynical. Or rather, they remained at least convinced that Rocard's ambitions could be harnessed for genuinely radical ends. Pragmatism and principle are by no means entirely exclusive political instincts; but they must be reconciled if either disposition is to have any positive bearing on events. Rocard, a consistent advocate of a radically 'reinvented' left long before his current difficulties, looked to be an altogether better prospect than some of the career politicians waiting patiently in the wings to take over the Socialist Party in the post Mitterrand era. It was Rocard, after all, who had kept alive the hopes of undogmatic and creative socialist ideas after Mitterrand had imposed his 'grand seigneur' vision on the party. He had first challenged Mitterrand in the 1970s and had continued to advocate an altogether more radical brand of social democracy than Mitterrand, especially after the latter had adopted a 'national' strategy of deflation, wage control and welfare cuts after 1983.[68] With this progressive track record to trail, there was clearly more than mere opportunism in Rocard's appeal to progressives to unite behind a new agenda. As he did when he told a PS campaign rally at Creteil that "no party, no organised group can alone sustain all our hopes. We must unite", and appealed to a broad church, from trades unionists to intellectuals, and radicals of every progressive hue to create "an alliance of partners, with common goals and a precise timetable".[69] Unfortunately, this option largely fell on deaf ears within the broad left. The Greens derided it as 'a flop', even though it contained key measures - cutting the working week for example - to tackle unemployment favoured by pragmatic Greens such as Voynet, who subsequently fashioned her own 1995 Presidential campaign around the idea that "ecology must also be a social issue". She presented a programme - health, equal rights for women,[70] social measures - entirely compatible with Rocard's modernist vision.[71] However, preoccupied as they now were with their own narrow ideological schism and personality clashes, the warring Green factions turned away from the realignment option and again paid the inevitable electoral price at the European elections.

In spite of a massive rejection of the governing Socialist Party (down to 14.5 per cent from 23.6 per cent in 1989), and a less than enthusiastic embrace of the conservative alternative (the UDF/RPR took only 25.5 per cent compared with 28.9 per cent in 1989), the inflated protest vote that these elections usually encourage went almost anywhere than to the Greens. The clear mood of hostility to the political mainstream especially among the young, where the Greens expect to do best, was split - on one side between the nationalist right in the shape of the anti-Maastricht L'Autre Europe movement (Other Europe - 12.3 per cent) and the overtly xenophobic Front-National (FN) party (10.5 per cent). Those committed left voters looking for a suitable alternative 'home' gave the iconoclastic Bernard Tapie's pro-Europe Energie Radicale (a refashioned version of the small Mouvement des Radicaux de Gauche - MRG) 12 per cent of the vote. The Greens barely registered on this Richter scale of protest, polling only 2.9 per cent (down from 10.6 per cent in 1989) - a result that deprived them of any seats. They were, by any measure, clear losers, in spite of the use in European elections here of a system of proportional representation and a national list that should, in theory, have enhanced their prospects.

The bitterness engendered in the ecology movement during the run-up to the Euro-poll was carried over into the 1995 Presidential campaign. Generation Ecologie was by now as fragmented as Les Verts and exhibited these differences over its choice of a Presidential candidate. The Party Congress held at Laval did eventually choose Lalonde and opted to present a separate GE 'reformist' ticket, but some delegates preferred a joint campaign with Les Verts behind the candidacy of Dominique Voynet. Another group drew on their socialist roots and, in spite of Rocard's political demise, preferred an alliance with the then likely PS candidate, Jacques Delors.[72] Lalonde was eventually persuaded of the folly of splitting what was certain to be a miniscule Green vote. He withdrew his candidature and backed an eclectic campaign that avoided narrow ideology and, in a vain attempt to maximise support, claimed "not to be 100 per cent Green". The damage was already done and, indeed, had been inflicted long since. Voynet's broad church strategy failed to heal the breaches in the movement. In spite of an energetic campaign, aimed particularly at disaffected youth and disenchanted socialists, and with a volatile electorate expressing multiple discontents to aim at, the protest vote potential that resides in the Presidential first round largely passed the Greens by. Neither of the front runners managed to record even a majority of the total first round votes between them. Lionel Jospin, the Socialists' eventual choice, led Jacques Chirac (RPR) and Balladur (UDF) by 23.3 per cent to 20.5 per cent and 18.58 per cent respectively. The fact that Jospin's vote was some 10 per cent down on Mitterrand's first round tally in 1988, and was the lowest for any Socialist candidates since 1969, before the present Socialist Party was formed, gives some measure of the Greens' failure to impact on the current mood of discontent amongst otherwise radically inclined voters.

A significant minority of these first round votes went to parties outside the political mainstream. This outcome underlined the extent to which the dominance of the mainstream parties of the left and centre right over the governance of the Fifth Republic, continues to depend at least as much on the existing electoral rules as it does on stable and continuing patterns of partisanship. In the first round, in the 1995 poll, when political choice is optimal, some two fifths (37 per cent) of the electorate preferred the candidates of parties of the outside left or far right. Another thirty per cent of the electorate refused to vote at all. This was by any yardstick a powerful protest against 'the system'[73] These first round 'protest'votes were distributed between a wide range of parties, representing all manner of discontents. On the far right the FN polled 15 per cent, its highest national vote to date, and an anti-Maastricht maverick took 4.9 per cent. Amongst the alternative left and new politics parties on the other side, the PCF took 8.8 per cent, the Trotskyist candidate 5.4 per cent. Dominique Voynet, the standard bearer of a barely united Green movement, standing on a Convergences Ecologie

Solidarité ticket, won only 3.3 per cent (1,011,488) votes. In the second round run-off between the two leading candidates, the Green vote mostly went to Jospin, who deliberately courted the support of the residual left with a promise of reinstating the measure of PR in national elections[74] that Prime Minister Chirac had abolished in 1986.[75]

It is clear from this most recent episode in Green turbulence, following on from the electoral débâcles of 1994-95, that Les Verts, even under Voynet's measured leadership, has failed to re-establish its credentials as a likely, let alone as an effective, player in any realignment that might yet occur on the left. Whether this occurs under Jospin, who is far from being a neolithic or old guard leftist and is as amenable as Rocard was to some restructuring or realignment amongst progressive opinion, or his likely successors - for instance, the modernist Martine Aubry, whose sterling efforts helped to salvage the Socialists' apparently hopeless position before this election. If political realignment is indeed on the cards in France, radical socialists rather than progressive Greens are the more likely to carry it off in the foreseeable future. For regardless of Voynet's ready acknowledgement that ecologism in France needs to acquire a proper and realistic social perspective, in order to connect with the recent expansion in new social movements that have displayed a remarkable capacity to politicise, engage and mobilise the apparently 'disenfranchised' young, the Greens continue to remain very much on the margins of these developments. The dilemmas that continue to confront them are the same ones the movement faced at the outset. The need to connect with, and tap into, an altogether deeper well spring of discontent than any one progressive party can represent, suggests a broad based not an exclusive political strategy - an eclectic rather than an insular approach to ideas and issues. The nuclear issue - and its potency as a focus for galvanising the moral outrage which must sustain any genuinely radical politics - shows how near yet how far, too, the Greens are from building a secure bridgehead to the new politics in contemporary France. The Greens here drew much of their original momentum from this issue, only to dissipate this radical energy as divisions over ideology, political strategy and style overtook and debilitated the movement during the 1980s. The decision by the Chirac government to recommence France's nuclear testing programme on Mururoa atoll in the Pacific, as a short cut to establishing his Gaullist credentials after what he condemned as 'flabby' socialist diplomacy,[76] provided an ideal opportunity for the Greens of every hue to find common cause with all manner of radical and new politics movements. Voynet's articulate condemnation of Chirac's decision[77] failed, nevertheless, to rally the levels of mass anti-nuclear protest in France that would have put what is unmistakeably an ecological issue at the very centre of the broad left opposition to neo-Gaullism. While this would by no means ensure a Green revival, it would have done much to reinstate the ecology movement's radical credentials, and to facilitate the rapprochement with the new politics cause that could only help the Greens to a position of some influence in national politics.

The Greens were active in the national campaign to collect signatures for a petition against the Mururoa tests. But Voynet at this juncture remained curiously candid and even pessimistic about the likely impact of 'people politics', acknowledging that in the political culture of the 5th Republic, it has been customary, since de Gaulle set the precedent, to accede to the 'reserved domains' of Presidential prerogatives on foreign policy, so that the public have "not (been) used to forming their own views about defence and foreign affairs". This was a curious concession for any radical politician to make to Caesar's realm, let alone someone whose entire political raison d'être was conceived as a fundamental challenge to the complacent nostrums of normal politics.[78] It is hardly the stuff from which an effective or inspirational, or indeed an effective radical politics, could be fashioned. It might be the case that even this early in her leadership career Voynet, or indeed those pragmatic Greens who shared her strategic vision, had their eye on the longer game. Convinced of the damage done to Les Verts by its remoteness from public concerns, and taking account of how little interest there appeared to be, at least on the left, in an anti-nuclear stance, Voynet may have calculated that there were more promising issues on which to find common cause with the left. She was certainly far less reticent about identifying the Greens with the national campaign against air pollution - a major urban problem, particularly in Paris. The Greens published a draft law well before Chirac's new Environment Minister, Corinne Lepage, got around to it. Chirac's strategy of trying to depoliticise the environment issue seemed to have succeeded. The national agenda was dominated by those materialistic concerns - the costs of shaping the national economy to the stringent convergence criteria for European Monetary Union - that are preoccupying most western European governments. But agendas change, often unexpectedly and sometimes quickly. Or they can be refashioned by astute politicians to meet alternative, even radical purposes. The inauguration of a period of government by the right was always likely to bring quality of life issues to the fore, and before too long. Voynet's strategy, and indeed the mark of her success as a pragmatic leader, has been to ensure that Les Verts are well placed to play their part in the opposition to any negative environment impact that may follow from the remorseless pursuit of the free market ideology.

She found a sympathetic echo in Jospin, the PS leader, who was searching for populist causes to rehabilitate his party with the electorate after its electoral humiliation in 1993. The electoral pact agreed between the PS and the Greens in March 1997 - by which the Greens would represent the PS in 29 constituencies and the PS would represent Les Verts and the Radical party in 77 seats - was, nevertheless, an unsteady compromise which was bound to be tested - perhaps to breaking point, should the two parties find themselves in government as a result of it.[79] This outcome came more quickly than either side expected when President Chirac called parliamentary elections a full year before the end of the present Assembly's mandate - a political gamble (and a reckless one as it turned out) calculated to minimise the expected losses for the right a year hence, as his conservative government wrestled with the heavy costs of monetary integration and the EMU convergence criteria on the French economy.

The main Green Party, for the first time, found itself fighting national elections in a formal electoral alliance with other radical and leftist groups - in itself a major turning point in its political history. But one, too, that raised as many questions - about strategy, policy preferences and ideological compromises - as it settled. On the one hand, this remarkable outcome signalled the arrival of Les Verts as part of the political mainstream - a situation underlined by the invitation to Voynet, after the left alliance won these elections, from the new Prime Minister, Jospin, to sit in the new cabinet as the Minister for the Environment and the Regions.

On the other hand, this electoral compact - and its future consequences for the Greens in government - is based on the sort of compromises that are bound to induce tensions, not only within the new government between the 'old' left represented by some PS members, but especially the two Communist Party members and the representatives of the 'new' politics - Voynet herself, Chevenement, leader of the MDC (citizens movement) and Zuccarelli, of the Radical Socialist Party - but also within the ranks of the Green Party itself. The hastily concocted electoral pact of May 1997 that enabled these leftist parties to share out the electoral turf to their best advantage vis a vis a right irrevocably divided between the conventional conservative parties and the FN, certainly maximised the broad left's vote in both the first and second rounds. Above all, there was consensus of sorts on the left - albeit a negative one - over their opposition to the government's squeeze on welfare and jobs in its efforts to ensure that the economy converged with the Maastricht criteria for EMU. Jospin referred to this "red, pink, green" alliance as a pact between "the parties of progress".[80] They represented a loose - some might say unstable - common denominator as between Euro-scepticism, the concern to put employment before monetary and other market driven criteria of national economic efficiency, and a desire to protect welfare benefits against the neo-liberal forces that threaten the collectivist state. The Greens, however, subscribe to only part of this political bargain. The party's doubts about EMU and its endorsement of the welfare state notwithstanding, there may well be a residual tension between its deep reservations about the virtues of growth and the 'old lefts' conventional materialist and productionist preferences for reflationary measures to 'kick start' the economy out of its current recession. There may be rather more mileage for cooperation in the left's receptiveness to Les Verts' ideas about job sharing and a reduced working week.

To admit to ideological difficulties is not, however, to question whether some sort of political trade off might not be feasible. One that will lead in time to the Greens taking their place amongst reformed and progressive left. The French Socialists carry more historical and ideological baggage from their past than most of western Europe's socialist parties. The PCF, likewise, was the most reluctant of the western Communist parties to embrace the "historic compromise" with social democracy and other progressive political forces. But the once fixed pole of Marxism has shifted its axis since 1989 and the PCF, by its very willingness to bargain with once despised 'bourgeois idealists' (the Greens) and 'class traitors' (the PS) are as ripe as they have ever been for embracing a new broad-left politics of compromise and accommodation. To that extent, the radical politics of France mirrors the same degree of flux that is visible in Italy and elsewhere. It is a situation that promises the French Greens, if they approach it realistically, an unprecedented political opportunity. For this reason, the 1997 election marks a turning point for the movement as the eventual outcome confirmed.

The change in the Greens' fortunes was apparent in the initial results. There were some notable Green successes in the first round: Voynet led the poll as the left-unity candidate in the Dole constituency in the Jura (31 per cent), helped by her much publicised opposition to the Rhine-Rhône canal project; her leadership colleagues Yves Cochet (27.01 per cent in Val-d'Oise) and Jean-Luc Bennahmias (29.97 per cent in Roisay-sous Bois, near Paris) both ran RPR candidates close in 'le premier tour' and were selected as the standard bearers of the left alliance. There were other notably successful Green Party candidates - Guy Hascoet in Roubaix Est in Nord-Pas-De Calais (30.26 per cent, ahead of the RPR) and Giles Buna (26.42 per cent, ahead of the RPR challenge) in Lyon. There were also some independent ecologists who, on the basis of local reputations gained by diligent service to the community on ecological and other related issues, came through the first round in some style - for instance, the prominent anti-nuclear campaigner, Noel Mamère (President of the CES - Convergence écologie soilidarité) in Bordeaux Sud in the Gironde, standing for the EC (Ecologie citoyenne), who won a remarkable 34 per cent under his own steam; and Michèle Rivasi - standing on an independent leftist ticket ('neither left nor green'), but deliberately unopposed by Les Verts and the PS in the spirit of the new entente - who with 33.03 per cent fought a virtual dead heat with the PRP in the Valence constituency in Drôme.

These successes notwithstanding, the usual phenomenon of Green pluralism in the first round ensured that the ecology vote was split across the country between what many commentators now referred to as 'sensible ecologism', or "l'ecologie progressiste",[81] and

Voynet's rather disparaging reference to the fragments of "les petits morceaux d'ecologistes eparpilles".[82] To some extent the state funding of electoral activity encourages quite small parties to enter the fray. But green fractionalism is reinforced by an embedded culture of exceptionalism which the movement has found it difficult to overcome. The polling figure reveal that out of a total vote for ecology candidates of 1,724,122 (6.86 per cent) - respectable enough given that the campaign was dominated by 'old' politics issues rather than those central to the agenda of 'new' politics movements - Les Verts picked up 910,253 (3.59 per cent). With the rest of the Green vote divided between the GE (432,354 - 1.71 per cent), Waechter's MIE (trailing with 0.73 per cent) and sundry independent greens and alternativists (such as the Alliance rouge et verte - AREV, which allied with Les Verts in this election, on 0.29 per cent). The fact that Les Verts benefited electorally from its participation in the broad left alliance, so that some twenty Verts stood in round two, does not alter the fact that this continuing fragmentation of the green vote undermines the electoral appeal of the movement and weakens its potential impact on French politics. Almost half as many again of Les Verts' votes in round one were cast for 'other' ecology candidates. One cannot claim in any democracy that this exercise of voter choice 'wastes' votes. The right to protest, to pursue singular, even obscure, electoral preferences, is the essence of democratic politics. But from the strategic point of view, there is little doubt that a concerted Green initiative to overcome what are arcane differences of principle or personality as much as unbridgeable chasms of ideology, would maximise - and possibly even increase - the total Green vote. And in the alliance situation that Les Verts currently find themselves in, such an approach might well be calculated to improve their bargaining power vis a vis their new found allies on the left. There is certainly little to be lost, and much to be gained, by trying to bring iconoclasts like Waechter and Lalonde back into the sort of Green alliance that the movement briefly managed to achieve in the early 1990s. Not least to the benefit of the supporters of GE and the MEI, for neither of these parties managed to secure a single candidate on any constituency ballot in the second round.

The second round did see the election of Les Verts candidates to the National Assembly for the first time, standing as candidates on the left-unity slate. Voynet took her constituency in the Jura, as did Cochet his in Val-d'Oise, Hascoët in Nord, André Aschiéri in the Grasse constituency in Alpes-Maritimes, M-H Aubert (Eure-et-Loir), and with J-M Marchand winning Saumur-Sud in Maine et Loire as a joint AREV-Verts candidate. Two other 'divers ecologistes' - Mamère and Rivasi - won their seats with PS/Verts endorsement. The election of 8 - and diverse - ecologists shows that electoral cooperation, even between ideologically discrete but broadly complementary movements on the radical-left, is possible to organise and sustain in the heat of electoral battle. While this tactical liaison might be altogether more difficult to maintain under the unremitting pressures of government, the fact that the new PM invited Voynet to sit in the cabinet, with a brief to halt the ecologically damaging Rhine-Rhône canal project, launch a thorough review of the nuclear energy programme, and with a promise, finally, to close the Superphenix fast-breeder reactor, indicates that the Greens have made a significant political - and indeed psychological - breakthrough. What they do with this unprecedented opportunity, to some extent depends on how they behave in Parliament and in government - whether they continue to search for areas of cooperation with their allies and how they respond to the inevitable compromises, disappointments and defeats of being in office. An early and searching test of the new coalition, and indeed the grassroot Greens response to the party's inclusion in the system, has come within weeks of taking office. Scientific evidence that the nuclear plant at Cap de la

Hague on the Cherbourg peninsular is emitting dangerous levels of toxic effluent into the sea - and thence into the local food chain - prompted calls from Green MPs such as Cochet for their new Minister to raise the issue at cabinet level as a matter of urgency. The tension between the government's productionist instincts - nuclear power provides cheap domestic and industrial sources of energy - and Green demands for a halt to the programme will be heightened even before the government has time to find its feet. Nevertheless, the initial responses from Green party spokesperson indicated a constructive rather than a shrill or dogmatic approach to the problem.[83] The evidence from Les Verts' recent pragmatism under Voynet's stewardship indicates that the party is as well placed as any of Europe's other realist Green parties to seize its opportunity and to make the most of the mainstream left's receptiveness to the politics of radical renewal.

The Greens have undoubtedly travelled some way from their early, marginal role in French politics, and they are shaping to become the effective voice for ecologism within the political system that some other European Green parties have achieved, albeit in more favourable political environments. Recent events serve to confirm that, even in the face of daunting political obstacles and less than favourable opportunity structures, a carefully calibrated strategy appropriate to the circumstances they face can pay the Greens electoral dividends. Nevertheless, such compromises are less easy to carry off, let alone to sustain, under the pressures of the inevitable suboptimal bargains that shape government decisions everywhere. The Greens already have much further to travel down this road to compromise politics than the conventional parties they are now 'trading' with. Ideals are not driven out by the new found realism, but coexist - and frequently compete with them - in ways that promise unpredictable, and possibly traumatic or turbulent outcomes. A statement by Voynet, even after she had embraced the notion of an alliance with the broad left, underlines the potential for future conflicts with current allies. Her bold assertiont that "choosing the militant life is not to make changes in the short term but to satisfy one's dignity as a human being and resist destructive forms of reasoning",[84] is as much a motto for political obscurantism as it is a plausible rallying cry for resilient radicalism. Or at least, it may prove so to be, if the imperative to be radical for its own sake is not tempered or modulated by a shrewd acknowledgement that what can realistically be achieved depends on sustaining political alliances with 'significant others' on the progressive side of politics, as much as it does on ploughing the pure green furrow regardless. At the time she made this comment, it was a defensive gesture by the leader of a movement outside the political mainstream and effectively isolated - perhaps, in the circumstances pertaining then, a fitting epitaph for a movement in decline, and shorn of a meaningful or effective role in the politics of realignment. In view of what has happened since it might be construed in an entirely different light, as a rallying cry to a movement struggling to find a meaningful place in a changing political scene, but one that is still dominated by the classical left-right adversarialism of post-Revolutionary French politics. The dilemma facing Les Verts is much the same then as that confronting realist but radical Green parties everywhere; not so much a question of whether to compromise their bedrock principles but how far, and in exchange for what concessions in policy matters from the established parties they find themselves cooperating with. The answer to this conundrum, as far as Les Verts is concerned, will depend on whether they can resolve, once and for all, the persistent dilemmas over their appropriate place in French radical politics that have dogged them from the outset in their mission to put ecologism firmly on the map of national politics.

Notes

1. See J. Hayward, 'Ideological Change: The Exhaustion of the Revolutionary Impetus', Chapter One of P. A. Hall, J. Hayward and H. Machin, "Developments in French Politics" (Basingstoke, 1990) at pp. 15-32.

2. W. Saffran, "France", at p. 139 in M. D. Hancock, et al, (eds), "Politics in Western Europe" (Basingstoke, 1993).

3. R. Pronier and V.J. le Seigneur, "Generation Verte: les ecologistes en politique" (Paris, 1992).

4. T. Chafer, "The Anti-Nuclear Movement and the Rise of Political Ecology" in P. Cerny (ed) "Social Movements and Protest in Contemporary France" (London 1982); also, D. Nelkin and M. Pollak, "The Atom Besieged: Extra parliamentary Dissent in France and Germany" (Cambridge, Mass, 1981).

5. D. Nelkin and M. Pollak, "The Political Parties and the Nuclear Energy Debate in France and Germany", Comparative Politics XII (1980) at pp.127-41.

6. J. Bridgeford, "The Ecological Movement and the French General Election of 1978", Parliamentary Affairs 31 1978 at pp. 314-328, see also, J. Ardagh, "France Today" (Harmondsworth 1990), and J. Frears, "France in the Giscard Presidency." (London 1981).

7. Jolyon Howorth, "Foreign and Defence Policy: From Independence to Interdependence", Chapter 11 of P. Hall (et al) op.cit (1990), especially at pp. 204-208; see also Sudhir Hazareesingh, "Why No Peace Movement in France?" chapter 7 of "Political Traditions in Modern France" (Oxford, 1994), pp.178-206.

8. C.M. Vadrot, "Historique des Mouvements ecologistes" (1980).

9. J. Bridgeford, op.cit, (1978); and D. Boy, "Le Vote Ecologiste en 1978", Revue Francaise de Science Politique Vol.31(2) 1981, pp.394-416.

10. B. Prendiville, "France:Les Verts" in F. Muller-Rommel op.cit (1989) at pp. 89-90.

11. T. Chafer, "The Greens and the Municipal Elections", Newsletter for the study of Modern and Contemporary France 11-16 (1983).

12. T. Chafer, ibid (1983) at p. 205.

13. Ibid at p.207.

14. B. Prendiville & T. Chafer, "Activists and Ideas in the Green Movement in France", in W. Rudig (ed), "Green Politics One" (Edinburgh, 1990).

15. A. Cole and B. Doherty, "France, Pas comme les autres - the French Greens at the crossroads", in D. Richardson and C. Rootes, (eds), op.cit (1995), at p.51.

16. P. Hainsworth, "Breaking the Mould: The Greens in the French Party System", in A. Cole (ed), "French Political Parties in Transition" (Aldershot, 1990).

17. H. Kitschelt, "La gauche libertaire et les ecologistes", Revue Francaise de Science Politique 40 1990, pp.339-65.

18. F.L. Wilson, "When Parties Refuse to Fail: The Case of France", in K. Lawson and P. Merkl, (ed), "When Parties Fail" (Princeton, NJ, 1988); and A. Cole (ed), op.cit (1990), at pp.3-24.

19. A. Cole and B. Doherty, op.cit (1995), at p.46.

20. R. Ladrech, "Social Movements and Party Systems: The French Socialist Party and New Social Movements", West European Politics 12(2) 1989, pp.262-79.

21. G. Sainteny, "Les Dirigeants Ecologistes et le Champ Politique", Revue Francaise de Science Politique, Vol.37(1) 1987, at pp.21-32.

22. The impact of these 1985 changes should not, however, be exaggerated as subsequent results revealed. See A. Knapp, "Proportional but Bipolar: France's Electoral System in 1986", West European Politics, 10(1) January 1987.

23. B. Prendiville, "The Return of the Elusive Social Movement? Le Printemps de Decembre", Modern and Contemporary France 29 1989, at pp.19-24.

24. The Socialist Party (PS), or the Gaullist (RPR) and UDF (Radical) conservative coalition.

25. The 1981 study by F. Muller-Rommel and H. Wilke identified a similar generational profile, and particularly the adherence to alternative lifestyles or post-material values that was apparent in the Greens' political clientele across Europe. This demographic trend towards social marginality was confirmed in the later study by T. Chafer, who identified in the French Green vote a higher than average level of educational attainment, but also a distinct shortfall in the employment and career achievements. See F. Muller-Rommel and H. Wilke (1981), "Socialstruktur und postmaterialistische" Werdorientierungen von Okologisten: Eine empirische Analyse am Bespiel Frankreichs", Politische Vierteljahresschift 22,1981, at pp.385-97; and T. Chafer, "The Greens in France: An Emerging Social Movement", Journal of Area Studies 10 1984 at pp.36-43.

26. Financial Times, 17.6.89.

27. Les Verts' campaigned in the 1989 European elections under the manifesto "Les Verts et l'Europe. Pour une Europe des regions et des peuples solidaires", which contained an indictment of the divisive, insular and ecologically damaging consequence of the Single European Market and the bureaucratisation and elitism of the Single European Act.

28. F. Muller-Rommel, "The Greens in Western Europe", op.cit (1985), at pp.491-92.

29. A. Cole and B. Doherty, op.cit (1994), at p.52.

30. G. Sainteny, "Le vote ecologiste aux elections regionales", Revue Politique et Parliamentaire, No.927, Jan-Feb 1987.

31. J.L. Bennahmias and A. Roche, "Des Verts de toutes les couleurs: histoire et sociologie du mouvement ecolo" (Paris, 1992), at pp.74-75.

32. G. Sainteny, "Les Verts: limites et interpretation d'un success electoral", Revue politique et Parliamentaire, No.940 March-April 1989.

33. J. Bridgeford, "The French municipal elections of March 1989", Parliamentary Affairs, 42(3) Summer 1989.

34. The reality fell some way short of this rhetoric. In November 1989 the French National Assembly had debated environmental provision in the annual budget. Only 0.08 per cent of total expenditure was allocated to this policy area. This ensured that France continued to lag behind many other EC countries in environmental protection. Water and atmospheric pollution levels were high and several hundred tons of industrial waste were dumped annually at poorly monitored sites. Critics of the Government's efforts had also estimated that the sulphur dioxide levels in Paris were twice those of either New York or Tokyo. OECD statistics indicated that West Germany was currently investing six times as much as France on research into more efficient anti-pollution technology and waste disposal techniques.

35. Reuters News Service Report, 15.3.89.

36. Financial Times, 15.6.89; The Economist, 24.6.89.

37. The outcome of the 1989 European elections not only enhanced Les Verts' European profile, by taking them to Strasbourg for the first time. It also gave them a sound base (with 19 seats) from which to challenge Die Grunen's radical strategy in the European Parliament. As a direct result of this shift in ideological emphasis within the European Greens, the Parliamentary Group severed its links with the diffuse but radical Rainbow Group and created a more cohesive ecological group to operate at the EC level. Waechter himself acceded to the chair of the European Parliament's important Regional Policy and Planning Committee.

38. Jacques Régniez, "Political cockpit of the northern plains", The European 14/17 October 1993.

39. See G. Ross and J. Jenson, "French Rainbows: Towards a New Left in France?" Socialist Review Vol.18(1) 1988.

40. J.R. Pronier and V.J. le Seigneur, op.cit (1992), at p.198.

41. When the Greens had risen to the heights of a projected 15 per cent level of support in the pre-parliamentary election opinion polls in 1991, and similarly seemed to threaten the right's chances of sweeping the Socialists from office, the RPR likewise began a similar tactical game, making encouraging but unspecific noises about the prospects for Centre-Right/Green cooperation in government.

42. This intense rivalry between Waechter and Lalonde did not mean that Waechter or his party precluded either local or even national arrangements with other progressive groups or parties, including the Socialists. Although these were always more likely to occur at the local than at the national level. A formal governmental alliance of the sort Lalonde negotiated with Prime Minister Rocard was discounted as either political heresy or naivety. Nevertheless, Les Verts did occasionally collaborate, or enter into alliances, with leftist and non Green organisations; for instance, the left wing trades union, the Confederation Francaise Democratique du Travail. It cooperated, too, with the independent anti-racist lobby of the collectifs anti-racists, gathered under the national umbrella of 'SOS Racisme'. The criteria for such alignments were purely tactical - in the latter case it suggested the most effective way of defeating the National Front's local candidates. The immediate objective was to cement effective working relationships between the local party membership and compatible groups, in pursuit of common objectives. This strategy was easily reconciled with the party's highly decentralised and grassroots ethos; one in which the party was construed as being a far from professionalised, hierarchical or remote oligarchy, but was rather a flexible transmission belt of ideas, interests and concerns, capable of linking up adjacent causes into winning alliances of principle, rather than merely for electoral convenience. By their very nature, these alliances would vary from one region or district to another, depending on local agendas and circumstances. Above all ecologism, rather than any other progressive ideology, would provide the cement or common denominator of such political networks.

43. Reuters News Service Report, 3.3.92.

44. Reuters News Service Report, 11.3.92.

45. Reuters News Service Report, 3.3.92.

46. C. Barbier, "Generation ecologie: la galaxie Lalonde", Le Point, 29.2.92.

47. C. Boggs, "The Socialist Tradition: From Crisis to Decline" (New York, 1995), at chapters 5 and 6.

48.   There is a growing literature on this subject. See, for instance, David Miliband (ed), "Reinventing the Left" (Oxford, 1994) - especially Miliband's introduction and Chapter one, Anthony Giddens, "Brave New World: The New Context of Politics"; C. Lemke and G. Marks (eds), "The Crisis of Socialism in Europe" (London, 1992); E. Hobsbawm, "The crisis of today's ideologies", New Left Review (192), 1992, pp.55-64; and F. Scharpf, "Crisis and Choice in European Social Democracy" (Ithaca, N.Y., 1991).

49.   Reuters News Service Report, 11.3.92.

50.   The Greens uncompromising stance on the nuclear issue in both of its aspects - security and energy policy - was almost certainly a premeditated attempt to deflect this insistent courtship from the left. The security both of energy supplies and the independence of a national nuclear deterrent have been central bi-partisan themes of establishment politics in France over several decades. In the aftermath of the 1973 oil price shock administered by OPEC, French governments of every political complexion have sought to avoid overdependence on external energy sources in an increasingly unstable world. One of Giscard's first and most symbolic acts as President, had been the setting up of the most extensive nuclear energy programme anywhere in Europe. Mitterrand, every bit as much a nationalist as he was a Socialist, had continued with that policy. So much so that, by 1980, 80 per cent of the country's electricity was generated by nuclear power. And while this proportion had dropped slightly (to 72 per cent) by 1991, as some of the older stations neared the end of their useful - and safe - lives, France remained the most nuclear dependent country in the world, after the USA, and its second highest producer of nuclear power.

51.   The Guardian, 10.4.92.

52.   Reuters News Service Report, 3.2.93.

53.   Ibid 3.2.93.

54.   The Guardian, 19.2.93.

55.   The Guardian, 12.2.93.

56.   The Guardian, 29.1.93.

57.   Libération, 23.3.93.

58.   Reuters News Service Report, 24.2.93.

59.   Reuters News Service Report, 16.2.93.

60.   A. Cole and B. Doherty, op.cit (1994), p.62.

61.   Ibid (1994), at p.53.

62.   Le Monde, 1.12.92.

63.   Reuters News Service Report, 26.6.93.

64.   The Guardian, 31.8.93.

65.   The Guardian, 15.11.93.

66.   The Guardian, 18.4.94.

67.   Journal de Dimanche, 17.4.94.

68.   J.W. Friend, "Seven Years in France: Francois Mitterrand and the Unintended Revolution" (Boulder, Col, 1989), at pp.64-69.

69.   Reuters News Service Report, 8.6.94.

70.   See C. Duchen, "Feminism in France: From May '68 to Mitterrand" (London, 1986).

71.   Leyla Boulton, "Dual Forces for Change", Financial Times, 16.8.95.

72.   Financial Times, 21.6.94.

73.   The Independent, 21.4.95.

74. The Economist, 29.4.95.
75. See A. Knapp, "Proportional But Bipolar: France's Electoral System in 1986", West European Politics, Vol.10(1) 1987, pp.89-106.
76. Sunday Times, 10.9.95.
77. M. O'Neill, "The Pursuit of a Grand Illusion", European Brief, Vol.3(1), October 1995, pp.22-24.
78. See "Green Runner Charms the Bretons", The Independent, 4.4.95.
79. Reuters Textline, 30.4.97.
80. Financial Times, 3.6.97.
81. "Les Verts devraient avoir des élus à l'Assemblée nationale", Le Monde, 27.5.97.
82. Ibid.
83. Le Monde, 14.6.97.
84. Financial Times, 16.8.95.

6 Green Lists and Federations in Mediterranean Europe

1.   Italy

(i)   Green roots

Italian postwar politics has been dominated by the issues generated by the traditional regional, religious-secular and socio-economic class cleavages which reflect the country's historical experience of nation building and political modernisation.[1] The country's multi-party system was primarily a political map dominated by the traditional cleavages of class and productionist politics, superimposed on continuing regional divisions; or those between church and state in a society where the pervasive influence of the Catholic hierarchy and the extensive political leverage exerted by the Papacy had continued to influence the politics of an otherwise modern and secular state.[2] Ecologism had little place in this crowded landscape. New politics, let alone environmental issues were, until quite recently, largely peripheral in a political scene dominated by two powerful hegemonic parties.   The culture of Italian party politics reinforced this tendency. Instead of operating instrumentally as machines for vote maximisation, parties functioned here as inclusive communities touching almost every area of a member's life.[3] On the one side of the political divide, at the very centre of national political life, stood the party most favoured by the Vatican, the Christian Democrats. It was opposed by the PCI, one of Europe's most successful non-Stalinist Communist parties. These party hegemons between them monopolised the loyalties of the large majority of citizens. They were either the fulcrum of governing coalitions (the DC), or else the principal focus of opposition (the PCI).[4] The animus between them largely shaped the national issue agenda.[5] This remained the situation, even after the emergence of new issues and alternative foci for politics in the late sixties and seventies.

The new politics as it was practised in Italy was less novel than it was elsewhere. It continued to address those perennial debates - for instance, on political corruption, civil liberties or the abuses of power - that had been central concerns of the Italian political community since the establishment of a new Republic on liberal democratic principles after the second world war. Italian politics continued to revolve, albeit in a less rigid sense, around the primary ideological axes of left and right that had shaped it since the beginning of the century.[6] Ecologism hardly impacted on this well-established agenda.[7] Apart, that is, from occasional and barely significant campaigns over specific issues. There were a few exceptions to this general rule - for instance, the protests that eventually led to the cancellation of the national nuclear energy programme; the defeat of a government coalition that attempted to rescind that decision;[8] eutrophication in the Adriatic; traffic congestion; or excessive emissions of smog-forming pollutants from the industrial cities in the north, which saw the relocation of some industrial plants; and not least the public concern raised in 1976 by the escape of dioxin from a factory at Seveso near Milan.[9] None of these issues generated sufficient momentum, however, to put ecologism firmly on the political agenda. The aftermath of Seveso illustrated the limitations of political ecologism at this early stage. Ecologists in Milan found it difficult to capitalise on public concern in order to organise a unified radical protest movement. In one important sense, the exclusion of ecologism from the political mainstream in Italy actually helped the Greens in the long run. The movement acquired a virtual monopoly over the issue, sufficient to make it their own distinctive electoral territory.[10] Only latterly have other political newcomers (the Radical Party and the Workers Democracy Party in particular) attempted to impinge on the Greens' territory here, with rival pro 'ecology' lists standing in some cities such as Turin.

As the issue gained in political salience, some of the traditional parties began to include assorted 'pro-ecology' candidates (or 'ambientalisti') on their electoral lists. In so far as the issue had acquired any political significance, the Greens tended to be given the credit for pioneering ecology matters. The Greens, nevertheless, have not enjoyed a clear run on this agenda. They have faced an insistent threat to their monopoly of the issue from the Workers Democracy (Democrazio Proletaria) party - a party with a particular appeal to the 'new politics' electorate. The DP's preference for campaigning politics, with its cellular structure of local branch activists, persuaded its strategists to compete with the Greens for the same post-materialist, alternativist and radical constituencies. The DP has organised campaigns on appropriate issues that have challenged the Greens' monopoly of the modest new politics constituency. As it did, for example, on both the anti-hunting and anti-nuclear issues. This rivalry from a party at least as well versed in the arts of political organisation as the more fragmented Greens, has certainly cost them a measure of electoral support although how much in sum is unclear - for these organisational resources have also counted against the DP. The party's Marxist orientation, and especially its emphasis on party discipline and the 'party line' did alienate many of those free thinkers and libertarians - the young and the intellectuals and the new social movement activists attracted to the new politics - precisely because of its loose structures and anti-disciplinarian demeanour.

The issue with the greatest potential to galvanise this radical clientele into a political movement in the early days was the government's decision to develop a nuclear energy programme. Even then, the impact of this issue and its importance as a radical catalyst needs to be put into proper perspective. Ecologism took much longer to impact on Italian politics than it did in many other neighbouring countries. The movement had its roots in the early days of the anti-nuclear campaign. Italy was amongst the first western European countries to countenance a nuclear energy strategy. The initial proposal to commission 20 nuclear reactors by 1985, with another 22 or so by 1990, raised concern in the progressive but small Radical Party. Opponents of the decision, which was a matter of widespread public concern in view of Italy's susceptibility to earthquakes, formed an Anti-Nuclear League, although the campaign was far from united over either tactics or objectives. It remained a diffuse social movement and concentrated on direct action politics, rather than embarking on any more formal organisation. Amongst the movement's most notable achievements was a well-supported demonstration against official energy policy in Rome in May 1959, and a march of some 20 thousand people on Montatto di Castro - the site of one of the planned new reactors.

One tangible effect of this concerted protest was the decision by the state authorities to cut back their reactor building programme to 12 installations. By 1977 this movement had transformed itself into a fully fledged ecological pressure group - Amici della Terra (the Friends of the Earth). The *Amici* continued to concentrate on a lobbying strategy. It organised, in May 1977, an international anti-nuclear conference in Rome, chaired by the prominent ecologist Aurelio Peccei, the founder of the Club of Rome. Close collaboration between academic specialists - particularly scientists and lawyers - and ecological protest on the ground was a distinctive feature of Italian ecologism. These contacts with scientific practitioners provided the movement with one of its abiding strengths - the credibility that comes from the authoritative appeal of 'expertise'. These moderate ecologists also built some useful bridges with the alternative left that gave the movement wider popular appeal, and enhanced its capacity to keep the issue on the radical agenda. The Amici della Terra, for instance, developed close contacts with the Radical Party - an energetic purveyor of 'new politics' causes.

The nascent Green movement continued, in spite of these modest successes, to suffer the inhibitions and limitations of its inchoate movement status. It remained a disjointed network of local protest and action groups that concentrated on issue based campaigns. Amongst its diffuse support the conservationists of the anti-hunting lobby concentrated on collecting signatures for national referenda opposed to hunting as well as on the nuclear issue. Other local campaigners attached themselves to the emergent green movement, attracted as much by its loose arrangement and non-hierarchical disposition as by the publicity and purchase won for disparate single issue causes by sheltering under a broad ecological umbrella movement. Green campaigners in Florence, together with a 'Friends of the Bicycle' group enjoyed some success after lobbying the left-dominated city council. Further modest but tangible successes followed this increased profile for political ecologism - an agreement, for instance, to close down an incinerator, and renewed momentum behind local referenda on hunting and traffic pollution. Even in the far south - a region not noted for widespread environmental sensibilities - green activists in Palermo endorsed the local Socialist-Christian Democrat campaign against mafia corruption. A more overtly political input came from dissident Marxists who quit the Communist Party (PCI) in protest against its pro-nuclear stance. A notable recruit here was Gianni Matteoli, a subsequent leader of the Italian Greens. Some of these disgruntled Marxists in 1980 organised an Environment League (Lega per l'Ambiente). This move represented a significant step towards the consolidation of a national Green party from its diffuse local roots. Although the League was conceived as an independent pressure group, it acquired a markedly political outlook from its close, albeit indirect, contacts with the Community Party (PCI), as well as through its links with the official Communist cultural organisation, the ARCI. These affiliations also introduced into green politics, however, those distracting tensions between a pure ecology and red-green outlook familiar elsewhere. The League remained hostile to the idea of pure ecology and cultivated continued links with the official Communist Party. This, in turn, alienated those ecologists who defined political ecologism as a movement outside and beyond conventional political allegiances.

The danger of unwanted entanglements with established parties that threatened to smother at birth any chance of an independent green politics persuaded pure Green activists to adopt a more overt political strategy. In 1978 in the Northern Region of Trentino-Alto Adige, two electoral lists with a strong preference for green issues contested the municipal elections, each winning one seat. This modest success encouraged these local movements to confirm their green identity. One of these groups - Nuovo Sinistra - eventually became the Lista Verdi. The other, Neue Link List, became the Lista Alternative.[11] In the Emilia Romagna region, too, the Lugo di Romagna, another radical list of ecologists, Catholic radicals and assorted leftists, adopted as their logo in 1989 the Danish anti-nuclear movement's peace symbol. They failed to win any seats, but the banner of an independent green politics was raised in the country's capital city. Elsewhere, mixed lists tinged with various shades of green stood in city council elections in several towns. Success was counted here in modest terms, as the slow spread of independent green lists rather than by any sharp rise in their vote. The next stage saw an attempt in 1981, at informal local coordination and improved information networking of information to increase the chances of electoral success. The 'Arcipelago Verde' was set up as a focus for national coordination. Encouraged by this, representatives of Italy's green lobby met at Mestre in 1982 in an attempt to further consolidate the national green movement. The resistance encountered here from activists reluctant to formalise the movement's loose networks into a party structure prevented further progress on this front. Instead, in a compromise that fell a long way short of embracing normal party politics, the representatives merely established an educational initiative - an ecological 'university' - to further encourage ecological awareness. The Federazione Universita Verdi Italia was successful enough in its own limited terms. So much so, that it was eventually accorded proper educational status by the Ministry of Education. The resistance, however, witnessed at Mestre to embarking on a national political initiative, served to illustrate the depth of ideological divisions within Italian ecologism - notably between pure greens and those with leftist preferences. As well as laying bare an equally persistent tension within both camps, between those activists who counselled proper party status as the way forward, and those who saw this strategy as a defeat for the spontaneity of local, issue-based campaigning.

(ii) Party formation

These local green groups continued to proliferate. By 1983, the number of local lists contesting local elections had risen to 16, but with limited success. The Alternative List in Balzano province, for instance, took 4.5 per cent of the vote in local elections. The national movement consisted of no more than a diffuse network of groups loosely coordinated on local issues by the Friends of the Earth, who used its organisational resources to direct campaigns on 'appropriate' issues. The *Amici* also organised conferences and commissioned reports on, amongst other issues, nuclear safety - a strategy that maintained the ecology movement's strong links with the academic community. At the same time, those greens who counselled the need for a stronger national structure to consolidate the movement and increase its impact on national policy outcomes continued to push their arguments at every opportunity. The breakthrough experienced by Green parties elsewhere in Europe, notably in West Germany, began to tip the balance in favour of this outlook. Representatives of several green groups met at Trento in October 1983 to pursue this debate. They convened there with members of the pro-ecological Radical Party, alongside delegates from both the Austrian and West German Greens, brought in precisely to share their own experiences of party building. An agreement to review this issue represented a breakthrough of sorts. Yet the sheer breadth of ideology and differences of political disposition represented at Trento, ensured that the case in favour of full party status was far from decisive. There were further unsuccessful attempts to organise a national party at conventions held in Florence in November 1984, in Florence,

Pescara and Bari in 1985 and again in Pescara in May 1986.

The pressure in favour of some degree of national coordination increased as the green lists continued to make their mark in local contests. At the same time, they paid the price of their continued dislocation. The 1985 administrative elections saw some 150 separate Green and Alternative Lists stand across the country, 12 of them at the Regional level. They polled 2.1 per cent of the votes in the constituencies where they stood (a total of 636,000 votes) which yielded 141 seats in the various assemblies (10 at Regional level, 16 at Provincial level and 115 in the city councils). This was hardly a green wave but it was a modest success in otherwise unpropitious circumstances. As such, it added to the impetus of the electoralists in the movement, who anticipated an even greater yield of seats from a properly organised national Green party. The prospect of national elections in 1987 played their part in propelling the issue once again to the front of the green agenda. Green activists were also impressed by the success elsewhere of Green parties in the 1984 European elections. Widespread disillusionment with the conduct of the mainstream parties added to the momentum for an entirely new politics. The rising sense of a radical opportunity constructed around a new issue agenda was underlined by successful single issue campaigns focused on national referenda on social issues such as divorce and abortion.[12] The established parties acknowledged this challenge. The Socialist Party leader, Craxi, tried to manipulate the campaign on the anti-nuclear referendum for narrow party advantage. Cooptation of radical movements is a familiar response by old left parties to the challenge presented by the new left. In Italy, too, both the Socialist and Communist parties sought to placate and absorb the new radical mood by running 'ecologists' on their own party lists. The Italian Greens rode out this challenge and events continued to favour them.

The impact on public awareness of the Chernobyl disaster in April 1986, which inflicted considerable damage on Italy's domestic food supplies, gave a further boost to those greens convinced that ecologism was now an issue with considerably more political potential than was indicated by recent elections. The mass support for an anti-nuclear demonstration in Rome in May 1986, organized by the Lega per l'Ambiente, helped to reinforce the claim that there was a reservoir of latent public support disposed to green party politics. The sense that a turning point had been reached on the political front was confirmed by the overwhelming support of the ecological lobby for two national referendum - on hunting and nuclear power - instituted by the Radicals and Proletarian Democrats. The rising salience of ecological issues was well illustrated by the turnout figures. In the nuclear referendum some 80.8 per cent opposed the installation of nuclear plants; whereas, 79.7 per cent rejected subsidies for local authorities who allowed such installations; and 71.8 per cent opposed Italy's collaboration with foreign governments on joint nuclear projects.[13] The final breakthrough in the protracted series of negotiations to put the green movement on a national political footing came in October 1986. A national delegate congress meeting held at Finale Ligura, near Genoa, agreed official statutes for a national party (La Federatione della Liste Verdi (Federation of Green Lists), albeit cast in the highly decentralised mould favoured by many local activists. Resistance to any notion of party hierarchy was as prevalent as ever.

The national organisation, such as it was, was intended to merely coordinate local campaigns. There was no formal criteria for party membership and local party meetings remained open to anyone who shared the movement's broad aims. This aversion to formal party hierarchy, discipline and control from the centre was a deliberate attempt by those groups who joined the Federation to avoid unseemly and destructive factional infighting for control of party structures. As much as an ideological gesture, this anti-party ethos was also a practical acknowledgement of the sheer diversity contained within the Green Federation. Without agreeing to abide by such a minimalist common denominator, even this tentative attempt to coalesce Green activists under a national party banner would have ended in certain failure. Even so, by no means were all of the new party's members happy with this compromise. Some critics attacked this lack of structure from entirely the opposite perspective, as a recipe for organisational chaos. The argument from this point of view was that such openness of party structures, combined with a reluctance to impose any semblance of decision-making coherence on the party, opened it to obscurantist, subversive and unrepresentative elements, more interested in negative protest than in positive politics. The available evidence seems to suggest that these fears - while not entirely unfounded - were overplayed. And that without the adoption of a minimalist organisational framework, a national Green party would never have emerged from the motley of radical and alternativist groups who populated its ranks.

The strong autonomist tradition of the Italian new left has ensured that local party groups retain their political independence. There has been since then, staunch resistance to any attempt to professionalise or centralise the party. The 'sovereignty' of the rank and file has remained paramount. Local party lists continue to regard their direct links with their own communities as the principal raison d'être of radical politics. Moreover, elected representatives - whether members of the national parliament or councillors elected under the Federation's auspices - continue to enjoy autonomy from any nationally imposed party discipline. These are inhibitions about playing party politics according to the conventional rules as these apply to Italy, that have, as we shall see, prevented the party from cashing in its potential for influence during the recent political upheavals and the party realignments that have followed on from this. These anti-party inclinations have remained entrenched at the heart of the party's organisation. Inasmuch as the Green Federation retains a conventional party political rationale - winning parliamentary seats and increasing its leverage over national policy - it also has the function of being a conduit for the state funding which accrues in Italy to any party contesting elections. In the formal sense, the national party structure takes the shape of a Coordinating Committee (of eleven members), with a one year mandate or stewardship over party affairs. This Committee has the principal responsibility of coordinating national and other election campaigns. There are, nevertheless, clear limits to the exercise of this executive prerogative. Any attempt to control the party through this Committee is resisted, on the grounds that it represents a style of leadership that is anathema to grassroots activists. Although the component regional and local city lists do have formal representation in the Federation's national meetings, as well as control over speaking and voting on policy proposals, any individual member enjoys the right to attend such meetings in order to hear what is being decided in his name.

The new party format was hardly greeted with unqualified enthusiasm throughout the green movement. Although 76 of the local lists whose representatives met at Genoa felt able to approve these statutes immediately, others took time to reflect on the constraints involved. The ambivalence that surrounded the new party was even more apparent in the response to the loose federal arrangements covered by the statutes. Local groups retained considerable independence from the 'centre'. Likewise, local green lists which felt able to endorse the party statutes were permitted to join the Federation, after approval by the national coordinating group and a delegate Conference. Even so, it remained a step too far for some groups anxious to retain their freedom of action. Although over 140 lists did eventually embrace the new organisation, the prospect appealed more to those red-green elements whose links with leftist parties ensured they had fewer inhibitions about the notion of party discipline. Many groups of a pure green disposition took the decision to stay outside the Federation - a decision which has, on occasion, caused some green lists to compete against one another with adverse electoral consequences.[14] The moderate environmental protection groups such as Italia Nostra, the Federazione Pro Natura, the ornithology and anti-hunting lobbies (LAC) and the World Wildlife Fund, were particularly reluctant to embrace a movement whose political demeanour was overtly radical and even leftist. These pressure groups were concerned lest a more overt political stance should unduly compromise their painstakingly acquired lobby status. For the most part, they preferred instead to liaise with parliamentary representatives of the centre parties (the Social Democrats, Liberals and Republicans) or the Socialist party. Many of these groups depended, too, on state funding to fund their research and educational activities. As such, they preferred to continue what was an effective working relationship with officialdom, rather than to engage in electoral politics. And with good reason, for this status had afforded them a degree of influence over policy outcomes which they were loath to jeopardise by unpredictable flirtations with radicals. The most these environmental lobbies were prepared to entertain on the political front was selective cooperation with kindred spirits on specific local campaigns. The division within the national green movement over strategy undoubtedly reduced the new party's impact. There was, at the same time, a more positive outcome. The separation between pure greens and those of a more radical persuasion did at least pre-empt the protracted and debilitating civil wars that were waged within many other Green parties. Moreover, the party's federal structure was ideally suited to the more or less peaceful coexistence of groups with altogether different ideological priorities within the party itself.

The prevailing federal structure has, nevertheless, by no means ensured that the Italian Green party has been entirely spared the sort of tensions that have occurred in other Green parties. But it has tempered the occasional, sometimes intense outbreaks of hostility between the party's various tendencies - whether about policies and tactics, or over the choice of party candidates. There have also been disputes over positive discrimination in favour of women candidates, as well as resistance by some local lists to the recruitment of prominent or 'star' Greens in an attempt to cultivate popular support. Another source of conflict has been a continuing tension between pro-Communist sympathisers in the Front organisation, the League for the Environment, who tried in typical entryist fashion, to use the Greens as a respectable front for a more militant agenda, and independent greens who suspected them of political subversion aimed at a takeover. The party's federal structure did at least maximise cooperation amidst such continuing diversity.

The new Green party was undoubtedly assisted by Italy's gathering political crisis in its efforts to represent a distinctive issue agenda, as the old party system collapsed under the weight of inefficiency and endemic corruption. The taint of corruption touched the entire political establishment, regardless of ideological armour. This crisis of confidence in the 'old' politics helped to strengthen the Greens' appeal with the new social movements who might otherwise - following the logistics of Italian clientelism - have been tempted to align with the parties of the 'old' left or radical centre. Recent political dealignment has helped to confirm the Greens' electoral base amongst a social constituency that might have remained more resistant to new parties when the old left (especially the PCI) was still able to legitimate their progressive credentials by basing their radical appeal on the cachet of populist Marxists of real stature such as Gramsci and Berlinguer. The ensuing political change meant that the Greens were able to build an electoral base not dissimilar to that of Green parties throughout western

Europe. In a country that had remained deeply divided between the largely modernised northern and central regions and the economically backward and socially conservative south, it was to be expected that the appeal of a new post-material and anti-productionist movement would be limited within both the country's agrarian and industrialised sub-cultures. The Greens' political appeal was confined, rather, to those progressive and post-materialist elements amongst the 'new' and better educated middle class for whom an untainted PCI might well have retained its political appeal.[15]   As it turned out, the Greens' support was concentrated, by and large, in these progressive pockets of the most socially developed and urbanised areas: Turin, Milan, Rome and some of the smaller but prosperous municipalities. In the 1985 local elections the Green lists won only 10 of their 141 successes in the south; and in the 1987 parliamentary poll there were no gains and minimal support from that region. The Greens likewise attract disproportionate support from younger voters, who tend to be much less rooted in one of Italy's traditional political sub-cultures, and are therefore more willing to shift their political allegiance. The social roots of an emergent Green constituency were discernible, even before the recent political upheavals confirmed them and added to its momentum.

The evidence for partisan dealignment as a factor in an emerging Green vote also became clearer in these polls. The Greens recruited many of their new voters from the disillusioned electorate of other radical parties. Most of them had been, before 1985, voters of the Socialist, Radical or Republican parties. The picture here is, nevertheless, complicated by real differences between the political dispositions of Green party voters and activists. Green voters tend, by and large, to be rather less oriented to the left than either its full party members or activists.   The new party tapped into a well-established radical tradition embracing old and new left causes - community politics, social issues, libertarian themes, civil liberties, feminism, youth culture, peace politics and so on.   A contemporary sociological study of Italy's Green vote by Biorcio[16] identified a more amorphous group of opinions and political predispositions than that represented by the movement's activists. What this survey did reveal was a propensity for the Greens to attract a share of an increasingly large protest vote, discontented with the established parties ineffectual attempts to manage the liberal state. Biorcio catalogued a significant protest vote amongst the 'Green electorate' from the outset - estimated at some 71 per cent in the May 1985 election.   It is debatable whether or not this type of support is durable enough to build on. After all, this core 'Green' vote did rise significantly - from a scant 4.8 per cent at the outset, to 27.5 per cent over a relatively short period of some eighteen months (May 1985 to December 1986).[17] As such, it had all of the hallmarks of an ephemeral protest vote. More recent research, however, has confirmed that this pattern of support is a surer prospect. Mario Diani felt confident enough to predict the electoral consolidation of a distinctive Green constituency; that "we can conclude that, at least as far as electoral choices are concerned, the cross-cultural nature of ecological issues seems to have proven effective in mobilising a heterogeneous constituency which would be hard to place on a strict left-right scale.   In fact, the moderate political background of this constituency differs greatly from the leftist background of the (Green) activists. Thus, a political alliance is created between radical and moderate sectors of society which is rather unusual, if not totally new, in the Italian political arena, while being quite common in northern European countries".[18]

(iii)   Political developments

The Green Federation's abiding preference for decentralisation was apparent in the conduct of its affairs from the start. The resistance to any notion of strong control over party affairs from the centre was highlighted in some notable policy decisions. Not least the decision to channel forty per cent of the state funding it received in exchange for its 971,728 votes in the 1987 national elections into a campaign to reinstate the planned referendum on nuclear power precluded by these very elections. When the referendum was held, the Greens made much of the fact that even this most critical of national policy decisions - whether or not to construct a nuclear power station- should remain a matter for local decision.[19] Similarly, in November 1987, the Liste Verdi assembly meeting near Rome decided to endorse the campaign of the World Wildlife Fund to make Italian agriculture chemical free, but to leave it up to local campaigns to pursue this broad goal in their own way. The localised anti-party elements who dominated the internal politics of the Federation continued to resist any attempt by the party's national meetings to impose central decisions. This rubric was applied even to those limited functions allowed by the party's statutes, which political common sense had abrogated to the executive group. Some activists, for example, resented, on the usual anti-party grounds, the Federation's decision to set up an action committee to better coordinate the 1987 election campaign. There were fallouts, too, over the choice of candidates, disputes over appropriate gender quotas, and a simmering tension between local activists and the group of 'professional' politicians who invariably began to emerge within the party's national structures. The strength of this residual anti-partyism was illustrated by the depth of the resistance, in December 1987, to an attempt by pragmatists in the party to make the Federation the sole legal representative of the Liste Verdi. The pretext for this change was the legal requirement for proper accountability introduced, as an element of proposed changes in the state funding arrangements for political parties. Both opponents and supporters of the change in party procedures saw the move as a thinly veiled attempt to consolidate a formal Green party structure.

The Greens learned to live with these tensions even if they could not resolve them. The Green Federation stood as such for the first time in the national elections in 1987. It polled 1 million votes (2.5 per cent of the total), but with better than average results (up to 6 per cent in some districts) in some of the more politically progressive urban areas, which have always been the party's best electoral prospects.[20] They were helped to this modest achievement by the electoral rules then in operation. Italy's format of pure proportionality- a version of the imperiali system - favoured, or at least did not unduly penalise, minor and even poorly coordinated parties, provided they can win a full quota in at least one electoral district.[21] This particular condition sustained those 'anti-partyists' who saw electoral advantage in consolidating their existing power bases in some of the larger metropolitan constituencies, where there was considerably more support for ecologism and new politics issues. Even a modest vote here secured the Greens 13 representatives in the lower assembly (the Camera dei Deputati) and 2 seats in the Upper Chamber (the Senato). This outcome was in many ways the culmination of a steady momentum built up on the basis of effective community and single issue campaigns, and assisted by international events. Here, too, was a case where a national opportunity structure favourable to small parties - enhanced by quite generous state funding of parties - has worked in the Greens' favour.[22] This success at their first attempt on the national stage has nevertheless to be put in context. There was at this juncture a fa ~urable wind behind ecologism and other radical agendas. Apart from the general mood of discontent with established politics that assisted every Green party at this time, the cumulative crisis in the Italian state severely undermined the usual patterns of partisanship. The Greens also benefited from the impact of Chernobyl on public opinion, as they did from the presence in the movement of a capable, well informed and articulate cadre of 'leaders', many of whom were acknowledged national or international experts in the ecological field.

The increasing salience of ecological issues in Italian politics was further underlined by the passage of a spate of environmental laws and regulations - most notably the 'Galasso Act' - which imposed severe restrictions on environmental damage, permitted citizens to go to law against polluters, and reinforced the government's somewhat lax adherence to EC environmental directives.[23]   The setting up of an Environment Ministry, and even the incorporation of an environmental dimension by the trades union movement, were further indications of this agenda shift. The rising concern with lifestyle issues began to pay electoral dividends for the Greens.   In the 1988 round of municipal elections the Liste Verdi stood in only 431 districts (approximately 20 per cent), but polled an average of 3.7 per cent that brought them an additional 61 seats. They also won two additional Provincial seats - at Pavia in Lombardy and Ravenna in Emilia Romagna, with 4 per cent and 4.4 per cent respectively. The party followed up this steady success in June 1988, with further gains of 3 Regional, 3 Provincial and 10 Municipal seats in Friuli-Venezia-Giulia and won its first seat on the Valle d'Aosta regional council.   In November 1988 the list took additional seats in Trentino-Aldo Adige.

These victories provided the Greens with a sound platform for the 1989 European elections. The Italian political establishment was by now entering a period of unprecedented turbulence with the once dominant Christian Democrats about to poll their worst postwar result, with much worse to follow. Moreover, the European electorate was apparently proving to be more receptive to Green issues than ever before. In Italy the anticipation that preceded these elections in the Green camp was in stark contrast to the disappointment that followed. The Greens proved unable to fully capitalise on their opportunity. The residual legacies of the disputes over party format and ethos that accompanied the setting up of a national Federation, finally spilled over into open warfare. Two separate Green lists competed at this election, instead of working together to maximise the Green vote. A red-green list - the Verdi Arcobaleno (Rainbow Greens), consisting of new leftists and ecologists drawn in the main from the Radical and Proleterian Democracy parties - secured 2.4 per cent (and 2 seats at Strasbourg). A straight or pure Green list polled 3.8 per cent (and won 3 seats). A combined vote of 6.2 per was, on the face of it, a considerable achievement. But the impact of this success was heavily qualified by the perpetuation of divisions that prevented a national Green party claiming what would, by any yardstick, have been the remarkable feat of becoming the fourth largest party in Italy. The leader of the main Green list, Gianni Matteoli, was quick to claim that this surge in support demonstrated a palpable demand for change in the Italian body politic.[24] This much was beyond dispute; but there was much irony in his conclusion that "Italians are fed up with the continuous duel between the Christian Democrats and the Socialists and policies constructed around images", whereas "electors prefer to concern themselves with concrete and immediate problems".[25] For the fresh outbreak of feuding within the Green movement was hardly a testament to political realism, let alone a convincing signal to a disconcerted electorate, that they were ready to play their part in brokering an entirely new consensus on the progressive side of Italian politics. Indeed, these perpetual divisions merely contributed to the left's failure to respond to the incipient national crisis, and allowed the right to seize the initiative. By showing their hand and then refusing to reach out beyond narrow ideological obsessions, the Greens allowed the old politics to pre-empt their challenge. The establishment response took a predictable course. A fist of new environmental laws were implemented to head off the Green challenge in the wake of the 1989 result. The Socialist Environment Minister, Giorgio Ruffola, set up the Adriatic Authority to deal with the excess of algae which had begun to build up on the Adriatic coast at least three years previously, and now threatened the lucrative tourist trade. The government also legislated on urban and industrial waste disposal, soil conservation, as well as establishing an intensive two year programme of environment measures (scheduled for 1989-91), and funded by an impressive allocation of 2 per cent of GDP. Ecologism may have arrived at the centre of the national agenda, but the reluctance of its political standard bearers to represent it there in the shape of an organised, purposive party, severely weakened the Green movement's political leverage. And it did so precisely at a time when party realignment offered them at least the prospect of an unprecedented electoral breakthrough.

The Greens' response to this challenge was tepid and largely defensive. They maintained that the mainstream parties' ecological credentials were fraudulent, pointing out that funds previously earmarked in 1988 for an environment programme were never actually spent. Green campaigners made much of independent statistics which indicated that some 247 thousand acres of land had been burned in 1990 (double the 1989 figure); that one third of the country's beaches suffered from erosion; that the government was remiss in failing to apply EC directives on protected species; and that in spite of a host of new national laws and agreed EC directives, Italy remained the EC's most polluted country. Official Commission statistics indicated, for instance, that some 19 per cent of its long coastline was wholly unfit for sea bathing; many of its principal rivers, including the Arno and the Tiber were heavily polluted; and that only 15 per cent of the country's annual total of 20 million tonnes of solid urban waste was recycled - barely a half of the EC's average. The Greens questioned, too, the sincerity of government commitments on energy conservation and criticised them as little more than a cosmetic exercise conducted primarily in the interests of Italy's powerful, state owned energy and oil corporations. In effect, any real prospect indicated by the increased Green vote in 1988, of wounding the established parties as the Italian polity buckled under the weight of revelations about institutionalised corruption and graft was largely squandered.[26]

By pursuing their staunch anti-party dispositions, the Green movement could not hope to emulate the political clout, let alone to play a decisive role in reshaping national politics, of those Green parties elsewhere who were prepared to confront this critical issue. Unable to resolve these dilemmas and settle on their place in a rapidly changing political environment, the Italian Greens made a virtue of necessity by carrying on much as before. They concentrated their various energies on particular issue-based campaigns, instead of evolving a cogent national strategy. Local green groups, for instance, confronted Italian car manufacturers with questionnaires on pollution and demands for the immediate introduction of catalytic converters and lean burn engines. Green groups also continued with their demand for a new law on hunting to safeguard inadequately protected species, and for another referendum to follow the one on hunting in 1987, which had failed because of minimal support - as well as contributing to a campaign waged in the European Court on bird protection. Green activists were prominent in three national referenda launched in 1990 against hunting and the environmental damage inflicted by the use of pesticides - although in each case, they failed to mobilise the majority required because of low turnout. There was some evidence too in these campaigns that the green issue was becoming discounted as the Italian electorate focused attention on the altogether more critical issues facing the country. Various referenda held on environmental issues in 1991 were likewise defeated. Whereas in 1992, the powerful hunting lobby easily saw off proposed restrictions on their access to national parks.

The Italian Greens continued to plough their particular parochial furrows as the country became engulfed by a trauma which, even in this crisis ridden polity, was on an unprecedented scale. The Greens, of course, tried to link their narrow concerns with the wider picture. The party, in so far as a national strategy was possible, responded to the failure of the Italian state by portraying themselves as clean politicians concerned with the 'real' needs of citizens. They even gained some notable converts for their moral crusade against political failure and corruption. The former Socialist Minister and EC Environment Commissioner, Carlo Ripa de Meana, quit the scandal ridden Socialist party after resigning his government post in protest at the decision to reduce the punishment regime for politicians found guilty of corruption.[27] At the Green Federation's national congress in Montegrotto Terme, in March 1993, he was elected by a majority of delegates (209 out of 350) as the Party's national spokesman. This was a reluctant accommodation by this majority to one of the tenets of conventional party organisation. But it was hardly enough to put the Greens at the centre of the shift that was underway in Italian radical politics. For what was equally clear was the absence of a single issue capable of unifying a still disparate movement around the ecologist cause, in the same way that the emotive anti-nuclear stance in the mid 1980s has provided the focus for the emergent ecology movement. Continuing divisions in the Green movement enabled other radical parties, better organised and equipped to broker deals that encompassed the new issue agenda, to impinge on what the Greens regarded as uniquely their own political space. Both the Radical and Socialist parties, for instance, had some success in incorporating ecologism into their own programmes for change. The Italian protest vote may well have increased, but so has the competition for it amongst a host of radical parties.

The Greens have faced stiff competition even on their own ideological ground - initially from Craxi's rejuvenated Socialist party, which denied the Greens a sizeable share of the younger, radical and post-materialist middle class constituencies it depends on for its support base. After the Socialists had imploded, the Greens faced equally stiff competition from all manner of new radical lists and coalitions - from the anti-corruption, anti-Mafia network (La Rete); the former PCI Rifondazione Communista; and Proletarian Democracy groups - who now speak for much of the new left. The regionalist lists (the Northern and Lombard Leagues) also managed to open a new territorial axis that cut across the Greens' appeal to community and localism as the basis of political identity. It is much more difficult to corner the market in political novelty in a landscape crowded with radical and reformist groups, each one appealing to a disconcerted electorate yearning for easy, painless solutions to the deep seated legacies of a failed past. Nor were the Greens particularly well equipped, with their issue-based politics and commitment to anti-party status to take full advantage of the opportunities presented by the unfolding crisis. The Greens remain not so much insulated from the major shifts that are steadily breaking the mould of Italian party politics, as unable to turn these clear opportunities to any real political advantage. As one recent commentator has argued, "by the 1990s, the Italian Green movement had succeeded in creating a united political force, in forging a position for itself within a highly competitive party system and in gaining some access to political decision-making. Nevertheless, the movement has found it difficult to sustain a distinct identity, separate from its roots in both 'old' and 'new' left parties".[28]

There was more to this problem than merely bad political judgement - although this contingent factor played its part in determining outcomes. There were also structural reasons behind the Greens' political difficulties that reflect the complex patterning of Italian politics. Green parties everywhere, however well they accommodate to established procedures, are essentially political outsiders. Their political opportunities are shaped as much by prevailing circumstances and political culture as they are by self determination. Of course, the Italian Greens have hardly helped their own cause. Nevertheless, deep laid structural factors largely beyond their control continue to shape their political destiny. In Italy, as we have seen, the political landscape has been marked by some seismic shifts which occurred at precisely the time ecologism emerged as a grassroots social movement with political aspirations. This fact, paradoxically, both facilitated an independent Green politics and limited its impact. Sartori's classical model of Italian party politics, rooted in a system of 'polarised pluralism', with poles of ideological coherence on both the left (around the PCI) and the centre right (with the DC as the focal point), and reinforced by the rigid clientelist political culture, had always provided some limited space in the interstices 'between' these party families for small alternative parties.[29] When this prevailing pattern of privileged party politics was rapidly eroded by the forces of social-economic modernisation and political change that occurred throughout western Europe during the 1960s, and was replaced by an altogether more fluid system, the continuation of a reciprocal clientist ethos favoured established parties at the expense of newcomers. The constellation of political forces shifted at this stage, without being replaced by entirely new configurations. The Socialists, the Christian Democrats and eventually even the Euro-Communist PCI under Berlinguer began to entertain a 'new' politics of compromise, cooperation and even coalition.[30] The prospects for a truly radical shift remained modest, until the credibility of these reform minded parties was severely dented by the collapse in public confidence in system politics in the late 1980s, as short term deals and party opportunism became a symbol of accelerating national decline.

In these circumstances the Greens, along with other new politics and radical forces, did enjoy a greater opportunity to shape the new Italian agenda. As we have seen, the Greens were, however, less able or equipped to take advantage of the opportunity. A legacy of exclusion and a deep rooted introversion - as much an effect as a cause of insularity - had saddled the party with a preference for local, grassroots and issue-based campaigns ill suited to maximising their chances in the new political milieu. The unfolding crisis opened up a space on the left for small parties, fired by the 'betrayal' of progressive ideas perpetrated by the parties of the 'old' left, by a more positive enthusiasm for an altogether new type of alternative politics. These pragmatic Greens (a majority in the party by 1988 as the election of Ripa de Meana to the leadership indicated) with sufficient realism to look beyond the next local campaign or referendum, accommodated themselves to this new political climate. As they did, too, to the fact that the scope in these circumstances for carving out a distinct green constituency entirely remote from broader radical concerns was little more than wishful thinking or ideological self indulgence. For realists in the Green Federation, the only practical option was a clear choice between cooperation, implying compromises struck with other radical parties; or isolation and almost certainly obsolescence - with other radical parties quite willing to take on the green mantle. This political flux in some degree facilitated political cooperation, and in another sense frustrated it. The boundaries between ecology and other more deeply rooted ideological families (the Socialist or Communist left) have become blurred. Crossing these boundaries has certainly become easier. Yet it remains, at the same time, a prospect as likely as ever to divide the Green movement and thereby to dissipate its political energies. Some Green activists continue to see this option as a trap that threatens political extinction. Whereas for others it suggests an opportunity to bring the movement across the threshold of 'normal' party politics. The uneasy tension between these options continues to reverberate through the Liste Verdi, perpetuating its internal division into pure ecologists and red-greens. The Greens were certainly part of the restructuring of Italian politics that followed on from this national crisis. Whether or not they will play a significant part in any future party realignment depends as much on how long they can sustain their tentative links with the reformed centre-left, as it does on the continuing salience of ecologism as a central issue in the new radical consensus.

(iv)   Prospects for political change

The crisis of confidence in Italy's failed party system gathered pace during the 1980s, encouraged by the disclosure of a raft of endemic corruption, scandal and inefficiency amongst the country's political elite. One outcome of this volatile political mood was a degree of electoral dealignment as the once firm support bases of the established parties eroded. The scope for protest politics has thus increased apace. The 'flow' of votes after 1987, both between the new and old parties, and between the new ones, too, confirmed the existence of a green constituency.[31]   At the same time, the Green party has been by no means the only party to benefit from this new politics cleavage. The Greens have certainly profited from the flux that has opened up the Italian party system to new and radical alignments, but it has proved difficult for the Greens to consolidate this new politics electorate.[32] The Greens have not entirely helped their own cause here. Continuing divisions within the ecology movement have perpetuated a damaging factionalism - with separate electoral lists appearing even after 1987.   The impact of these divisions on the party's sense of common political purpose, and their negative effect on a growing number of voters in the post-material middle class, and amongst the young who see ecologism as an element in the broader radical shift underway in modern Italy, has certainly cost the Greens votes. But these divisions should not be over-exaggerated. The Green party's federalist structure was, after all, deliberately created to manage internal differences, and to soften those rigidities of party structure that seemed to be a denial of a genuinely new politics. Indeed in some ways, the Greens' coalitional culture is an ideal grounding in the new rules of engagement in which Italian party politics and government formation is rooted. Much will depend on the usual exigencies of politics, on the particular configuration of centre-left forces the Greens are obliged to deal with - on personalities too. And not least, on how successful or relevant the Greens will deem future policy outcomes to be, in relation to their own priorities.
        If the Greens do get close to real power, the compromises and difficult choices imposed on a party of government may yet activate the movement's latent ideological divisions. The recent victory for the centre left 'Olive Tree' coalition, endorsed by the Greens, will present the party with the greatest test yet of its political maturity. Commentators aware of the party's existing fault lines, see as much scope here for crisis as for compromise; that there is, for all of their recent ideological moderation, a deep fissure waiting to open up in the party. In the Greens case "the persistence of the division between the pure-Greens (or *verdi doc*), and those with a New Left commitment to wider social issues, in particular pacifism, anti-racism and the north-south divide" lies dormant but unresolved; and "this split tends to mirror that between the supporters of demonstrations and grassroots activism (the *piazza*) and the advocates of national lobbying and parliamentary politics (the *palazzo*)".[33] From the far reaches of opposition, these quarrels were restricted, by and large, to disputes over the

228

selection and allocation of candidates on the party lists. The pure greens, who have far less in common with the leftist orientation of the new government, are the more likely to break ranks. This faction has constantly felt aggrieved - as it did in both the 1987 and 1992 election campaigns - over the dominance of the new left in the party. This is a familiar story in Green party politics. Moreover, it is one with fairly predictable consequences, if it is allowed to fester. If such resentments are not resolved - or prove to be insurmountable as the prospect of a share, however modest, in national governance sharpens old jealousies - the party faces a potential crisis with serious implications for its future status.

Divisions amongst the party's grassroots have been replicated, with at least as much potential for damage and certainly less excuse, within the parliamentary leadership itself. The dominant group in the national party's 11 member coordinating committee, centred around the prominent and pragmatic Green, Francesco Rutelli, remain firmly committed to the idea of welding the Greens to the broad radical coalition that is reshaping centre-left politics in Italy. They envisage a new coalition - one that links ecologism with wider social movements ranged against racism, and in favour of social justice, tackling the crisis of structural unemployment, positive European integration, gender politics, civil rights, anti-corruption measures, and social renewal. As these realists see it, none of these radical measures can be carried out in isolation from the others. Ecologism is, in these terms, part of the radical renewal of the Italian state, its political arrangements and socio-economic relations. Moreover, in this 'realist' account, the necessity for a cooperative approach is reinforced by the logistics of party politics as conducted under the new electoral rules. These arrangements require that three quarters of both houses are elected from single member constituencies by a first past the post system; with the other quarter allocated by proportionality. Even this modest gesture to the chances of small parties, is tempered by a four per cent threshold designed precisely to avoid the proliferation of micro parties, and to ensure a degree of parliamentary coherence that has been absent from Italian politics since the war. If the Greens want to participate in this radical politics of renewal, and wish to be taken seriously, they have little option but to build rather than burn their bridges to the other parties on the centre-left. A cursory survey of the impact of Green divisions on their electoral prospects, even under the previous electoral rules that were more favourable to micro-parties than the new arrangements, points firmly to the logic of cooperation rather than to isolation.

Green parties are not, of course, always as well atuned as they need to be to the obvious rules of 'normal' politics. The *verdi doc* or pure green option continues to find favour in some sections of the Federation, concerned that 'deep' ecology should not be hijacked or misappropriated by unscrupulous opponents pursuing unsuitable causes. The anti-partyists remain convinced that the party's political soul continues to lie within grassroots movement or street politics[34] - a position summarised in the slogan "less politics, more ecology".[35] These instincts for a separate politics continue to be expressed in independent lists and candidatures that perpetuate old divisions and weaken current prospects. At least 10 variants of Green lists stood amongst the 54 separate parties and 471 other movements which contested the 1992 national elections. Even the official 'Green' list remained divided over their tactics, policy and overall direction, along the pure green and red-green fault line.[36] These divisions contributed to the party's failure to take full advantage from an otherwise promising political situation. The unfolding political imbroglio threatened to undermine the old patterns of political allegiance, and represented an unprecedented crisis for the postwar party establishment, from which the Greens - as a 'clean', anti-corruption movement - might profit. It proved to be a lost opportunity. The poor performance of the Green List saw only a modest rise in their vote for lower house seats - from 2.5 to 2.8 per cent (with an increase of 3 to 18 members), and a similarly small rise in their upper house support (up from 2 to 3.1 per cent), which gave them four senators (up from 2 seats). The Greens, meanwhile, performed particularly badly in the more developed central and northern regions where the cracked mould of Italian politics, and widespread disillusionment with the old parties, should have maximised their appeal to represent an entirely new politics with no links with the failed past. The most that can be said about these and more recent electoral performances, is that the Greens have at least confirmed their presence as a national party. They are still in the political game - if barely so. What is more encouraging, in a country where power has begun to be devolved from the centre, and a federal constitution might eventually be the price of holding the regions together within a single state, is the Greens' continuing strength at the sub-national level.[37] For this reason alone, their bigger potential national allies have to take them seriously. They have already cooperated with the parties of the left to mutual advantage in power sharing arrangements at the municipal, provincial and regional levels. In addition, there are encouraging precedents from elsewhere that reinforce this coalitional logic. The degree of national credibility that can follow on from such pacts contributed to both the consolidation of Die Grunen as a national party and enhanced its leverage over the major parties. The fact that the Italian Greens remain well placed to poll to their local strengths became even clearer in recent elections. In June 1993, the Greens made significant gains in the regional elections in Valle d'Aosta on 7.1 per cent of the vote, even rivalling the Northern League (7.6 per cent). They have performed well in other local and provincial elections across Italy, repeating this steady consolidation of their local bases in the municipal elections in November 1993 - including the historic and symbolic capture, after negotiating a deal with the left parties, of the mayorality of Rome.

These are notable achievements for a party with such residual doubts about the virtues of playing 'normal' politics at all. But there are limitations on the Greens' capacity to be a power broker in the system of bargained pluralism that is modern Italian party politics. The Greens remain a minor factor in this equation. It has been left to other, mostly regionalist or more formally constituted radical parties, ranged along a much revised but still recognisable left-right axis, to contest the electoral space left by the collapse of the discredited Christian Democrat and Socialist parties.[38] Of course, this reformulation of the classical left-right spectrum that continues to pattern Italian politics by no means precludes a role for the Greens. In a situation of political uncertainty, the Greens' image as a progressive party, because of the continuing salience of its key issues with many of the young and new middle class voters who may not vote Green but are amenable to lifestyle issues, sharpens their electoral appeal and on that basis, enhances their political leverage. The new multi-party coalition formed in April 1993 as a government of national salvation by a former Governor of the Bank of Italy, Azeglio Ciampi, saw the prominent Green realist Francesco Rutelli appointed as Environment Minister.[39] These establishment concessions are less significant than they might appear on the face of it, but they are not entirely without importance as a sign that the Greens have at least arrived on the national stage of Italian politics. The new Ministry's record was disappointing. It remained inadequately resourced - both in terms of manpower and funding - for the tasks that faced it, and its record of effective action was much less than it should have been.[40] The Ministry's apparent intention to encourage representations from the wider Green movement, delivered much less direct influence than was initially promised. Some commentators hold to the view that the Ministry has merely provided a distraction - one that has undermined as much as it has strengthened the Green party's claim to speak for ecologism. Green movements everywhere divide their energies between lobbying and electoral politics. In Italy, the clientelist habits of a bureaucracy attuned to narrow, priviledged constituencies has discouraged many ecologists from seeking the insider's route into the policy universe. Instead, these negative expectations of lobbying tend to throw Green politicians back onto two competing strategies. On one side, a realist view that concentrates on building a national coalition with like minded radical parties; and a more sceptical view that continues to trust in local, issue-based and grass roots campaigns. These are as incompatible now as ever they were. Rhodes identifies in this persistent dilemma over strategy and political purpose, the continuing fault line and the Achilles heel of Green politics in Italy; that "there are still many mobilising issues at the local level, but these can be dealt with most effectively by local action and the use of local referendums, dispersing both Green activity and Green identity at a time when there has also been a widespread loss of faith in national politics and government".[41] The provision in the Italian Constitution for calling a referendum, if a half million signatures can be gathered in support of an issue continues to reinforce the views of those activists who see the Greens, above all, as a campaigning social movement. The success of the anti-nuclear referendum in 1987 provided them with a legend to be cited in defence of their position. Nevertheless, an established Green movement with the capacity to exert real influence on national policy, demands something more than the occasional exercise of public opinion on single issues. Such campaigns may be good for the radical soul, but as the similar practice of *votations* in Switzerland confirms, they also expose the Greens to powerful and better resourced movements who use these opportunities to reveal the limits of green idealism to expose the movement's internal divisions. At best, referenda campaigns offer periodic platforms for flying the ecology kite. On their own, however, they lack the potential to connect the Greens to the critical issues of public concern on the national agenda.

In these perplexing circumstances, the Italian Greens have struggled to carve out for themselves a distinct niche in national politics. The prospect of an election in 1994, held under Italy's new first past the post rules, obliged its minor political parties - and not least the Greens - to make some difficult choices in order to ensure their continued representation in the national Parliament. There was no alternative here, other than organising interparty alliances built around the electoral axes of the dominant parties.[42] The Greens showed willing by practising the strategy with a degree of success in the 1993 Regional elections. An arrangement with the reformed Communist Left - the PDS - brought it a notable victory when Rutelli - after resigning his government office - won the mayoralty of Rome.[43] The central question here, is whether the Greens can respond to the political opportunities presented by the unprecedented flux of Italian politics. The choices became clearer as the crisis of the state deepened - whether, on the one hand, to embrace the pure green preference for independence; or instead to adopt a wider coalitional strategy, including the exercise of local government responsibility and direct involvement with a national government of the broad left. There are clear risks in either approach. Cooperation implies cooption - a short step away from political oblivion to critics of this strategy. Whereas continued aloofness threatens a similar fate in the realist outlook. On balance, however, only the latter holds out any real prospect of exercising a degree of influence over the future shape of national policy.

On the evidence of the general election result of March 1994, the prognosis for a Green breakthrough seemed less than favourable. The Green vote of 2.7 per cent represented a drop of 0.1 per cent on 1992.[44] As a junior partner in a Progressive Alliance of six parties, the Greens seemed no nearer to making even a modest showing. Of course, the Greens do occupy a crowded political landscape and must compete for a limited new politics constituency with the Radical and Proleterian Democracy parties.[45] But this should not preclude a coherent Green party, sure of its identity, from securing its due share of this radical constituency. Green parties elsewhere have faced similar difficulties and survived. The Green realists drew some comfort, too, from the circumstances that surrounded the 1994 elections. The populist right, led by Berlusconi's 'Forza' movement, were in the ascendance, and the elections were held in a political climate that was far from conducive to a leftist let alone to a post-materialist agenda.[46] There were, however, salutary lessons to be drawn from this election. The limits of an insular, alternativist politics disengaged from wider radical agendas were clearly underlined at the polls. Ecologism continues to struggle for a hearing from the Italian electorate alongside more pressing issues. Eurobarometer surveys indicate only modest support for the environment as a public good worthy of major resource allocations let alone sacrifices. The Italian electorate, in what Denis Mack Smith has characterised as an archetypal 'right of centre' polity,[47] have been preoccupied instead with the fall out from the recent corruption scandals and the rolling crisis of the state. Not far behind on the national issue agenda are those issues - economic competitiveness, labour costs, welfare reform - associated with the latest phase of European integration. The mood of public concern and discontent was, at this juncture, translated into support for a loose alliance of right of centre parties promising to clean out the national stables.[48] The odds against this unstable coalition delivering effective government were such that it eventually collapsed, and it was replaced by an interim, non-political or technocratic administration. After a brief interlude, during which the forces on both sides of Italy's left-right divide manoeuvred to consolidate their coalitions, a left dominated government recently took power. The Green party has taken part in these byzantine coalitional arrangements. It may be that they will be better placed in these circumstances of flux to influence the national policy agenda than any other Mediterranean Green party. At the same time this expectancy should not be exaggerated. The 'Olive Tree' alliance of centre-left parties is a no more stable prospect than the centre-right government that preceded it. Within that progressive coalition the Greens are a minor element with modest influence and little political clout. The 'new' Italian left is, in effect, a reconstructed version of the old left. It consists of parties still dependent on electoral clients, whose interests are frequently far removed from those of the new politics and ecology agenda; and not least, wedded for the most part to the materialist priorities of their predecessors. The most that can be claimed for Green prospects here, is that they are at least a player, however minor, in the mainstream of national politics. This role presents opportunities as well as dangers. Involvement in the complex multi-party bargains that are necessary to preserve the coalition is a resource that even a small party in an unstable and fragmented polity can play to some advantage. At least, the opportunity for exerting leverage on policy is available, if the Greens can resolve some of the dilemmas that persist in the party about playing 'normal politics', and dealing with the left. They are, however marginally or ambivalently, now playing within the political system. And that, in itself, presents them with a useful political resource in a volatile and fractured polity.[49]

The Greens continue to face some difficult choices in the new politics of Italy. The manifold pressures discussed above would seem to indicate that political ecologism, if it is to become an effective presence in national politics, must resolve its own doubts and settle its internal differences over strategy and political direction. Above all, it must do so if it is to accommodate to the broad political coalitions encouraged by recent electoral reform that operate at every level of the political system. With further changes designed to encourage better party discipline and clearer lines of representation and government stability likely to follow, these questions have taken on a new urgency. The resolution of these questions will almost certainly pose, in even starker terms than before, the same perplexing choice between pragmatism and ideologism that has overshadowed the party throughout its brief political life. Pragmatism comes uneasily to a movement that grew out of a wholesale rejection of the follies of 'normal' politics. If the Italian Greens take such accommodations in their stride, this will almost certainly take the party down a red-green rather than a pure-green route. Accommodating to the political forces on the left does not, however, necessarily mean an abandonment of ecologism. The Greens may, if they take the pragmatic route, have little alternative but to embrace political cohabitation within a broad radical alliance. This does not in itself, however, require a complete loss of identity, let alone cooption by, or merger with this alliance's dominant parties. The essence of the new coalitions that currently dominate Italian politics is that of a series of multiple bargains between distinct party groups clustered around the principal axes of left and right. Within the broad left constellation to which the Liste Verdi is currently attached, the party remains free to pursue a distinctive ecological agenda. The threat to their political independence comes less from other predatory parties than from the Greens themselves. If the Greens prove unable to resolve their continuing doubts over strategy or ideology and fail to subsume their factionalism in common cause they will become distracted from the task at hand. A reversion to narrow factionalism is a luxury the party simply cannot afford. Weakened by such experiences, the Greens would then, indeed, become prey to splits and secessions to adjacent leftist parties, and ultimately to political obsolescence.

The Green party has so far avoided such perils. Indeed, they have begun to adjust almost as well to the logistics of coalitional politics as any other Italian party. The party participated in the 1994 national elections as part of the broad Progressive Front, orchestrated by the Democratic Party of the Left (PDS), the former Communist Party now committed to a social democratic orientation. This alliance drew together a medley of new left and radical groups - left Christian Democrats from the divided Popular Party (PPI), the Democratic Alliance, Socialists and Christian Socialists, the hard left Rifondazione Comunista, and the anti-mafia network (La Rete). Although this coalition lost that election to Berlusconi's right wing alliance, the polarisation of Italian politics revealed at this election confirmed to the Green party's strategists the imperative of attachment to a multi-party network, in order to secure any national representation.[50] Standing alone in splendid isolation - as some green purists would have preferred - the party would have won no seats whatsoever. A number of the Greens were unable to win any representation on their own account. Whereas some Green candidates who stood on the joint left lists were elected. The Greens won eleven seats in the Chamber of Deputies (down from 12 in 1987) and secured 7 Senate seats (an increase of 4 on 1987) on barely 2.7 per cent of the national vote.[51] The lesson of pragmatism was reinforced by subsequent events. The party took a decision in April 1994, to formalise the Greens' role in the alliance of progressive parties formed to fight the upcoming national elections. Whether the Greens continue to adopt such a realist position will depend on the party's present leadership holding their line against the objections of some of the rank and file. For the time being, the omens seem favourable. The Greens' presence in local and regional politics has provided them with a useful resource to be traded with their current political allies on the mainstream left. The Greens may not always win seats at whatever level they stand, but their activists have energy and commitment and are experienced campaigners with effective organisational networks to call on. There is sufficient leverage available to them under present circumstances to make the Greens useful partners. And the bargains that ensue are enough to cement the progressive alliance, both as a viable electoral force but also as a credible government. These are two sides of the same coin, for the Green realists see the electoral pay off not as playing 'normal' politics for its own sake, but rather as the only feasible route to exerting any influence over policy.

The electoral pay off from this strategy of accommodation speaks for itself, with Green councillors in local and regional government across the country, a presence in both chambers of the national parliament and seats in the Strasbourg Assembly, and even a modest if brief role in government. This amounts to a real achievement for a small party that would otherwise face electoral oblivion had it not set out its stall accordingly. This calculus has helped to consolidate the pragmatic over the utopian vision in the party's ranks. The party's institutional presence ensures that ecologism will remain a factor in the Italian political equation for the foreseeable future. The Liste Verdi is now sufficiently ensconsed to ensure that there is an awareness of environmental issues at every level of society, reinforced by the increasing salience of the issue in the programmes of the EU.[52] The notable success of Rutelli, the former if short lived Green environment Minister, in defeating with broad left support the neo-fascist National Alliance (Alleanza Nazionale) candidate for the mayoralty of Rome, and his energetic and imaginative efforts to tackle that city's housing, traffic and related environment problems, illustrates both the social relevance and the political potential for ecologism. The Greens - and most notably their nominal leader, Carlo Ripa de Meana - were prominent, too, in the national opposition to the previous right wing government's cavalier approach to the environment. The party did much to publicise the wider political significance of the decision by National Alliance's Environment Minister, Altiero Matteoli, to pander to the gun lobby by opening the national parks to hunting. The Greens may well be a minor political force; but by careful manoeuvring and shrewd bargaining they continue to suggest that they do have a political future rather than merely a turbulent past.

As things presently stand, the Greens' place in the progressive Olive Tree coalition has, if anything, improved these prospects. The balance of power tipped more firmly in the left's favour after Berlusconi's brief tenure ended in December 1994 in the familiar stew of corruption, and propelled by quarrels within his own right wing bloc between the hard right National Alliance and Forza groups, compounded by the regional demands of Bossi's Northern League (Lega Nord). The right wing coalition lost electoral favour precisely because it failed to meet the insistent mood for change that had brought it to power. Berlusconi's government behaved with much the same insouciance that de Tocqueville once detected in the French Bourbons, who had neither 'learned nor forgotten' anything from a failed past. The government elected in 1994 fell apart in quarrels over the future of welfare spending, devolution from Rome and, not least, Berlusconi's own autocratic variant of the Mussolini complex and his naive insistence on ignoring the lessons of postwar corruption. Instead of real change he preferred to substitute a smug populism; one that substituted a shallow, media driven charisma for the carefully calibrated bargains necessary for building consensus around the reforms and the difficult policy choices facing the country.[53] The Progressive Alliance, led by Romano Prodi - a left inclined christian democrat - overtook the right as the dominant electoral force; until an unlikely victory for Berlusconi in a referendum held on the issue of whether he should continue to hold a virtual monopoly of Italy's private broadcasting media, returned a familiar immobilism. The political deadlock was only broken after another electoral contest in 1996, between the two broad constellations of parties. With some minor adjustments, the electoral scales this time were tipped in favour of the left.

The outcome of the 1996 general election turned less on the charismatic bluster of Berlusconi than on the left's promise of real reforms. The Greens found it relatively easy in these circumstances to shelter under the 'Olive Tree' coalition (whose slogan was firm roots, many branches). Led from the centre by a widely respected moderate, Romano Prodi, and keeping its distance from the hard left Rifondazione, the 'Olive Tree' coalition had continued to challenge the right's claim to be the government best equipped to preside over the widespread reforms necessary to re-legitimise the state.[54] The outcome of the contest between these competing blocs was determined - and ironically 'brokered' in the conventional way of things - by three minor political forces who stood outside them. The rump of the old and discredited Christian Democratic Party (now the Popular Party) and the former PCI hardliners - the Rifondazione - who rejected the social democratic route of the PDS, were hopelessly divided over who to endorse. In the PP's case, the dilemma was whether to jump to the left or right.[55] Whereas the Rifondazione agonised over whether to join the revisionist camp and support the centre-left, or retain what they saw as their ideological integrity and militant soul. The solid bloc of Northern League support on the other hand - which grew to loathe Berlusconi more than it feared the left[56] - played fast and loose, and eventually weighed in its parliamentary favours with the new government because it regards it as the more likely to federalise the state.[57] The prospect of further electoral reform also played its part in these machinations. The two blocs had collided over this issue. Berlusconi proposed a more majoritarian system based on the British model, with constituency based MPs, and removing all vestiges of proportionality in pursuit of strong, centralised government rooted in party discipline. His preference for a directly elected, quasi-presidential Prime Minister - understandable enough given his dominant personality and the ready-made 'charisma-vehicle' afforded by his control over much of the national mass media - is altogether less appealing to more progressive minds.

On the other side of the debate, the left endorsed instead the recommendations of Professor Ettore Gallo, the former President of the Italian Constitutional Court. According to Gallo's proposed model of the political process, parliamentary discipline, stable governance and proper representation are better ensured by a balanced system that combines, along the broad lines of the German system, elements of both the proportionality and majoritarian systems. These proposals also envisaged a two stage election which owes much to the French experience. In the first round a clear run for every party would fully cater for the 'protest itch' and ensure a real degree of minor party influence - a trade for votes - over the two leading blocs in the second or run off election. The Greens clearly have more to gain from the second rather than the first of these procedures. In view of what is at stake here, the resultant stalemate and the time scale involved in legislating such complicated reforms, it is unlikely that far-reaching changes in the electoral rules will occur before the next national elections.[58] The Greens, nevertheless, knew what was at issue here and had every incentive in the circumstances to work hard for a Progressive Alliance victory - as they had to take their place in the ranks of the new government, in order to ensure that whatever procedural changes do occur, help rather than hinder their cause to remain a presence in national politics.

This goal was duly achieved, although the overall outcome was far from conclusive. The Olive Tree alliance won a majority in the Senate and a small majority in the Chamber of Deputies - the first time the left have been the dominant force in Italian politics since 1946. The main player in this eight party centre alliance - the PDS - emerged as Italy's largest party with 22 per cent of the vote. Nevertheless, it required the support of other radical or progressive parties - the PP, Lamberto Dini's moderate Italian Renewal movement, and the modest contribution of the Greens, in spite of the fact that the party's influence was further reduced when their most notable member, Carlo Ripa de Meana, lost his seat.[59] Equally significant was the fact that Umberto Bossi's populist Northern League decided to fight alone in its electoral heartland, increasing its share of the poll largely at the expense of the right, and winning 11per cent of the national vote. It was clear from the outset that the new government - in which the Greens are represented - would have to rely for a secure parliamentary majority on the Rifondazione (former Communists), whose hardliners may prove to be intractable on many of the serious 'reforms' in the public sector, wages policy, budgetary and welfare area that confront the new government. In these circumstances, the government's survival options will depend on how far it can satisfy the League's urgent demands for constitutional reforms and a serious measure of political federalising and fiscal devolution.

The government - and the financial markets - have been encouraged on this score by the culture of cooperation and dealmaking that already exists amongst the centre-left parties at both the regional and local levels of governance.[60] The extent of disaffection by younger voters against the 'old' corrupt politics of *'tangentopoli '* ('bribesville') suggests that a serious generation gap is opening up in Italian politics.[61] This rejection of the establishment parties of both left and right presents the Greens with an opportunity and a challenge. Overcoming the depth of current electoral cynicism suggests, however, that they face a daunting task in extending their support base, in this as in any other direction. The Greens are part of the reconstruction of Italian politics. Not so much because they are the beneficiaries of the fundamental shifts and dealignments that are underway there, but precisely because they have accommodated themselves to the situation in which they now have to operate. They have, accordingly, seized on the opportunities that resulted from a massive discontent with an inefficient and corrupt postwar order. The new government of Romano Prodi, dominated by Massimo D'Alema's Democratic Left, is embarked on a massive reform programme that addresses mainstream concerns with the budget deficit, constitutional reform, anti-corruption measures, improving the quality of public administration, educational and other social reforms.[62] The most the Greens can expect in these circumstances, is to consolidate their newfound place at the centre of the politics of renewal - to build bridges towards their allies in the governing coalition; to gain experience of 'normal' politics and, with that, to sharpen their leverage and increase the respect that accrues from participating in effective governance. This promises to be the most effective way of fighting their corner, whether on green or those other monumental issues that confront this beleaguered polity. And thereby to maximise their modest but real opportunity to influence public policy as a small but responsible cog in the progressive movement that is seeking to refashion politics and reform society in contemporary Italy.

2.   Greece

(i)   Green roots

A combination of high concentrations of urban pollution and rural/coastal environmental degradation caused by unplanned industrialisation, deforestation and damage to habitat to accommodate poorly planned tourist infrastructure, ought to have provided Greece with the best (or worst) foundations for a thriving Green movement. In fact, apart from occasional activities by local groups - such as the Ecological Initiative, a Green newspaper published in Athens, and an ecological club based in Thessalonika - there were few signs of the sort of sustained ecological movement which occurred in most western European countries during the eighties. The reasons for this reticence are understandable enough, within the context of the country's pattern of economic and political development. After a period of repressive military dictatorship (from 1967 to 1974), the movement for restoring democratic freedom attracted those very elements amongst the progressive intelligentsia and the new middle classes who, elsewhere in Europe where liberal democracy was more secure, have provided the support base for alternativist and green causes.[63] Greece is also one of the poorest countries in western Europe. Low levels of industrialisation have not wrought the same level of environmental damage experienced elsewhere, although inadequately controlled emission levels from the country's outdated and small scale industrial plants did put the issue on the national agenda.[64] Neither has the environment movement received the same injection of political awareness the nuclear issue gave it in other European countries, because Greece does not generate nuclear energy. A 'catch-up' and pro-developmental ethos finds favour here with all of the major parties across the ideological spectrum. This mood was strongly reinforced after Greece joined the European Community in 1986. EU membership has brought fierce pressures, both from within the country and without, for economic convergence and improved competitiveness. Community policies have thereby added to the 'rush' to develop. The EU's structural funds have encouraged infrastructural developments with adverse consequences for the environment, alongside their more obvious benefits; whereas the financial structure of the Common Agriculture Policy, regardless of the protestations of the EU Commission to the contrary, has encouraged changes in farming practice in pursuit of excessive production, that have inflicted immense damage on the landscape. In the underdeveloped, largely peasant based agricultural economy of Greece, the lucrative subsidies available under the CAP have encouraged the farming community to 'slash and burn' large areas of virgin land and forest. Although environmental damage is widely reported in the media, it has largely been discounted as a political issue. While the electorate is aware of the issue - and the difficult choices posed for public policy makers by the very idea of environmental controls - they continue to place other concerns higher on their scale of political priorities.

In spite of these constraints, some two hundred environmental 'clubs' and associations were founded from the mid seventies onwards. Most of these were local campaigning and single issue groups of limited duration and modest impact. They did not amount as such to an effective social movement with real political clout.[65] Although something more than an elitist fad, the movement was tentative rather than strident. The moderate ethos of the Greek ecological movement was reinforced in this formative period by the prominence in it of apolitical technocrats and scientists. The new left and libertarian alternativists who launched green movements in many other European countries focused their energies instead on the pro-democracy campaign. Green issues were raised here in the altogether more ethereal world of the academy. It was scholars rather than militants who fought its corner. Even when this concern did acquire a degree of 'public' salience - as it did from the mid 1970s - with action mobilised in specific local campaigns against industrial infrastructural developments, its character was essentially protectionist rather than radical. It was concerned, with environmentalism rather than 'deep ecology', and employed the usual tactics of demonstrations, media campaigns and strikes.[66] The entrenched clientelism of the political system discouraged the adoption of a party format. The centralised nature of the policy process encouraged groups to attach themselves to, or otherwise work through, the established parties.[67] For it was they, as Demertzis points out, "who, during the 1970s, first taught and brought into Greek universities and other institutions the environmental problematic in a scientific and systematic manner".[68] This narrow group was much less concerned about stimulating eco-awareness as a lever for political change than as an expression of deeper cultural instincts - the virtues of nature preservation in the homeland of classical antiquity, as yet largely unspoiled by mass industrialism. There was, even in this early campaigning, a degree of fraudulence or self indulgence. As Demertzis sees it, "ecologism was used as a pretext for more selfish motives" and was "frequently stimulated by sheer economic motivations by vested material interests, glossed up ideologically by appeals to tradition and homeland". In short, "the environment was not consistently recognised as a societal value at all".[69]

After 1981 Greek ecologism did take on a more overtly political - and radical - demeanour. Local initiatives in both the provinces and in Athens, with its high concentration of enlightened, more highly educated opinion and whose receptiveness to eco problems was heightened by Chernobyl, were complemented by a rising interest amongst alternativist elements.[70] Nevertheless, the nascent green movement fell a long way short of the 'take off' point reached by green movements in Europe's more economically developed polities. The fragmentation of a movement of widely dispersed local groups, and the cultural handicap of a national mindset shaped by the traditional hegemony of the established parties over most expressions of political interest, discouraged green activists from the idea of going it alone. The initial stirrings of interest in 1984 in an independent green party, had to contend with these unfavourable circumstances. The first attempts by greens at electoral politics in the 1986 local elections were half hearted and ineffectual. By 1988 an inchoate 'Citizens Union' (*Enosi Politon*) tried to launch a debate about the prospects for a more concerted green presence in Greek politics. The resistance from vested interests, and an electorate with high levels of partisan commitment to existing parties, meant that progress on this front was slow. A modest breakthrough only came some two or more years later, with the country's first experience of European elections. Before we pick up the threads of Green party development, we need to put this reluctance to embrace new ideas into its sociological perspective. The Greek electorate are by no means natural post-materialists, even if enough of them share radical instincts. For one thing, many of them are either dependent on agriculture for their livelihood, or come from families with continuing roots in the countryside. Similar materialist arguments apply to the cognitive investment of many Greeks in the massive expansion of the tourist industry, particularly on the Aegean Islands. The desire for prosperity touches every social class. This is not a nation particularly receptive to arguments in favour of economic restraint, or readily mobilised against practices that promise economic salvation.[71]

In such unfavourable circumstances, the Greens in Greece were not only thin on the ground; they also reserved their energies for local campaigns against more obtrusive developments, and showed little inclination to contest elections at any level. At least until the end of a decade, when electoral successes by Green parties elsewhere had indicated the advantages of a national political strategy. Political culture played its part in determining this early strategy. In so far as they wished to influence the national policy agenda, ecologists had little choice but to work with the established parties and accept their dominant role as the political gatekeepers of the policy making system.[72] The prevailing practice of politics mitigated against any effective collective action outside this system. A weak liberal tradition and a fragmentary civil society - a legacy of a history of political authoritarianism, reinforced by the individualistic mores of peasant society[73] - combined to sustain an insular rather than a socially aware civic culture. Modernisation is by no means a singular experience. It is everywhere moulded by the host culture which experiences it. The public mind here, in so far as an agreed sense of purpose does exist, reflects individual wants or family interests, rather than any universal notion of the 'common good'; and as Demertzis has observed, "these have been expressed through an ever-moving stream of consumerism and greedy material prosperity which makes it difficult for the environment to be protected and accorded a central place in public interests. Under such circumstances, the environment is not conceived as a public good or as something endowed with its own inherent value but as a field and means for maximum economic exploitation".[74]

It was hardly surprising, in the circumstances, that the greens chose to make their first foray into electoral politics on the European rather than the national stage. A group of green activists, encouraged by the success of Germany's Die Grunen, and drawing directly on their expertise - as the Spanish Green party did in similar circumstances - tried against heavy odds to form a 'party' in anticipation of the 1989 European elections. The absence of any properly established organisation, compounded by personality clashes and serious divisions over ideology between pure Greens and extra-parliamentary alternativists and leftists undermined the project. Those involved were persuaded to forego any attempt to build a party proper in the limited time available, and to concentrate instead on fielding an agreed slate of candidates. Even this more modest aspiration seemed beyond them. For in the event, this decision merely brought into the open and legitimised factional infighting, and led to three competing lists and the fragmentation of what was, at best, a minimal vote. The Greek Democratic Ecological Movement polled a mere 1.1 per cent (and won no seats); the Alternative Ecologist list also won 1.1 per cent; and the inaptly named Ecological Movement-Political Renaissance secured a mere 0.4 per cent. These unwarranted divisions and the political self indulgence they betrayed almost certainly cost the Greens a seat in Strasbourg, given the very generous electoral national threshold of 1.36 per cent for securing a Euro-seat.

(ii)   Party formation

This lesson was quickly assimilated. These fractions did manage to submerge their differences for the national elections of November 1989. The Greens were helped by the fact that these elections took place during a period of excessive atmospheric pollution over Athens - which houses almost half of the country's total population.[75] A concentration of smog - known in local parlance as 'nefos' (the cloud) - forced the authorities to cut industrial production by 50 per cent. Schools were closed, respiratory illness increased and private cars were prohibited from using the city centre. By uniting into a federal party under the Alternative Ecologist banner (the Federation of Ecological Organisations) as a coalition of pure and red-green ecologism, including over 90 groups in all - from a Society of Bicycle Lovers and anti-vivisectionists to transvestites (the Kraximo ray group), and all manner of other eco-groups - they did manage to win one seat, albeit with only 0.58 per cent of the total vote. Not that this reconciliation was easy to accomplish or to maintain. The Greens were unable to capitalise on this situation, as became apparent during the electoral aftermath. The resulting electoral deadlock meant that the Greens' single parliamentary seat became indispensable for confirming the Socialist-led coalition in office. The Prime Minister, Andreas Papandreou, openly courted the Greens. He even offered them the environment portfolio in the new government. But they refused all overtures of negotiation, and were preoccupied with consolidating their own tenuous coalition of groups, by apportioning their one seat between the various component parts of the new party. Committed as they were to an anti-party model, they opted for annual rotation. A 'party' spokesman, Giorgos Karabelias, observed that "we don't like deputies who are isolated within the political game, away from society". This studied isolationism was as short-sighted as it was principled, given that this new, tentative party had turned down what would have been the quickest elevation to national office of any European green party!

The perpetuation of internal tensions saw the postponement of the nascent party's founding Congress on four occasions between December 1990 and January-February 1992. These strains indicated the extent of ideological tension within the Green movement. The lack of consensus also dictated the new party's federal format. Delegates eventually agreed a loose arrangement consisting of an unwieldy but ultra-democratic coordinating secretariat, with an equally large presidency of nine members - and with assorted committees to work on issue campaigns, research and support for the occasional parliamentary representative. The rotation principle was vigorously applied - with a three month turn around, unless there were no replacements willing to stand in the stead of incumbents. The 'realo'-'fundi' cross-currents, about the purposes of party politics, compounded by differences between red-green and pure-green dispositions, were as ingrained here as in any other nascent Green 'party'. So much so that a dozen or so of these constituent groups - especially those with a preference for eco-socialism - withdrew from the congress and turned their back on the Federation. The crisis was disruptive enough to persuade the Federation's one national parliamentary representative to announce her rejection of the Green party label and to adopt an independent status. The majority of the Federation persevered and tried to find some political cement to consolidate such a fragile internal unity.

(iii)   Political developments

The Greens avoided the temptation - almost certainly fatal at this stage - to frame an agreed party programme. In spite of its abiding divisions, the Federation took full advantage of the publicity that came with national representation. In line with its grassroots ethos, it set about lobbying for environmental change, outside parliament as much as within. The Greens campaigned on the ground in favour of specific issues; reforestation; nature conservation - highlighted by the threat from rampant tourism to the nesting grounds of the sea turtle on Zakinthos, and the dangers of toxic chemicals used in farming on seabirds after a mass poisoning on Lake Ioanniana; for a review of industry permits and an attempt to ban cars from the city centre to protect the health of its citizens, and to preserve its ancient monuments; opposition to the government's bid to host the 1996 Olympic Games, which drew attention to that scheme's intolerable environmental impact; curbs on uncoordinated tourist developments on the main holiday islands, and to promote the environmental benefits of cycling or walking. In the event, this proved to be the least divisive strategy available. The party raised its profile and, at the same time, managed to avoid exacerbating its divisions. With the political establishment still gripped by immobilism, the Greens tried to broaden their base, particularly among young and women voters, but only marginally succeeded in doing so. At the 1990 general election they barely increased their vote to 0.8 per cent, although under the proportionality system they retained their parliamentary seat. Not surprisingly, for a party composed of multifarious local groups whose political impact has been confined to local and single issue campaigns, the Greens have fared better in sub-national elections. In the 1990 municipal and regional elections they won seats on the municipal councils. But even at this level, their impact remains modest and their cause continues to seem eccentric or esoteric rather than popular in the extent of its appeal. The Greek Greens have also experienced the same inconsistency, as between a stated interest in the environment amongst the electorate at large - especially in the congested and smog ridden urban conurbations - and in direct contrast, its marked reluctance to vote for Green candidates.[76]

(iv)   Prospects for political change

The future of political ecologism in Greece will depend as much on national social and political developments as it does on the Greens' own behaviour. As long as the main electoral preoccupations are with materialism - growth, development and 'catching up' - the very real environmental problems associated with rapid socio-economic modernisation are unlikely to galvanise significant electoral support.[77] In these circumstances, the party's principal tactic, of reserving most of its political energy for particular campaigns on selective issues, is probably the approach best suited to raising ecological consciousness and winning policy concessions. It is also an approach dictated by the sheer diversity of groups who shelter under the Green Federation's umbrella. The reluctance to finally resolve these differences has, paradoxically, kept the Federation intact. The pressures imposed on more organised Green parties by electoral success, and the increasing salience of green issues in national politics, has hardly arisen here. And therein lies a threat to the Federation's future viability. Should ecologism ever gain the political momentum it has enjoyed elsewhere in Europe, the pressure to resolve differences over the party's political orientation and to assume some of the organisational demeanour of a party proper, could well lead to the sort of civil wars that have so debilitated other Green parties. This is unlikely, however, to occur for the foreseeable future. While the Greek party system and the social cleavages that sustain it remain 'frozen' or time locked with traditional preoccupations, any significant dealignment, let alone far-reaching political change - in a post-materialist or any other direction - remains an unlikely prospect. Of course, no political system is static. Change is part of the natural order of things and Greece's participation in the EU, and the impact of economic shifts brought about by what Rosenau has called the "cascading interdependence" of modern globalism,[78] are bound, sooner or later, to make inroads into old habits and partisan loyalties.

There are some, admittedly modest, signs that these shifts are underway. A recent commentator in a survey of Greek society detected an underlying mood change; that "after three decades in which many Greeks became city residents for the first time, while attaining a standard of living comparable to that elsewhere in southern Europe, attitudes are undergoing a radical change. Social and environmental problems, ranging from drug use to atmospheric pollution and the dumping of toxic waste, assume a much higher profile. The urge to modernise cuts across political boundaries".[79] Papadopoulos, too, has seen this movement reflected in shifts in ideological affinity. Citing Eurobarometer 19 data (from Spring 1983), he observed that the ideological distance between the two dominant parties of the left (PASOK - Panellinio Sosialistiko Kinima - the Panhellenic Socialist Movement) and the right (ND - New Democracy) had "the highest value among the 12 EC member countries". Although this was reducing, as an underlying consensus emerged "on such fundamental issues as the (republican) regime", nevertheless, the traditional political style remains confrontational.[80] While it is the case that the liberal faction of New Democracy and the pro-European Union technocrats - who have done much to convince the traditional PASOK leadership to grasp the awkward nettles of fiscal reform and budgetary discipline, if the country is to even close the gap opening up between Greece and the rest of the EU - do share a modernising agenda, these cross party affinities should not be exaggerated. Party politics in Greece remains locked in a bipolar time warp. Recent attempts by the PASOK government to address these serious structural issues - to cut the country's crippling public deficit (13.2

241

per cent of GDP), reduce the spiralling public sector borrowing (11.4 per cent of GDP in 1994), curb runaway stagflation (at 12.1 per cent annually), introduce a modern and equitable taxation system, root out patronage and inefficiency - have merely underlined the deep inertia of the prevailing political system. There are simply too many clients of the major parties to risk any drastic change. The immobilism of a party system rooted in vested interests only serves to signal the urgent need for real change and, at the same time, to highlight the heavy odds stacked against it. The depth of the problem was revealed in the unfavourable contrast between Greece and the EU's other new southern members, Spain and Portugal, neither of whom had suffered the economic ignominy of a continued fall in prosperity compared with the other EU states.

The combination of a durable political culture and a staid political regime that the major parties regard as their prerogative to tamper with in order to improve their own electoral fortunes leaves little scope for a breakthrough by any new political movement. As Papadopoulos identifies the predicament facing new parties here, "the abiding problematic of the Greek polity is the ideological distance between the major parties and polarised bi-partyism rather than the presence of any presumably 'anti-party' system".[81] The odds are thereby stacked as high here against the emergence of a new politics dimension, represented by a viable alternative party, as they are anywhere in Europe. Political change is much more likely to come from realignments within the major party families and the smaller parties that revolve in their ideological orbits, than it is from any wholesale realignment. There are no real signs of an emergent fault line that will open up even the modest post-materialist cleavage visible elsewhere. The Green prospectus here has to assimilate these facts rather than ignore them. If there is to be an environmental locale in contemporary Greek politics, it will be a modest and moderate one, linked closely with a widespread desire to improve lifestyles and conserve rare natural resources.

The Greens have long assimilated these lessons and they draw some comfort from the fact that there are already signs of public concern over these issues on which they might build their campaigns and frame their electoral appeal. The tentative approach, for instance, by authorities more concerned to appease a narrow constituency than they are to take difficult decisions in the wider public interest, can be seen in the worsening urban traffic crisis. Emissions from traffic and the blight caused by tourist development underline decades of official complacency and neglect. Vested economic interests are never far from the surface when these issues are discussed. More recently, a start has been made to address these issues because public opinion, 'educated' in part by ecological pressure groups, has begun to place a higher value on lifestyle issues that now gives these matters a degree of political gravitas. The government has had to tread carefully where tourism is concerned, not least because the sector accounts, directly or indirectly, for some 7 per cent of GDP and 10 per cent of employment. At the same time, mass tourism and especially the unplanned, illegal or indiscriminate developments that have accompanied it has attracted a degree of public censure. The pressure of this opinion, to which the Greens have made a signal contribution, has forced the government to announce a plan to balance 'quality' and well-planned tourist infrastructure with its continuing economic benefits. This policy shift has to be counted a success for the Green movement. Above all, it has reinforced the arguments of the movement's moderates - whether of a pure or red-green disposition - that political change can be achieved, and is more likely to ensue in this political culture by making common cause with other groups; and that lobbying within the system combined with effective compromise measures does suggest a viable political strategy.

The plans to address the equally difficult issue of urban pollution - particularly in Greater Athens - have followed a similar pattern of compromise. A balance has been struck here between the interests of commercial and industrial sectors, and what ecologists regard as the inalienable human right to the collective public good of minimum health standards. The Environment Ministry has, for instance, recently agreed to stagger working hours in order to reduce air pollution from traffic by a planned 15 per cent. They have likewise adopted measures to prohibit car usage in the central zone with less than 3 passengers on days when air quality is poor, to tighten up controls on vehicle emission tests and certification procedures, and to improve public transport in the city. The local Green groups have contributed much to raising the public awareness that has brought about the pressure for these changes. These developments do not in themselves represent a dramatic victory for a post-materialist agenda. Green obscurantists may readily dismiss them as minor concessions by a rampant productionist and materialistic culture, and condemn those Greens who dignify or legitimise them as mere quislings. It is certainly true that these modest adjustments are far removed from the confrontation with Prometheus that figures in the dark green discourse. But a green 'revolution' of that ilk is not even a remote prospect in Greece as things currently stand. The Greens have fewer options here than they have in almost any other western European polity. It is a question of compromise - the tactic of carefully nurturing concessions by working with allies at every level of the system - or bust. It is also a question of the movement's moderates biding time - of waiting for the gradual thawing of deep-seated and conservative political instincts to be brought about by a slowly shifting pattern of realignment - a movement in which post-material and new politics issues are at best only matters of minor significance. The Greens may well contribute to these shifts, but as allies of other progressive forces rather than as the principal harbingers of change.

This incipient momentum can be seen in the modest yet, in the context of Greek party politics, notable rise in support for small parties such as the Left Coalition and Political Spring. The signs here are by no means indicative of an imminent seachange. In the municipal elections and the Euro-elections held in 1994, palpable unrest with the complacency of the established parties was qualified by the fact that these were second order elections with comparatively little at stake. Even so, the signs of any emergence of a 'new politics' force of any description were minimal. The welcome given by a leading member of the Left Coalition to reforms in the structure of PASOK hardly represented a breakthrough towards a new radical agenda. There is little sustained evidence from recent electoral behaviour to suggest that the electorate are disposed to any major shift in the political landscape, let alone to corroborate the excessive claims of the political scientist, Dimitris Dimitrakos that "people are thirsting for fresh faces and new ideologies", or indeed that "there is a feeling that things are not going at all well and that after twenty years, the two party system has yielded as much as it is going to (and) many believe the time has come for new political formations".[82] The electoral data in support of this prognosis remains less than convincing. In the 1994 elections for the Strasbourg Parliament both PASOK and New Democracy certainly lost support (down some 9.24 per cent and 6.6 per cent respectively), compared with their performance in the 1993 national elections. In spite of the hyperbole employed by spokesmen for the smaller parties who benefited from this manifest electoral disenchantment - with both the new right Political Spring, (a breakaway from ND), and the Left Coalition improving their 1993 performance - this outcome should be given due perspective.[83] It represented more of a protest vote against a government trying to push through unpalatable and far-reaching budgetary reforms, rein back public expenditure, and cut the biggest budget deficit in the EU, than it heralded an imminent realignment of politics. These reforms hit PASOK's bedrock constituencies hard. They precluded the Government making generous inflationary pay and pensions awards to the public sector, and likewise prevented it from maintaining, let alone increasing, the public sector fiefdoms of job creation and other patronage which had been one of the main props to its support. The same can be said of equally disruptive plans to curb a 'black economy' accounting for some 45 per cent of GDP, and costing an estimated 45 million (US) dollars annually in lost tax revenues, by introducing tax reforms that hit hard its own support base amongst farmers, many of whom organised their affairs to avoid taxation altogether! These election results likewise indicated a distinct lack of enthusiasm for an opposition party whose former leader and Prime Minister, Constantine Mitsotakis, was caught up in a major corruption scandal. They may have dented the mould of Greek politics; they did not break it.

A similar pattern of protest was evident in the 1994 municipal elections, and largely for the same reasons. Both major parties were penalised for perceived policy failures and broken promises. The minor parties picked up modest but far from spectacular gains. In fact, the picture was patchy rather than clearcut. The Left Alliance did well in places, notably Athens, as a focus of a protest vote, whereas Political Spring lost ground there. The Socialists were heavily punished for their national stewardship as stringent budgetary reforms in 1995 loomed nearer. But the Greens were by no means beneficiaries of the protest quota. Indeed, they fared badly in their most favourable milieu of community politics - in the contest for 434 mayoralties and the 54 Prefectures who oversee the disbursement of state funds in the regions. Their poor showing here was accentuated by the fact that this was precisely the type of political contest ideally suited to their campaigning style, their fragmented organisational structure, and to their modest resources. The political odds in their favour should have been markedly improved because of the considerable publicity that surrounded the consequences of the torrential storms which coincided with the contest for the mayoralty of Athens - regarded as the second most important political office in the country. A generation or more of poor urban planning, deforestation, and haphazard and illegal building, had blocked natural water courses for relieving flood waters and lives were lost. Nevertheless, the Green candidate failed to reap the electoral whirlwind.

The recent general election (September 1996) both confirmed these broad trends and shed more light on the unfolding pattern of party politics. A closely contested campaign, fought over economic issues - and focused especially on the consequences of PASOK's policy under its new leader, Costas Simitis, to improve the country's prospects of qualifying for the first round of EMU membership, as well as Balkans dispute with Turkey[84] - saw PASOK (41.5 per cent and 162 seats) returned with a slim but workable majority. Although both major parties were divided over these issues, New Democracy (38.2 per cent and 108 seats) were harmed more by the defection of many amongst the business community impressed by the Simitis government's fiscal prudence - including the incipient privatisation of utilities. New Democracy's leadership relied on an unashamedly populist campaign that pledged to reinstate unpopular cuts in welfare subsidies, restore tax breaks and to pursue a firm line in relations with Ankara. Uncertainty over these issues benefited the smaller radical parties as much as it did ND. The Democratic Renewal Movement (DIKKI), formed earlier in 1996 by disenchanted PASOK supporters and led by former Finance Minister, Dimitris Tsovalas, promised to put back the clock by expanding the public sector, subsidise small businesses, and use EU funds to create rural employment.[85] This appeal to the status quo ante enabled the minor parties - DIKKI, along with SYNASPISMOS (an alliance of former Euro-Communists) and the unreconstructed Stalinist Greek Communist Party (KKE) - to occupy for the first time seats in the national Parliament. The 1996 election was hardly a landmark in the realignment of Greek party politics, inasmuch as it reflected an already well-established pattern. What it did underline was a transition in the pattern of conventional party politics; in particular, a distinct shift of emphasis within PASOK, marking a clear step in its 'reinvention' under a new, modernising leadership, as a social democratic party in the mainstream western European mould. The re-election of a government whose already published budget promised even stiffer fiscal medicine - further cuts in the deficit, a cap on local government spending and recruitment, and compulsory welfare audits[86] - was a testament to a 'new' politics only in the sense of an uncertain public mood reluctantly embracing the larger, unavoidable constraints imposed on the country by regional and global circumstances. In these conditions, the 'new' politics of ecologism or its related radical issues hardly figured, either in the campaign or in determining its outcome. Even when 'green' issues were raised for debate, these only 'played' in the negative sense. Many island voters, for instance, objected to the government's delays in funding projects to boost tourism - including a proposal to build a sewage plant with additional EU structural funds, and to undertake a drilling programme for fresh water.[87] The Greens' impact on the 1996 campaign was entirely peripheral and has raised awkward questions about political strategy and ideological orientation that the movement must address if it is to avoid irrelevance or even outright obsolescence.

The Greek party system since 1981 has consolidated into two broad ideological 'families', each with its own firm support base.[88] There is much less evidence in recent Greek elections of the discontent and electoral volatility that has shaken up the established party systems in Europe's more developed polities.[89] This solidity - reflected in much lower levels of undecided voters in national opinion polls - has persuaded some commentators to describe the party cleavage here as 'frozen'.[90] Although there are some modest signs of changes afoot, these have occurred as much from generational conflicts within the two main party groupings as from the emergence of any new mold breaking force. Where clientelist politics and the state patronage it gives rise to are so well entrenched in political culture and practice, it is difficult for new parties to emerge, let alone to put down firm electoral roots.[91] The recent picture of Greek party politics largely reaffirms this conservative outlook, although there are some tentative signs of electoral discontent, especially amongst a new generation of technocrats across the political spectrum - the very group which has provided a reliable base of support for new politics and Green parties in other European societies. The signs of any far-reaching change leading to the 'unfreezing' of the prevailing cleavage pattern are negligible indeed. The political and party systems remain closely tied to the interests of key socio-economic groups, and the major parties remain as dependent on them - as much as they act as their agents in the policy arena. Parties and their principal client groups remain tightly locked together in a cycle of mutual advantage. The perceived benefits to both sides of maintaining this system, are reflected in the way the various parties give priority access and consideration to the interests of their respective clienteles.

The rules of the electoral system - favourable in principle to representation by small parties - have failed to overcome this legacy of expectations about how politics should work in practice. The actual threshold is low enough. Until 1993 parties with only 1 per cent of the total vote were automatically entitled to one seat - whereas parties or alliances that fielded candidates in a minimum of three quarters of all constituencies, and received up to 2 per cent secured three seats from the 288 non directly elected (constituency) seats. In spite of changes in 1993 that instituted a 3 per cent threshold - due to blatant manoeuvring for electoral advantage between the mainstream parties (in this case PASOK were the culprits) - this was by no means a high barrier by European standards; especially for a small party able to tap into particular public discontents. The Greens were unable, however, to take full advantage of this otherwise favourable opportunity structure because the culture of entrenched clientelism continued to work against them. The recent changes in the electoral rules - which now combine different types of proportionality - have done little to alter the public mindset, or to change the dynamics of party politics.[92] By and large, the well organised and established party 'families' continue to dominate the national party game - a situation reinforced by the prevailing ethos of Greek party politics as a classic adversarial struggle between competing ideologies. The level of disquiet has risen in recent years, as national governments have faced the unpalatable choices that confront all contemporary European states. The corruption scandal that surfaced in 1988, and exposed the shortcomings of the political elites, fanned this disaffection. But ecologism has barely showed on this rising scale of discontents, and the Greens have been unable to capitalise on the recent disruptions to the normal allegiances and pattern of party politics registered by the younger, more modern and better educated urban groups. This unease - and not least its future significance as a cause of political change - should not be underestimated. As yet, however, it has not begun to erode the bedrock support for PASOK or its conservative opponents in the New Democracy party.[93] Failure in government by either of these mainstream adversaries tends to benefit their main opponents most, with only a modest if palpable protest vote accruing to the 'new parties', who themselves conform to the rigidities of the prevailing system of party families, by occupying a place in the dominant cleavage pattern alongside PASOK or New Democracy; notably the Left Alliance and, on the right, the modernist nationalists of the Political Spring Party.

The Greens have made little progress in attracting this discontent vote. The Greens' response to their predicament has been to turn their back on the conventions of the party system and retreat from what many of them regard as a lost cause. This is a predictable response to their limited political opportunity, even if it is far from being the most rational answer to their immediate let alone their long term political plight. It reflects the intense frustration of outsiders marginalised by an inhospitable political culture, and confronted with a closed and quite rigid party system. The comparable predicament of the British Greens comes readily to mind here.   The Greek Greens have, predicably enough, turned these frustrations into factional disputes. Some Green activists have simply abandoned ecologism in these circumstances as a lost cause, and joined up with other parties - particularly the Left Alliance - as the most effective way of getting the green message across. In the light of the Left Alliances' close connections with PASOK, this collaborationist strategy might, in the short term, have something positive to commend it. It may offer the most direct route, the surest way, of bringing green issues into the policy arena. This coalitional approach may also be the best available prospect for representing ecologism in national politics. At the same time, it runs the attendant risk, associated with any political cohabitation between a minor and a more dominant partner, of being manipulated, tamed or coopted by the principal ally for altogether more selfish ends.

Nor is it certain that the dominant parties either want or need the support of a minor party with minuscule support, and whose programme is almost entirely antithetical to their productionist and materialist agendas.   The Greens have been ill placed so far, and less than favourably disposed, to negotiate the sort of suboptimal bargains or to engage in the kind of political networking that had enabled the Left Alliance (itself amenable to ecological concerns) to build bridges with PASOK. The Italian and Portuguese Greens, in similar political cultures and faced with likewise unfavourable opportunity structures, have already adopted the same sort of pragmatic approach. The Greens in Greece will almost certainly have to follow suit if they want to cash in on and shape, the modest but rising public concern with lifestyle and related issues. Otherwise, they will surrender by default valuable political ground to those other leftist parties which already have PASOK's ear and, as such, are closer to power. In the meantime, the verdict of one close observer of Green affairs, that their situation here contrasts "sharply with the experience of western Europe where, in most cases, Green parties have been the outcome of a deep rooted set of social needs expressed through potent movements and ruptures of political cleavages",[94] provides an apt summary of the Greens' continuing predicament in contemporary Greek politics.

Notes

1. Raphael Zarinski, "Italy: The Politics of Uneven Development" (Ilinois, 1972), at Chapter One.

2. See Norman Kogan, "A Political History of Italy: The Postwar Years" (New York, 1983); on the coalitional shifts in Italian politics, see Alberto Marradi, "Italy: From Centrism to Crisis of the Centre-Left Coalitions" in Eric Browne and John Dreijmanis (eds), "Government Coalitions in Western Democracies" (London, 1982).

3. G. Galli, "Il Bipartismo imperfetto: Communisti e Democristiani in Italia" (Bologna, 1966).

4. See R. Leonardi and D.A. Wertman, "Italian Christian Democracy: The Politics of Dominance" (London, 1989).

5. P. Farneti, "The Italian Party System 1945-1980" (London, 1985); and Guiseppe Di Palma, "Surviving without Governing: The Italian Parties in Parliament" (Berkeley, 1977).

6. The reduction in ideological polarisation has been noted by more than one close observer of these events. See the discussion in R. D. Putnam, R. Leonardi and R. Y. Nanetti, "Polarisation and Depolarisation in Italian Politics", American Political Science Association Conference, New York, September 1981 and cited in Yves Meny, "Government and Politics in Western Europe" (2nd edition, Oxford, 1993), at pp.111-12.

7. In spite of a national tradition of seminal writings on the subject. See for instance, Ugo Leone, "Polluted Italy" published in 1970; Antonio Cederna and "The Destruction of Nature in Italy" (1975).

8. P. Ceri, "The Nuclear Power Issue: A New Political Cleavage Within Italian Society?" in R. Nannetti, R. Leonardo and P. Corbetta (eds), "Italian Politics: A Review" Vol.2 (published in London for the Instituto Cattaneo, 1988), pp.71-89.

9. D. Alexander, "Pollution, policies and politics: the Italian environment", in F. Sebetti and R. Catanzaro (eds), "Italian Politics: A Review", at pp.90-111 (published in London for the Instituto Cattaneo, 1991).

10. F. Muller-Rommel, op.cit (1982); W. Rudig, op.cit (1986).

11. S. Parkin, "Green Parties: An International Guide" (London, 1989), at p.154.

12. A. Panebianco, "The Italian Radicals: New Wine in an Old Bottle", in K. Lawson and P.H. Merkl (eds), "When Parties Fail: Emerging Alternative Organisations" (Princeton NJ, 1988), pp.110-36.

13. D. Hine, "Governing Italy: The Politics of Bargained Pluralism" (Oxford, 1993), at pp.155-156.

14. See G. Lodi, "L'azione ecologista in Italia: dal protezionisma storico alle Liste Verdi", in R. Biorcio and G. Lodi (eds) "La sfida verde: il movimento ecologista in Italia" (Padova, 1988), pp.17-26.

15. N. Magna, "Le quattro Italie del voto europeo", Politica ed Economia 10 1989 pp.33-43.

16. R. Biorcio, "L'elettorato verde" in R. Biorcio and G. Lodi, op.cit (1988), at p.197.

17. Ibid (1988), at p.182.

18. M. Diani,"Italy: The 'Liste Verdi'", in F. Muller-Rommel op.cit (1989) at pp.117-119.

19. P.V. Uleri, "The 1987 referenda", in R. Leonardi and P. Corbetta, "Italian Politics: A Review" Vol.3 (London, 1989).

20. D. Sassoon, "The 1987 elections and the PCI", in R. Leonardi and P. Corbetta (eds), ibid (1989).

21. G. Pasquino, "Il Sistemi elettorali" in G. Amato and A. Barbara (eds), "Manuale di diritto pubblico" (Bologna, 1981).

22. G. Pridham, "Italian Small Parties in Comparative Perspective", in F. Muller-Rommel and G. Pridham (eds), "Small Parties in Western Europe: Contemporary and National Perspectives" (London, 1991), at pp.71-94.

23. D. Alexander, "Pollution, Policies and Politics: The Italian Environment", in F. Sebetti and R. Catanzaro (eds) "Italian Politics: A Review" Vol.5 (published in London for the Instituto Cattaneo, 1991), pp.90-111.

24. See Giacomo Sani, "The Political Culture of Italy: Continuity and Change" in G. Almond and S. Verba (eds), "The Political Culture Revisited" (Boston, 1980), at Chapter 8.

25. Reuters New Service Report, 19.6.89.

26. See Carlo Donolo, "Social Change and Transformation of the State in Italy", in Richard Scase (ed), "The State in Western Europe" (London, 1980).

27. Reuters News Service Report, 21.3.93.

28. Martin Rhodes, "Italy: Greens in an overcrowded political system", in D. Richardson and C. Rootes, (eds), op.cit (1995), at pp.168-69.

29. G. Sartori, "European Political Parties: The Case of Polarised Pluralism", in J. LaPalombara and M. Weiner (eds), "Political Parties and Political Development" (Princeton NJ, 1966), pp.137-76.

30. P. Farneti, op.cit (1985), at pp.182-89.

31. R. Biorcio, op.cit (1988), pp.194-95.

32. S. Tarrow, "The Phantom at the Opera: Political Parties and Social Movements of the 1960s and 1970s in Italy", in R.J. Dalton and M. Kuechler (eds), "Challenging the Political Order: New Social and Political Movements in Western Democracies" (Cambridge, 1990), pp.251-73.

33. M. Rhodes, op.cit (1995), at p.186.

34. M. Rhodes, "Piazza or Palazzo? The Italian Greens and the 1992 Elections", Environmental Politics 1 1992, at pp.438-39.

35. Cited by M. Rhodes, op.cit (1995), at p.188.

36. M. Rhodes, op.cit (1992), at pp.437-442.

37. See David Hine, "Federalism, Regionalism and the Unitary State: Contemporary Regional Pressures in Historical Perspective", in Carl Levy (ed), "Italian Regionalism:

History, Identity and Politics" (Oxford, 1996), pp.109-129.

38. See Joseph LaPalombara, "Democracy Italian Style" (New Haven, 1987).

39. Agence Europe, 30.4.93.

40. R. Lewanski, "La politica ambientale", in B. Dente (ed), "Le politiche publiche in Italia" (Bologna, 1990), pp.179-208.

41. M. Rhodes, op.cit (1995), at p.183.

42. For a general overview of the new mood for change, see Arturo Parisi and Gianfranco Pasquino, "Changes in Italian Electoral Behaviour: The Relationship between Parties and Voters" in P. Lange and S. Tarrow, "Italy in Transition: Conflict and Consensus" (London, 1980) at pp.6-30.

43. Financial Times, 23.12.93; ibid 6.12.93.

44. The Guardian 30.3.94; the Greens failed to win any of the 155 seats in the 630 seat lower house reserved, under a proportional electoral system operating with a 4 per cent threshold, and based on party selection. They did, however, pick up some of the Progressive Alliance's 213 seats elected, under Italy's new and complicated electoral rules based on a first past the post system.

45. For a guide to Italy's new political constellations, see Robert Graham, "On the planet of the unholy allies", Financial Times, 27.1.94.

46. Financial Times, 25.3.94.

47. See the interview with Denis Mack Smith, The Guardian, 30.3.94.

48. Financial Times, 15.3.94.

49. R. Graham, op.cit Financial Times, 27.1.94.

50. R. Graham, "Italy's voters look set to put new political alliances to the test", Financial Times, 25.3.94.

51. A. Hill, "Voting system leaves small groups in cold", Financial Times, 30.3.94.

52. For a discussion of the European policy dimension of environmental issues, see Sonia Mazey and Jeremy Richardson, "EC policy making: an emerging European policy style?", in J.D. Liefferink, et al (eds), op.cit (1993), at pp.114-125.

53. Financial Times, 24.12.94

54. R. Graham, "Italian parties limp to the starting line", Financial Times, 18.4.96.

55. R. Graham, "Italian parties fight for Catholic vote" Financial Times, 17.4.96.

56. R. Graham, "Italian poll fuels hopes for independent north", Financial Times, 9.4.96.

57. R. Graham, "Elections may not bridge that gap", Financial Times, 23.3.94.

58. R. Graham, "Prodi's plan to end 'paralysis'", Italy: Financial Times Survey, 4.7.96.

59. Financial Times, 24.4.96.

60. R. Graham, "A toe hold on power", Financial Times, 23.4.96.

61. R. Graham and A. Hill, "Old politics fails to fire young voters", Financial Times, 13/14.4.96.

62. R. Graham, "At last the chance of a greater role", Italy: Financial Times Survey, 4.7.96.

63. See K. Featherstone and D. Katsoudas, "Political Change in Greece: Before and After the Generals" (New York, 1987).

64. N. Mouzelis, "Modern Greece: Facets of Underdevelopment" (London, 1978).

65. N. Demertzis, "Greece: Greens at the periphery", in D. Richardson & C. Rootes (eds), op.cit (1995), at p.194.

66. Ibid, (1995), p.195.

67. See C. Lyrintzis, "Political Parties in Post-Junta Greece: A Case of Bureaucratic Clientelism" in G. Pridham (ed), "The New Mediterranean Democracies: Regime Transition in Spain, Greece and Portugal" (London, 1984).

68. N. Demertzis, op.cit (1995), p.195.

69. Ibid (1995), p.195.

70. For a topical account of these developments, see G. Karamalis, "The Ecology Movement has a Future", and K. Plassara, "The Present and the Future of Greece's Ecological Movement", in C. Orphanadis (ed), "The Ecological Movement in Greece" (Athens, 1987) - published in Greek and cited in N. Demertzis, op.cit (1995).

71. For a discussion of a common 'Mediterranean Syndrome' as it applied to all of the four countries discussed in this and the following chapter, see Antonio La Spina, and Guiseppe Sciortino, "Common agenda, southern rules: European integration and environment change in the Mediterranean states", Chapter 12 of J.D. Liefferink, P.D. Lowe and A.P.J. Mol (eds), "European Integration and Environmental Policy". These authors explain the tardiness of the Mediterranean countries to produce public goods, such as environmental policy, in terms of cultural factors such as 'amoral familism', and structural constraints such as a "viscous, fragmented, reactive and party dominated legislative process"; see especially at pp.219-222.

72. See Y. Papadopoulos, "Parties, the State and Society in Greece: Continuity Without Change", West European Politics 12(2) 1989, pp.55-71.

73. N. Demertzis, "The Greek Political Culture in the 80s", in "Elections and Parties in the 80s: Evolution and Prospects of the Political System", (Hellenic Political Science Association, Athens, 1990) - published in Greek and cited in N. Demertzis, op.cit (1995), p.206.

74. N. Demertzis, op.cit (1995), pp.197-98.

75. P. Gillman, "A Touch of the Vapours", Sunday Times Magazine, 14 October 1990.

76. Demertzis cites an opinion poll - conducted before the 1990 elections - in which 8 per cent of respondents ranked the environment as their principal concern, compared with total electoral support for the Greens of a mere 0.77 per cent.

77. See P. Nikiforos Diamandouros, "Greek Political Culture in Transition: Historical Origins, Evolution, Current Trends", in Richard Clogg (ed), "Greece in the 1980's" (London, 1983).

78. J. Rosenau,"A pre-theory revisited: world politics in an era of cascading interdependence", International Studies Quarterly 28 1984, pp.245-305.

79. "Survey of Greece - European Prosperity Proves Elusive", Financial Times, 14 November 1994.

80. Y. Papadopoulos, op.cit (1989), at p.63.

81. Ibid, at p.68.

82. Reuters News Service Report, 29 November 1994.

83. The President of Political Spring, Antonis Samaras, claimed that "Today is the beginning of the end of the two old parties", Reuters News Service Report, 13 June 1994.

84. Financial Times, 11.9.96.

85. Ibid, 21/22.9.96.

86. Ibid, 24.9.9٠.

87. Ibid, 16.9.96.

88.   See G. Mavrogordatos, "The Emerging Party System" in R. Clogg (ed), "Greece in the 1980s" (London, 1983); and A. Lijphart (et al), "A Mediterranean Model of Democracy? The Southern European Democracies in Comparative Perspective", West European Politics 11(1) 1988 at pp.10-11.

89.   G. Mavrogordatos, "The Greek Party System: A Case of Limited but Polarized Pluralism?" West European Politics 4(2) 1984 pp.156-169; and P. Nikiforos Diamandouros, "Transition to and Consolidation of, Democratic Politics in Greece 1974-83: A Tentative Assessment", West European Politics 4(2) 1984, pp.50-71.

90.   S. Verney, "Between Coalition and One-Party Government: The Greek Elections of November 1989 and April 1990", West European Politics 13(4) 1990, pp.131-138.

91.   C. Lyrintzis, "Political Parties in Post Junta Greece: A case of "Bureaucratic Clientelism"?" in G. Pridham (ed), op.cit (1984), pp.99-118.

92.   G. Pridham and S. Verney, "The Coalitions of 1988-90 in Greece: Inter-Party Relations and Democratic Consolidation", West European Politics 14(4) 1991, pp.42-69.

93.   K. Featherstone, "The 'Party-State' in Greece and the Fall of Papandreou", West European Politics 13(1) 1990, pp.101-115.

94.   N. Demertzis, op.cit (1995), p.205.

7 The Iberian Verdes

1. Spain

(i) Green roots

The politics of Spain have been as deeply divisive as those of anywhere in Europe. Since the re-establishment of liberal democracy in the late seventies, Spain has exhibited all manner of multiple cleavages which have complicated its political geography during this formative period of socio-economic modernisation. The classic pattern of cleavages which made Spanish politics turbulent throughout the contemporary era, continues to be represented in its recent politics of democratic transition, albeit in a more institutionalised format. Divisions persist between capital and labour, urban and rural interests, and between the metropolitan centre (Madrid) and a periphery of regionalist and sub-national movements. These traditional cleavages are compounded by tensions between reactionary elements nostalgic for an ordered past, and progressives entirely happy with the new democracy; as well as between the Catholic interest opposed by a new secularism. There have been signs of change in the traditional patterns of political partisanship since the re-emergence of democratic politics. The social determinants of political allegiance are less predictable or deeply rooted than they were during the pre-Franco Second Republic. A new generation of better educated, more socially mobile Spaniards appears to embrace some of the cynicism of modern electorates everywhere about ideological politics, and to have taken on some of the instrumental values that make for a greater degree of electoral detachment and even volatility.[1] A recent survey of the sociological foundations of modern Spanish politics suggested that the sheer complexity of these social patterns has made for multiple identities, and thereby ensured a much greater ambivalence about political allegiances. To this extent, "the cleavage structure in Spain is not only labile but multi-dimensional... Not all cleavages smoulder at white heat. Moreover, the electorate is now twice the size it was during the Second Republic. Recognition of sheer complexity has encouraged an incrementalist style among members of the elite... But in Spanish political culture or, more precisely, in the sub-culture of absolutes that some Spaniards still cultivate, the politics of imperfect bargains smacks of the betrayal of a triumphalist destiny".[2]

The experience of rapid social change after the time warp of the Franco era has, nevertheless, coincided with the impact of generational change to accelerate a break with the past. As McDonough and Lopez-Pina have observed: "Age is also a cleavage itself. Young Spaniards are, or claim to be, more progressive than their forebears. Yet they have only vicarious memories of the structural matrix from which traditional ideological antagonisms have arisen in Spain. The 'historic mission' that leaders on both the Left and the Right sometimes recall as their patrimony does not ignite the young with equal passion. And more of the young belong to the middle class than did their predecessors. The structural and organisational bases of combat have been transformed. The liturgy of polarisation hangs on, but its resonance is limited; its social roots have floated free".[3] The prospects for political change are certainly apparent, but it would be facile to exaggerate them. Although the impact of the traditional cleavage patterns that moulded political identities in this fragmented country has softened over time, with many younger Spaniards adopting a less ideologically dogmatic and a more open minded approach to politics, the break with 'the past' has not been - and never is in complex societies - entirely clean or complete. A troubled past continues to shape the political outlooks and loyalties of many Spaniards of whatever generation. The prevailing patterns of party identification are rooted, however tenuously, in a bipartisanship between left and right - with an overlay of cultural regionalism which predates the new era of democracy.[4]

These legacies are reflected in party preferences, with even young voters recruited to partisan loyalties that transcend the generations - ensuring a pattern of alignments that seemingly leaves little scope for a new politics cleavage.

In these circumstances, advocates of alternative or new issue politics have found it difficult, though not impossible, to establish a niche in contemporary Spanish politics. Politics - and therefore government - continues to be dominated by the agendas of the 'old' politics of productionism and materialism and, not least, the enduring struggle to distribute its 'spoils' and benefices amongst the respective claimants. The dash for growth that has preoccupied all recent governments, regardless of political colour, is more than an economic stratagem. It underpins a massive cultural shift that has challenged and replaced traditional values and mores for an increasing number of voters. For in Recio's view, "industrial growth nourishes a culture of modernisation which trusts in the limitless possibilities of technology to grant sustained material expansion: Northern Europe is seen as a model to be emulated. This is true for all social groups, but particularly for the new middle class sectors born from this very process".[5] Industrialisation was accelerated in the 1960s under the Francoist regime, in order to generate high per capita income as a bribe to prop up the dictatorship. It was continued by the first democratic governments as a means of legitimising and consolidating a fragile regime. More recently, as democratic legitimacy became firmly rooted, industrialisation and all that ensues from it in terms of employment prospects, increases in per capita income and improved consumption, has become quite simply the epitome of everything that a modernised society stands for.[6] In these circumstances, concern for post-materialist or environmental concern figures as a very low priority, either with political elites or the electorate at large.

There have been some discouraging signs in this situation for those who took an entirely different view of this equation of progress with production. The first parliamentary debate to address the environmental costs of economic development was only staged in December 1992, and even then it only attracted some forty deputies. Even after the government began to acknowledge the issue and to implement some environmental legislation - partly in anticipation, and as a consequence, of Spain's membership of the EC - the lack of any serious enforcement by the authorities called even this notional intent into doubt. Nor was there any notable grassroots pressure - as there had been from extra-parliamentary and grass roots campaigners in defence of the environment elsewhere on the continent. The new middle class and radical youth constituencies, in so far as they existed here, were otherwise engaged in different causes. The consolidation of democracy and the race to 'catch up' took priority over utopian or ethereal causes. While there has been some concern expressed about the impact of accelerated development, this has by no means tapped into a wider movement for a new politics or alternative lifestyles that has buoyed up Green movements elsewhere. At best, concern for amenity or habitat remains modest and equivocal. Survey evidence indicates a persistent ambivalence about this issue. On the one hand, general concern about environmental deterioration does register in the polling data. But this is belied by a lack of support for, or involvement in, green movements at every level of society. A survey conducted in 1992, for instance, revealed that only 27.7 per cent of respondents rated 'the environment' as a national priority - with a mere 8.1 per cent ranking the issue in first place. The issue increased its salience for respondents, however, as a matter of global importance - with some 42 per cent identifying it in these terms. A kind of convenient transference, or shifting of blame, appears to be at work here. For this scant response mirrors a mindset that is typical of societies undergoing rapid development. According to the 'free rider' mentality that pertains in such circumstances, the right to catch up more than excuses the pollution caused. Whereas other societies who started earlier and are more advanced are perceived as the real culprits anyway. In short, according to this logic, pollution is principally the fault of the world's main industrial powers - a convenient historical demarcation between the 'real' perpetrators and their victims, which thereby avoids taking any responsibility for a problem that largely originates beyond the national boundaries. This poll provided some evidence that something akin to moral abdication does prominently figure in the Spanish outlook on the problems facing the 'global commons'. Environmental depredation was identified here as the serious climatic changes - ozone depletion and so on - that have been wrought by the early industrialisation of 'others'. Domestic 'pollution', on the other hand - depleted rivers, car emissions, waste disposal - were largely discounted as a matter for serious concern. The closer the issue came to home, the greater the reluctance of respondents to acknowledge it as a matter they should take responsibility for.

The attitudes of younger respondents on these questions were not markedly different from those of older cohorts; a general 'awareness' of the issue (measured at some 80 per cent) contrasted again in this group with a widespread reluctance to change behaviour on ecological grounds.[7] A study of voting intentions in the 1993 general election confirms that the young here are by no means as amenable as they are elsewhere to radical politics in any form, let alone to ecologism. The findings of this survey confirmed a propensity amongst younger voters to support the right wing Popular Party, rather than the leftist PSOE or United Left. The evidence suggests that the younger generation of voters is far from being receptive to a new politics and remains, by and large, wedded to the post-Francoist materialism. Previous generations, meanwhile, continue to be influenced by their own formative ideological influences of the civil war and its aftermath. These sociological factors conspire to prevent the rise of a new post-materialist cleavage. The pursuit of economic security remains an attractive prospect across the generations, in a country which under fascism had remained out of the European mainstream of development. For similar reasons, the desire for political stability reinforces the hold of the mainstream parties over the electorate.[8] There is little political space left for ecologism, or any other variant of new politics, to colonise. Green politics has flourished best in societies that are secure in their democratic traditions and prosperous enough for young and middle class voters to consider alternative or post-materialist agenda. None of these preconditions apply to Spain: or at least not sufficiently to make any real difference to Green prospects. Green politics also requires a level of political development that has yet to evolve in this new democracy. It responds best to a highly developed pluralism that encourages widespread participation rather than the sort of narrow clientelist politics that exists in contemporary Spain, where the sense of civic orientation fosters only limited participation in secondary associations outside the family or other primary networks.[9]

In spite of these considerable handicaps, groups with an interest in various aspects of ecologism did begin to show even before Franco's demise. These green movements have continued to maintain a limited presence during the politics of democratic transition; unlike the greens in eastern Germany, not as a distinctly radical component in a wider movement for political change, but with the altogether more modest aspiration of plugging the limited issue space left vacant by the major parties. During the Dictatorship, environmentalists, for the most part consisting of biologists and other scientists, formed in 1969 ANAN (Amigos de la Naturaleza de Navarra (Navarre Friends of Nature) - a movement dedicated to environmental protection that was barely political. ANAN concentrated on conservation matters, including the protection of the natural habitats of rare species.[10] In spite of limited membership and low political salience, the number of green groups had expanded by the mid eighties to over 300. The Green movement here covered the usual diversity of purpose and endeavours to be found amongst ecologists everywhere: from nature protection lobbies of conservative demeanour - such as the Spanish Association for Planning of Land and Environment (AEORMA), which was allowed to exist during the Franco era - through to the further reaches of radical ecologism of both a dark green and red-green persuasion. As the political climate improved, 'mere' environmentalism began to evolve into a more overtly political ecologism, and attracted in turn all manner of anarchists and independent minded militants, who saw in the movement a genuinely radical alternative to the somewhat tamed and staid 'old' left Socialist Party.[11] These autonomists and utopians shared an anti-industrial vision that romanticised 'nature'. It was, nevertheless, a visionary ideal that had little appeal, let alone any political purchase, beyond its radical constituency. This was, in essence, a reactive or instinctive politics, ill-suited to the bargains or accommodations of the conventional political game. Moreover, it represented a view of Green politics much closer to the fundamentalist than the realist tradition of ecologism.

As such, it substituted emotive slogans and single issue protests for a comprehensive political programme. The 'Bases de Daimiel', a loosely connected 'wish list' of favourite causes, agreed at an early 'national' meeting of interested groups held in 1978, was typical of this unfocused approach. This manifesto included a commitment to the autonomy of communities, criticism of capitalism and male patriarchy, third world solidarity, and many other noble but essentially vacuous and non specific generalities. They amounted, as such, to radical gesture politics, rather than a cogent and politically plausible programme. This 'programme' of radical discontents was certainly not the basis for an organised national movement, even as that political option was considered by various Green groups during the 1980s. Other Green activists - radical by disposition but aware of the minimum requirements of discipline for effective politics - began to confront these issues. A more refined version of political ecologism, framed in terms of a red-green or leftist discourse that was re-emerging at this time, appeared in the journal 'Mientras Tanto', started in 1979 by the radical philosopher M. Sacristan as a forum for the exchange of radical ideas and the development of critical theory. The debate gathered pace in other radical journals such as 'Ecologia Politica'.[12]

There was a general commitment here to the idea that ecologism belonged as an integral theme of a critical discourse. At the same time, there was by no means any consensus about how the movement should engage in politics. Many of the Green groups that began to be involved in politics, but by no means all of them, preferred a loose network arrangement rather than submerging their distinctive identity in a formal, disciplined and highly structured organisational party format. There was more to this resistance than an anti-party disposition. The cellular model had been a requirement of political survival - a 'safe' form of political organisation for opposition groups - during the dictatorship, when, as Recio points out "active grassroots activity was valued and bureaucratic structures mistrusted", and indeed threatened danger to those involved with them.[13] This instinctive mistrust was carried over to the democratic transition, and it presented a real obstacle to the national coordination necessary to put the Greens on the national political map. The particular appeal of this cellar factionalism under the conditions of political repression are precisely, as Recio notes, "its weakness in the mass politics of modern liberal democracy".[14] There were other centrifugal legacies in the 'Spanish labyrinth' that compounded the problem of Green political organisation. The usual ideological tensions between pure ecology and all manner of left alternativists, were further exacerbated by entrenched regional differences. These territorial rifts encouraged the emergence of distinctly regional Green movements, each with their own local priorities.[15] In the Basque country, for example, local ecologists were particularly exercised by the campaign to have the nuclear reactors at Lemonitz shut down - and by the protest against the Leitzaran motorway. In Castilla-La Mancha the principal issue was the opposition - successful in the end - to installing a European firing range at Cabaneros, instead of its preferred use as a nature reserve. Greens in Castilla y Leon had less success trying to block the Riana dam project, and in Andalusia the regional ecologists devoted their energies to preserving the Coto de la Donana National Park. All Green movements have to start somewhere. And while there is no inconsistency as such between waging energetic local campaigns, and harnessing the momentum and experience garnered here behind an effective national movement, under Spanish conditions localism was a symptom of a cultural instinct - an abiding resistance amongst many of the alternativists attracted to these movements to the very idea of conventional party politics with its snares and corruptions laid to ambush unwary radicals. There was also, amongst these Green pioneers, a deep-seated antagonism to a 'hegemonic' nation state. In the view of one such activist, Jordi Bigas, "the (Spanish) ecologist movement has rejected the arena of the state as a valid framework for the self determination of the peoples subjected to the nationalism of the Spanish state".[16]

The Spanish Green movement was by no means monopolised by activists with either red-green, regionalist or fundamentalist preferences. The picture was further complicated by the existence of altogether more formal organisations, usually involved with conservationist matters. These practised a more structured but less militant politics. They had properly constituted rules of membership, were financed by subscriptions, published group newsletters and conducted their affairs according to the conventional procedures of the lobbyist and consultancy groups they essentially were. The most important organisation here was the Coordinadora de Organizaciones de Defensa Ambiental (Coordinating Committee for Organizations for Environmental Defence - CODA). The groundwork for this type of focused lobbying had been initially laid, however, by the Coordinadora para la Defensa de las Aves (Coordinating Committee for the Protection of Birds). The Spanish arm of Greenpeace tried to bridge the gulf between the conventional lobbying activities of these moderate conservationists and the overtly political aspirations of more radical groups. The need to synthesise both types of activity became more urgent during the 1970s with the government's adoption of a nuclear energy programme to meet the country's rapidly rising energy needs, as it embarked on industrial development at a time of hugely inflated oil prices. The important symbolism of the anti-nuclear issue for launching a viable national Green politics can be seen from its conspicuous role in those other places where the emergence of Green parties was sparked by the nuclear catalyst. The nuclear issue was, however, a test which the Spanish Green movement failed. The government's nuclear programme certainly had the potential to be the catalyst for the 'take off' of Green politics it became in many other European polities. A large majority of public opinion consistently opposed the nuclear energy option, which indicated the potential to politicise a much broader constituency on the left in favour of Green ideas than the conservationists, who had dominated the ecology movement, had so far managed. In spite of this public support for the anti-nuclear cause, the Green movement failed - unlike their colleagues in France or Sweden - either to get the three existing nuclear power plants closed, or to prevent the government from building five more. This defeat was a turning point of sorts, although by no means the only reason for the Greens' future shortcomings. Thereafter, much of the radical political energy drained away from the Green movement, and relocated itself within both the peace and new left movements.

Divided against themselves, the Greens made an easy target for their opponents in mainstream politics to present ecologism as "the 'enemy of the good life'".[17] It became more difficult in these circumstances for the Greens to break out of their isolation, and to mobilise on any other than a local basis. After the initial euphoria and relief that accompanied the reinstatement of democracy, many citizens withdrew into a privatised world, with aspirations limited to individual or familial advancement, and more often than not couched in terms of conspicuous consumption. This cultural resistance to new politics issues is only part of the story of Green political impotence. After all, the other parties had to cope with the same limitations and managed, albeit with better political resources at their disposal and from a more promising starting point to build political support bases. A large part of the problem for the Spanish Greens lay in the diffuse and fragmented nature of a movement caught between single issue and localised campaigning on one side, and anarchistic and autonomist groups, ill disposed to the necessary disciplines of party politics, on the other. These problems haunted the movement from the outset, and they have persisted, in spite of efforts throughout the 1980s to draw the disparate regional groups into an overarching national federation, in an attempt to rationalise the movement and thereby to increase its national leverage. The Spanish 'Green Pages' directory continues to list over 700 green, ecologist or environmental campaign groups; from conservationist, animal rights and naturalists, to those concerned with deep ecology.[18] Similar variety exists everywhere - and this in one sense is a sign of a flourishing movement. In the Spanish context, however, this inclination to separatism and insularity is a clear reaction to the particular legacies of national history and political culture discussed above. The principal instinct of these groups is to look inwards rather than to build outwards and upwards - to disaggregate rather than to connect. In a society where ecologism is already heavily discounted for reasons of political culture and political economy, this introversion merely handicaps the Green movement more than it needs to be.[19]   National organisations such as the Coordinadora Assembliearia Movimento Ecologista (CAME), the Coordinadora Estatel Anti-nuclear (CEAN) and the Coordinadora de Organizaciones para la Defensa Ambietal (CODA),[20] were early attempts at providing national coordinating mechanisms.   But these, apart perhaps for CODA, whose coordinating office enjoyed some executive independence, were essentially loosely structured arrangements that facilitated a useful exchange of information and experience, rather than providing an effective means for focusing green pressure on the policy making elites.   The coexistence of several of these competing or at least overlapping 'national' bodies, merely deepened the tensions between 'moderate' conservationists and 'deep' ecologists within the Spanish Green movement, and encouraged the respective factions to resist what they saw as a 'take over' by rival organisations.[21] The international ecology movement, led by Greenpeace-Spain (founded in 1983), Adena (the World Wildlife Fund, 1984) and Friends of the Earth (1979), have recently tried to coax these disparate groups - particularly the pacifist, anti-nuclear and some conservationist groups at the far ends of the green spectrum to work more closely together, in order to maximise their political impact. Regionalist rivalries   and ideological tensions continue, however, to fragment the movement and dilute the effect of political ecology at the national level.

The Greens can certainly be indicted for contributing to their own difficulties. As Recio sees it, "the movement itself must shoulder part of the blame" for its own failure to mark out a viable space for itself in Spanish politics. An obsession with organisational and political splintering has impeded the movement's growth and dulled its political cutting edge. The resistance to working together, as well as the fact of an even greater antipathy to looking for allies further afield on the traditional left, has limited the Green movement's scope for attracting an audience amongst those sectors of society whose receptiveness to new ideas and a tradition of activism makes them prospective allies.[22] Recio is particularly critical of the Greens' reticence about building political networks, especially with a well mobilised peace movement whose myriad connections with an active tradition of left wing militancy that enjoys useful connections to at all levels of society, could bring the Greens the sort of political dividends recently experienced by the Italian ecologists. This culpability is, however, mitigated in some measure, by the special circumstances of the national political culture as well as by recent experience.

(ii)   Party formation

Resistance to effective networking goes back to the earliest initiatives to build a viable Green party in Spain. The fate of these initial attempts to address this organisational deficit provided a telling diagnosis of the extent of the problem, rather than any ready cure for the endemic disease of factionalism. The Green Alternative (Alternativa Verde, established in Catalonia in 1983, was an unlikely, because regionally focused, attempt to synthesize both ecologism and Catalan nationalism. This regionalist ethos was equally apparent in parallel attempts to merge local groups into a national Green Federation. An initiative to this end was eventually launched, in May 1983 - and then almost incidentally, with external encouragement from prominent German Greens such as Petra Kelly and Lukas Beckmann. The intention was to coalesce the disparate ecological groups into a national organisation capable of giving the movement some national profile.   The opportunity came at an Ecological Film Festival in Tenerife. A manifesto was issued - the

Manifesto de Tenerife - endorsed by many of the Green groups present. Even this manifesto amounted to little more than a statement of broad intent which committed the signatories to merely set up a provisional commission to discuss the prospects for a Green party. The momentum begun at Tenerife carried over, in December 1983, to a congress attended by some 50 or so local Green groups, which finally agreed to call the first national convention of a Green party - Los Verdes - at Malaga in June 1984; before dispersing to canvass the idea, but just as surely, to reinforce the elemental idea of a 'bottom up', loosely organised party of local groups that was never intended, even by its strongest advocates, to amount to anything more than a federal arrangement.

The Malaga conference did, however, get as far as endorsing a decision to formally register Los Verdes as a party under Spanish constitutional law. The sheer variety of groups represented in the Spanish Green movement, to say nothing of their divergent ideological preferences, determined this minimalist model and the adoption of a federalist structure. The Federation's principal organisational focus was as little more than a round table of representatives drawn from the local organisations and electoral lists. Although the Federation was formally set up in October 1984, considerable ambivalence remained about reconciling such diverse tendencies under a common political umbrella. There were doubts, too, about the chances of a Green party exerting any real influence on a polity dominated by entrenched interests, and whose patterns of partisanship were shaped by existing social cleavages. Deliberations continued along these lines, and it was not until the inaugural congress of the party, held at Cardedeu outside Barcelona in February 1985, that the Federation's statutes and programme were finally endorsed.

The absence of any effective sense of national coherence in the movement was revealed almost immediately. A minority of alternative, radical and pure ecologist groups rejected the compromise negotiated at Malaga and formally instituted at Cardedeu. They did so, in spite of the limited constraints imposed on local party groups by the federal format - which amounted to little more than conforming to the minimum requirements of the Spanish Constitution for the formal registration of any political party. These disputes continued to belie the very idea of a truly national party. In the 1986 national elections, for instance, three entirely separate Green lists stood on the ballot. Los Verdes' efforts to represent ecologism was challenged by an Alternative Verde List - originally a Catalan faction which split from Los Verdes over organisational and personality differences - as well as by a right wing group, Vertice Espanol de Revivindicacion del Desarrollo Ecologico (VERDE) - the Spanish Vertex for the Reclaiming of Ecological Development. The electoral consequences of these divisions for Los Verdes prospects were underlined by the party's inability to contest more than 52 constituencies, from which they polled a paltry 89,000 votes. This propensity for excessive fragmentation was further exhibited when a faction of Alternative Verde, linked with another local group centred on Madrid, (Los Assemblea Verde de Madrid), formed yet another Green fraction - Los Verdes Alternativos. The Alternativos subsequently transformed themselves, in 1986, into a Confederacion de los Verdes. These divisions were less a reflection of deep-seated ideological divisions than they were of a culture of oppositionalism for its own sake, compounded by excessive personal egotism. Many of these splinter groups revolved around the political ambitions of one of Spain's most prominent ecologists, Santiago Vilanove I Tane, who was determined to resist what he claimed was a drift in Los Verdes towards the hierarchism of conventional party politics contrary to the decentralised model negotiated in Tenerife.

(iii)   Political developments

The intensity of these divisions, which far exceeded what might have been expected from otherwise quite modest differences over ideology, says much about the weakness of Green politics in a political culture still dominated by traditional norms and materialist preferences. Limited prospects for impacting on national politics tend to increase frustration and turn it inwards, and to divert political energy into factional squabbles. These difficulties are unlikely, as things currently stand, to be easily resolved. There are other structural factors, too, which mitigate against the sort of political discipline and aptitude for compromise, necessary if minor parties are to maximise their electoral opportunities. The electoral system has hardly been conducive to the efforts of niche parties with a narrow constituency to win the levels of representation that might persuade their members of the advantages of playing the 'normal' game of politics. The Spanish electoral system was designed during the transition to democracy, precisely to encourage political stability. The principal concern here was to accommodate large, mainstream parties - initially the Union of the Democratic Centre - and to maintain its hold on power. The Socialist Party (Partido Socialista Obrero Espanol (PSOE) which subsequently took over this mantle as the dominant system party, and which has won frequently and usually convincingly under this system, felt little inclination to change it. The main obstacle to the representation of small parties is a 5 per cent threshold for local or municipal seats. The same barrier applies for elections to the autonomous regional parliaments. In addition, a three per cent barrier - a formidable hurdle for small, regionally dispersed parties such as Los Verdes - operates for entry into the national parliament, the *Cortes Generales*.

The daunting combination of an unfavourable opportunity structure and persistent factionalism ensured that the Greens' impact on national politics would be limited indeed. Not that the Greens have helped their own cause. The various Green political organisations all stood competing lists at the 1989 European elections. Even a combination of their respective vote tallies (2.8 per cent) - with Los Verdes winning 1.1 per cent (164,577); the Ecological greens (161,933) 1.0 per cent, VERDE (58,697) 0.4 per cent and the Green Alternative (47,250) 0.3 per cent - would not have yielded a single seat at Strasbourg. These divisions were carried over into the campaign for the national elections in 1989, and led to bitter acrimony and a lively trade in insults. Not surprisingly, the 3 per cent outcome which resulted from their combined efforts failed to secure even one seat for any Green list. Nor were there any signs that the lessons of continuing division had been learned. The Green List spokesman, Luis Hidalgo, in his campaign postmortem, justified his List's unilatralism in the adversarial language of a turf war - that the principal objective of the campaign had been "to show their distinction from other Greens". The leader of the Green Ecologists, Felix Herrara, displayed a similar sectarianism with his claim that "we are the real Greens. The others are false ecologists". This narrow vision of politics as an ideological crusade against heresy, is wholly inappropriate for the practice of effective politics in any liberal democratic milieu. It was even less rational in the sociological context of Spanish politics - rooted as it is in a social system where a pre-civic political culture requires that political participation, if it is to be at all effective, should be channelled through formal political organisation rather than dissipated in intensely competitive networks of the same party family. The resultant factionalism was bound to weaken a movement already handicapped by the prevailing values and policy preferences of the electorate. It could only further marginalise the Greens on the remote fringes of national politics.

The impact of these squabbles between the contending Green groups wrought damage within the movement itself. They merely served to intensify the differences within what was still a tenuous Green Federation. It was only in 1991 - some seven years after its formal launch as a 'truly' national party - that Los Verdes, at their fourth national congress, could agree their first coherent national programme, and were finally able to stand candidates in every region (*comunidades autonomas*) of the country. The onset of a degree of coherence within the main Green group, by no means ensured the end of factionalism within Los Verdes, let alone any accommodation with the wider Green movement. Indeed, the prospect of Los Verdes operating as a truly national party merely served to intensify the resistance of some grass roots members to what they saw as an 'unhealthy obsession' with electoralism, and reinforced the opposition to Los Verdes' 'hegemony' by Green groups outside the Federation. The consequences of putting these arcane divisions before the common goal of creating a single national party were apparent from the results of successive elections. None of the Green groups managed to corner even one per cent of the national vote in any of the six general elections held between 1977 and 1993, in spite of a modest incremental increase in the total "Green vote" - from 31,909 (0.16 per cent) in 1986; 153,514 (0.79 per cent) in 1989; to 218,108 (1.36 per cent) in 1993. The Greens' best results by far, have been achieved in second order elections. In the 1989 European election, faction divisions again prevented any Green group from winning a seat, although a minor leftist party (Izquierda de los Pueblos) did win a seat in Strasbourg, and chose to sit there with the Green fraction. In the 1991 municipal elections, a Green councillor was elected for Rivas Vaciamadrid in the Madrid region, and six other Greens were elected elsewhere.[23]

The negative impact of these continuing divisions did, eventually, bring the Greens to their political senses. After nine years of election defeats at every level, they prepared to re-open the question of Green cooperation. In anticipation of the forthcoming national elections later in the year, a unification congress was held in March 1993, albeit without any positive outcome. To some extent, the movement is the victim of a political situation that provides little incentive to adopt a rational approach to factionalism. A post-materialist movement marooned in a society obsessed with economic growth and the politics of materialism is hardly likely to impact on events, however sensibly it behaves. At the same time, the movement's continuing divisions ensure that political impotence is assured, and this factionalism undoubtedly alienates potential radical voters who must look elsewhere for a political vehicle to represent new politics issues. There is a small if growing market for such issues in a rapidly modernising society The political naivity of a movement out of touch with these radical undercurrents in contemporary Spain was aptly illustrated during its founding congress. With more critical and socially relevant issues to address, the new party confirmed the prejudices of its establishment critics and prospective supporters alike by agreeing to abolish the national sport of bullfighting![24]

Political change is by no means an entirely remote prospect in modern Spain, but the Greens remain too far out of touch with the moods and anxieties that feed it to contribute much to the radical momentum. As the Greens turned in on themselves, the radical space in a society experiencing a rapid modernisation that raised all sorts of anxieties and discontents was yielded too readily to other parties. When the Socialist Party (PSOE) took power in 1982 with a working majority, there was a sudden explosion of, mostly unrealistic, expectations. The PSOE, drawing on the prestige it had gained as a consistent opponent of the Falangist dictatorship, and promising to deliver sweeping reforms in a country thirsting for economic development and cultural renewal, became the principal vehicle for every type of progressive aspiration. The PSOE became a ready magnet for a coalition of labourist, social democratic and new left groups. For the time being, other radical groups were marginalized and the PSOE's untarnished radical appeal contributed to the peripheral status of political ecology. The PSOE, fashioned by classical *ouvrièrist* principles that embraced the industrial paradigm, was never enthusiastic about ecologism. Some Greens, unattracted by the prospects of working with the Communist Party and disconcerted by the failure to launch an effective national Green party, had tried to make overtures to the PSOE - but with little by way of an enthusiastic response in return. The state of the environment remained of limited concern to the PSOE - a matter of interest to some middle class sensibilities, but expendable in the pursuit of economic growth at almost any cost.[25] The PSOE was cast in a different radical mould entirely. It was a party led, for the most part, by young, energetic modernisers, committed to creating employment in order to please its trade union affiliates, to attract inward investment, and thereby to further its main project of catching up with northern Europe's most developed economies. Nothing much has changed in this regard over recent years. Nor is it likely to, even though the PSOE now finds itself back in opposition. As things stand, there seems little chance of the PSOE embarking on a green direction. The party has been consistently wedded to a growth agenda through European integration. It sees its political future through the clear lens of conventional social democratic politics - a mix of economic justice for its key urban and rural constituencies, tempered now by the fiscal disciplines required to remain as part of the European mainstream by joining EMU at the earliest opportunity. This chasm of ideology between the left and the Greens continues to be matched by one, just as wide, over political sensibilities. As a consequence, the PSOE has little in common with the ecology constituency. It regards the Greens as ideological utopians whose occasional direct action campaigns against the authorities challenge public order, and even threaten to undermine properly constituted democratic procedures. Bigas reports some telling evidence of this immense lacuna in political empathy between Spain's red and green politics. The PSOE's first meeting to review the options for the environment, "devoted a good part of its time to devising a 'black list' of ecologist groups to be excluded from all government grants. On many occasions ecologists have been criminalised, repressed or come under surveillance." The ecologists in Valencia - the Accio Ecologista-Agro, a reputable and locally well supported campaigning group - were ludicrously accused by a prominent PSOE spokesman of being "involved in politics".[26] This is hardly the stuff of serious or sympathetic discourse, let alone of political reconciliation. If the Greens do decide to take the parliamentary route more seriously than they have done so far, they will need to find political allies far more receptive to their ideals than the mainstream left currently is.

Other developments on the left have further undermined the Greens' tenuous place in the politics of democratic transition. The translation of the Spanish Communist Party (PCE) into a Euro-Communist party open to progressive alliances or 'historic compromises' with former ideological enemies - on the alternative left and amongst what old style Leninists would have disparaged as 'bourgeois progressives' or mere utopians - eventually culminated in an energetic leftist politics; and the emergence of a radical coalition of parties and groupuscles that filled the new politics space Los Verdes and its Green rivals have been unable to make up their minds to occupy. The PCE had already begun to bid for the support of radical ecologists disaffected by the Greens' endemic factionalism. The PCE worked hard to connect with green socialists disconcerted by both the PSOE's disinterest in environmentalism and deterred by Los Verdes' half hearted commitment to a radical social programme. Tentative political links were forged here between pacifists, radical ecologists and the 'hard left'. After all, these groups had worked together in the 'no' camp during the national referendum on NATO membership in 1986. The refreshing experience of cooperating in a common cause that overcame ideological differences and produced some political dividends stood in marked contrast to the Greens' own deepseated divisions. These links were eventually and formally cemented in 1989, as part of the Spanish 'hard lefts' response to the final implosion of Communism. The United Left Coalition (Izquierda Unida - IU) showed just how far the Greens had squandered a real opportunity to represent an alternative agenda. Successes in local, regional and national elections made the IU the country's third political force. This was achieved by campaigning on a progressive agenda that included green issues. This development, in turn, has denied Los Verdes support (both from activists and voters) it can ill afford to lose. It also points to their own shortcomings in the arts of practical radical politics.

The choices facing Los Verdes may well be similar to those which have confronted the Italian Greens in very similar political circumstances - that is, with a small post-materialist constituency to call on and with alternative radical groups competing for the same electoral territory. Los Verdes, like their Italian counterparts, have the negative option of continuing to stand aloof from these political realignments, with little expectation that they can in the circumstances corner their share of the new politics constituency, let alone win it over completely. On the other hand, the party might - as the Italian Greens have done - face the severe constraints of its situation and throw in its lot, not only with other Green groups, but also forge a broader radical alliance with parties that presently deny it any real share of or access to the radical constituency. This suggests a degree of realism the Spanish Greens have yet to bring to their own affairs, let alone to their relations with other parties. Such a strategy would require them to engage in a degree of political brokering they have so far been hostile to. The portents are not particularly encouraging for the prospect of the Greens linking up with a new radical third force, and thus to speak for ecologism within its ranks. The continuing resistance to ideological compromise is a very real obstacle here, given Los Verdes' prevailing commitment to dark green rather than red-green ideas. But the Greens have little choice in the long or even the medium term. Los Verdes have much greater need of the IU than the hard left have of them. Nor will these potential allies come to them as supplicants. A radical realignment cast in this mould will not be readily welcomed by IU activists, suspicious as they are of the motives of 'bourgeois idealists'. Any realignment here would also require concessions on both sides that are unlikely to come about with any ease. The Greens will have to exhibit a much greater political humility than their track record so far indicates. The IU, for its part, would also have to alter its political tune to encourage the Greens to countenance such an approach: not least, to temper some of its 'hard left' rhetoric. The presence of ecologists in the IU, even if they are of a red-green disposition, might facilitate the reconciliation for both sides, although on past evidence it by no means ensures it. As things stand, then, a realignment on these terms is improbable but by no means entirely out of the question. For the Greens, above all, it requires a degree of realism and political courage that has so far eluded them.

(iv)   Prospects for political change

The 1993 election underlined just how peripheral ecologism is in contemporary Spanish politics. The issue hardly registered on the intense left-right battle. Nor was it raised in any of the televised debates conducted between the leading politicians. The campaign was dominated instead by the 'old' politics agenda - the impending economic crisis, and the aptitude of the PSOE and especially its leader and Prime Minister, Felipe González, to deal with a host of national crises and party scandals. The Green Federation, for its part set itself the modest goal of securing a toehold in national politics, by winning a seat in the Lower Chamber - an 'honour' allotted to Francisco Garrido who headed the Federation's list in Madrid. With a total national vote of 125,855 (0.78 per cent) the Greens failed to achieve even that modest goal, and finally began to resolve some of the deep ambivalence about playing at 'normal' politics. They even began to adjust to an altogether unpromising political milieu, by tentatively reopening channels to the old left. There was even talk of building bridges to the PSOE via contacts with the United Left (IU), a party that was altogether more receptive to ecological issues. The Greens based this strategy on an assumption that the dominant left party was badly wounded - a legacy of economic mismanagement, internal strife, corruption and a general loss of faith in González. The Green pragmatists took the view that this reduction in electoral support and the prospect of defeat would oblige the PSOE to seek political allies. This, too, proved to be a miscalculation and, as things turned out, the putative broad-based radical coalition failed to materialise. González preferred instead to consolidate his tenuous hold on power by reaching an agreement with the regionalist parties (the CIU in Catalonia and the PNV in the Basque country). Even if the Socialists had been inclined to look further left for allies, it is hard to imagine what leverage the Greens - without any national representation in the Chamber of Deputies - could expect to have over this well-organised and widely supported governing party.

The Greens' cause was also weakened by the Federation's lack of resources. They have been unable over the duration to raise sufficient monies to begin to compete in the expensive and technologically sophisticated marketing of political ideas that has become the norm for modern electioneering. In spite of a conservative estimate by one close observer of these affairs, that some 15 million pesetas "would be the minimum required to reach the electorate", the Greens spent barely 5 million pesetas - a sum raised, not from the wealthy corporate interests that bankroll the mainstream parties, but collected from their own small membership and support base.[27] Just as debilitating has been the continuing failure of the national party to absorb all of those groups that continue to insist on standing local lists under the ecological banner. The official Greens had only a very limited success here, in that they successfully resisted the claim of a dubious sect, La Communidad de Silo - with a reputation for nefarious financial practices, and which received support from the PSOE controlled Ministry of the Interior to establish itself as a legal presence in order to divide the Green vote - to usurp the 'official' Green label; only to find that a group standing as 'Los Ecologistas' (the Ecologists), attracted enough votes (68,851) to cut into the Greens' own national tally. Los Verdes continue to share the very limited political space for ecologism with other regional Green factions who continue to resist all approaches to throw in their lot with the Federation. Los Verdes did manage to bring together some nineteen separate groups under a common banner, but three eco-pacifist Basque groups chose to opt only for observer status in the party, and the Catalan Greens refused to adopt even that semi-detached status. This is a degree of factionalism that the Greens can ill afford. In the 1993 general election, for instance, Los Verdes de Andalusia polled a modest 23,372 votes on their own account - a cache of votes that would have been more usefully weighed if they had been recorded for the national Verde list. The problem of factionalism carries over into the Federation itself. Ideological tensions have by no means been stilled by this nominal 'unification'. The 'realo'-'fundi' divide continues to distract the party from the daunting task of consolidating an effective Green presence in national politics.

This is, of course, a familiar pattern elsewhere in Europe. The Spanish Greens, even with their particular disadvantages, may yet be following, albeit at a pace dictated by the exigencies of their situation, a path to political realism trodden, sooner or later, by most Green parties with a serious political intent. The process of radical party politics does tend to start everywhere with discordant movements engaged in disparate single issue campaigns. There is no guarantee, however, that this will lead to eventual coalescence upwards. On the contrary, in Spain single issue movements may have emerged as "the byproduct of burning ecological issues",[28] but they tend to dissipate when the issue that gave rise to them is resolved or otherwise runs out of steam. For instance, Green councillors were elected in Riano after a local valley was threatened by government plans to erect a dam there. The Greens have also been active in the debate over the proposed national park at Covadonga in Cantabrica, which threatened to put intolerable strains on the local environment. They have been prominent, too, in the debate over water shortages in the Mediterranean coastal regions, and the subsequent diversion of that increasingly scarce resource from central Spain in 1994.[29] The water issue certainly holds some potential for the Greens, but only if they have the political will to capitalise on it. On the face of it, the issue is more a matter of supply, of the quantity of the resource, than it is one of ecological concern over its quality. Nevertheless, this is precisely the sort of resource issue that provides Green politics with a distinctive and salient agenda. To connect with public concern - and even the self interest that underlies it - has, after all, been the source of much effective political leverage and radical momentum. The recent drought - the longest for a century, and made worse by a growing demand - ensured that this issue has become a central concern on the contemporary national agenda. The continent's changing climatic pattern will raise the profile of this issue even higher in the scale of national priorities - especially if recent predictions by scientists of future desertification come to pass. Providing water in sufficient quantities is bound to have important environmental implications. The National Hydrological Plan, devised for this very purpose and which envisaged massive infrastructural developments over some two decades, failed to pass through Parliament. It has now been revised as a matter of national priority.[30] The Greens cannot fail to enhance their political profile - whatever is decided in the details of this Plan - as this proposal finds its place on the new and subsequent governments' legislative agendas. But its impact and their leverage on events will be that much greater if they can settle the persistent divisions in their ranks which continue to diminish their political competence and weakens their moral claim to speak for 'the future'.

So far none of these modest local successes have facilitated the next stage in Green political development - the coalescence of single issue and community based campaigns, capable on their own, of little more than briefly raising local awareness of ecological threats into a national political movement capable of registering a sizeable vote and impressing on the national policy agenda. If the Green Federation is to occupy a viable place in Spanish politics, it must somehow break out from single issue politics, and at least challenge the IU for the Green space on the map of progressive politics. The best opportunity here for the Greens to share a platform with the broad left, and to find a receptive ear with public opinion per se, lies in their hostility to present EU arrangements, and particularly the burdens for ordinary Spaniards, in contrast to the promised benefits of integration in a regional Community that favours the large northern European multinationals and the Brussels technocracy, at the expense of the poorer members on the periphery. The Greens also subscribe to the left's critique of the EU's autarchic commercial policy. There is the promise of common ideological ground in their view that regional economic growth has been at the expense of the world's poor - that it has inflicted damage on a balanced ecological and global development, and particularly on Spain's north African hinterland in the Mahgreb. Ramon Fernandez, a Green spokesman for the grassroots campaign launched in 1995 - at the time of Spanish Presidency of the EU's Council of Ministers - stated the movement's aim was to fight this centralisation of power.[31]

These are, then, real points of contact with potential political allies, yet there is less mileage in them than Green realists would prefer. The current issue agenda, dominated as it is by the traditional if modified left-right and regional-centre cleavages of Spanish politics, does not seem on the face of it, to be particularly amenable to the Greens' still modest appetite for playing serious politics. The recent crises that faced the outgoing PSOE administration - a mixture of scandals and endemic corruption[32] after some fourteen years of continuous government, and of the social costs of facing hard political choices over European monetary integration[33] that imposed a fiscal retrenchment whose effects fell heavily on the PSOE's natural constituencies - have done little to make ecologism appear more relevant to a growing number of malcontents. The prevailing image of the Greens is of a party committed to issues that appear at best irrelevant, or whose solutions threaten to increase industrial costs, raise even higher an already unacceptable level of unemployment, and oppose what all the main parties regard as 'necessary' economic development. Spanish public opinion is certainly more ambivalent now about the value of European integration than it was when the country optimistically acceded to full EC membership in 1986 - even if a majority still exists who prefer to be part of a wider European project, regardless of the short term economic pain. The Greens' deep opposition to European integration has so far won them little political kudos and even less electoral support. Yet there are enough opponents of regional integration, and sufficient issues with an ecological dimension to them, for the Greens to make more political capital out of their anti-EU stance than they have done so far. There is scope here, on a number of particular issues - over fishing policy, agricultural subsidies and structural funding that favours agro businesses rather than smaller family or peasant farms, and the anticipated shift away from support for Mediterranean convergence and towards East/Central Europe - for aligning Green hostility to global capitalism with the IU's complementary campaign to renegotiate the terms of Spanish membership. The IU have taken up a similar position to the Greens on this issue. They, too, seek a reform of the EU in order to minimise the economic consequences of further integration on one of the EU's poorer members, and to ensure that Europe avoids becoming an economic fortress rather than the focus for positive economic and social development in the EU's neglected southern Mediterranean hinterland and beyond. Whether the Greens manage to raise their profile on this promising issue, or whether instead they yield the running - and the anticipated political pay off - to other new left groups, remains to be seen. If they do build on this issue, their political salience will surely increase and their electoral fortunes could well improve. If on the other hand, they fail to capitalise on the issue, it will provide a further testament to their endemic factionalism and of their self defeating resistance to playing liberal democratic politics according to the usual suboptimal rules of cooperation and compromise.

There are other ecological issues, too, which have some potential for encouraging a realignment of the progressive political forces in Spanish politics. Tourist blight, deforestation, water shortages, traffic pollution, urban sprawl resulting from rapid, poorly planned development, are all issues that typify the Mediterranean development syndrome and likewise threaten public health or otherwise reduce amenity. There have been some occasions when these issues have revealed their political potential. Tourism is a case in point. Conflicts over infrastructural developments have raised the profile of ecologism, as they have done in Greece. Tourism has become a major source of revenue and especially of 'hard' currency. At the same time, this sector's contribution to the national income has to be weighed against the costs of rural blight and the despoilation of the coastline. The priority given by government to concrete infrastructure (especially motorways and airport terminals) stands in stark contrast to the lack of investment in sanitation and alternative rural development. The issue of traffic emissions and the accompanying noise pollution also stems in no small part from an absence of proper urban planning procedures. There is, of course, no certain political advantage to be had from opposing the automobile revolution. The convenience and freedom brought by modern transport is part of the popular social revolution that has occurred here as elsewhere over recent decades. But these clear gains have to be weighed against their less obvious shortcomings. And while there is far from being any mass protest against the motor car, there is a feeling in some quarters - and thereby some political mileage - that government has too readily acceded to the automobile lobby to the detriment of the wider public interest. Government itself has tried to restore some balance here, but only by tinkering with the problem. The '*Plan Renove*' scheme - to give fiscal incentives to replace older vehicles with new ones - was motivated as much by a desire to boost flagging consumer spending in a keynote industry during a deep recession, as it was with environmental matters.[34] It was attacked as such by Los Verdes as "anti-social and anti-ecological".[35] The Greens predictably argued for more investment in technology to reduce petrol consumption and cut emissions from existing vehicles. This issue, too, gave some clue to the Greens' new if tentative realism. The green lobby, per se, successfully linked up with Izquierda Unida and formulated an alternative traffic scheme that included a plan to close city centres to private vehicles. This proposal was the subject of a voluntary referendum in Madrid.

It won the support of several hundred thousand respondents and encouraged similar movements in other cities.

The Greens have also been active on a range of conservation issues that have put them at the forefront of other popular campaigns and citizen initiatives. They spearheaded the successful campaign in the Coca de Barbera - a depressed agricultural hinterland in Catalonia - to halt plans by the regional Catalan government to set up an industrial waste treatment and disposal plant. Although there were many other political groups working in support of this campaign, the Greens again experienced the virtues of networking across ideological boundaries, in order to raise the profile of ecological issues in a political milieu otherwise unsympathetic to post-material concerns. There was a similar outcome from the campaign to mobilise the substantial local support for closing the obsolescent nuclear plant at Vandelios, south of Barcelona, after an accident there. This campaign took the form of a people's legislative initiative - the only mechanism provided for in the 1978 Constitution, that permits direct citizen participation. A half million signatures were collected within the six months deadline, for a proposal that called on the government to declare the country a nuclear free zone - only some 37 thousand short of the total required to have the matter debated in parliament. The campaign attracted widespread support from all sections of the community - including community groups, left wing parties and the trades unions. It also reactivated the campaign to close all nuclear plants.[36]

These single issue campaigns suggest then, a feasible strategy for Los Verdes - a way out of the political cul de sac in which they have found themselves ever since the Federation was formed. The party has by no means resolved its deepseated ambivalence about political engagement. Nevertheless, the tensions between realists and those who prefer ecologism to stay aloof from the compromises and snares of 'normal' politics have been apparent in these debates over strategy. The success of joint campaigns with other radical groups has strengthened the case of those Greens who prefer to take a more flexible view of party politics. The essence of their case, translated into this particular national context, is a familiar one in every Green party; that they are unlikely to consolidate an effective presence in regional, let alone in national, politics, unless they cash in the credit won in successful campaigns, and continue to network more effectively with potential radical allies - with a view to overcoming their ideological isolation in what is likely to remain, for the foreseeable future, an unfavourable political culture for minor parties committed to new politics and a post-materialist agenda. The route to any practicable accommodation with the PSOE is closed - at least for the time being. The most likely option for radical bridge building currently available to the Greens lies, then, with the one political group - the IU - already amenable to radical ecological ideas. As one commentator sees it, the Greens must continue to network in order to "generate collaborative experience to cut through this (current) isolation and help to build a residual network able to tackle the problems in store".[37]

The recent defeat of the PSOE in the 1996 national elections and the installation of a right wing Partido Popular (Popular Party) government, committed to renewed fiscal stringency, will be much less a test of the stability of Spanish democracy than it will be of the coherence of the left.[38] Over some fourteen years of continuous government, the Socialist party had eventually lost its way in a mire of unseemly scandals, corruption charges and policy compromises. These caused as much tension on the left - within the PSOE and between it and the IU - as these events did between the left per se and the opposition right wing and regionalist parties. The defeat of González was, nevertheless, less comprehensive than expected (a total loss of 18 seats), and this is likely to encourage the PSOE to believe that it can bide its time and wait for the tensions within the new centre-right coalition government, to present it with another opportunity to convince public opinion that only the PSOE can provide political stability.[39] As long as the PSOE believes that a return to government is imminent, any far-reaching political realignment on the left is unlikely. At the same time, the PSOE cannot take any, even modest, electoral success for granted. The party has proved by its conduct of affairs over recent years that it is, at the very least, a jaded rather than an entirely spent force; that its radical cutting edge had become blunted by the complacency that eventually settles on all longstanding parties of government; and that it is in need of rejuvenation.[40] It is too early to say whether this recent defeat confirms the broad trend noted by Boggs in northern Europe, of an ideology and movement in decline. According to this revisionist account, something has changed - or begun to change - in the continent's political landscape. This does not, Boggs avers, imply by any means the end of radical prospects, but the need to revisit them. For "while many leftists try and explain away socialist failures and disasters as a function of passing historical conditions and fads, I argue that anti-system movements on a global scale are now leaving behind the socialist paradigm with its universalist, class based, productivist vision of change". In this perspective, to have any chance of success, future strategies for radical change must adapt to a rapidly changing political matrix, where disparate situations of conflict and sources of change negate the socialist penchant for identifying single or 'leading' agencies of transformation.[41] Whether or not this prognosis applies to the Spanish left is less important in the medium term than the fact that its main political expression - the PSOE - refuses to accept such a negative historical assessment of its prospects. The PSOE's political dominance and its continuing, if reduced, electoral strength prevents it for the time being from abandoning its singular claim to embody the only feasible radical option in Spanish politics.

The interlude in opposition, meanwhile, presents the old left with an opportunity for strategic reflection as well as for political renewal, much as electoral defeats did for social democratic parties elsewhere in Europe. To be effective in opposition, however, requires that the PSOE cooperate with other parties - in this case the IU - who gained 3 seats in these elections, even though it failed to reach its earlier levels of support. Together these two leftist parties command 162 seats in the chamber, six more than the governing Popular Party (PP) on its own. Cooperation in parliament will inevitably foment ideological debate. The IU will bring ecological issues onto the oppositions' agenda,[42] thereby raising their profile. Whether the Greens will benefit from this cooperation or remain entirely incidental to it, is more problematical. The PP's attempts to pursue a new right agenda, and to implement the levels of fiscal retrenchment and deflation that they see as necessary for Spain to play its full part in the next stage of European monetary integration, are the issues that are much more likely than ecologism per se to dominate the parliamentary battle.[43] At best, the opportunity for the Greens to exert any influence on an opposition agenda - let alone to contribute to refashioning its fundamentals - will be modest. Even this outside chance is premised on some fairly remote prospects. For one thing, it assumes that the Greens are amenable to the prospect of participating in such a political shift. As we have seen, realism may be gathering momentum in the Green party, along with an awareness of the need to look for allies outside the movement's ideological citadel. But so far this flexibility has been confined to local and single issue campaigns rather than to any major strategic review. And perhaps just as problematical - even more so, given the balance of political forces involved - the prospect of a major left realignment that includes the Greens depends on the dominant and minor parties of the left who continue to make the running in the radical camp, inviting the Greens on board. The PSOE for its part, continues to see them as largely an irrelevance. The PSOE is unlikely to embrace ideas that would alienate its usual productionist constituencies amongst industrial and rural workers, the public sector and the prosperity conscious middle class. The IU's claim to adequately represent ecologism within its own ranks looks to be, in these circumstances, an altogether more likely route for the Greens.

The prospects for ecologism on the political agenda may look more promising than they did even a few years since - which will strengthen the hand of the Green realists and encourage them to be even more accommodating. But this does not ensure that Los Verdes will be principal beneficiaries of this modest value shift. At best, any political realignment that does accrue will be a two stage affair. The PSOE, spurred by parliamentary logistics, may show a greater willingness to make pacts and deals with the IU. There are already signs of this occuring at the regional level. Meanwhile, both the Greens and the IU may be prepared to bury old suspicions and build on some tentative but successful cooperation in single issue campaigns that have already brought the two movements closer together than either had anticipated. This offers the Greens a surer but by no means a certain way forward. Even if the PSOE does decide that its preferred political option is staunch adversarialism vis a vis the new PP government, and thereby chooses to stand aloof from any short term electoral or parliamentary manœuvres that appear to draw what remains a mainstream and ideologically quite conservative party too far to the left, the Greens' best option would still seem to be one that develops its albeit tentative political linkages with the new and radical third force IU coalition. There are better prospects here for effective cooperation. Apart from some shared affinities over the importance of ecologism - which offers the two parties a point of ideological contact as much as it sharpens their electoral rivalry - the IU favours a change in the present electoral system that would make it easier for small parties to secure representation. The IU want a more proportional system per se, as well as an increase of some 50 seats in the size of the Congress of Deputies.[44] The two dominant parties have responded to this issue by merely proposing a modification of the current d'Hondt system, that would make individual candidate choice within the existing regional party lists somewhat easier. The situation holds some modest potential for the Greens to break away from the cycle of political failure that has gripped them from the outset - an unfavourable political culture compounded by a singularly unrealistic approach to politics, which merely confirmed their marginal appeal on the fringes of a new politics of democratic transition and economic modernisation. On the other hand, there is little choice for Green politics here, other than to make such accommodations. For the obstacles that remain in the way of a Green breakthrough continue to weigh heavily against the party. Bigas has prescribed the conditions necessary for such a shift, both to take place and to be successful, as the "need for a new socio-ecological climate, necessarily of the left; one that prioritises social questions, understands the need to develop an egalitarian, anti-racist and anti-fascist culture rooted in solidarity. It definitely needs to be based on the understanding that there will not be an improvement in the environmental situation without social change, without a culture of participatory democracy and non-violence, and a culture that acts as repository of the emancipatory traditions of humanity".[45]

It is easier, of course, to state what is required to bring about such a radical breakthrough here than it is to ensure that it happens. There are, however, some inexorable facts that the Greens will ignore only to their considerable cost. In order to be part of such a political seachange, Los Verdes will have to show a receptiveness to change, a much greater realism, and a degree of ideological flexibility that has so far eluded them. Even then, the outcome will depend far more on how the established and new left itself responds to their new circumstances of opposition and the growing respectability of right wing politics, than on anything the Greens can do to convince their prospective allies that they are ready to seriously entertain, and to participate, in some kind of radical realignment. If this option is closed off to them, or by them, for whatever reason, the Greens' electoral prospects look bleak indeed in a political culture and a national opportunity structure that continues to be heavily stacked against them. We, and indeed Los Verdes themselves, will be in a much better position to estimate the chances of such a change occurring when Spain's post-socialist political landscape has settled down, and the mainstream left have made their considered response to their recent electoral defeat.

2.   Portugal

(i)   Green roots

Portugal is another state that fits the generic category of those economically less developed new Mediterranean democracies, whose post dictatorship (and in this instance post-colonial) politics has focused primarily on maximising economic growth, creating a modern industrial and welfare infrastructure, and generally catching up with those societies which make up the developed core of the European Union. For the reasons already outlined above, in these circumstances of political transition and economic modernisation, the appeal of post-materialist politics tends to be minimal. The support base for political ecology in Portugal can be counted in hundreds rather than thousands, and even where it has showed, its emphasis has been localised, issue specific, and its impact marginal. The way the green movement has responded to its plight has hardly helped to improve its political prospects. The movement remained deeply divided between competing green factions working in isolation, and without any concept of a national strategy. This encouraged the absurd luxury of four entirely separate national Green organisations; the Amigo de Terra (Friends of the Earth - a national embodiment of the international pressure group); the Liga Para a Posteaccao de Natureza (League for the Protection of Nature); the Grupo de Estudos de Ordenamento Terratori e Ambieta (Study group for the Planning of Land and Environment) and Quercus, a small group of nature preservationists. All of these groups were essentially conservationist or pure green in orientation, and primarily concerned to access the political system by lobbying on specific ecological issues as circumstances demanded. The green ethos was fashioned by a preference to engage in lobbying rather than party politics per se. One of their most notable and promising campaigns, in terms of raising ecological consciousness was centred on opposition to the Spanish government's proposal to build a plant for disposing of nuclear waste on the border at Aldeadaville, as well as to extend its military range at Alcochete, as part of the Spanish contribution to NATO.[46]

These groups were either unwilling or unable to make the transition to party political status. This reticence vacated the small political space available to ecologism to other conventional party groups. The Partido Popular Monarquieco, a nominally pro-monarchist but primarily an anti-dictatorship party with roots in the opposition to the dictator Salazar, was the first national party to identify with environmental issues - albeit in a partial and far from radical manner. In 1980, the PPM had joined in a coalition with the Christian Democrats and Social Democrats, and thereby became isolated from the mainstream left. Ecologism provided them with a convenient political tool as the party tried to maintain its progressive credentials from within a conservative government. They chose to keep a watching brief from inside the government over environmental issues, including infrastructural developments such as motorway building and deforestation. They did so with some success. Not least, they used their leverage to influence the government's decision against adopting a nuclear energy programme. The PPM was eventually overwhelmed, however, by intense factional disputes over its commitment to the restoration of the Portuguese monarchy - an issue of more moment for the party than ecologism per se.

The Movimento Democratico Portuguese (MDP), which had its spiritual roots in post-dictatorship politics, was also riven by deep factional divisions - this time between Communist and Socialist sympathisers within the movement. After it had managed to divest itself of these early Marxist influences, ecologism began to play an instrumental role in providing the party with an alternative radical issue around which to unite. A combination of factors - an effective populist grassroots organisation, in touch with social movement politics, a party which was particularly attractive to the intelligentsia who, as elsewhere, were disproportionally interested in ecologism, and the need to coalesce around a suitably radical agenda - all pushed the party in the direction of ecologism. The MDP nurtured these radical green credentials by developing close international links with red-green groups such as Die Grunen.

(ii)   Party formation

The only party that could reasonably claim the status of an independent Green party was the Partido Os Verdes. The development of Os Verdes parallels in some ways that of the MDP. This party, too, began its political life under the aegis of the Communist Party. The Communists, who tended to make a tactical virtue of forming and then orchestrating popular fronts for their own political advantage, set up an electoral coalition - the Coligacao Democratica Uniaria (CDU), the United Democratic Coalition - to broaden their appeal outside the hard left in the 1987 national elections. Os Verdes and other dissident leftist groups were incorporated into this front organisation specifically for this purpose. The 'united front' strategy undoubtedly made good political sense for the Communists, who had lost much of their earlier cachet as a focus of anti-fascist opposition leading up to the 1974 revolution. As such, they needed to improve their appeal beyond the party faithful and thereby widen their electoral net, by attaching themselves to all manner of new politics and progressive issues. The element of electoral calculation here was not entirely one sided. There was a degree of realism in the decision of the Greens to accept Communist tutelage. It was quite clear in the prevailing electoral circumstances, that ecololgism faced a bleak prospect in its own right, unless it found political allies closer

273

to mainstream politics. By leaning on its leftist credentials and using the disciplined local organisation of the Communists, Os Verdes did manage to win 2 seats in the national parliament. Although Os Verdes stood on the CDU list for the 1989 European elections, only 1 of the 4 seats won by this list was allocated to the Greens. The fact that the party appears, regardless of its name, a captive of better organised and politically shrewder forces, is only part of its problem. In spite of the sincerity of its commitment to ecologism, unlike the MDP, Os Verdes remained a small, insular and elitist party, controlled by a small leadership faction. The reluctance to cultivate a free-ranging debate on political options merely confirmed the general impression, that the party remains little more than a colony of the Communists and their successors.

(iii)   Political developments

Green politics in Portugal has, in these circumstances, remained disjointed, unfocused and limited in its impact. In a country that has experienced multiple revolutions within a brief timespan - decolonisation, democratisation, rapid economic development, EC membership and the intrusive social change wrought by all of these experiences - it is unlikely that the 'Greens' could have done much more to improve the salience of the ecological issue, or to increase their own leverage over national policy, other than to float in the slipstream of such massive transformations; exerting influence, or at least voicing predictable concerns about the pace and direction of socio-economic change, whenever events permitted. The same strategic questions apply to the Greens here as elsewhere - of whether to take part in electoral politics on their own account, or to settle for a degree of influence by working through other parties; and the equally difficult choice between taking a pure ecology or a red-green approach to their ecological goals. There were some tensions within the movement over both issues. Sara Parkin, in an early commentary, saw little future in perpetuating these continued divisions, and counselled unification. If these disparate groups are to capitalise politically on the unavoidable ecological consequences of such rapid and cumulative changes, they will, as other Green movements have discovered before them, need to address the key question of organisation and political purpose. Parkin saw distinct advantages in such a coordinate strategy: for "although very different, each party has something that the others don't have. The rather anarchic PPM has the affection and the trust of many Portuguese people; the MDP has intellectual curiosity and a substantial local organisation; Os Verdes has the most developed programme and two young, attractive members of parliament. When each has explored its own road a bit more they could eventually become a politically potent combination".[47]

This strategy was easier to prescribe than it was to deliver, given these groups' diverse social and ideological origins. Combining moderate and radical greens (including a party with at least one foot in Marxism) proved to be difficult. The demise of international Communism and the opening up of the hard left to a new radical prospectus have favoured the realists in the movement and reinforced the idea of cooperation. But these trends have not brought about, or even much encouraged, a resolution of the continuing differences within the green movement. Nor have they persuaded the main Green group, Os Verdes, to break away from its cohabitation with the hard left. This link with a small but disciplined party may, however, prove to be of benefit to ecologism in the long run. To see why this might be, we need to look at the wider developments in

Portuguese politics over the past decade. Portuguese politics seems to have settled down to a period of relative stability. The main party contests here focus on a familiar confrontation between centre left and centre right formations, each addressing the same issues, but offering rather different solutions to them. The tenure in government of the Social Democratic Party (Partido Social Democratica - PSD) between 1987 and 1995, consolidated the new pattern of Portuguese politics. During this period Portugal joined the EC and the Social Democrats presided over a national commitment, endorsed by the other mainstream parties, to a modernisation strategy based on European integration. The European project was overwhelmingly accepted by mainstream public opinion, as the only alternative to geographical isolation. According to this scenario, it offered the best hope of inward investment; a necessary spur to commercial competitiveness, and not least, promised a vital source of funding for infrastructural development. The PSD likewise embraced, albeit with some reservations, the project for European Monetary Union and for the same reasons, regardless of the pain inflicted on less developed economies by the Maastricht convergence criteria. EMU was seen, in essence, as a logical extension of this drive for national economic modernisation. In the initial stages, this approach seemed to pay dividends. An unprecedented economic boom was generated, in part by generous EC funding - estimated at some Es 2,700 billion (£10.75 billion) - most of which was used to finance infrastructure (including 1,700 kilometres of new roads). There was a significant shift, too, in employment patterns from farming to primary and secondary industry, as well as to the service sector, which led to a rise in real wages of some 2 per cent. Unemployment fell to quite low levels by current European standards, largely because equally low comparable labour costs (Portugal was the cheapest region of the EU in which to employ production workers) encouraged, in turn, increased labour mobility to other parts of the EU as well as increased inward investment. Volkswagen and Ford, for instance, have built a new joint venture production plant at Palmela, south of Lisbon which, on its own it is estimated, will increase national exports by some 15 per cent and create up to four thousand new jobs. In the eight years since EC membership average growth reached 2.9 per cent pa, annual inflation fell from more than 19 per cent to barely 5 per cent pa, and GDP per capita rose from 51.4 per cent of the European average (in 1985) to 64 per cent. Boosted by the spurt in economic growth, the expansion of new middle class wealth, economic liberalisation, and improvements in consumer choice and standards, Portugal overtook Greece and left that country with the unenviable status as western Europe's poorest relation, measured by a 'basket' of lifestyle indicators - for instance, a doubling in the number of automobiles, up to 54 per cent of the population; and a similar increase in telephone installations, running water, televisions and other consumer durables. The Socialists (Partido Socialista - PS), a party cast in the European social democratic mold, adopted this European policy after they took office. Only the marginal parties - the right wing nationalist Partido Popular (CDS-PP) and the post Communist United Democratic Coalition (CDU), to which Os Verdes remains attached - adopted an unequivocally anti-EU stance. The Greens have given an ecological gloss to their opposition to the EU, but the overwhelming support for the modernisation strategy adopted by the country's two major parties has hardly enabled radical parties who stand outside this mainstream consensus, to seize the political initiative.

The limited popular appeal of what seemed to the majority of the electorate to be a negative and backward looking approach to the country's deepseated commitment to economic modernisation yielded the far left-green alliance little political purchase. The alliance stood on this platform in the 1994 European elections, and lost one of the four

Strasbourg seats they had won in 1989, polling 11.2 per cent compared with 14.4 per cent in 1989. Even this modest vote was much less an endorsement of alternativist, let alone of ecological concerns than it was a residual expression of loyalty to the hard left - boosted in part by the rejection by principled socialists of what they saw as two 'identikit' establishment parties, and especially a sense of betrayal by some former PS loyalists of that party's radical heritage. The biggest protest recorded in these elections came from the large number of abstentions: mostly from an electorate unattracted to what they felt to be the far left opposition's negative anti-Europeanism, but at the same time protesting *in absentia* as it were against their sense of relative deprivation - a perceived shortfall in economic gains, after the rising expectations of the previous decade and the government's failure to maintain these higher standards of personal consumption and job security.[48] The United Left has attracted support in recent elections from rising concerns with this strategy of 'necessary' and 'enforced' modernisation that follows in the wake of European integration - a feeling that became more palpable, as the government wrestled with the dilemma of imposing the Maastricht convergence criteria on an economy that was ill equipped to carry them without considerable social costs, or unleashing widespread resentment amongst a population that was becoming used to real material improvements in its living standards. These pressures notably increased after April 1992, when Prime Minister Anibal Cavaco Silva put the escudo into the fiscal corset of the Exchange Rate Mechanism as a positive signal of the government's intention of joining the EU mainstream. The slowdown in economic growth that accompanied the 1993 recession and a tepid recovery throughout 1994 which deterred private investment, badly hit personal consumption, reduced disposable income and increased the unemployment level from 4.5 per cent to 7.1 per cent.

The United Left's position on Europe has become less marginalised than it used to be, especially after the Single European Market has showed up the serious weaknesses in Portugal's competitive position. The recent association agreements to ease the transition of the former Warsaw Pact countries into the pan-European economy, and as a preface to a prospective enlargement, have also added to Portugal's economic woes. These shifts in the focus of EU commercial policy have particularly undermined Portugal's markets in clothing and textiles. The proposal to divert to the candidate member states in east and central Europe, the lion's share of the generous structural and convergence funds that have so far softened the pressures on Portugal of joining the Community, and eased its commitment to EMU integration, has also begun to introduce cracks in the once solid edifice of Portuguese 'Europeanism'. What is clear from these opinion shifts, is that the Greens and their allies now at least have an issue that they can trade on and even use to increase their support. The United Left, in contrast with assertive nationalism and Euroscepticism of the far right CDS-PP - with whom they compete for this expanding constituency - do not recommend the outright rejection of the EU. They call instead for drastic changes in its present arrangements. They advocate, for instance, a more genuinely democratic, less autarchic and insular community. They envisage a union that is not dominated either by the big member countries or by Europe's leading multinational companies. This is a balanced and, in the circumstances, a credible position that avoids the impossibilism of a withdrawal from the EU (wholly implausible and politically untenable), yet tempers economic realism with a critique that reflects widespread public anxieties. It is a platform that has given the United Left and their Green partners a fingerhold on parliament, without denting the strong moderate left-right adversarialism that continues to shape Portuguese party politics.

## (iv)	Prospects for political change

The 1995 general election was fought on the very same issues as the Euro-election, but with a more decisive outcome. The Socialist Party, with 43.9 per cent (112 out of the 230 seats and a clear lead over the Social Democrats of some ten per cent of the popular vote - their biggest ever share of the national vote) formed the new government. The state of the economy and the impact of impending EU developments - all very much productionist concerns -were the key issues. There was considerable public unease over the impact of the Maastricht convergence criteria on living standards and levels of personal consumption, and not least the fact that neither of the two main parties differed all that much in their intention to prescribe the unpleasant fiscal palliatives they saw as necessary to bring about the long term benefits of economic and structural convergence. All that the Socialists could promise, to appease their supporters amongst the less affluent sectors, was a vague commitment to exert its influence in the EU's councils to protect the country's share of the convergence and structural funding necessary to soften the worst impact of these changes. The electoral contest was typically adversarial - a choice for most electors between two competing visions of how to manage a market economy. This complementary discourse filled the media and dominated the airwaves. It was bound to minimise the publicity for, and dull the appeal of, the more radical parties and their prospectuses. The former Socialist minister turned academic political scientist, Antonio Barreto, drew the obvious conclusions from this trend. He observed that "we are edging towards a two party system".[49] National elections, inasmuch as they offer stark choices, tend to be less open to a meaningful protest vote, and the 1995 Portuguese election was no exception in this regard. Indeed, in this instance, the PS vote was actually boosted by some former United Left supporters - determined to avoid the almost deadheat outcome of the 1994 Euro-poll and the unpalatable prospect of 'wasting' votes that might help to keep the centre-right in power. They did so in spite of their ideological reservations about a revisionist Socialist party in the soft left mold that had long since jettisoned the classical leftist shibboleths of state ownership and the use of stringent interventionist means for national economic management - even to the point of embracing elements of the PDS's neo-liberal privatisation programme.

An emergent political pattern was discernible from this, as from the two previous elections. The apparent preference of the electorate was for stable, single party government, even though the electoral system was not deliberately designed for ensuring that end. Unlike the situation in many other western European polities, the majority of the Portuguese electorate now vote for one or other of the two mainstream parties and tend to shift their support between them. Minor parties, which tend anyway to be outside the moderate left-right mainstream, are squeezed in the process. The use of a proportionate list system here ensures that the two main parties do not by any means monopolise the ballot. At the same time, the division of the country into 20 electoral districts does put a premium on high levels of national party organisation, or at least on a strong regional concentration that neither the far left nor the Greens enjoy. The present arrangement of large multi member constituencies (Lisbon has 50 members out of 230) is well suited to the larger parties. They possess the resources (publicity, finance, manpower) to cover the ground, get their case across, and are able to attract prominent names to favourable positions on their lists. The small parties do, at least, have an opportunity to negotiate a place on the list of a major party by arrangement - the principal raison d'être for the ecologists originally throwing in their lot with the Partido Communista Portugues (PCP), and maintaining the same arrangement with the PCP's successor, the United Left. The recent decision to review the electoral system, with a view to instituting single member constituencies in order to breathe new life into Parliament - for the most part, a rubber stamp for government legislation - and to make deputies more accountable to their constituents, is unlikely to improve the prospects for minor parties. An electoral system of single member constituencies, even under proportionality rules, is likely to spread the resources of minor parties much more thinly, and thereby to further consolidate the hold of the major parties. The United Left has opposed these changes as a cynical attempt to install obstacles to wider representation in what is already an unfavourable electoral system for minor parties. There is no prominent third or discontent party capable of building a strong support base on a new cleavage or of drawing on a set of alternative interests or causes, other than a residue of negative or disjointed minority issues - for instance concern over Europe, ecologism, ideological atavism or local issues. This pattern is unlikely to encourage any widespread partisan dealignment, let alone ideological adventurism that might destablise the new democratic system altogether. Electors, whatever their genuine worries about impending changes and the new insecurities that have arisen over the impact of the EU's current direction, continue to show a commitment to a system that stands in marked contrast, both to what went before, and to the uncertainties of the years of flux that immediately followed the dictatorship years which produced 16 governments in barely 13 years. The Socialist leader, Antonio Guterres, gave voice to the strong mood of bipartisanship that now prevails in Portuguese politics, when he observed that "in a modern society, political ruptures generally lead to disaster. Policy differences today are a matter of degree."

In these circumstances, the prospects for any widespread, let alone consistent support for any form of alternative or radical politics that might jeopardise the political transition and economic modernisation of Portugal remains modest indeed. However, to say that ecologism is entirely discounted in Portugal, even in such unpropitious circumstances, is to take no account of the growing salience of the issue for key social groups. Not least, where the political significance of environmental issues is closely linked with the critical socio-economic issues at the centre of contemporary politics. A number of environmental issues have illustrated the potential for the Greens to build local support; and by this means to raise the profile of the issue, even if there is no thriving post-materialist constituency in this country - where the new middle class are more nouveau riche than they are worried about the global commons or exercised by new politics concerns. There is, at least, sufficient grassroots support for local area concerns to keep the issue on the political agenda. At the time of the 1994 Euro-elections, disturbances were reported in the northern electoral district of Alveiro, as thousands of voters boycotted the polls in protest against a plan to store industrial waste. The Greens were too weak and poorly organised to be able to harness this issue to any great effect, and the campaign went little beyond a grassroots protest against an unpopular government decision, linked to similar protests over a motley of loosely connected discontents in favour of better sanitation and in opposition to the planned closure of local coalmines and post offices, as well as against the importation of Spanish fish supplies.

The same can be said about other issues with some potential for raising ecological consciousness. Public protests on a number of fronts have failed to raise any widespread ecological consciousness and even lost much of their green resonance as they became assimilated into the agendas of the other parties. Green politics continues to lose out on issues that a resourceful, well organised and independent Green party, with a secure support base, would either make its own; or else would use to bargain for a more complementary issue agenda with other radically disposed parties. The public protests caused by the 50 per cent increase in tolls for Lisbon's only bridge over the river Tagus provides some indication of squandered opportunities in this regard. The protest had an ecological resonance but whose potential got lost in the public and political clamour. The substantive issue went much deeper than the nominal amounts involved, and was much more about appropriate infrastructure and the transport problems of a fast expanding urban society. This issue has had only a marginal ecological impact so far, but the exponential increase in private automobile traffic in the urban centres - and especially in Lisbon - will ensure that the issue returns and acquires the political salience it now enjoys in other Mediterranean cities such as Athens and Rome. The Greens are better placed than the materialist, growth-oriented parties to capitalise on this issue, as long as they avoid an inflexible or dogmatic fundamentalist stance that will alienate them from the very public they seek to educate and influence. The same logic applies to the other infrastructural issues that invariably accompany the levels of economic development associated with Portugal's participation in a regional and global economy. The expansion of the port of Lisbon is another useful illustration of how materialist agendas overlap in rapidly developing economies. The ambition of a mobilised business community, supported by the political establishment, to turn Lisbon - the last European port of call before the Atlantic - into a deep-sea port and trading hub of southern Europe raises all of the environmental and related issues that have exercised the ecology lobby in the Netherlands over plans to expand port facilities in Rotterdam. Even before such developments were mooted, the port in 1984 already shifted some 54.63 million tonnes of freight - including a large increase of some 90 per cent in its roll on-roll off cargo trade in only a few years. Whether the Greens can capture this issue from the current productionist agenda whose terms of reference are wholly materialist - and are discussed primarily in terms of investment, planning, manning levels and so on - and give it a green gloss capable of winning support for them in those communities whose amenities and quality of life will be most affected by the proposed changes is entirely another matter. The Greens may be too weak to seize such opportunities, but those chances do present themselves and will continue to do so.

The one issue on the current national agenda that does offer more convincing evidence of ecological salience, is the critical matter of water supply. Water is an increasingly urgent problem across Iberia and especially in Portugal. After four years of the worst drought conditions this century, public opinion is now highly sensitive, both to the amount and quality of water available, and to the way government plans in Spain and Portugal to use this resource may cause long term damage to the environment.[50] The critical issue here is unavoidably one of the eco system; for as one close observer of Iberian affairs has noted, "geography has made things uncomfortable. The amount of water generated within the country in a normal year is put at 31,000 cubic hectometres of which 18,800 comes from the Portuguese sections of those rivers shared with Spain".[51] Although the two Iberian countries have operated a joint agreement on this sensitive issue since the days of the dictatorships (beginning in the 1960s), the recent drought has caused Madrid to develop a National Hydrographic Plan - a major project to dig an elaborate canal system to divert some of the head waters of the three major rivers that rise in Spain and flow to the sea in Portugal. The issue has taken on added urgency because 76 per cent of all water used in Portugal is utilised for agricultural purposes, with the rest is divided between Portugal's hydro-electric and other industrial usage and domestic consumption.

This is a case where economics, ecology and the public interest clearly converge. There could hardly be in this drought-ridden country, and threatened by far more severe climatic conditions over the next half century or so, an issue with greater political potential for ecologists. So far, however, most of the political capital from this issue has, in the usual way of things in this adversarial polity, accrued to the established parties. The influential Water Institute - an adjunct of the national Environment Ministry - has engaged in negotiations with Madrid under Ministers of both recent governments. The head of the Institute, Cunha Serra, has been careful to balance the requirements of water for the usual industrial and public uses, with politic references to "environment conditions". The potential still remains here, nevertheless, for a distinctive Green contribution to this debate. Especially so in the light of recent privatisations of domestic water supply under the usual public utilities regulations of the Single Market, which has seen a degree of ownership over this precious and politically sensitive commodity pass from local municipal control into the hands of foreign companies - including, ironically, some vested in Spain. The Greens and their tentative allies on the new left have, in what will continue to be a crucial issue in Portuguese politics, an ideal opportunity to harness public discontent and connect ecologism with public fears in a way that avoids the prevailing impression so far, that Green politics is a matter for more developed societies: or that it has little or no place in a polity wrestling with the twin and immensely demanding problems of consolidating the democratic transition and ensuring economic modernisation.

Notes

1. See the analysis in P. McDonough and A. Lopez Pina, "Continuity and Change in Spanish Politics", Chapter 12 of R. J. Dalton (et al), "Electoral Change in Advanced Industrial Democracies" (Princeton, 1984) at pp.365-396.
2. Ibid, at p.395.
3. Ibid, at p.391.
4. S. Del Campo, J.F. Tezanos and W. Santin, "The Spanish Political Elite: Permanence and change", in M. Czudnowski (ed), "International yearbook of elite studies" (Illinois, 1983).
5. A. Recio, "The Ecologist Movement in Spain - Boomerang of the Development Model", in Maria-Pillar Garcia-Guadilla and Jitta Blauert, (eds), special edition on social movements and development of the International Journal of Sociology and Social Policy Vol.12 (4/5/6/7), 1992, at pp.162-63, for a summary of ecological depredation in Spain as a direct consequence of this.
6. See A. Recio, ibid (1992), at p.163.
7. For a summary of this evidence, see S. Aguilar-Fernandez, "The Greens in the 1993 Spanish General Election: A Chronicle of a Defeat Foretold", Environmental Politics Vol.3 (1) 1994, at p.155.
8. See E. Moxon-Browne, "Political Change in Spain" (London, 1989).
9. P. McDonough, P. Lopez-Pina and S. H. Barnes, "The Spanish public in political transition", British Journal of Political Science Vol.11 1981 at pp.459-79.
10. J. Bru, "Las Ciencias Sociales ante la problematica Medioambiental", in Mientras Tanto 34 (Barcelona, 1988).
11. X. Garcia, J. Reixach and S. Vilanova, El Combat Ecologista a Catalunya, Edicions 62, Barcelona, 1979; and J. Puig, "L'Ecologisme" (Ed Barcanova, Barcelona, 1991).
12. J. Martinez Alier, "Ecologia y Economia", Edicions 62, Barcelona 1984; J.M. Naredo, "La Economia en Evolucion" Siglo XXI Madrid, 1987.
13. A. Recio, op.cit (1992), at p.165.

14. Ibid, p.165.
15. O. Piulats, "Una Historia Reciente del Movimiento Verde", in Integral (112), Barcelona, 1989.
16. Jordi Bigas, "Ecologism in Spain: Commentary on the Spanish Case", in Maria-Pillar Garcia-Guadilla and Jutta Blauert (eds), op.cit (1992), at p.178.
17. A. Recio, op.cit (1992), at p.168.
18. J. Bigas, "Paginas Verdes. Guia de Recursos Ambientales" (Editorial Integral, Barcelona, 1991).
19. B. Varillas, CODA, la Supraorganizacion del Movimento Ecologista Espanol, CODA, (Coordinadora de Organizaciones para la Defensa del Medio Ambiente), Madrid, 1990.
20. This was originally the Coordinadora de Defensa de las Ares referred to above.
21. J. Araujo, "La muerte silenciosa. Espana hacia el desastre ecologico" (Ediciones Tema de Hoy, Madrid, 1990).
22. A. Recio, op.cit (1992), at p.168.
23. S. Aguilar-Fernandez cites the evidence of various El Pais yearbooks that illustrate the Greens' best regional results as follows; in Catalonia in 1988 - Alternativa Verde (0.16 per cent), EPS Verdes Ecologistes (0.33 per cent); Los Verdes (0.30 per cent); partit Ecologista Catalunya (0.22 per cent); in Gallicia in 1989 - Os Verdes de Galicia (0.24 per cent), Os Verdes Ecoloxistas (0.21 per cent); in Andalusia in 1990 - Verdes de Andalusia (0.51 per cent), Los Verdes Ecologistas (0.46 per cent); and in the Basque country in 1990 - Los Verdes Ecologistas (0.42 per cent).
24. The Observer, 23.5.93.
25. J.J. Damborenea (ed), "Desarrollo y Destruccion: una introduccion a los Problemas Ecologicos de Espana", (Libros de la Catarata, Madrid, 1990).
26. J. Bigas, op.cit (1992), at p.81.
27. S. Aguilar-Fernandez, op.cit (1994), at p.154.
28. S. Aguilar-Fernandez op.cit (1994), at p.158.
29. T. Burns, "Water Gets Political in a Very Dry Spain - Access is Dividing Regions", Financial Times, 27.7.94.
30. D. White, "Danger hides in the depths", in Financial Times Survey: Spain, 24.6.96.
31. Reuters News Service Report, 26.6.95.
32. I. Traynor, "Blame in Spain stays mainly with the EU", The Guardian, 14.6.95.
33. D. White, "Crowd bays for González's blood", Financial Times, 14.9.95.
34. Financial Times, 22.9.94.
35. El Pais, 6.10.94.
36. See A. Bosch et al, "Algunas Reflexiones sobre la Campana 'Vivir sin Nucleares'", in Mientras Tanto, (46), 1991.
37. A. Recio, op.cit, (1992), p.174.
38. Financial Times, 26.2.96.
39. Financial Times, 4.3.96.
40. John Hooper, "Felipe viva", The Guardian, 5.3.96.
41. C. Boggs, "The Socialist Tradition: From Crisis to Decline" (London, 1995), at p.x.
42. Financial Times, 5.3.96.
43. Q. Peel, "Spain joins drive for EU 'great leap forward'", Financial Times, 8.6.94.
44. Financial Times, 26.2.96.
45. J. Bigas, op.cit, (1992), at p.184.

46. S. Parkin, op.cit, (1989), at p.241.
47. Ibid, (1989), at pp.244-45.
48. See "Portugal - Country Profile", The Economist Intelligence Unit, London, August, 1994, pp.1-46.
49. Guardian, 18.2.95.
50. D. White, "Dispute over fluid frontiers", Financial Times, 8.11.95.
51. Ibid, 8.11.95.

8 The Green Party in the United Kingdom

(i)   Green roots

The oldest Green party in Europe was formed as the People's Party in Coventry in 1973. It based its programme on the four principles of the influential ecological text, "Blueprint for Survival".[1] This proposed a strategy for human survival which involved the minimum disruption of ecological processes; the maximum conservation of materials and energy; a population in which recruitment balanced loss; and a social system in which the individual citizen was content with, rather than constrained by, the first three conditions. The new party drew on an already widespread and deep rooted tradition of environmental concern,[2] and recruited from amongst those disparate groups and individuals broadly concerned with environmental matters. Even at this early stage, deep divisions were apparent in the party between pure ecologists and those who preferred an explicitly socialist approach to ecologism.[3] Some party members had already joined the Socialist Environment and Resources Association (SERA), founded in 1973 with a view to influencing the Labour Party - or at least those new leftist elements in the party who were ideologically in tune with new politics and social movement issues. However, in the British context it was noticeable that both the radical peace movement and the long established and more conservative environmental protectionist groups chose, by and large, to become involved in socialist politics rather than with the green movement per se.[4] From their very different perspectives, both of these movements were concerned that any direct involvement with even a minor political party would diminish their potential as lobbyists, or reduce their leverage on the main political parties.[5]

The People's Party stood in five constituencies at the February 1974 general election - polling an average vote of 1.8 per cent, with its best result, 3.9 per cent, in Coventry North West. They followed up this minimal showing by polling a much lower vote - an average of 0.7 per cent in 4 seats - in the October 1974 election. In 1975 the party changed its name to the Ecology Party, to reflect the overwhelming preference of its young leadership for a pure green approach which transcended the usual ideological divisions that were later to wreak havoc in many other parties as between their dark green and red-green factions. There was, however, already a strong anti-partyist disposition that ensured that the other main faultline of Green party politics - a split between fundamentalists and those realists convinced of the need to adopt a more conventional party format - would be hard to avoid. At this stage in its development, the new party was able to indulge its fundamentalist outlook. It firmly rejected what it saw as the hierarchical social system and materialistic economic paradigm perpetuated by the British political establishment. Critics of this radical demeanour - inside the party and outside - took a more disapproving view of such moral absolutism. For although the commitment to pure ecologism did at this stage save the party from disintegration, this fundamentalist approach did cause it at the same time to embrace a political creed, confirmed in a new Constitution adopted in 1977, that gave the party little resonance in a conventional and deeply partisan political culture that had been firmly wedded to class politics and well organised party machines for most of the present century. The preference of the Ecology Party, both for a political discourse couched in apparently ethereal terms and for a style of politics that encouraged direct action and poor discipline, merely helped to further distance the party from the 'accepted' norms of the party political game which continue to shape expectations about how politics should be practiced.[6] This handicap was confirmed on the ground; it had scant success in the local elections it contested during 1976 and 1977. As Byrne has observed, "the Green Party's emphasis on idealism, seeking long term solutions, and taking a global rather than a democratic perspective may be disconcerting to an electorate noted for its pragmatism and aversion to political change".[7]

The British ecologists faced additional political liabilities too. In common with Europe's other new Green parties, its radical bent and a preference for grassroots or movement politics, distanced ecological activists from potential allies in other parties. They were essentially ill disposed towards what they saw as the electoral short-termism, the hypocrisy and the politics of easy promises and quick fixes that they associated with the normal political game. Under these circumstances, the survival of an independent ecology party was less than certain; at least until the national issue agenda began to shift perceptibly in the party's favour during the seventies.[8] The various economic and political crises of that turbulent decade opened a debate on energy resources which has never returned to its earlier complacency. Nuclear energy, too, became a matter of serious debate.[9] The 1977 Windscale Inquiry at the end of that decade, focused increasing public attention on the issue of nuclear waste reprocessing through organisations such as Energy 2000.[10] Both of these issues contributed to the determination of many activists concerned by these issues to support an independent ecology party.

The new Conservative government added momentum to this mood after 1979, when it embarked on the expansion of the nuclear energy industry - as it did, too, with its support for NATO's policy of modernising Britain's nuclear deterrent by acquiring the Trident weapons system. These twin decisions did much to energise an already well-established and radical green and pacifist protest movement. The Campaign for Nuclear Disarmament (CND), a largely middle class lobby,[11] was transformed from only a few thousand activists into a mass movement of over 100,000 by 1983: and one with even more diffuse social roots. Although this political ferment helped to sustain the emergent Green party, and provided a source of steady if modest recruitment, the ecologists continued to remain aloof from the increasingly militant leftist orientations of CND. One historian of these radical social movements has identified a source of competition, if not irritation, between the Greens and these other movements. The proliferation of green radical and pacifist groups almost certainly inhibited the party's growth. They were competing on the same political ground for the limited resources of activist commitment and funding that are indispensable to the success of any political movement, but which are crucial for the survival of radical movements.[12] There were, however, distinct benefits from this continuing separation. The weakness of the Green Party in an unhelpful opportunity structure deterred many far left 'entryists' from infiltrating the party, and thereby from fomenting deeply divisive and damaging arguments over arcane ideological issues. Instead, as Rootes has observed, "the environmentalist movement was largely left to its own devices and its moderation was never seriously challenged".[13] The party did not escape other equally debilitating internal arguments. It opted for an holistic, dark green approach: one at least as radical in its commitment to a grassroots model of participatory politics as any other western European party, regardless of its position on the pure-green/red-green discourse. The rationale here was not to trust in high politics to ameliorate the symptoms of environmental degradation, but instead to tackle its causes directly through specific campaigns. This, in turn, generated a style of politics that was anti-hierarchical and ultra-democratic. As tensions developed between those who saw the Green Party - as it subsequently became - as a living embodiment of a new lifestyle, and others in the party who preferred a more measured and pragmatic politics, the British party was not spared the same damaging internecine squabbles that occurred in Europe's other Green parties. The rising militancy not only cost the party access to important support networks; it also deterred many moderate voters and potential activists, alienated by the spectacle of futile gesture politics.[14]

Although the favourable shift in the national issue agenda and the party's increased electoral profile, helped to raise membership figures from 650 in 1979 to some 6,000 by 1981[15] (where the figure stabilised more or less, until a further but brief surge in support at the end of the decade),[16] the party remained as a marginal force in British politics. [17] In the 1979 general election, for example, its candidates won only 1.6 per cent of the vote in the 53 seats contested, in spite of claiming a free national election broadcast. It polled only slightly better in the 1979 European elections, nominating 3 candidates who averaged 3.7 per cent of the vote where they stood - and this at a time when British politics seemed ripe for a degree of realignment. The breakaway of the SDP from the Labour Party in 1981, and the recent success of regional parties in Wales and Scotland seemed to offer some evidence of incipient change in British politics. The Greens were not one of the beneficiaries of this discernible shift in partisan loyalties. In fact, there were few tangible signs of British marginal voters being attracted by ecologism, other than as an occasional vehicle of mid-term protest.[18] The ecologists secured only minimal support in both the 1983 general election, where the party polled an average of 1.0 per cent in 106 constituencies, and at the 1984 Euro-elections, where the Ecology Party candidates won an average of only 2.6 per cent in their constituency contests. The resurgence of a climate of possessive individualism on the back of the Thatcherite neo-liberal 'revolution' underlined the immense cultural lacuna between the hard nosed and optimistic individualism that had transformed political expectations, and the idealistic concern of anti-materialistic ecologism with unpalatable futures and unavoidable sacrifices. The ecologists had more than hostile political values to contend with. The evidence of a large membership of various green pressure groups suggests that many British voters rejected rampant hedonism and favoured a degree of asceticism to save resources or indeed the planet itself. The discrepancy between this large constituency and the paltry vote for ecology candidates, is explained in some measure by the persistence of the 'wasted vote' syndrome in Britain - an electoral system whose rules are uniquely unfavourable to all small parties without a regional base in which to concentrate their vote.[19]

(ii)   Party formation

The party's decision in 1986 to change its name yet again to the Green Party - with regional but affiliated parties for Scotland and Wales - in an attempt to cash in on the wave of support for Green party politics across Europe, could hardly overcome these persistent handicaps. It had little apparent effect on the conservative British electorate.[20] In the 1987 general election the party stood 133 candidates, who only managed to poll 1.4 per cent (a total of 90,000 votes) in the seats contested.[21] A further breakdown of these electoral statistics offered little comfort to the Greens. The British Greens managed barely 2 per cent in 10 seats and its best constituency performance was only 3.5 per cent. These figures suggested an absence of those local or regional strongholds which Green parties in France, Belgium, Germany and elsewhere have been able to exploit to advantage. Germany again provides the clearest example of what can be achieved by a Green party harnessing potent social issues and organising local campaigns, to tap a clear vein of environmental concern running through social attitudes; on the basis of grassroots campaigns, to build up resources, recruit membership, gather political experience and achieve political visibility; and, moreover, to use those resources as an launching pad for a more effective role in national politics. None of these advantages accrued to Britain's Greens.[22] On the contrary, the peculiarities of national political culture, a centralised polity and administrative system, and a highly unpropitious opportunity structure for minor parties, precluded a strong base for the Greens in both regional or local politics. This legacy in turn, made an effective national role even less likely.

The Greens were also victims of an unfavourable electoral system. British electoral law discriminates against small parties in elections at every level - and particularly so in parliamentary elections. The requirement of a £500 deposit in order to stand on the ballot - and the prospect of losing it, unless a requisite percentage vote is obtained - is a big disincentive to any small and poorly resourced party considering whether or not to run a sufficient number of candidates, in order to raise its national profile. The near certainty of surrendering large numbers of deposits is something no party can face with equanimity. This is a situation that does not confront small parties in altogether more favourable opportunity structures. In many other European democracies the Green parties have enjoyed the benefits of proportional systems, as well as ready access to public funding to defray their campaign costs. The overall consequences of the British 'opportunity structure' were an added burden for a party already suffering the usual reticence of the electorate faced with untried and inexperienced politicians. Many potential Green activists chose to support an active green lobby, but to vote for other, more established parties. Prospective green electors, likewise, continued to regard the party as a classic case of the 'wasted vote'.[23] The electoral payoff spoke for itself here. By the end of the 1980s - even after almost two decades of continuous existence - the Green Party had not advanced beyond holding a handful of council seats (many of them at parish level), compared with Die Grunen's impressive haul of 2000 seats at every level of West German politics.

The failure to make a breakthrough on the Parliamentary front - or even to poll a sizeable and consistent protest vote - did little to help the party's development, let alone improve its internal cohesion. This continuing marginality merely turned the party in on itself. Energy that is expended, even in moderately successful parties, on contesting the political turf with rivals, tends in fringe parties to be channelled into arcane ideological disputes, all the more damaging for their close focused intensity. The party's structure merely aggravated these quarrels. The abiding preference for local party autonomy, and thus for a loose party structure, together with an almost obsessive preoccupation with the rites of party democracy, prevented effective coordination by the party's national organisation. In these circumstances, the party was ill equipped, either for engaging in the usual inter-party adversarialism that is the meat of British party politics, or for running effective national election campaigns. Just as damaging in a political culture that prefers moderation to extremism, and pragmatism over utopianism, was the prominence given in the party's affairs to small factions led by prominent activists intent on pursuing parochial and in some instances bizarre causes - in one notable case, a party member claimed to be the 'Son of God', and there were many instances, too, of the usual gamut of politically correct causes (anti-racist, anti-sexist and so on) which sit uneasily with British mores and which contributed to the party's eccentric image.

What turned out to be a deep and protracted division between the fundamentalists who saw the party structure as an arena for grassroots action over radical causes, and their opponents who defined the party as a vehicle for articulating a cohesive Green programme capable of winning electoral support and influencing the national policy discourse, was accentuated by these quarrels. These divisions were apparent in the party's very origins.[24] The British party was the first national Green party as such, to emerge anywhere in Europe. The unfavourable political opportunity structure told on the party's electoral prospects from the start. The pattern of party growth was slow and essentially rooted in local cells. Those activists who continued to hope for a national presence based on a better electoral performance pushed for a more coordinated party organisation. The key to success in this perspective was a shift from parochialism, in order to better confront the political system on its own terms. The critical assessment of the party's shortcomings by a leading Green pragmatist, Jonathon Porritt, was couched in precisely these terms. He noted that while "our primary concern is at the local level, and our primary goal is to start winning seats on local councils", circumstances in Britain dictated a need for a national political drive. For "such is the power of our centralised media and power structure that we cannot possibly achieve this (breakthrough) without a stimulus and equally strong commitment to politics at the national level".[25] Porritt saw a distinct political advantage in adopting a less confrontational stance towards the political establishment and, indeed, favoured the adoption of some of its procedures.[26] The fault line in the party came to be defined in essentially these terms. In the early stages, the party did respond to its poor electoral performances with an attempt to improve internal procedures. A compromise between the anti-partyists and pragmatists saw the party set up a Party Organisation Working Group (POWG), and the appointment of two party convenors. The POWG's recommendations for suitable constitutional amendments to resolve the confusions over the proper channels of authority and communication between the local and national parties, and the nature of the mandate of any elected Green representative, were placed before the February 1986 national conference. The balance of forces within the party against these modest compromises with conventional procedures, was revealed when the conference rejected these reforms. In part because they seemed too elaborate, but in essence because they touched a raw ideological nerve in the party. This was the first battle in what became a protracted war over the style and format of Green Party politics. It was a conflict that deeply divided the party thereafter, and confirmed its political ineffectiveness.

Even at this stage, feeling ran deep over the issue. The conference was moved to postpone any serious attempt to confront this issue or to push hard for its resolution, in spite of periodic attempts by the party's convenors - mostly of a pragmatic persuasion - to persuade it otherwise. Any initiative, however oblique, to professionalise and routinise party procedures, was regarded with immense suspicion by the anti-partyists. The sudden and largely unexpected success of the Greens in the late 1980s - when the party won an unprecedented 14.9 per cent of the total vote (2.25 million votes), and took third place behind the two main parties in the 1989 European elections, without taking any of the 11 Strasbourg seats they would have won under a proportional list system because of the mathematical inequities of the plurality electoral system - merely buried these organisational issues under the general euphoria that gripped the party at this outcome, but without resolving them. The Green Party tried to accommodate both tendencies within an unobtrusive party framework. Compromises were enacted, although over time these, too, became subject to considerable stress. A London headquarters was established in Balham, and its full-time staff performed most of the usual administrative and coordinating functions required of modern parties. The Balham organisation was seen as the minimum price to be paid for conducting national election campaigns. Although the anti-partyists went along with this, they resisted any notion that this organisation amounted to the bureaucratisation of party functions. Diversity remained the central axiom of the party's organisational ethos and arrangements. Independent political action was not only permitted: it was seen as a positive virtue. Green CND, for example, contributed its own evidence to official inquiries - for instance, the one instituted to examine the impact of the construction of the Sizewell B nuclear power station. Local Green groups arranged their own participation in, and support for, the peace camps at Greenham Common and Molesworth. Independent publications were also tolerated. The wouldbe centralisers were unable, at this stage, to muster enough power at party congresses to bring these autonomous local power centres under effective control.

The salutary experience of an equally rapid decline in electoral support on top of yet another dismal performance in the 1992 general election brought the reform issue back to the centre of Green party politics. The pragmatists continued to canvass with a new urgency the reforms of party procedures that challenged head on the fundamentalists' defence of party democracy. This latest attempt to make a realistic adjustment to prevailing circumstances launched the party on its most divisive debate so far about the essence of radical party politics. The inclination of the anti-party fundamentalists was to concentrate their main energies on issue-based campaigns and grassroots activity. The electoralists, on the other hand, saw a credible Green Party as the best hope for putting ecologism on the national political agenda and representing it on its own terms, and in a way that precluded other parties from colonising or trivialising it.

(iii)   Political developments

The outcome of the 1989 European elections was an important catalyst for change in the Green Party's uneven development. The party's various tendencies each found some vindication of their respective positions in the events of this, the best year so far in the party's history. They were initially encouraged by some patchy successes in the 1989 local elections, which helped to raise the party's national profile. The Greens fielded some 600 candidates, secured an average vote of 8 per cent across the board, and took 13.6 per cent in Somerset and Dorset West and 14 per cent in Hereford and Worcester. The party faced the forthcoming European elections with an unprecedented degree of expectancy. They stood on an anti-EC platform which in itself was not the public flavour of the moment - yet managed to reconcile this position with an anti-centralist approach to continued integration which easily chimed with the abiding British preference for limited EC encroachment in British affairs. In the event, policy matters per se were much less the cause of the Greens' remarkable success than a mid-term mood of deep disillusionment with the Conservative government and its embattled leader, Margaret Thatcher. The Green Party stood confidently in all 78 British Euro-seats on a 'common statement' endorsed by their 'sister parties' throughout the Community. This included the usual range of ecological issues, and took issue with the growth targets and the accompanying environmental damage of the impending Single Market. The manifesto also promised the outlawing of wasteful packaging, harmful pesticides, ozone depleting CFCs, shipments of hazardous waste and dumping at sea. It advocated, too, the phasing out of nuclear waste; the transformation of the CAP into a system of chemical-free food production to meet essential local needs; special protection for European parks; a non-aligned and nuclear weapon free Europe; land redistribution, and a basic income scheme to allow for flexible working and to sustain a small scale farming industry.[27] The close links forged during this, the best moment ever, for European Green party politics, between the Green fraternity, were further cemented by the decision of the 30 strong Green Group in the European Parliament that emerged from these elections, to allow one British Green party representative to join the group's 8 strong executive. The Belgian and Italian Greens each allocated one of their two votes and some of the group's funds to the British representative, Jean Lambert, a prominent Green Party 'realist'.[28]

The unexpected success in the European elections, with the largest percentage turnout for British Green candidates of any previous Euro-election, had mixed consequences. It was helpful in boosting political confidence and raising the party's profile. The Greens became the focus of fear or loathing for parties that had previously ignored them. The Liberals were the Greens' principal victims. The Liberals polled a mere 986,000 votes - less than half the Green total, causing them to suffer a string of lost deposits - and fell back into fourth place. The result also occasioned a surge in party membership, which rose at the rate of 50 a day throughout the campaign, and reached an unprecedented total of 18,000 by the end of it. The bald facts of this success need, however, to be put into perspective. This was always a tenuous rather than a signal achievement; a momentary breakthrough on the back of a favourable following wind, but hardly a seachange. For one thing, the Greens had clearly taken over the usual role of the Liberals as the party of the residual protest vote in what was, after all, Britain's least important second order elections. They were helped, too, by the Conservative Party's less than enthusiastic approach to the European Parliament - the particular object of this electoral exercise - and the Government's more obvious failure to sustain the economic boom of the mid 1980s. This is not to discount increased concern in some quarters with the damaging environmental consequences of this economic upturn, and not least with what some commentators defined as "the number of motor vehicles on the roads, especially in the already highly populated southern England", where the Green vote was largely concentrated; or with "a development boom which markedly increased the pressure upon the environment".[29] Environment pressure groups enjoyed a surge in membership on the back of such concerns; Friends of the Earth grew from 31,000 to 125,000 members and Greenpeace from 150,000 to 281,000 during 1988-89.[30]

The Green Party polled over 20 per cent in 17 of the Euro-constituencies, with their best performances in West Sussex (24.5 per cent) and Somerset and Dorset (23 per cent). They took second place in 6 seats in front of Labour and took third place, usually at the expense of the Liberals, in every other English and Welsh Euro-constituency except two, polling particularly well, with some 50,000 votes in Devon alone, in traditional Conservative strongholds.[31] They could hardly be expected to hold on to these votes in a general election campaign, where the protest vote would either revert to the Conservatives or to their main party challengers. The Liberals' disarray, following that party's recent troubles in its turbulent alliance with David Owen's SDP, could not be guaranteed to last. Moreover, the Greens' failure to make any significant, let alone a permanent, inroad into the established British pattern of two and a half party politics, was underlined by their inability to challenge Labour for the radical left vote - either in Labour's traditional urban strongholds, or in those marginal seats in which there was a straight Labour-Conservative contest.[32] The Greens' success in the Euro-poll in 'natural' Conservative territory in the south was not matched in those regions where other parties - either Labour or nationalist parties - offered a more established protest vehicle. Chris Rootes has identified a qualified post-materialist effect at work here, underpinning Green support in relatively affluent regions, but diminishing it outside the south of England.[33] He noted that, apart from Cornwall and Devon (a traditional centre of Liberalism), "the Green vote declined quite consistently with distance from the relatively affluent, Conservative-dominated south: in the south it averaged 20.3 per cent, in London 16 per cent, in the Midlands 14.7 per cent, in the north 12 per cent. In only three English divisions, all Labour strongholds in the north east, did the Greens poll less than 10 per cent". Whereas in Scotland, the Greens averaged only 7.2 per cent and came in behind all of the main parties and the nationalists in every one of that country's eight seats.[34]

The Liberals initially responded to this strong challenge to their third party status by openly courting the Greens, with a view to encouraging some sort of electoral pact. As Green support began to evaporate as quickly as it had risen over the ensuing months, the Liberals reverted to tactics similar to those employed by the other mainstream parties. In short, the Green's 1989 Euro triumph was dismissed as a mere flash in the pan. The Greens faced illconcealed derision from the established parties and their policies were subjected to greater critical scrutiny than ever.[35] Chris Patten, the Foreign Office Minister, dubbed the Greens during the campaign as 'Zen Fascists'.[36] Paddy Ashdown was hardly more charitable, dismissing them as a political fad. For Labour, Dr David Clarke chided them for being 'simplistic' and 'utopian'.[37] There was, however, as much latent concern over Green electoral potential as contempt in such criticisms. The major parties revealed their underlying concern with the political potential of environmentalism, in much the same way as established parties elsewhere in Europe. They tried to appropriate Green credentials by incorporating ecological measures into their own policy programmes.[38] There was more strategic calculation in this belated conversion than sincerity. But it worked against the Greens and saw them outflanked by more politically astute rivals. The most notable convert here to 'green awareness' was that otherwise unreconstructed free marketeer and exponent of possessive individualism, Prime Minister Thatcher. Mrs Thatcher had rather ambiguously signalled her belated 'conversion' to green values in a much publicised speech to the Royal Society, in the autumn of 1988.[39] She followed this with a decision in March 1989 to host a 124 nation conference on the growing threat to the ozone layer.[40] Conservative Ministers took their cue from this lead and, in response to concern over lost votes and prompted by the novelty of a spate of motions inspired by environmental awareness at the 1988 Party conference,[41] began to press for tighter EC rules on exhaust emissions. Ministers likewise agreed to withdraw their objections to the proposed European Environmental Agency,[42] as well as endorsing the EC's ban on the ivory trade. The Prime Minister included in her leader's speech to the annual Conservative Party conference positive references to a national environmental strategy. Michael Howard, the Minister of State for the Environment, followed up what was a blatant appeal to win back former Conservatives who had switched to the Greens, by outlining the Government's current list of environmental schemes - from encouraging household waste recycling to examining the idea of marketable permits for emissions. The new Energy Secretary, John Wakeham, likewise broached higher fossil fuel prices as an energy consumption measure.[43]

In the event the Green revival proved to be as much of a mirage as the belated conversion of the political establishment to environmentalism. The ephemeral quality of what amounted to little more than a mid-term protest against an unpopular government was soon revealed. The Greens' average poll rating was halved within a month of the European elections, and fell thereafter, until by 1991 it was deemed to pollsters to be insufficient to merit recording in its own right. The party's electoral rating was lumped together with that for other 'fringe' parties as its position deteriorated on the ground. Where the Green Party contested seats at all in the 1991 district elections, it won barely 6 per cent of the vote;[44] and with only 13 district council victories to its credit, managed to make an impact on only one district council - Stroud in Gloucestershire - winning only occasional seats in other rural areas (notably in Hereford, Worcester and Avon).

The volatile and unreliable quality of the Green 'protest' vote was underlined by the polling evidence. Many 'Green' voters remained blithely unaware of what the party actually stood for. The polling data did indicate that the Greens had tapped into a widespread unease about the environment, and the need for its greater protection - against a background feeling that the main parties had simply not taken the issue seriously enough.[45]   At the same time, the positive response of all three mainstream parties to the environment question indicated the electorate's fickleness. It also indicated the relative ease with which they could be won back from the Greens once this issue received some attention in the area of policy priorities. The Greens were vulnerable on other counts too. The polls showed that the more voters knew about the Greens, the less they actually identified with them - a fact which the party's opponents used to advantage in their urgent campaign to win back lost votes. Only 41 per cent of those polled, for instance, actually knew that the Greens favoured a marked reduction in personal consumption; or that serious conservation measures would entail significant changes in lifestyle.   Only two items on the Green Party's 1989 policy programme - the banning of factory farming and the diverting of a significant proportion of defence expenditure into improving the environment - received positive endorsement from a majority of their voters. Even more damaging were findings that underlined the ephemeral nature of Green support and especially the party's dependence, not on Green converts but on the protest vote quota[46] - and that confined, by and large, to second order elections whose outcome was always of little consequence for the national balance of power in this conservative and highly centralised state.[47]   The great proportion of the Green vote fully intended to revert to more familiar partisan loyalties in the next general election.[48]

The Greens failed to capitalise on their 1989 success because they were as unprepared for it as their opponents. The party had settled, before their brief resurgence for the marginal role in British politics which its loosely structured and anti-party preference had consigned it to. Many of the party's 'realists' had long despaired of changing this fundamentalist outlook, even if they continued to challenge it in the party's institutions. These 'realists' had joined the party out of a residual loyalty to the ecology cause, but reserved their real energies and most effective campaigning for the parallel green network of pressure groups which was actively, and to a degree successfully, engaged in lobbying governmental and other policy making agencies. At the same time, the favourable disposition of the Liberal Party - and for the brief time of their separate existence as a party, the SDP - towards environmental issues, denied the Greens a firm and unchallenged support base amongst Britain's 'new politics' constituency.[49] The British Green Party had largely settled for such a peripheral political role, until the 1989 outcome suddenly opened up altogether new horizons. At least this event whetted the political appetite, and indeed the ambitions, of some of the party's more pragmatic elements, who felt increasingly concerned that the party was organisationally ill equipped to take full advantage of, let alone to build on, their electoral windfall. The Euro-elections left another legacy: they reopened the debate on party status and strategy. Events raised to the top of the party's agenda the prospect of adopting - or resisting - the electoralist strategy already being followed by other European Green parties, albeit under rather more favourable circumstances. The failure to hold on to this unprecedented level of support only served to intensify the debate, and galvanized the party's pragmatists to redouble their efforts to move the party away from anti-partyism and towards a 'realist' strategy that involved adopting a better coordinated party organisation and more conventional political goals. The realists saw this as the indispensable prelude to convincing those prospective Green voters who had recently flirted with the party in unprecedented numbers, that the Greens were indeed a serious party - one that was capable of pursuing sensible policies, exhibiting a degree of political responsibility in the process, and thereby worthy of support. For the time being, the momentum was with the realists, who were disproportionately represented in positions of 'leadership', or at least enjoyed significant influence in the party organisation. A group of prominent realists formed an internal pressure group - Green 2000 - and used this forum to lobby within the party's internal structures, for what they saw as necessary reorganisation and constitutional change. They were confronted from the outset by determined resistance within the party's grassroots, opposed to any compromise with decentralisation, anti-partyism and the loose or non-existent leadership that characterised the Green Party.[50]

The reformers' initial aim was to professionalise the party by routinising its ramshackle decision making procedures. It was part of this plan to enhance the party's electoral appeal by sharpening its policy focus. Aware of the certain opposition to any changes that smacked of a more hierarchical or formal party status, these modernisers tried to maximise consensus around a pure green version of ecologism. The intention here was to build agreement in favour of reform - in the circumstances by no means an easy objective to accomplish - without opening up the parallel divisions over ideological orientation that had both diminished and delayed the impact of Green parties in national politics elsewhere in Europe. The attempt at a trade off here was by no means successful. The pursuit of moderation and the common sense that infused the efforts of the realists, took precedence over the need to placate the ecocentric sensibilities of the party's purists. This bargain proved difficult to carry off and was not, in the long run, a recipe for successfully balancing the interests of the competing factions.

The party's modernisers tried to fashion ecologism into a distinctively radical but realistic alternative to the 'failed ideologies' of the established parties.[51] A leading party spokesman at the time, David Spaven, was quick to equate the revived drive for 'realism' exhibited at the 1989 Annual party congress with the Party's consistent commitment to its pure Green legacy. Spaven's statement here was a clear testament to the rising revisionism amongst some leading elements in the party. According to this outlook: "We don't want to go back to the caves, we don't dream of imaginary rural idylls, and we're certainly not a bunch of modern Calvinists .... As for hair shirts, the best place for them is on the backs of political leaders who have manifestly failed to capture the public mood .... We are not a no growth party. We are not an anti-technology party. We've demonstrated that Green economics is all about sustainable economic development - meeting everyone's needs instead of pandering to the profit driven mass consumption which has brought our world to the brink of disaster. As a forward looking party we're committed to the use of technology to eliminate drudgery and assist the battle to save the planet. But the technology has to be appropriate for real human needs instead of the out of control monster which diminishes and degrades so many lives".[52]

The reformist wing managed, on the basis of a direct appeal to a refined but unmitigated pure green ethos,[53] to at least secure the party's tentative agreement to a review of what they regarded as its unwieldy arrangement of six co-equal national spokespersons. Reformism gained impetus as the Liberal Democrats passed the Greens in the opinion polls for the first time since the Strasbourg elections. At the 1989 Conference hostility from the entrenched anti-partyists on the floor was at least contained, even if they were not won over to the revisionist cause. The modernisers managed to deflect the brunt of the most insistent criticism - that they were about to impose an oligarchic and elitist party format on Britain's only 'genuinely' democratic party. An outbreak of overt hostilities was only averted when they modified their own preferences for a proper party status. The proposal, for instance, for a reduction to four elected speakers - with other specialist speakers coopted as required, and three party co-chairs - was little more than a scaling down of the existing cumbersome arrangements, and some way removed from the conventional model of party management. The same rationale was offered for their proposal to turn party conference into an all delegate affair, with tighter voting arrangements and a more streamlined approach to policy making. Advocates of even these drastic changes, including Porritt, argued that they would not reduce the abiding sense of a party driven by its membership but would, nevertheless, send out a more coherent message to the electorate. The principal aim here was to remove the damaging perception of an ill-disciplined party presiding over incoherent and even inconsistent policy. Without diluting the party's a priori commitment to grassroots participation, these procedural changes would contrast favourably in the public's mind with the present arrangements, whereby anyone could attend conferences.[54]

The relative success of the party's reformers in 1989 to persuade the conference to at least consider these proposals encouraged them to increase the tempo at the party's spring conference in 1990. On this occasion the principal issue under consideration was a proposal to further modify the leadership function - to inaugurate two new salaried posts, a national speaker and a national political coordinator. Although this proposal was prefaced by strong disclaimers that the occupants of these posts would merely be party figureheads and not national leaders per se,[55] the suspicions of the fundamentalists were fanned - not least because they were endorsed by the party's full-time staff at the Balham headquarters. These functionaries complained that organisational incoherence had lost the party valuable electoral ground, even in the successful 1989 poll, because it had proved unable to respond, either quickly or convincingly enough, to media requests for authoritative interviews or statements. The desire to become a serious force in national politics depended, in this realist prospectus, on replacing the inexperienced National Council spokespersons - who exerted little direct control over party policy or affairs - with an altogether more focused party format. The case of one pro-reformist speaker, that these changes did not, as such, threaten intra-party democracy - that "we are talking about a professional who is responsible to the party, not someone who is taking decisions ahead of the party" - did little to mollify the fundamentalists. On the face of it the reformists drew what they regarded as merely obvious conclusions from the party's recent experiences; that to create a political space for ecologism and maintain it under the conditions of mass electoral politics requires a professional leadership cadre capable of taking incisive executive actions. And one, moreover, with whom the public and the media alike can identify. The fundamentalists, for their part, saw this as a subterfuge for the adoption of a model of party politics entirely alien to the practice of grassroots democracy that was inseparable from ecologism per se. The anti-party tendency resisted these blandishments and objected that the reformist case was not only intellectually dishonest and wholly unnecessary, but also a dangerous distraction from ecologism's essential roots in locally based and fully participatory politics. The fundamentalists, with support throughout the party but particularly concentrated at the grassroots, saw in the revisionist case a covert attempt by elitists and careerists to subvert party democracy. One of the leading critics of the reform agenda, Janet Aulty, staunchly defended open decision making, widespread participation by members at every level, and the virtues of talking until a consensus was reached, as the only democratic way of making policy: "We don't", she argued at a party meeting in 1990, "decide our policies amongst a few people behind closed doors, then present the membership with a fait accompli. We want to involve as many as want to be involved. In Green politics everyone has a right to have a say".[56]

The discord over these issues set the scene for an increasingly disruptive internal battle which raged within the party over the next three years.[57] The first signs that this conflict could not be safely contained under the convenient guise of a 'mere' modification of existing practice came to light at the party's 1990 spring conference. Insistent support for a call to hold a special conference to consider all the questions raised by the reform agenda alarmed the fundamentalists - who felt that they were in danger of yielding the initiative to their opponents. They fought back and vehemently signalled their opposition to the proposed changes. Perry Kemp, a former co-chair of the party, issued a clarion call that rallied the opponents of change at this conference, with his defiant cry that "I see the Green Party as an anti-party.... We are about empowering people".[58] The opponents of reform had, nevertheless, yielded rather too much ground to immediately win back the initiative. In spite of waging a militant campaign against change on the floor of both of the 1989 party conferences, for the time being the reformists were in the ascendancy. The inconclusive outcome of the special conference, called in July 1990 to consider reform, indicated not only how finely balanced was the equilibrium in the party between the antagonists but how, in these circumstances, it was easier to do nothing - to block reform than to enact it. Although this conference endorsed in principle the idea of change, the anti-partyists were able to muster sufficient support to challenge the legality and the legitimacy of the decision and thus to have it rescinded. Thereafter, the reformers pushed harder for change. At the conference held in September 1990, the reformist group, Green 2000, which had continued to lobby more urgently on behalf of reform as it faced such entrenched opposition, attempted to resolve the impasse by pushing for the concrete changes that would ensure, as they saw it, a strengthening of the party's organisational coherence and an improvement in its electoral image. The essence of these proposals was enshrined in the argument that the party must accept, however unpalatable, "the need for leadership as a function" even though it was proposed that this would "be in a democratically elected and accountable team".[59] There was a sense, too, of a gap opening up between the party's most prominent and publicly sanitised figures, and the rank and file with their roots in local politics. The party's de facto leadership elite stood squarely behind the case for reform. Jonathon Porritt, for example, read an uncompromising lesson in what he saw as incontrovertible political realities, to the 1990 Party Assembly. It contained an incisive critique of persistent anti-partyism as naive, misguided and essentially infantile. "The Green Party", he observed wryly, "seems to attract an awful lot of people who don't like politics. These are strengths in that you get fewer opportunists but there are real drawbacks. You have no depth of experience in the political process, you have not got the staying power".[60]

In spite of rising support in the party for the pragmatic idealism of those such as Porritt, who had proved that green ideas could receive a fair hearing in the media and even a respectful one from erstwhile political opponents - and not least at a moment when the party was sinking fast in the opinion polls[61] and with its membership and revenue falling back sharply - the sheer disorganisation of existing party procedures enabled a determined anti-party rearguard to successfully bloc the Green 2000 initiative. There were in these circumstances, palpable signs of intense frustration or worse amongst the realists. Not least from Porritt, who finally seemed to lose patience and appeared to be on the verge of abandoning reform altogether as a hopeless cause. In the event, and in spite of blandishments and a much publicised appearance at the Liberal Democrats' annual conference, he merely threatened to 'reconsider' his party membership if the party refused to pull back from what he and other leading Green realists saw as its abiding fantasy - that any significant political influence could be exerted without the party undertaking a thorough reform of its procedures. Porritt underlined the senselessness of the party's present course by arguing that while the 1989 Euro success should have signalled the end of the 'fantasists', the party continued to shun political reality. It preferred instead to live with chimeras, by maintaining the luxury of its "wholly irrational abhorrence of political leadership. They (the purists) seem to have an approach to the media and to party organisation that makes the architects of the tower of Babel look like reasonable people".[62] Other party notables weighed into this debate along similar lines. Sara Parkin, another prominent realist, recorded her rising annoyance at the prospect of a party slipping rapidly down the polls, and yet seemingly facing the political oblivion that awaited it with equanimity, even though it had, as she believed, the solution to its problems in its own hands.

As on previous occasions, the party seemed more willing to review the options for constitutional change than it was to implement them. The spring conference of 1991 provided yet another example of 'much heat signifying nothing'. The party toyed with the modest proposal to adopt a 'shadow cabinet' model, as a concession to a more conventional leadership strategy. But it chose instead to reject any measures that would have limited the power of the party's grassroots over its policy procedures. The only sign of compromise here came when the conference overturned, by a card vote, an earlier decision agreed ad hoc on the floor - and predictably condemned by the realists as 'the route to anarchy' - that would have permitted any 3 members to declare themselves to be a policy group of the party. The party seemed to observers as determined as ever to jeopardise its own already negligible electoral credibility, and to resist the reform agenda dangled before it by an increasingly frustrated 'leadership' group. The prospect of an impending general election and a likely electoral humiliation galvanised the reformists to make one more concerted effort to break the reform impasse at the September conference of 1991. The conference was persuaded to endorse, after the usual divisive debate, some procedural changes, with a view to improving the party's ability to fight an effective electoral campaign. The conference voted to abolish the Green Party Council and to replace it with a more focused Regional Council, representing the area parties, and with an altogether more coherent leadership structure. This consisted of a party Executive of 9 voting and 2 non-voting speakers. It was further agreed that all party officers were to be elected to specific party posts or portfolios, and by a postal - and therefore secret - ballot of the membership. With a general election imminent, the conference took the opportunity to endorse advance arrangements - notably for two principal speakers - Jean Lambert and Richard Lawson - to handle the major London press conferences - and with two other equally well-known moderate Greens, Sara Parkin and Jonathon Porritt, designated to launch the manifesto and deal with the inevitably unsympathetic or hostile media grilling. The conference also endorsed the reformists' proposal that party conferences should be recast as more structured delegate assemblies, in the place of the open, disorganised, often chaotic fora that currently prevailed. The present arrangement had prevented national meetings from being the positive advertisement for alternative politics - disciplined arenas for lively debate but coherent policy making - that would be more likely than the current spectacles of disorderly debate and frequently inconclusive posturing to remove the apprehensions of at least some of the electorate.[63]

These proposed reforms were carried overwhelmingly and the reformists were jubilant at what they took to be a major breakthrough for political common sense. Sara Parkin, for instance, pronounced that "we are now in serious business". Even more hyperbole followed from otherwise sensible people who, apprised of the odds against electoral change, should have kept more cautious counsel. It was predicted in some quarters that there would be a Green government by the year 2010. The signs of a backlash were apparent even as these reforms were accepted. For they were not embraced with equanimity, and they were forced through against the instincts of many party members, only after repeated resignation threats by reformists such as Porritt. This deterrent certainly helped to carry the day, but it also unleashed a festering resentment and offered a hostage to the future should the changes fail to deliver an improvement in the party's fortunes. The defeated anti-partyists determined to bide their time, ready to regroup, and strike again should the Faustian bargain of an exchange of the principle of democratic control over the party leadership for electoral success fail to materialise at the forthcoming general election - as it was almost bound to do under the current electoral rules. The anti-partyists did not have long to wait before springing their trap. In spite of a much better coordinated 1992 general election campaign, the Greens were unable to sustain anything like a convincing electoral performance. At a time when the electorate was preoccupied with the usual material issues and concerned with the impact of recession,[64] the Greens were caught in the normal pincer movement of adversarial politics.

The party's strong showing in the European elections had held out some expectation that the major parties might be squeezed. In the event, in the closest general election for almost two decades, and one dominated by two well-funded party machines - both of which expended record amounts on advertising and enjoying a virtual monopoly of media coverage - it was the Greens who were squeezed. The sizeable third party protest vote they had successfully attracted away from the Liberals in 1989 deserted them in droves.[65] The Greens started the three week campaign at barely 3 per cent in the national opinion polls. The actual Green vote was cut to barely 1 per cent on polling day - a figure below even the party's modest 1987 turnout. The Greens put up a record 256 candidates (almost double its 1987 total of 133, and well in excess of 106 nominations in 1983), polled a modest 170,000 votes nationally, and lost 254 deposits at a cost of £127,000, in a campaign it was forced to fight, because of its severe shortage of funds, on a shoestring budget. The party managed its highest constituency percentage in Islington North (3.75 per cent). The closest the Greens came to success was the contribution made by Green tactical voters to secure the election of Cynog Dafis, a joint Plaid Cymru (Welsh Nationalist Party) and Green Party candidate, for the Welsh seat of Ceredigion.[66] The party's 1992 election result was poor even by the mediocre standards reached by minor parties in British general elections - and a far cry from an earlier and flattering description of the Greens by Robin Cook, a leading Labour front bencher, as "the slumbering giant of British politics".

In the bitter aftermath of this great disappointment, the party ended its truce and re-embarked on its barely abated civil war. The reformers, for their part, took the scale of the 1992 defeat as confirmation that even more far reaching changes were necessary if the party was ever to win the electorate's trust and become a credible party. Porritt continued to challenge the fundamentalists. He regarded complacency as even more damaging to ecologism than bold reform in the long run, because "denying political reality is as dangerous as denying ecological reality". Porritt also accused the anti-partyists of "almost breathtaking superficiality" and argued that their self indulgent claim to be merely above the ideological fray meant little as such; for "being non-party political is no excuse for being politically inadequate - a charge which the left has consistently levelled against the Green movement, and which may well be justified".[67] The brunt of Porritt's stinging rebuke fell on those in the party he regarded as self indulgent posturists. He repeated his insistence on the need even for radicals to face up to and make difficult choices; that in order for ecologism to amount to anything more substantial than wishful thinking, vacuous rhetoric, or merely nebulous protest, it had to connect with the anxieties of real voters - to reach outside the movement and speak to everyday concerns in a way that makes ecologism relevant rather than merely eccentric. In short, ecologism must be applied to life in ways that actually touch the concerns of ordinary people. The essence of Porritt's critique was that the Green Party must shed its political naivety along with its economic illiteracy or perish. Porritt used the existence of a well-supported green lobby to substantiate his case against the revanchists in the Green Party. The remarkable fact was that there were more successful ecological pressure groups in Britain than in any comparable European country. This lobby had flourished and exerted influence over policy, precisely because it had made meaningful contacts with policy elites at every level, and had developed, through its successful campaigns, a resonance with environmentally minded public opinion. The stark contrast between a rapidly declining Green Party, with a membership down by this time to below 7000 - less than half the total in the heady days of 1989 and early 1990[68] - and effective campaigning groups such as the Friends of the Earth, which boasted a relatively steady support base of 240,000 members, seemed to Porritt to point to the folly of the party's narrow obsessions with 'principle' over 'power'.

The contrast between the green lobby and the party was most apparent at the strategic level. The Green Party seemed incapable of developing much beyond the negative doomsaying or obsession with democratic 'rights' that preoccupied the fundamentalists in the movement's grassroots. The green lobby, on the other hand, had never shared this insular ghetto mentality. There were, of course, divisions and much debate between managerialists and activists over strategy, but the lobbyists were altogether more focused on specific policy issues. By operating in the real world of campaigns and interest articulation, these eco-lobbyists had evolved effective tactics, and a pragmatic philosophy firmly rooted in the achievable goals of environmental protection. It was Porritt's over-riding ambition to import a similar pragmatism into the Green Party. He launched in 1992, along with Sara Parkin, a "Realworld" initiative to strengthen the tenuous links between the party and the eco-lobby. The objective was to agree a common agenda with a range of campaign groups from environmentalists to the aid lobby (Christian Aid and Oxfam) and the homelessness charities. Porritt envisaged the members of these grassroots organisations joining the initiative on an individual basis, in order to avoid the legal prohibition on registered charities overtly engaging in politics. Porritt's notion of linking the Green Party with the broader movement that was emerging behind civil rights and new politics issues, was much in tune with parallel developments from other quarters. The Director of Friends of the Earth, Charles Secrett, similarly endorsed a joint campaign by the environmental and development movements "to become a mature political force" so that environmental organisations could "address their fundamental failure - an inability to move environmental concerns to the centre stage of British politics".[69] The Green Party's fundamentalists remained unmoved by any such project and preferred to cling tenaciously to obscurantism.[70]

The situation in the party worsened to the point of crisis. It seemed as if Porritt would lead an exodus of discontented pragmatists out of the party, in order to concentrate their talents and energies on the more politically astute and effective green lobby. He announced his decision not to stand for re-election as the chair of the party's executive, and threatened to quit the party altogether if it refused to embrace a further reform package devised by the Green 2000 group - to be debated at the forthcoming September conference. The new reform demand met with a pent-up resistance from the fundamentalists. All of the party's familiar fault lines re-emerged, magnified by the trauma of electoral defeat. Sara Parkin used the opportunity of presenting the party with its formal election report to add her political weight to the call for real changes in outlook and procedure. She openly condemned the party for its conservatism, its obsessive navel gazing and, above all, its sheer reluctance to face unpalatable facts and to accommodate a new political landscape.[71] Parkin's critique brought the simmering crisis to a head, precisely because it avoided the anodyne language of appeasement. The current attempts at reform were, as she saw them, feeble and wholly inadequate. Parkin's report put the blame for the election defeat squarely on the sheer amateurism of a party preoccupied with democratic protocol, and seemingly incapable of operating in the political world as it is, not as these out of touch idealists might prefer it to be. With the world's governments and key interest groups about to embark on the major review of the ecological issue at the forthcoming UN Rio Summit, Parkin - and the realists in general - despaired of a party that refused to break out of its self imposed ideological ghetto, and face real issues that could only be tackled by involvement in serious politics. Parkin backed up her stinging rebuke with hard evidence. She cited the findings of an independent survey on the effectiveness of the British Green Party, undertaken by a research group from Strathclyde University. As she chose to interpret it, the evidence suggested that many former Green Party supporters - both activists and voters - had deserted the party precisely because it lacked effective leadership, acted indecisively, and was apt to engage in futile factionalism.[72] Parkin drew conclusions that were as damning as Porritt's: that the party as it was presently constituted was at the end of the road, in so far as it offered a viable channel for effective political action. "Sadly," she argued, "I have been forced to the conclusion that the Green Party has become a liability to Green politics. Instead of being a standard bearer, the Green Party as it now is only provides its detractors with regular proof of its unfitness to contribute to the rapidly evolving political debate".[73]

The party was in no mood for candor, and even less receptive to appeals for realism in the aftermath of a heavy election defeat. The anti-partyists seemed to be incapable of absorbing these critical messages. Indeed, they inverted the argument and blamed the compromises with fundamental ecological principles for alienating Green voters. For the most part, they regarded the rebukes of Porritt and Parkin with deep resentment and saw them merely as the excuses and alibis of careerists who had mistakenly been given their head at earlier conferences, and had simply failed to deliver on extravagant electoral promises. The resignations or withdrawal from the fray of those who had 'blackmailed' the party before the election simply left the fundamentalists unmoved. Setpiece confrontations thus, between fundamentalists and realists, are hardly uncommon encounters in European Green party politics. But rarely have these feuds been conducted with the venom or vigour, and above all with such debilitating effects, as they were in the British party after the 1992 election. The issue still remains essentially unresolved, with the realists marginalised and the party, for the time being, largely dominated by anti-party and fundamentalist elements of various dark green and alternativist persuasions. The anti-partyists reoccupied their essentially negative position as the resistors of change in the vacuum left by the self imposed exile or disengagement of the modernisers. Both sides now seem to be locked together in a party whose outer skin remains green, but who represent very different visions of an ecological future. This is much less an active civil war than a resentful stand off that periodically breaks out into hostilities - between frustrated progressives, who have chosen, for the moment, at least, to opt out of party activity; and an inchoate group of local activists and eco-anarchists, for whom ecologism offers a source of emotional fulfilment and even psychological sustenance, as much as it is a cause for determined policy networking and practical politics.

There are a few encouraging signs that the realists may not have entirely surrendered the ground to their opponents. They continue to put their faith in the revival of interest by mainstream politicians on the centre-left in changes in the electoral system, as part of a wider package of constitutional reform. The experience of Green parties elsewhere does tend to suggest that a combination of circumstances - for electors of a radical bent the practical inducement not to waste their votes on hopeless parties, and for activists both the discipline that tends to follow from a real prospect of winning seats, and the realism that comes with the political experience gained from such success - does much to help resolve these tensions in favour of a pragmatic strategy. And thereby to transform the style and conduct of Green party politics accordingly. The defeated realists in the British party have continued, albeit from the sidelines rather than the fulcrum of the party, to publicise the hard choices that confront the Greens, rather than to abandon the party altogether. Porritt and Parkin, regardless of their damning criticism of its continued impotence, both decided to stay inside the party, at least for the time being. The realists are down but by no means out of the game. They continue to pursue the goal of reforming the party along the lines of those more effective Green parties which have begun to cohabit with progressive political forces elsewhere on Europe's political landscape. Porritt and his allies have taken their own independent initiatives here. They launched a more broadly based movement, precisely to underpin the alliance of Green and environmental groups, with a view to regaining the political initiative squandered, as they saw it, by the British Green Party. This "Green Realignment" opted, at the outset, to issue a joint manifesto or shopping list, to be put before the main political parties, as a means of bargaining with them for Green electoral support. There may well be some mileage in this tack, in spite of the reluctance of the established parties to overtly indulge in electoral pacts. No political party can afford to entirely turn its back on ecologism, although the recent recession has hardly helped to restore post-materialist or other ecological concerns to the place on the political agenda they enjoyed during the late 1980s.[74] Some British parties - most notably the Liberal Democrats, but also elements in the Labour Party[75] - are even more amenable to a closer working relationship with progressive Greens, and have courted Porritt and other Green 'emigrés' in recent years. The motives of these other parties may well be dubious. But the fact that some of their own key constituencies - among the young, the new middle classes and women voters - place great store on quality of life issues, should enable a well-organised green movement to extract some policy concessions. New Labour has shown signs that it regards the Green vote as an important constituency in its attempt to break out from it's undue reliance on the productionist vote, and in the important task of building a new middle class constituency.[76]

The Greens may yet find another route into the mainstream of radical politics, more in tune with their own progressive instincts. There are tentative but as yet no firm or substantial links between the Labour left and British ecologism.[77] There may well be scope here for exploring a red-green axis further to the left of the spectrum, if Labour fails in its project to build a new centre party and, in the process, to recapture sufficient support from amongst those 'materialist' constituencies (especially the skilled working class) who have deserted the party in unprecedented numbers since the 1960s. The effect of a successful Blair 'revolution' is likely to deflect Labour away from this kind of radical revision, although its only real test will come in government, where a notoriously ideologically sensitive and fractured labour movement has, under the pressure of making tough policy choices, come unstuck at the seams more than once. The Green Party may benefit in the long run from 'new' Labour's discernible shift to the right, by winning over disenchanted and 'disenfranchised' leftist voters, unattracted by the spectacle of a party steering by the fickle lodestone of electoral success rather than by the firmly anchored 'north star' of socialist principles. This may well be the case with those campaigners who stayed in the Labour Party throughout the 1980s and who are now showing signs of feeling marooned in what has become a mainstream social democratic party. There were already some signs of modest disaffection on the left with Kinnock's unremitting drive to modernise Labour, amongst unilateralists, pacifists, anti-nuclear campaigners, and all manner of alternativists and radical eccentrics. The Green Party tended to attract some of the leftist protest vote even in natural Labour territory. While Arthur Scargill's new Socialist Labour Party will present some competition here, the rigid discipline and centralised nature of that organisation is unlikely to appeal to many left alternativists or utopian socialists. Blair's revolution has not only modernised what was still a socialist party; it has, in effect, broken the mould forged by earlier generations of Labour leaders. The uneasy tension within that party, and amongst some of its erstwhile supporters, is bound to surface in government. The Greens may be one of the main beneficiaries of these changes. The Liberal Democrats, for their part, had more immediate and perhaps cynical reasons for coopting the Greens into their own radical project. Even a modest Green Party vote in the 1992 poll, in competition with the Liberal Democrats (in 35 constituencies), had damaged the latters' prospects, in spite of its revival from the 1989 electoral nadir. There is, in these circumstances, something still to play for - if the Greens can resolve the persistent predicament facing any radical 'outsider' party bent on organizing to bring about change.

(iv)   Prospects for political change

The Green Party may be poorly placed - both in terms of a political opportunity structure that cripples the chances of small parties, and because their own continuing and deep factional divisions about adopting a practical approach and playing the conventional political game - to become established as the minor but persistent 'force' in national politics achieved by some Green parties on the continent. In the circumstances, its 'successes' have been largely confined to modest gains in local politics. Even here the picture is variable and far from convincing; from a high water mark of a vote of 8.64 per cent in the 1989 local elections when green issues were at their most fashionable, down to a 3.82 per cent average in 1992, rising modestly to 5.7 per cent in the 1993 County Council elections. The Green Party has never managed to win more than a handful of local authority seats. Whereas in Ireland, where similar conditions shape the political culture, but an altogether more favourable electoral system operates, the Green Alliance has been able on occasions to trade second preference votes with other parties: and on that basis, to convert a modest but reliable community support base, rooted in effective campaigning on local and national issues alike, into a degree of leverage in local and national politics, and even to a limited extent to impact on the national policy making process. This is not to say that the political conditions that prevail in Ireland replicate those of the United Kingdom. The scope for building an effective bridge between the local community and national politics is much reduced in both states by the centralised nature of the policy process. In the UK, however, the reduced competencies of local government over recent decades, an entrenched political culture of adversarialism and, of course, the mathematics of an electoral system that overly discriminates against small parties, continue to undermine the community base for the sort of coalitional politics in which European Green politicians figure, everywhere from Ireland to Germany. Nevertheless, the opportunity does exist for a disciplined, well-organised and determined 'local' Green party politics to influence, however modestly, community outcomes. The Oxford Green Party, for instance, after standing 21 candidates in the 1993 County Council elections, (and who averaged a commendable 9.56 per cent) did make their influence felt on the local council with the selective exploitation of targeted green issues. This strategy, in turn, brought them good publicity and an increased political profile.

There have been similar limited successes for the Green Party in the counties of Gloucestershire and Hereford and Worcester. Recent shifts in the map of local government have helped to sharpen the impact even of minor party groups. More British Councils than ever are 'hung' between the major parties. With no outright control, the scope for a small party to negotiate policy concessions in exchange for votes is accordingly increased. This is far from being a promising Green breakthrough, but it does offer a way forward that suggests a model for cooperation on the national level if the Green Party, on the back of electoral reform, ever manages to win representation at Westminster. This at least suggests a plausible strategy for mobilising the undoubted appeal of ecologism that exists amongst the younger and new middle class cohorts of the electorate.[78] This is not to simplify what will, even under the most favourable circumstances, still be a difficult and daunting political task. The onset of recession and the accompanying shift in both public perceptions and policy priorities[79] has not, it has to be said, been the only reason for the decline in support for Green parties. The British Green Party, however, has added to its own woes. While every other Green party has confronted similar difficulties in this regard - with the political agenda shifting against them - many of those parties which adopted a realistic strategy, and steered a pragmatic course managed to carve out a niche as effective political actors at both the local and national levels. The critical factor here seems to be a difference in outlook - certainly compounded by an unfavourable electoral system - between the obscurantism of the British Green Party and those parties where a degree of realism prevailed.

Other contextual factors have also played their part in determining political outcomes. A situational factor - and quite possibly a structural one that says much about British political culture and the instrumental values that sustain it - seems to operate to ensure British 'exceptionalism' here.[80] This is what Rootes has identified as "the relatively low salience of new social movements in Britain, which in turn, depresses radical instincts and the youthful articulation of post materialist values".[81] Support for the new left, alternativist and radical social movement agendas of the post 1968 period, has been altogether more modest in Britain than in many other European countries. The British left remains conservative rather than radical in its outlook and instincts, largely because it is principally 'captured' by a labourist coalition and by other disciplined and even authoritarian traditions further 'left' - rather than by innovative or spontaneous social movements.[82] Britain has certainly produced a well-supported peace and anti-nuclear movement, as well as other radical causes - from women's liberation, gay rights, anti-racist and civil rights organisations such as the Anti-Nazi League, and Charter 88, alongside grassroots single issue campaigns (the Anti-Poll Tax and Criminal

Justice Bill movements are the most notable examples here). These movements have, however, either drawn their ideological sustenance from more traditional leftist, libertarian, or even liberal credos:[83] or else they have resisted capture by any political party, however loose or democratic its internal arrangements. This residual militancy - a potent political resource in the right circumstances - was not, as it was elsewhere, channelled into support for, and has certainly not coalesced into, a successful Green party. The principal political focus of British environmentalism has been those single issue campaigns that have remained largely insulated from any broader political debate; or those umbrella 'green' lobby organisations that have steered a wide berth around the tribulations of Green Party politics, and are concerned above all with 'facts' not factionalism - with 'irrefutable scientific evidence' and 'better' technological solutions than those currently on offer, rather than with the narrow pursuit of ideological exclusivism. The success of both types of lobbying depend on winning public support in order to put pressure on policy elites. The 'compromise-oriented strategies'[84] organised by Greenpeace, Friends of the Earth, or the WWF,[85] are by no means discouraged in the relatively open British policy process,[86] with its receptiveness to informed interest articulation weighed in by moderate movements[87] - those with a keen eye for good publicity, but also conducted in a managerial style that maximises their limited resources. These lobbies campaign on - and gain their support - precisely on the basis of practicable solutions to immediate problems, rather than by peddling the arcane and distant utopias apparently preferred by many active members of the British Green Party.

On the face of it, it seems as if no single factor accounts for the underdeveloped nature of Green party politics in Britain. A combination of structural factors (especially discouraging opportunity structures), unfavourable cultural legacies, and the contingent factors that operate in politics everywhere, have conspired to arrest the 'usual' process, whereby movements eventually became transformed into political parties.[88] Nevertheless, these situational factors and legacies, which help to account in part for the Green Party's abiding problem of the 'wasted vote' syndrome, as well as the sheer costs of political campaigning compared with its likely pay off for small parties in a single member, majoritarian electoral system, can only explain so much. Other Green parties have faced unfavourable opportunity structures and managed to make more room within them for an effective Green electoral strategy than has been the case here. Certainly, Green moderates such as Porritt have criticised the Green Party for putting rigid ideology before practical politics - and thereby passing up the chance to build effective alliances with adjacent political parties and movements to further the ecological cause. It is easy, of course, to apportion blame. The fundamentalists' case rested on more than a determination to remain free of political entanglements with other movements on the grounds of principle alone. Fear of cooptation, of being sucked into a vortex of compromises with bigger, better resourced parties that would lead to their own oblivion has, understandably enough, figured in their political calculus. This is the very essence, after all, of the radical predicament. Whether or not they have made the correct decision is another matter entirely. In the teeth of one of the least hospitable opportunity structures anywhere in western Europe, this principled stand has probably done the Green Party's cause more harm than good. By resisting the logic of collective political action as it works in advanced democracies, the Green Party has conspired in its own political impotence. This choice is not, however, irreversible. The green issue may well be discounted under present circumstances, but it is far from becoming redundant. A litany of public concerns - caused by all manner of pollution, emissions and spillages, public health scares, food impurities (or worse in the recent crisis over BSE in cattle), suggest a potent agenda with real political possibilities.

The British Green Party, regardless of its resource limitations and a political opportunity structure that is unfavourable to small parties of whatever ideological persuasion, does retain some capacity - if it can resolve its principled objections to playing practical, suboptimal politics - for making effective political alliances on the ground. And by doing so, for influencing to a degree policy outcomes. Failure to capitalise on these limited prospects - and the apparent desire to confuse, as radical parties with a militant purpose so often do, ideological intransigence with the more pragmatic strategy of staking out viable political territory - is a sure recipe for perpetuating political impotence. It may be guaranteed to nourish the radical soul, but it is just as likely, in the case of the Green Party, to surrender a promising political space to those other parties looking, at a time when partisan loyalties are eroding, to widen their own electoral appeal. One sure way of staking a claim here is to strengthen contacts with the green lobby. In comparison with the green movement elsewhere in western Europe, these linkages in Britain have by no means been pursued as vigorously as they might have been. The self inflicted isolationism of the Green Party from the wider social movements that continue to enjoy widespread support and a membership of over 5 millions - most of whom, of course, are also voters - is a matter of choice for both sides. The Green Party continues to plough its own furrow here. But what it does, the choice it makes here, also influences the perceptions and responses of this powerful lobby and its supporters. So far, the impact has been less than salutary. For what this critical audience sees, instead of reliable allies with a constructive outlook on the political front, is an unhelpful image of intense, negative and bitter factionalism, which encourages the many green practitioners who actually want to change things, to reserve their political energies for green lobbying.[89] This response largely flies in the face of the Green political experience elsewhere.

The closeness between Die Grunen, for instance, and green pressure groups that is part of the strength of the German movement, and one of the reasons for its success, is largely absent in Britain.[90] Yet establishing effective networking between the two branches of the green movement is imperative if Green party politics is to survive let alone to prosper as a credible electoral force. There is more to this than a one-sided bargain to rescue the Green Party from political extinction. The wider ecology movement is bound to benefit, as it has in Germany and elsewhere, from a Green Party that is a focal point, a clearing house, for bargaining joint initiatives amongst the myriad single issue campaigns and the many local and national lobbies of which the green movement consists. The fear - understandable enough in any 'outsider' radical movement - of being drawn into the inclusivist weft of conventional party politics, with its enticedments and ambushes, has to be balanced by the advantages that come from taking risks by making such connections. The analysis of these dilemmas by Rootes is accurate and to the point; in effect, that the Green Party does have something that is distinctively radical to preserve, for "only the Green Party has a strong value-commitment to democratic mass participation; the rest of the British environmental and ecological movement is more narrowly success-oriented". As such, the 'reformist' environmentalism, as practised by the green lobby, "has relatively little to contribute to the broader process of democratisation simply because so much of its limited energy and resources is channelled into the process of institutionalised consultation and negotiation (and) energies and resources channelled in that direction are unavailable for popular mobilisation".[91] There are dangers, certainly, in any strategy that involves working with elements who do not share the same broad values and outlook. Nevertheless, there is more to be gained than lost from a strategy of measured cohabitation. Cooperation does not have to mean abject surrender: political bargaining is a two-way street.

To attract support, any political party has to be seen to be effective - or at least potentially so - by its target voters. This requires something more than the winning of seats. 'Influence' may be defined more broadly, as part of a longer term goal to influence political discourse and shape the values that underpin electoral choice. Even small radical parties that do not register a high count on the electoral seismograph can still influence outcomes if they set out to do so. A party that rates higher on the 'protest' scale than it does on a straightforward quantitative count of council or parliamentary seats has to offer at least some tangible evidence of a viable strategy - a calculus that is premised on the cashing in of support for a degree of influence over policy outcomes. Otherwise it will fail to attract and hold on to its share of the larger numbers of discontent votes available to alternative and radical parties within any modern electorate.[92] The significance of the remarkable vote for the Greens in the 1989 Euro-elections should not be over exaggerated here. Certainly, many of these votes were borrowed from other parties while the Liberals, the usual vehicle of protest in British politics, were otherwise engaged in their own internecine wrangling with the SDP. Yet it is too easy to dismiss even this remarkable event as a 'one off' protest. The very fact that such large numbers of 'ordinary' mainstream voters felt able to vote Green did at least indicate the existence of a residual vote for change; a reservoir that the Greens have since largely alienated by their own antics.

None of this is meant to underestimate the daunting odds facing even a pragmatic, well organised Green party in contemporary British politics. The Greens do confront the double indemnity of a conservative political culture - and one which gives scant regard to eco-engineering at other than a nominal level[93] - and an unhelpful opportunity structure. Yet, as we have seen, neither hurdle would be quite the insuperable obstacle it presently appears to be, if the Green Party was more prepared to accommodate the compromises required for effective participation, and abandoned its passé preference for tilting at illusory windmills![94] Establishing closer linkages and good working relationships with the broader ecological movement - whether over local and single issue campaigns, or with the big lobby organisations - would at least show a serious intent here and assist, if by no means ensure, that widespread support for green causes might more easily translate into votes for Green Party candidates. There are some modest signs that the British green lobby is at least receptive to the idea of such networking. One active campaigner for this broad front approach has argued that, "it may be that, rather than regarding the Party as weak due to its lack of political presence, the environment movement may decide that a strong Green party would be very useful in any strategy of accelerating change, and closer links might be formed".[95] Or rather, they would be, and the green lobby would be even more convinced of the practical advantages of such political cohabitation, if the Green Party showed signs of taking itself more seriously than it has so far managed to do. The making of practical accommodations here is the necessary starting point for building a wider green consensus - one that can be translated both into support for Green party candidates, and for building coalitions with other parties that have the same sort of vested interest in the constitutional changes that will accord Green votes the same electoral weight they would acquire in a proportional system. In the end, the success of Green party politics in Britain does depend on this basic change in the rules. Without it, the Greens are certain losers at every level. But the Green Party on its own, however plausibly it presents its case, cannot bring about these constitutional changes without securing allies in other parties. The assessment of one observer in 1991 remains as pertinent now as it was then; that "without the concrete gains of parliamentary seats the Greens will remain peculiarly vulnerable to shifts in popular sentiment" that have since left them beached as a credible political force - and thence electorally squeezed and easy prey to other parties who 'cherry pick', adapt, distort and dilute the radical import of their particular demands for change.[96]

Pragmatic voices within the Green Party have already drawn their own conclusions about the need here to build radical networks. Jean Lambert was an active supporter of the broad campaign for constitutional reform that crystallised around the radical Charter 88 movement formed in 1991. Although acknowledging the obstacles in the way of collaboration on both sides - the Greens' fear of cooptation is as readily matched by the labour movement's reluctance to deal with rootless utopians or esoteric and precious middle class elitists - Lambert has recommended a joint strategy as an elemental part of an effective new politics of liberation that might, if it is successfully carried off, transform the 1990s into what she calls the "turnaround decade"[97] - a new era for politics in which the ideological gap between both the red and green factors of the radical equation has already become much narrower, due to widespread public anxieties over risks to health, and labour's gradual acceptance that sustainable development may present no more of a threat to job security, let alone the job satisfaction associated with the 'dignity' of labour, than the recent experience of acceding to ruthless market forces that relocate jobs where labour costs are lowest, propel people from the labour market as new technologies accelerate, and threaten all manner of new insecurities. There is, under these quieter, if not entirely 'silent revolutionary' conditions, a foundation for a red-green dialogue that was much less apparent even a short decade ago. The recent acknowledgement by the open minded green thinker, Jonathon Porritt, that 'new' Labour's commitment to a modernised 'stakeholder' economy is indeed fully compatible with sound eco-practice, is a good example of where such common ground might be found.

The Green Party already has some ambivalent experience of this political 'trade'. What seemed to be successful experiments in building coalitions for mutual political advantage in celtic Britain - leading Porritt to advocate a general strategy of promoting tactical voting for sympathetic MPs on the basis of their Parliamentary voting records[98] - eventually came up against the atavistic instincts of Green fundamentalism in the English Green Party. The tactical support of the Greens in the 1992 election for the Plaid Cymru candidate, Cynog Dafis, in the Westminster constituency of Ceredigion and Pembroke North, ensured the seat's capture. This particular example illustrates the continued pitfalls as well as the potential for radical 'alliance' politics. Tensions between local Greens, who were mostly happy with this arrangement, and with Dafis's voting and speaking record in the House of Commons, and a fundamentalist 'Green dragon' faction, who saw themselves as the 'last defender of earth now awake and alert for the final confrontation with the machine', led to the untimely end of this alliance - the Greens only real connection with Parliamentary politics.[99] Porritt and Parkin saw this quarrel as typifying the worst kind of irrational utopianism. Indeed, Porritt deliberately went far out on a political limb and endorsed the Plaid candidate (who was opposed by an official Green) in the 1994 European polls - a gesture which eventually caused him to be vilified as a "green Tory", arraigned before the Party's Regional Council, and threatened with expulsion.[100] The logic of Porritt's position was straightforward enough and entirely consistent with the pragmatism he exhibited throughout his years as a Green Party activist: in short, that parties with a weak electoral base under Britain's discriminatory electoral rules need to make accommodations with other radical parties. As Porritt put it in this particular case, "there are ways we can work with other parties, through special arrangements and tactical voting.... to promote policies of ecological sustainability, democratic renewal and social justice".[101] Porritt's subsequent apologia for his provocative action was one couched more in regret than anger with his critics in the party. But it did contain an implicit valediction for a party that had, in his view, finally lost all touch with political reality. As he chose to put it, "I shall miss the finely balanced schizophrenia that allows Green Party candidates to go on hoping it will be all right on the night, even though they know for sure it won't be. And I shall miss that unlimited capacity to make out things are a tiny bit better than they were last time round.... Pollyanna is alive and well in the Green Party".[102] Parkin, already by now outside the Party mainstream but who, like Porritt, had kept up her subscription, "nursing.... a micro-hope that it would re-enter the real world of the politics", was more scathing than sentimental about this event. The entire episode merely confirmed for her "that the earplugs are screwed in more tightly than ever.... that the national party should connive with such nonsense and not only fail to build on their one bit of good news since 1989 - the election of Cynog Dafis - but actively seek to divorce themselves from him, surpasses understanding.... the post European election wash of self delusion (has) painted over the total eclipse of Green politics in the UK".[103]

The discounting by these pragmatic but progressive elements in the Green Party, whose small but by no means quiet voices of reason in a party that had all but sidelined them, provides some measure of how far the Green Party has yet to travel before it arrives within touching distance of contributing to a prospective radical realignment of British party politics. The continued preference for posturing and factionalism has, for the time being, ensured that the leadership of the ecology movement has passed from the Green Party to the green pressure groups. As Parkin has argued, the Greens have contributed to their own problems by wearing "virtual reality goggles" and ignoring the basic precepts of party politics by offering the electorate "a journey without maps". Her advice, offered in a public letter to a party she believed had not so much lost its way as never having found it, was straightforward; "first, be a political party. You do not have to be an encounter group, or a direct-action cell, or a campaigning pressure group. Other bits of the Green movement do these things perfectly well. Your job is to field confidence inspiring candidates backed by a sensible Green programme at election time. Green issues are off the UK agenda because you are. Second, Green parties have no divine right to the votes peeling off the big traditional parties. They have to be earned."   In this regard, the British Greens stand in direct contrast to the "well marked stepping stones and clear leadership" presented by the German Greens.[104] Before the British Greens can make even the sort of political impact of green parties elsewhere, they must face some unpalatable facts about their own weak position. Parkin's analysis of events might even pass as an epitaph rather than a critical rebuke, except that she retained a vestige of hope that the situation facing the party might yet be directly confronted: for "the truth is that no one has any experience of turning a dying industrial society into a sustainable one. We need a political realignment, that is true, but we also need a realignment inside the Green Movement.... deconstructed as it now is, makes it less rather than the sum of its parts".[105]

Developments in Scotland, too, where the 'ancient' constitutional firmament was more in motion than it was in England, were altogether more promising for a form of tactical politics from which a constellation of minor parties - including the Greens - might benefit. The Scottish Green Party - with its own constitution, council, executive body and policy agenda - was cast in a rather more pragmatic mould than its English equivalent. Since the 1992 election it had joined other opposition parties and constitutional reforms organisations in advocating a Scottish Parliament elected by a form of PR, that both more fairly represented minor parties and gave them every incentive for working together on joint policies. The party had produced a "Highland Manifesto" as long ago as 1989 that shared many of the ambitions of the other Scottish parties for regional initiatives to revitalise rural communities and hill farms, support reforestation, as well as a distinctive and radical policy of land reform by encouraging common ownership. It advocated nothing less than "an environmentally sustainable human scale and economically just society". The complex logic of the Scottish constitutional reform movement further inclined the Scottish Greens to the politics of compromise. They were fully aware of their dependence on the Convention pact between the Labour and Liberal Democratic parties, as they were on Labour winning the next general election, if these radical changes were to come about. Consensus rather than narrow exclusivism offered the only sensible way forward. And while many Scottish Greens were realistic enough to accept that even the proposed electoral reforms - a system of 8 regional party lists - would induce divisive rivalry within the Party for favoured places near the top of these lists, and that its limited resources would further reduce the number of candidates the Party could afford to stand - and with that the extent of its representation - the Scottish Greens have professed themselves ready, by and large, for the challenge of constitutional change and post revolution politics, if and when it arrives.[106]

On the face of it, the ferment that is underway on the progressive side of British politics looks to be a direct challenge to the Green Party's claim to be the sole political expression of ecologism. Parkin has been explicit about this loss of salience. In a situation in which, as she sees it, there are even more genuine Greens now located outside the Green party than there are inside it, and with "too many Green Party members - themselves unreconstructed deconstructionists, unable to move beyond whatever the single issue they favour", the way seemed clear for progressives attracted by a new political route for British ecologism to reform into a new Green party. When the Green Realignment Movement met in London in the early 1990s, such a move was certainly on the agenda. Nor could it have expected much resistance to such a political challenge from its longer 'established' rival. The signs of political decline in the party were palpable. The opening of the September 1993 Green party conference had to be delayed because it was inquorate. Only forty members arrived for the first plenary session. Party membership, too, was barely a quarter of what it had been only some three years previously. Even so, however attractive this prospect may be to frustrated pragmatists, they have so far resisted it. The scope for two competing Green parties under Britain's electoral rules would be even less than it is in polities whose opportunity structures are altogether more conducive to small parties. Arresting this decline has been no less easy to achieve for all this modest display of realism.

The Greens have been in apparent free fall ever since the 1992 general election. The 1994 European poll (the surest test since then of the party's national electoral standing) showed just how far short they are of being an effective presence in national politics. They polled an average of merely 3.2 per cent in the 84 seats in which Green Party candidates stood - some way short of the party's own modest target of 4 per cent, and below their recent 5 per cent average in the May 1994 local elections. Only 3 of these candidates actually crossed the 5 per cent threshold to enable them to hold onto their deposits.[107] Jean Lambert produced the best result (6.4 per cent) with a campaign consciously based on sensible moderation in the London North East constituency. The candidates in Herefordshire and Shropshire and Sussex South and Crawley also both saved their deposits, with 5.6 per cent and 5 per cent respectively. The party lost a total of £81,000 in surrendered deposits, and although this money was raised by local parties, there was less insouciance and more than a hint of sangfroid in the comment of its national election agent, that "we regard it as (money) spent well in promoting our case".[108] Complaints that the media had marginalised the Greens, or that the public broadcasters had disallowed air time their 1989 turnout had entitled them to,[109] were less convincing than explanations which point to a combination of agenda changes - with social and economic issues taking precedence in a recession over post-material matters[110] - and, not least, the Greens' own apparently determined pursuit of political demise. The latter element seems to be more pertinent here than the former. Green parties everywhere have been squeezed by a mixture of recession, and the fact that other parties have paid them the dubious compliment of moving onto their territory and stealing some of their ideological clothes. In many of these cases, Green parties have survived and, by accommodating to the rules of the conventional political game, have even consolidated at the community, regional or national levels of politics. The British Greens, faced with one of the most unhelpful opportunity structures sent to try the patience of small radical parties anywhere in Europe, have felt collectively disinclined to temper their politics, or to seek accommodations with other parties.[111] This does not mean, however, that all is lost to them. Indeed, if they were to change their collective mind and to adjust their approach to accommodate the pragmatism recommended by the vociferous minority of realists in the party, they could yet reap some clear political benefits. Social and ecological issues, as Porritt pointed out above, are by no means entirely exclusive agendas. The decline of the social environment, community breakdown, unemployment, racism and other expressions of social discrimination, now take priority on the national political agenda of the mid nineties. But not to the abrogation of concern with the environment, whose present and future importance continues to be signalled by serious Green commentators[112] and mainstream opinion formers alike.[113] The indisputable correlations between poverty, unemployment, community breakdown, crass materialism at the expense of adequate social provision, or of a creative economic thinking that is concerned with sustainable development and an ecocentric regard for resource and habitat conservation as well as with public health, are legion in contemporary public policy and well represented in the political and academic discourse that reflects on these current agendas.

These linkages contain, too, a political potential which has yet to be fully exploited. Boggs, in his perceptive account of the modern radical agenda has made the case in similar terms for a resilient green politics across the advanced industrial world. As he sees it, time is on the side of the Greens, as long as the rising tide of ecological concern finds its expression and best outlet in organised politics: for "we have reached a point in worldwide industrial development where global ecological crisis, worsening by the day, forces serious appraisal of political methods, strategies, tactics and even goals. If local movements reveal the shrinking capacity of normal politics, they nonetheless remain parochial, diffuse, and ideologically unfocused. Loose grassroots networks can win adherents and lay the foundations of community, but they lack the strategic direction and flexibility required for political effectiveness. The values of autonomy, identity, and spontaneity are not always compatible with norms endemic to the struggle for power which have more in common with the bureaucratic model".[114] The issues on which to build an effective Green politics exist in every advanced industrial society, not least in Britain. The recent crisis over mass agricultural production fostered by government complacency and the food industry's relentless pursuit of the profit motive in disregard of both nature and the requirements of public health provided a poignant reminder of the potential for connecting ecology with the broader social dimension. And in ways that offer the Greens a clear way forward, and connect them with a much broader radical agenda on the progressive side of British politics - if they would only abandon their claim to be the sole voice of ecologism.

Greens of a more pragmatic disposition have discerned in these recent changes in the political climate the potential for an altogether new politics: one which, with careful positioning, the Greens could readily assimilate, benefit from, and, if not dominate, certainly influence.[115] As Porritt identifies this prospect: "I cannot help believing that there is a 'new politics' emerging somewhere out there. It involves people of all parties and of none, and keeps popping up in 101 different ways (from road protests to ethical investment, from organic farming to telecommuting) that all but defy analysis. That is the natural territory for the Green Party. But to tap into it requires a transformation at least as profound as that which the Labour Party has undergone. Deprived of power, neglected or ridiculed by the media, the easy way out for what is left of the national Green Party has been to take up on the task of Keeper of the Holy Green Grail, defining with involuntary arrogance what is or not truly Green".[116]

The option here is not so much for a unilateral Green breakthrough, but rather to settle for ways of connecting the party with this underlying and growing concern with environmental issues - with deepening the party's capacity for exerting influence on a realigned, progressive political landscape. This prospect was identified in no less an influential organ of establishment opinion than the editorial columns of *The Times* newspaper, which argued that "it is this piecemeal approach that appeals more to the average environmentally conscious voter than the all-encompassing, quasi-religious message of the official Greens. In its apocalyptic warnings and promises of redemption, the Green gospel has much in common with established religion. But most people want merely a Green tinge to existing policies. Depending on the constituency, this is as likely to be achieved by voting tactically as by remaining pure".[117] Although it identifies a prospect for Green influence, this advice is less sagacious than it ought to be from this experienced source. Fragmented, issue led green politics is by no means the best way forward for ecologists who want to influence contemporary agendas. On the contrary, it is more likely to keep the movement disorganised, and thereby to ensure its continued political impotence. To be truly effective, local campaigns and issue based politics need an effective Green Party to give them a parliamentary voice and a political focal point. As Boggs has more appropriately observed, "local action, to be sure, cannot be dismissed as a complete failure. It does promise a rekindled sense of community that the chaos of urban life so often denies.... The problem is that local victories will mean little in cases where negative outcomes (for example, toxics) are simply transferred elsewhere.... All local forces eventually collide with, or become submerged by, social forces they cannot control.... The failure of local groups to expand outward to engage the public sphere - to generate a transformative politics - testifies to the highly depoliticised nature of much ecological thought and action today. The discourse of political strategy is inevitably enfeebled. Local 'knowledge' is a vital ingredient of this equation, but without strategic form it becomes dissipated in the manner of enclave consciousness.... In modern history the struggle to globalise local movements has become the domain of political parties, which have attempted to mobilise diverse interests for the purpose of winning and exercising state power.... The realm of normal politics includes elections, coalition-building, party manoeuvres, and of course, compromise, which always introduces the risk of institutionalisation".[118]

This analysis serves both as a gauge of the predicament confronting Green movements everywhere and suggests a recipe for its further success. Most of the European Green parties have resolved this quandary in the direction recommended by Boggs - a delicate balance between local, urgent community needs and the requirement of effective national action. That this issue continues to be the principal preoccupation of the British Green Party says much about the development of green politics in this island. On the other hand, as we have seen, the lessons are being slowly if painfully absorbed into the green psyche. The Greens have a long way yet to travel down the route of compromise and cooperation - amongst themselves, let alone with other radical forces. But even here, a tentative start has been made. The cross party cooperation between the 'green' Welsh nationalist Cynog Dafis and some 400 MPs of other parties, supported by large number of local authorities and campaigning groups, on the promotion of an Energy Conservation Bill - which only just failed to make the statute book - showed what could be achieved here. The apparent conversion of 'new' Labour to an even more sweeping environmental programme "In Trust for Tomorrow" - the result of the party's Policy Commission on the Environment - placed the environment at the core of every area of policy, and encouraged some Greens to consider the prospect of working with Labour in a new progressive politics. This new agenda has certainly appealed to moderate Greens. If only a fraction of a new Labour Government's policy recommendations make the statute book, it would, at the very least, signal a major shift from that party's productionist past - and a change, however tenuous, in its long standing image as merely another party committed to unlimited economic growth, regardless of the consequences for amenity or environmental wellbeing. The document was a cornucopia of positive and imaginative environmental thinking. It included an emphasis on job creation in accordance with 'Green regulation'; improvements in public transport, and a switch from road to rail freight; cycling and pedestrian schemes for towns; new, tougher air quality targets and powers to prohibit cars from cities; a six month moratorium on new road building; and the cancellation of some planned motorway developments; strict environmental impact assessments for all infrastructural projects; an Environmental Bill of Rights including a right to clean air and drinking water; citizen access to open country; and the setting up of an environmental division of the High Court, with legal aid for citizens taking on big corporations. It further proposed a Parliamentary Environmental Audit Committee, with powers comparable to those of the Public Accounts Committee; a Green New Deal, to encourage stringent regulatory standards to promote 'greener' technology; a national energy programme to foster energy efficiency and create some 50,000 new jobs; an end to power station building; an expansion of the Environmental Agency to include a Nuclear Installations Inspectorate; a Drinking Water Inspectorate; and on the European plane, CAP reform and more environmentally sensitive employment measures.[119]

This document represents a major advance on Labour's commitment to the environment to date, and extends its sustainable development and eco-friendly energy and transport programmes. It goes some considerable way beyond the party's endorsement of the key Green fiscal principle, of making the polluter pay, and the precautionary measure by which potential polluters are obliged to show that their emissions offer no risk to health, amenity or environment.[120] Labour has also undertaken to foster a nationwide consultation exercise, with the principal aim of reforming national accounting methods by the end of the century. Official statistics - the most reliable measure of the actual greening of public policy - are also to be adjudicated by an independent agency in order to avoid political manipulation. Moreover, Labour promises in government to develop a new measure of National Income - to be published alongside existing measures of GDP - as well as reformulated indicators of National Economic Welfare to gauge resource depletion and pollution, as part of a social, or non-monetary, accounting of economic growth.[121] Labour's official policy has gone further here than any prospective British governing party has ever gone to date, in undertaking commitments to a major infusion of ecological thinking into public policy and national economic management. It is, of course, easy both to plot and to promise policy seachanges from the safe and distant haven of Opposition. Even with a following political wind, economic fair weather, the lucky avoidance of those vagaries which sidetrack and often shipwreck the best laid plans of the most well-intentioned of governments, such reforms in economic and administrative culture will be difficult to implement, against the natural conservatism and parsimony of strategic vested interests in the business, political and administrative sectors. These powerful gatekeepers, driven by altogether narrower motives, retain an inordinate capacity to waylay official good intentions and bloc radical reforms that threaten their interests.

The Green Party has a part to play in this political scenario and a clear choice to make here. Whether to continue to stand on the sidelines, clinging to the purity of its principles - and with that, the certain demise of any realistic expectation of participating in the gradual tilt of the national policy agenda in an ecological direction; or else to welcome even the modest reforms that will result even from Labour's bold Opposition prospectus, once it experiences the constraints of government. The Green Party's choices could not, after almost a quarter of a century of disputation, be clearer: to face certain sterility, or work at whatever level is available to Green politicians, in order to shape and influence such reforms, by building alliances for progressive change in the community at large and, by extension, in politics too at every level. The Labour Party may seem to many Greens an unreliable and fair-weather convert to the sustainable development cause.[122] But its commitment will be even more ephemeral once the winds begin to blow that propel all governments off course in some degree; unless, that is, the Greens and other progressive movements get involved with the project, accept its suboptimal limitations, and stick with it to resist the inevitable backtracking that will be induced by establishment resistance, and the pull of rival policy priorities and fiscal constraints, when these reactionary forces begin to take their toll on outcomes, as they invariably will. The concept of an Environment Agency provides a useful marker here, of the gap between intent and action, that can devalue promises for real changes in procedure. The idea of a single, comprehensive Agency is hardly new. It has had bipartisan support ever since it was initially mooted by the Conservative Government in the aftermath of Mrs Thatcher's belated 'conversion' to the green cause, was signalled in the 1990 White Paper - "The Common Inheritance" - and was subsequently established. This innovation notwithstanding, words are devalued currency unless action follows. As Dieter Helm saw it, "however good the idea (of an Agency) in theory, its practical effect will depend upon its design and the purposes to which it is put. Initial steps have been dogged by Whitehall infighting, and a battle over jobs and functions between the pollution regulators and bodies with pollution responsibilities.... An environmental agency, soundly based, with a clear answer to those who focus only on the costs and with a system of pollution charges to support it, is within the government's grasp. But if traditionalists stick to their conventional tools, if the Treasury stands in the way of pollution charges.... and if utility regulators are allowed pre-eminence of costs over benefits, then the new agency may prove.... a missed opportunity".[123] The Green Party could play a useful part in ensuring that the case for ecology is well expressed, and in resisting any official temptation to backsliding. It cannot, however, undertake this task in isolation from other progressive forces.

Whether the Green Party is yet sufficiently versed in the British method of politics as 'the art of the possible', to play this type of compromise politics is, on the current evidence, less than obvious. But without learning that crucial and often painful lesson, the Greens are unlikely to improve their political position, let alone to enhance their bargaining potential for leverage over public policy. It is hard to disagree with the assessment of the prospects for a Green strategic rationalism, which has argued that the main stumbling bloc to this accommodation lies in the remoteness of the British Green Party from even the outer margins of official politics, that is ensured by more favourable electoral systems or in the non-adversarial political cultures that flourish elsewhere in western Europe. The Greens are not entirely to blame for their isolation and impotence here. Even those moderate Greens who have lost the battle, for the time being to take the party into the arena of 'normal' if new politics that is opening up on the centre left in Britain, would face an uphill struggle if ever they seized back control of the party from the fundamentalists. As one cynical commentator sees this task, "even as they shape our political agenda, the Greens will always find themselves uneasy insiders, paid lip service.... but never quite absorbed, and told as St Augustine might have put it: 'Dear Lord make us Green, but not quite yet'".[124] Nevertheless, it is precisely these unfavourable and demanding circumstances that require the British Greens to abandon their splendid isolation and join in the political fray - if they are ever to exert even a modicum of influence over the issues they place at the centre of their political canon. The defeat at the party's 1996 autumn conference, of an emergency motion to 'disengage' from electoral politics altogether until the electoral system is reformed, was an indication that a current of realism - if not yet a tide - is still running in the party. The fact that the issue was debated at all is, likewise, a measure of the continuing battle for the party's ideological soul.[125] The issue of the party's disposition to 'normal' politics is, however, far from resolved, let alone in the direction of a conventional party model.

The party's continuing confusion over its orientation to the political system - a combination of ideological reticence and its awareness of the very real constraints imposed on the party by discriminatory electoral rules - were just as evident during the 1997 general election. Candidates stood on the official Green ticket in only 84 of the 651 constituencies scattered across the country - and with no palpable success and barely any impact on the national campaign. The total Green vote was a mere 54,912, with many lost deposits; the 'best' single constituency result - 3415 votes (5.48 per cent) - came in the Green's 'heartland' in Stroud. There seems, even after more than twenty years of national campaigning, to be little prospect for the Greens' electoral breakthrough in what remains a hostile political opportunity structure. But Green issues are now more firmly placed on the political agenda, if only in part as a result of the Green Party's efforts. The party has little option, if its members decide to continue to put their faith in a parliamentary or electoralist strategy after such a poor showing, other than to build bridges towards green empathisers in the other 'progressive' parties; and to lobby along with these and other radical forces for electoral reform. This, in turn, requires that the party adopts a less exclusive demeanour - that it listens to, as well as chastises, those radicals in other parties without whose support and good favour the Green Party will continue to be an electoral irrelevance. Political dependence makes for some strange alliances, and there are, of course, dangers as well as opportunities in pursuing such a strategy. But until the Green Party grasps this awkward nettle and confronts its desperate plight head on, it will have little expectation and no sure foundation on which to make an effective contribution to the new radical politics of the millennium.

Notes

1.   "Blueprint for Survival" (Harmondsworth, 1972).
2.   J. McCormick, "British Politics and the Environment" (London, 1991).

3.   A. McCulloch, "The Green Party in England and Wales: Structure and Development: The Early Years", Environmental Politics 1 1992, pp.417-435; ibid, "The Green Party in England and Wales: Branch Organization and Activity" Environmental Politics 2 1993, pp.20-39.

4.   See R. Taylor, "Green Politics and the Peace Movement", in B. Coates, G. Johnson & R. Bush (eds),"A Socialist Anatomy of Britain" (Cambridge, 1985).

5.   S. Parkin (1989), op.cit at p.219.

6.   See Dennis Kavanagh, "British Politics: Continuities and Change" (Oxford, 1985), especially Chapter 4 at pp.52-56.

7.   P. Byrne, "Great Britain: The 'Green Party'", in F. Muller-Rommel (ed), op.cit (1989) at p.109.

8.   For an assessment of the extent of the switch from a materialist to post-materialist agenda in Britain, see A. Heath, R. Jowell, J. Curtice and G. Evans, "The Rise of the New Political Agenda?" European Sociological Review 6 (1990), at pp.31-48.

9.   G. Boyle, "Nuclear Power: The Windscale Controversy" (Milton Keynes, 1978); see also B. Wynn, "Windscale: A Case Study in the Political Art of Muddling Through", in T. O'Riordan and R. Turner (eds),"Progress in Resource Management and Environmental Planning" Volume 3 (Chichester, 1980), at pp.165-204.

10.   P. Lowe and J. Goyder, "Environmental Groups in Politics" (London, 1983), at p.34.

11.   F. Parkin, "Middle Class Radicalism" (Manchester, 1968).

12.   P. Byrne, "The Campaign for Nuclear Disarmament" (London, 1988).

13.   C.A. Rootes, "Political System, The Green Party and The Environmental Movement in Britain", International Journal of Sociology and Social Policy Vol.12 1992, at p.219.

14.   C. Hughes, "Greens pin their hopes on the power of ideas", The Independent, 21.9.89.

15.   H. Kitschelt, "The Logics of Party Formation: Structure and Strategy of Belgian and West German Ecology Parties" (Ithaca, 1989) at p.35, maintains that such important networks enhance new parties' infrastructures. He reveals that Die Grunen drew on a diverse and highly mobilised social movement sector.

16.   Compare this to the figure for the German Greens, of some 38,000 members by the mid-eighties.

17.   W. Rudig and P.D. Lowe, "The Withered 'Greening' of British Politics: A study of the Ecology Party", Political Studies (34) 1986 at pp.262-84.

18.   R. Inglehart and J.R. Rabier, "Political Realignment in Advanced Industrial Society", Government and Opposition 21 1986, pp.456-79.

19.   See M.N. Pedersen, "Towards a New Typology of Party Lifespans and Minor Parties", Scandinavian Political Studies (5) 1982.

20.   For a review of these developments, see J. McCormick, "British Politics and the Environment" (London, 1991).

21.   P. Byrne, op.cit (1989), at p.104.

22.   Chris Rootes, "Britain, Greens in a cold climate", in Richardson and Rootes, op.cit (1994), at p.67.

23.   W. Rudig and P. Lowe, op.cit, (1986).

24.   Ibid, (1986).

25.   J. Porritt, "Seeing Green" (Oxford, 1984), at p.9.

26.   J. Porritt & D. Winner, "The Coming of the Greens" (London, 1988), at p.15.

27.   The Independent, 26.5.89.

28. Ibid, 1.8.89.
29. C. Rootes, op.cit. (1994), at p.70.
30. J. Curtice, "The 1989 European Election: Protest or Green tide?" Electoral Studies 8 1989, pp.217-30.
31. P. Kellner, "Decoding the Green Message", The Independent, 7.7.89.
32. The Independent, 7.7.89.
33. See A. Adonis, "Great Britain", Electoral Studies 8 1989, p.267 on the high correlation between the 'middle class' and the Green vote.
34. C. Rootes, op.cit (1994), at p.74.
35. The Conservative Research Department put together a pamphlet of selective quotations from Green Party publications,"The Green Party and the Environment", which referred to what it called a "hidden agenda" and to the Green's concealed "extremism".
36. The Sunday Telegraph, 28.5.89.
37. Financial Times, 14.6.89; for similar criticisms, see also the Daily Telegraph, 20.6.89; Financial Times, 20.6.89.
38. M. Robinson, "The Greening of British Party Politics" (Manchester, 1992).
39. A. Blowers, "Transition or Transformation? Environmental Policy under Thatcher", Public Administration, Vol.65 1987 at pp.277-94, and P. Lowe and A. Flynn, "Environmental Politics and Policy in the 1980s", in J. Mohan (ed), "The Political Geography of Contemporary Britain" (London, 1989).
40. Sunday Telegraph, 28.5.89.
41. A. Flynn and P. Lowe, ""The Greening of the Tories: The Conservative Party and the Environment"", in W. Rudig (ed), op.cit (1992), pp.9-36.
42. Sunday Telegraph, 23.7.89.
43. See M. Robinson, op.cit (1992).
44. C. Rose, "Lessons of the 1991 Local Government Elections", Econews (British Green Party, No.57, April 1991) at pp.5-6.
45. The Independent, 20.6.89.
46. E.Gene Frankland, "Does Green Politics have a future in Britain?" in W. Rudig (ed), "Green Politics One", (Edinburgh, 1990), at pp.7-28.
47. W. Rudig and M. Franklin, "Green Prospects: The Future of Green Parties in Britain, France and Germany", in W. Rudig, op.cit (1992), pp.37-58.
48. Ibid (1992), at p.43.
49. C. Rootes, "The new politics of the new social movements. Accounting for British exceptionalism", European Journal of Political Research 22 1992, p.176.
50. C. R. Rootes, "The Greening of British Politics?" International Journal of Urban and Regional Research, 15 1991 p.295.
51. The Observer, 24.9.89.
52. Quoted in The Independent, 25.9.89.
53. The party kept faith with this pure green approach to policy throughout the period under review. For a summary of its particular proposals see Financial Times, 19.3.90; Guardian, 24.9.90.
54. Financial Times, 23.9.89.
55. The Independent, 8.4.90.
56. Financial Times, 6.4.90.

57. B. Doherty, "The Fundi-Realo Controversy: An Analysis of Four European Green Parties", Environmental Politics 1 1992 pp.95-120.
58. The Guardian, 9.4.90.
59. The Guardian, 21.9.90.
60. The Guardian, ibid.
61. A poll in The Observer in the new year showed the Greens at a mere 1 per cent of the total vote. See The Observer, 20.1.91.
62. The Guardian, 16.3.91.
63. S. Goodwin, "Greens Face Split Over Attempt to Change Leadership", The Independent, 19.9.91.
64. Financial Times, 10.7.92.
65. C. Brown, "Party aiming for 'visible protest vote'", The Independent, 16.1.92.
66. N. Carter, "Whatever Happened to the Environment? The British General Election of 1992", Environmental Politics 1 1992, pp.441-447.
67. Reuters New Service Report, 26.9.92.
68. A. Mitchison, "Hugged out of Office", The Independent Magazine, 26.9.92, p.25. This figure fell to below 5000 in 1993 and even further thereafter to a small, dedicated rump of committed activists, with little sign of any revival in fortunes to shore up, let alone boost, membership.
69. The Observer, 12.6.94.
70. This juxtaposition between green realism and green absolutism was reinforced by the impact of the recession on the green lobby. The experience of severe financial constraints and even of a temporary shortfall in funds merely served to induce a greater sense of realism. The Friends of the Earth were forced to shed one fifth of its full-time staff, with membership falling and green issues slipping down the political agenda. Similarly, the World Wildlife Fund lost 10 per cent of its staff in 1992, with further cuts in 1993, because of a shortfall in its global income of some 3 million dollars between 1989-92. Greenpeace International was also forced to make severe staff cutbacks in 1992 in response to a drastic drop in income. The global public at the same time, showed signs of 'doom fatigue'. In short, these groups did not turn their back on, or retreat from these unpalatable facts, however disagreeable. Instead, they fine tuned their message and campaigning methods in order to better respond to them.
71. The Observer, 6.9.92.
72. The Independent on Sunday, 13.9.92.
73. Reuters News Service Report, 27.8.92.
74. For a discussion of the continuing 'green' debate within the Conservative Party, see B. Maddox, "Green sheen on Whitehall machine", Financial Times, 23.2.94.
75. N. Carter, "The 'Greening' of Labour", in M.J. Smith and J. Spear (eds), "The Changing Labour Party" (London, 1992), pp.118-132.
76. See the discussion of this issue in Stephen Tindale, "Sustaining Social Democracy: The Politics of the Environment", in D. Miliband (ed), op.cit (1994), at pp.192-206.
77. John McCormick, "Environmental Politics", in P. Dunleavy, A. Gamble, I. Holliday and G. Peele, "Developments in British Politics 4" (Basingstoke, 1993) at p.281.
78. See D. Fuchs and D. Rucht, "Support for New Social Movements in Five Western European Countries", in C. Rootes and H. Davis (eds), "A New Europe? Social Change and Political Transformation" (London, 1994).

79.　K. Young, "Interim report: rural prospects", in R. Jowell, S. Witherspoon, and L. Brook (eds), "British Social Attitudes: The 5th Report", (Aldershot, 1989); and K. Young, "Living under threat", in ibid (eds), the 7th Report, (Aldershot, 1990).

80.　C. Rootes, op.cit, European Journal of Political Research 22 (1992), at p.180.

81.　C. Rootes, op.cit (1992), The European Journal of Political Research 27 1992, at p.177.

82.　For a 'classical' account of the shallow roots of British radicalism, see P. Anderson, "Components of the national culture", in A. Cochrane and R. Blackburn (eds), "Student Power", (Harmondsworth, 1969), at pp.214-215.

83.　R. Taylor, op.cit (1985); and R. Taylor, "Against the Bomb" (Oxford, 1988).

84.　D. Jahn, "Ecological Discourse in Decline? Changes in the Political Agenda in Sweden and Germany between the 1970s and 1990s"; paper delivered at the workshop on "Green Politics in the New Europe", at the 24th Joint Session of Workshops of the European Consortium on Political Research, Oslo, 29 March - 3 April, 1995.

85.　See Hein-Anton van der Heijden, Ruud Koopmans and Marco G. Giugni, "The West European Environmental Movement", Research in Social Movements, Conflicts and Change Supplement 2 1992, pp.1-40.

86.　See J. McCormick, op.cit (1991).

87.　M. O'Neill, "Oil on the troubled waters of Greenpeace", European Brief, Vol.2(8) 1995, at pp.82-84.

88.　C. Rootes, op.cit (1992), at p.181.

89.　C. Rootes, "Political System, The Green Party and the Environmental Movement in Britain", International Journal of Sociology and Social Policy Vol.12 (1992), at p.224.

90.　J. McCormick, op.cit (1991), pp.123-124.

91.　C. Rootes, op.cit (1994), at p.84.

92.　For a discussion of the propensity to partisan dealignment in British politics, see B. Saarlvik and I. Crewe, "Decade of dealignment" (Cambridge, 1983); R. Rose and J. McAlister, "Voters Begin to Choose" (London, 1980); with a revisionist perspective presented by A. Heath, R. Jowell and J. Curtice, "Trendless fluctuation: a reply to Crewe", Political Studies 35 1987, pp.256-77.

93.　D. Pearce, "Green Britain wilts in a cloud of hot air", Observer, 23.1.94; and Bronwen Maddox, "Green sheen on Whitehall machine", Financial Times, 23.2.94.

94.　See Melanie Phillips, "Greens aren't always good for you", The Observer, 24.3.91.

95.　J. Lambert, "Origins, Praxis and Prospective - The British Environmental Movement", International Journal of Sociology and Social Policy Vol.12 (1992), at p.214.

96.　C. Rootes, "The Greening of British Politics" (1989), at p.296.

97.　J. Lambert, op.cit (1992), pp.204-215.

98.　The Observer, 12.6.94.

99.　The Times, 25.8.94.

100.　The Independent, 1.6.94.

101.　Quoted in The Times, 25.8.94.

102.　J. Porritt, "Regrets for the Greens", Observer, 28.8.94.

103.　The Guardian, 28.8.94.

104.　Sara Parkin, "Dear Green Party", The Independent, 29.9.94.

105.　Sara Parkin, "How Fresh-Look Greens Could be Good for You", The Guardian, 3.6.93.

106.　The Scotsman, 1.11.95.

107. The Guardian, 14.6.94.
108. Financial Times, 14.6.94.
109. The Independent, 1.6.94.
110. "Green Pastures for a Wilting Environment", editorial, The Independent, 3.6.94.
111. The Observer, 12.6.94.
112. See Porritt's commentary in "We need more shades of Green", The Independent, 29.8.94.
113. The Guardian, 15.6.94.
114. C. Boggs, op.cit (1995), at pp.235-36.
115. See P. Ghazi, "Green economy could create 700,000 jobs", The Observer, 20.11.94.
116. J. Porritt, ibid, 29.8.94.
117. "A Tinge of Green", editorial, The Times, 25.8.94.
118. C. Boggs, ibid (1995), at pp.237-38.
119. Daily Telegraph, 20.7.94.
120. The Guardian, 20.7.94.
121. Financial Times, 27.7.94.
122. Larry Elliott, "Forget Capitalism versus Socialism. Now Capitalism Confronts Environmentalism", The Guardian, 22.6.95.
123. Dieter Helm, "Design for an environmental agency", Financial Times, 27.6.94.
124. "Green Wave", The Guardian, 2.8.94.
125. The Guardian, 21.9.96.

9 Comhaontas Glas in Ireland

(i)   Green roots

Green politics in the ecological rather than the nationalist sense came late to the Irish Republic. Surprisingly so in view of the island's largely rural make up, the splendour and indeed the economic value of its scenery as a tourist attraction, and the absence of the sort of concentrations of heavy industrialisation likely to reinforce the anti-conservationism found amongst the vested interests and political establishments of Europe's more advanced economies. On the other hand, Ireland has long been a highly conservative society, reluctant to embrace radical change.[1] Until recently, when generational and social changes have introduced an unprecedented degree of volatility into electoral behaviour, Ireland's politics remained frozen in the traditional mores and expectations of what was once a classic peasant society, tied to what Patrick Commins has called 'rural fundamentalism'.[2] Latterly, social and economic change, accelerated by Ireland's membership of the European Community has begun to impact on both the values and expectations of its citizens - and, in turn, to repattern the country's politics. The Greens have been a relatively minor but persistent factor in this shift. It was only in December 1981 that Christopher Fettes, a Dublin schoolteacher, established the Ecology Party of Ireland (EPI) on familiar grounds. He felt that the already flourishing network of local ecological groups seemed less likely to bring about any significant degree of change, without the national focus provided by a political party.

The Ecology Party was organised from the outset along the lines of a conventional party. Although a central committee was set up to coordinate the network of local branches - for the most part established in urban centres, with the primary but not exclusive centre of activity in Dublin - the preference of ordinary members for a loose, decentralised format was fully acknowledged in the party's structures and procedures. The party retained its flexible pattern by organising itself as an alliance of the constituent and local ecological groups of which it was comprised. These units, in turn, retained their freedom to pursue their grassroots campaigns and local networking, as circumstances allowed, cooperating in the process with all manner of compatible single issue groups and social movements - most notably with CND, the Irish Peace Council, Earthwatch, Friends of the Earth and so on. The Ecology Party's discernibly pure green ethos was underlined by its reluctance to build any contacts either with organised labour, or the emergent alternativist and radical movements of the left. Ireland's late dash for industrialisation was broadly endorsed by the left, which shared the productionist ethos of every European labour movement. Whereas the country's social movements, although sharing some common cause with the Greens - for instance, the anti-nuclear and peace agenda - were regarded with equal caution by the ecologists as primarily 'red' and, therefore, as too ideologically driven.

(ii)   Party formation

The Ecology Party changed its name and reformed into the Green Alliance (Comhaontas Glas) in 1983, in order to better reflect its pure green and decentralist preferences. This loose framework continued after the Alliance again changed its name to the Green Party in 1989, but not without some ambivalence over the same issue. Recent successes in national politics have caused the party to address some of the very same organisational issues that have exercised national Green parties elsewhere. Every constituent group pays a subscription to the party and accepts its broad principles as an a priori condition of membership. A degree of internal coherence is ensured by these arrangements - not least the sense of belonging to a national party. This is hardly, however, a restrictive formula which curbs local autonomy. The Green Alliance was organised along classical anti-party lines. The emphasis on decentralisation was quite deliberate and, by and large, remains so. Each group retains its own rules or constitution, and operates with a real degree of semi-independence from the party's central institutions. The party headquarters in Dublin was established as a necessary compromise with movement politics - part of the logistics of party status, rather than as the bureaucratised hub of a centralising party machine. The party's 'offices' operate largely as a conduit, or at most provide a means of facilitating party activities across the board. It is staffed by volunteers rather than by party functionaries in the formal sense, and is funded by private donations. This latter arrangement underlines its continued dependence on grassroots members and 'ordinary' party workers. The party charges only a small mandatory levy for any of the organisational services provided for those constituent groups who use its services to assist with their own 'sovereign'activities. The funding of the party's election campaigns is also a matter for local constituency parties.

The party's membership arrangements follow much the same informal pattern. It was agreed when the party was formed not to hold a central membership list or to publish actual membership figures, precisely to discourage any idea that this was a national party in the usual sense. It might be debated whether this continued preference for decentralisation was a cause, or merely an indirect response to the party's failure to make an early electoral impact. More recent successes in both national and European elections have certainly raised for more urgent debate, the very same issues that have exercised other parties. But so far, without the same degree of acrimony or divisiveness within this party's ranks. The general consensus in the party over its pure green and community based politics has kept at bay many of the bitter squabbles that debilitated other Green parties. Even so, the party has paid a price of sorts for its ultra democratic preferences. This overt and deepseated attachment to localism from the outset may have hindered the party's ability to project to the electorate an image of decisive or focused leadership. This is always a critical consideration where the inconclusive outcome of elections fought on the Single Transferable Vote system might lead - as they have tended to do in Ireland's recent electoral history - to a period of hard bargaining prior to coalition formation.[3] In these circumstances the electorate, and of course the media who inform them, focus on party leaders and national political personalities. They require the sort of reassurance provided by decisive political leadership. The Green Alliance's emphasis on community rather than national politics, and on the grassroots movement instead of a leadership cadre, did tend to marginalise them in these terms. More recently, a degree of electoral success has opened this issue to renewed debate inside the party.

The existence of a formal party organisation in the formative period was, by and large, the minimum response necessary to accommodate Ireland's constitutional requirements. The regulations that apply to party status here demand that any would-be party must register its officers. In the case of the Greens, these were a Treasurer, a European representative, the editor of the party newspaper, and three party 'coordinators'. Apart from this, no one individual was obviously in a command position in the party and it is still the case that there is no formal leadership position similar to that of every other Irish party. The party's central administrative body, the Party Council - which meets irregularly and infrequently, every second month or so - reinforces the abiding ethos of localism. It consists of one delegate from each of the constituent groups, together with one observer. The party's officers sit in the Council as ex officio members and their legitimacy or 'mandate', such as it is, rests with these local representatives. They are usually nominated after consultations and close networking amongst the active membership. Even so, the Council enjoys no formal rights over decisions - other than in emergencies, where urgency demands speedy administrative action. The Council's main task was not conceived of in a formal executive sense, but rather as providing a forum in which the various groups could discuss issues as they arose. Of course, in any party where democracy is taken as seriously as it is here, politics is bound to lead to disputation, and even this highly participatory arrangement has failed to prevent occasional outbreaks of factionalism similar to those in ultra-democratic Green parties elsewhere. In 1986, for instance, the mainstream ecologists who had long been in the ascendance in the party, were briefly challenged by a minority of anarchistic and more radical fringe elements. These alternativists tried to push the party to embrace more militant expressions of direct action campaigning. They failed, however, to undermine the moderate consensus and were obliged to leave the party. The party remains committed to 'moderate radicalism' and pure ecologism. In genuine anti-party fashion, all the party's policy decisions remain devolved to the full membership, meeting in the party's most authoritative decision making body, the National Convention, which all members may attend. Such an unstructured decision making model can only work in a party as small, as loosely organised, and as ideologically unencumbered as is the Green Alliance. Disputes, when they do occur, whether as personality clashes or over doctrine, are not deeply disruptive affairs. Indeed, they are resolved by the only technique available in parties whose centre of gravity lies with the members rather than with professional functionaries or elected representatives - that of building intra-party consensus. This can be a painstaking process as it has been here. Each individual member is entitled to a say in decisions, with ad hoc and local groups taking it upon themselves to research and propose policy ideas to the party. The various drafts of these prospectuses are circulated within the party, with the prime intention of maximising agreement. Each local party group retains the ultimate sanction of exercising a veto on any such proposal. Without a large residue of good will, and not least an absence of deep factional divisions or ideological discord, this 'system' would undoubtedly implode into impasse or even chaos.

The decision to form an independent Green party was both assisted and hindered by the opportunity framework of the Irish polity. On the negative side of this equation,

Irish electoral politics was ossified into a fairly rigid post-civil war cleavage, which inclined the majority of voters to orientate their political choices around one or other of the two dominant, and broadly conservative, nationalist parties.[4] On the positive side - and opening up some prospect of political change - was the existence of an electoral system based on the Single Transferable Vote (STV) version of proportional representation. This voting system facilitates not only coalition government, but also minor party representation in the national parliament. It encourages, too, a lively 'trade' in second preference votes at the constituency level, which has enhanced the influence of small parties over the final outcome of elections in Ireland's multi-member constituencies. The sense of political flux, and even of a degree of partisan dealignment, is easier to register in an electoral system altogether more sensitive than the plurality model to the shifting sociological undercurrents of politics.[5] The leverage that was already becoming available to small parties on the increasingly fluid ground of Irish politics was indeed one of the main causes of the party's initial launch. In 1981 a recently elected minority coalition in imminent danger of collapse encouraged a small band of ecologists to believe they could actively exercise some effective purchase on future close electoral outcomes. The objective here was to achieve a say in the balance of power in subsequent coalitional negotiations - and, in the process, to bargain hard to win concessions for ecologism which were otherwise unavailable to the movement. In the event, the party's political inexperience and lack of organisational resources at this early stage in its development counted against it. The Greens were too slow off the mark to take advantage of Ireland's latest mood of political uncertainty. The government fell in February 1982 and ordered fresh elections before the Greens could adequately respond. The party stood no candidates at these elections and took no direct part in them, other than to issue a leaflet of their intention to stand in future elections! In the contemporary climate of political instability this opportunity arrived within the year. When another short-lived coalition government collapsed in November 1982, the Greens were able to stand 6 candidates. They polled a minuscule 0.22 per cent of the total national vote (amounting to only 1.26 per cent in the 6 constituencies concerned), with their best result - some 1500 votes - in the Cork South Central constituency. This was hardly an outstanding result and it is partially explained by the prevailing mood of electoral mutability in what was the third general election to take place in eighteen months.[6] Under these circumstances, voters exercised considerable caution in making their choice. They were more concerned to focus their attention on those mainstream parties able to provide the desired outcome of a stable government; and much less inclined to experiment with parties who might further destabilise the political equation.

Within the narrow ideological context of Irish politics, the Green Alliance might easily be taken for a disruptive influence. In fact, as Green parties go, this one was hardly a radical force. The new Green Alliance's constitution, and its initial programme, reflected its essentially conservative pure green credentials. It adhered to the basic principles of environmental protection and the conservation of natural resources; and it endorsed a decentralised model of decision making; committed itself somewhat vaguely to 'international peace' and to the redistribution of global wealth in favour of the third world, whilst emphasising self help rather than open-ended aid. The imprecision, and indeed lack of imagination, in the new party's economic thinking was revealed by its inability to put together a distinctive economic programme: one which would demarcate the party from other conventional parties as a genuinely radical prospect in the cosy, conservative consensus that prevails in both the practice and discourse of Irish politics. While the party managed to at least say some positive things about the environment issue, the sheer difficulty under the party's loose organisational format of imposing a coherent policy explains why it took until 1987 for the Green Alliance to sufficiently refine its policy here, in order to be able to put together a distinctive Green programme for the general election of that year.

The 1987 programme was another eclectic mix of ecological policies. It endorsed anti-nuclearism and anti-pollution; energy conservation and alternative energy sources; urban conservation; bans on animal testing; ecologically friendly transport; the promise to each individual of a guaranteed basic income; a move towards labour intensive and locally based production; support for organic farming; the end to bank monopolies; tax equalisation; and the rescheduling of Ireland's national debt. The party grafted onto the economic element of its programme a complementary checklist of progressive social policies. These included educational reform - to increase training and post-school education - as well as support for more eccentric issues: positive discrimination to favour Gaelic speakers; the teaching of Esperanto; and a greater emphasis on preventative medicine and nutritional diets. The party also incorporated the usual libertarian and civil rights measures identified with Green parties across Europe: the commitment to reducing gender and other forms of discrimination and support for a freedom of information act - which reflected the party's reliance on a liberally inclined urban, middle-class support base. The new party did disproportionately attract the young, urbanised and better educated cohorts, with a strong preponderance of science and humanities graduates amongst their number. To this extent, they proved to be politically attractive to precisely those harbingers of post-material values who were drawn to the green movement throughout Europe. There were also more men than women amongst Irish Green voters - a fact which reflected the male bias of Irish politics per se,[7] but which has recently been challenged by the association of Irish feminism with progressive social issues. The party's radical 'political' stance on economic and ecology issues was predictable enough. There were, however, signs that the party shared some of the prevailing values that have shaped Ireland's distinctive international position. On the Ulster question, for instance, it favoured a non-sectarian approach, jointly agreed with the British Greens, but hardly radical in the context of Irish party politics. On defence matters, too, the party embraced continued Irish neutrality - along with every other party - although it went further and advocated disarmament. Neither of these policy positions amounted to a dramatic political gesture in this non-NATO country, which has never fought a foreign war and had managed to remain formally neutral in the two major European wars of this century. Much of this package amounted to slogans and lip service paid to 'good' causes. Despite being far from unremarkable as the usual diet of political ecologism goes, it did nevertheless appear to be eccentric in a country which, in spite of accelerated social change over recent decades, was for the most part deeply conservative. The national political agenda certainly lacked any obvious stimulus for widespread movement politics of the sort that the nuclear energy issue had provided elsewhere in Europe.

The Green Alliance achieved, in these circumstances, only a modest political impact. It reserved its greatest energies for local campaigning initiatives. Nevertheless, its decision to adopt full party status has been accompanied by its regular appearance at the polls at every level. The Green Alliance stood in the European elections of 1984, when the party's founder was its only candidate for the Dublin constituency and polled barely 2 per cent. In the 1985 local elections, in anticipation of the usual mid-term protest vote against an unpopular government, it ran 34 candidates in urban areas (28 in Dublin alone), but secured a miserly 0.55 per cent of the total vote (2.2 per cent in the constituencies where it stood), with only one success in the Killarney urban district of County Kerry. At the 1987 general election, it put up candidates in 9 of Ireland's 41 parliamentary constituencies but with a scant return, again securing a bare 0.4 per cent of the national vote (1.7 per cent where it ran candidates - which actually represented a marginal drop from its showing in the local elections in the previous year). This shortfall was a significant factor in persuading the Alliance in 1989 to adopt a clearer identity as a political organisation with a change of name to the Green Party - although the party's Irish language designation (Comhaontas Glas) still translates as Green Alliance which, in itself, suggests a movement still caught in two minds as to its political direction. The party's perseverance, and its determination to confront the multiple disadvantages that stand in the way of new, small and radical parties in this political milieu did, however, eventually pay off. It managed to win a seat in the 1989 general election, when it profited from its concentrated vote in the Dublin region, in spite of running a poorly funded campaign. Of course, the Green Party was hardly geared up for widespread electoral success, then or now. The progressive, anti-productionist and post-material preferences which characterise political ecologism have hardly been consonant with what, for the most part, is an unreceptive Irish political culture, with its ingrained conservatism, the continuing influence of the Church over the issue agenda, and the prevalence of rural concerns. The central discourse of Irish politics tends to be one conducted between the rival claims of interests exercised as much by pre-modern as against modernisation concerns, and hardly at all by the post-modernist agenda of ecologism.

This prevailing climate has hindered the development of the Green Party in one obvious sense. Several commentators have drawn attention to the absence in Irish society of any clearly defined social bases. The political frame of reference here tends to be personalised, narrowly clientelist or localised. Cognitive abstractions that shape political identity, such as idealistic causes or ideologically defined movements, while not entirely absent, are by no means significant sources of political allegiance or widespread mobilisers of political engagement. Such sharply defined and politically well articulated categories of identity and identification are indispensable to any party looking to consolidate a reasonably firm electoral base.[8] This situation has been both a blessing and a hindrance for the Greens. On the one hand, it has prevented the emergence of those divisive ideological battles that have rendered some Green parties politically impotent. At the same time, it has closed off the small but ideologically committed reservoirs of support available to many other Green parties. The Greens have been obliged to build electoral support on altogether more ephemeral foundations - the shifting sands of local issues and concerns. The absence, for instance, of a distinctive right-left cleavage in Irish politics, which has yielded a querulous but active red-green constituency in most other European countries, has to date been largely absent in Ireland. The Greens clearly preferred it that way - the low ideological salience of Irish politics, at least in these terms, has preserved the party from factional splits.

But there has been a price to pay for this lack of intra-party ferment. In spite of some recent evidence of de-alignment and generational shift in the contemporary Irish electorate,[9] the peculiarities of the country's political history and a unique electoral sociology forged by these experiences, has continued to ensure the electoral dominance of those centre-right parties whose principal electoral appeal remains a singular mix of residual traditionalism.[10] Even the recent modest breakthrough of the Progressive Democrats and the remodelled Labour Party under its popular leader Dick Spring did come about not from any seachange in electoral loyalties that signals a major political breakthrough - but rather, as the result of a more modest shift within those traditional patterns of support, and primarily between the established parties themselves.[11] These sociological issues are of considerable importance for the future of 'new politics' in Ireland and we shall return to them later in the discussion.

(iii)   Political developments

The pattern of politics in Ireland is, of course, far from static. There has been a discernible shift over recent elections, which might indicate a better prospect for those parties which stand outside the post-civil war animus that has continued to cast a long shadow over the country's politics. Irish electoral behaviour has become more fluid, without as yet becoming volatile. Support for minor parties - including the Greens - has risen, especially in the urban milieu, and even in those rural fiefs which were once thought of as the impregnable bastions of the 'civil war' parties. This gradual flux has become more discernible in successive general elections since the turmoil of the early eighties, and deprived Fianna Fail (FF) of an overall parliamentary majority in both 1987 and 1989.[12] In 1990 this movement for change produced its most tangible outcome so far, with the election of Mary Robinson as Ireland's first woman President. Nevertheless, parties other than the Greens were the most notable beneficiaries of these changes. This social ferment has begun to convert the Labour Party from its relative political isolation in both its urban heartland and rural enclaves into a much more modernised and progressive party, capable at least of tapping into a broader radical constituency in Irish politics.[13] The Labour Party may have been at the centre of this recent shift in political alignments, but other factors, too, have played their part in the 'freeing up' or unfreezing of Ireland's traditional social cleavages and, with that, the movement in the patterning of its party politics. The broad direction of political change here, may be sketched as follows - the traditional electoral supremacy of the two 'catch-all' nationalist parties, not least of the once dominant, ultra Catholic, Fianna Fail party, has begun to crumble, opening up all manner of new right and neo-liberal parties on the centre-right (notably the Progressive Democrats), and a medley of new forces on the centre-left (including Labour, the Democratic Left (DL) and the Greens). As a result, Irish elections have become much less the predictable oscillations between the two mainstream parties - even though the process of dealignment is slow and by no means inexorable on the present evidence. The secession of a group of liberal minded and anti-Haughey members from Fianna Fail in 1985, and the subsequent failure in 1990 of Fianna Fail to prevent the election of a radical and female President by accusing her of holding 'anti-Irish' values, was the first of a series of electoral events signalling an opening up of the political landscape. Fine Gael, standing too long in the shadow of its main rival - and after suffering similarly from shrinkage in its own conservative support base - contributed to the flux in party politics by courting the idea of a new progressive politics. After flirting with the Progressive Democrats as their natural ideological allies, this realignment has recently culminated in a 'rainbow coalition' of the centre left, with the election of a Fine Gael (FG), Labour and Democratic Left government. The position of the Labour Party in this ferment has become more pivotal as Labour's electoral base has both consolidated and expanded, with the party more than doubling its share of the national vote (yielding 33 Dail seats in the 1992 election compared with only 16 in 1989). In the process, it denied Fianna Fail an overall majority, and seriously damaged Fine Gael's position as Ireland's second largest party - especially in Dublin where FG dropped behind Labour for the first time in a popular vote - and thereby continuing a trend first apparent in the 1990 local elections.

The future of the Green Party as an element in the national political equation will almost certainly depend on its willingness to seek some sort of political understanding with the revitalized if not yet resurgent parties of the left - Labour and also with the Democratic Left - with whom it competes for a share of the 'principled radical' and 'discontent' vote. This is likely to be a more difficult strategy under Irish conditions than it would be if the party shared some ideological affiliations with the left. The Green Party's resistance to red-green ecologism will make any prospect of cooperation here less easy to construct with these leftist parties, let alone to sell to the party's grassroots. All the same, there seems to be no realistic alternative to some form of cooperation between these progressive forces if the Greens are to reap any advantage from the new currents in Irish electoral politics, and to become a more electorally significant force in the national parliament (the Dail) than they have managed to date. A modest base in local politics, where the party consolidated a small but persistent base with the election of 13 councillors at the 1991 local elections, and the recent impressive, but for all that an essentially protest, vote in the 1994 Euro-elections, will not in itself guarantee the Greens a secure place in Ireland's changing political firmament. The indicators here remain mixed. The chances of the Greens increasing their national bargaining potential are less than they seem on the evidence of secondary (local and European) polls. The failure of a local and popular candidate to take the seat in the 1994 by-election in Cork South Central suggests an abiding reluctance even by a disconcerted electorate to place their trust in minor parties in elections that have some significance for the shape of the governing coalition. The Greens have certainly acquired some status as a 'home' for residual protest votes in second order elections. Protest votes won in mid-term polls, however, are far from a reliable indicator of any party's real standing in the national political order - let alone any guide to their performance in a general election. The Greens are unlikely, then, as things stand, to take Irish politics by storm. But this does not mean that they have no relevance in modern Irish politics. Nor are they excluded from exerting a degree of influence on the complicated machinations that are now the normal preface to installing governments in Dublin. They will not, however, enjoy these perquisites unless they make some adjustments to the political milieu in which they have to operate.

If the Greens manage to resolve their own dilemmas concerning their purpose in national politics, consolidate a mainly middle class support base around moderate policies that speak to widespread local concerns about environmental depredations, and effectively organise to maximise their influence with other parties at every level of politics, they clearly are capable of becoming a small but persistent element in the increasingly delicate equation of national power brokerage. Whether this will provide them with a reliable basis for long term support is much less clear. The eminent political scientist, Basil Chubb, has observed that Irish politics has spawned a host of ephemeral, short lived or 'fad' parties over the years since independence, none of which have long survived.[14] Irish electoral politics and governance continues to revolve around the country's three established parties (FF, FG and Labour). The Greens do at least have the potential advantage here of representing a new social cleavage of middle class concerns and rising post-materialist discontent with the increasingly visible impact on amenity and habitat of rapid development - along with the new, intrusive global forces that impinge on a rapidly modernising, secular and urbanised society. At the same time, they do not by any means have a monopoly of these concerns and aspirations. The most likely route for the Greens in these circumstances is to make alliances with other parties that harbour similar concerns. The Greens' options here are constrained by the political baggage carried by the other parties. Fianna Fail is simply too conservative to entertain such notions, even in its present chastened mood after a serious drop in its support base. Whereas Fine Gael is more open to radical ideas, but only in a neo-liberal or new rightist sense. Neither of these two traditional conservative parties - each moving at variable speeds to embrace a modern variant of European Christian Democracy - has much to offer the Greens by way of radical policy commitments. The best hope for a radical alliance amenable to progressive ecological ideas lies, then, with Labour and the Democratic Left.

Not that this will be easy either to build or to maintain. The prospects for a new radicalism, built around Labour's solid urban core, promises ideological difficulties and political tensions for the Green Party, even if it overcame its own reticence about dealing with the conventional left. Labour is, after all, a party that remains as committed as its conservative rivals are to productionist preferences and a conventional growth model as the principal source of jobs and prosperity - although its trades union roots puts a redistributive and a progressive gloss on Labour's policy outlook. The current political calculus of Irish politics points to only a modest potential for a major shift in party arrangements. As things stand, Labour's best chance of sharing in government has come from maximising its appeal and even more, its usefulness vis a vis the tight parliamentary arithmetic of contemporary Irish politics, to one or other of the two dominant parties. Labour's bargaining potential, and its most likely route to government, means that it is more likely to seek accommodation with either Fianna Fail or Fine Gael - as it has done with both parties over recent years. The Greens were no more encouraged by the formation of a FG-Labour coalition than they were by the outgoing FF-Labour administration it replaced. A fundamental political realignment seems on recent form to be no more than a distant prospect. The Greens have voiced criticism of Labour's opportunism, as setting back by years any likelihood of a radical refocusing of Ireland's politics. Nor has the emergent Democratic Left Party offered any surer prospect on this score.[15] The DL leader, Proinsias De Rossa, with his own mind firmly set on a centre-left realignment in place of more familiar permutations, settled in the event for merely a minor role in a misleadingly named 'rainbow' coalition with Fine Gael and Labour. The pivotal coalitional axis continues, thus, to revolve firmly around the two dominant parties and Labour.

While this triangular coalitional calculus has had some positive benefits for environmentalism these have been incidental rather than axiomatic to the enterprise of radically changing the national political agenda. In 1992, for instance, Fianna Fail, desperate to reinforce its weakening grip on power, made some suitably progressive noises to entice Labour into government. In the area of social policy they promised to fund a centre for battered wives and, on what might loosely be called 'the environment', they courted Labour's increased concern with over-development, by abandoning plans to build golf courses in Kilkenny national park. The sincerity of Fianna Fail's commitment to far-reaching environmental reforms was, however, soon underlined by their condemnation of the Green Party's concerted opposition to re-zoning schemes, and the infrastructural development that ensued from the re-zoning of land use, as the actions of 'fanatics'.[16]

Although Labour's own commitment to 'real' environmental concern might just as easily be doubted, the party's radical fringe has at least identified with the very same concerns of the Greens with careless re-zoning, greenbelt erosion, and speculative development programmes that ignore or override local concerns. Labour's radicals do tend to oppose these policies on ideological grounds, that draw more on the party's socialist roots than on ecological persuasions per se. But this has not prevented, *quand même,* a meeting of minds over these increasingly contentious issues. Green activists have joined with local Labour Party groups in opposing some of the worst excesses of development blight to stem from the country's cumbersome and centralised planning procedures. Councillors from both parties - especially in Dublin - have cooperated in opposing careless development. Both parties, too, while competing for the same post-materialist middle class electorate, have good reason to coordinate their appeal to this constituency, and thus to maximise the support for progressive candidates in the transfers of votes under Ireland's STV electoral system. A strict electoral calculus prevails here, more than any real meeting of minds. Nevertheless, making common radical cause wherever possible, to deny seats to more conservative candidates, does become habit forming. Regular contact leads to compromise and thus to the identification of mutual purposes. Political realignment is hardly guaranteed by such a strategy, let alone the emergence of a cohesive radical project. Yet, given the coalitional logic that sustains Irish governments, it has the potential for at least increasing the Green Party's leverage over these outcomes. The movement in the patterns of political identity that underline these shifts might, in time, assist the Greens to harness social groups that are in the process of becoming detached from former allegiances to one or other of the dominant 'system' parties. So far, however, the party has failed to respond to these opportunities by looking much beyond its narrow pure green preoccupations, in order to attract the support it needs to become part of such a progressive coalition. After the inconclusive outcome of the 1992 general election, the Greens were unable to do much more than retain their single seat in the national parliament - a forum where the member (TD) manages little by way of exerting influence than confronting the other parties with their 'misappropriation' of the Green 'mantle'. The party has fared better in both local and European elections. Even then, it has had to fight hard to retain its modest foothold in national politics, and has been restricted, in an intensely competitive electoral climate to consolidating its existing, but for all that modest, local bases.[17]

The Greens have pleaded as mitigation for their lack of clout a political innocence that they assume will pass as they acquire experience of the game. At the party's Annual Congress in May 1993 a leading local activist, Dan Boyle, claimed that the Greens were learning fast and had shed much of their political naïvety. "In the early days", said Boyle, "we felt that we could 'green' other political parties. We know now that although they speak our language, other political parties cannot be depended on to undertake Green issues".[18] This defence is less plausible than it seems if we consider that the Green Party has been contesting elections for over a decade - that is, for at least as long as many other

Green parties elsewhere in Europe, who have far more to show for their efforts by way of parliamentary seats and political gravitas. The hostile political culture and unhelpful opportunity structure that prevail here, provide only a partial alibi. By far the biggest handicap facing the Irish Greens is self imposed - the party's continuing insistence on pursuing community politics, rather than putting some of its energies into a concerted national strategy. Of course, as the experience of many other Green parties has showed - notably Die Grunen, Les Verts, and the Italian Green Federation - these are by no means mutually exclusive strategies. But neither one can be pursued to the exclusion of the other. An intensely localised form of pure green politics has certainly yielded some dividends for the Irish Greens. The party's grassroots activists have been at the centre of some very successful local campaigns: for instance, on waste disposal, public transport and housing. This is not, however, sufficient in itself to reach out to other parties, let alone to attract the sort of viable electoral base capable of exerting real leverage on the centre left parties as a traditional political culture opens up to new issues and agendas.[19]

The Greens were reluctant to learn these lessons and remained convinced that they were merely playing to their strengths. There have recently been more encouraging signs that things are beginning to change on this score. The modest breakthrough in 1992 - even though it yielded only one Dail seat and 1.4 per cent of the total first preference votes - gave the party's pragmatists both a taste for national politics, and increased their conviction that localism should be complemented by a broader strategy. At the 1993 national party convention Trevor Sargent, the newly elected Dail member, used his influence to urge the Green party to show that it was a national party rather than merely a narrow issue-based or community movement - and that its policy agenda covered the usual gamut of national concerns; including health, education, agriculture, employment, energy, transport, the economy, international affairs and Northern Ireland. At the same time, he wrapped up this call for realism in a distinctive ecological leitmotif, and refused to entertain the cynical 'catch-all' quality that political idealists disdainfully associate with the mass parties' sordid scramble for votes. Instead, Sargent outlined what he saw as a principled pragmatism. But one that he believed would appeal, at the same time, to those radicals of other political persuasions looking to revamp Irish society and realign its politics. He challenged the use of traditional technology or the conventional economic growth models which continued to drive Ireland's development, called for "an end to unecological, ignorant, and anthromorphic arrogance," and advocated 'mother nature' as Ireland's most reliable 'contractor'. This ecological theme was also pursued when the Greens - under greater pressure by now from media and opponents alike - turned their attention at their 1994 annual convention to the problematics of financing this alternative development model. Sargent's keynote address on this occasion - the closest thing in this highly decentralised party to a leadership mission statement - proposed the replacement of income tax with pollution taxes; for instance, a charge on fossil fuels. The reasoning here was a mix of ecological, progressive and even leftist ideas; a rejection of the 'futility' of market generated economic growth advocated by every other Dail party. This prospectus included the abandonment of outmoded production techniques that both pollute and destroy jobs; a shift in the burden of taxation away from labour; and a fairer redistribution of available work, underpinned by a guaranteed basic income. In addition, the supply side payoff of job sharing was deemed sufficient to counter rising alienation and to prevent social breakdown.

These bold precepts, whilst appealing to party stalwarts, did little to achieve the purpose for which they were, in part, designed. They failed to enhance the Green Party's credibility amongst the mainstream parties with which it had to negotiate and deal, either in council chambers or the Dail itself. In truth, the party's sudden 'success' had caught it as unawares as its opponents. There were clearly some hard choices to be made and the party - although not as deeply riven ideologically as many other European Green parties along either the red-green or 'realo' 'fundi' fault lines identified in Chapter One - did begin to experience some internal tensions as these dilemmas were confronted. The tension between realists and idealists, which became apparent in the 1993 Dublin national convention, in spite of Sargent's eclectic attempt to advocate a radical agenda that would appeal to both camps, amounted less to civil war than to an intense debate about the purposes of party politics. Even here, there was more heat than venom, with the balance of the argument being in favour of the realists, anxious to build on rather than squander the new opportunities that seemed to be opening up for the party in mainstream politics. Dan Boyle, the party's local government spokesman, caught the new mood of realism when he advised the party that political success brings with it difficult decisions; and that accordingly "we have had to leave many assumptions behind us (and) many more will follow in their wake".[20] The most obvious predicament here was over organisational arrangements. After the 1992 elections the party had assembled a ten strong 'think tank' to advise the new Dail member for Dublin North. The balance in this forum was evenly divided between his constituency party and the national party - a sign that the party was at least attempting to reconcile its endemic localism with some of the demands of its new found national party status. Nevertheless, the party remained, for the most part, reluctant to accede to any idea of a parliamentary elite or of a hierarchical party 'led' from Parliament. Even the realists in its ranks remained convinced that the only effective base for the party lay in its commitment to localism and direct democracy. Party stalwarts had been quick to remind the Greens' first MP, Roger Garland, that the media's description of him as a 'leader' was entirely misplaced and Boyle, now the voice of principled pragmatism, refuted the false humility of the other parties, and what he called their 'sham' commitment to transparency and proper accountability. He agreed that it was "because of this, the ideas (of local democracy) become polluted, the language becomes corrupted. Consultation does not consist of involving people in a process only to ensure that their opinions are not given any weight. Decentralisation is not about the moving of an office bloc, but is the dispersal of functions within that office bloc".[21] The abiding commitment to intra-party democracy underlined in this commentary was further reinforced by the example - and the precedent - set by the Greens' new MP, when he relinquished his seat on Dublin County Council in order to avoid 'collecting' offices or involvement in more than one level of government simultaneously, and thereby to give someone else the opportunity to serve. In the context of Irish political culture, this sacrifice was a break with an established routine, whereby Dail members - and until recently, even government Ministers - cling to local office in order to enhance their chances under the STV electoral system, of using their local prominence to rack up the transfer votes that are frequently necessary to secure a parliamentary seat.

These were relatively straightforward organisational changes to undertake, because they went entirely with the grain of the grassroots' preferences for anti-partyism. There were other proposals - put to the 1995 party convention - that were far more divisive, and which reflected the predicament of every Green party caught between its ultra-democratic disposition and the organisational requirements facing any party competing in the elaborate 'game' that is Irish national politics. The issue was highlighted by the new Green Lord Mayor of Dublin, John Gormley, who recommended that the party appoint two full time officers to organise recruitment, service elected party functionaries, and to help draft policy. He went further and advocated a new party constitution, to be drafted by professional lawyers and drawing on the experience of the successful, because well organised, policy-coherent Green parties of Germany - of which he had had direct experience - and of Sweden and Finland. The essence of Gormley's appeal was a plea for political maturity over enthusiastic amateurism, and for the party to capitalise on, and to consolidate, its growing support in order to become a serious 'party of government'. The evidence in support of Gormley's aspirations was equivocal to say the least, in spite of the fact that the Green Party had emerged from the very fringes of Irish politics to become a factor in the new calculus of party political manoeuvring. In 1987 the party had been little more than a pressure group centred on Dublin, whose highest constituency vote was barely 3 per cent. By 1989, after a cash starved general election campaign, and with barely 600 members to call on nationwide for electioneering purposes, the party took its first Dail seat (in Dublin South) with 8.8 per cent, largely due to favourable transfers; and its candidate was narrowly beaten to a seat in the Dublin South East constituency, with an impressive 10 per cent of the first returns. Another Green candidate lost out in Dublin North but with a commendable 11.6 per cent.

The Greens had maintained this electoral momentum in the 1991 Council elections on the back of a major defection of support, especially in the capital, from both Fianna Fail and Fine Gael. Fianna Fail lost control of 14 of its 17 councils (and 68 seats) across the country, and retained outright control of only 12. Its total vote dropped by 7 per cent to 38 per cent - the lowest it had ever recorded. Likewise, Fine Gael lost seats to the left, particularly in Dublin. Although Labour was the principal beneficiary of these shifts - almost doubling its vote - the Greens (with 2.5 per cent nationally) nevertheless gained their first foothold in local government, winning 14 council seats; four in Dublin, two each in Fingal, Dun Laoghaire, Rathbone, and one each in South Dublin, Cork City, County Kildare and County Wicklow. These developments hardly amounted to a seachange in Irish politics, but they did underline the rising mood of electoral volatility, especially amongst urbanised and affluent voters who represent an increasing proportion of the Irish electorate. A seasoned commentator on Irish politics, Dick Walsh, the political editor of the Irish Times, detected an emerging pattern here that prefaced a prospective, if tentative, realignment. As Walsh read the situation, social change and the value shifts consequent on it, were slowly but surely altering the political landscape. Moreover, "the movement has accelerated and, in ever-widening arcs around the cities - in towns too, which had once been thought the unvarying centres of rural strongholds - support for Labour, the Progressive Democrats, the Workers' Party and the Greens is spreading. The movement is part of a pattern which has become clearer with each election since the mid-eighties. In 1990 it elected President Mary Robinson. It has converted Labour.... into a much more vigorous and cohesive party, with a widening urban base. The local elections (of 1991) have added, perhaps more modestly than expected, to the advances made in Dublin, Cork and Waterford by the Workers' Party; and they have proved emphatically that the Greens' performance in 1989 had more substance than many thought at the time".[22]

Other commentators saw in these changes much less an incipient realignment than a cumulative volatility - a feature of a rising discontent with traditional governing parties apparent everywhere on the European electoral landscape. Richard Sinnott, for example, the Director of the Centre for European Economic and Public Affairs in Ireland, found evidence here of protest rather than of an inexorable erosion of old and durable patterns of partisanship; in short, that voters were less than radical, but more than ready to punish at the polls those power holders who failed to meet their rising expectations. The key to Sinnott's analysis here was the Labour vote, rather than support for the Greens or the alternative left. Labour had done well in the early 1990s as the main focus of electoral protest against the mainstream 'governing' parties, culminating in a large increase in its support in the 1992 national elections. The Labour upsurge in 1992 swamped the Greens and even halved their overall share of the total vote in the Greens' Dublin 'heartland' - and this in spite of the fact that a creditable tally of some 2500 transfer votes saw the Greens take one of the Dublin North seats. These electoral movements emphasised both the extent to which Ireland's 'new parties' depend on an ephemeral and ultimately an unreliable discontent vote; as well as the intense competition for that protest quota, especially in an electoral system that is acutely sensitive to inter-party competition and to a tactical voting that reflects both local circumstances as much as it does the wider national calculus. The ephemeral quality of these shifts was further underlined by the outcome of subsequent elections. Participation in government, with its inevitable complicity in some unpopular decisions that compromised the party's radical image, saw much of Labour's newly won support evaporate after 1992, as the results of the 1994 Euro-elections revealed. Although the underlying electoral currents that are clearly in flux in Irish politics will not be properly uncovered, or their patterns adequately mapped, until a long cycle of elections has passed, Sinnott has maintained that the available evidence so far does indicate that the electoral fickleness that characterises recent elections is "not the stuff of which major realignments are made".[23]

We might reasonably conclude that both the radical and the tentative interpretation of these electoral eddies may each contain an important element of truth. There may be less evidence here to support the case for a thorough-going party political realignment. At the same time, a volatile electorate, and one that is undergoing the intrusive and far-reaching changes that have affected Ireland over recent decades, may well be more amenable than previously to new ideological preferences, and to the changes in political partisanship that reflect them. The electoral flux of the past decade, of which small parties such as the Greens have been the main beneficiaries, does suggest that something politically significant is afoot here than a mere episodic protest. The 'big three' parties win and lose support from one another across the country, depending on a medley of issues, and the usual interplay of political personalities. At the same time, the Greens have been the only party to show a steady if modest pattern of gains across all constituencies by comparison with previous electoral cycles. Moreover, the evidence from the Euro-barometer surveys continues to show the increasing salience of environmental issues - helped in particular by widespread concern across all demographic groups and social classes about the expansion of Sellafield across the St George's channel. The protest quotient began to work in the Greens' favour, once Labour became identified with unpopular government decisions. This trend was certainly apparent in the 1994 European elections. The two coalition parties experienced a sharp drop in first preference votes, and the Green Party was the principal beneficiary of this shortfall. There was, however, more to this than a negative protest against the tribulations and compromises of coalitional government. The Greens presented themselves for the first time on the national stage, as a positive force for change. They put up candidates, again for the first time, in every constituency and despite a resources shortfall campaigned effectively on a national programme. Although ecology remained the central plank of the campaign - with Sellafield and the Thorp project the principal vote winner, especially in the Dublin and Leinster constituencies along the eastern seaboard where the Greens were most successful - they campaigned, too, as a wider front, canvassing the issues of unemployment, emigration, the need for sustainable development and the neutrality issue raised by the proposal enshrined in the Maastricht Treaty for a European Defence Identity. The party exceeded even its own best expectations, and took two seats in the Strasbourg Parliament - admittedly in an election regarded as a mid-term referendum on the state of national politics that presented an ideal opportunity to register a protest against the political establishment, as it did in every EU member state struggling with the economic consequences of new and disruptive global forces. Voters tend to be less forgiving and far more anxious about the impact of these immensely complex and intrusive forces on their life chances, than either political pundits or professional economists. Along with the other opposition parties, the Greens took full advantage of the mood of widespread discontent. The Greens also took local council seats in the counties of Dublin, Wicklow, Cork, Kildare and Kerry, and polled a commendable 7 per cent in the Dublin South Central by-election for a vacant Dail seat held on the same day. The destination of their transfer votes undoubtedly influenced the eventual outcome, obliged the other parties to court first preference Green voters, and accordingly raised the profile of ecological issues. The successful Green candidate in Leinster observed, whether naively or disingenuously, that "people want to get out of that political cynicism and are tired of the traditional parties. They see the Greens as an alternative".[24]

The Green Party spokeswoman on human rights, Patricia McKenna, topped the poll in the Dublin constituency where the Greens stormed into the lead on the first count with a vote of 40,000 - some 20,000 ahead of the leading Fine Gael candidate and 3,000 in front of the nearest Fianna Fail challenger. And while the Fianna Fail candidate made up ground with heavy transfer from his two running mates, the Greens went on to head the poll by the tenth count - a remarkable result, by any standard, given that the party had only anticipated 14 per cent at best, of first preferences - and had expected at the outside, to take only the third seat in the constituency. Even more remarkable, a Green Party councillor on Wicklow County Council, Nuala Ahern, used her strong base in local politics, where she had a reputation as an effective community campaigner - saving oak trees in Coolattin woods and opposing the re-routing of the Arklow bypass through a gypsum dump for example - to secure the last seat on the tenth count, ahead of a Fianna Fail candidate, in the Leinster constituency, on the back of favourable transfers. In the Connacht-Ulster constituency, Richard Douthwaite (author of "The Growth Illusion") polled a steady 8,628 votes, and established a useful base for future elections. While the Greens have not maintained this support in subsequent by-elections for Dail seats, their performance has been good enough to maintain pressure on the other parties. In a by-election contest for the Cork South Central seat, for instance, the Green candidate, Dan Boyle, cashed in his local community credentials to equally good effect, and campaigned on a mixture of ecological issues (pollution and over development of Cork harbour) and social concerns (housing), to force even Fianna Fail to try and occupy his ground by laying claim to green credentials. A Fianna Fail party spokesman announced, for instance, a ban on bituminous coal to upgrade air quality in Cork, improvements in the water quality of the rivers Lee and Bandon, and the siting of the Environmental Protection Agency there as a further incentive to good, environmental management. The Greens profited as much from the publicity resulting from this agenda as their rivals, and markedly improved on their previous best performance in both seats. Green transfers there, after a solid vote of 16 per cent, affected the eventual destination of the seat (a win for Fine Gael), and persuaded one leading commentator to refer to the Greens as "the hottest political property around".[25] Dan Boyle saw this as further evidence of both the Greens' 'arrival', and as a reward for their political maturity. He was moved to observe that "we have performed as anticipated and we have laid down a marker for the next election".[26] In the adjacent seat of Cork North Central, a Green return of 4 per cent dented the Labour vote - and reminded that party that the Greens could no longer be ignored in the increasingly complicated electoral equation. Green transfer votes here also helped to give the seat to the Democratic Left Party. In a more recent by-election in Wicklow (in May 1995), the modest but firm Green vote, built around an active presence in community politics, and drawing again on Sellafield and local environment issues of concern (road building and high density housing programmes,[27] and plans to locate a 'super dump' for waste in Wicklow[28]) also played its part in determining the outcome. Dan Boyle drew comfort from this steady but unspectacular improvement in the party's electoral performance at every level, and spoke for the Green electoralists who now had the ascendancy in the party, when he said that this record of success demonstrated how far the Greens had come in a short time down the road of political moderation; that they had "come through the barrier - (because) people are no longer afraid to vote Green".[29]

This may well be true. What is at issue, however, is what this electoral record really amounts to. Whether the Greens' recent electoral successes are anything more than a protest vote, or reflect instead the shifting undercurrents of national politics, is certainly debatable. The Greens did intend to use the Euro-elections as a way of increasing the party's national profile, in order to consolidate a 'Green' constituency as a base from which to increase its strength in the Dail.[30] The profile of the Green vote tells a less emphatic story. The Greens took the bulk of their votes from disgruntled former Labour supporters, angry at what they saw as that party's complicity in Fianna Fail's conservative economic policies, and not least the lack of effective action on unemployment. The Greens were, however, particularly appealing to a persistently growing constituency of 'soft left' middle class voters, exercised by moral disquiet across a range of progressive social issues. A number of this small but articulate and disproportionately influential constituency - but by no means all - were 'post-materialists', searching for a viable anti-establishment vehicle. Nevertheless, this pivotal constituency of opinion formers who help to provide the radical 'grit' in the politics of every modern liberal democracy, were not 'owned' by any one party. The Greens did not have a monopoly of either of those constituencies most receptive to radical appeals and susceptible to electoral volatility. They had to compete hard with other small parties who also appealed to some common radical elements, and likewise engaged the instincts for real change that mobilise such cosmopolitan, middle income, urban voters.[31] On the left, the Democratic Left party, and on the right the part

Thatcherite, part 'yuppy' Progressive Democrats - who held on to a swathe of the liberal middle class vote in spite of internal party discord, and sought to deflect attention from their own strife - presented equally attractive, radical alternatives to the Green party. Both of them, too, found good reason for attacking the Greens for being a 'loony' or "motherhood and apple pie" party, as a convenient deflection from their own internal troubles.

The Greens' modest electoral success has failed to settle other intra-party dilemmas that became more urgent matters, precisely because of the party's recent achievements. Not least, the question of the party's future political orientation, or the equally pressing issue of party organisation. The electoralist wing - now in the ascendance but by no means without opposition - have become more determined, after the taste of success in 1994, to push for further reforms on this still contentious issue. As one leading commentator on these events sees the situation, the "lack of organisation, structures and a consistent (party) profile has led to an erosion" of the party's surge in support in Dublin and further afield by the early 1990s; moreover, that while this "solid electoral cushion" did promise further growth, the Greens remain vulnerable to counter attack, especially from their main rivals for the anti-establishment vote. The mainstream parties may have been caught unawares by the Greens' initial 'surge', but have since assimilated that threat, even absorbed some of the distinctive 'green' message and in consequence have put the Greens under the severe scrutiny only reserved for parties deemed to be a threat to entrenched party political interests. The political gradient facing the Greens, hereafter, will certainly become a much steeper one. The prospect for a modest consolidation of their niche position in the ever more complex electoral equation was - and remains - a viable one for the Greens. But only if the usual compromises that confront all radical parties engaged in mainstream politics are seriously addressed. According to the assessment of one authoritative commentator on these events, "unless professionalism, competence and clear policies on the use of power are harnessed, the party will miss out on its potential".[32]

The persistent critique of amateurism and indecisiveness in the party was by no means the sole preserve of 'outside' pundits. It has surfaced, too, within the party as it tried to come to terms with its improved electoral fortunes. The call for realism - both in party organisation and political strategy - was a central plank of the case put before the party by its own pragmatists. John Gormley, fresh from his own first-hand experience of governance as the mayor of Dublin - an arrangement which came about as the result of a power sharing 'rainbow' alliance of progressive and minor parties (Greens, Labour, Independents, Workers' Party and Fine Gael), to counter Fianna Fail's dominance of the city's politics, and which had negotiated a 15 point civic charter for the city's development that gave prominence to environmental schemes[33] - reminded the party that community success was only the first step to a national status that it should not turn away from. As Gormley put it, "we are a party that wishes to govern. The Greens are on an upward curve and we will continue to build and progress if we can maintain the momentum of our latest successes and we are willing to face up to the challenges that face us". In line with his own electoral strategy in Dublin where, as a supporter of the German 'realos',[34] he spearheaded a light-green ecological platform (local production, anti-smog measures, sensible transport policies pursued with political pragmatism), he reminded his local supporters that "politics is the attainment of power to implement your policies. Elections are about getting elected. If you don't want to get elected, don't stand".[35] Gormley also warned the 1995 national party convention that it must overcome deepseated prejudices if it expected to be taken seriously and trusted with responsibility, at a time when the old nationalist and the more recent left-right political cleavages were decreasing in significance. In short, the choice facing the Greens was between continued marginality and lack of influence or political engagement - and in effect to be "a party of government.... a party that wishes to govern and .... a party that after the next election would like to be a party of government on our own terms",[36] or to court oblivion.

Gormley spoke for a faction that remained convinced that the Greens were clearly part of an emergent realignment underway in Irish politics. The objective here was to achieve full national party status. He maintained that with proper attention to detail, the party could realistically target up to 9 parliamentary seats by maximising the rising discontent vote, and thereby more effectively play the transfer vote 'game' essential to the success of this strategy. The realists, including Gormley, by no means underestimated the formidable task that faced the party in this regard. Power broking in Irish coalition building is a consummate art[37] that requires a degree of leadership that the party at this stage in its development was ill prepared for. As such, the prospect of playing 'normal' politics and the high stakes involved were bound to test the Greens' democratic credentials almost to breaking point. Gormley reminded the party that, to this extent, they held their fate in their own hands: that they had to face up to and respond to these tests, or risk squandering an historic opportunity to play their part - and sooner rather than later - in a centre left coalition. The force of his case was reinforced by the mainfest benefits that had already accrued to the Green Party by joining - originally with the eight Democratic Left and Independent members of the Dail - to form a 'technical group' with access to specific parliamentary privileges and resources such as private members' time, priority questions, representation on committees, and full participation in whips meetings.[38] The addition of another Democratic Left member to this group after the Dublin South Central by-election in 1995, increased this 'coalition's' access to parliamentary privileges and made the group larger in the Dail than the Progressive Democrats. There was, of course, some predictable resistance to this realist prospectus from those party members who preferred a more decentralised party format that kept the party in the hands of its grassroots activists, and thereby ensured priority was given in its councils to community politics and local issues. Gormley's prescriptions motivated these anti-partyists to reject his "objectionable observations".[39] These tensions surfaced again, albeit less disruptively than they might have done, in the dispute over the support the former Green MP, Roger Garland, had given to an independent 'Green' who stood against the official candidate in Leinster in the 1994 Euro-election. After much internal prevarication, a specially convened Party Council decided to expel Garland, by a margin of 75-25 per cent. The conflict here between party discipline and freedom of action was resolved in favour of the former, and provided some conclusive evidence that the party was finally prepared to gear itself to the possibilities and rigors of a new style of coalitional politics.

(iv)   Prospects for political change

The promise of the fundamental political realignment on which the realists' agenda was raised, momentarily in tempo and improved when endemic tensions within the Fianna Fail-Labour coalition led to its mid-term collapse in 1994. After long drawn out deliberations between the parties that opened up the prospect of a centre-left realignment - and motivated not least by the determination of all of the major party players to avoid a parliamentary dissolution that would, on the Greens' current electoral form, have almost certainly increased their representation in the Dail and improved their national bargaining position in any subsequent coalitional negotiation - John Bruton (Fine Gael) headed the centre-left 'rainbow coalition' he had floated from opposition some two years previously. The Fine Gael, Labour and Democratic Left government was described by the new Prime Minister as "a government of renewal".[40] The Greens remained outside this 'rainbow'. This might be counted a lost opportunity, and maybe something more serious as the Greens have initially slipped back in the polls and the new coalition - helped initially by the optimism that surrounded the Ulster Peace process and the profile this gave to Ireland's international status - presided over a more benign domestic politics. The rising stature of the Labour leader, Dick Spring, has also contributed to a slowing down of a mood favourable to national political realignment. Under Spring's leadership Labour has been sufficiently confident of its place as a front player in Ireland's new politics to have claimed the Taoiseach's mantle in the recent coalitional bargaining that preceded the new government's formation.[41] Political realignment may still be in the air but it is a less imminent prospect now than it appeared to be in the early 1990s as the outcome of the recent (1997) national elections underlines. If change of any magnitude is to occur, Labour is as likely to figure in any prospective alignment with the emerging centre left that might result from the further fragmentation of the once dominant post 'civil war' coalitions, as they are to be tempted by a more risky and unpredictable liaison with the Greens, although the now regular occurrence of tight, often indecisive electoral contests, with resulting 'hung' parliaments - what one Irish political scientist refers to as 'hung hung' Dails - might help to bring the Greens into the post-election calculus. As it almost did on this occasion.[42]

These prospects, too, increased the pressures within the Green party, as between its realists and those determined, if not quite militant, anti-partyists who prefer that the party should concentrate on consolidating its base in community politics. Even if this choice is resolved in favour of the former group, as seems likely on current form, the party will by no means easily secure its place as a significant political player. There are yet more hard choices to confront. In these circumstances, the onus is more on the Greens to make the best accommodations indispensible to coalition formation than it is on the left parties. The choice facing the Greens goes to the very heart of what we have identified here as the same radical predicament that, sooner or later, confronts all radical parties operating within the 'normal' game of party politics: whether to recognise the volatility of the protest vote which they continue on to depend for their best results at every level of electoral politics; or to move towards pragmatic adjustments with those parties better placed to bring about a radical dealignment in national politics. This is a less straightforward strategy in the present circumstances of Irish party politics than it might seem on the face of it to be, given that the small radical parties here are in direct competition with each other for the discontent and anti-establishment vote. The STV electoral system and Ireland's multi-member constituencies does, nevertheless, present an opportunity structure in which the mutual accommodations linked to the trade off in transfer votes are not only desirable per se, but are the only way that any of these small radical parties can maximise their political influence. Of course, this can also count against small parties, which are either squeezed by more organised, better resourced parties, or otherwise fall foul of changes in political fashion.

The realignment underway in Irish party politics, if such it is, will be a protracted and untidy affair by any standards. It is likely to encompass, as much as any fundamental shift in the balance of the country's political forces, a change in the position of the mainstream traditional parties as they fight to maintain their shrinking support base, and to reorientate themselves to the sensibilities of an electorate experiencing those far-reaching socio-economic changes and value shifts that invariably accompany such rapid modernisation. Fianna Fail and the Progressive Democrats, for instance, have already tried to respond to these movements in the political landscape by modulating their commitment to "the culture of business and towards the left".[43] The Progressive Democrats' commitment, as part of this politics of renewal, to genuine ecologism might well be skin deep and indeed be suspect, given that party's ideological enthusiasm for free market principles and the 'laws' of market forces. Yet the Progressive Democrats' support for prohibitions on detergents using phosphates in order to guarantee water quality, and its call for recycling as a solution to waste disposal, is testament in part to a remarkable shift in the lexicon of Irish politics, brought about by a recent surge in public awareness of ecology.[44] Convenient political clichés can, of course, mean whatever their advocates choose them to mean. The Bruton-led Government, aware of its vulnerability on its left flank and amongst the new middle class, was also active on the environment front, even if its contribution had been equally selective. It did signal an interest in environmental policy and at least manages to sound, from its position closer to the centre-left, rather more convincing than did the previous Fianna Fail led government when it broached its own variant of a reformist agenda.

To date, the extent of any realignment of Irish politics has been modest. What is most noticeable here is the replacement, as the ideological mainspring of national politics, of the insular and conservative nationalism that was the principal legacy of the civil war, with its previous concordat between Church and State, by a more socially aware and outward looking brand of European Christian Democracy. A future settlement of the North of Ireland question might even bring Fianna Fail and Fine Gael closer together and encourage a centre-right coalition that has so far been precluded by the historical legacies of the partition of the island.[45] A reconciliation on these terms would undoubtedly present a major obstacle to a centre-left alignment. On the other hand, it would equally propel the minor left and the radical parties into their own electoral arrangements, to counter the threat of a centre-right hegemony at the polls. This prognosis is purely speculative. It does suggest, however, that the future patterning of Irish politics is far from being a foregone conclusion - and that any number of permutations are possible amongst the existing party players. Meanwhile, the established parties continue to pressurise the Greens on their own political territory, in order to reduce even their indirect effect on electoral outcomes. Yet, while all three of the main parties challenge the Greens for their ecology mantle, they have each proved to be its less convincing wearers in practice. The Green Party remains, then, the surest repository of radical ecologism and is well placed, whatever its other handicaps, to secure most of whatever electoral credit exists amongst that niche constituency. There is a degree of political promise in this position, as well as the obvious liabilities that accompany the Greens' continuing intra-party divisions over strategy, alongside the continuing prevalence of materialist issues as a focus of the national political agenda. As long as the Greens accept their own limitations, position themselves in order to play the electoral game to their own best advantage by bargaining and reaching compromises in joint local campaigns that raise ecological awareness and maximise the radical and protest vote, they will continue to have a distinctive rather than a decisive role to play in Irish politics. Pragmatism has to be the Greens' watchword here - playing the system for what it is, warts and all, rather than as the party's idealists might prefer it to be.

The extent to which environmental issues per se offer a firm basis for the bargaining and trade offs that are the essence of coalition building remains an open, but nevertheless a critical, question. It is one which can only really be answered by the Greens themselves. So far, they have treated ecologism as little more than a symbolic talisman, devoting much of their energy to delineating their own 'purity' on this issue, and distancing themselves from what they see as the cynical misuse of the issue by other parties. This obsession has tended to distract them from an altogether more cogent strategy. It is, as we have seen, a familiar dilemma that faces Green parties everywhere. Some other parties have fared rather better in dealing with this quandary than the Irish Greens. Unable to turn a convenient 'blind eye' to what they see as hypocrisy, they have not exploited their principal issue as a bridge, nor used it as a common denominator, to forge effective, issue-based alliances of mutual advantage, as Green party pragmatists in Belgium, Germany, Finland, France, Italy, Portugal and elsewhere have managed to do. The opportunity to take this realist route still exists, and whether or not it is seized upon may yet determine the future of the Irish Greens. For a whole range of environment issues will undoubtedly become salient as this small, sparsely populated country continues, under the impact of global macro-economic forces, encouraged by its membership of the Single European Market and eventually EMU, and assisted by EU regional and other structural funds, to develop its industrial and technological base as well as to further expand its tertiary and services sector. This is not to say that the cause of the environment will rise easily up the national agenda, or without challenge from powerful vested interests. Moreover, the increasing significance of the environment issue, here as elsewhere, has attracted as much opportunism as serious commitment from the mainstream parties anxious to exploit it for their own ends. After the modest success of the Green Party at the 1989 European elections, Prime Minister Haughey made much of Fianna Fail's new-found commitment to 'environmentalism'. He promised that the forthcoming Irish Presidency of the European Community, beginning in January 1990, would be a 'Green Presidency'. He talked, too, of developing a common transnational environment strategy, with progress signalled on water quality, waste management, wildlife protection and preparation for the forthcoming Montreal Protocol on the ozone layer. Apart from a short term desire to outflank a rising Green vote, with a potential to damage Fianna Fail in the complex transfer procedures of Ireland's proportional electoral system, Haughey's good intentions were also motivated by more naked political ambitions - his vain bid to secure for Dublin the prestige of locating Europe's new Environmental Protection Agency. The Chair of the EC Environment Committee was less impressed with this rhetoric than he was aware of the stark fact, as he communicated it to Ireland's Environment Minister, of a notable reluctance in Dublin to implement even the EC's existing environmental directives!

The Irish Government continued, nevertheless, to plough a green furrow. Spokesmen argued at the time, that a raft of measures for environmental management was already planned. A case was even made for the apparent tardiness in this policy area, on the grounds that nature had already endowed Ireland with a relatively 'clean' environment, and that the lack of any serious initiative here might be excused, both by the nature of Irish economic development and the country's relatively favourable geography. There was a grain of truth in this: but not enough to excuse, as the Greens saw it, some of the blatant abuses of amenity that had begun to accompany the recent spurt in economic growth. To date, the usual forms of environmental pollution had hardly been a matter of any serious concern in a predominantly rural country of barely 4 million citizens, spread over 69,000 square kilometres - the least densely populated state in the EC. The prevailing winds, by and large, carry any industrial smog or other man-made pollutants away from Ireland's main urban concentrations. On the other hand, there have been other, more insidious, threats to amenity and public health that the Greens have fastened on, and which do contain some real political potential. The pristine nature of the Irish environment and its prime economic or market value - in a country where tourism is a major industry - has provided the spark for an ecology movement with a capacity for reaching out politically towards and connecting with other social movements. Under these circumstances, the green issue may eventually develop an even more powerful resonance than it currently enjoys. Smog scares, especially in Dublin, toxic emissions which threaten air quality and the beauty of landscape and urban architecture alike, traffic congestion, offshore and river pollution,[46] are all issues that could well furnish the Irish Greens with a potent series of political causes. These are issues with immense political potential, should the party at large decide to follow the advice of its realists, and break out of its largely self imposed political ghetto by building alliances with other progressive parties. A start, however tentative, has already been made in this direction. The Greens have made some political capital out of several issues with the potential to raise environmental awareness and to mobilise support at the local community level. The decision, for instance, of the Dupont Corporation to build a large toxic waste incinerator in Donegal, as the most 'efficient' and 'environmentally favourable' way of disposing of some 20 thousand tonnes of hazardous waste, both in liquid and solid form, from all over Ireland - and despite the company's agreement to undertake an environmental impact assessment - raised considerable local opposition. Although the campaign originated with a local protest movement - the Derry Environmental Alliance, an amalgam of some 66 local groups - it was taken up by Greenpeace Ireland, who complained that the proposed technology was unsafe. The level of public concern was sufficient to eventually persuade the Environment Minister to rescind the plan to spend £40 million installing a central waste incinerator. He redirected the money instead, towards more environmentally friendly options such as recycling and re-use. Greenpeace also used the publicity generated by this issue as a lever to press for the rescinding of Environmental Protection Agency licences, awarded to five other major Irish companies to operate incinerators. The Minister's denial of any link between this decision, taken in October 1994, and the surge in support for the Green Party at the European elections, was less than convincing to political pundits and gave the party's realists much cause for political optimism.[47]

Greenpeace also led the campaign to embarrass Forbairt, the State Science body, for its pandering to the anti-environmental needs of the chemical industry, thereby undermining the work of local authorities in monitoring pollution levels. They particularly singled out the Pharmachem industry in Cork city as a source of serious water pollution and air emissions damaging to public health. Local campaigning groups here based in residents associations, and representing some 14 thousand tenants, objected to the proposal for an £85m sewage treatment plant to be built on one of the few remaining greenfield sites left in Cork harbour. The level of opposition was such that the City Corporation rescinded the proposal - a requirement under EU law - and were obliged to search for an alternative site. Finally, two serious fires at chemical plants caused some 150 thousand gallons of chemically contaminated water containing carcinogens to spill into Cork harbour and its environs in August 1993, drawing attention not only to the hazards, but also to a clear failure in the procedures of the new Irish Environmental Protection Agency in this, its first major crisis, to adequately police them. The green movement - including the Green Party - pressurised the Ministry to make an order under the Environmental Agency Protection Act to enable it to carry out a full investigation, with the right to summon witnesses. The Minister's failure to do so exposed the weakness of the Agency and its lack of independence from government. Dan Boyle, the local Green Party councillor, rejected the official investigation as wholly inadequate and called for a proper public inquiry to restore public confidence. The Green Party pressed the authorities further, for a detailed account of current national policy on monitoring industrial hazards in Cork and of the regions' current Major Accident Plan.[48]

These local campaigns raised both local and national awareness of the environmental dimension of Ireland's rapid economic development. There was also a direct political spin off. The Cork harbour incident, for instance, raised the Green Party's electoral support in the city. Similar anti-pollution and pro-environmental campaigns increased the Greens' political profile in community politics across Ireland. A small local action group in Galway tried to prevent developers destroying the only greenbelt left in the city. Mussel farmers in Bantry took on the government in an effort to curtail oil shipments and storage facilities in the bay where repeated spillages had damaged local livelihoods without adequate compensation. Road and motorway expansion, and related infrastructural developments, encouraged similar grassroots residents' movements that complemented the Green Party's community style of politics in Kildare and County Dublin.[49] The acrimony that surrounded the passage of Dublin's controversial County Development Plan (1993) enhanced the party's political profile, both at the community level and in the Dail itself. The political payoff that accrued from an alliance with local residents, alerted other parties whose green credentials were rather more doubtful, and encouraged them to make common cause with the Greens. This issue, in particular, illustrated how community politics could interface with national politics - an ideal synthesis of what has remained for the Green Party two competing instincts about how to play the political game to the best advantage. Labour and the Democratic Left, too, were eventually moved to criticise this plan as "developer driven" and lacking proper consideration for residents' interests. Labour linked the recent "frenzy of re-zoning" - the redesignation of greenbelt for infrastructure development projects - to the establishment parties preference to put short-term material gain before public welfare.[50] Overall, the Irish government - taking full advantage of generous EU co-financing packages while they are still available - planned to spend some £226 billions on road projects up to the year 2000.[51] Green Party councillors and campaigners, in alliance with the Democratic Left and other opponents, were at the forefront of a locally based protest movement against the steady erosion of greenbelt in County Dublin, as property developers and council officials, overwhelmed by an unprecedent growth in population, moved to 're-zone' land for housing. The anti-development campaign resisted the official claim that rezoning was necessary and demanded more democratic transparency in the planning procedure.[52] All of these issues illustrate the continuing political potential for the Greens, of linking infrastructural development with rising environmental awareness.

The nuclear issue has already underlined the prospects for an effective citizen based politics which Green parties elsewhere in Europe have already tapped to advantage. A proposal to build a nuclear generating station in Ireland was briefly mooted during the late seventies, but was subsequently dropped after signs of deep public unease. Nevertheless, this issue has retained its political potency, at one remove as it were, as a focus of continuing protest by ecologists and other groups against the polluting capacity of British nuclear stations across the Irish sea. The Sellafield issue has long been a source of concern to Irish ecologists. The recent proposal by UK Nirex Ltd to expand this plant and build a large underground nuclear waste disposal facility and dump, and a Thermal Oxide Reprocessing Plan (THORP), have rekindled the issue. This has undoubtedly provided the Green Party with an emotive campaigning issue that has sharpened its national profile. Although all the mainstream Irish parties have opposed this scheme, the issue was tailor-made for the Greens and they have taken full advantage of it.[53] Greenpeace Ireland organised a concerted action programme in which Green Party members were prominent, calling on the Irish government to pressurise London to abide by the agreed guidelines of the Paris Commission on the Prevention of Marine Pollution (PARCOM). As a result, some 60 thousand individual objections were received by the Irish government. For their own reasons, Irish Governments have endorsed this protest, just as the mainstream Irish parties have found it convenient to expropriate other ecological issues, such as waste recycling, to improve their own green credentials. Nevertheless, this agenda has increasingly favoured the Greens. As the electorate has become more ecologically conscious - an inevitable outcome of accelerated modernisation and growth everywhere in Europe - and the Irish Government became a signatory to an ever-expanding range of commitments under international and European Community treaty arrangements (the EC 5th Action Programme for instance), the scope for orchestrating rising public concern about environmental issues has grown accordingly. The Greens are the more likely political beneficiaries of the increased salience of this issue in public opinion. And the more so if they continue - as they have thus far - to remain at the forefront of effective and occasionally successful campaigns, to halt initiatives that threaten public health or amenity.

The Green Party has already begun to identify those issues which, if properly handled, will sharpen the public resonance of ecologism and will, in the process, potentially enhance their leverage over policy and electoral outcomes in Irish politics. They have defined, for instance, in the inexorable flight from the land and the rush for economic growth which has accompanied it, as Ireland's industrial and social modernisation continues apace, another significant threat to the environment. More people have recently quit the land than at any time in Irish history since the great famine. Nor are the human or environmental consequences of this trend likely to be much more palatable now than they were then. Mary O'Donnell, a Green Party spokesperson on rural development, noted with some alarm that, "not since penal times have farmers been banned from farming, fishermen banned from fishing and cooks banned from selling food. This is a job destruction programme in operation, particularly targeting the small-scale food producers".[54] Leaving aside the emotive use of language here, the issue is a highly pertinent one for a party searching for a relevant issue agenda; especially one that will give it the same degree of purchase in contemporary Irish politics that Green parties elsewhere have begun to experience. Ireland's transition to economic modernisation is clearly not going to be painless or without heavy social and environmental costs. The Greens, if they bide their time and respond appropriately, are as well placed to capitalise on this fact as any other party. All forms of socio-economic change wreak havoc with both the natural and human environments. In Ireland's case, the ecological damage caused by rapid economic development is compounded by the steady dismantlement of the rural infrastructure - the closure of its hospitals, schools, post offices, churches and so on.

The corollary of this has been urban overcrowding, poor housing conditions and a rise in crime and other social problems.[55] The Greens' standing in local politics has caused them to draw attention to the social consequences of rapid urbanisation, including the link between youth unemployment and a rising drug problem. The potential for widening this social agenda, in what is still an essentially conservative society where the Catholic hierarchy retains immense influence over moral issues, suggests that the Greens will enjoy rather less purchase over this part of the social agenda. But there has been a rising challenge to the power of the clergy from a new secular agenda with its roots in a better educated, more cosmopolitan and new middle class - the very constituency which provides the support base for new politics elsewhere in Europe. The Greens have begun to network with this constituency. They have resisted the temptation of purists and more fundamentalist ecologists, to cleave only to deep ecology. The Greens have, for example, linked up with other progressive secular groups to campaign for the liberalisation of lifestyles: to urge, amongst other things, the government to conform to the European convention on Human Rights by lobbying for the decriminalising of male homosexuality. There are few votes in this courageous stand, and indeed the risk of losing some of those it has already won over. The support for abortion law reform and other women's rights issues are no less difficult for the party in a society where Catholic values are still pervasive, and where the two traditional and dominant political parties have thrown much of their considerable weight against significant changes in lifestyle. But there are opportunities here as well as risks. Ireland these days is by no means an unreflective theocracy. The Greens, with their special talent for community politics, could utilise some of these controversial issues as a conduit to tap into the rising social concern of the young, the better educated and the new middle classes. There are sufficient votes amongst these constituencies to at least consolidate the Greens on the stage of national politics. After all, they are hardly aspiring to be a mass party, but rather to speak for an altogether new politics. The Greens have certainly tried to harness the support in some quarters for these issues, in order to improve their support base, but with variable success. Some of these issues, however, are more likely to yield electoral payoffs than others, and careful choices will have to be exercised if the Greens are to gain from the undoubted social unrest that has accompanied recent modernisation. Community based issues still seem to offer the best option for the party. Campaigns waged effectively in localities where development clashes with the community interest has already proved to be a source of improved electoral support.

Although by no means a leftist party, the Greens have also identified other radical issues with the potential, both to widen their appeal amongst a more cosmopolitan audience, as well as with other progressive groups it might expect to cooperate with in order to radicalise the national political agenda. The question of Irish neutrality or even militarism per se is a much less divisive issue in national politics in Ireland than it would be in a polity with a history of international engagement. The Greens did not reap the same opprobrium from its stand, along with Labour, against any Irish involvement in the Gulf war; or when it objected to this decision, in January 1991 to permit, under the terms of the UN Charter, allied planes to refuel at Shannon airport en route for the Middle East. Public opinion broadly endorsed this decision, but the Green MP, Roger Garland, by no means went out on an ideological limb when he warned of the risks therein to Ireland's neutrality status. Indeed, he was very much in tune with public opinion on that reading of the event. Trevor Sargent, another Green MP, was on equally sure ground when he pointed out in 1996, the same risk to neutrality posed by the EU's Intergovernmental Conference decision to consider a prospective common European Defence Identity. The question of European Union membership continues to cause the Irish Greens as many problems as it does any other European Green party. The party is much less convinced of the long term benefits of Community membership. It campaigned for a 'No' vote in the national referendum on the ratification of the Maastricht treaty, and remains dubious about the real advantages of the country's 'supposedly' generous share of EU structural funding. Along with a number of green lobby groups and other leftist parties such as the Democratic Left, the Green Party has favoured decentralised expenditure on locally based, rather than the prestigious infrastructural, projects - such as improvements in the national rail network - that have ensued from Euro-funding. The Greens continue to canvass the installation of a light rail transport system to relieve traffic pollution in Dublin, the abandonment of the city's proposed eastern bypass scheme, urban renewal (particularly improvements in the housing stock), and the development of Green tourism. The party has also rejected the unduly centralised and bureaucratised allocative and disbursement systems for managing these Euro-funds, and has continually reminded the authorities that under the Maastricht treaty, member states undertook an obligation not to spend structural funding in an environmentally damaging way.[56] The Greens likewise resist the dangers, as they see it, of the narrow autarchism of 'fortress Europe', and prefer to take what they see as a genuinely international stance. The party's criticism of recent budget cuts in Ireland's overseas aid programme indicates that the party is by no means wedded to a narrowly conceived ecologism. It prefers instead to reach outwards to an altogether wider new politics agenda.

The Greens have thus worked hard to dispel the most telling criticism levelled by their opponents - not least those in the other radical parties, and competing for much the same electoral constituency of younger, more idealistic or secular voters, concentrated for the most part in Dublin; namely, that they are a one-issue pressure group rather than a serious political party.[57] The party's manifesto for the 1997 elections covered the sort of agenda addressed by every modern party in contemporary western European democracies: from fiscal policy and crime, to European and other foreign and security issues; and from social policy (health, welfare, education) to criminality and the arts. Of course, this programme gave particular emphasis to the environment (everything from pollution control and waste management to animal rights and traffic management, energy, water policy and ethical investment) and Comhaontas Glas' special claim to be a 'new politics' party (open government, subsidiarity, transparency in decision-making and so on). The fact that the 'rainbow parties', especially those on the left, shared many of these progressive preferences indicates a narrowing of the political space between the Greens and their most likely political allies. Even so, there is still some way to travel before this widening of the 'rainbow' leads to anything like a firm prospect of electoral or other forms of political cooperation.

The politics of radical accommodation is, necessarily, a two way process. The Greens have begun to make the transition that will break down some of the barriers between the party and other radical groups. But in order to take full advantage of these accommodations, the Greens will certainly need to abandon their own exclusive claim to be the only party with anything constructive to say on ecological issues. They must, therefore, be prepared to broaden their outlook on their own principal issue, and to entertain the prospect of making flexible alliances with the other progressive forces in Irish politics. There is, as yet, little enough political space for these radical forces to afford the Greens the luxury of closing off creative networking with other political groups broadly moving in the same direction. The claim in the 1997 manifesto, that "the Greens cannot be placed anywhere on the usual Left-Right axis", that the party "is unlike all established Irish parties; it is structured differently, advocates very different policies and is working towards a very different kind of society" is more than a radical flourish. It also represents a continuing self-image of exclusivism that is hardly conducive to the politics of accommodation favoured by the pragmatists in the Alliance's ranks; almost a defiance of the established party system - a response that is altogether less favourable to the realignment into progressive and conservative blocs that has recently begun to unfreeze an increasingly irrelevant post-civil war cleavage.

There had been some signs, latterly, that the political climate might be more favourable to such radical accommodations, and that ecologism in its widest sense, might yet contribute to a more permanent realignment of Irish politics, rather than merely remaining as a minor and peripaheral element in the present flux. The contribution of the Labour Party to the national policy agenda has been particularly promising in this respect. A number of recent policy changes indicate that the present centre-left government has begun to accord environmental management a new priority. The Minister for the Environment, Brendon Howlin, undertook, in reply to protests by the environmental lobby, to amend state regulations governing freedom of access to information on the environment. In particular, he reduced the official response period, following his Department's publication of a review of how these provisions had operated since their introduction in 1993.[58] Howlin, acknowledging that the country's growing waste and especially packaging, was the "unacceptable face of consumer society", also published a Waste Bill that provided for a comprehensive approach which consolidated commitments made by previous governments to update the framework of statutory regulation in line with the EU's 'best practice'. The changes envisaged therein included rationalising existing regulatory structures by increasing the scope and powers of both the Environmental Protection Agency and local authorities - although the preferred emphasis here remained with self regulation, and compulsion was only seen as a last resort.

Nevertheless, this is progress of sorts. 'Polluters' will, at least, be obliged to provide a detailed listing of their output of toxic waste materials. Howlin, moreover, did threaten to take "the statutory route" if industry failed to agree a reasonable voluntary code. The Bill also addressed the "waste of waste" - the problem of recycling - and anticipated that, by the year 2000, the amount of recycled or composted waste would increase from the current derisory figure of 7.4 per cent, to some 20 per cent.[59] The Minister kept an open mind, too, on the question of disposal - wherein a conflict exists between the ecologically viable method of incineration, the norm in environmentally progressive EU countries where new reliable but expensive technologies were available, and landfill dumping. Both methods have already raised local opposition in Ireland, but the Minister was at least aware that cost and convenience had to be balanced against public concern, including an appropriate "national sustainable strategy" which must include getting across "the notion that we really mean business about having sustainable development that runs across Government departments and all national plans and policies".[60] Each one of the Government's economic Ministries established environmental units, coordinated by the Environment Department, to encourage environmentally sound initiatives and to encourage best practice. The successes of this scheme have included a Rural Environmental Protection Scheme, the establishment of an Irish Energy Centre to promote energy conservation in business and industry, and the inauguration of an eco-label for tourism.[61]

The Minister's strategy in recommending sustainable development, also depended on equating environmental quality, not "as a negative obstacle to economic progress and job creation", but rather as a source of an estimated 155,000 new jobs. Howlin, whose own political credentials included an earlier involvement in ecological campaigning - against the ESB's plans to develop a nuclear power station at Carnsore Point - also addressed the adjacent issues of Dublin's traffic congestion, dumping at sea,[62] as well as sustainable development and Sellafield. On the latter issue, Howlin, whilst openly conceding that the United Kingdom government was unlikely to abandon its multi-billion pound investment, was at least the first Irish Environment Minister to tackle the issue decisively. He did so by instituting an inter-Departmental committee - drawn from all Ministers whose policy remit was affected by the plant, with participants from the Taoiseach's and Attorney General's offices - to formulate an effective national strategy; and thence, to formulate a basis for legal action, both under international law as enshrined in international treaties, and in the common procedures of the international fora (the OSPAR Convention and the non-nuclear proliferation agreement for instance) to which both Ireland the UK are signatories. All of these measures underlined the increased commitment of government to enforcing a more stringent environmental management policy than that of any previous administration.[63] This may, of course, be bad news for the Greens as other parties rush to challenge their tenure of what 'real' ecologists see as their distinctive political territory - thereby diluting the distinctiveness and sapping the urgency of the Greens' own message. On the other hand, this positive response by the political establishment owes just as much to the effectiveness of the Greens' politically astute strategy of raising the profile of the environment on the national issue agenda. Whether or not the party continues to capitalise on the situation will remain as much a matter of their own making as it is merely a residual response to the machinations of the other parties.

The Green Party has certainly moved much closer to the political centre of gravity during the 1990s. The obstacles that remain in its path as it tries to consolidate its tenuous hold on the Irish political imagination remain, for all that, formidable. Not the least of these challenges are the constraints imposed on the party's manoeuvres by the country's political opportunity structures. The rules of the political game continue to inhibit more than they encourage the electoral chances of the minor parties. A provision was included, for instance, in the Electoral Bill published in 1991, to increase election deposits from £100 to £800, although these are refunded where a candidate receives over a quarter of the quota, compared with the present ratio of one third. The risk factor here is greatly increased for small parties, and especially for a party such as the Greens which remains dependent on large numbers of protest votes and only has a small 'natural' support base. The cost of elections likewise operates as a severe stricture on parties with small memberships. In the Euro-elections, for instance, it has been estimated that the minimum cost of running an effective campaign is around £60,000 for a Dublin seat. The European Parliament after 1989, ended the practice of apportioning monies to the Parliament's political groups, to be disbursed to the national parties for their campaigns according to seats held in previous elections - adjusted for votes won in the succeeding election. Under the present rules, the Strasbourg Parliament only funds, on the same proportionality principle, party groups for 'information work', and even then the practice ceases prior to elections. Those parties already represented - and especially the larger ones - are considerably more advantaged by these resource allocations. The two successful Irish Green candidates in 1994 did, however, reap a modest benefit from the special provision of Commission funding to the Council for the Status of Women and Women's Political Associations, in order to promote women candidates in European elections. Sitting MEPs, of course, also enjoy the bonus of 5 years generous salaries and expenses which help to defray election expenses. The Greens in the 1994 poll had to find this funding from their own meagre resources and it clearly disadvantaged them, compared with the resources available to the main parties.[64]

The constraints imposed on Green party politics by this, at the very least unhelpful, political environment, are hardly balanced by the putative advantages of a favourable electoral system. Elections in Ireland are conducted according to a proportionate system based on the Single Transferable Vote formula. STV is a system which occupies, on the spectrum of proportionality - and therefore of fairness - a place in between the gross mathematical distortions of British plurality, and the extreme proportionality of some other European electoral systems.[65] This has the direct outcome that smaller parties do not enjoy the same degree of equity enjoyed by minor parties in more fully proportionate systems. The system does encourage voters at least to pause for thought; and it provides them with multiple chances to influence the eventual electoral outcome,[66] inasmuch as electors indicate their preferences for all the candidates on the ballot, regardless of party. In what are frequently shrewd or calculated tactical trade offs, which even the minor parties can influence, electors transfer their preferences down the electoral list until all the seats are filled. The STV system, however, by no means automatically favours the Greens, or indeed any other minor party. Nevertheless, in the recent climate of electoral volatility, with more parties active on the ballot, the often utilitarian and tactical logistics of these political trades does tend to enhance the impact of quite small parties such as the Greens, and thereby to increase their political clout. Close scrutiny of these multiple preferences also allows some useful insights into the typical Green voter - information which should reinforce the pragmatic, outward looking strategy favoured by the realists currently at the centre of the party's affairs. For the Green voter is most noticeably not staunchly partisan or ideologically dogmatic, in that he or she identifies exclusively with one or other side (left or right) of the traditional ideological spectrum.

To an extent, this notional pattern is reinforced by the minimal salience of a left-right cleavage in Irish politics. The available electoral evidence, based on patterns of partisanship and political identity, overlays the recent emergence of conventional notions of left and right with all manner of other identities (regional, rural-urban, 'old' and 'new' politics, secular-clerical) that complicate the electoral map. This complex weft of identities confirms the wisdom of the Green Party in resisting any narrow ideological identity. The Greens in their intra-party deliberations may exhibit a radical or progressive demeanour, but they refuse to become a party of the left or the right. Indeed, in these sociological circumstances, they simply cannot afford to do so, even if that was their inclination. This ideological pliancy, in turn, increases their appeal to disconcerted voters from other parties - as well as maximising their own bargaining potential over second preference votes. Green votes have tended to transfer, just about evenly, to both of the major centre-right parties (Fianna Fail and Fine Gael) who have dominated post partition Irish politics, and to the 'new' centre-right Progressive Democrats, as well as to the Labour, Democratic Left and Workers' parties on the left. The fact that the centre-right parties receive proportionately more votes from these transfers than the parties of the left reflects the resilience of the traditional pattern of party dominance, and the pull it still exerts on the Irish political imagination. The fact, too, that only a relatively small percentage - some ten per cent - of the primary Green vote refuses on principle to transfer their vote, whereas the bulk of it does so precisely to avoid wasting its influence on the final constituency outcomes, says much about the underlying pragmatism of the Green electorate. These facts confirm that the Green vote is in no sense a 'ghetto' vote, and is indeed well integrated into the prevailing political culture. Above all, it is an electorate well versed in the rules of the electoral game. At the same time, the promiscuity of this vote confirms that the Green electorate is less surely mobilised behind any cogent or unambiguous project to realign Irish politics in a clearly radical direction.

There are important messages in this electoral data that the Green Party would do well to assimilate. On the one hand, it indicates that the party's realists may be ahead of their electorate in their preference for building working arrangements with other progressive forces in pursuit of a genuinely new and radical policy agenda. At the same time, the evidence of a support base that remains eclectic about its political preferences, and refuses to subscribe to narrow ideologism, is good news for the party's strategists. For it implies a way out of the party's present impasse. An electorate which is amenable to making its own bargains with other parties across the spectrum will surely tolerate, and almost certainly reward, those politicians who likewise show signs of open-mindedness, tolerance and political flexibility. By the same token, it is just as likely to punish ideological rigidity. The Irish Green Party is in a transitional phase. On the one hand it has not managed to resolve, to the satisfaction of its own realists let alone of its prospective allies in a changing electoral milieu, those awkward predicaments that confront any small, radical political newcomer to a party system hostile - or at least unsympathetic - to its insistent challenge. On the other hand, the Green Party has begun to confront this 'radical dilemma', and to assimilate the lessons of its past. It is now more prepared to look outwards and to build alliances at both the community and national levels. It has also begun to engage those adjacent parties with whom it can make common cause, however difficult the compromises involved. And there are signs that some of these parties have begun to take the Greens seriously. Every party in the recent election campaign had something to say about the environment.[67] The prospect of another inconclusive election persuaded the Labour leader to give credence during the campaign to the Greens joining a new 'rainbow' government. A very modest shift in the actual voting pattern in this election - if the Labour vote had held steadier than it did, for instance, thereby tipping the balance of advantage in this knife-edge contest towards the 'rainbow' parties - would almost certainly have seen the two Green TDs on the government benches, with one of them in the cabinet. This prospect is now, at least, thinkable in Irish politics and more than likely after some future election. In short, the Green Party has opened itself out by degrees to other progressive forces on the landscape of Irish politics, and in the process, the pattern of party politics is beginning to accommodate it. The more that the Green Party continues to pursue this political tack, the more likely it is to play its part as an agent of the political realignment which must eventually follow on from the climate of socio-economic change; and to benefit from the shifts in the pattern of electoral allegiance which will inevitably accrue from the changing dynamics of contemporary Irish society.[68]

The evidence of the latest Dail elections confirms these broad political trends. The once familiar domination by the two traditional parties seemed to resurface - but only if the point of comparative reference here is seats won rather than voting patterns. FF and FG took 131 out of 166 seats between them. FG did poll its best ever tally (27.9 per cent) on the back of a sound campaign by Bruton and his growing reputation as both a statesman and a good economic manager. Ireland's economy has recently emerged as one of the most successful in the EU with GNP growing to 6.5 per cent in 1996-97 and inflation stable at 1.5 per cent - a performance marred only by high relative levels of unemployment and personal taxation. However, this apparently rooted pattern of political partisanship must be put into proper perspective. For the FF vote barely improved on the party's worst ever showing with the relative collapse in its support in 1992. Its seat tally in 1997 was as much a testament to the political skills employed by its local campaign managers and a vote management strategy that successfully maximised the party's second preferences, as it was due to FF's reinstatement as the dominant 'catchall' party of Irish politics. FF's alliance and prospective coalition partner, the neo-liberal PDs, also saw its vote shrink (to 4.7 per cent and 4 seats), largely because of its unpalatable prospectus of welfare cuts and other harsh remedies for cutting public expenditure. The two conservative parties were only able to install themselves as a minority government in what one commentator on the day of the count called a 'double hung' Dail,[69] because of a near spectacular collapse of the Labour vote (down to 10.4 per cent and 17 seats). Again, this was due less to any clear ideological shift than it was to a belayed protest by erstwhile Labour voters - particularly in that party's Dublin heartland - against what many saw as its unduly cynical coalitional flirtation with the ultra-conservative FF between 1992 and 1994.

The recent phenomenon of electoral pluralism (32.8 per cent of the total vote and 35 seats went to seven 'other' parties and a host of independent candidates) has remained very much part of the Irish electoral scene. This complicated patterning serves to increase the prospects for small parties, not only to sit in the Dail but, given the parliamentary arithmetic of regularly 'hung' Dail's, also to play their part in the bargaining that must invariably precede and sustain the multi-party coalition governments that have become the norm here.

The 1997 election also confirmed another, parallel, trend which likewise increases the opportunities for small parties to operate on the inside track of Irish politics. Low turnout levels (barely 66 per cent - 62 per cent in Dublin and only 60 per cent in the working class areas of the city) underline the model of change in the electorate[70] - a combination of indifference or outright cynicism about the perceived 'graft' of some machine politicians. The post-election analysis confirmed this degree of flux and revealed a much greater propensity amongst the electorate at large, whatever their original political affiliations, to switch their votes. Some 25 per cent of voters in both the 1992 and 1997 elections changed their party first preferences - a lessening of old loyalties and habits which has significant implications for the trade off in second preferences. In addition, 49 per cent of voters in 1997 only made up their political minds during the campaign itself and 55 per cent identified themselves as 'floating' rather than firmly partisan voters.[71] A leading commentator has concluded from this telling evidence of political change that the Irish party system is undergoing a transformation with "an increased fragmentation at the lower end and a series of successive failures (by the once dominant parties) to sustain an electoral breakthrough."[72]

The Greens made a point in the campaign of trying to capitalise on this undercurrent of discontent by highlighting their commitment to a 'new' politics - making a virtue of the party's commitment to decentralisation, parliamentary and local government reform, transparent decision making and reform in the rules on political funding. The Green Party did strike some chords with young and alienated voters, particularly in Dublin where they took seats in the Dublin North (Sargent) and South East (Gormley) constituencies. But in an election dominated by 'old politics' issues - notably taxation and crime - the tendency to increased partisan dealignment have benefited the established parties as much as it did the minor parties. In the event, the Greens were squeezed by other parties and failed to receive enough transfers to increase their representation. From opinion poll ratings of up to 7 per cent on the back of their success in the European elections and pockets of apparently solid support just prior to the poll, the party's eventual national vote slipped to 2.8 per cent (2 seats) - better than any previous national performance yet a disappointing outcome, nevertheless, given the widespread expectations of commentators that the party would secure "a large and dynamic Green group in the Dail" of up to ten seats.[73]

Any benefit that accrues from the apparent loosening of old patterns of party alignment are likely to bring long term rather than immediate gains to the Greens or any other small party. But sustained political breakthroughs require both resources and effective strategy and the Greens, like most small parties without a secure base, have found the former difficult to acquire (the Greens had barely 20,000 pounds to finance their entire national campaign and little by way of a professional party organisation to call on) and the latter hard to formulate, in view of the preference in this still essentially grassroots party for internal democracy and a continuing reluctance to fully embrace a conventional model of party organisation. Both are essential requirements for political profile in a political system that puts a premium on deal-making and inter-party trade-offs in the business of coalition formation. Whatever the mood of rising discontent with established politics, most of the electorate still inhabit a mindset that looks to the Dail as the focal point of political influence and expects parties to organise and deal in a way that maximises their impact therein. Comhaontas Glas' image as a new type of party has, in these terms, proved as much of a hindrance as a help. The Greens' prospects in national politics will improve only if the party can address and resolve the particular difficulties some grassroots elements still have with playing the conventional game of party politics.

The party, under the guidance of pragmatists such as Gormley and his allies, has continued to confront this predicament and even to make some headway. Irish politics has recently begun to be refashioned around an admittedly inchoate radical-conservative cleavage. The 1997 election was, in effect, a choice between the governing 'rainbow' alliance and the conservative-liberal coalition. The contest between individual parties was overlaid with a secondary or implicit choice between two governments with competing if not entirely exclusive policy agendas. This, in turn, concentrated the electorate's minds and influenced, to an extent, the exercise of second preference votes and the direction of the resultant transfers. The Green Party clearly lost out in this stark choice between governing options, as it did, too, from an abiding image amongst many electors of the Greens as idealists rather than 'fixers' capable of securing their interests in the 'pork barrel' politics of the Dail. In this 'trade off' of advantages, the appeal of idealism and principle - Labour and the DL's main concern about Green incursions into their radical constituency[74] - lost out to a much broader instrumentalist electorate concerned above all to elect Teachta Dala (MPs) capable of having their interests represented by 'fixers' and pragmatists. Not that, as their electoral star rose after the 1994 Euro success and improved poll ratings, the Greens had entirely eschewed the demands of an effective role in national politics. The party's realists, and especially those members with some experience of electoral success, continued to argue for accommodation with the system in order to consolidate a 'soft' support base. The party responded positively to the Labour leader's tentative suggestion at his 1997 party conference that, with support for his party waning, the shortfall in Dail support for the 'rainbow' coalition might be made up by Green TD's,[75] by putting in place a strategy that Gormley described as "preparation for government".[76] This included a 'shopping list' of ecological and radical social measures to be negotiated as the price of cooperation; and a 5 person negotiating team - small enough to be cohesive but broad enough to be accountable to the wider party - of TD's and representatives of the party's officers and Council, to pursue these demands with any prospective coalition partners. A concession was made to grassroots sensibilities about secret deals and elitist leadership with the provision for a special delegate conference to be called to ratify any coalitional formula and endow it with democratic legitimacy.[77]

The acknowledgement here of the imperatives of horse trading in order to secure a share of political power, in itself represents a breakthrough in the Green Party's approach to the political game. At the same time, disquiet remains in the party's ranks in the country about any such compromise with its political scruples. Moreover Comhaontas Glas - a pure Green party with little ideological empathy with either the left or the right - remains unsure about its preferred coalitional options. On the one hand, its progressive policy preferences suggest it has more to gain from aligning with the 'rainbow' parties. But on the other hand, it has studiously avoided courting either of the available coalitions. Standing aloof from the two alternatives, the Green Party is in danger of remaining a marginal influence on either of the alliances that compete for power here. The Greens will have to revisit these awkward dilemmas and, indeed, resolve them if continued electoral flux puts them in a position to join a future governing coalition. This is by no means a far fetched proposition. The vagaries of the STV system and the discernible shifts in the patterns of political allegiance in this rapidly modernising country could, had the Labour vote held firmer than it did and FF's vote maximisation strategy proved less successful than it was, quite easily have presented the Greens with this very opportunity in the aftermath of the 1997 election - even with its modest tally of only two seats. If the pattern of electoral flux continues to unfold in future elections, the Irish Green Party is as likely to figure in the same post electoral calculus here as its sister parties have recently done in France, Italy, Finland and Germany. When that signal moment arrives in Ireland the Greens will enter uncharted political territory. They will be faced with a situation that presents them, in equal measure, with a challenge and an opportunity.

Notes

1. See M. Bax, "Harpstrings and Confessions: An Anthropological Study of Politics in Rural Ireland", (Assen, 1976); see also, R.K. Carty, "Party and Parish Pump: Electoral Politics in Ireland" (Ontario, 1981).

2. P. Commins, "Ireland: A Sociological Profile", in P. Clancy et al (eds), "Ireland: A Sociological Profile" (Dublin, 1986), p.52.

3. J.F. Ross, "The Irish Electoral System: What It Is and How It Works" (London, 1989).

4. M. Gallagher, "Political Parties in the Republic of Ireland" (Dublin, 1985).

5. For a review of the changing political sociology of Ireland, see P. Clancy, S. Drudy, K. Lynch and L. O'Dowd (eds), "Ireland: A Sociological Profile"; and H. Peillon, "Contemporary Irish Society: An Introduction" (Dublin, 1982).

6. H.R. Penniman and B. Farrell (eds), "Ireland at the Polls, 1981, 1982 and 1987: A Study of Four General Elections" (Durham, NC, 1987).

7. The Guardian, 2.6.94.

8. J. Whyte, "Ireland: Politics without Social Bases" in R. Rose (ed), "Electoral Behaviour: A Comparative Handbook" (New York, 1974); see also R.K. Carty, "Ireland: From Predominance to Competition", Chapter 10 of S. Wolinetz (ed), "Parties and Party Systems in Liberal Democracies" (London, 1988) at pp.222-245.

9. M. Laver (et al), "Patterns of Support" in M. Laver, P. Mair and R. Sinnott (eds), "How Ireland Voted" (Dublin, 1987); see also M. Gallagher, "The Outcome", ibid (1987).

10. J. Sinnott, "Party Politics in Spatial Representation: The Irish Case", British Journal of Political Science 16 1986, at pp.217-41.

11. M. Gallagher, "The Irish Labour Party in Transition: 1957-1982" (Manchester, 1982).

12. M. Laver, P. Mair and R. Sinnott (eds), "How Ireland Voted: The Irish General Election of 1987" (Swords, 1987); and M. Gallagher and R. Sinnott (eds), "How Ireland Voted 1989" (Galway, 1990).

13. K.A. Kennedy (ed), "Ireland in Transition: Economic and Social Change Since 1960" (Dublin, 1986).

14. B. Chubb, "The Government and Politics of Ireland", (3rd edition, 1992), at p.95.

15. Irish Times, 30.1.93.

16. Irish Times, 19.2.93.

17. Irish Times, 22.5.93.

18. Ibid, 24.5.93.

19. See P. Bew, E. Hazelkorn and H. Patterson, "The Dynamics of Irish Politics" (London, 1989).
20. Irish Times, 24.5.93.
21. Ibid, 24.5.93.
22. D. Walsh, "Eire: Shift of Power Continues", Irish Times, 1.7.91.
23. Richard Sinnott, "Government's Loss is Not Oppositions Gain", Irish Times, 24.6.94; see also R. Sinnott, "Irish Voters Decide: Voting Behaviour in Elections and Referendums 1918-1994" (Manchester, 1994).
24. Irish Times, 13.6.94.
25. Irish Times, 12.11.94.
26. Ibid 12.11.94.
27. Ibid, 19.6.95.
28. Ibid, 28.6.95.
29. Irish Times, 13.11.94.
30. Dan Boyle, "Today Leinster, Tomorrow Cork South Central?" An Caorthann, 1994, p.22.
31. "Embattled Progressive Democrats Struggle to regain political profile", Irish Times, 10.9.94.
32. Irish Times, 8.5.95.
33. This included rescinding the plans for an Eastern bypass; a moratorium on other road building projects - until comprehensive land use and transportation studies had been completed; an amenity area for Dublin Bay; a full review of city organisation and local amenities.
34. Sunday Times, 31.7.94.
35. Quoted in "Bicycling Green Mayor Plans Green City", Irish Times, 14.7.94.
36. Quoted in the Irish Times, 8.5.95.
37. See M. Laver,"Party Policy and Cabinet Portfolios in Ireland 1992-93: Results from an Expert Survey", Irish Political Studies Vol.9 1994.
38. Irish Times, 2.2.93.
39. "Leaderless Greens Need Direction on Path to Power", Irish Times, 8.5.95.
40. Fintan O'Toole, "Gael forecast for Ireland", The Guardian, 13.12.94.
41. Irish Times, 16.12.94.
42. M. Laver, quoted from the Financial Times, 29.6.97.
43. J. Murray Brown, "Calm hand at helm of uneasy coalition", Financial times, 16.12.94.
44. Irish Times, 19.5.95.
45. Irish Times, 26.12.94.
46. Irish Times, 2.2.88.
47. Irish Times, 18.10.94.
48. Irish Times, 13.8.93.
49. Irish Times, 20.9.93.
50. Irish Times, 11.12.93.
51. Irish Times, 16.4.94.
52. Irish Times, 15.7.93.
53. D. Clancy, "Sellafield II - Can the Law Protect?", An Caorthann, 1994, p.35.
54. Quoted in the Irish Times, 24.5.93.
55. Ibid.

56. Irish Times, 19.8.92.
57. Irish Times, 8.5.95.
58. Irish Times, 17.4.95.
59. Ibid, 23.5.95.
60. Ibid 23.5.95.
61. Ibid, 3.11.95.
62. The 'Dumping at Sea' Bill was published in November 1995. It awarded the Irish Naval Service considerable powers of search and arrest, and included the imposition of unlimited fines and even custodial sentences for illegal dumping at sea, from 12 to 350 miles off shore, depending on the depth of the Continental Shelf. See Irish Times, 9.11.95.
63. Irish Times, 24.7.95.
64. Irish Times, 5.3.94.
65. M. Gallagher, "Disproportionality in a Proportional Representation System: The Irish Experience", Political Studies 23 (1975).
66. P. Mair and M. Laver, "Proportionality, PR and STV in Ireland", Political Studies 23 (1975).
67. Irish Times, 5.6.97.
68. See J. Murray Brown, "Old certainties die in economic transformation"; and ibid, "Europe's new 'miracle' recovery", in Financial Times Survey: Ireland, 24.6.96.
69. A. Adonis, The Observer, 15.6.97.
70. R. Sinnott, "Seeds of Election Result were sown long before campaign", Irish Times, 9.6.97.
71. Ibid.
72. Ibid.
73. Irish Times, 6.11.96.
74. "Party will hope for a place in the sun", Irish Times, 7.4.97.
75. Irish Times, 31.5.97.
76. Ibid.
77. Ibid.

10 The Green Association and the Miljopartieten of Scandinavia

1. Finland

(i) Green roots

Green politics in Finland is, on the face of it, the very obverse of the experience of the Irish movement discussed above. It has its roots firmly in the new left and, for the most part, in the student radicalism of the late sixties and early seventies. The 'new left' movement, which elsewhere in Europe challenged the 'old' guard Marxists of the official Communist parties, in Finland remained largely under their political domination. Those free thinkers and student radicals who reacted against this heavy handed imposition of hardline Marxist-Leninist dogma decided to go their own way. Some of this radical energy found its way, during the late seventies into an eclectic if uncoordinated network of new social movements - from feminism and the disabled lobby, to vegetarianism, the anti-nuclear movement, and eventually into a distinctive Green movement. Ecologists made their earliest entrance into Finnish politics as nature conservationists. They organised to protect the famous wild bird sanctuary on Lake Koijarvi and employed an effective direct action campaign to prevent the authorities draining the lake.[1]

Neither this movement's roots in radical protest, nor its experience of a highly successful direct action campaign, precluded it from developing a taste for electoral politics. An ecological list had stood, unsuccessfully, in the municipal elections in Helsinki in 1976. In 1980 this list marginally improved its earlier performance with 1.7 per cent of the vote, taking 1 seat. By 1983, a motley of alternative movements came together, less than convincingly, as a common Green list to contest 7 of the 15 constituencies in the national elections of that year, including all the most populous constituencies in the south of the country. Nevertheless, the outcome of an electoral system which is more favourable than most to small parties determined that a nominal 1.5 per cent of the total vote, conveniently concentrated for the most part in the constituencies of Uusimmaa (3.3 per cent of the constituency total) and Helsinki (4.5 per cent), saw the Greens comfortably over these requisite electoral thresholds. The Greens therefore won two seats in the 200 seat single chamber assembly, the Eduskunta. One of these was allocated to the representative of a disabled group and the other to the leader of the successful Koijarvi protest.

This outcome represented a modedst breakthrough for a 'party' which hardly existed as a formal entity and did not even register as a party proper until 1987, being content to operate largely as a loosely coordinated electoral list to which the numerous alternative movements nominated candidates. The fact that the Finnish electoral system requires no candidate deposits, and independent candidates may be treated as a party in their own right, contributed to this reluctance to organise.[2] Under these circumstances, neither of these members of parliament proved to be a particularly effective or active representative - an approach to parliamentary politics which also reflected an unmistakable ambivalence in the ecology movement about the value of the parliamentary route for achieving radical ends. Green activists showed a stronger preference for extra-parliamentary protest. The working groups and congresses which met at Jyvaskyla in 1983 and Oulu in 1984, commended the role of direct action in the green armoury. On the other hand, the movement's inclination for an active campaigning role did pay handsome dividends, with the alternative lists winning over 80 local council seats. On that basis, it had built a secure platform in community politics by 1986.

With the Greens now represented in the Eduskunta, however, they were obliged to address the difficult and divisive issue of their role in conventional party politics, and in particular their disposition to parliamentarianism per se. The resolution of this dilemma did not come easily or quickly to the Finnish Greens. Anti-party tendencies were appealing to an organisation firmly wedded to alternativism. These instincts encouraged intense debate, and led to confusion at meetings where these groups convened to decide how to respond to even the minimal requirements of electoral politics - for instance, the order of the candidates on the lists, and which policy commitments to put before the electorate. One obvious response to this obligation was to settle for only a low common denominator of agreement. At the congress called before the 1985 national elections, for instance, the Greens accommodated their persistent divisions over the meaning of ecologism, by conveniently agreeing a minimalist programme of four demands, more akin to a set of single issue goals than a party manifesto as such. They agreed to call for the reduction in sulphur emissions; a moratorium on the building of new nuclear power stations; a halt to the expansion of the wood processing industry which threatened Finland's forests; and the inclusion of a vague endorsement of autonomism and self determination close to the ideological heart of all alternative movements, and which means all individuals should be allowed to take control of their own working arrangements. The other 'details' of this Alternative electoral programme were to be left to the various local component groups to 'fill' in as they felt appropriate. This, in turn, led various Green candidates and their close allies to stand on an eclectic platform which included some bizarre notions. One local list, inspired by the radical ideas of a prominent nature conservationist, Pentti Linkola, went so far as to urge that Finland should become a one party state in which a 'Green Vanguard' party would be the ruling party.[3] These slogans hardly amounted to a party programme in the conventional sense of that term. Moreover, the image of chaos and extremism conjured by them was hardly calculated to woo even the most sympathetic and progressive voter. Another abortive attempt was made to resolve these difficulties in 1986. But it was only in February 1987, with another national election pending, that Finland's amorphous Greens agreed to establish a national 'Green Association' or 'Union'. And even then, this tentative arrangement fell some way short of full party status. Not least, because this loose-knit organisation had to bridge the movement's deep ideological and personality differences, as between the pure green or ecological tendency and a more radical, leftist inclined, 'social' tendency.

The Greens' poor showing in the 1987 elections was a further confirmation of the disaffection amongst even the radical part of the electorate with a movement that seemed unable to act in concert. On the face of it, the Greens improved on their 1983 showing, more than doubling their vote to 4 per cent - which gave them 4 parliamentary seats. This achievement was immediately discounted, however, by the fact that the coherence of this Green bloc was severely undermined by its division into 2 pure ecologists and 2 radical members. The electorate had already taken note of these internal divisions. After reaching 8 per cent in the opinion polls, the Green vote fell far short of its initial promise. Many pro-Green but otherwise moderate voters abstained in the 1987 poll, and there was a noticeably low turnout amongst those younger voters who were amongst the Greens' principal target groups.

(ii)   Party formation

This fundamental schism within the Union of Greens rumbled on into 1988. Although both factions were by this time convinced of the need to take the next decisive step and transform this interim 'alliance' into a full blown party under the terms of the Finnish Constitution - by collecting 5000 signatures to register as a party, and thereby have access to state subsidies towards their organisational costs - they could not in the end agree to cohabit within the same organisation. The pure ecologists split from the more radical groups and formed a group called the 'Greens' (Vihrea). The radicals, likewise, collected their own signatures and formed the 'Green Association' (Vihrea Litto). This Union did little more, however, than bring together under one loose-knit umbrella organisation various regional lists and organisations - for instance, the Green Feminists, and the Environmental Policy Association - without actually imposing on them anything remotely approaching a coherent party structure. Each local section continued to enjoy its own semi-autonomy within the overall framework.

Although differences over ideology played their part in fomenting this factionalism, with the 'social' tendency more often endorsing the Communist Party's demands for improved child care, greater social equality, and better public transport, these issues were less critical per se - at least on the evidence of the two factions' complementary voting records in the Eduskunta - than they were a convenient excuse for clashes between the personalities involved. The lack of any meaningful ideological space between these two 'parties' was underlined, too, by the active cooperation between their Parliamentary representatives. Political culture rather than ideological schism per se kept the two Green factions from burying their differences within a single coherent party format. Not least, the impact of what some commentators have referred to as Finland's "more or less permanent crisis of parliamentarianism". Rapid turnover of governments as well as considerable coalitional flux,[4] tend to detract from any sense of strong party discipline and similarly encourages factional strife. This aspect of the political culture has certainly influenced the way the Greens of both tendencies operated. Politics, in these circumstances, takes precedence over governance. Even when the Greens achieved a presence on local municipal councils, they tended to behave as outsiders and oppositionalists, rather than adopt a more constructive outlook to the business of policy making. Greater damage still was done to the Greens' reputation by their refusal to play a more constructive role in the resolution of the 1989 political crisis. They passed up the opportunity to cooperate in the formation of a new four party coalition government, much in line with the earlier precedent of a government of national salvation set up for the first time in 1987, as a way out of the country's deep political impasse. The Greens seem not to have been unduly disturbed by the opprobrium they reaped for this refusal to maximise their leverage and enhance their electoral credibility. On the contrary, many Green activists saw this overt refusal to join the system as a testament to their enduring radicalism. Some Green strategists even remained convinced that this self exclusion would reap its own political rewards -that a principled anti-politics role would attract the support of those electors disgruntled with consensus politics, as well as those former Communist supporters amongst the intelligentsia who the Greens courted in order to enhance their reputation as a seriously radical movement with something important to contribute to the national political discourse.

(iii)   Political developments

Whatever the causes of these internal splits - or the political raison d'être behind them - their political consequences were certainly costly for both Green parties. The electorate gave its own verdict in the 1988 local elections - with a paltry 2.4 per cent of the vote going to Green candidates. These early election results showed the Greens the costs of indulging what were, after all, quite narrow ideological differences. These arcane divisions have persisted, nevertheless, even though the Green Association now represents the majority of ecological opinion. There is certainly insufficient political space in Finland, or for that matter in any other European democracy, for two separate Green parties running against one another at the polls. The prospects for Green politics in Finland might be improved, as was the case in France, by a decision by the two rival Green parties to sink their deliberately exaggerated differences. By showing such political maturity, and working more closely together for what are, regardless of important differences of emphasis, still essentially common purposes, the Finnish Greens are much more likely to secure their niche constituency amongst those social groups who are attracted to ecologism. There is more at stake here than merely an electoral calculus. After all, the pure Green Ecology Party mustered only a minuscule 0.3 per cent vote (and 1 seat) in the 1995 national elections, compared with the Green Association's 8.7 per cent (and 10 seats). The perception amongst the electorate, however, of exaggerated and jealously guarded divisions, may easily deter some radical but pragmatic voters from committing their support to a movement incapable of a properly coordinated electoral effort. The fact that after the 1995 poll, the Ecology Party's sole parliamentary representative was able to endorse the tough coalitional programme negotiated between the governing parties - when even some Social Democratic MPs abstained because they regarded it as too punitive on the welfare state - merely reinforces the impression of Green posturing rather than of any unbridgeable ideological chasm. If the Greens continue to turn their back on conventional politics by refusing to confront these dilemmas, or to resolve their own internal differences, they can hardly expect or deserve to maximise their electoral potential.

The potential for Green party support, in spite of these shortcomings, was underlined by the outcome of the national elections of March 1991, fought under the shadow of an economic recession made worse by the collapse of the Soviet Union - Finland's major trading partner. The uncertainty helped the cause of the opposition parties. The centre right Conservative Party (Kansallinen Kokoomus-Kok) and the agrarian Centre Party (Suomen Keskusta-Kesk) capitalised on this mutability and formed a coalition with some of the minor parties (the Christian Union and Svenska Folkpartiet-SFP, the Swedish People's Party). The Greens, too, in an electoral climate dominated by anything but post-material concerns (economic and military security were at the very heart of this campaign), nevertheless produced a combined green vote of 6.8 per cent, which brought 10 Green members into the Eduskunta. Green issues were raised during this campaign, but were by no means of paramount public concern. Indeed, the potential for a post-materialist agenda remains modest, even though the Green constituency has become firmly established in Finnish politics. It was boosted in the late 1980s by the damage wrought by the Chernobyl disaster on the Finnish environment, and not least its food chain. It was subsequently reinforced by widespread pollution fears and a deep-seated concern about "the depreciating aesthetic value of nature and environments"[5] amongst Finland's population. This level of support was broadly maintained in the 1992 local elections.

The steady electoral support for Green issues in successive elections at every level emphasises the political potential for the Green movement. They have been helped in this by the reluctance, so far, of the mainstream parties to seek to challenge the Greens in their own issue area, or to impinge on the Green agenda in a search for additional, fringe, votes. So far, the major parties, preoccupied with the fundamental structural issues which have overtaken the Finnish economy (with national GDP falling by 6.5 per cent in 1991 alone, and precipitating a major economic crisis), have left what they see as the 'peripheral' ecological issue largely to the Greens. The Greens, in spite of their nominal differences over ideology, have managed to successfully concentrate their political energies on a range of ecological issues which they have made their own. They have at least gained some electoral credit for their purposive pursuit of these issues amongst a clearly defined constituency, by prosecuting the idea of pollution controls and green taxes, waste recycling, as well as environmental protection in critical economic sectors such as forestry. Their success in consolidating this constituency may, however, increase the political pressures on them in the longer term. For when the recession slackens - as it has done in something approaching spectacular fashion since the country joined the EU - it is unlikely that the established parties will continue to give them such a clear run in issue areas that are likely to gain in electoral salience as prosperity and economic growth increase. Once they are confronted with political competition on this ground, the Greens will have to work even harder to keep hold of the progressive vote they have so far cornered for themselves on these issues.

The Greens will also need to cope with what Liisa Uusitalo has identified as the tendency to 'inner inconsistency' of attitudes on the environment question. What is at stake here is the classic 'free rider' mentality which calls into question the depth of individual commitment to any real changes of lifestyle needed to bring about a better environment. In short, environmental preferences coexist - and compete with other interests - in the mind of the same political actor and in ways that encourage ambivalence. On the one hand a positive response to green questions, perhaps even a green vote, but with no real expectation that ecological reform measures will seriously restrict the same individual's lifestyle or consumption patterns. This is surely *the* acid test that awaits any Green party that secures enough political power to be able to influence national policy. The cognitive and behavioural paradox at the root of this ambivalence is frequently expressed as an "individual utility versus collective welfare dilemma", in which individual wants may easily take precedence over public goods; and where environmental preferences survive, if at all, as a much more nebulous option. Uusitalo's detailed survey of environmental attitudes in Finland found clear evidence of this political 'pitfall' confronting the Greens. Especially when economic downturns bring private wants and collective goods into greater conflict. This is a situation, by no means unique to Finland,[6] whereby "despite desiring the collective good - environmental quality - each individual often tries to shun own sacrifices and wishes that others will bring about the collective good".[7] In these difficult times, when ecologism stands discounted, or even when the economy improves sufficiently and it becomes the subject of competitive bids from other parties, the Greens will need a greater degree of pragmatism and common sense than they showed when they first took part in national politics. There have been recent signs that the pragmatists in the movement have begun to register these tactical requirements. The Greens have at least taken some strides towards addressing these issues. Their decision after the last election to join the government, and the presence of a Green member in the Cabinet, are positive moves towards acquiring 'normal' political status. The real test will come, of course, when the Green parliamentary party is confronted with policies and agendas that conflict - as many must do in a rainbow coalition spanning the ideological spectrum - with their elemental green preferences. For the time being, at least, a decision to identify with the mainstream parties' search for ways out of what threatened to be a national crisis of unprecedented proportions has turned the Greens away from their cult of febrile oppositionalism and strident anti-partyism. The Greens are now at least regarded, by their own activists as much as by their opponents, as a 'national' party.

In the matter of their disposition towards the political game, the Greens hold their electoral fate in their own hands. Some of the changes they have adopted have resulted from the lessons of experience that all new parties must learn, sooner or later, if they are to consolidate their place in the game of party politics and survive as an effective player in national politics. Yet other practical adjustments have been imported by a kind of osmosis, from the Green experience of participating in 'normal' politics elsewhere. The Finnish Greens have strong links with the wider European Green movement, where the very same organisational and ideological dilemmas are being confronted, and in many case addressed, by a pragmatic response. It was indicative of the Finnish Greens' receptiveness to these common experiences that they hosted, in the early 1990s, a meeting of those Green parties represented in the European Parliament, in conjunction with 'Europe's Green Coordination' - the 26 Green parties of western and eastern Europe. The main issue under discussion here was a prospective Federation for all of Europe's Green parties. The convention heard the chairman of Finland's Green Union, Pekka Savri, recommend unity as the best means of exerting political influence. This message has been assimilated, at least by the factions within Finland's main Green Party, and the political reward was evident in the outcome of the 1995 national elections.

These elections took place against the background of the worst slump since the 1930s. The collapse of Finland's important export market after the breakup of the Soviet Union, on top of another international recession, and the collapse of a domestic credit boom, saw the national economy - one of fastest growing anywhere in the 1980s - contract just as sharply, by 15 per cent, between 1991 and 1993. GDP fell in successive years (by as much as 7.1 per cent in 1991), and the unemployment level rose from 3.5 per cent in 1990 to a record 20 per cent in 1995. A devaluation of the markka in 1991 helped to sustain a modest recovery and the economy returned to growth in 1994. But not before this economic free fall had brought about a seachange in Finnish politics. The shock administered by these events fomented a debate over Finland's external policy in general, and the country's pending membership of the EU, as a way of replacing these lost markets, attracting inward investment and retaining domestic funds. There was also a security dimension to this issue. Finland shares an 800 mile frontier with Russia, and it felt increasingly exposed in the post-Communist milieu to political uncertainties there. EU membership offered a better prospect than continued isolation - a sentiment that was accelerated by the rash promise by the ultra-nationalist Zhirinovsky to re-establish Russia's regional hegemony. Pekka Visuri of the Finnish Institute of International Affairs has observed, "that there has been a close correlation between the Finnish attitudes (towards EU membership) and Russian political development".[8] The attraction of EU membership intensified during the early 1990s, culminating in the referendum of October 1994 that endorsed accession by a majority of 57 to 43 per cent.

This outcome launched a number of complementary debates. For instance, over the impact of Community membership on the relatively privileged position enjoyed by farmers, whose heavily subsidised commodity prices were already some 60 per cent higher than those enjoyed by the EU's farmers under the CAP. As well as the implications for a generously funded welfare state system, of attempting to abide by the budgetary discipline necessary to accommodate the Maastricht requirements for EMU, which the centre-right government elected in 1991 had acceded to. And, not least, the implications for Finland's neutral and nonaligned foreign policy of the common security architecture emerging from the latest stage of European political integration.[9] The European issue was by no means as internally divisive here as the debate over the very same issues was for the other Nordic applicants. The end of the Cold War had, in fact, the very opposite implications for Finland compared with its neighbours. It removed the most enduring historic threat to the country's independence, wrested in 1917 from Tsarist Russia and defended during world war two with German assistance, in two regional wars against Soviet incursions. The uneasy truce with this powerful neighbour was enshrined in the 1947 treaty of friendship and cooperation, by which 'Finlandisation' traded neutrality for peace. The fall of Communism promised new beginnings - an opportunity to join the European mainstream for the first time. At the same time, these considerations were hedged with persistent doubts about Finland's special status relations with its dominant neighbour, and not least an awareness of Russia's sensibilities about Finland's command of the Baltic approaches to St Petersburg. This situation encouraged a guarded approach to Finland's acquiescence to any proposals for western European defence initiatives, or it's participation in NATO. EU membership was recommended less as a taunt to Moscow than as the chance to stabilise the Baltic, with Finland providing a diplomatic bridge between Brussels and Moscow. These strategic questions undoubtedly weighed as heavily with the Finnish electorate as the anticipated economic advantages of EU membership. Opinion polls regularly cited concern with political instability across the border, and its likely consequences for Finland. Pertti Salolainen, the deputy Prime Minister in the centre-right government that negotiated Finland's terms of entry, summed up the national mood on EU entry thus; "no one can say Russia is a country of stability today. There is a certain hazard in Russia .... so it is a question of security. The mere fact of being a member of the EU will give security because then you are untouchable militarily - without having to make any new military arrangements. The EU could never accept any aggression against one of its members".[10]

The economic arguments were, however, the paramount attraction of this new approach to external affairs. As the economic crisis deepened, the material arguments tipped the balance firmly in favour of EU membership - much less as an idealistic conversion to the advantages of European integration, as what one commentator aptly described as a "defensive pragmatism".[11] It was this materialist agenda - a compendium of the 'old' politics in every sense - that dominated the domestic political discourse up to the 1995 elections. In so far as ecology figured at all in this debate, it was only as a second order issue. The Greens contributed to, although by no means instigated or monopolised, a subsidiary debate about how far EU membership would dilute Finland's existing high environmental standards. Or whether instead, membership might better facilitate Europewide eco-regulations, by incorporating already high Nordic environmental standards within the Community's policy structures. Environmental concerns were, however, no more than incidental on the national policy agenda. The 1995 budget had raised energy taxes - already higher than equivalent taxes in Sweden. There was an environmental bonus from this measure, which added to the costs of the forestry and base metal sectors on which 80 per cent of exports depended. Nevertheless, this fiscal mechanism was introduced, primarily to raise revenue rather than with the greening of industry in mind. The national agenda was dominated by the usual materialist concerns. There was a gathering consensus between the mainstream parties in the run up to the election, about the need to cut social spending to prevent the budget deficit racing out of control, in order to reduce the social costs on employers as a means of encouraging job creation, and - with EU membership in mind - as a way of attracting inward investment.

The 1995 budget tried to distribute the pain equitably between the main social partners - agriculture, labour and capital - with the increased energy costs balanced by a reduction in unemployment benefits. There was also a proposal - subsequently rescinded - to abolish the tax deductible status of trades union subscriptions. Proposals to compensate farmers for a projected fall in income after EU membership by national subsidies led to conflict within the centre-right government, between the agrarian Centre Party and the urban-based Conservatives, who opposed such 'feather bedding'. The central issue here, as it was in the other Nordic 'model' welfare states, was the 'trade off' between social harmony and competitiveness based on balanced economic growth in the rapidly changing economic circumstances that confronted all advanced western European states. Every contemporary state now faces hard political and social choices as a result of the constraints imposed by global competitiveness. This amounts to a critical dilemma that threatens the civilised balance on which the political legitimacy and, ultimately, the social stability of these societies, has rested for a generation and more. The growing tension here is between the role of private industry, as the motor of economic growth, now facing unprecedented challenges to its competitiveness from a global market place; and, on the other side of the equation, "a deep seated determination to maintain the welfare state even at the cost of tax rates which would be unsustainable in other western countries".[12] This discourse, and the unpalatable choices it entailed, has been as evident here as it is in every other liberal democratic polity in western Europe. It has dominated the national political debate, yet the differences between the main parties have been more those of degree than substance or principle.

Finland's SDP nominated President Ahtisaari, underlined the broad national consensus over this issue. He appointed a national committee which recommended sweeping reductions in state expenditure of some 16 billion markka by the end of the century, to put the economy back on track. The main opposition party, the Socialidemokraattinen Puolue (Social Democratic Party - SDP), the most likely winner of the upcoming election, embraced its own version of fiscal rectitude as the only solution to the escalating problem of unemployment. The leader of the SDP, Paavo Lipponen, advocated a modified supply side strategy for economic renewal. This included the nurturing of conditions conducive to a competitive economy, but with rather more emphasis on smaller scale enterprise. He proposed "a real paradigm change (for) ours has been an economy of big companies, big cooperation, big banks, big wholesale companies and, if you like, big government. There has not been a role for a citizens society".[13] In essence, Lipponen envisaged the switch from a public sector ethic to an economic model which balanced affordable welfare with an enterprise culture of the kind that was at the centre of the revisionist Social Democratic project elsewhere in Scandinavia and beyond. The reasoning behind this revisionism on the left was, for Lipponen, a matter of facing unpalatable economic facts - because "the public sector cannot employ more people and the export sector is already efficient. So it is mainly in the small service companies that future employment will come. We have to get more flexibility and reduce labour costs - and social security costs".[14] There was, in these circumstances, a broad consensus between the mainstream parties over the principles, if not the precise details, of a national medium term strategy to restore fiscal credibility, rationalise the state finances, constrain public expenditure, stabilise the public debt-GDP ratio, and curb the growing budget deficit, over the period of the new Parliament. In order to sustain non-inflationary growth, reduce unemployment and make the economy ready for EMU membership at the earliest opportunity.

The Greens, predictably enough given their commitment to the civilised virtues of the Finnish welfare system, initially stood outside this broad policy consensus. In 1994, for instance, they utilised the usual Parliamentary procedure of initiating a no confidence vote against the centre-right government over its economic strategy. The Greens were much less exercised by these conventional arguments about economic viability, than they were about the economic justice of reducing welfare or the pursuit of fiscal practices that enhanced environmental protection. They refused to distinguish between economic policy and good environment management. Sustainable growth remained the key theme of their programme for national recovery, including the use of what they called 'economic guidance tools' such as eco-taxes, to meet 'appropriate' levels of economic growth. The Greens regarded the conventional growth targets of the other parties as both undesirable and unattainable per se. Unemployment, as they saw it, was a social evil, but one that could not be cured by traditional measures. It required, instead, a radical eco-strategy that involved a shorter working day, work rotation schemes, recreational vacations, and the creation of jobs in "less competitive" sectors such as the recycling, environmental protection, waste management and service industries.[15] The Green programme also recommended forestry improvement - a matter of considerable public concern in Finland - by reducing export subsidies that favoured the big companies who exploited these resources, and encouraged instead good environmental practice. Moreover, cuts in municipal grants - which featured in the public finance plans of the major parties - did little, as the Greens saw it, for the environment. The key to this alternative fiscal programme was the proposal of a novel way of raising public finance to pay for these ambitious green schemes. Instead of advocating sweeping reductions in welfare spending, the Green Association's chairman, Pekka Haavisto, recommended a more 'humane' way to manage the public finances, that required instead a continued, heavy public expenditure; a basic guaranteed income combined with a daily unemployment allowance minus the earnings related element, to encourage people to take short term work; with this scheme to be balanced by continued generous national pensions and student grants, housing provision and child care support. This programme would be financed by far-reaching shifts in the tax burden to lower the price of work, cut tax evasion in the black economy, the introduction of a range of green taxes (on carbon dioxide emissions and energy use), while lowering personal income tax by up to 3 per cent. There would also be a commensurate shift in the burden of the internal cost distribution of the corporate sector, away from labour intensive and towards capital intensive sectors, to ensure that the highly automated and high energy using export sectors would carry their appropriate share of the costs of the country's welfare and employment commitments.

The Finnish Greens were also out of step with the broad national consensus on the EU issue. They shared the reservations of Green parties elsewhere about the European Union as an exclusive trade bloc. There was a domestic edge to this hostility t the European project, as well as an international dimension. The Greens were as concerne by the likely impact of

EMU on employment levels, as they were by the prospect of a trading arrangement structurally designed, as they saw it, to concentrate prosperity in Europe's economic core at the expense of a neglected periphery. The Greens remained unimpressed, too, by the consensus amongst pro EU opinion in the country and even in the green pressure groups, that Finnish membership - along with that of the other Nordic candidate members - would somehow strengthen the environment lobby in Brussels, which already consisted of Germany, Austria, the Netherlands and Denmark. Sweden, for instance, was certainly ahead of every other EU state with regard to curbing sulphur emissions, ensuring air quality standards, and imposing carbon dioxide taxes. With the Council of Ministers votes available to the Nordic states and the rest of this informal 'green alliance' under the rules of Qualified Majority Voting, they would be well placed, either to block environmentally harmful, or to promote ecologically sound, legislation. The Greens, however, remained convinced that the EU project was driven by altogether narrower productionist concerns that would ensure that deep ecological matters - other than as a merely cosmetic exercise - remained heavily discounted in its policy agenda.

This resistance to regional integration was both principled and pragmatic. The decision to represent the case for peripheral regions found considerable resonance in this sparsely populated but geographically remote country, where 35 per cent of a population of barely 5 millions lived in its far-flung rural areas.[16] The Greens, of course, did not have this issue by any means to themselves. Concern over rural depopulation and neglect, as with the Greens' reservations about the impact of lower EU farm prices on agricultural incomes, was an issue that played even better for the agrarian Centre Party. The Centre Party had capitalised on it during government negotiations - in which they were a junior partner - for EU membership. They had asked for Finland to be treated as a special case because of its severe sub-arctic climate, but had to settle instead for a compromise arrangement that divided up the country into areas (covering a majority of its territory in the event) which qualified for compensatory regional subsidies as Less Favoured Areas (LFA). In addition to the normal EU price support - an arrangement which excluded those more southerly areas that produced most of Finland's cereal and vegetables. The Greens were thus denied a small but useful support base as the representatives of rural interests. The Centre Party, although by no means opposed to EU membership per se, was better placed to harness whatever electoral potential existed for a sceptical or even an anti-EU constituency amongst Finland's rural population.

(iv)   **Prospects for political change**

With so much consensus around, the 1995 election was a relatively dull affair! It was conducted in a political climate, and around an agenda that, on the face of it, offered little scope to the Greens - other than to appeal to their small niche constituency amongst those sections of the better educated, urbanized and 'new' middle class who were attracted to radical and post-materialist ideas. The Greens certainly courted this limited constituency. The party's best claim to political innovation took the form of an attempt - unsuccessful in the event - to drastically increase the number of women in the Eduskunta, by fielding a large number of female candidates. The result of the election, in terms of party placings, was hardly more remarkable than the campaign. Although support for the Social Democrats slipped back somewhat as the poll approached (to 28.3 per cent but up from

22.1 per cent in 1991, which yielded 63 seats compared with 48 at the previous election), they polled their best performance since 1945. The Centre Party, the SDP's principal opponents, performed less badly than predicted - with 19.9 per cent and 44 seats - down from 24.8 per cent and 55 seats. The Conservatives took 17.9 per cent (39 seats), a slight fall from its 19.3 per cent share (and 41 seats) in 1991. Of the minor parties, the Swedish Peoples Party more or less held its own on 5.1 per cent (11 seats). The former Communist Leftist Alliance marginally increased its vote to 11.2 per cent (22 seats). Whereas the Green Association, too, at 6.5 per cent (and 9 seats), barely shifted from its earlier performance and actually dropped a seat - although most of this 'lost' vote shifted to a pure green Ecology Party which took one seat.

After an opinion poll rating of over 10 per cent in May 1994, support for the Green Association steadily declined as the national debate focused on an issue agenda that was some way removed from its own radical policy preferences. They were squeezed, in the event, by parties better placed to exploit the prevailing public anxieties outlined above. Nevertheless, in an election with no overall winner, and in a political system designed to encourage coalition government, the Greens found themselves better placed than on previous occasions to trade their small bloc of seats in the post-election negotiations that inevitably follow Finnish elections, for a place in the new Government and a modest degree of influence over its policy programme and direction. The Social Democrats' leadership, to whom the task fell as the strongest party to negotiate the composition of the coalition, considered every possible combination - from a 'grand' coalition with their main Centre Party rivals (precluded in the end because of continuing disagreement over the issue of special subsidies for local farmers), to the 'rainbow' coalition that eventually emerged, and which included representatives from the Conservatives, the Swedish Party, the Leftist Alliance and the Green Association. The decision to participate in a rainbow coalition was much less surprising than might be suggested by the apparent chasm between the Greens' election programme and the broad consensus amongst their rivals on European and fiscal matters. For one thing, the Greens were by now sufficiently experienced in the machinations of Finnish party politics to separate the apparently unbridgeable policy positions paraded in election campaigns, from the altogether more pragmatic trade offs necessary to sustain workable governments. There was evidence, too, in the Greens' post election calculus, of tactical thinking in pursuit of clear political (and policy) objectives. The Green Association's chairman, Pekka Haavisto, had already expressed a wish to avoid any participation in a red-green government. This would be strongly dependent, he felt, on the trades unions and, as such, would be altogether too cautious and predictable, and thereby unable to address the serious policy shifts needed to ensure a sustainable growth model. It would, in short, "slow the (necessary) changes needed in work and working hours". Whereas he maintained, "the best government base, in the view of the Greens, bridges the left-right bloc divide and is not on the leash of either employers or agricultural producers".[17]

Haavisto had already trailed the idea of a broad-based government that would reflect the balance of the country's competing social interests. Although this prospectus greatly exaggerated the likely influence of the Greens on the policy process, a rainbow coalition was in fact the eventual outcome of the post-election negotiations over the composition of the new coalition. The incoming Prime Minister's reasons for constructing such a coalition (controlling 145 seats in the Parliament), was the key requirement of commanding as much support in the chamber as possible for pursuing an economic programme that promised to challenge old shibboleths and the complacent assumptions about the direction of public policy. The new administration projected instead sweeping cuts of some 20 billion markka (£2.87 billions) in public expenditure.[18] The Green Association's moderate Parliamentary leadership - in spite of deep reservations amongst some of its Eduskunta members, to say nothing of party activists and supporters in the country - felt able to endorse the programme of retrenchment on which the new coalition was negotiated. In part, because this was unavoidable, but primarily because it was negotiated on the basis of a national package in which the sacrifices would be equitably spread amongst the country's various social interests. The stark facts of unemployment and a public sector deficit at levels that threatened long term economic security and social stability had already softened the left's resistance to retrenchment and made it amenable to the idea of cutbacks. The country's conservative forces, too, were already on board with the reform package. The Greens, who had even more ideological ground to cover before they came within touching distance of this apparently conservative agenda, showed just how far they had developed - one is tempted to say 'matured' - into a party now in tune with these awkward choices and complex realities. As well as one able to reconcile both the constraints and opportunities afforded by a role in national politics.

The prospect of becoming the first Green party to win representation in a national government anywhere in Europe (apart from the Italian Greens' brief twentyfour hour sojourn) with the offer of the Environment Ministry - combined with responsibilities for Development Cooperation and a proposed new national forest plan - was a chance to exert a degree of political influence the party leadership could not abjure. Cabinet status amounted to a political bonus of symbolic importance that outweighed, any continuing doubts that existed in the party about being compromised by association with a materialist agenda; one that included a more or less conventional growth strategy, deeper integration within the EU and welfare retrenchment. The Leftist Alliance, who also joined the coalition, shared this ambivalent outlook. It was, however, a testament to the newfound pragmatism of the Green Association, that these pervasive reservations about the fairness of the Government's programme have caused more obvious disconcertion in other coalition parties than amongst the parliamentary Greens, at least to date - within the Leftist Alliance, for instance, (over budget cuts, EMU and the threat of nonalignment), and even on the left of the Social Democratic party.[19] Although two Green Association parliamentary members did oppose participation in the coalition, they were over-ruled by the party's leadership and the decision was endorsed - albeit with distinct unease - by the party's rank and file. Moreover, this potentially divisive matter was dealt with in an orderly and disciplined way - a fact which adds to the impression of a party that has moved some way to embrace a conventional model of party organisation.

The party appointed a negotiating team - the usual procedure for participating in coalition formation here - consisting of a leader of the Parliamentary group and party spokesperson, Tuija Brax, and a first and second deputy, along with the party chairman, deputy chairperson and the party secretary. The common sense pragmatism that informed this monumental decision by the Greens to embrace governance, was aptly summarised by Heidi Hautala, the Green Association's candidate for the European Parliament. Hautala recommended that the Greens should take up this role in government because they had no other choice if they wanted to be taken seriously in national politics. Participating in 'normal' politics is, in the realist perspective that now pervades strategic thinking in the party, indispensable. Not only for extending the party's credibility, but also as a means for influencing the policy agenda, instead of having to respond from the political fringes to one set by the other parties.[20] The Green Association's accommodation to government has, moreover, been a relatively smooth transition, although it is too early to claim that it has conclusively established the party in the political mainstream, let alone resolved any residual tensions in the party about embracing the constraints of conventional party politics. The combination of fortuitous circumstances - a rapid upturn in Finland's economic fortunes in response to the end of the European recession, a boost to national economic growth, and a discernible prosperity brought on by EU membership - have so far given the 'rainbow' government a relatively straightforward ride. Food prices had decreased by some 11 per cent by the end of 1995, long term interest rates were falling, and one of the strongest economic recoveries in the EU was well underway.[21] It is by no means certain that this situation will continue. The latent tensions within the rainbow coalition - and the continuing doubts within the Green Association, at every level, about the wisdom of being associated with a government whose ideological and political centre of gravity is so far removed from that of even this moderate and pragmatic Green party - may yet rise to the surface in less favourable circumstances. Especially so if difficult, politically divisive and unpalatable policy options have to be faced. So far, the pressures on the Government have been eased by Finland's improved economic fortunes. Unemployment has begun to fall, if modestly rather than spectacularly. The idea that even such a broad based coalition as this can ensure a full economic recovery, or preside over the sort of far-reaching and painful structural changes that will challenge head on the expectations of a population used to enjoying the fulsome benefits of the postwar Nordic model of welfare capitalism, without encountering opposition, is fanciful.

The coalition may yet fall out over the competing claims of its various natural constituencies, as it continues to wrestle with the immense challenge of rationalising the welfare system and gearing the country up to the rigours of a competitive European Single Market and Monetary Union. Wide differences over ecological matters also continue to divide the coalition partners. The Conservatives, the second largest coalition party, chose the nuclear energy option at its 1995 annual congress, as the preferred basis for meeting Finland's future energy requirements. The scope here for a political fallout with the Greens clearly remains considerable. According to the Conservative Party's constitution, this decision merely commits the Party's Board, but only 'recommends' its Parliamentary and ministerial representatives to adopt the policy.[22] The Social Democrats, with a radical wing of their own to consider, are unlikely to risk the fragile unity of the coalition by pushing such contentious issues to the top of the national agenda. Meanwhile, there are more pressing matters to occupy the Government. A common sense compromise to head off conflict on this - or any other issues that threaten a cabinet crisis - in order not to distract the Government from its main agenda, is the more likely outcome. Either way, the Government, minus its one Green member, and the nine Green parliamentary votes, is hardly likely to fall over the issue. But if the Greens begin to feel politically uncomfortable in the rainbow coalition for whatever reason, they may choose to fall back on such convenient ideological alibis as a principled passport back into Opposition. The fact that, so far, the Greens have continued to constructively play their part in a government for which ecologism is hardly a primary matter of concern, without any undue problems, is a testament to an abiding mood of realism and a moderation in the Green Association, that continues to stand it in good stead in Finland. The party is hardly likely to break out of its current status as a niche party. At the same time, its practice of moderation and its willingness to shoulder a share of responsibility in a Government of national endeavour, can only add to its electoral credibility. This experience provides, too, a unique yardstick against which to measure the performance of similarly placed and moderate Green parties elsewhere in Europe.

2.   Denmark

(i)   Green roots

Concern with conserving natural habitat and preserving the environment, although represented by an influential lobby of urban middle class activists from 1911 onwards in the Danmarks Naturfredningsforen - the Danish Society for the Preservation of Natural Amenities,with its influential connections with the public authorities, was not a major political issue until the late 1960s. The emergence of radical student politics on the back of a generational shift during that decade, led to the creation of a social movement -NOAH - that combined ecological concern with demands for social change. This organisation spawned upwards of 80 local and ad hoc committees during the following decade. This development did not, however, crystallise into a national Green party. The launch of a Green party was also pre-empted, in part, by effective government action in this field. For instance, the establishment in 1971 of a Department of the Environment, which oversaw (in 1973) a Law of the Environment that was, at this early stage in environmental management, one of the most extensive environmental legislative measures anywhere in Europe. There was every indication by the early 1970s that the environment possessed little potential as an issue capable of mobilising widespread public support.

The emergence of the debate over nuclear power ensured that this issue did at least retain political salience. Denmark had adopted a nuclear power strategy during the 1950s. Although a Nuclear Energy Commission was appointed in 1955, and a nuclear research centre was instituted between 1956 and 1958, the nuclear option was not adopted. The onset of the energy crisis in 1973-74 propelled Denmark into the same politically charged debate over energy policy that was underway in many other advanced societies. After ELSAM - the country's largest group of electricity power suppliers - had sought official permission to install a nuclear plant, opposition against the proposal began to gather momentum. The Organization for Information on Nuclear Power (OOA) became the principal focus of this opposition. It demanded a referendum on the issue, prefaced by an immediate and wideranging public debate on the nuclear options before the government sanctioned any irrevocable decision. The success of the OOA campaign and the extent of its public support was evident from parliament's positive response - an agreement to postpone the final decision; to launch a public information campaign; and to pass only a small part of the complex enabling legislation. Only a minor party, the Left Socialist Party, was equivocally opposed to nuclear power. A rebellion by the grassroots members of another minor party, the Socialist People's Party, gave the nuclear issue greater political salience in a highly fragmented Parliamentary situation, where even small parties can exert some leverage over the policy agenda, especially on issues that enjoy public support. The mounting public concern generated by the nuclear issue - not least because of the importance of this issue to young (and especially student) voters - filtered through to the Social Demokratiet (the Social Democratic Party). The Social Democrats, one of the linchpins of governing coalitions during this period, depended on this youthful constituency to maximise their turnout.[23] The vulnerability of the party to the disaffection of this radical constituency had already been underlined by desertions from the ranks of Social Democrat voters and was underlined by a further loss of support after the party's endorsement in the 1972 referendum campaign on accession to the EC. What the nuclear issue did signify was the potential in Danish national politics, for altogether new issues to impact on the political calculations of the mainstream parties. The issue also helped to define an emergent post-materialist agenda in which ecologism became a persistent and central theme. This green momentum lasted beyond the settlement of the nuclear issue by 1980, and concentrated attention on such issues as air pollution, toxic waste dumping and the nitrate pollution of ground water. The increased salience of the environment in national politics undoubtedly contributed to the moves that followed to set up a Green party.

The Greens were handicapped in their attempt to make political space for themselves, by both the structure of the Danish polity and the nature of its political culture.[24] Until 1960 the political system had been dominated by four parties, each of which reflected a pervasive aspect of Denmark's currently stable socio-economic make up, ranged over a longstanding pattern of economic class/rural-urban cleavages.[25] A schism in the Communist party in 1960, and the emergence of the Socialist People's Party, slightly modified the prevailing pattern of party politics, but hardly deflected the national issue agenda from the conventional postwar Keynesian preoccupations of every western European liberal democratic state, with a mixed economy geared to steady growth and tempered by a generous and moderately redistributive welfare state.[26] The cumulative prosperity encouraged by this conventional model of political economy did, however, eventually bring in its train new stimuli for change. The gradual emergence of a prosperous middle class which had both experienced and expected high levels of consumption, but whose incomes also attracted what they came to regard as punitive rates of taxation, began to feel that they carried a disproportionately unfair burden of financing an increasingly expensive welfare system. The new materialist middle class became more receptive to the appeal of new right wing parties, whose neo-liberal ideologies promised a renewed emphasis on enterprise, self-help, low taxation, and anti-state as opposed to alternativist libertarianism.[27] The abrupt end of economic prosperity that followed in the wake of the major disjunctions in the global economy in the early seventies[28] introduced unprecedented levels of volatility into Danish politics.[29] This overt mood for change was accentuated by the current government's decision in 1973 to move away from an insular Nordic orbit, and to embrace EEC membership. The European issue injected a further cause of political turbulence into Danish politics which has persisted ever since. All of these politically potent issues - of class interests, political economy and national identity - have retained a far greater potential for realigning Danish party politics than ecologism.[30] The salience of the environment issue - which ironically enjoyed its most influential years before De Gronne became active - has been severely discounted by other productionist issues: for instance, unemployment, the future of the generous welfare system, budget deficits and economic competitiveness in the global market place. The Danish electorate was thus confronted with several causes of discord over a relatively brief timespan, but which owed much more to the old politics than to the new.

The first sign of these disruptions to the underlying political consensus came in the most politically disruptive election in Denmark's recent history. Some forty per cent of a normally stable electorate switched their political allegiance during the two years preceding the 1973 election. The number of parties represented in the Folketing markedly increased and an unprecedented degree of volatility and party fragmentation was introduced into Danish politics - with the direct outcome that minority governments have become a more normal occurrence.[31] At the same time, this dealignment has not imported into the party system those excessive levels of ideological polarisation in which extremist or anti-system radicalism might flourish. The system remains fluid but stable, as far as the underlying commitment to civic culture and democratic politics goes. Borre's research on the demographic make-up of the Danish voter reveals little more than modest shifts entirely consistent with a changing sociology of modern politics apparent in every advanced liberal state. The sudden volatility in patterns of party support after the early seventies was matched by a noticeable decline in class-based voting. This was due, in some degree, to what Borre identified at the time as the "erosion of bourgeois support within the middle classes".[32] Key groups of voters, once closely tied to class-based parties, became available, in these more turbulent times, for recruitment to new and even radical party 'homes'. This did not mean, however, that the more or less predictable world of Danish party politics was turned upside down. Or that these politically 'promiscuous' voters were attracted to options or issue agendas which were altogether outside the political mainstream. In spite of these otherwise momentous electoral shifts within and between the electoral clienteles of the mainstream parties, Danish political culture has remained quintessentially pragmatic and its principal issue agenda and policy discourse have focused on those same productionist, materialist and national identity questions that have occupied electors and fashioned electoral politics across the continent. Ecologism and other post-materialist or 'new politics' issues have not been entirely excluded from this discourse. But neither have they enjoyed the salience required to increase its profile on the contemporary scene. The coalition governments that have occupied the centre ground of politics in Denmark over recent decades have concentrated their principal energies on trying to resolve those increasingly urgent questions thrown up by this materialist agenda.[33] As an endemic sense of unease gripped the electorate, a political space did open up on the margins for radical groups and new social movements, convinced that the productionist preoccupations of the political centre were simply misdirected or irrelevant to 'real' social needs. Ecologism was a central element of this persistent critique of the 'old' politics.[34] The Greens, when they did eventually set up a political party, did not have this political constituency entirely to themselves.

(ii)   Party formation

An independent Green party had been mooted by Danish ecologists from 1980 onwards. In the initial stages of the project, however, indecision was rife. The various local ecological groups and factions who addressed this issue were unable to make up their minds, about whether or not to crystallise the political potential for green issues to the extent of setting up a full blown party. This hesitation was, in part, informed by practical considerations - not least, how such a party, without an obvious social base of support to draw on, could be electorally viable. On the face of it, this seemed to be a curious cause for concern, given the widespread support for the green lobby. The membership of Danmarks Naturfredningsforen had steadily grown throughout the 1970s, and had doubled by ,1980. With some 200 thousand members by 1983, DN was already well on the way to becoming the largest nature preservation society in Europe, with a larger membership than that combined of all of Denmark's political parties. Nevertheless, it was the case here as elsewhere, that support for the green lobby by no means translates into votes for Green parties. A poll conducted in December 1981 had identified barely 2 per cent of the electorate as potential Green voters. The formation of a Green party was also delayed by the usual ideological divisions. There were quite deep differences both between red-greens and deep ecologists, and between those on both sides who contested the virtues of forming - or the need to form - a political party at all. Many Green activists resisted what they saw as the risks and the compromises with radical principles required by party status and inflicted by the parliamentary route to ecology. The electoralists on the other side, took the pragmatic view that a party committed to ecologism was the most effective way of keeping the issue in the public mind and raising its profile in national politics. According to this optimistic account of the prospects for a viable Green party, such a party would provide a magnet for an extensive but so far an unfocused constituency.

In the event, the electoralists carried the day. They did so, however, only after three years or so of febrile debate that allowed other political parties to put their own mark on the ecology issue. The issue was resolved in favour of party status once it was accepted in the Green camp, that none of these other parties which had laid claim to represent the issue, were other than Green imposters. In spite of increasing environmental damage, and an effective campaign spearheaded by the DN lobby to persuade the government to adopt more stringent measures to protect the environment, the Green activists decided that only a Green party could effectively fight the cause of ecology at the parliamentary level. After a period of lively debate within the green movement over these issues, two Green parties emerged. The larger of the two, De Gronne, represented a pure green programme and was launched in October 1983, after the collection of the mandatory 20 thousand signatures required to register any party intending to participate in national elections. De Gronne became the vehicle for those activists who wanted to carry pure green ecologism into the mainstream of national party politics. Another, regionally based, Green party, with minuscule support - the Danmarks Miljopartiet (The Environmental Party of Denmark) was also founded in Jutland after a convention in Aarhus in September 1984. These continuing divisions between the pure greens compounded those between deep ecologists and red-greens already active in the alternativist and new leftist parties. Needless to say, they further undermined the movement's political coherence, let alone its chances of developing a coherent national strategy. These are divisions that the Green movement can ill afford to perpetuate in such a crowded political market place. The delay, and the fragmentation in the movement that was merely encouraged by it had important and negative consequences, both for the type of Green parties that eventually emerged, and for their future electoral prospects.

The legacy of infighting within the Green movement was less damaging as such, than the fact that it had prevented party formation and allowed other radical parties to usurp the green label. The fact, too, that De Gronne did not actually contest national elections until 1987 confirmed the party's difficulties vis a vis its surrogate 'green' competitors. Militants, radicalised by the nuclear issue, had already been drawn to new left parties which readily assimilated ecological demands into their 'rainbow' programmes. Support for these radical parties steadily increased - from 10 per cent in total in 1988, to 20 per cent by 1987; and this, during a period which, in most other countries, had seen the formation of Green parties as the main repository of ecological values and the beneficiary of this new politics vote. The Socialist People's Party and the Left Socialist Party, in particular, had become closely identified with the anti-nuclear and ecology issues,[35] especially amongst the extensive new left and alternativist constituency. Both of these parties undoubtedly benefited from the prolonged absence of a Green party on the political scene. Nor was ecologism by any means the sole preserve of the left. In the absence of a Green party to contest their claims, other parties, too, positioned themselves on the ground of ecologism. The Danish political establishment had adopted a cautiously receptive approach to environmental issues, if only because of their increased political appeal after the success of the anti-nuclear lobby. Denmark had eschewed the nuclear energy option and successive governments and their policy advisers continued to show sensitivity to the social consequences of energy policy. Although Denmark did join NATO, 'ts governments of every political colour, exhibited the usual Scandinavian discretion over .r:ilitarism, and managed to avoid having any nuclear weapons stood on their territory or NATO troops deployed there. These were significant policy concessions measured against the standards of the time. By accommodating public concern over ecology, they helped to soften the rigid demarcation between Green and conventional politics. The Radical Liberal Party, a progressive centre party which had supported the centre-right coalition that took office in 1982, had also tempered its enthusiasm for conventional market-driven economic policy, and identified with 'practical' environmental measures. Even the centre-right Christian People's Party saw political advantage in putting forward positive environmental proposals. The Social Democrats, aware of the appeal of the nuclear issue, especially to their left wing supporters, also jumped on the 'green' bandwagon. The blue collar vote here was by no means entirely unreceptive to good environmental practice, although much depended on their occupations, skill levels and precise position in the productionist system. The trade unions' support for the anti-nuclear campaign in the 1970s, as well as the fact that the DN, and even many OOA activists, adopted a sensible approach to ecology, and rarely endorsed the extreme zero growth option of some deep ecologists, helped to sanitise the issue and facilitate its place on the 'normal' politics agenda. Jorgen Goul Andersen has identified here the unusual phenomenon of "the greening of the labour movement".[36]

Other electoral shifts, too, encouraged the Social Democrats to court the Green vote. The loss of some of its traditional working class support to the centre-right, and even to the populist Progress Party, who made much of the argument that the Social Democrats had betrayed the interests of production workers and become a party of intellectuals and public employees wedded to utopian causes and high taxation (by no means an unusual phenomenon in the complicated patterns of electoral support in advanced democracies), merely added to the difficulties of the Greens in consolidating the ecology vote. As Andersen has identified the dilemma confronting De Gronne, "when 'left' and 'green' become almost indistinguishable in the public consciousness, the prospects for a green party are worse".[37] De Gronne's electorate was thus restricted, by and large, to pure-greens - by no means the dominant ecology constituency in Denmark. In short, the ecological issue has become assimilated into the conventional left-right cleavage in Danish politics, rather than being appropriated by a strong, independent Green party as the basis of a sound support base; for "to the extent that 'environmentalism' affects party choice, it does not cut across the traditional left-right polarisation between the parties; on the contrary, it reinforces it".[38] In so far as this is the case, the prospects for a viable Green party in Denmark remain heavily discounted. The 'failure' of Green party politics in Denmark was largely determined by the political climate that preceded - and delayed - its formation. The blame for this outcome does not lie entirely with the Greens, although their prevarications no doubt contributed to the plight of De Gronne when it did latterly embark on a parliamentary stratagem. The virtual monopolisation of the ecology issue by other parties - most notably those on the left - did inhibit the party's formation. The longer that this green territory was yielded to the left, the more likely it was that any Green party that did manage to form, would fail to capitalise on the wide support at every level of society for those environmental measures encouraged by an immensely successful green lobby.

(iii)   Political developments

De Gronne, when it did form, was squeezed electorally from the start and the new party decided not to contest the general election of January 1984. In fact, the party had to wait almost two years before flying the green flag in a national election. Meanwhile, it did manage to win small pockets of local support. It secured 12 municipal council seats and 6 provincial council seats in the 1985 local elections on a 2.8 per cent share of the total vote. The legacy of its delayed formation, the virtual exclusion of an extensive red-green constituency, and continuing doubts within its own ranks over its purpose in national politics, merely added to the party's electoral woes. De Gronne made a poor showing in its first national election and polled a mere 1.5 per cent of the total vote (and only 20 thousand votes), compared with a combined vote of almost 20 per cent for the two radical parties already closely identified with the green cause. And this, in spite of the fact that the Socialist People's Party, which had drawn much of its support from the public sector component of the 'new' middle class, and was closely identified with radical causes such as opposition to NATO and the EEC, and strongly supportive of pacifism and ecologism, suddenly decided to modify its uncompromising opposition both to NATO and EEC membership - a policy switch that opened up to it the prospect of joining the new coalition formed by the Social Democrats. De Gronne repeated this poor performance when new elections were held in May 1988, and again failed (with 1.5 per cent) to cross the modest 2 per cent threshold needed to take any seats in the Folketing. The electoral cost to the party of the surrender of the red-green constituency was quite apparent from the outset. The party was simply unable to remove the widespread feeling amongst the alternativist and post-materialist constituency, that the new left parties were much better placed to represent green issues in Parliament.

The shortcomings of De Gronne's performances stand in stark contrast to an opportunity structure that is otherwise favourable to minor parties. Elections for the 195 Folketing seats are contested according to a proportional formula (a modified Sainte-Lague system that does favour larger parties slightly more than does the 'largest remainders' system, but less so than the d'Hondt system that was abandoned in 1953) based on party lists in eighteen constituencies. The system also operates a 'complex districting' formula - with 'higher tier' constituencies "to iron out discrepancies arising from lower level constituencies".[39] The degree of proportionality in the electoral system is further enhanced by reserving some 40 additional seats for allocation amongst any party reaching a nominal 2 per cent threshold.[40] This, and the absence of any requirement for financial deposits from candidates, together with the provision since 1987 of state funding to 'match' votes won in previous contests at every electoral level, and public assistance in making election broadcasts, makes for an electoral playing field as level as that anywhere in western Europe. The Green Party's continuing mediocre performances says much more about its poor start in an otherwise favourable political milieu, than it does about a discriminatory opportunity structure.

De Gronne's marginal standing in Danish politics is further emphasised by the party's low membership - less than 2 per cent of its modest electorate. Denmark's radical and leftist parties are noticeably poor recruiters. They face a kind of cultural resistance typical of radical organisations elsewhere. The target group of these radical parties is a clientele - predominantly young, anti-authoritarian, iconoclastic, well educated and disposed to spontaneity rather than the discipline and bureaucratic procedures of more conventional political associations. Formal structures and the usual constraints and obligations of party politics, are widely regarded amongst this cohort as hierarchical restrictions on democratic vitality. The pure greens were as resistant to the rigours of organised politics as the new left. De Gronne has deliberately pursued an open and direct democratic political style by ceding considerable autonomy to local party branches; both in the selection of candidates for its lists as well as in the matter of policy formation. The party indulges this preference for grassroots control by holding regular national conferences - up to three times in a single year. These conferences are attended by one local delegate for every 10 members. As a gesture to political realism the conference decisions are not held to be legally binding on Green members of parliament. Nevertheless, the party places great store on the notion of a direct mandate from the grassroots, and there is continual pressure on party functionaries and elected members at every level to abide by these democratic precepts. These legitimating principles have extended to the party's general outlook on the purpose and practice of governance. The party favours subsidiarity; all policy decisions should be devolved to those who are directly affected by their consequences. It may be argued by cynics or realists, that this generous interpretation of the democratic idea ignores the immense complexity of modern governance, as well as the sheer interdependence of decision making, which applies even in the smallest polity - Denmark has a population of only 5 million or so. Whether this preference amounts to gross simplification, or is a genuine reflection of the civic purpose which all radical parties lay claim to, it has done little either to increase the Green Party's appeal to the new politics electorate, or to help it to agree a coherent programme capable of winning over those mainstream Social Democrat or Radical Liberal voters attuned to environmental concerns. De Gronne's policy preferences differed little at the outset from other pure-green parties with a decided fundamentalist orientation. The party's manifesto consistently advocated the virtues of deep ecology - grassroots democracy; anti-bureaucracy in the conduct of the party's affairs; the regular use of referenda as an aid to democratic governance, even on the most complex policy issues; and the inalienable civil right of citizens to resist unwarranted authority by the state.

De Gronne soon strayed off this pure green agenda once it embarked on serious campaigning. In part, this was a belated attempt to compete for the alternativist and new politics electorate the party had yielded to other leftist parties by delaying its launch. It was a sign, too, of the progressive discourse that pervades Danish politics. De Gronne's programme included a social programme some of whose issues were more usually associated with red-green parties - for instance radical measures to address poverty and social deprivation. The progressive content of De Gronne's policy programme was similarly boosted by its radical stance on international issues. De Gronne has always emphasised the moral imperative of non-violence and exhibited a preference for the consensual rather than the confrontational conduct of international relations. The party's roots in the anti-nuclear campaign have continued to place it much closer to a red-green outlook on many of the issues essential to its political identity as a force for change - a position that eventually persuaded the party to throw in its lot with displaced leftists and propel itself even further down the red-green trajectory. From the start, De Gronne endorsed a policy of unilateral disarmament and a positive effort to end the 'artificial' confrontation of the Cold War by foreclosing on both NATO and the Warsaw Pact. These were, of course, hardly controversial issues in Danish politics given the minimalist interpretation by its governments of their international commitments. The Green Party found the issue of European integration even less useful to it in its search for a distinctive political niche. Although De Gronne opposed the EC as an 'exploitative' and 'artificial' entity, dreamt up by bureaucrats and politicians to divide the continent's peoples in its pursuit of atavistic, ecologically damaging and narrow commercial interest, this was hardly a novel stance in Danish politics. Many other parties or factions of parties were equally ill disposed towards 'Brussels'. The Greens did play an active part in the two referenda called in 1992-93 to ratify the Maastricht Treaty of European Union. They were, however, unable to distinguish themselves from other parties better placed to effect the outcome on this issue. The most that can be said for De Gronne's anti-EC stance has been its consistency, and the fact that it has not done the party any particular harm with its target electorate.

Green politics in Denmark amounts to nothing less than a remarkable and by now familiar paradox. This is a society where the electoral ground, and the political discourse which has shaped it, seemed ripe for the success of a Green party. Yet, at the same time, it is a situation where a combination of political ineptness and poor timing saw the Greens yield these apparent advantages to other parties. The persistent legacies of this unsteady start have continued to marginalise the Green Party on the fringes of politics, even though the ecological issues the party seeks to represent have retained a higher salience in public debate without dominating it.[41] The continuing uphill struggle facing De Gronne was illustrated by the events surrounding the 1989 European elections. At a time when even small and previously insignificant Green parties elsewhere in the European Community reaped unexpected and unprecedented electoral rewards, the Danish party failed to put up a single candidate on their own account, and resorted instead to endorsing surrogate greens running on the Anti-Common Market list. This absence of a distinctive Green platform and campaign for a parliamentary assembly where Green politics had a real presence was a failure by any yardstick. It undoubtedly helped to detract from the party's already modest appeal. De Gronne's poor showing (0.8 per cent) in the general election the following year, confirmed the party's weak position[42] - that an independent green politics was alive, if barely so, but at a time when the movement was flourishing in almost every other EC state. The party continued to be overshadowed by the rival 'green appeal' of other parties. In Andersen's judgement, "Green politics is new politics, but new politics in Denmark has been picked up by old politics".[43] It was a belated acknowledgement of this position that persuaded the Greens to broaden their appeal, in an attempt to win back for the party the progressive constituency that currently resided with other parties. The Greens have cooperated since 1989 with former Communists and assorted leftists in a Green Unity List (Enhedaliste de Rod Gronne/Green-Left Unity List) - the obverse in some ways of the strategy of those Portuguese Greens who started life in a political network fronted by the Communist Party. This has echoes, too, of the recent cooperation between Italian Greens and their electoral partners in the Olive Tree alliance. This was, however, a marriage of convenience as much as compatability. Each side had need of the other for different reasons. For the Greens, the ecological issue had lost some of its electoral salience with the settlement of the nuclear issue. Unable to find their own political space on an already crowded political landscape dominated by a left-right cleavage, the Greens required allies. They were attracted, too, by the organisational capacities of their partners, who came from an altogether more disciplined political tradition. These leftists were also in need of allies. The collapse of international Communism, culminating in the symbolic fall of the Berlin wall in 1989, had deprived them of a firm political base or ideological orientation. They were liberated from dogma but cut adrift from a clear political identity. Like many revisionists, they settled for a novel mix of conventional socialist and ecological ideas. The Unity List brought together an unlikely blend of pure greens, hippies, former hardline Marxists and anarchists. Its principal bastion was the densely populated new age commune of Christiana in Copenhagen.

So far, this belated response to persistent political failure has done little to rehabilitate De Gronne as an effective force in national politics. Nothing that has happened in Danish politics in the turbulent years since 1989 has improved the chances for this new red-green alliance. The Green Party remains a largely peripheral force. Concern for ecological values continues to figure in the preferences of the electorate at large, but it by no means enjoys the levels of salience experienced when the anti-nuclear issue was at its height. Ecologism also continues to suffer the same degree of ambivalence amongst Danish public opinion as it does in any other advanced Scandinavian democracy. The central concern of public policy and opinion alike, is to balance economic growth, encourage enterprise and prosperity on one side of the policy equation, with quality of life issues on the other. The onset of recession has reduced the salience of the latter objective, without burying it altogether. Post-material values have been discounted, although by no means entirely displaced. Other issues have risen up the national agenda and in the discourse of Danish politics during this current period. The two dominant and closely linked issues of recent years have been much the same here as those concerns which have pervaded politics elsewhere in Scandinavia. The conflict between the centripetal pull of traditional Nordic insularity, and the centrifugal pressures of globalism with their regional expression as deeper European integration, stands alongside an equally urgent preoccupation throughout the region with fundamentally materialist concerns. Not least, how to make national economies more competitive in the new European and world economic systems; and whether or how far these same economic pressures can be reconciled with the generous Nordic system of welfare and an economic model that has traditionally been heavily dependent on an expansive public sector. The Greens have addressed these critical issues, along with every other Danish party. At the same time, this is an agenda that is not easily accommodated to their post-materialist preferences. And while Danish politics has been turbulent in response to these debates, other parties better ideologically attuned to the anxieties and expectations raised by these issues have dominated national politics. A brief review of the current political landscape serves to illustrate how far removed the Greens remain from the focal point of national politics - a fact that, as such, underlines their limited prospects in the foreseeable future for improving on this situation.

(iv) Prospects for political change

The centre-right Conservative-Liberal coalition that continued in office under Poul Schlueter in 1990, following the logic of its commitment since 1982 to embrace strict fiscal discipline and to cut public expenditure in order to make for a more internationally competitive economy,[44] committed Denmark to deeper European integration. This decision, as much as its failure to curb state spending (still above 60 per cent of GDP after a decade in office), proved to be its undoing, although the government eventually fell from power on another international matter entirely. The question of national identity, raised by the requirement to implement the European Treaty of Union agreed at Maastricht in 1991, was a matter of some concern in a polity where state sovereignty continued to be seen as a positive political value. A deeply divisive debate opened up over the issue of national identity, once the constraints on national sovereignty included in the Maastricht treaty became a matter of political concern. An increasingly febrile debate culminated in a very divisive referendum campaign in 1992, which resulted in a clear vote against the ratification of the Maastricht treaty. The damage done to the government's standing by this rebuff weakened the Prime Minister's personal authority, eventually causing him to resign after a judicial inquiry found that he had misled Parliament in 1987 over an illegal curb on Tamil immigrants. The coalition immediately unravelled and in the resulting power vacuum, Poul Rasmussen, the leader of the Social Democratic Party, pieced together a centre-left alternative that was able, after negotiating important opt outs to the Maastricht Treaty at the Edinburgh European Council in December 1992 - notably on joining the first phase of the proposed European Monetary Union, a full commitment to participate in the Western European Union's mutual defence arrangements, and common policies on home affairs and justice policy - to win a second referendum in 1993 that ostensibly settled the question of Danish political identity.

At the same time, neither Rasmussen's government nor Danish public opinion could afford to ignore the insidious pressures of economic interdependence that were at work in the wider regional and global processes. The results of the 1994 European elections in Denmark - the first opportunity in a national poll since the Maastricht débâcle and the subsequent mid-term change of government, for the electorate to register its verdict - underlined the deep unease with both the present and previous governments' handling of these critical policy issues. Although the Social Democrats paid the usual price of most incumbents in European elections (a vote down to 15.8 per cent from 23.3 per cent previously), the outcome was hardly a ringing endorsement either of their mainstream rivals on the centre-right - who won only modest increases in their votes. The Greens (with a reduction from 9.1 per cent in 1989 to 8.6 per cent - enough only to retain its solitary seat) certainly did not benefit from the widespread inclination of voters to register a protest against the widely perceived complacency of the political establishment. And this, regardless of the fact that the principal campaign issue - Euroscepticism - was indisputably a 'strong' issue for the Greens with their consistent opposition to the EU. Other movements, more ephemeral and even less organised than the Greens, outran them on this issue. The June Movement (*Junibevaegelsen*) and the People's Movement Against the EU (FB) took a remarkable 25.3 per cent between them on an increased turnout (52.2 per cent), and won 3 of the 16 available seats. The result showed a nation as divided as ever over its national identity and future direction. In these circumstances, post-materialist issues were bound to be heavily discounted, and the Green Party with them.

At the same time as public opinion was expressing its deep anxieties about the European project, the government was obliged to confront the rising economic costs of Denmark's version of the Nordic welfare state. The whole question of economic futures dominated the 1994 general election. The Social Democrats were caught in an uncomfortable pincer. The non-ideologism of a Social Democratic party well versed in the exigencies of government had persuaded them that the old welfare model now placed an unbearable burden on the public purse - with the highest levels of taxation (49 per cent of GDP) in the OECD. On the other hand, the party's electoral fortunes continued to depend on support from its traditional blue collar base that remained, in turn, heavily reliant on various expressions of welfarism - state transfer payments, high expectations for a fully state funded health service, the provision of care for the elderly, public education - and just as much on public sector employment in a society where government expenditure accounted for 64 per cent of GDP. The Social Democrats had little room for manoeuvre, given that 44 per cent of the population - many of them natural Social Democrat supporters - depended on some form of transfer payment or state employment. They promised a modest retrenchment, but not quite enough to satisfy the markets.[45] The red-green Unity list was forced by events to move onto the agenda dictated by these public anxieties. Its campaign gave as much prominence to the 'Europe' and 'welfare' questions as did those of the mainstream parties. Overt ecological themes did figure in the Greens' campaign, but the Unity List's very modest vote (3.1 per cent and 6 seats) owed more to its appeal as a vehicle for leftist anti-Europeans who wished to defend the welfare state - hardly a large constituency. The fact that the Unity List was obliged to resort to negative campaigning was a measure of its continuing marginal status in national politics. The List's distinctive theme in 1994 was essentially negative from the start, reflected in its 'Vote for the Anti's' slogan. It stood against the establishment options - anti-Europe, opposition to privatisation, the bridging of the Onesund, to NATO and much else - rather than 'for' ecologism. The left Socialist People's Party (Socialistik Folkparti - SF) - which also exhibited some ecological tendencies - continued to win the votes of those 'greens' who preferred a more positive vision of ecologism. To this extent, the Green Party's past continues to haunt it. The Greens were unable to take advantage - a familiar and recurrent coda in Green politics here - of the modest opportunity to exert a degree of influence over the formation of the next government that this volatile electoral mood presented.

It seemed that the excessive fragmentation of Danish party politics - encouraged by a modest electoral threshold of only 2 per cent - might inflate the significance of the smaller leftist parties in the uncertain aftermath of the 1994 election. With a combined vote of 10.4 per cent - barely up on the 10 per cent it won in 1990, but yielding a useful bloc in a hung parliament dominated by the Social Democrats (34.6 per cent and 62 seats, but some way short of a governing majority) - the ecological left and their leftist allies seemed about to exert an unprecedented degree of parliamentary influence. In the event, the ideological dynamics of Danish politics worked against them, and has continued to marginalise the Green left ever since. The Social Democrats were insistent from the outset of the election campaign that they would neither include the far left in any likely coalition government - preferring instead to govern as a minority, a quite normal occurrence here - nor that would they yield these radicals any undue influence over policy. They had no intention of being held to ransom by irresponsible parties likely to tie their hands in government, and to bloc any necessary policy measures offensive to their utopian preferences. Political culture worked in favour of this resistance. The Danes do not perceive hung parliaments as the sign of political crisis that they are in more adversarial party systems. On the contrary, the Danish system makes a virtue out of its excessive pluralism. The system works on deals struck between parties of different ideological persuasions, as long as they share some underlying precepts about the purpose of government as the basis of their political bargain. The incoming Prime Minister Rasmussen was not inclined to bargain a share of power for unsustainable policies. As he saw the situation, "we do not fear a minority government. These are often the case in Denmark and we have become good political craftsmen. We can handle the situation".[46] No single party has enjoyed an overall parliamentary majority since 1914, and the outgoing administration had been the first since 1971 to govern with the 'luxury' of a majority over the combined opposition parties. All of the signs pointed to the exclusion of the radicals and the installation of a coalition drawn from the political mainstream. Rasmussen did, nevertheless, include the leftists and the Greens in the usual wide-ranging consultations that precede coalition formation. Not, however, because of their green or post-material credentials, but rather because they represented part of the anti-EU vote, and he wanted to establish "the broadest possible support" for Denmark's national negotiating position at the forthcoming IGC of the EU.

After protracted negotiations, Rasmussen assembled much the same centre-left coalition as the outgoing one - minus the Christian People's Party which had failed to cross the parliamentary threshold. Although he needed - and received - the support of the leftist parties in his 'election' to the premiership, he made it clear from the outset that he intended to govern according to the lights of a modest reform programme - "A Common Future" - based on a conventional growth strategy negotiated with his two coalition partners (Radikal Venestre - the Radical Liberal Party and Centrum Demokrateme - the Centre Democratic Party). This programme sought to strike a fine balance between a strong underlying economy (with relatively low inflation, interest rates and firm economic growth), and some measures to cure unemployment. While the new government refused to accommodate the centre-right opposition's preference for the usual package of stricter fiscal discipline, welfare cuts, more privatisation, and so forth, in order to reduce the budget deficit, it did resist even more firmly, the green-left's demands that fiscal policy be relaxed altogether, in order to increase the quality of welfare and finance public sector (and socially useful, ecologically sound) job creation.[47] Neither the Green left nor the Left Socialists managed to exert any real leverage over either the composition of the new government or its policy programme. The radical parties' hands were, in effect, tied. The alternative to endorsing a centre-left coalition was the even less palatable option for the left, of a centre-right government. One much less enthusiastic about the environment, and even keener than the incumbents to retrench on welfare and to privatise the extensive public sector. The most the Green left managed to extract from the government, as part of Rasmussen's consensus strategy, were some vague and largely worthless promises - to bear the environmental impact of policy making 'in mind'. The Greens may have reassured themselves, as they considered this one sided 'deal', that the centre-left had already acquired some modest 'green' credentials during its previous administration. Its 1994 budget, for instance, had set up a job rotation scheme to encourage paid sabbaticals for studying and child care. The 1995 budget likewise included new measures for green taxes, a proposal to prepare 'green' national accounts, to extend wider powers to environmental audits, and to coordinate all government policy through the Environment Department.[48]

This limited 'package' of proposals, nevertheless, amounted to little more than a token - the lipservice paid by a government fully aware of the volatility of the national political mood, and its acknowledgement of the need to court any constituency that might be won over to its brand of progressive pragmatism as it confronts some very difficult choices. These 'eco-measures' were in no sense a political trade off with the green left, or even an acknowledgement of the government's minority status. For one thing, this green constituency continues to extend well beyond the Green Party, to include voters of almost all of the centre-left parties. Even the Radical Liberals, who are coalition members, draw heavily on 'green' votes. Modest ecological measures here reflect, at most, a modest greening of politics - the pursuit of an environmentally managed society which finds broad national endorsement - rather than any calculated attempt to buy short term parliamentary support. The governments' efforts to stay in office depend far more on securing the support base of its own parties, or even the acquiescence of the main opposition parties, as underlined by its prudent budgetary philosophy,[49] than it does on reaching out to what are essentially fringe parties. As things currently stand, the radical realignment of Danish left wing politics is far from being a central priority of the dominant Social Democratic party. The Prime Minister's post-election statement, that "there is no room for proposals which increase net spending or decrease net state income", and that "to use money in one area, corresponding savings must be made in another area", was clearly designed to build a stable consensus that reflected the government's continued dependence on the parties of the centre-right who continue to hold the parliamentary balance of power, than it was motivated by any prospect of realigning the left.[50] This essentially conservative consensus was eventually enshrined in a budget accord which projected a cut in the budget deficit, promised cutbacks in all manner of social benefits - including the job rotation programme, a measure that angered the green left - and a semi-privatisation scheme for national rail and postal services.[51] This package, which has set the tone for public policy for the foreseeable future, received overwhelming cross-party support in the Folketing. It was only opposed, for entirely different reasons, by the populist and far right Fremkridtspartiet (Progress Party) and the far left and Green parties. The fact that the most effective opposition to these relatively modest welfare cuts came from within the Social Democratic Party, and the fact too that the debate over Denmark's economic future continues to be couched primarily in the language of social welfare rather than ecological politics - the lexicon of the old rather than the new politics - says much about the continuing political weakness of political ecology in Danish party politics.

The Rasmussen coalition, as so often with governments in this pluralistic polity, has failed to satisfy the competing constituencies that stand behind it. Although the government worked hard with the opposition Conservatives, who cooperated with it in parliament to ensure the passage of a budget designed to trim public spending, it failed to satisfy an increasingly restive and sceptical business lobby - one that demanded a more positive commitment to European integration as the only feasible source of balanced economic growth, and a continued input into the rules that frame the operations of an increasingly interdependent regional economy. Public opinion, too, has moved more in favour of the EU, with the accession of Finland and Sweden in 1995 and the prospect of a Nordic bloc pursuing mutual sub-regional interests within the Community's decision making councils. There were signs from the centre-right camp, and particularly the Liberal Party, that even participation in the revived scheme for monetary union and the Union's defence arm, the WEU (in which Denmark only had observer status), was preferable to the self imposed exclusion adopted as a necessary compromise to ensure the passage of the diluted EU treaty in the second referendum in 1993. The prospect of a third referendum to implement the proposals for closer integration underway in the IGC process of 1996-1997, promises to re-open the barely healed wounds on this controversial and politically damaging question.[52] The Social Democratic government faced deep internal dissent over both the European issue and their budgetary proposals to cutback welfare spending by, as Rasmussen put it, finding "new ways of doing things",[53] in order to reduce the social costs that continue to threaten economic competitiveness.[54] Political volatility is likely to be a persistent feature of national politics. The Greens, or for that matter their far left election partners, are unlikely, however, to be the principal beneficiaries.

The politics of Denmark - and the place of the Greens in it - in many ways mirrors the situation in Norway and, to an extent, Sweden. A paradox is clear in each case. On the one hand, these are progressive societies with a widespread public concern about the environment and the need to balance quality of life issues with material prosperity. The salience of ecological issues has, nevertheless, to be put into its appropriate perspective in the Danish situation. The success of the green lobby in accommodating the green cause to the public mood means there are green votes to be won by almost any party. This is a country where the green constituency - whether dark green or red- green - has by no means been confined only to Green parties. There is an intense competition for the green vote between the mainstream parties spread across the conventional left-right spectrum, and distinctive ecological parties. This is a competition that has recently seen the Greens squeezed, on occasions almost to oblivion, when the current shift in the political discourse - mirrored in parallel debates on national identity, regional integration, the politics of welfare and the cumulative global pressures on commercial competitiveness and the affordability of welfare - have marooned the Green Party some way from the political centre of gravity represented by the new discourse on the old politics issues. Green politics is by no means obsolescent. At the same time, it remains marginalised. Its preferred agendas are far removed from the prevailing concerns of Danish national politics as it is presently conducted. In these circumstances the Greens have to confront choices as unpalatable to them as to any other radical party for whom the political times are out of joint. At least, it does if it prefers political survival to ideological isolation. Whether this is a temporary condition, or whether and in what ways, the Greens might harness these rising uncertainties to their own advantage remains to be seen. In some ways the Greens might anticipate the same prospects for participating in a radical realignment as green parties in other advanced democratic societies undergoing the very same socio-economic changes. Yet in other ways, the Danish Greens remain less well placed, let alone equipped, to cash in on these prospects than their sister parties. Although they have overcome their own resistance to working with other eclectic radicalisms in pursuit of a progressive agenda, the legacy of those wasted early years continues to haunt them and to disperse what might have been a far more substantial Green party vote drawn from those other parties whose essential priorities remain wedded to the agenda of the old rather than the new politics.

The failure of the Greens here and in neighbouring Norway, to make the best of an otherwise favourable cultural climate does, however, have about it a degree of exceptionalism. A case not of too little to say about the deep national dilemmas facing these far northern countries, but of parties too late arriving on the scene. Too late, that is, to claim the political territory more surely appropriated elsewhere by Green parties, but ceded here to other radical (and not so radical) parties. If the Danish Greens are to survive as a viable force in national politics, they will have to address these issues, and sooner rather than later. They have made a start by accommodating radical and red-green elements previously excluded from the party's ranks. This is almost certainly their only available option. Given the political lie of the land, the Greens will need to perfect the art of compromise that is indispensable for exercising political influence in this polity. The Greens must begin to build bridges to those groups on the centre-left who share some of their concerns for the future of the global commons. The relative absence in this movement of any rigid red-green dogma should facilitate this process, although ideological resistance in the movement to playing the 'sordid' game of politics, may also hinder it. A residual anti-partyism - that is, continued resistance to a disciplined and pragmatic approach to political organisation, let alone to the idea of making 'squalid' bargains with other parties, implying a dilution of first principles - remains as a heavy liability, even in a party that continues to struggle to make its mark in national politics. This is a legacy that presents abiding obstacles to the sort of political realism required even by radical parties in the contemporary multi-party politics of Europe's advanced democracies. To this extent, the Green Party holds its fate in its own hands. At least it does for the immediate future. Whether the other mainstream parties will be receptive to - or will at some stage need to reach out to the Greens and their leftist allies - is another question entirely. The recent experience of coalition making provides equivocal evidence on this score. If the Green Party does manage to consolidate its 'natural' constituency - or a larger proportion of it than hitherto - under its own banner, there is no doubt that the party's bargaining stock would rise accordingly. But 'if' is, of course, an altogether more contingent, let alone elusive, moment than 'when'.

3. Norway

(i) Green roots

The Green Party of Norway (Miljopartiet De Gronne) was a latecomer to national politics, and by comparison with ecology parties elsewhere has been the least successful. It shares some of the handicaps of the Danish Greens discussed above. There are distinct parallels between the situation of Green party politics in Denmark and Norway. Not least the same paradox of widespread public concern for environmental matters, alongside a reluctance to express this as support for a distinctive Green political party. There was no participation by a Green party in Norwegian national elections until 1989. Ecologists had participated in local elections in 1987, but in only two of the country's 19 provinces (taking 0.4 per cent of the vote in Oslo and 0.8 per cent in Akershus). The new party's performance was hardly an electoral breakthrough![55] In the years since its appearance, the party has failed to make even a modest impression on national politics. To some extent this is hardly surprising. The Norwegian political agenda has recently become dominated by the same critical issues as those which are current elsewhere in Scandinavia; especially the question of national identity - the delicate relationship between an entrenched sense of nationhood and the commitment to political independence and continued control over national policy that accompanies this. Together with the anxieties raised by the strong centrifugal global pressures that are pushing all of Europe's small and medium sized nation states into new forms of regional interdependence. Norway has responded to these transnational pressures with a surprising insouciance. The country has now rejected, after deeply divisive referenda, the opportunity to join the European Union on two separate occasions, in 1972 and 1994. In the circumstances, post-materialist concerns tend to be replaced by the preoccupation with a different concept of political 'futures'.

Although the debate over how Norway could best orientate itself in a rapidly changing world order did touch on a general concern to maintain the country's high environmental standards, this issue was far from being the central theme in this discourse. Nor was the Green Party, when it eventually formed, the only organisation representing the environmental dimensions. The delay in establishing a Green party allowed other organisations and parties to occupy the territory ahead of it. When the Green Party was launched in 1988, it faced two distinct handicaps. In the first place, the Miljopartiet De Gronne arrived on the political scene only to find that other and better established parties had already incorporated environmental concerns into their own agendas. The front runner here was the Liberal Party, which had broken up in the aftermath of the divisive referendum on EC membership in 1973, and used the environment issue as a rallying cry for rebuilding the party on a platform which had electoral appeal beyond the class and regional cleavages that have traditionally shaped Norway's patterns of political partisanship. Not that this strategy was particularly successful. At a time when the environmentalism was less crowded by rival issues, the Liberals failed to give the issue any political resonance. The Socialist Left Party, which also raised the green standard, alongside other progressive concerns, enjoyed rather more political success with it; but only because it avoided the Liberals' error of becoming identified with only one issue of limited electoral salience, and managed to tie ecology into a broader radical programme.

The Miljopartiet suffered another severe handicap. The environment can never be an 'outdated' issue. But it is one whose electoral salience is affected by the usual cycle of political fashion and the pressing concerns of economic and other forms of primordial security, that have a more immediate impact on party support and electoral competition. The Green Party emerged at a time when Norway's political agenda was already dominated by potent issues that loomed much larger in the political imagination than the environment per se. Denied the favourable following wind that provided many other European Green parties with their early political momentum, the Norwegian Greens' arrival on the national scene coincided with the displacement of the ecology issue by more immediate and essentially materialist issues. The intense debate that raged in the country during the early 1990s over its economic orientation, the future of the welfare state, and its place in Europe, all severely disadvantaged a party whose primary raison d'être was an issue only remotely connected in the public mind with the imminent public concerns about commercial success, employment prospects, living standards and the welfare issue. To an extent, the Greens were also disadvantaged by the fact that the political establishment had already taken the environment issue seriously and enacted extensive 'green' legislation. Environmentalism was widely acknowledged as a public good. Unlike many of Europe's more heavily industrialised countries, there was little deep or instinctive resistance here to protecting habitat or amenity - and only a minimal concentration of industrial or urban pollution. The absence, too, of any strong social movement campaigning against nuclear power, or of notable battles over local single issue campaigns, denied the green movement the sort of *cause célèbre* status that had helped to launch Green parties elsewhere.

The environment issue had only briefly encouraged social movement politics, as when the development of the hydro-electricity industry raised the political tempo in the 1970s. A mass protest and 'sit down' was launched against the installation of a new hydro-electric dam that threatened some spectacular waterfalls at Mardola, a place of considerable natural beauty in North West Norway. The protest attracted interest from youthful rebels seeking a cause. It was led by prominent academics who employed the fashionable Gandhian tactic of *satyagraha* - a refusal to accept the power of authority by means of direct action and overt confrontation. It would be misleading to exaggerate the radical angst that motivated this cause. At the same time, it exhibited a trendy cachet, and it did draw some of its vital political energy from rebels in search of a suitable cause. The new leftist and alternativist modus vivendi to be found in anti-nuclear protests elsewhere in Europe were less important in this movement than an abiding concern to preserve a natural habitat with an outstanding amenity value. The protest against the building of dams and the sacrificing of natural beauty took on a potency that sustained Norway's ecology movement, much as the anti-nuclear issue did elsewhere. The movement acquired a pure green ideological resonance; a refusal, in essence, to accept the prevailing governmental ethos - subscribed to by all the mainstream parties of both left and right - that economic growth and industrialism must take precedence over the considerations of habitat.

There were periodic demonstrations over the issue; notably a much publicised protest in 1980 over the construction of the Alta dam in the remote region of Finnmark. In spite of some conveniently exaggerated fears by the political establishment, that such outbreaks of direct action and protest politics posed a threat to the country's democratic stability,[56] these dam protests were neither extensive enough or sufficiently well organised to become the platform for either a radical new left politics nor a viable Green party. The low political salience of the environment issue and the unpromising prospects for political ecologism, might be summarized as an enigma - the high public value attributed to habitat and quality of life, which evoked a positive response from political elites, thereby diminishing both the incentive and the political potential for an independent Green party. One observer of these trends has identified four closely connected and mutually reinforcing factors at work here; the minimal exposure to serious environmental hazards or accidents in this spacious northern country, without heavy concentrations of industry dependent on antiquated technologies; an eco-system (both habitat and amenity) widely regarded with pride and cherished as a national asset, to be safeguarded as an important national resource; low energy needs in a small country with only small pockets of concentrated industry; and the absence as a catalyst of green militancy of nuclear power or the hazards associated with it, in a country rich in 'clean energy' - the immense potential of hydro-electric and with bountiful oil reserves available, and conveniently out of sight, in the North Sea.[57] In so far as Norway did experience environmental problems (most notably air borne acid rain that affected the country's lakes and rivers and damaged fish stocks and forests), these were widely perceived of as having external origins - a perception which helped to reinforce in the public mind resistance to 'unnecessary' entanglements with 'careless' economic organisations such as the European Community.

In the event, the dam protests had the opposite effect of depoliticising the environment issue in so far as they restricted it to an eco-movement or lobby without a firm political base or electoral potential. The political establishment's response also played its part in containing the movement, by closing down any political space that might have been available to an independent Green party. The Liberals - in search of a new raison d'être after their 1973 referendum débâcle - and the Socialist Left party (Socialistisk Venstreparti (SV)) founded in 1975 - took vacant possession of the ecology issue and adapted it to meet their own particular political requirements and ideological ends.[58] The Liberals, after their re-launch in 1973, became, in effect, Norway's first Green party. The pure ecologists undoubtedly missed a promising opportunity in a political system and opportunity structure that is far from discouraging to new or small parties. The fluidity of the relatively open political system did not present the sort of obstacles that were faced by many Green parties elsewhere. It is not especially difficult to launch new parties in Norway. Norway was the first Nordic country to abandon the region's traditional five party model.[59] The open electoral system, a PR list system based on 20 multi-member constituencies elected according to the modified Sainte-Lague formula that favours smaller parties, and with a complex 'districting' arrangement whereby 8 national seats are added to ensure a greater degree of proportionality, favours multi-party competition. As a consequence, up to 15 parties compete in national elections with a comparatively large number (up to 7) frequently securing representation in the Storting. Moreover, the country's pattern of multi-dimensional social cleavages, and the regional distribution of Storting seats, positively encourages quite small parties to secure an electoral niche. At the same time, there are clearly some abiding rules to be observed here. Any party that seeks to establish a political presence has to demarcate and take possession of its critical issue, before other parties occupy its territory.

The Norwegian Green movement failed to do this. It continued to prefer local direct action campaigns to formal political organisation, and even failed to mark out ecology as its distinctive niche, allowing other parties on to its ideological ground. Some of the mainstream parties, aware of the political salience of the issue, included environmentalism in their party programmes.[60] Environmental protection was assimilated as readily and as early into Norway's mainstream political discourse as it was anywhere in western Europe.[61] The issue was diffused throughout all of the political parties and the electorate at large. The environment was not identified as a special niche issue reserved to a discrete Green party with its own distinctive constituency. This fact illustrates both the success and the failure of environmental politics in Norway. Public opinion has long been favourable to positive measures to safeguard the environment, a fact that was readily acknowledged by the mainstream parties - even by those committed to conventional models of economic growth and industrial development. Survey data, however, continues to endorse the fact as one commentator sees it, "that the Norwegian public seems to be less inclined to support post-materialist values than the publics in other Nordic countries. This also applies to the relative ranking given to environmental protection. Norway is on a par with those countries which are relatively low with respect to the prevalence of post-materialist values".[62] In so far as the issue did possess even modest political potential, other parties appropriated the issue long before the Green Party arrived on the scene. At the same time, this strategy closed off a route to Green Party formation that had been successfully followed elsewhere - whereby establishment indifference encouraged the mobilisation of a small but distinct green constituency. After a Green Party was formed here, the diffusion of the issue onto the conventional political agenda has made it all the more difficult for the Miljopartiet De Gronne to compete for the 'green' vote.[63] The Liberals had already acquired the ideological freehold on environmentalism, and by no means merely as a cosmetic or secondary issue, alongside the usual agenda of a conventional 'system' party. In the intensely competitive and crowded market place for ideas in Norway's multi-dimensional polity, the Liberals managed - more successfully than any other party - to become identified as pure green ecologists. The Socialist Left Party ran the Liberals close on this issue; and with the additional advantage of appealing to a small but highly politicised red-green constituency. They exhibited a brand of ecologism that synthesised the usual leftist and populist causes - anti-capitalism, opposition to Norway's bipartisan foreign policy including NATO membership and the endorsement of its nuclear shield, and a progressive social agenda - with a distinctively radical ecologism.[64]

(ii)   Party formation

The political potency of the ecology issue fluctuated in response to events. A relatively active interest in environmental causes - notably the 'dams' protests - in the late seventies, had been replaced by the mid eighties with issues that had more resonance with the materialist and productionist agenda of the mainstream parties. Most particularly, a rising concern about the viability, at a time of a severe economic downturn, of the country's generously funded welfare state commitments. When the grassroots ecology movement eventually decided, during the course of the eighties, to circumvent what it saw as these ecologists manqué, and put the green case directly to the electorate - encouraged in particular by the public concern that followed the fallout from Chernobyl - its chances of success were bound to be minimal.[65] The electoral costs of the delay in forming an independent Green party became apparent in the first election the Greens contested. The additional competition for a modest constituency fragmented the Green vote. Neither the Green Party nor those other parties that flagged the issue, performed well. This came as a surprise to the ecology movement. The polling evidence had indicated a different outcome. It suggested that the environment issue had regained much of its earlier salience after a spate of environmental scares - including an invasion of seals in both the north and south of the country, and in 1988 a serious surfeit of coastal algae. The issue continued, on the contrary, to rank as a secondary concern - trailing welfare provision and related issues - in the electorate's order of priorities.

This inconsistency between attitudes and electoral behaviour, apparent in many other advanced societies, can be explained by the difference between the 'hard' or primary issues that determine political choices, and those ephemeral, or self indulgent preferences that might be better accommodated once the primordial matters of material security have been resolved. The spate of ecological 'crises' failed to turn genuine concern with quality of life issues into an immediate priority that ranked with the altogether more urgent problems facing the electorate. The environment issue was, in effect, the victim here as elsewhere of a cyclical process. A process in which every public issue, and especially those secondary matters whose salience fluctuates in response to fashion or events, enjoys only a limited interest span with the public, whose political motivations are primarily driven by material concerns. These second order issues more easily reach a saturation point, unless their political profile is raised by notable events that reinforce their sense of urgency. For, as Aardal has identified the Greens' dilemma, "in order to maintain public interest, a problem must be dramatic and exciting". The environment issue was thus confronted in Norway, as it was elsewhere, by two related problems. Modern political agendas consist of first and second ranked issues. A combination of acute self interest does coexist with strong moral preferences. These represent the basic and optimum preferences of most electors. These are by no means mutually exclusive concerns. They may coexist, uneasily and without any ideological consistency or coherence. Until or unless, that is, they are brought into stark conflict in the minds of electors confronted by dilemmas and hard choices over resource shortages, or faced with specific crises. In these circumstances, moral indulgence often come a poor second to the utilitarian and instrumental considerations of self interest. Aardal has observed, of this tendency to discount ecologism's preference to give a higher priority to long term futures over short term considerations of self interest, that it is "one thing to recognise that environmental problems are important. It is quite another to change traditional political values and goals in order to improve the environment and prevent environmental disaster".[66]

(iii)   Political developments

The disparity between a widespread public concern for the environment, and an equally apparent reluctance to direct scarce economic resources to it, or to undergo privations by changing materialist priorities to accommodate it, was as much a feature of the 'green paradox' in Norway, as indeed it has been in many other advanced and materially comfortable societies. This reticence to put ideals before interests explains much about the failure of the Miljopartiet De Gronne to consolidate a distinctive electoral niche in this environmentally aware society. There has been a marked disparity in Norway between a consistent expression of concern with 'the environment', and the shortfall in support for political parties calling for the sort of sacrifices - reduced living standards or resource conservation - required, according to the green canon, to bring about a notable shift towards an ecologically sustainable economy. The prevalence of these persistent concerns with materialism over post-materialism, has been the central theme of Norwegian politics during most of the recent past. A glance at the map goes some way to explaining why material issues have dominated Norway's political discourse. Most of the issues which prevail on the national issue agenda stem directly from persistent concerns with political identity in a rapidly changing world. Stein Rokkan's model of the Norwegian polity identified spatial factors as a persistent influence which continue to shape the electorate's political preoccupations. They provide the key to understanding the direction of national politics.[67] An enduring belief in the virtues of standing alone confronts a modernist agenda that puts the case for joining the European mainstream, if the country is to continue to prosper. Both sides of this debate put their respective cases essentially in terms of material costs and benefits. On one side, a mixture of pride in special national attributes - open government, high levels of welfare, and political independence - in contrast to the amorphous, centralising bureaucracy of 'Brussels'. The case here was underpinned by the availability of abundant natural resources - oil and natural gas in particular.[68] The 'realists', meanwhile, aware of the centripetal, globalising forces at work in contemporary political economy, have continued to argue the very opposite of this 'splendid isolation' scenario - and to maintain that myopia about its national options is a luxury that the country can no longer afford. As they see it, remoteness is not a choice for Norway, and that the longer this fact is denied the more painful the adjustments to reality will be in the medium and longer term.

This discourse lay at the heart of the recent campaign over EU membership. What is clear from these events is the secondary importance of other issues. The environment has figured in this debate, but only in a derivative sense. A concern for the future of the national environment surfaced in the EU campaign as a minor coda in the symphony of arguments brought to bear by protagonists on either side of the critical question that divided the country. The 'yes' side in the recent EU referendum argued, amongst other things, for an approach to environmental protection based on the recognition that pollution respects no frontiers; and that the problem can be better tackled on a regional rather than a national basis. The Greens, however, did not endorse this interdependent outlook, and sided instead with those groups who used this issue merely as a substitute for altogether narrower and atavistic concerns. The Green Party has thus found itself in some strange political company on this issue. The anti-EU camp brought together a motley of rural groups from the remote northern regions who depended on natural resources (fishing, forestry and farming communities) for their livelihoods; and those urban groups (especially in greater Oslo, where one third of the country's population resides)[69] who resisted the idea of foreign entanglements for a mixture of instrumental and ideological reasons.[70] The Greens were active in the 'no' camp and gave what they saw as a progressive gloss to the nationalist case, by highlighting the EU's 'weak defence' of the environment - from contaminated drinking water to the allowance of growth hormones in animal husbandry. But ecologism was never more than a minor theme in the case against the EU, and the Green Party was only a small voice in the general populist clamour. The running here was made - and far more effectively - by other parties. Most notably by the agrarian Centre Party, the Socialist Left and even by an anti-EU faction within the Labour Party itself - all parties far removed on the ideological spectrum from the Greens.[71] The Green Party did little to extend its narrow support base by hitching the environment issue to this negative side of what was primarily a materialist agenda.

(iv) Prospects for political change

The environmental issue continues to be an issue of limited political salience in a deeply divisive debate over national identity and the best way to ensure economic and strategic security. Ecologism remains heavily discounted by other more prevalent issues. This is very much the legacy of a party that came late into the electoral lists. Other parties less obviously committed to ecologism, and searching for convenient issues to restore their own flagging political fortunes in the face of the dealignments that invariably occur in the politics of advanced societies, put themselves in the market for green votes. The emergence of a debate over national identity continued to marginalise the relevance and appeal of the Green Party, even when it did emerge. The Greens have had to compete on these unfavourable terms and have showed little sign of breaking the stranglehold of the 'old' politics over the 'new' politics they exist to advance. The judgement of one observer, that "despite expectations of an emerging 'New Environmental Paradigm' transcending political cleavages, the Norwegian experience shows that environmental awareness can to a large extent be assimilated into the political system", remains appropriate in these circumstances.[72] But this is true here in spite of rather than because of the Green Party's efforts. Not that any of the ecologists manqué who beat the Greens to the electoral draw on this issue have shown any signs of being much better able to improve the standing of the environment on the national political agenda.

This was illustrated by the way the Liberals, who share a positive concern for environmentalism and acquired credibility at the 1985 election as exponents of an entirely radical or alternative politics with the small new politics constituency by endorsing the Labour Party's (Det Norske Arbederparti - DNA) radical prospectus, squandered that reputation after the 1989 poll when it changed sides and backed a 'bourgeois' coalition. The Socialistik Venstreparti (SV - Socialist Left) which also incorporates ecologism into its eclectic leftist programme, has fared rather better because of its defence of the welfare state and its opposition to privatisation. These essentially materialist concerns, rather than ecologism per se, remain the principal reasons for the SV's increased support. The logistics of Norwegian politics have continued to ensure the predominance of 'old' over 'new' politics, even amongst the radical constituency of this party. This calculus was the main reason why the SV chose to endorse the minority social democratic administration of Gro Harlem Brundtland, along with the rural based Centre Party (Senterpartiet), rather than allow a centre-right government dominated by the Conservative (Hoyve) to take power. Realignment based on a new politics, let alone an ecological agenda, has hardly figured in these political calculations. If Green politics has any role to play in the continuing debate on Norwegian futures, it will almost certainly not be represented by the Miljopartiet de Gronne, but rather by the leverage exerted on any future government by the Socialist Left which took 7.9 per cent of the national vote in the 1993 elections - or by the Liberals, whose steady if modest support (6.3 per cent in 1993) makes it likely that they will figure in future coalitional arrangements. The Green Party, meanwhile, polled a mere 0.1 per cent, took barely 3,000 votes, and won no seats in an electoral system that is inordinately receptive to even fractional parties - requiring only 0.67 per cent of the national turnout to qualify for parliamentary representation. This is a derisory vote which suggests that the Green Party has fallen between two stools. The Greens are simply unable to win any credit from mainstream voters for weighing in on the side of national interests in the Europe debate - where other parties can always play the retrenchment card and easily outbid it. Nor are the Greens able to win over the wider green constituency that presently inhabits the electorate of other minor leftist parties. In these circumstances, the Green Party, per se, will continue to be a marginal actor and, with only a handful of local councillors to its credit, continues to fall some way short of any claim to the status of a national party compared with the Green parties of neighbouring Sweden or Finland.

In the aftermath of the 1995 referendum on EU membership there are few encouraging signs for the Greens. The irresistible impact of regional integration and global interdependence requires all serious political movements to engage with, rather than to retreat from, this critical issue. Radical movements with something positive to contribute to this debate might be expected by contemporary electorates to have something constructive to say about the challenges and opportunities of encroaching interdependence; to respond critically to its worst socio-economic or ecological excesses and its positive incentives to restructure the political economy of nation statehood, rather than to simply offer outdated platitudes, or to engage in the negative politics of denial. Some Green parties have taken up this intellectual and political challenge. They have begun to offer a critique of the current phase of European integration. And in the process to suggest alternative and more equitable ways of organising the regional project, rather than settling for the autarchy of 'fortress-Europe'. The Norwegian Greens have not been amongst their number. Instead, the Miljopartiet de Gronne have taken up a stance on the EU debate that owes as much to traditional instincts as to a modern outlook based on progressive values. The Greens reflect a deeply conservative mood here - one that the prominent pro-Europe campaigner, Roy Jacobsen, identified as a legacy shaped by Ibsen's drama and motivated by romantic delusion and "self inflation".[73] It looks backwards rather than forwards. To this extent, the Greens' critics believe it has little by way of impetus to offer to the ecology cause the party exists to further. The Environment Minister, Thorbyn Bernstein, censured the Greens' almost stubborn lack of vision here with an observation that is altogether more in keeping with the facts of the case, when he said that "it is ridiculous to pretend that we can defend our environment outside of the EU" given that 90 per cent of Norwegian pollution originates there. Moreover, that Norway "must be in the EU to get effective action to tackle cross-border pollution".[74] It can be seen, even on this issue, just how much 'old' rather than 'new' politics still pervades Norway's political agenda.[75] It is the politics of national identity - the deeply divisive split between modernisers (both on the mainstream left and right) and assorted traditionalists - with its inherently materialistic concerns with security and welfare issues, rather than any radical, post-materialist agenda, that continues to dominate Norwegian politics. There are few signs from recent events that this situation is likely to change for the foreseeable future.

4.   Sweden

(i)   Green roots

In contrast to its near neighbours in Scandinavia, Sweden is a progressive society where both the political elites and public opinion came to regard environmental management as a matter of priority, almost as soon as the issue began to appear on the international agenda from the late 1960s.[76] Sweden, after all, was the place where the current fashion for ecological navel gazing had begun, with the occasion of the 1972 Stockholm international conference on the environment. The Swedish Green Party - Miljopartiet de grona - was founded in September 1981 from an amalgam of provincial green and local alternative groups. Ecology groups had already secured a small base of electoral support throughout the seventies. Following a pattern already visible elsewhere in Europe, these disparate groups had rallied in opposition to the controversial use of nuclear energy. There was widespread aversion to the way this issue had been dealt with by Sweden's political establishment. The critical catalyst here was the considerable disappointment amongst its erstwhile supporters with the way the Centre Party had compromised its staunch opposition to nuclear power while it was in government from 1976 to 1978.[77] The nuclear issue sparked an intense ethical debate that gave ecological questions much wider currency and superimposed a quality of life dimension on the conventional productionist agenda of national politics.[78]

Until that moment, Swedish politics had conformed to the conventional pattern of socio-economic and class-based cleavages that prevailed in other advanced industrial democracies - although its party politics were complicated by the existence of 5 major parties and 1 minor party (the Communists) brought about by its proportional electoral system.[79] This system - a variant of the modified Sainte-Lague system - also encouraged further electoral fragmentation favourable to minor parties; by reserving 39 of the Riksdag's 310 seats for redistribution amongst parties making the relatively low national threshold of 4 per cent of the national vote and 12 per cent in any one the 28 electoral constituencies - and by operating a 'tier formula' whereby a lower tier of 26 geographical constituencies returns 310 of the 349 deputies, with 39 seats held back for allocation in the higher or second tier, and distributed in a way that facilitates a higher proportionality quotient, subject to the 4 per cent threshold.

This structural incentive to minor parties was belied by the continuing dominance of the Social Democratic Party in the party system. Political sociology and history rather than the liberality of the electoral rules per se, determined the pattern and outcome of party competition.[80] A novel configuration of an enlightened society, a nonaligned state, and a high spending welfare democracy,[81] together with entrenched divisions within the centre-right opposition, had ensured the Social Democrats' pivotal role as the normal party of government from the Great Depression in the nineteen twenties until the mid seventies.[82] Even this remarkable dominance suffered the unusual strains that faced political elites everywhere during the late nineteen sixties and early seventies - and for much the same reasons, as altogether new agendas, compounded by the usual discontents of established socio-economic groups, impacted on the political status quo. In Sweden this mood for change drew on the same discontents apparent throughout western Europe. The Keynesian and social welfare consensus - designated here as 'the Swedish model' - suffered from the inflationary pressure of OPEC's unilateral hike in energy prices. These hardships were compounded by the impact of rather more localised issues. The nuclear issue, for instance, also caught the attention of radical protesters and likewise threatened to import more disruption into the political system. The concern raised by a proposed nuclear energy scheme - reputedly the largest in the world measured on a per capita basis - was bound to be of political significance in a society where public health figured high on the list of social priorities. The political system was obliged to address this issue and, as the mainstream parties took up positions in favour of or opposition to it, there were signs that this ecological issue had gained sufficient momentum to disrupt the normal pattern of party politics. The Social Democrats, for instance, found themselves on the same side as the right of centre Liberal Party (the Folkpartiet), and the right wing Conservative Party (Moderatera). The Communists and the rightist Centre Party, formerly the Agrarian Party which had some roots in conservative environmentalism, and which had initially endorsed Sweden's nuclear energy programme, changed their mind on the issue after1973 and opposed it.[83]

The nuclear issue was, in one sense, a demonstrably 'new politics' issue. At the same time, it also reflected some of the abiding concerns of the conventional productionist agenda. It certainly did mirror those doubts already expressed in Sweden about the development of the country's political economy.[84] The nuclear issue thus reflected and deepened an emergent cleavage between the 'old' materialistic politics of growth and production, and the 'new' politics of post-materialism, concerned to highlight alternative issues and to increase ecological awareness.[85] The 'old' politics - which had presided over Sweden's postwar prosperity and the development of its extensive welfare state - appealed both to business and trades unions alike.[86] The 'new' politics, meanwhile, appealed to new social groups outside the traditional socio-economic structure; most especially to the younger and better educated cohorts of the population - groups who felt unrepresented by the political establishment.[87] Alternative networks, radical groups and protest movements, mostly based in local communities and in the universities, began to represent a vociferous and active lobby outside the conventional political system. The nuclear issue was a signal moment in the development of this radical politics. It provided this progressive constituency with an important catalyst - with a cause through which they could confront the establishment at the level of national politics and the public policy process. The nuclear issue certainly gave a timely boost to an expansive green lobby. Ecological issues - a campaign, for instance, to resist despoiling the forests and 'wilderness', by driving more concrete infrastructure (roads, hydro-electric dams, mining projects or airports) through it, and widespread concern on public health grounds over the use of chemical pesticides and fertilisers in the farming industry - all played their part in giving momentum to 'new' politics in Sweden.[88] The nuclear issue, however, was the critical catalyst here. It galvanised attention and eventually encouraged important political realignments when, after the election of 1976, and for the first time in two generations, the Social Democrats lost their grip on power and were replaced in government by a three party coalition based on a new centre-right majority in the Riksdag.[89] These events helped to shape Green party politics, as much as they were shaped by it.

The impact of an unconventional 'post-materialist' issue, outside the mainstream productionist agenda which had fashioned Swedish politics since the mid 1920s, was well illustrated by the extensive support the Centre Party's anti-nuclear stance drew from across the class cleavage. A 'green' constituency which consisted of various ecological and alternativist groups coalesced around the stated intention of the Centre Party's leader, Thorbjorn Falldin, to phase out Sweden's nuclear energy programme by 1985. The Centre Party, in the event, became caught up in the usual compromises demanded by coalitional politics and failed to deliver on this extravagent promise. Although it maintained a radical rhetoric on this issue, the Centre Party in government provided few tangible signs that it would dismantle Sweden's nuclear energy programme. Nevertheless, the expectation that conventional politics provided the key to a successful outcome here was enough to launch the green lobby on the road to parliamentary and party politics. This determination was increased, in no small measure, by the effect on public opinion of the nuclear accident at Three Mile Island. The exigencies of party competition also played their part in these developments. The Social Democrats, now painfully aware that there was no inexorable law that ensured them permanent success in politics, responded shrewdly to these public concerns. The Social Democrats took advantage of the deep sense of betrayal amongst progressive opinion at the Centre Party's apparent betrayal of trust, and likewise shifted their position on the nuclear issue. Although the subsequent coalition formed by the Social Democrats was far from united over this controversial issue, the Social Democrats themselves, aware that another general election was imminent, agreed to hold a national referendum on the issue. When this referendum eventually took place in March 1980, the Centre Party was back in government. There was a distinct sense in these machinations - at least to committed ecologists - that the issue was becoming a convenient pawn in the new game of party manoeuvres. Each of the major parties presented its own cocktail of options. These ranged from a complete if incremental phasing out of nuclear power altogether, endorsed by both the Communists and the Centre Party and supported by 'The People's Campaign Against Nuclear Power', which gained 38.7 per cent support; through to more cautious variations on the broad theme of resisting the expansion of the existing twelve reactors - for which the pro-nuclear Social Democrats secured 39.1 per cent, and could claim to have 'won' the referendum on the basis of a 'sensible' compromise. Only the right wing Conservatives (Moderatera) had supported the continuation of the existing nuclear programme - and won 18.9 per cent of the referendum vote for what was now widely seen on all sides as the least ecologically sound and most extreme policy option.[90]

(ii)   Party formation

The inability of the Centre Party to deliver its promise to curtail the nuclear programme did much to undermine its support amongst 'deep' ecologists. In the aftermath of this referendum, the nuclear programme was actually expanded, with four additional nuclear stations signalling a significantly increased dependence on nuclear sources of electricity supply. This provided even more momentum for an independent Green politics. A former Liberal member of the Riksdag, Per Gahrton, who had joined the anti-nuclear movement, decided to circulate his own ecology manifesto amongst those radical and alternative groups which had already established a base for Green politics in local council elections. This led, in turn, to the formation of an organising committee which met at Orebro in September 1981 and founded the Ecology Party (Miljopartiet). In marked contrast to the unpromising conditions facing the Greens in neighbouring Denmark and Norway, the situation in Sweden was altogether more favourable to Green party politics. For one thing, green issues had entered the political consciousness due to the impact of the anti-nuclear campaign. Moreover, the mishandling of this issue by the mainstream parties alienated many of their progressive voters, and played into the hands of the ecology movement. The only mainstream party which had identified with progressive opinion on the nuclear issue, and threatened - as other parties did in Norway, Denmark and the Netherlands - to occupy the green space that was opening up in national politics, had lost its advantage here by an untimely compromise. The Centre Party's prevarication on the nuclear issue opened the way for the Greens. It has been estimated that up to 30 per cent of the Miljopartiet's initial membership was drawn from this particular source. With as many recruits again coming from disillusioned and radical Social Democrats who had also lost patience with that party's cynical misuse of the nuclear issue for short term party political advantage.[91] The Ecologists also attracted disaffected Liberals and Communists, albeit in smaller numbers.

The new Ecology Party enjoyed some advantages that enabled it to consolidate its place in national politics. The Miljopartiet was imbued, above all, with an abiding sense of political realism from the start. A combination of factors - the fact that voters and activists attracted to the Greens were less well disposed to a leftist, let alone a fundamentalist radical ideological orientation, and the fact, too, that even the SAP remained in a position to the left of Greens on the conventional left-right axis[92] - gave the Miljopartiet a 'green reformist' demeanour.[93] Gahrton provided the new party with competent, experienced and decisive leadership. He was well equipped for his new role, having already acquired a considerable reputation as both a capable organiser, but also as a principled opponent of what he claimed, as a 'reformed' political insider, were the corruptions and patronage that pervade the conventional world of politics. The new party was thus able to plausibly combine principle with pragmatism. A leader respected for his inside knowledge as much as his idealism, with a small but solid support base drawn from across the ideological spectrum, enabled the Miljopartiet to avoid being marginalised in either a pure green or new left ideological ghetto. The party was more able than many new green parties to reach out to a broader constituency, and even to present itself to voters disillusioned with the main parties as a residual protest party. To an extent, these political advantages were neither fortuitous nor planned, but were rather a direct expression of national political culture. Progressive politics in Sweden has tended to be pragmatic rather than utopian in its ideological orientations. The impact of new social movements on public policy making in Sweden has always been tempered by a concern to connect with, rather than to alienate, public and political opinion. The well-planned and astutely targeted efforts of the nuclear lobby reflected this realism - above all, that there was little virtue and even less political mileage in occupying a marginal role as principled outsiders.

The structure of public policy making served to reinforce this mood. The Swedish system is by no means closed to effective lobbying by interests other than those of the corporatist establishment. The Greens responded in kind. Jahn observes in his study of the nuclear issue, that even those radical movements which took on the state, were essentially "pragmatic, reforming, consensus-oriented" and goal oriented rather than utopian, inasmuch as this campaign was "not aimed so much against public institutions, but rather (focused) on specific issues".[94] The Swedish Ecology party displayed a tendency to pragmatism much less in evidence in many other Green movements; in fact, the very opposite of the usual pattern of radical ecologism. The anti-nuclear and ecological lobby in Sweden drew its activists from the ranks of those already politicised by earlier (and more moderate) environmentalist groups - from the new left and from other political parties with a less than militant demeanour. Activists from these backgrounds who found their way into the Miljopartiet were already attuned to a realistic rather than a detached or utopian view of politics.[95] All of these influences worked in favour of political moderation. There were even some party members who defined the essence of radical politics as that of working to fully incorporate the ecology movement into the milieu of mainstream party politics and even of governance, rather than impotently confronting it from without. The openness of the Swedish polity and its receptiveness to progressive ideas encouraged the ecology movement to work within these conventional political channels. This abiding legacy of liberal statehood, combined with an enlightened corporatism, was influential in shaping both the style and conduct of Green party politics here. For as Jamison maintains, "more than in other countries, the movement was listened to and allowed to participate in the making of energy policy". In return, "the movement accepted the knowledge perspective and frameworks of the established political culture".[96]

These particular advantages did not, as such, ensure the Greens either a clear run or a flying start in electoral politics. Neither the party nor its distinctive message were excluded from the party political debate. The Greens were squeezed, nevertheless, by the movements that had started to 'unfreeze' the political landscape from the 1970s onwards. The party also suffered, as new and radical parties do, from distinct disadvantages. The shift in the party political equation that followed on from the decline in partisan alignment that spelled the end of the Social Democratic hegemony, introduced an unprecedented uncertainty into elections. These have tended to be closer run affairs than previously. With so much at stake in elections, and an intensified competition between the mainstream parties, the smaller parties tend to be squeezed, as the Ecology Party soon found to its cost. In the 1982 national elections, for instance, the Green vote only amounted to a minimal 1.7 per cent - well below the modest 4 per cent national threshold required for any party to secure seats in the Riksdag. The new party found itself confronted with more persistent electoral loyalties than it had anticipated, on the basis of real movements in the underlying pattern of social cleavages. In particular, it experienced difficulty in shifting the focus of political debate away from 'old' politics and productionist issues. The 'old' redistributive agenda of left-right party politics - principally the wage earner's fund - dominated the 1982 election campaign.[97] Even more surprising, the Ecology Party performed little better in its early forays into local politics. While it did gain an average of 3 per cent of the vote, this only put it fractionally above the modest threshold needed to hold county (*lan*) seats). The party did manage to win some 167 of these seats, spread throughout 96 of Sweden's 284 municipal councils in these early contests. In part, this was due to the party's inexperience and lack of local networks, compared with its more established opponents. The party worked hard to improve its deficiencies here. Between 1982 and 1985 it built up its local networks and established a lively, campaigning party newspaper (*Alternativet*) which provided a useful focus for policy debate and for publicity. '*Alternativet*', in common with party newsletters in other similarly inchoate movements, also provided a much needed 'notice board' for information regarding events, meetings and campaigns of various kinds.

The Miljopartiet was essentially a pragmatic party, but one that was committed to working within the system to bring about radical policy changes. This radical intent was made clear in the way the new party formulated its procedures. The party structure that evolved during this preliminary period confirmed the members' desire to avoid an over-centralised party format. The new organisational arrangements emphasised the importance of participation at every level; of transparency and proper accountability in its decision making procedures. Moreover, it endorsed the use of the rotation principle - which, in turn, confirmed the memberships' preference for a style of politcs that was not professionalised but was something akin to a civic duty. The party's procedural rules, agreed after much debate, did permit members to belong to other political organisations - underlining the notion that membership was a matter of rational choice rather than merely party tribalism. In short, the new party opted for an internal structure that emphasised direct democracy and grassroots power over more conventional hierarchical arrangements. The meetings of the National Congress - the party's supreme national decision making forum - are held far more frequently than similar gatherings of Sweden's mainstream parties. Moreover, this Congress also maximises local (geographical) representation - with each of the 28 national constituencies represented by two delegates, irrespective of the size of the local membership - although the principle of equity is underwritten by the fact that additional representation is accorded in the Congress on the basis of one additional delegate per 100 members. Delegations to Congress are also rotated - after a three year maximum term - in order to discount any tendency towards entrenched elitism or party cabals. Motions may be submitted to Congress either by local parties or by individual members. In either case, they are subject to review by a Committee of Congress, elected openly by the delegates themselves. While this procedure maximises democracy and participation, it also fragments decision making and makes a common position more difficult to arrive at. As does the further subdivision of the party's procedural organs into a biennial National Council (made up of geographical representation) and no less than 4 national committees. Any national committee may participate in the Council, but may not vote on its proceedings - on the ultra-democratic grounds that no one may be a full member of more than one party organ at one and the same time. National coordination and policy continuity was further weakened by the rule which divides the party's administrative functions into a political committee - which confirms the party's general policy programme - and an administrative committee charged with managing its budget. Both committees are elected by the Congress for one year only - with no member being permitted to stand for a longer consecutive term than 6 years, and with one quarter of the membership renewed each year. The Greens confirmed their anti-party disposition by adopting a notion of collective leadership favoured by most other Green parties. The convenorship of the supervisory political committee circulates amongst its membership for brief three-monthly periods of 'office'. This is a process quite deliberately designed to minimise the conventional elitist party formula of an identifiable leadership. Latterly, however, this extreme democratic instinct has been modified, not least in response to less than satisfactory electoral performances since 1982. Nevertheless, the prevailing instincts in the party still favour a decentralised structure, rotation of office, non-simultaneous office holding, and a non-oligarchic or hierarchic pattern of leadership.

(iii)   Political developments

The Miljopartiet set out is political stall from the start, as a pure green party prepared to embody its belief in the need to radically refashion politics, by establishing a party format that embodied its progressive instincts. At the same time, its underlying pragmatism has enabled it to make adjustments to its organisational arrangements, in response to a public perception about its inability to play an effective role in national parliamentary politics. The party convenors adopted the more formal role of administrative agents, and there were further compromises in 1985 to meet the electorate's expectations of what a coherent and effective party should look like. A system of national spokespersons was introduced to stand alongside the convenorship. Two spokespersons - one of each gender (a principle of equity which is extended throughout the staffing of the party's committee apparatus) - are elected annually. These changes, undertaken to improve the coherence of the party's policy focus, particularly with a less than sympathetic mass media in mind - a crucial considedration during election campaigns - have been partially offset by the decision to keep these spokespersons under the democratic control of the National Congress. The same intent is also apparent in the fact that neither of them is required to be a member of the party's political committee.

With new national elections in the offing, the Miljopartiet tried in 1985 to sharpen its political image. In an attempt to attract a diffuse green constituency, and directly influenced by the recent success of the German Greens - much publicised in Sweden's media - the Miljopartiet national congress altered the party's name to Miljopartiet de grona. The name change contributed little to the party's electoral fortunes. Although the Greens had established themselves in local politics (winning 237 seats on 148 local councils in 1985), they were unable at this stage to translate this local base into an effective presence in national politics. And this after what had seemed, on the face of it, to be promising times for Green party politics. The economic boom of the mid eighties had highlighted quality of life issues.[98] A national poll conducted by the Research Group for Social and Information Studies in 1988, indicated that 53 per cent of respondents believed that a sound environmental policy was more important than whether one or other of the main party groups achieved power.[99] Yet, when it came down to actually making choices, the electorate confined its attention to the programmes on offer from these mainstream parties. The Greens were again squeezed by these parties in another closely fought election in 1985, in much the same way and for largely the same reasons as they had been in 1982. The party polled scarcely 3 per cent, which again failed to yield any seats in the Riksdag. However, the party did make some progress. It was beginning to achieve a degree of public recognition as a national party. More voters preferred the Greens in this election as their second choice party (4.5 per cent) than had done so in 1982 (2.7 per cent).[100]

Some Green apologists blamed the mass media for their failure, with its focus as they saw it, on the 'outdated' old politics agenda of the mainstream parties. There was a strong feeling in the Miljopartiet de grona that some of the media had even deliberately distorted the party's election programme. Negative media coverage is bound to take some toll of any party's electoral support. Radical parties with novel messages invite a hostile press. In the search for convenient scapegoats blame was also laid at the door of the opinion pollsters, on the grounds that they failed in their questionnaires to take proper account of the Miljopartiet, or to treat it as a party in its own right. It is hard to say whether a different polling methodology would really have made any great difference, let alone 'discovered' additional support that failed to show in the ballot boxes! Certainly, when the major broadcasting companies and polling organisations responded to the party's complaints after 1985 and improved their coverage the Miljopartiet de grona did show a modest rise in its level of support. This was, however, much more likely coincidental. For the polling evidence itself indicated that the Greens had gained some extra support because of an increasingly nervous publics' concerns with nuclear safety after Chernobyl; and likewise the much publicised effect on the country of other sources of airborne pollution - acid rain on the southern forests, the build-up of algae in lakes, the death of seals on the west coast, and the scandal of milk supplies contaminated by dioxin. The public perception of cover-ups over environmental scandals was sharpened, too, by the 'Carlsson affair' - with official collusion in the investigation into the murder of the former Prime Minister, Olaf Palme.[101] A much more plausible explanation for the Greens' poor showing in 1985 can be laid at the party's own door; the fact that the Greens' prevailing anti-partyist tendency, the excess of direct democracy in its internal affairs - the obsession with grassroots accountability - added to its confusion over policy and detracted from its organisational coherence. All of which ensured that it sent out a garbled message, and guaranteed that it ran what was a poorly organised election campaign.

The party drew similar conclusions from these events. The 1985 election failure provoked a major review of the party's operations and rationale. The party's pragmatic founder Per Gahrton, was one amongst a number of realists in the party's ranks who took this defeat to be a timely lesson in practical politics. This group was certainly amenable to the view that the Miljopartiet's inability to benefit from a growing concern with environmental issues said as much about the party's conduct and orientation as it did about the political system per se. There was also a parallel move from some elements within the party to position it closer to the left - a practical response to the coalitional prospects opening up in what looked to be a potential dealignment of Swedish party politics. Gahrton took the initiative here and urged the party to adopt an unequivocal red-green line as a clear signal to progressive voters who remained unsure of where the party stood between the two major party blocs. The party seemed unable to grasp this opportunity and prevaricated - in part because the Social Democrats' loss of popularity made such a move to the left less attractive. This reticence reflected, in some measure, the rising tension between the pure greens, and those party members more inclined to commit the party to a strategy that involved working with other radical parties. This impasse over political direction remained unresolved. The pure greens were by no means without a persuasive case to argue. As they saw it, a move to the left would close off as many electoral opportunities as it opened up. In the circumstances, it seemed easier to do nothing, rather than damage the party by openly confronting the issue. The Miljopartiet were thus caught in a dilemma familiar to that facing some other pure green parties (in France and the UK for example); of whether to expand their electoral base by adopting a broad leftist demeanour, but to risk, in the process, alienating the pure green voters on whom the party relied for its core support.[102] The inability of the party to grasp this awkward nettle merely reflected the social eclecticism of the potential Green vote. The Centre Party's legacy to the Greens had been to make a much broader cross-section of the electorate far more aware of the impact of ecological issues, whether or not they actually translated this into a direct vote for the Greens. The pure green faction, therefore, saw its principal task in these circumstances, as that of maximising that diffuse vote, rather than narrowing the party's electoral appeal to only one side of the political spectrum. The national party congress at Karlskroga thus decided to keep its options open until after the 1988 election, rather than risk these divisions inflicting even greater electoral damage.

Persistence eventually paid off. The 1988 election did mark a turning point in the fortunes of the Green Party. Environmental concern was palpable and indeed cumulative. The aftermath of Chernobyl, anxieties about a belt of toxic algae that threatened marine life, and a virus that decimated the wild seal population on the west coast, all helped to raise awareness of the issue. In spite of polling only half of its best opinion poll ratings, the party did secure 5.6 per cent of the popular vote, which translated into a useful bloc of 20 Riksdag seats.[103] The extent of this success should not be underestimated in either the context or culture of Sweden's electoral politics.[104] It was a measure of the Greens' achievement here that they became the first new party for some seven decades to break into the country's 'frozen' party system.[105] The Swedish party system had not changed its 5 party configuration - ranged along the classic left-right continuum - for well over half a century.[106] The recent increase in electoral volatility has seen an acceleration in party competition in this once stable party system. The entry of new parties other than the Greens - most recently New Democracy and the Christian Democrats on the new right, as well as a Womens' Party - combined with the relatively modest 4 per cent threshold for parliamentary representation in an increasingly fragmented party system is bound to make for even less predictable electoral outcomes in future. This, in itself, does not ensure electoral success for any particular minor participant in the party system. An increasingly capricious electorate and a decline in partisan alignment, may just as easily count against minor parties without a securely established support base, as it might work in their favour. The Greens are a case in point here, for much of their support comes from residual protest votes as it does from an entrenched constituency sympathetic to their programme. This is an ephemeral electorate - and one that is much less likely to stay with them when political fashions change, or the mainstream parties strike more telling chords with the electorate's preferences. The evidence of Swedish voting patterns after 1988 underlines the endemic problem for the Green Party. The pattern of electoral volatility by no means represented an inexorable shift towards an altogether new politics agenda. Instead, it reflected a combination of slippage in once secure loyalties - a degree of dealignment (which clearly is not the same thing as realignment); alongside some rather ambivalent support for particular elements of a new politics agenda in which green issues, on the back of recent health and nuclear safety scares, enjoyed an unprecedented degree of electoral resonance. In other words, there was evidence in Sweden, as in many other advanced European democracies, of the coexistence of new politics issues within the prevailing 'old' politics agenda, rather than the straightforward replacement of the former by the latter.[107]

This situation suggests mixed news and promises fluctuating electoral fortunes for the Greens. There are unmistakable signs here of an emergent post-materialist constituency. But this is by no means a coherent electorate with a clear sense of ideological purpose. Nor is it one that is clearly delineated from the 'old' productionist politics that characterises the left-right cleavage that continues to pattern Swedish party politics. The constraints on any imminent or full blown realignment of Swedish politics, let alone an irrevocable shift to a post-industrial discourse, are as apparent in Sweden as they are elsewhere. Persistent doubts about national identity - of a suitable orientation in a rapidly changing regional and global landscape - continue to shape the inter-party debate in Sweden much as these same issues do in the other Nordic and western European states.[108] The mood of anxiety and ambivalence - and a sense of looking backwards as much as forwards - has been reflected in the discourse of Swedish politics into the nineties. This national dilemma merely serves to underline the fragile roots of the 'new' politics in Sweden. The salience of ecological issues has fallen dramatically during the present decade compared with the eighties, as other - for the most part traditional - concerns have continued to dominate political debate and the national policy agenda. This has made the Greens' electoral situation even more uncertain, without entirely making it hopeless. A Green constituency continues to exist, but at each successive election it tends to be twice as large, measured in terms of expressed second preference votes, as the actual Green vote - a statistic that is a measure of the Greens' problem in translating a vague endorsement of its aims into solid support at the polls. The fluctuation in the party's support - which is merely another manifestation of the ephemeral quality of the green constituency - is yet another barrier to building a stable base and thereby operating as an effective force in national and parliamentary politics. Bennulf and Holmberg's study[109] of the sociology of the Green vote in Sweden indicates a party that remains dependent on precisely that constituency that is least receptive to deep-seated, partisan commitment. The Greens draw disproportionately on that critical, often fickle, group of voters who perceive political choice to be less a matter of tribal allegiances than a reflective, rational and reciprocal activity. This is a recipe for volatile rather than steadfast support. Unconditional loyalty is not a political resource the Miljopartiet de grona - in common with most other Green parties - can expect to rely on. This was not an entirely bleak picture; but it was one that required a degree of serious strategic thinking the party was apparently unable to engage in - until the serious electoral setback in 1991 obliged it to rethink its political strategy.

The party's modest breakthrough in 1988 put most of these issues on hold, instead of encouraging them to be resolved. The party's cooperation with the Social Democrats was largely a matter of parliamentary tactics, rather than the start of a political realignment. The same short term considerations applied to the Greens' cooperation in the Riksdag with other parliamentarians broadly sympathetic to green issues, most notably those in the Centre Party and the Left Party. These arrangements were never formalised.[110] The party also began to improve its performance in local elections. It took 13 per cent and some 698 seats on 260 out of 284 councils across the country, thereby becoming the effective power brokers in 40 local councils. It likewise consolidated its regional base with 101 seats spread over all 24 county councils. In spite of the party's tenuous position in parliamentary politics, it quickly became established in a reasonably effective base in local government. This power base was so secure in some regions - notably in the university cities of Goteburg and Uppsala - that the Greens found themselves operating a balance of power which eventually led to a local coalitional arrangement with each of the major party blocs.

The Green Party adopted a pragmatic response to its new position that drew it more surely away from its once rigid anti-party stance. In effect, the party learned how to maximise its tactical advantages. It converted even these modest levels of support into useful political leverage in the increasingly competitive circumstances of Swedish party politics. The efficacy of this strategy was revealed in 1990 when the minority Social Democrat-led coalition, faced with a deteriorating economy - steep inflation, rising unemployment and increasing industrial action - seemed to be in real danger of losing office, and being forced to call new elections in an unfavourable political climate.[111] The government depended on support from the Greens in Parliament for their survival. As part of this political quid pro quo the government legislated a timely revision of the official energy policy. The deal included revisiting the nuclear issue and the less than conclusive outcome of the 1980 referendum. In what was a major concession to Green Party expectations, the government agreed to close Sweden's 12 nuclear power plants by 2010 and brought the closure of the first two installations forward to 1995 and 1996 respectively. It also proposed to make up this massive shortfall in energy supplies, by expanding the country's capacity for manufacturing hydro-electricity. The fact that this was less a coherent energy policy than a response to immediate political constraints became clear from additional measures aimed at appeasing the Greens. The decision to oppose any development of Sweden's four unspoilt northern rivers, and to reduce carbon dioxide emissions to 1988 levels - in a determined bid to cut down on homegrown acid rain - actually contradicted the decision to rely on hydro-electricity to meet the nation's energy needs.[112]

The Greens made the most of their presence in the Riksdag. This advantageous position was not to last. The onset of recession shifted the focus of the political agenda back towards the materialist agenda of the 'old' politics.[113] In the 1991 election the Greens were again squeezed between the big parties. In spite of polling forecasts that predicted the Greens would hold their support above the 4 per cent threshold, their total vote dipped marginally below, falling to 3.4 per cent. Again they fared better in the local elections where these critical issues counted for less, and managed to retain many of their local seats. After only a brief parliamentary 'honeymoon', Green strategists were once again confronted by some perplexing and unresolved questions. The Greens could hardly be expected to break the durable mold of Swedish party politics. At the same time, their expectation of exerting the degree of parliamentary leverage experienced after 1988 depended on them confronting the very issue raised by Gahrton and his supporters, when the party had initially embarked on the parliamentary road to ecologism - in essence, where the Greens actually stood on the ideological spectrum. On this pivotal issue they continued to send out mixed - and confusing - signals. Although their decision before the 1991 election not to support the Conservatives if they won power suggested that the party had moved in favour of a red-green orientation, which in turn reduced its appeal amongst those centrist or even Conservative voters who might possibly vote Green, the party continued to cultivate the preferred option of standing aloof from the conventional ideological extremes. This was much less a matter of sound tactics - an evenhandedness that was calculated to maximise their influence over policy - than it was a reflection of the continued dominance in the party of a pure-green demeanour. The party has consistently adopted a middle way between these ideological poles. The primary concern has been to endorse whichever of the major party programmes offers the most to ecologism. By this yardstick, the Greens usually displayed greater hostility to the Conservatives and their increasingly neo-liberal policies; but this has by no means ensured a favourable response to, let alone a permanent endorsement of, the Social Democrats and their parliamentary allies.

The Miljopartiet de grona, along with many other green parties in western Europe, thus represent a curious political paradox, and one which has provided them both with opportunities, as well as exerting constraints on their freedom of manoeuvre. To an extent the party is a victim of circumstances beyond its immediate control. Yet it has clearly squandered some of the fortuitous opportunities provided by these prevailing circumstances. The overriding constraint here - as elsewhere - is the persistence in both the political imagination and on the electoral ground of old politics (productionist) issues and patterns of partisanship that reflect well-established social cleavages, and the left-right ideological preferences that follow on from this. The scope available to Sweden's Greens to establish a sizeable support base remains circumscribed by these circumstances. This is not to deny that changes have begun to alter the perceptions on which these arrangements rest; and, in the process, to erode these political loyalties. The rise of a post-materialist and new politics constituency, including an ecological agenda, has contributed to these changes, but it has by no means supplanted the 'old' politics. One recent study of Sweden's political sociology concluded that, "opinions on questions about government influence over private business, income distribution and social justice tend to be correlated with one another in ways one would expect on logical or ideological grounds; the level of inter-item correlations is sufficiently high to make it reasonable to talk about the existence of a left-right dimension among Swedish voters".[114]   It is difficult to contest these facts. By and large, the recent turbulence in Swedish politics has been the result of uncertainties, anxieties and discontents which either reinforce or encourage shifts in political identity, but that have been expressed in the usual lexicon and by the conventional agendas of left-right politics.   In these circumstances, the scope for a genuinely 'new' politics remains limited indeed.   This does not mean, however, that the Green Party must be an entirely hapless victim of circumstances.   Yet the Greens have continually failed to respond to their own shortcomings, or at least less so than Green parties elsewhere - notably in Germany .   They seem to have concluded that any serious attempt to confront the really awkward questions might worsen their situation rather than resolve their predicament.

The critical issues here - as they have been for other Green parties facing the very same dilemmas - concern the party's response to the awkward choices and inevitable compromises that face all parties which choose to play normal politics and to operate in the parliamentary arena.   To operate an electoral strategy requires both discipline and realism.   The Miljopartiet de grona certainly adjusted well to its first experience of the Riksdag.   At the same time it avoided settling the really difficult questions of party organisation, policy formation and leadership.   The parallel issue, of whether or not to adopt a pure or red-green strategy, was hardly even confronted, let alone resolved. Amongst these perplexing issues was the question of the leadership function.   There is evidence from opinion surveys that the Greens suffered electoral damage in the 1991 election from the widespread perception that they lacked a proper leadership and, for that matter the degree of discipline needed to operate as an effective parliamentary party.[115] The Miljopartiet de grona was unable in its councils to decide whether it was content with the minimal role it had so far achieved in national parliamentary politics.   Or whether, if it adopted new procedures and a more positive outlook, it might carve out a more influential role for itself on the back of an electorate that was by no means unfavourably disposed to its core issues.   Gahrton's original reservations about the party's long term political orientation proved to be prescient indeed; for the party has proved unable on its own to shift the ideological fulcrum of Swedish politics, and that to improve on this position it must therefore participate in the building of a progressive alliance on the left, including the still powerful Social Democrats.[116] At the same time, this red-green option has threatened to alienate many of the party's pure-green supporters and, by reducing its electoral base, to make it less viable as a parliamentary partner.

There are no easy solutions to this persistent dilemma facing the Green Party, and these choices were no less easy to confront as the 1994 election approached.   The Swedish Greens had reached the stage in their political evolution whereby the issues they represented were at least recognised as critical, if not the dominant, issues confronting the electorate of this advanced industrial polity.   This was an achievement of sorts - a landmark in its political development - regardless of whether the party itself had made the best of it.   The 1994 election represented something of a political comeback for the Greens, although this claim has to be put into proper perspective.   One way of looking at this situation might have identified this upturn in fortunes as leading, sooner or later, to the sort of political consolidation experienced by the German Greens - that is as a political breakthrough, the end of the beginning as it were and a prelude to the next stage in the party's development.   A more pessimistic account saw these events as little more than a cyclical blip in a long if slow decline - the beginning of the end for a political phenomena unable to come to terms with political reality. This conundrum was only partially resolved by the outcome of this election. We will surely have to wait for a much longer electoral cycle before we can answer this question with any degree of certainty. The Greens certainly started out in this election campaign with more handicaps than advantages. They were unrepresented in the Riksdag - a fact that emphasised their marginal status. Moreover, their main agenda was also discounted because the environment had been overtaken in the list of public concerns by more pressing issues - for instance the future of the Swedish model of welfare capitalism in an increasingly competitive and globalised economy, the related question of national identity, and the virtues or otherwise of continuing with what now seemed to many to be an unduly introverted policy of international neutrality, tempered only by the country's involvement in regional (Nordic) cooperation. Sweden now faced an unprecedented fiscal crisis as the recession accelerated into a full depression. This deterioration in circumstances provoked a frenetic debate about the future of what was one of Europe's most generous welfare systems. The conservative government after 1991 had already moved towards entrenchment; to dismantle what Prime Minister Bildt had called an 'obsolete' model, by embarking on privatisation, welfare cuts and fiscal reforms designed to reduce the amount of GDP committed to state provision. The rapid onset of recession momentarily curtailed these reforms and the welfare edifice seemed immovable. By the time of the 1994 election, the economy was dominated as much by *étatism* as ever. It faced an unhealthy deficit of some 11 per cent of GDP; a spiralling public sector debt (equivalent to 100 per cent of GDP) with public expenditure accounting for the highest proportion (at 73 per cent, compared with an average of 50 per cent for most small European countries) of GDP of any OECD country; and a public sector that employed 30 per cent of the workforce (some 50 per cent higher than most small European countries). These issues dominated political debate, and the environment was little more than a peripheral concern in the minds of voters faced with more pressing worries. The Greens also lost some of the moral ascendancy that had helped them in the late eighties. Sweden now continued to enjoy better levels of environmental management and higher eco-standards than most other industrialised countries - a level of commitment that was widely endorsed by all sides of the party political spectrum.[117]

Ecological interest may have waned, but it has not entirely lost its relevance in the current political discourse. Rather, a significant degree of adjustment or prioritising has crept into the assessment. The issue has had to compete, latterly, with other matters that have more immediate relevance to the electorate's concerns. There are still, however, some encouraging signs for the Greens. The continuing deliberations and deadlock over whether, for instance, to build a bridge across the Oresund, to connect Sweden with Denmark by what would be one of Europe's biggest and most spectacular infrastructural projects, illustrates how material and post-material agendas continue to interface. The Conservative government's commercial preferences, endorsed by most of the other mainstream parties, as they were by employers and trades unions, to reduce the country's physical isolation and to link it more closely with the European economic heartland, had to accommodate widespread environmental concern. And not just from the Greens. The Centre Party, indispensable to Bildt's fragile coalition - and whose leader, Olof Johansson, was also the Environmental Minister - raised environmental objections to the project. As did a significant minority of public opinion concerned that the main sections of a bridge would interfere with currents into the Baltic, and thereby cause further deterioration of that already heavily polluted waterway.[118] Feelings ran high and, in the event, Johansson resigned from office, rather than compromise his environmental principles. The Centre Party permitted Johansson's three party colleagues - who also objected to the project - to stay on in the government to avoid a political crisis. Other environment issues exercised policymakers on the bridge issue. Objections were raised about meeting the projected exhaust emissions levels agreed by the two governments at the Rio Earth Summit and the Swedish government undertook costly design alterations to the bridge to take full account of its environmental impact.[119]

There was a continuing disquiet, too, over the long established agreement to terminate all nuclear energy installations by 2010. The tension here between what had been a firm political commitment and economic expediency, grew with the onset of the recession and the subsequent heavy pressures on public finances. Some economists began to argue that a phase out by the agreed deadline made little practical sense while most of the plants - some of which had undergone expensive repairs - were nowhere near the end of their technical lifespans. Especially so as the technology for harnessing renewable sources of energy, such as wind and solar power, were not yet viable at the required economies of scale.[120] The nuclear issue enjoys an almost symbolic status in national politics. After all, the referendum had been a defining moment in the country's self image as a progressive society and a democratic state. With this legacy to contend with, any delay in implementing what had been regarded as a firm commitment was bound to raise the profile of environmentalism. The perception of treachery, or even back tracking on a firm guarantee, activated the Green lobby including the Miljopartiet de grona.

Environmentalism was also a prominent theme in the rising debate on European integration that gripped the public mind in the early years of the present decade. Sweden has some of Europe's strictest standards on waste disposal, emissions, and the control of acid rain - which threatens the delicate eco-balance of its forests and lakes. In spite of the resistance of a powerful industrial lobby - in an economy dependent on energy intensive industries such as steel, paper and pulp manufacturers - to environmental audit regulations that might unduly threaten their competitive advantage in international markets, fiscal constraints and eco-taxes (such as a carbon dioxide tax) have been implemented. By and large, the Federation of Swedish Industries has cooperated with 25 of the country's leading companies (including Volvo and ABB) to implement an environmental dimension to product development. During Sweden's accession negotiations and since the country's full membership of the EU, official negotiators have been in the forefront of the lobby for tougher Community environmental restrictions - whether for their own sake or to improve their competitive position against members with slacker eco-regimes. The Green Party, for its part, has resisted these arguments for more stringent environmental controls by way of a common approach, and continues to maintain that EU membership would merely compromise the country's relatively high eco-standards. These concerns were reflected in the views of Karen Nielsen, an opponent of EU entry at the Environment Federation of Sweden, who maintained that free trade was the very reverse of progress; and that "the possibilities to lead the field decrease (with membership)". As she saw it, "the big environmental problems are with products, but within the EU free movement across borders is what counts", for "only on an exceptional basis can individual countries forbid unwanted products".[121] These developments show that environmentalism is a far from peripheral concern of informed opinion and policy makers alike. At the same time, the issue has become heavily discounted, and with it, the profile of the Miljopartiet de grona as a force for serious political realignment, as other, more pressing matters have come to dominate national politics. If there are signs of a tentative shift underway in the pattern of party politics, this is more likely to come from sources other than the Greens. Meanwhile the Green Party is a much less determinative actor in these events than an uncritical reading of the new politics paradigm here would indicate.

(iv)   Prospects for political change

The Social Democratic Party (Socialdemokratiska Arbetareparti - SAP - which had enjoyed a virtual political monopoly throughout most of the century, and had built a powerful electoral base and a public policy agenda on a conventional productionist-redistributive platform - began to lose its dominance in national politics during the 1980s. The party divided into two broad camps - a split that became more pronounced after the 1991 'defeat'. Neither of these factions, however, moved much beyond the sort of debate over the production and distribution of material resources that had exercised, over a different set of priorities, the Conservative and new right opposition parties. The SAP's 'modernisers' advocated the reform - a trimming rather than an abandonment - of their own Swedish model. Monica Sahlin, the influential SAP Secretary, and a leading exponent of this reformist tendency, saw the economic crisis as a portent, awakening the party as much as the country from "a fairy tale where we were sleeping without realising what was really going on. We have tried to stop pretending that everything can be kept. We are trying to see what is the essence of the Swedish model, to see which parts we can keep".[122] The message here for the Greens was stark if disagreeable; that they must either respond to an agenda that did not reflect their own preferences or priorities - or else risk complete marginalisation as a factor, however modest, in a changing political equation. In order to survive in this unpalatable political climate, the Greens had to address the prevailing agenda of issues that was at the centre of the current political discourse, and attempt to consolidate a constituency around them. This was a less than easy endeavour for a party whose principal raison d'être was the pursuit of an entirely new politics. Ironically, it made for some curious ideological liaisons that compromised this fresh image. This amounted to an appeal to dated if not conservative preferences - the defence of the welfare state against global capitalism and the endorsement of national identity against 'pernicious' integrationist tendencies - alongside some more obviously progressive themes - democracy against bureaucracy and small-scale business against the multinational enterprises.

The 1994 national election and the interim poll in 1995 to fill Sweden's seats in the European Parliament, provided some revealing insights into how the Miljopartiet de grona was coping with an agenda that was by no means favourable to its mission of establishing itself as a new party addressing contemporary issues in a novel way. On the face of it, the Green party looks to have restored its position in national politics. What is less apparent from the outcome of these elections is the precise significance of this achievement, let alone its import for the future pattern of party politics. The evidence is far from reassuring for the Greens. The party's relative success in these recent elections drew on a strong element of protest against the mainstream parties, and reflects the way they have responded to the hard choices and difficult dilemmas facing the country, more than it was a positive endorsement of ecologism, let alone a demand for a major political realignment. This is, however, only a partial explanation of these events. Post-materialism does clearly enjoy a small but entrenched following amongst the electorate. By no means enough to ensure a political realignment, yet sufficient to ensure that environmental concerns retain enough salience to continue to figure in electoral politics. But only if the Green Party can come to terms with the awkward choices and dilemmas that involvement in serious politics imposes on any political party. The starting point of an effective strategy here is, of course, an aptitude for political realism - to see the situation for what it actually is rather than idealising it. The Greens have come some considerable way on this count, but by no means far enough. The party's activists, naturally perhaps for a party that had disappeared from the Riksdag in 1991, tended to make more of their comeback than the evidence will sustain. The party's co-spokeswoman, Marianne Samuelsson claimed, for instance, that the 1991 defeat was merely an aberration caused by internal disarray, because "we simply did not have our act together", rather than a sign of a signal shift in the national political landscape that had left the party effectively beached as the post-materialist tide ebbed. The Greens likewise drew altogether more positive conclusions from the reversal in their fortunes in 1994; that the balance in favour of the environment cause had been restored by an electorate finally aware that it needed the Greens, because no other party could represent the issue purely for its own sake. As Samuelsson put it,"when we were out of parliament the last time, people genuinely missed the fact that environmental issues had disappeared from the debate".[123]

The Greens, understandably enough, chose to put a favourable gloss on their vote. They saw it as not so much a protest at the failure of the big parties to restore the complacency and well being of earlier decades, but rather as a positive indication of durable support for a new politics - particularly among young and women voters who were more inclined to vote Green than other social categories. According to Samuelsson, the increase in the Green vote in 1994 represented a rising concern amongst these key constituencies, not only with the preoccupation of Bildt's conservative government with outmoded agendas, but also with the SAP's studied vagueness over its longstanding pledge to close down the nuclear power plants.[124] This, too, was a partial account and selective reading of the Greens' modest 'revival', and as such was no more true than the sceptical account. The actual picture was altogether more mixed and even ambiguous. The Greens did clearly benefit from widespread disillusionment with the mainstream parties, as they did, too, from a degree of dealignment that has accompanied social change in every advanced European polity. The outcome of the 1994 election was, however, far from conducive to any major shift in the foundations of the body politic. The bald facts of the election by no means paint a clear picture. The right lost the election and the left - including the Greens - were its principal victors. Yet this broad trend disguises some variable tendencies. The Bildt government fell, not so much because the Prime Minister's Moderate Party reaped a radical whirlwind - it actually achieved a small increase in its 1991 vote - but rather because its coalition partners, the Liberals (with their second worst vote on record) and the far right Christian Democrats and New Democracy (who were largely wiped out), lost heavily on the back of their demands for even more stringent cuts in public expenditure.

The record swing to the left - at 67 per cent, the largest overall vote for leftist parties since 1948 - also contained some important differentials. It was much less a resounding victory for the SAP (who nevertheless took an impressive 45.3 per cent in an increasingly competitive party system), than it was an aggregate victory for a wide range of parties who benefited because they were not identified with an unpopular right of centre government that threatened to push the country into the unfamiliar territory of neo-liberal reform. Several parties benefited from this resistance to change, including the Vansterpartiet, whose highest vote since the 1940s (6 per cent) gave it 23 Riksdag seats. The Greens (with 5.2 per cent and 18 seats) also came into this category of parties that gained from the protest vote.[125] Jahn's analysis of the changing dynamics of Swedish party politics suggests that there are some clear limits to how far the Greens can go as things currently stand. The new politics space remains occupied by other parties that might prove more attractive to - or at least a rival for the votes of - the new middle class and post-materialist constituency. Indeed the Greens may well be further 'squeezed'. The Left Party continues - as recent elections have indicated - to win a share of the alternativist and new left vote. The Centre Party remains attractive to moderates with ecological sympathies. Whereas the rising ideological divisions within the SAP - especially on the issue that currently defines radical intent - European integration in its present format - suggests that the Miljopartiet de grona will continue to find "difficulty in occupying a genuine political niche in the Swedish party system".[126] The Greens at least have the virtue of a residual and long-standing political realism to enable the party to adjust to these constraints. On the other hand, they will have to share the dealigned vote with other parties. By the same token, as the evidence of recent elections suggests, that vote is increasing. The new politics vote is notoriously fluid and unreliable - as the Greens' 1990 election failure indicated. Nevertheless, the recent improvement in fortunes suggests that the party is capable of winning back enough support to at least keep it in the game, but almost certainly as a minor player.

What is apparent from the aftermath of this election is the extent of realism in the Green Party's ranks; a determination to resist squandering its electoral good fortune and to put the opportunity presented by its restoration to the Riksdag to better use than it did when tthat prospect first presented itself in 1988. This may, in turn, help to deliver the stable Green support base that has so far eluded the party. The evidence of a party that uses even its modest position in the Riksdag to pressurise government and win policy concessions, may encourage some voters to desert the party. But at the same time, to persuade others - who were once deterred by the party's refusal to compromise, or to work with the political grain, to secure marginal policy adjustments, and thereby concluded that a Green vote was a wasted vote - to support it. This is some way from the 'revolution' many Miljopartiet de grona activists came into politics to further, but it seems to be the most they can hope for under present circumstances. A Swedish political scientist, Jorem Holmberg, has identified realism as the party's best resource, observing that "the leadership of the Green Party has become more seasoned, more experienced and less fundamentalist than in their earlier years. They have shown that they are a party with whom political deals can be struck".[127] The growing perception of a party prepared to adjust to the usual exigencies of parliamentary politics, has done the Swedish Green Party some interim good at a time of widespread uncertainty. This image of common sense was reinforced by the alacrity with which the Greens reconvened their parliamentary duties, occupying their place in 16 of the Riksdag's 18 committees.

Of course, this prudence only takes the party so far. Whether it is a secure or sufficient base from which to launch a concerted radical challenge to the 'old' politics, as the Greens would prefer, is another question entirely. The Greens continue to be optimistic about their chances as the party system becomes less dominated by previous configurations. The party's co-spokesperson, Birger Schlaug, although fully aware that the 1991 elections were dominated by materialist issues, believed that the mainstream agenda by 1994 had moved much closer to the Greens' preferred territory. Indeed, that there was now considerable potential for harnessing prevailing concerns about national 'futures' - not least the critical question of EU membership - with the related ecological issues raised by the regional project.[128] The Greens believed that EU membership - a rubicon by any standards in Swedish history - would certainly have negative ecological consequences, and that this could be linked to a wider public perception about the costs of European integration to the national interest. This convenient issue linkage could, then, be made to count against the political establishment. In the short run, they managed to win a share of the protest vote exercised by these wider concerns, although not necessarily for the reasons they would prefer to be the cause of their improved political fortunes. The Greens built a modest political revival on the back of these national anxieties. What is more uncertain is the extent to which their increased vote in 1994 was a straightforward reward for a party that has consistently opposed EU membership on both ecological and social grounds[129] - an economic power seen to be responsible for high pollution levels, trade distortions and armaments manufacture - from the moment Ingvar Carlsson's SAP government lodged a membership application, and a position the party sustained throughout the Conservative government's negotiations. There is no doubt that the whole question of national identity, and particularly of how those parties that have so far dominated Swedish politics throughout the present century respond to this massively changing situation, retains considerable potential for further political dealignment. The end of the Cold War has altered Europe's political landscape almost beyond recognition. In Sweden's case, as Svasand and Lindstrom point out, this monumental event has, as much as anywhere, "removed the supporting rather than the restraining structures of its identity as a nation state".[130] In much the same way as it did in Denmark, Finland, Norway, as well as in the United Kingdom, Germany, Italy and the other Mediterranean members of the EU.

The Greens were helped here - as were Sweden's other minor anti-EU parties such as the former Communist Left Party (Vansterpartiet - VP) - by the clear public perception of the heavy costs the mainstream parties were prepared to inflict on Sweden's people in order to meet the convergence criteria for EMU membership enshrined in the Maastricht Treaty. These are tough enough for every aspirant member, but they will be crippling for Sweden with its large budget deficit and high levels of welfare spending. The Greens were also able to exploit to advantage the severe compromise of Sweden's neutrality of any commitment to the common European Defence Identity contained in the same treaty. In short, the Greens profited as much as any other opposition party in the 1994 election from widespread doubts and anxieties raised by an agenda dominated by old rather than new politics issues. Although the Miljopartiet de grona stood on a conventional pure Green programme not dissimilar to its 1991 manifesto - that called for stiffer eco-taxes, traffic reductions, a smaller working week to cut unemployment, the promotion of recycling, and opposition to current plans to build an installation for disposing of hazardous waste - its modest electoral improvement was built at least as much on negative (anti-EU) votes, as on a positive pro-ecology platform. The Greens cashed in on these redolent anxieties and undoubtedly profited from the pervasive scepticism, in some quarters in this geographically remote and culturally insular country, about its future prospects within the EU.[131]

The outcome of the 1994 election has given the Greens more influence over the conduct of parliamentary business than the party enjoyed in their previous time in the Riksdag - but not significantly so. The SAP lacks an overall parliamentary majority - a remarkable change in fortunes for a political party that used to dominate Swedish politics, and has governed for all but 6 of the past 32 years. The recent shift in voting patterns does provide a yardstick against which to measure the degree of political change underway here. The SAP has lost to the parties of the right a significant proportion of its once solid bluecollar vote - and especially to the new right that have, in common with right wing populist parties elsewhere, taken advantage of palpable public anxieties, to play up the appeal of issues shaped by national chauvinism or worse.[132] In 1966 some 73 per cent of this constituency had voted for the SAP. By 1991 this bedrock *'ouvrièrist'* constituency had shrunk to 52 per cent - a firm majority, but much less than the impregnable electoral bastion it used to be.[133] While there was a modest increase in the SAP's bluecollar vote in 1994, it was clear that the party was becoming - in common with so many other European Social Democratic parties - a party of the new professional and even post-material middle classes. This shift in the sociological profile of the party's support base has had one important consequence for the Green Party's electoral prospects. For it has closed off to it an important source of progressive votes. The SAP has continued to limit the Greens' impact in even more direct ways. The SAP's leader, Ingvar Carlsson, refused to entertain a formal coalitional arrangement - either with the centrist or left parties. Aware that the one clear message in the otherwise confused signals that resulted from the 1994 poll was a loss of legitimacy by the centre-right government, the SAP felt able to govern in their own right, mustering ad hoc support from the Centre Party, the Liberals, the Vansterpartiet and the Greens, behind specific legislation, as the occasion demands. This has prevented the Greens from enjoying a place in government, with the immense boost to their credibility and political experience that would undoubtedly have followed from that breakthrough. The situation here stands in marked contrast to the situation of the Miljopartiet de grona's sister party in Finland. The SAP, for their part, were determined to avoid any undue dependence on parties further left. Not least, because this would almost certainly have widened the ideological rifts within the party, between its modernising and traditionalist wings, over the future of the Swedish model and the full implications of European integration.[134] The Greens continue, then, to exert only a modest degree of influence over the legislative programme - but not on the really critical issues. Nor in any way that is likely to contribute to a major shift in the balance of public policy. The Greens' frustration with the SAP's 'pick and mix' approach to government was reflected in Marianne Samuelsson's condemnation of an opportunistic 'smorgasbord' government.[135] The Greens may reject this muddled formula for government as entirely unsatisfactory; yet they are powerless to change it. There are few signs that, as things stand, they can anticipate any significant improvement in their political fortunes let alone an increase in their influence.

The post-election agenda has certainly been dominated by the SAP's attempts to modernise the economy and equip Sweden to compete better in the increasingly integrated economy of the EU and beyond. Successive budgets have undertaken a reappraisal of existing welfare commitments, but so far have avoided any drastic surgery - much in line with the approach to this issue of the outgoing government, and for much the same reasons.[136] The SAP continues to be led from the centre by its modernist wing - Carlsson was replaced by his former finance minister, Persson, in 1996 - who have tried to stem public expenditure without splitting the party irrevocably. This compromise has staunched the upward drift in public expenditure, which peaked at 70 per cent of GDP in 1995. The constant fear of a political Armageddon being visited on the party by a pincer movement, both from the political right and the far left, has caused Persson to promise to "stick to the welfare society as we have built it". As long as this can be reconciled with the application of the fiscal discipline required by the markets, alongside the strictures that will be imposed by Sweden's proposed membership of EMU.[137] This is old politics in a new format. But it is not without a positive pay off for environmental standards, which gives the Greens good cause to sustain the government in office. The government has so far tried to square this circle, by calling on the EU to level the commercial playing field by adopting for the EU as a whole - as part of the major review underway in the current IGC - those same high (cost push) standards on health, safety and environmental standards already operated by Swedish industry. Not that the putative realignment of politics held out by such policy bargains promises to be straightforward or easy to accomplish. The prospects here for a more permanent or consolidated red-green alliance remain blighted by other aspects of government policy that fly in the face of the Greens' preferences. Not least, when the government followed up this demand with a parallel call for a greater proportion of the EU's structural funds be devoted to employment creation and infrastructural schemes that are calculated to lessen the pervasive antipathy of the Swedish electorate to EU membership - which had risen to 61 per cent against EU membership[138] less than a year after they had narrowly voted (53 to 47 per cent) in the 1994 referendum to join the Union.[139] The Greens were one of the political beneficiaries of this change of mood but they remain deeply at odds with the SAP modernists' aspirations to overcome the culture shock wrought by this scene shift, and to assimilate Sweden into the European mainstream as soon as possible.

With these major obstacles to overcome, the likelihood of a major realignment on the centre-left of Swedish politics, including the Greens, remains a distant prospect indeed. The problematic nature of a red-green consensus on the back of the European issue was clearly visible from the outcome of the country's first European elections. A deepseated sense of doubt and betrayal pervaded these elections in September 1994 to fill Sweden's 22 designated seats in the European Parliament.[140] The fact that this was a second order election with little at stake encouraged a significant degree of disengagement from 'usual' party loyalties. The result was undoubtedly an interim referendum on the EU. Above all, it was a safety valve for the rapid disenchantment that soon settled on the country after so many hopes had been raised and so much had been promised during the referendum campaign. Prices, particularly for food, had remained high, as had interest rates, and there were few signs of the promised jobs bonanza. The SAP - by now openly divided on the issue and standing two separate lists - polled only 28.1 per cent - the party's worst showing in a national election since 1911. The right-wing parties fared little better. All three mainstream centre-right parties that had campaigned unequivocally for EU membership, including the Moderates and the Liberals, took less than 32 per cent. The clear winners were the Left Party, standing on outright opposition to a European 'super state', and the approval of EMU membership subject only to national parliamentary approval,[141] and the

Greens, who between them took 30.1 per cent - almost three times their combined vote in the 1994 general election. The low turnout (41.3 per cent) in the country's first European elections was almost as significant as a commentary on prevailing attitudes to the EU as the actual breakdown of the vote. The special circumstances that surrounded this second order election produced a result that is unlikely to be repeated in any election to the Riksdag. At the same time, the outcomeof this election showed that, even as a party of merely residual protest, the Greens do have a role in national politics; and indeed, some potential as a vehicle of both progressive and traditional concerns. The electorate did, after all, have a range of protest options to choose from - not least a SAP list wholly opposed to the EU. The result of these elections indicates that the Greens do enjoy the potential to exploit the anxieties that surround those deepseated rifts in Swedish society that threaten the support base and remain highly divisive for mainstream parties in general, and the centre-left in particular. The SAP is more vulnerable to dealignment than any other single party, if only because it has more bedrock support to lose. It is no longer the monolithic and disciplined party able to rely on a deep reservoir of bluecollar votes, or to exploit the straightforward ideological and class cleavage that used to pervade and pattern Swedish politics.[142] The party's electoral base is now altogether more volatile. It contains a significant minority of new middle class voters amenable to new politics issues, and thereby capable of being won over by other parties if it fails to deliver. Environmental issues have continued to play an increasing part in this electoral calculus and will undoubtedly continue to do so. Particularly so in circumstances where increased party competition enables what were once minor movement parties, outside the parliamentary system, to consolidate a discernible constituency - and thereby, in increasingly 'hung' parliaments, to use their leverage therein to influence public policy. If this degree of electoral flux is to be the future pattern of Swedish politics, the present contrast between the situation of the respective Swedish and Finnish Green parties may become instead comparable if not quite convergent, with the Miljopartiet de grona following the example of Finland's Vihrea Litto into a centre-left coalition - but not for the foreseeable future.

For the time being, the Greens will have to settle for an altogether more limited and conditional role as the ecological grit in the productionist oyster. Nevertheless, there is much that the Greens can do, even in these straitened circumstances, to improve their political profile. And, indeed, there is much they have already done to consolidate their place in national politics as the Green conscience in an otherwise materialist milieu. One issue stands out here as a beacon of potential cooperation and the basis for a workable political bargain between the Greens and the left. Fiscal constraints, and the fast approaching deadline of 2010 agreed after the 1980 referendum on the future of the country's 12 nuclear reactors, have caused the SAP pragmatists to reopen the energy debate. Nuclear power still accounts for half of the national supply of power, and to honour the 1980 commitment on switching to alternative technologies will be both expensive and administratively daunting. A prominent commentator, Siegfrid Leijonhufurd, writing in the leading journal, *Svenska Dagbladet*, has identified the energy question as the "single most important issue" facing the SAP government. For "decommissioning by 2010 would jeopardise the whole of the government's efforts to clean up the state finances".[143] Given the tight time-scales involved in any replacement energy programme, the issue is imminent in policy terms and cannot afford to be further delayed. Current economic strictures - the pressing need to stabilise a total public debt that would

411

still, even at 85 per cent of GDP compared with the EMU target of 60 per cent, leave a mountain to climb if Sweden is to join the Euro currency club from the outset - point in the direction of a major policy reversal - in short, one of continuing with nuclear energy. But only at a high political cost - with the Miljopartiet de grona and other green lobbies clamouring for immediate action, and for the government to keep faith with its earlier commitment.[144]

All the signs are there for a breaking of that faith. 'Experts' are already pronouncing sagely on the 'safety' of nuclear energy and arguing that 12 of the extant reactors have another generation of 'useful' life left in them. Aware, however, of their reliance for the time being anyway on Green Party support in the Riksdag, the SAP has been obliged to dress up this economic short-termism in an ecological garb. What the government hopes will be reassuring 'green' noises about the virtues of a relatively clean technology, compared with the emissions from the coal fired or gas alternatives, or the negative environmental impact of damming more rivers to develop hydro-electricity sources, have accompanied recent official statements on national energy policy. The fact that on this particular issue the bluecollar trades union constituency is significantly more ecologically sound than it tends to be on other issues where greening the economic agenda clashes more overtly with their employment creation and economic growth priorities spells further trouble for the SAP.[145] At the same time, however, these awkward dilemmas do offer an increased opportunity for the Green Party to exert parliamentary leverage. Not least because the Centre Party - on which the SAP minority government depends on occasions to pass legislation - and the Left Party, too, are both hostile to any backtracking on this headline 'radical' issue. Some sort of parliamentary compromise will almost certainly be reached on this issue - a partial retention of the nuclear option is the most widely canvassed option. Either way, this issue will play much better for the Greens than it does for the SAP or the other 'old' left or centre parties.[146]

The same potential for a more progressive politics is even discernible on those mainstream issues that, on the face of it, seem to be much less favourable to the Greens. Amongst these is the continuing debate on the future of the public sector and the welfare state. This issue is much less a reflection of any clearcut left-right cleavage in Sweden than it is in many other European countries. To the extent that it is still seen as a 'class' issue, it favours the left less amongst its main constituencies than it used to do. For the SAP's bluecollar vote has already largely discounted this issue in its broad electoral calculus. In other words, the SAP receives no extra credit for defending the Swedish model, and actually loses votes, both from amongst its traditional support base and in the post-materialist constituency on which it has increasingly come to rely to maintain its position as Sweden's dominant party. This shortfall reflects the apparent willingness of the party's modernisers to adjust welfare expenditure in line with the requirements imposed by other economic, commercial and foreign policy objectives - notably EMU membership and the pursuit of international competitiveness through fiscal prudence.[147] There may well be scope on both of these critical issues for the Greens to negotiate on terms with the government - support in parliament in exchange for policy concessions. Whether the Greens can bring themselves to bargain and compromise over what will be, in either case, the fundamental principles on which the party has built its political base, and indeed pitched its claim to represent a novel political idea over the past decade, remains to be seen. To this extent, the Miljopartiet de grona confronts, in its own special political milieu, those very same dilemmas that confront similarly placed Green parties everywhere in Europe. How well they respond to this predicament will be a gauge of the party's growing political maturity. The extent to which the Greens make room for manoeuvre here, without exposing their own internal fissures, or losing the support of their radical voters and activists as they negotiate the hazards and pitfalls of political compromise, will be the ultimate test of the Green Party's political development, and thus provide a telling measure of its staying power in a polity as ripe for change as any other in contemporary Europe.

Notes

1.   T. Jarvikovski, "Alternative Movements in Finland: The case of Koijarvi", Acta Sociologica 24 1981, at pp.313-320.

2.   M. Laakso and R. Taagepera, "Proportional Representation in Scandinavia: Implications for Finland", Scandinavian Political Studies 1 1978, at pp.43-60.

3.   Jukka Paastelo, "Finland: The Vihreat", F. Muller-Rommel, op.cit (1989) at p.84.

4.   See R. Helenius, "The Finnish Social Democrats", in W. Paterson and A.H.Thomas, "Social Democratic Parties" (London, 1988), at p.273.

5.   Liisa Uusitalo, "Are Environmental Attitudes and Behaviour Inconsistent? Findings from a Finnish Study", Scandinavian Political Studies 13 1990, at p.218.

6.   See W. Lafferty and O. Knutsen, "Postmaterialism in a Social Democratic State", Comparative Political Studies 17 (1985), pp.411-30.

7.   L. Uusitalo, op.cit (1990), at pp.223-224.

8.   Quoted in Reuters News Services Report, 6.10.94.

9.   "Neutrality Fades", The Economist, 11.6.94.

10.   Quoted in The Guardian, 18.10.94.

11.   H. Carnegy, "Into the EU's Arms", Financial Times, 11.10.94.

12.   H. Carnegy and H. Barnes, "Welfare Dilemma for Nordic Social Democrats", Financial Times, 23.9.94.

13.   Financial Times, 9.11.94.

14.   Ibid.

15.   Reuters News Service Report, 23.2.95.

16.   H. Carnegy, "Rural Finland Holds out against EU", Financial Times, 14.10.94.

17.   Reuters News Service Report, 23.2.95.

18.   Reuters News Service Report, 13.4.95.

19.   H. Carnegy, "Rainbow Coalition is chasing a pot of gold", Financial Times, 9.10.95.

20.   Reuters News Service Report, 13.4.95.

21.   Financial Times, 9.10.95.

22.   Reuters News Service Report, 12.6.95.

23.   See Jorgen Goul Andersen, "Denmark: Environmental Conflict and the 'Greening' of the Labour Movement", Scandinavian Political Studies 13 1990, at p.187.

24.   O. Borre and D. Katz, "Party Identification and Its Motivational Base in a Multi-party System", Scandinavian Political Studies 8 1973, at pp.69-111.

25.   O. Borre, "Recent Trends in Danish Voting Behaviour", in K. H. Cerny (ed) "Scandinavia at the Polls" (The American Enterprise Institute, Washington DC 1977) at pp.3-37.

26.   J. Fitzmaurice, "Politics in Denmark", (London, 1981).

27. A. Thomas, "Parliamentary Parties in Denmark, 1945-1972", (University of Strathclyde Occasional Papers, No.13, 1973).

28. R. A. Isaak, "International Political Economy: Managing World Economic Change", (Englewood Cliffs, 1991), especially at pp.49-55.

29. O. Borre, "The Social Bases of Danish Electoral Behaviour", in R. Rose (ed), "Electoral Participation: A Comparative Analysis" (California, 1980).

30. O. Borre, "Denmark" in I. Crewe and D. Denver (eds), "Electoral Change in Western Democracies" (Beckenham, 1985) at pp.372-91.

31. O. Borre, ibid (1985).

32. O. Borre, op.cit (1977), at p.20.

33. J. Fitzmaurice, "Politics in Denmark" (London, 1981), at p.96.

34. O. Knutsen, "Materialist and Postmaterialist Values and Social Structure in the Nordic Countries", Comparative Politics 23 1990, at pp.85-101.

35. F. Muller-Rommel, "New Social Movements and Smaller Parties: A Comparative Analysis", West European Politics 8 1985, at p.41.

36. J. Goul Andersen, op.cit, (1990).

37. Ibid (1990), at p.204.

38. Ibid (1990), at pp.202-3.

39. M. Gallagher, M. Laver and P. Mair, "Representative Government in Modern Europe" (2nd ed. London 1995), at p.275.

40. B. Saarlvik, "Scandinavia" in V. Bogdanor and D. Butler, "Democracy and Elections: Electoral Systems and their Consequences" (Cambridge, 1983) at p.122.

41. M. Pedersen, "The Birth and Life and Death of Small Parties in Danish Politics", in F. Muller-Rommel and G. Pridham (eds), "Small Parties in Western Europe" (London, 1989).

42. W. Rudig, "Green Party Politics", Environment Vol.33 No.8 (1991), at p.26.

43. J. Goul Andersen, cited by S. Schuttemeyer in T. Muller-Rommel, op.cit (1989), at p.60.

44. Financial Times, 9.9.94.

45. H. Carnegy and H. Barnes, "Welfare Dilemma for Nordic Social Democrats", Financial Times, 23.9.94.

46. Quoted in Reuters News Service Report, 21.9.94.

47. Reuters News Service Report, 26.9.94.

48. Financial Times, 4.10.94.

49. Financial Times, 30.11.95.

50. Financial Times, 4.10.94.

51. Reuters News Service Report, 21.11.94.

52. Financial Times, 27.11.95.

53. Quoted in "Scandinavian Election Previews", The Economist. 10.9.94.

54. Financial Times, 16.11.94.

55. T. Bjorklund and O. Hellevik, "Green Issues in Norwegian Politics", Politica 4 (University of Arhuus, 1989), pp.414-431.

56. See G. Hansen, "Civil Disobedience - A Threat to Representative Democracy?" in B. Hagtvedt (ed), "The Difficult Disobedience" (Oslo, 1981).

57. Brent Aardal, "Green Politics: A Norwegian Experience", Scandinavian Political Studies 13 1990, at p.148.

58.   S. Gronmo, "Conflict Lines in Party Politics, 1969-1973: Some Effects of the EC Struggle", Tidsskrift for Samfunnforskning 2 (1975), pp.119-153.

59.   See S. Rokkan and H. Valen, "The Mobilization of the Periphery", in S. Rokkan (ed), "Approaches to the Study of Political Participation" (Bergen Michelsens Institutt, 1962).

60.   T. Bjorkland and O. Hellevik, op.cit (1989).

61.   B. Aardal, "Energy and Environment: A study of voter attitudes and party profiles 1977-1985", (Oslo: Institute for Social Research 1991).

62.   B. Aardal, op.cit (1990), at p.152; for further discussion, see O. Knutsen, "The Priorities of Materialist and Post Materialist Values in the Nordic Countries - A Five Nation Comparison", Scandinavian Political Studies 12 1989, pp.221-243; and A. Jenssen and O. Lishaung, "Post materialism and Elections in Norway", Norsk Statsvitenskapelig Tidsskrift 2 1988, pp.154-171.

63.   B. Aardal, op.cit (1990), at p.158.

64.   See H. Valen, "Elections and Politics - A Changing Society", (Oslo, 1981); and B. Aardal and H. Valen, "Voters, Parties and Political Distance", (Social and Economic Studies, 69, Oslo: Central Bureau of Statistics).

65.   O. Tonsgaard, "Environmental Consensus?" in J. Elklit and O. Tonsgaard (eds) "To Folketingsvalg. Valgerholidinger og vaelgeradfoerd: 1987 og 1988" (Arhuus, 1989), pp.271-90.

66.   B. Aardal, op.cit (1990) at p.151.

67.   See H. Valen and S. Rokkan, "Norway: Conflict Structure and Mass Politics in a European Periphery", in R. Rose (ed), "Electoral Behaviour: A Comparative Handbook" (New York, 1974); H. Carnegy, "Oslo fears being Europe's odd man out", Financial Times, 11.10.94.

68.   The Guardian, 29.10.94.

69.   Financial Times, 30.11.94.

70.   Ibid, 28.11.94.

71.   Financial Times, 7.11.94.

72.   B. Aardal, op.cit (1991), at p.158.

73.   The Guardian, 29.10.94.

74.   Financial Times, 30.11.94.

75.   Ibid, 28.11.94.

76.   L.J. Lundqvist, "The Case of Mercury Pollution in Sweden: Scientific Information and Public Response" (Stockholm, 1974).

77.   O. Petersson and H. Valen, "Political Cleavages in Sweden and Norway", Scandinavian Political Studies 2 1979, pp.313-331.

78.   See D. Jahn, "Nuclear Power, Energy Policy and New Politics in Sweden and Germany", Environmental Politics 1(3) 1992, at pp.383-417 for an overview.

79.   B. Säarlvik "Sweden: The social base of the parties in a developmental perspective", in R. Rose (ed), "Electoral Behaviour: A Comparative Handbook" (New York, 1974), at pp.371-434.

80.   H. Heclo and H. Madsen, "Policy and Politics in Sweden: Principled Pragmatism" (Philadelphia, 1987).

81.   Gosta Rehn, "The Wages of Success", Daedalus Spring 1984; see also M. Donald Hancock and John Logue, "Sweden: The Quest for Economic Democracy", Polity

Autumn/Winter 1984; and Bernt Schiller, "The Swedish Model Reconsidered", in M.D. Hancock, J. Logue and B. Schiller (eds), "Managing Modern Capitalism: Industrial Renewal and Workplace Reform in the United States and Western Europe" (Westport Conn, 1991).

82. See F. Castles, "The Social Democratic Image of Society" (London, 1978); and G. Esping-Andersen, "Politics Against Markets: The Social Democratic Road to Power" (Princeton, 1985).

83. See B. Nedelmann, "New Political Movements and Changes in Processes of Intermediation", Social Sciences Information, Vol.23 (1984), pp.1029-48; and R.C. Sahr, "The Politics of Energy Policy Change in Sweden" (Ann Arbor, 1985), at Chapters 3-4.

84. O. Borre, "Electoral instability in four Nordic countries, 1950-1977", Comparative Political Studies 13, 1989, at pp.141-171; See also E. Anners, "Conservatism in Sweden", in D. Hancock and G. Sjoberg (eds), "Politics in the post-welfare state" (New York, 1972).

85. G. Therborn, "Swedish Social Democracy and the Transition from Industrial to Postindustrial Politics", in F.F. Piven (ed), "Labour Parties in Postindustrial Societies" (Cambridge, 1991), especially at pp.101-107.

86. H. Milner, "Sweden: Social Democracy in Practice" (Oxford, 1990).

87. See E. Vedung, "The Environmentalist Party and the Swedish Five Party Syndrome" in K. Lawson and P. Merkl, "When Party's Fail" (Princeton, 1988); see also Gosta Esping-Andersen, "Postindustrial Cleavage Structures: A Comparison of Social Stratification in Germany, Sweden and the United States", in Frances Fox Piven, op.cit (1991), at pp.147-168.

88. D. Nelkin and M. Pollak, "The Politics of Participation and the Nuclear Debate in Sweden, the Netherlands and Austria", Public Policy XXV 1977 at pp.333-57.

89. O. Petersson, "The 1976 election: New Trends in the Swedish Electorate", Scandinavian Political Studies 1 1978, at pp.109-121.

90. For a discussion of the terms of reference of these referenda, see D. Jahn, op.cit (1992), at pp.398-99.

91. H. Flam (with A. Jamison), "The Swedish Confrontation over Nuclear Energy - A Case of a Timid Anti-Nuclear Movement", in H. Flam (ed), "States and Anti-Nuclear Movements" (Edinburgh, 1992).

92. See A. Jamison et al, op.cit (1990), at p.55.

93. D. Jahn, op.cit (1993), at p.184.

94. D. Jahn, op.cit (1992), at p.404.

95. See A. Jamison, R. Eyerman, R. Cramer & J. Laessoe, "The Making of the New Environmental Consciousness Movements in Sweden, Denmark and the Netherlands" (Edinburgh, 1990), at p.55. See also H. Heclo and H. Madsen, "Policy and Politics in Sweden: Principled Pragmatism" (Philadelphia, 1987).

96. A. Jamison et al, op.cit (1990), at p.55.

97. D. Granberg and S. Holmberg, "The Political System Matters: Social Psychology and Voting Behaviour in Sweden and the United States" (Cambridge, 1988).

98. See Olof Petersson, "Democracy and Power in Sweden", Scandinavian Political Studies 14 1991, at pp.173-191.

99. S. Parkin, op.cit (1989), at p.192.

100. M. Bennulf, "Sweden: The rise and fall of Miljopartiet de grona", in D. Richardson and C.A. Rootes, op.cit (1995), at p.129; O. Lindstrom, "The Swedish Elections of 1985", Electoral Studies 5, 1986, pp.176-78.

101. For a discussion of Sweden's administrative/political culture, see T.J. Anton, "Administered Politics: Elite Political Culture in Sweden" (Boston, 1980).

102. D. Jahn, "The rise and decline of new politics and the Greens in Sweden and Germany", European Journal of Political Research 24 1993, at p.188.

103. M. Micheletti, "The Swedish Elections of 1988", Electoral Studies 8 1989, pp.169-174; and J. Worlind, "The Election to the Swedish Riksdag 1988", Scandinavian Political Studies 12, 1989, pp.77-82.

104. O. Borre, "Critical Electoral Change in Scandinavia", in R. J. Dalton (et al) (eds), "Electoral Change in Advanced Industrial Democracies" (Princeton, 1984), at p.331.

105. A. Affigne, "Environmental Crises, Green Party Power: Chernobyl and the Swedish Greens", in W. Rudig (ed), "Green Politics One" (Edinburgh, 1990), pp.115-152.

106. E. Vedung, op.cit (1988), at pp.77-109.

107. D. Jahn, "The rise and decline of new politics and the Greens in Sweden and Germany", European Journal of Political Research 24 1993, at p.187.

108. D. Jahn, op.cit (1996), especially at pp.12-14.

109. M. Bennulf and S. Holmberg, "The Green Breakthrough in Sweden", Scandinavian Political Studies, 13 1990, especially at pp.169-179.

110. P. Gaiter,"The Swedish Green Party. Responses to the Parliamentary Challenge, 1988-90" (Stockholm, 1991).

111. The Guardian, 12.2.90.

112. The Economist, 3.3.90.

113. M. Bennulf and S. Holmberg, op.cit (1990), at pp.165-184.

114. M. Bennulf, op.cit (1994), at pp.138-139.

115. M. Bennulf, op.cit (1994), at p.141 cites the study by M. Gilliam and S. Holmberg, "Valjarna infor 90-talet" (Stockholm, 1993).

116. For an account of the Social Democrats' attempt to respond positively to the tangible mood for economic and social change, see D. Sainsbury, "Swedish Social Democracy in Transition: The Party's Record in the 1980s and the Challenge of the 1990s", West European Politics 14 1991, at pp.32-57.

117. C. Brown-Humes, "Swedes have set tougher targets", Financial Times, 15.12.95.

118. Financial Times, 17.6.94.

119. H. Carnegy, "Stockholm tries to bridge gap over Danish Link", Financial Times, 13.1.94.

120. C. Brown-Humes, op.cit, Financial Times, 15.12.95.

121. Quoted in "Nordic Nationals would Boost EU's Green Lobby", Reuter's Textline, 8.11.94.

122. Quoted in Hugh Carnegy, "The Limits of Tax and Spend", Financial Times, 14.9.94.

123. Quoted in the Financial Times, 19.12.94.

124. Reuters News Service Report, 14.9.94.

125. Financial Times, 15.9.94.

126. D. Jahn, op.cit, (1993) at p.186.

127. Quoted in the Financial Times, 19.12.94.

128. Reuters News Service Report, 18.9.95.

129. For a general discussion of Green politics and European integration, see W. Rudig, "Green parties and the European Union", in J. Gaffney, "Political Parties and the European Union" (London, 1996).

130. Lars Svasaland and Ulf Lindstrom, "Scandinavian political parties and the European Union", in W. Rudig, ibid (1996), at p.210.

131. Financial Times, 19.12.94.

132. Hugh Carnegy, "Swedes count the European costs of bananas and whisky", Financial Times, 31 December/1 January 1995.

133. L. Svasaland and U. Lindstrom, op.cit in J. Gaffney, op.cit (1996), at p.214.

134. Financial Times, 22.9.94.

135. The Guardian, 23.9.94.

136. See Hugh Carnegy, "Sweden shows effects of painful cure", Financial Times, 8.11.93, for a review of the issue.

137. Financial Times, 24.4.95.

138. Financial Times, 6.9.95.

139. See Lionel Barber, "Positive vote for a bigger club", Financial Times, 15.11.94.

140. Financial Times, 11.11.95.

141. Financial Times, 19.9.95

142. The Guardian, 15.11.95.

143. Quoted in the Financial Times, 31.10.95.

144. G. McIvor, "Sweden set to grasp nuclear power nettle", Financial Times, 6.12.96.

145. Carl Bildt, "Importance of Nordic influence in EU", Financial Times, 22.11.94.

146. Hugh Carnegy, "Renewers still have battles to fight", Financial Times, 15.12.95.

147. See Hugh Carnegy, "Sweden's finance minister case as lion tamer", Financial Times, 10.4.9.6.

Part Three: New politics and Green parties: the problematic of political change

"If the doors of perception were cleansed, everything
would appear as it is ....."

William Blake, **A Memorable Fancy**

11 New politics for old? An overview of a changing political landscape

1. Identifying the Critical Issues

This study of Green party politics in western Europe has been organised around some critical issues. The purpose of this inquiry might be summarised in the following questions; where do Green parties come from and why do they emerge? Are they the organisational expression of an entirely 'new' politics, and how much is this 'new' politics an empirical reality rather than a prescriptive preference or idealised vision? Are Green parties an entirely new type of party organisation? How do they develop in the context of the political systems they seek to challenge yet, nevertheless, must adapt too, to some extent, in order to win the electoral support necessary to exert any degree of influence over policy outcomes? And are they a persistent force for change? In short, do Green parties have a political future? Considered singly or in sequence these questions contribute to an even more problematical issue that informs them - the prospects for, and the direction of, political change in contemporary Europe. The problematic of change stands at the very centre of every one of these questions. Moreover, it must be approached with considerable intellectual caution and indeed with a degree of humility.

Although this study is primarily concerned with the dynamics and development of Green parties within their respective national political milieux, a degree of transnational comparison is not only unavoidable but indispensable, if we are to make any sense of the Green party phenomenon. This comparative theme is implicit in each of the separate case studies. It is clear from these that we are confronting a political phenomenon that has common roots, shared goals and congruent forms of political organisation across the continent and beyond. In these concluding remarks it does seem appropriate to draw together some of the general themes that recur in the study of Green party politics. An overview of the Green party phenomenon, organised around some broad theoretical considerations which address these recurring questions, will obviously contribute that much more to our understanding of each national party. There are other potential benefits that accrue from a comparative approach. It is only through comparative analysis that we can begin to engage the challenge of explaining how far the Green parties have contributed to political change in western Europe. With these questions in mind, the line of inquiry will focus on the following issues: a brief review of the meaning of political change as a preface to considering whether there is any substance - to balance the rhetoric that usually accompanies the discussion of this

421

matter - to the notion of a 'new' politics agenda capable of mounting an effective challenge to the productionist, materialist and redistributive agendas of 'normal' or 'old' politics. These issues raise for consideration other important matters; for instance, whether or not 'quality of life' issues, including environmental concerns, do actually require an entirely different type of party to prosecute them in the political arena. And the extent to which other parties might be better equipped than Green parties to occupy this progressive space. All of these issues, considered in sequence, suggest an even more important question - and one that is correspondingly difficult to answer: how far does the presence of Green parties in every western European polity represent a significant force for political change? The case studies in Part Two present a variable response to this critical question. Clearly, the effectiveness of any political organisation depends on two distinct but closely related sets of circumstances. In the first place, internal structures, procedures, ideological preferences, even the power of particular personalities within these structures - all contribute to the overall resources and capabilities of any political party. Europe's Green parties share many organisational and procedural arrangements in common, but they are by no means identikit parties. Rather, they are also actual organisations that exist in real time and in particular national environments that shape these organisational characteristics and behavioural dispositions into unique patterns. This is as true of new and radical parties as it is of established and conservative ones - whatever the inclination of these newcomers to deny that fact.

To that extent, there has been in every case a dialetic between broad ideological preferences and the constraints imposed by their particular national political environments. One of the consistent themes in the comparative study of European Green parties is the extent to which the outcomes of this dialectic have encouraged the most persistent and urgent debate over the direction of Green party development in virtually every national party over the past two decades. The standoff between 'realists' and 'fundamentalists' - ranging from outright hostility to deep unease about how far to compromise the non-hierarchial, decentralised and highly participatory structures embraced by ecologists of every ideological persuasion as the Greens were obliged to come to terms with their predicament has been the principal internal dynamic and defining characteristic of these radical parties, operating as they do within established political systems largely unsympathetic to their urgent call for new beginnings and alternative policy priorities. All of these issues contribute to a better understanding of what Green party politics is about. But these structural questions take the analysis only so far. It follows that the question of 'how much change' a Green party might precipitate in its national milieu requires that we look beyond internal party organisation. However important this endogenous element is in providing indications of 'radical intent', it gives only limited clues. Political change can only really be measured at the level of the political system itself - or at least the party system in which Green parties must compete with other parties in order to win support, market their distinctive message and, wherever possible, win a degree of leverage over public policy.

To acknowledge the significance of the broader political environment on any political party, and especially on new parties struggling to put across a radical message and establish a core support, may seem to be a mundane observation. All parties operate within the nexus of competition that is the national party system. Every party system has its own distinctive rules of engagement, opportunity structures, procedures and conventions that may facilitate or constrain the efforts of the respective parties to play the political game to their own best advantage. Much of the previous work on Green parties has tended to utilise an endogenous focus - to concentrate on party structures and procedures, political style, ideological discourse and programmatic content. There are good reasons why this should be so. For one thing, much of the pioneering work on Green parties concentrated on selective and relatively successful examples of political ecologism - especially on West Germany's Die Grunen - and there is a tendency in this type of work to focus on internal dynamics. The seemingly unique style of Green party politics also encouraged this emphasis on organisational matters, with researchers perhaps intrigued by the sheer novelty of the Greens' claim to defy the laws of political gravity and to build a genuinely 'bottom up', non-hierarchic and ultra-democratic party organisation. The perplexing dilemmas and fallouts within these parties, faced as most of them have been with tensions generated within their own ranks as they came face to face with what Max Weber called the 'hard boards' of 'real' politics, also goes some way to explaining this preoccupation with internal party affairs.[1] Of course, these are all important matters in their own right and they contribute to our better understanding of 'the green wave'.[2] But, at most, they provide a one dimensional focus of what is a more complex phenomenon. And one that is insufficient if we are to engage the question of change - of how far these parties have really contributed to the 'greening' of European politics, and the true extent of their political impact, let alone their long term electoral viability. It is through these questions that the case studies in Part Two evaluates the prospects for Green parties in the context of the evolving pattern of national party competition. We offer there a cursory account of Green party futures. It is the theoretical import of these events that we now address in these concluding chapters. Suffice to say at the outset that, mindful of its pitfalls, this overarching or systems approach is indispensable to any measured analysis of these parties' long term prospects. We can only agree in part, then, with the observations of one leading analyst of Green politics, that while "future studies should focus more on the strategic interaction between Green parties and other competitors in the electoral arena", nevertheless "once the parties have arrived on the political scene, their maintenance or decline does not hinge exclusively on the actions of outside political forces but on the conscious, calculating strategies of their own voters and politicians".[3] This is certainly one factor in a complex equation, but a necessary rather than a sufficient one. To identify the research prospectus in these unduly narrow terms is to repeat the methodological constraints and biases of much of the previous research on Green parties. The electoral fortunes of these new parties only lie in their own hands - or even those of the electorate - to an extent. What these case studies do show is how far the long term prospects of Europe's Green parties depend, too, on the rules and logistics of the system of party competition that embraces them. All of these questions revolve around the concept of political change. And if, as the former Laureate believed, the "great world" does indeed "spin forever down the ringing groves of change", it is as well that we start our discussion with some consideration of this critical concept.

2. Hitting a moving target; explaining political change

There are no absolute certainties in the practice of politics, nor any infallible truths let alone 'iron laws' in political science. Politicians may speak or act without apparent doubt, but it is the task, nay duty, of academic political scientists to dispel such fallacies. And their natural caution is mirrored in the way they ply their trade. Circumspection replaces positivism as the watchword of the discipline. This maxim is nowhere more applicable than it is in the study of political change. Political change may be elusive rather than illusory. But in so far as this concept presents the observer with a moving target, it is one that is no easier to 'hit' with perceptive insights and effective methodology. Political change is precisely that; the most evanescent quality of the political universe - the star to which the most original intellects in the discipline of political science have tried to hitch their best theoretical endeavours. The intellectual task of explaining the meaning and course of political change remains as exacting as it was when Plato addressed the 'rhythms' of social and political development in his *"Laws"* twenty four centuries ago. Change remains the great conundrum, the critical problematic of the social sciences. It is much easier, however, to state the obvious, to identify change as the elemental fact of political life, than it is to adequately account for all of those 'necessary' circumstances and 'sufficient' conditions that dictate its momentum and shape its direction.

The most cursory glance at contemporary events in western Europe reveals that the continent's political affairs are redolent with every kind of change - demographic fluctuations, structural transformations, political developments, party and party system shifts, and those effective and cognitive metamorphoses in values, attitudes, expectations and social behaviour at both the individual and collective levels, that reflect changes at the macro level. Although it is a relatively straightforward matter of common sense to establish the ubiquitous quality of 'change', the prospect of properly accounting for the particularities of change raises immensely challenging questions. Change is as variable a quality as it is inexorable. It may take the form of a sudden and highly visible break with previous circumstances - an historic turning point or seachange when a revolutionary disjunction turns the world upside down. It is more usual, however, for change, even political change, to be an altogether more seamless affair. To amount, that is, to a modest incrementalism - a steady, even ambivalent, evolution rather than a spectacular eruption, and to be measured thus as modest adjustments not as monumental convulsions in the political landscape. Some of these theoretical issues have been touched upon during the course of this account of contemporary Green party politics. The implicit assumption throughout this study is that the Greens are a symptom or expression of an entirely new politics. It is an approach to the subject that is rooted in the very idea that change is underway in the European body politic. The widespread political phenomenon of the greening of party politics tells us much about the social and economic fabric of the modern state, the nature and dynamics of party competition, and the electoral make up of contemporary western Europe. Of course, there is no simplistic general theory or single overarching explanation of the 'green phenomenon'. Broad continental trends towards new political agendas and the parties that 'carry' them, coexist here with specific national configurations. The overall picture remains complicated if not confused. It certainly defies any simplistic explanation, let alone easy predictions.

To the extent that there is a 'new politics' underway in the continent's affairs, or even the potential for political novelty, the Green movement clearly reflects some of its common impulses, mutual concerns and shared assumptions. Even so, the case studies reviewed in Part Two do not suggest that there is anything like a cogent or inexorable radical force working consistently to alter the continent's political fabric - let alone a uniform green tide sweeping over and blunting the distinctive contours of the western Europe's national politics. What is evident instead is a palpable and a growing disquiet - certainly nothing more ineluctable or certain than that prospect. It amounts to a tension, if you like, between, on the one hand, those broadly shared characteristics of Europe's post-industrial societies that give rise to and sustain a new political impulse for change, with its associated post-material concerns that challenge the complacency of 'productionist politics'. And on the other hand those governing institutions, political parties and national policy agendas that embody this 'old' or conventional approach to politics. Both the demand for change in the prescriptive or ideological sense, and the embodiment of change as the objective outcome of the ensuing but as yet far from epic clash between the 'old' and the 'new' politics, have been persistent themes in the national case studies of the greening of European party politics. The Green parties, and what their emergence represents in socio-economic terms, are by no means the only or principal expression of contemporary political change. They are, however, one consistent element in the unfolding political landscape in every advanced European society. To this extent, the study of Green parties - their emergence, formation, development, contribution to national political life, and impact on the policy process - provides a useful lens through which to view at close quarters, the qualitative nature of contemporary political change. It helps, too, to uncover something of the impact, significance and direction of those altogether deeper shifts that may or may not be emerging within the fabric of western European politics.

Before we embark on a discussion of what 'new' politics is, and its impact on European party politics, it would be as well to put this debate into perspective. To juxtapose an 'old' and 'new' politics is not so much to exaggerate the differences of political style, disposition and goals between them - because these disparities do exist in the real world - but rather to ignore the extent to which these two political milieux continue to coexist and even to overlap. For it is clear, from the copious evidence of contemporary party politics, that 'old' politics parties are not wholly antagonistic to new agendas, regardless of what might be their underlying cynical motives for addressing them. Nor are 'new' parties precluded by their radical ethos, from at least adapting - if from necessity rather than conviction - to a style of politics from which their ideology and instincts might otherwise alienate them. Indeed, we might agree with Offe that there is a retrospective even a conservative instinct in some forms of ecologism, as much as a wholly progressive one. The juxtaposition between two mutually exclusive expressions of politics is thus misleading, because it rests on two false premises. On the one hand, that the fabric of European politics is durable, dominated by tradition and slow to change; or otherwise, that it is in constant flux, open to radical influences and essentially dynamic. These contrasting models of the contemporary political process represent two exclusive 'ideal types'. In the 'real world' neither condition is entirely evident. As we have seen in the discussion of the prospects for Green parties in the national profiles in Part Two, no singular model remotely begins to capture the complexity of politics on the ground. 'Old' and 'new' politics continue to coexist in every European polity, and are likely to do so for the foreseeable future.

These are not contradictory conditions so much as competing ones. The 'old' politics and the traditional political parties that pursue its productionist agenda and carry its materialistic message have showed remarkable staying power. These parties continue to hog the electoral limelight, to dominate governance, and to unduly influence the public policy process. At the same time, they have by no means remained static. Many traditional parties on all sides of the political spectrum have displayed remarkable ideological and organisational dexterity, in order to reposition or even to 'reinvent' themselves in a rapidly moving political landscape. But they remain, for all that, those vestiges of political ideas and practices that have showed, regardless of their pliancy, exceptional resilience over time. It is difficult to demur from Gordon Smith's observation that "a kind of halfway judgement is to say that the (old) parties have become more 'vulnerable', and whilst that is indisputable in terms of increasing volatility and declining party identification, it may considerably underestimate the capability of parties as 'adaptive actors'".[4] These adaptive qualities have ensured that the pattern of political change underway in western Europe's advanced democracies is a conditional rather than an exponential process. It is better conceptualised as incremental, rather than as a monumental shift of direction. Smith identifies here progress of sorts, a tendency to 'restabilisation' - the steady assimilation of new ideas, but something short of the seachange premised in the 'new' politics thesis. For this adaptive logic "will hardly mean that there is a reversion to the status quo ante, for the price of recovery is to make adjustments. Nor can 'core survival' be treated as the sole criterion; other central or contextual features may have altered out of recognition, and .... a party system may be 'transformed' with all the party actors still on stage but the changes less evident since they occur behind the scenes".[5] We must acknowledge this adaptiveness alongside the quality of persistence, if we are to give a plausible account of contemporary politics.

The 'new' politics which has emerged to challenge this orthodoxy, inhabits the very same landscape. And while its radical tribunes oppose almost everything the 'old' order stands for - its complacency, profligacy and sheer irrelevance in the face of the 'unprecedented crises' that confront humanity - they have yet to build sufficient momentum to drive out the old and replace it with an entirely new political order. Indeed, the parties that embody this radical agenda have struggled to impose themselves on the political landscape. We have seen above why this is so; a mixture of an unpalatable message that spells sacrifices, the problem of making organisational and ideological adjustments that might facilitate a more effective political role, and the resistance to the sort of radical shift in the patterns of partisanship alignments that would encourage dealignment and herald a signal breakthrough for 'new' politics. Instead, the 'old' and 'new' politics continue in an uneasy coexistence. In so far as the Green parties have enjoyed any real prospect of influencing policy outcomes or sharing power, these opportunities have come, more often than not, from adjusting their own political styles, and accommodating to those traditional parties - usually on the 'old' left - amongst whose elites and grassroots activists they have found a degree of common cause, and with whom they share a degree of commitment to progressive ideas. In short, the 'old' and 'new' politics are two sides of the prevailing currency of contemporary European politics.[6]

The coexistence of 'old' and 'new' politics has important implications for the meaning of political change. Clearly, political change does not have a uniform quality, although some general themes have been apparent in recent developments in western European politics. There has been a decline in support for the core parties of the western 'party families' - albeit more marked in some polities than others. The decline, too, in partisan loyalties has encouraged a degree of political dealignment. Yet the recent pattern of electoral volatility by no means amounts to a political meltdown or anything like it. The configuration of 'old' and 'new' politics varies from one country to another. The precise patterning here depends on a number of intervening structural variables - the type of political culture, the level of economic development, the nature of the existing party system, prevailing electoral rules and other opportunity structures. In order to make any plausible assessment about the prospects for radical political change in western Europe, we need to move from the polemics that characterise the new politics debate and examine some of these structural factors.

3. What is the 'new' politics?

Although there is a general acknowledgement in the literature on contemporary Green parties, that they and the social movements that contributed so much to their political emergence do represent a new force in politics,[7] there is much less consensus on the origins of these changes. Or indeed over their long term significance for the political order in contemporary Europe - not least for the changing complexion of the continent's party systems. Let alone any consensus on the durability of these new parties and their ultimate impact on patterns of partisanship and the framework of party competition, the effect of cultural change on political orientation, or the format of political participation, and ultimately on the content of public policy. Few commentators would deny that a 'new' politics - at least as a challenge to entrenched agendas and the usual ways of pursuing them - has been evident in the aftermath of the cultural flux of the 1960s. There has been over the duration an indifference to, and even a rejection by an upcoming generation, of the established procedures and the staid political practices of the 'old' order of politics that once presided over and shaped expectations during the modernising era that followed the twin European revolutions of industrialisation and nation building. There is nothing especially controversial or novel about this observation, at least in its most generalised expression. What we have here is a model which juxtaposes two ideal types of politics, neither of which exists exclusively or in complete isolation from one another in the 'real world'. On the contrary, as the case studies above suggest, the tension between these two conflicting outlooks and sets of aspirations provides much of the momentum that drives 'real' politics.

On one side of this equation is the 'old' political order, with its productionist agenda - a politics characterised, although by no means exclusively, by a left-right ideological cleavage, and underpinned by socio-economic or class divisions as the sociological roots of political and party competition. The modus vivendi of this conventional politics is an elitist political culture. Its principal agencies are hierarchically organised political parties managed by cabals of professional politicians - by and large, as this general caricature goes, middle class, middle aged and male as to their demographic profile. While this is an undoubtedly limited, even privileged form of democracy, it is by no means entirely closed or insular. It does, albeit in limited fashion, channel the usual impulse to participation as the alienable right of free citizens everywhere into disciplined parties that preside, at best, over an indirect and representative form of liberal democracy.[8] In its most complacent expression this model presents a positive - even positivist - vision of change. Indeed, its more exaggerated, even absurd, accounts have proclaimed the very end of change itself - a situation experienced, or rather 'enjoyed', in western style capitalist democracies; and one presumably to be attained eventually by less 'fortunate' societies, once they shake off the accumulated burdens of their past and fully embrace free markets and liberal ideas. In this deterministic account of historical change, 'history' as measurable progress finally reaches a terminus or 'end state' with the unequivocal triumph of pluralist politics.[9] This is a different utopia to the egalitarian vision of the socialist project that it eventually 'saw off' in the great war of ideas that has been waged over the past two centuries or so. It is a world without political conflict, where ideology as mere polemic is finally replaced by the 'truth' of common sense and objective science.[10] In short, in this positive version of what we might call 'bourgeois' or 'normal' liberal democratic politics, the dominant ideas of western liberalism ensure a structured, but by no means rigid, basis for mankind's normal competitive instincts. It takes its pre-eminent form in a polity in which social divisions based on primordial socio-economic interests encourage a healthy adversarialism. This is a response which is constructively channelled into political institutions that ensure that the 'centre' holds - and civilised life is thus guaranteed - instead of falling apart and surrendering to a Hobbesian chaos of a war of 'all against all'. Political conflict is by no means excluded from this model. On the contrary, it provides a healthy competitive edge. What characterises political competition here, in contrast to the classical conflict theories, is its non epic quality. Political conflict is supposedly confined to essentially pragmatic and small scale issues. The essential differences are now over the means not the end of politics, and are about the distribution of values or resources in an intrinsically materialist society. The outcome is a society whose success may now supposedly be measured, and its moral essence calculated by the canon of possessive individualism, rather than the impossibly utopian prescriptions of ascetics and visionaries who stand outside this prevailing consensus. Above all, it is a culture whose norms and mores are gauged by the objective indices of economic growth and material development.

A 'new' politics model has challenged this dominant paradigm as both misleading and complacent. Instead of a cosy consensus, deep contentions over ends as well as means continue, in this account, to shape political and ideological discourse, even - indeed especially - in the 'developed' or modernised societies so called. In essence, change in all of its aspects continues to unfold and 'history' retains its molten properties Uncertainty remains a natural political instinct and easy or optimistic prescriptions about 'futures' are the stuff of illusion. As the poet Goethe put it, 'the form flows' even as the 'flow forms'. The 'new' politics school is just as prescriptive as the 'old' politics model it confronts. But its advocates believe that they have found some evidence within existing liberal polities of an entirely new discourse, and of concrete movements for political and social change based on these radical ideas about why and how politics should be practised. The Green movement was a significant expression of this 'new' form of politics. In essence, these 'alternativists' rebutted the principal behavioural and cognitive assumptions that underpinned 'old' politics - not least, its highly structured, formalistic, bureaucratised and elitist properties. The practitioners of the new social movement politics have been obliged, however, to face some awkward predicaments in their efforts to bring to life this radical prognosis. As these alternativists have engaged the 'old' politics - not by principled rhetoric from the sidelines, but by becoming involved in 'real' politics in order to give their ideas a wider salience and to extend their constituency - they have confronted some challenging dilemmas. Especially, of whether or not to extend the politics of protest (an essentially negative if necessary activity in raising awareness of altogether novel possibilities) into electoral and other forms of direct engagement within the system of 'normal' politics itself.

The inevitable conflicts encountered in this predicament were most visible where social movements sought to engage and change the system, by forming political parties and becoming involved in electoral politics. While there has been no uniform outcome from this partial accommodation to 'normal politics' - as we have seen, a range of responses occurred depending on circumstances, political opportunity structures (for instance electoral systems) and other facilitating or inhibiting factors - the enterprise has about it a ubiquitous quality. For all of these Green parties confronted the same perplexing choices. Whatever their particular responses, their actions were motivated by a mutual and abiding ambivalence about the virtues of formal political organisation - not least party status - and about the benefits and costs of their involvement in conventional politics. Even as they engaged 'the system', they remained convinced that a 'higher' moral end somehow justified these less than ideal means. Moreover, the practice of party politics did not, as they chose to see it, compromise their political integrity or dilute their unmitigated opposition to an outdated and morally bankrupt order they wished eventually to see replaced. The practitioners of the 'new' politics remained dedicated to bringing about a fundamental shift in the political order. Political 'change', in these terms, encompassed not only alternative and utopian goals - that included a range of quality of life and social issues (peace, civil rights, anti-productionism, ecologism),[11] but an entirely new style of politics. As they became involved in the structure of a politics they wished to change, the 'new' politics practitioners exhibited alternative political values reflected, not least, in the way they managed their affairs and ran their party organisations. They manifested an open, democratic, participatory and citizen based politics - a model of party politics that is not driven by and for elites, but rather from below by the grassroots communities who provide these radical parties, both with their political raison d'être and with their political legitimacy. This model identified as the principal agencies of the 'new' politics those often spontaneous deeds (protests, demonstrations, boycotts) mobilized by social actors who were previously excluded, or self excluded, from the normal political process - notably, the young, the well educated, women and those socio-economic groups who are someway distanced from the production process.[12]

To acknowledge that a 'new' politics potential does exist in western Europe, and that it has begun to find its institutional expression in a new type of political party, is merely to point out what by common agreement is now a fact of political life. But this does not explain why this phenomenon has emerged, let alone its significance for the tenor of contemporary political life. Political commentators have recently begun to address these critical questions. A burgeoning and methodologically sophisticated literature has sought to place these developments in their wider sociological, cultural and structural milieux.

(i)   Political change as 'culture shift'

The most pervasive explanation of the rise of the 'new politics' has concentrated on primordial values as the key independent or causal variable. And especially on the assumption that changes or shifts in the basic value priorities that underlie cultural patterns and social structures, are responsible for new patterns of political behaviour. The critical causal connection in this model of political change is the purported linkages between perceptions of individual need - that shape value orientations - and political dispositions. The exponents of what is, in essence, a cognitive or political culture approach to the problematic of change, identify two broad sets of value responses to contemporary expectations. These, in turn, reflect distinct experiences of socialisation. This is a modern variant of utilitarianism - a theory of political behaviour that is driven by implicit, if competing, notions of individual welfare. Dalton identifies these elemental 'choices' thus: "many political issues, such as economic security, law and order, and national defence, tap underlying sustenance and safety needs.... In a time of depression or civil unrest, for example, security needs undoubtedly receive substantial attention. If a society can make significant progress in addressing these goals, then the public's attention can shift to higher-order values. These higher-order goals are reflected in the issues of individual freedom, self expression, and participation. These values are labelled as "post-material values".[13]

By far the most influential account of the shift to a new politics cast in this mold is provided in the opus of Ronald Inglehart.[14] Inglehart divides the predominant values that permeate contemporary societies into materialist and post-materialist orientations. Using this cognitive schematic, he discerns that the 'old' politics of materialistic or security concerns (economic growth, public order, national security and the stuff of conventional lifestyles) is persistently under challenge from alternative 'values' carried by social actors with entirely different experiences, expectations and goals. As Inglehart sees it, these new issues, and those who 'carry' them in their ideological armoury, pose a real threat to the existing political order. Instead of confirming the narrow agenda of the old politics - which for all of its endemic adversarialism remains focused on the best ways of pursuing the materialist goals of wealth creation and national security - the new post-materialist issues confront it in ways that refocus political competition. Nothing less dramatic than a 'silent revolution' is deemed to be underway in the social fabric of advanced democratic societies. Social change, fomented by a generational shift "firmly anchored in the socialization processes of individual value orientations, and slowly growing by generational turnover",[15] is creating those very conditions in which an entirely new politics can flourish.

Some other writers who draw on Inglehart's thesis, have tried to modulate his holistic, even positivist, view of social change. In one such revisionist account, the problem of separating out the multiple, far from congruent or mutually reinforcing influences that amount to 'social change', is resolved by introducing the more precise and time specific variable of 'period effects'. This is a cyclical rather than a linear or diachromic model of change. As such, it permits a perspective on 'change' that squares the long term and far from positive evolution of any social system, with short or medium term 'shifts' that might better account for social 'revolutions', silent or otherwise. The social transformation that is represented by the era of a new politics is seen here as a zeitgeist - clearly evident in contemporary politics but conditional for all that, and its outcomes possibly reversible. It all depends how the dependent variable, 'social change', is construed. For Chandler and Siaroff this transformation, to the extent that it has occurred, is also associated with a medley of other changes. Thus, while value change cannot be analysed in a vacuum, it can provide a means of conceptualising and refining the relationship between social structure and political forces. The difference between a change in social structure and value change is that, whereas social change is necessarily gradual with only long term effects, value change can be associated with 'period effects' - that is, accelerated by distinctive socialisation experiences such as war or peace, and depression or prosperity. These conditions may constitute crucial formative experiences for a given generation which are not easily explainable in terms of social change alone.[16] The 'period effect' Chandler and Siaroff identified in Germany represents one of a widespread disillusionment or *parteienverdrossenheit* which was "particularly fertile terrain for protest politics".[17] This current cycle of unrest represented "a new wave of protest potential (and) such trends, while generating a crisis atmosphere, may reflect the spread of political scepticism, even cynicism, that signifies a healthy basis for opposition politics". Viewed thus, "the 'Green phenomenon' (and protest politics generally) not only may signify a crisis of legitimacy but also may reflect a gradual maturation of the democratic capacity to criticise".[18]

A new lexicon of politics is required to explain this novel situation. What it is to be radical or conservative is thereby altered accordingly. The new radicals tend to be a fresh cohort, within a new generation, of well educated 'social and cultural specialists'.[19] The green movement was a principal agent of this political scene shift. For Inglehart, the "most striking finding" from an exhaustive trawl of social data, was the remarkable size of the potential green electorate across western Europe. Of course, he tempered his predictions with the usual caveats we would expect to find in any sophisticated social science endeavour. He observed, for instance, that potential green support was by no means a sign of an imminent political breakthrough, or that the greens were "about to become one of the major political forces in western Europe overnight".[20] Inglehart was well enough aware, too, that any 'revolution' is less about the wholesale replacement of one social order by another; that in any complex social system change amounts to trends that involve the usual adjustments, compromises and trade offs that blunt, or at least take their toll of, radical energy. This 'realism' extended to his awareness of the resource constraints that handicap new radical movements - not least, a reluctance to practise the sort of disciplined, strategically cautious, well organised politics required to channel raw, potent political energy in ways that maximise the electoral 'pay off' necessary to exert any influence over government and the direction of public policy.

Nevertheless, Inglehart remained convinced that far-reaching political change was in the air, inasmuch as "the rise of post materialism has placed existing party systems under chronic stress (and that) in most countries, these alignments do not correspond to the social bases of support for changes, or to polarization over the most heated issue".[21]

This exogenous model of political change has been widely criticised.[22] As a model of political change it takes too much for granted. Whereas, at the level of micro analysis it commits a familiar error of the deductive method: it draws too many particularistic assumptions about individual political motivation on the basis of a sweeping analysis of the putative macro dynamics of contemporary politics. In essence, it gives far too much explanatory weight to pre-adult socialisation patterns as the formative experiences of basic values. As such, it ignores both the variety and persistence of 'change inducing' influences - for instance the impact of higher education in shaping radical prospectuses.[23] As well as failing to account for the rich diversity of political cultural influences in otherwise adjacent polities at similar levels of development.[24] This is a refinement, nevertheless, of the value shift model. It avoids crude positivism, but in so far as it continues to regard values as the independent causal variable behind behavioural changes, it suffers the same methodological flaws as the socialisation thesis. Above all, it is a highly selective account. Kreuzer labels it unflatteringly as 'parsimonious' - implying that it is overly didactic, giving the impression that we are dealing with a universal, homogeneous and a less ambiguous phenomenon than the facts actually bear out.[25] There is clearly much about contemporary politics that confirms the general impression that a degree of 'real' change is underway, both in the pattern of politics and in the socio-cultural fabric that underpins the body politic. The inclination, however, to extrapolate from this 'hunch' and to be entirely convinced that the cause and direction of such changes lies in individual value shifts or socialisation patterns, can provide only a partial answer to the conundrum of change. To rely on accumulated 'survey' data about changing social, economic and cultural dispositions is by no means a sufficient basis for the explanation of their causes, or for the accurate prediction of future political trends. It is easy to identify the flaws in this approach, even though Inglehart's scholarship is impressive in its range and rigour. Indeed, he was subsequently sufficiently chastened by his critics to take more account of both structural and contingent factors. Nevertheless, these were minor adjustments grafted onto his values paradigm. The acknowledgement that pre-adult socialisation has to contend with continuous lifetime influences that modify the primordial experiences that shape 'being' and 'consciousness', does not alter the central conclusion that "the values of a given generation tend to reflect the conditions prevailing during its pre-adult years".[26] For one thing, we cannot afford to take the overt 'evidence' of radical inclinations at face value; 'facts' are by no means self evident and require interpretation. The very same values, mediated by different lifetime experiences, may just as easily lead to a conservative as to a radical disposition.

While this may not be the principal expression of non-material values there are, even so, non-radical greens. William Tucker was moved to write of the American environmental movement, that while environmentalism is perceived to be a 'liberal' cause, and is thereby more appealing to the left, this coincidence cannot be assumed a priori, but can only be properly explained by locating actual green movements in the social structures that shape them and condition their concrete political orientation. In America environmentalism took on a conservative as well as a radical demeanour because it served the interests of a privileged middle class to adopt an anti-industrial, anti-productionist outlook. Thus, "under the aegis of environmentalism, America's upper-middle class has learned to suspect technological change, to look askance at economic growth, to place 'spiritual values' over 'material progress', and to start looking down on industry and commercial activity as something vulgar and distasteful. All of these, of course, are ancient, well tuned aristocratic attitudes. The quality of self interest in the environment movement is something which the press has found absolutely impossible to grasp. The understanding of environmentalism as a protection of entrenched privilege makes this "anti-everything" position perfectly understandable. People who have reached a certain level of affluence and privilege in society inevitably turn their efforts away from the accumulation of more wealth and privilege, and towards denying the same benefits to others."[27]

We are as familiar in Europe with 'nimbyism' as are Americans, and the role of conservation and nature preservation societies in the wider ecology movement does indicate its altogether ambivalent outlook. Of course, Tucker's comments were made well before the European ecology movement connected with a deeper sense of radical discontent. Nevertheless, while it remains the case that the Green movement here has generally found greater ideological empathy with radical aspirations than it has with conservative instincts, the prevalence of pure green ideas, and the resistance in many national movements to a take over by leftists, does suggest a movement that is far from synonymous with the singularly progressive preferences identified by Inglehart as a political culture shaped primarily by a radical modus vivendi. This is a less familiar critique than it should be. Savage is surely closer to the mark when he connects the ideological tensions within the green movement to a complex mix of situational and structural factors largely overlooked by Inglehart. He concludes that "Inglehart's post materialists are not a unified group marching to the beat of a single drummer. There are important factions within the post materialists that have their origins in the pre-industrial and industrial divisions existing in Europe that are reflected in ideological disagreement and political conflict. These traditional cleavages are responsible not only for intergenerational antagonisms but intra-generational hostility as well".[28] Inglehart and his protégés took the visible symbols and verbal expressions of the radical intent apparent in contemporary society too much at face value. Ideological form was too readily confused with political substance - a persistent methodological error familiar to critics of the political culture or socialisation model of political change.[29]

Models of political change that concentrate on values as primary causes are inclined, then, to distort what is an infinitely more complex causal sequence. Not least, because they underplay the impact on politics of a host of structural, situational, institutional and even contingent variables. According to this more broadly focused account of change, it is much less a case of values conditioning political responses than of values themselves being mediated by all manner of situational influences, and through multifarious structural factors to produce variable outcomes and a far more complex and ambiguous pattern of politics than is allowed for by this altogether more didactic model. If we apply this methodological canon to the development and practice of Green party politics - the task to be undertaken in the concluding chapter - it soon becomes apparent, as the case studies indicate, that the political fate of these new Green parties has been determined much less by the certain allure of their message (the appeal to the values per se of their target constituency amongst the new post-material middle class), than by a host of structural, situational and contingent factors. In short, to identify values as the principal cause of change is to merely isolate one element of what is an altogether more complex equation. Particular configurations of national history and prevailing patterns of political culture certainly do help to determine why similar value preferences may enjoy a higher or lower political salience in some polities than they do in others. But these values would be ethereal and remain wholly disconnected from the social process, without those structural media or networks that provide them with conduits for social meaning. It is these nexus that give them their political salience. For even if it was the case that the reservoir of alternative ideas and radical values that express the contemporary impulse for 'change', was somehow its principal dynamic, this theoretical formulation fails to explain why it should be that these values are expressed as either ecologism or otherwise take a different ideological form. Claus Offe's critique of the values driven model makes the pertinent observation that "the predominant need for self actualisation could equally well lead to new and unconventional, but entirely private lifestyle and consumption patterns, rather than to new politics".[30] The sheer variety of the contemporary radical instinct, let alone the narrow preferences of those post-materialists who otherwise lapse into political apathy or mere self indulgence, calls into question, even in its own narrowly didactic terms, the explanatory virtues of a theory that cannot readily discriminate between the competing expressions of its essential dynamic.

Nor should we discount the significance of those contingent qualities that also help to shape political opportunities and determine political outlooks. The impact of seminal moments or climatic events on future political outcomes must be properly accounted. We saw above, in the various national accounts of Green party development, how important the Chernobyl disaster was in determining the electoral prospects of many Green parties. More local events too - from the Koijarvi lake protest in Finland to the Sellafield issue in Ireland - have impinged on these national developments. As have a range of other issues, political scandals and unforeseen events, at various moments in the electoral cycle, that have either facilitated or dulled the degree of ecological awareness in particular polities. It is by no means a trivial or irrelevant matter to acknowledge and audit such factors in determining the pace and outcome of political change - even if these are by no means its major causes.

(ii)   Structural models of change

Whereas Inglehart's account of political change focuses almost exclusively on value shifts, and regards the process as the cumulative and aggregated outcome of individual transformations, writers in the structural school focus instead on the macro dimension - the difference, as some analysts aptly put it, between a close up photograph and a wide angled, cinematic vision of the problematic of political change.[31] The advantage of using the structural model is precisely this width of focus. 'Structuration' is a conveniently ecumenical term that suggests a clutch of relevant variables here - from pervasive historical conditions, to those particular socio-economic organisations and institutional arrangements that mediate individual experience and impose collective patterns on behaviour.[32] Individuals respond to the social milieux that 'capture' them, and in which they play out their various roles. And while 'new' politics is an entirely conceivable response to recent and novel configurations of circumstances, and to how individuals and group actors perceive them, it is by no means the straightforward causal linkage identified by the value shift model. For these structures per se colour and cloak behavioural responses and invest them with a variety of both meaning and purpose. Several writers have focused on the political resources available to new social movements - or on the political opportunity structures[33] that either hinder or facilitate their emergence, and impact favourably or not on their political effectiveness, once they do emerge in a party political format. The mere potential for a new, radical politics is insufficient, on its own, to bring about any radical transformation of the political order. What is required instead, to translate this potential into effective action, are both available resources and elites capable of mobilising and employing such resources to good effect. Resource mobilisation theorists concentrate their explanatory efforts on this particular aspect of the organisational dimension. They distance themselves some considerable way in methodological terms from the didactism of the values paradigm. For as Kuechler and Dalton observe of this model, "the emergence of a social movement is an almost arbitrary event", whereas it is "the ideological bond of a movement (that) is manufactured and manipulated by elites".[34]

This emphasis on resources and deliberative action is apparent, too, in Kitschelt's explanation of new left parties. The critical variable here is less the prospect for change, identified as a cultural propensity to radicalism, than it is the availability of actual resources and those structural factors that determine how and to what extent the radical 'instinct' is actually operationalised. For "grievances and institutional change are endemic in most societies, but they are rarely translated into collective political action. Instead, the actors' skills and resources and the broader opportunity structures determine when individuals are able to engage in collective mobilisation. In particular, the choice of a specific vehicle of mobilisation, such as a political party, can be explained only in terms of actor's resources and opportunities".[35] A political opportunity structure that is relatively hostile to new politics - for instance an electoral system based on plurality - does influence the chances of new party formation and determines whether or not the radical impetus strikes out as an entirely new party, or concentrates its energies instead on an internecine fight for the 'ideological soul' of an existing 'leftist' party. Moreover, these are more than incidental tactical options that signify little for the tenor of national politics. It is clear from the above case studies that 'mere' tactical considerations do determine political outcomes.

There are other significant differences between these two paradigms. While the causal sequence of the value model posits a straightforward linkage between novel socialisation experiences and the values they induce and a new politics, the structuralist paradigm is less positivistic as to outcomes. For Inglehart the new politics is a phenomenon *au courant*. Whereas Offe's use of the structural paradigm, on the other hand - inasmuch as it allows values and propensities to be mediated by a clutch of complex structural milieux - is quite capable of allowing the paradox of a 'new' politics reflecting 'old', even conservative, values. And of explaining, for instance, the perplexing paradox we have seen amongst some Green parties: of why their Green activists or voters might well not be eagerly looking forward to a post-materialist world, but instead react negatively against the very idea of change - a fear or at least a reservation about the 'new' rather than its eager anticipation. Both the salience of new politics values and a resistance to them is deemed here to reflect the objective and frequently ambiguous circumstances in which all social actors play out their various and far from straightforward roles. This prismatic model offers an altogether more plausible account of the complexities of politics - radical or otherwise - than the value paradigms. As Frankland and Schoonmaker observe, "this political world is dense with tangible structures where individuals who jockey for tactical advantages wage real dramatic conflicts with ascertainable costs and benefits. Instead of relying on the profile of political values garnered through survey research, it emphasises organisational competition, political action, and more immediate conflict".[36] The subtlety of this distinction would certainly account for the differences between radical Greens and those pure Greens who are much less post-materialist in orientation, and more exercised by a concern to preserve nature, or to avoid, halt or ameliorate the worst excesses of rapid socio-economic change - without embracing the radical options favoured by Green party activists bent on a wholesale social transformation. This distinction is useful, too, in explaining some of the differences in motivation between Green party activists and green lobbyists.

If the structural variable has the advantages ascribed to it above, its very diffuseness also suggests some methodological drawbacks. These might be ameliorated, to an extent, by separating out specific elements for closer consideration. 'Structuration' is thereby disaggregated into a multivariate menu - a template for applied middle range research, rather than a fully fledged, grand theory of political change. With these constraints in mind, we would identify this menu as highlighting the following:

(a)   *Catalysts* that activate political discontent. There are wide variations within this sub-category. A political climate conducive to radical change - or at least to the mood of discontent or unrest that must preface it - might be induced by merely contingent factors. The Chernobyl nuclear accident, for instance, was a signal event in raising ecological consciousness across the continent. Protests against the nuclear energy option were, likewise, a significant factor in fostering the widespread disquiet that helped to mobilise Green and new movement parties in several west European states.[37] Some catalysts might also have a more organic quality; the demographic and generational changes that helped to foment unrest in the academies during the late sixties and early seventies were important synergists for the 'new' politics movement, but hardly a deterministic one.

If there is little to be said in favour of didactic or positivist 'general' theories, there is little more explanatory mileage in those 'hunches' about cause and effect that can only fasten on 'likely' contingent factors - plucked from the historical or sociological weft - and 'identified' a priori as primary causes of political change. Notwithstanding the significance of 'events', these are neither random nor freestanding. They are part of altogether more structured, composite and patterned arrangements. And while such contingencies do impact on outcomes, they do not entirely determine them. There is little, then, to be said for the account of the greening of European politics that identifies the nuclear catharsis of the Chernobyl disaster and its aftermath - the widespread public concern at airborne radiation - as a determinative factor in the development of Green parties. Affigne's study of the Swedish Miljopartiet, for instance, identified this accident as the principal factor behind the Green Party's breakthrough at the 1988 election.[38] Whilst acknowledging the salience of this momentous event in raising environmental consciousness across the continent after 1986, culminating in some spectacular performances by the Greens in the 1989 Euro-elections, these successes depended on more than this one event. They reflected, too, a deeper discontent with governing parties, and owe as much to the electorate's continuing obsession with materialist agendas as with ecologism per se.[39] Kitschelt, whose work focused on the contribution of anti-nuclear protest to ecological awareness and the radicalisation of politics, is altogether more measured in weighing the significance of such contingent factors. He notes that "it would be difficult to prove (such) a linkage between ecological deprivation and Green party performance in a cross national perspective".[40]

(b)   *Institutional factors*, as the evidence of the case studies indicates, may either facilitate or inhibit new politics parties. This variable includes the consideration of election systems, the formal rules of the political game (funding arrangements for instance), national political preferences and those cultural factors that shape the practice of politics: whether, for instance, the political regime favours an adversarial or a consociational or coalitional 'culture'. Of course, formal procedures (not least electoral rules) do help to condition these cultural propensities. But once in existence, these political preferences do, to a degree, take on a life of their own. Finally, the constitutional format can have a considerable impact - direct and indirect - on the conduct of politics. The degree of centralisation or the extent that power is devolved may raise or dampen political discontent, or channel it in a particular direction. This is an intricate topic with several facets, but one general conclusion we might draw from the case studies in this regard is that quasi-federal or fully federalised polities do encourage small parties, whereas unduly centralised regimes make life much harder for them. This does not mean that new politics parties will automatically flourish in federations - both Spain and Italy have devolved power to regional governments in recent years, and the main beneficiaries have been regionalist not new politics parties. But when other conditions are present - as they were in Germany - inter alia a suitable catalyst, demographic change, a favourable election system, and a sense of disillusionment with the main party of the left-federalism did provide a new radical party with a suitable base from which to consolidate, build its core support, and thereby to establish a firm bridgehead in national politics.

(c)   *Structural factors.* The social, economic and political arrangements beyond the institutional arrangements identified in (b) above, interact with these intermediate variables - opportunity structures, regime rules and resource factors - in ways that determine the broad tenor of political change in any particular society. The discussion by several analysts of class structuration,[41] new systems of production and political economy,[42] globalisation patterns [43] and, in sequence, the notion, however academically contentious, of a 'post-industrial society' covers the principal themes of this approach.[44] These exogenous or systemic factors are bound to feed back into and shape national political outcomes - as many of the national profiles above indicate. Because this study is about one particular expression of new radical politics, it is inevitably selective in its focus. We are more drawn, given the questions that were outlined at the beginning of this chapter, to the discussion of explicitly political variables - and in particular to the contribution of party and party systems to the prospects of a new politics and its contribution to political change. But we should not lose sight of these broader structural themes and their effect on our understanding of the greening of contemporary politics. The prospects for Green parties, their core electoral constituency, their ideological appeal, and their policy agendas, are all in some degree a manifestation of those macro-changes which are unfolding within the sociology and political economy of Europe's advanced societies.

This suggests a composite account of political change in which, as Poguntke sees it, "the overall political situation has an independent effect on the strength of new politics protest. The salience of environmental problems, the degree of permissiveness of society, the density of military installations in a country, and its geographical locations - to mention but a few factors - give more or less resonance to the political forces which mobilise upon such issues. Hence, the strength of the new politics segments of society varies cross nationally according to the quantitative extent of individual-level changes and the overall situation in the country".[45] In similar vein Kitschelt identifies what he calls the five key indicators which determine the prospects for 'significant' left-libertarian parties (including the Greens but not exclusively so). Bearing in mind that these indicators are time specific - and certainly are more relevant to the 1970s and 1980s than they have been subsequently - Kitschelt suggests that the following socio-economic circumstances are more, rather than less, conducive to the emergence and relative success of such parties: high per capita GNP; high levels of social security expenditure; low levels of industrial unrest (especially labour strikes); a significant role for left parties in national politics and even in government making; and a high intensity of controversy over the nuclear issue.[46]

There may well be very specific correlations between demographic and sociological and political outcomes, but this amounts to little more than a useful checklist - a starting point for formulating hypotheses about how these linkages actually work. Certainly, where the Greens are concerned this framework in itself is inadequate for explaining the greening of politics. Green parties have emerged and enjoyed a degree of success in countries where some or all of these factors are in place. But this is an indiscriminate model and hardly a predictive one, for these factors apply, in some measure, in almost all western Europe democracies. The principal differences are those of degree rather than of kind. What can be said with confidence, however, is that social structural variables do interact with political, cultural and even contingent factors, to determine the timing, circumstances, and type of Green party formation; as well as the pace and direction of their subsequent development and future prospects. The proper understanding of the Green phenomenon draws, thus, on the disciplines of sociology and economics as much as it does on political science.

(iii)   The 'party' variable; the endogenous (organisational) and exogenous (systemic) elements

Political parties are something more than passive conduits that merely 'channel' ideological preferences or mediate cultural values between civil society and the state. They continue to occupy a crucial intercalary position, and provide a focal point of the political communication, the legitimising functions, and of the political education that passes between citizens and government - and this in spite of a recent discourse that predicts their increasing obsolescence for either civic empowerment within the political management of advanced societies, where technology has apparently introduced more reliable points of contact between government and publics.[47] Parties are thus agents of change as much as of control. As one seasoned commentator on the Green party phenomenon has put it, "parties represent societal changes if they draw on distinct groups in the social structure and have unique political outlooks and dispositions to act".[48] Political parties have appropriately been identified as the 'crucibles' of political competition in nation states - the sine qua non of democracy.[49] To an extent, all parties perform these basic articulation and aggregation functions. Functionalists identify 'party' as the institutional embodiment or reflection of the social milieu that gives rise to them in the first place. In this model they are primarily, if not exclusively, reactive organisations. But they also take a more active role in shaping the political environment, inasmuch as they possess resources for mobilising what are often inchoate public moods, and for rousing latent or passive public interests. And they utilise these resources - albeit with varying degrees of success - in order to present a distinctive outlook on (and in the case of radical parties, to challenge) the political order.

Raschke's account of party development is, on the face of it, cast in the classic functionalist mold; thus, "parties (do) appear as bearers of societal interests, which are transformed into programmes by party organisations halfway democratised, and therefore are of lasting influence". They are "with respect to their programmes and policies, to a large extent determined by systemic imperatives" that "cannot in general be explained primarily by internal organisational circumstances".[50] While this is accurate, as far as it goes, it is a skewed and limited account of party politics. For it is also the case that this purely functional response to the social stimuli that give rise to party formation and development is by no means as uniformly reactive as the crude functionalist accounts infers.   If parties were merely a collective response to external stimuli, there would be little point studying the organisational, resource, procedural, leadership or any other endogenous quality of political parties. Neither leadership strategies, or factional strife, resource availability or procedural arrangements,

437

would have any determinative effect on the political fate of a party. The evidence suggests that this is simply not the case - that parties do improve, or indeed damage, their own political prospects by choosing particular leaders, by adopting certain procedures, embracing distinctive programmatic commitments, and not least by the general disposition they adopt to the political system per se. To suggest that there are no alternative responses available to them, or that these other options would have had no effect whatsoever on outcomes, is to countenance a determinism that ignores the rich and contingent history of the rise and fall of *real* political parties. None of these caveats, of course, gainsays Raschke's important point about the significance in this complex calculus of exogenous variables; that the prospects for political change do not merely require a radical impetus or a party dedicated to bring it about, but also a gathering sense of crisis in the polity at large. It is difficult to disagree with his general prognosis that the best prospects for a new politics do depend more than coincidentally on a rising mood of public discontent with the failures of the 'old' politics; a pervasive sense that "the established modern mass (*volksparteien*) parties have touched the limits of their effectiveness, which is impaired, inter alia, by (a) over adaptation to existing structures which prevents them from becoming vehicles of future-orientated, active change; (b) over-generalisation, which renders them increasingly incapable of representing the variety of qualitative societal interests; (c) over-institutionalised, which has estranged them from the participatory and also expressive needs of a growing number of citizens; and (d) overstrain as a result of no longer meeting the expectations which they themselves have created as well as those held by others. Such manifestations of party failure contribute to a form of instability in western party systems which cannot be detected with the aid of the usual party political indicators of crisis, and, therefore, is easily disputed".[51]

At the same time, it would be entirely misleading to suggest that whatever new political parties do to position themselves to take advantage of any climate of discontent, or to minimise the impact of their resource limitations, is of no real consequence for the political outcome of their radical quest. Parties are, then, important agencies of change: or rather, they mediate change. They are by no means passive agencies. How a party connects - whether it reflects or alienates, new social movements - does have significance for the pattern of national politics. And whether a new party presents itself as a plausible vehicle for new ideas or rising discontents can have a considerable bearing on the prospect for political change. For this reason, it is important that we precisely identify what is 'new' about new politics parties; who they attract into their ranks as activists and supporters; and how their ideological performance and programmatic choices close off, or otherwise open up, the potential for political realignment and dealignment in the prevailing pattern of national party politics.

The 'party' variable therefore merits close attention on its own terms. We divide it here into two distinct but closely related facets which mirror the critical variables identified in Chapter One as marking out a distinctive 'green' territory in contemporary party politics. Both variables have influenced how effectively Green parties have applied their energies and adapted their resources to the herculean tasks of bringing about political and social change. They are (a) 'party' as an organisational (endogenous) variable per se; and (b) the party system variable (exogenous) - how the prospects for the Greens, or any new or old party for that matter, are facilitated or circumscribed by the circumstances, procedures and operation of the broad system of party competition that envelopes them. The critical questions raised by the endogenous line of inquiry are whether, or to what extent, a new party type now exists alongside the 'mass' or 'catch-all' parties, and whether it has an entirely novel political rationale? In terms of ideological configurations, the question here is whether we can distinguish, in any meaningful sense, between the various new politics parties? Are the Greens all that different in their ideological preferences, organisational orientations, or in their overall disposition to the liberal political system, from libertarian, alternativist or new left parties? Von Beyme, for instance, awards the Greens a distinct category in his morphology of party families. Dalton and Kuechler recommend instead a broad category of 'movement parties' - an outgrowth of divergent but distinctive new social movements.[52] Kitschelt prefers to see the Greens as merely a species of a broader left-libertarian genus.[53] Whereas other writers have engaged in a persistent debate about the 'newness' or otherwise of Green and other radical parties.[54] These are more than matters of political classification. Establishing the particular impetus for any party's 'dynamic' or electoral momentum tells us much about the prospects or otherwise for its cooperation with other new parties - and even with some established parties over the medium or longer term.

The party organisation variable raises thus, some critical questions. Can we expect these 'new' parties, for instance, after an unsteady start, to offer any effective and sustainable challenge to the established political order? Or do they face instead a daunting and largely hopeless task for which they are poorly resourced, badly positioned - vis a vis other parties - and severely handicapped by their inexperience, utopianism, factional disputes over both strategy and ideology, and ambivalence at least - and in some cases outright hostility - to playing the political game according to the 'normal' rules? The central question here is the novelty or otherwise of these 'new' parties - the extent to which they see their principal purpose as bringing about a fundamental shift in the cultural and socio-economic order. If they are 'new' politics parties in the full meaning of that concept, they will be the more likely to retain a residual radicalism that even the exigencies of short term adaptation will not bury under an avalanche of compromise. On the other hand, 'newness' usually means fewer natural linkages, whether of a procedural or ideological kind, with established parties, particularly those on the old left. And such polarisation may well marginalise these parties at a time when the crisis of the old left and the urge to 'reinvent' the progressive side of politics is opening up all sorts of opportunities for new alliances and ideological cohabitation.[55] Nor are the Greens merely victims here. They possess resources and a potential, however constrained, to influence outcomes. How they carry themselves in this situation is likely to some extent to impact on events.

The way that any party conducts its affairs is bound to affect both its political effectiveness and its chances of electoral success. As we saw in Chapter One, Green parties do purport to be different - to abjure the conventional hierarchical arrangements, the top-down structures and the professionalised - and 'cynical' - politics employed by the mainstream, mostly 'catch-all' parties. Nevertheless, ideals do conflict with circumstances that require an unavoidable degree of adjustment - 'concessions', no less, to the organisational imperatives and the rigours of contemporary party politics as it is played in modern mass democracies. The Green parties have begun to address this problem, even if they have not by any means resolved it. To this extent, the party organisation variable provides us with a useful comparative focus for measuring the performance of Green parties against one other, and in relation to other parties in their respective national party systems. A contiguous problem here is whether the Greens - or any other variant of 'new' party - prefer to occupy a narrow niche status. We identified this option in Chapter One in ideological terms. There has been an intense debate in many European Green parties about their place on the conventional left-right spectrum. In essence, whether to plough a pure-green furrow, or otherwise to adopt a more eclectic view of ecologism that encourages a degree of accommodation with other radical parties, and especially those on the left with whom red-greens shared at least some ideological affinities. The evidence suggests that the manner in which many Green parties have approached these challenges and the predicaments that follow from them has, pace the functionalist account of party development, determined how far they have either squandered opportunities, or made the most of their limited resources.

The other principal element of the 'party' variable is systemic in character. It acknowledges that 'exogenous' factors - those external to the party organisation - must also be properly accounted; that no party, however resourceful, pragmatic, well led or adaptive, holds its political destiny entirely in its own hands. Parties in democratic societies inhabit a pluralistic and competitive environment with its own logistics. We must give due consideration to this systemic variable; to the way that national opportunity structures (the election rules, party funding from the public purse and broadcasting regulations for instance) affect the outcomes of party competition. The patterning of party politics is also an expression of deeper sociological factors - the history of ideological divisions and the degree of their polarisation, social cleavages, and constitutional or regime arrangements. These factors, in turn, determine the number of parties in any political system, as well as the spatial positioning of these parties along the system's ideological spectrum, and their adjacence to one another - all of which affects the scope for inter-party cooperation and the prospects for trade offs and coalition making. While there is nothing routine or automatic about this calculus - with every Green party making choices that reflect the dynamics of intra-party politics - and certainly no acceptance of the insular and deterministic logic of fullblown systems theory per se, it is hard to deny the importance for the prospects of the Greens, as for any political party, of the system of party competition in which these strategic choices are exercised.

The case studies again provide abundant evidence to show that, while a raw 'new politics' potential does exist, it may equally be constrained or encouraged - depending on the precise configurations of party competition in any particularly national polity. One cannot but agree with Muller-Rommel's observation that the Greens' "electoral success is not so much dependent upon the strength of new movements in a given country as upon the type of party system in which they operate".[56] The positive evidence in this account for the impact of the party competition regime on the formation, development and prospects for Green - and indeed other new politics parties - is quite conclusive; that "in polarised multi-party systems (Italy, Denmark and the Netherlands) with a proportional representation electoral law, the movement followers vote is distributed among several small left-wing parties, but also among larger parties".[57] There is more, in short, to the electoral calculus than electoral mathematics. Local political culture also plays its part in shaping the responses of the 'old' parties. In more flexible multi-party systems, for instance, where traditional parties are more receptive to the new politics agenda, and exhibit, for all sorts of reasons that we will discuss in Chapter Twelve, a willingness to incorporate some of their issues into their own programmes, these conventional parties may still retain the political initiative over the newcomers. Indeed, in some situations they may appropriate enough of the new politics potential to restrict support for alternativist parties to the very margins of the electorate. Whereas in multi-party systems, where more than two parties exist, but two party 'blocs' - Conservative and Social Democrat/Socialists, arranged along a straightforward right-left continuum - continue to dominate party politics, the logic of party competition tends to concentrate the minds of established political elites and publics alike on the centre ground, where electoral contests in most advanced democracies are usually settled.

The party variable in both of its expressions holds the key to unravelling some of the persistent enigmas of the new politics. In section (4) below we address the organisational question in greater detail; of whether, or to what extent, the Greens are an entirely 'new' type of political party. Or whether, instead, they are merely a variation on a radical theme that has deeplaid roots in the discourse and landscape of European party politics. The resolution of this conundrum - political novelty or a variant of a generic radicalism - helps us to uncover something of the meaning of 'greening'. Any discussion of party organisation - of how these new parties confront the political order and pursue their own agendas - requires that we audit the resources available to them and take note of the constraints they face. As we saw in Chapter One, part of their persistent predicament lies in the abiding tension between, on the one hand, a party model driven by elemental assumptions about 'political man' that have much more in common with Rousseau or Gandhi than with Hobbes or Hayek. And on the other, the continual need - a direct consequence of the decision to play electoral and parliamentary politics in the first place - to address those unpalatable adjustments and compromises with preferred positions that confront every party that opts for the routine game of politics. These dilemmas certainly impinge on Green party organisations and are most visibly - and sometimes destructively - played out in these parties' institutional fora. At the same time, the organisational or dispositional axis does not exist entirely in isolation from the system variable. The structure of party competition, which we discuss further in Chapter Twelve, pervades these deliberations over strategy and disposition as we saw in the national case studies. Moreover, by means of a reverse feedback, the developments and crises of the Green parties affected the ways that the other parties in the national party system responded in turn to them. Some critical issues were raised on this account. Whether, for instance, their core support could be won over by 'greening' a party's programme. How far the Greens were regarded as an electoral threat, an unreliable partner, or otherwise as an indispensable parliamentary ally with whom mutually acceptable policy deals could be struck and sustainable power trade offs negotiated. These are interesting questions for what they tell us about the dynamics of contemporary party politics. But they are of more than intrinsic academic interest. For an understanding of the logistics of Green party politics should enable us to better understand the potential for Green parties in western Europe in the foreseeable future, as well as their salience over the longer run. And by so doing, enable us to grasp something of the elusive dynamics of change in contemporary party politics per se.

4.   'New Politics' but a new party type?

(i)   The new politics model: ecologism as a 'famille spirituelle'

Green parties have appeared and engage in electoral politicsin every western European polity but they have become a significant force in national politics in only a very few of them. The Greens emerged in response to much the same discontents and continue to appeal to a broadly similar post-materialist constituency, consisting by and large of the younger, better educated and new middle class professionals employed in the service and public welfare sectors - groups both cognitively and, for the most part, spatially removed from the material production and wealth generating occupations of modern capitalism. Von Beyme, in his morphology of party types, identified the Greens as a distinct party group - a 'famille spirituelle'.[58] This generic listing is, however, misleading. It is a classification rooted in the idea that ideological affinity provides the main glue that holds these parties together.

In the case of the 'Green family', an otherwise eclectric mix of libertarians, new leftists, alternativists, anarchists and ecologists of various hues are assumed to share an underlying commitment to ecological values, with an affective investment in future rather than short term goals - one primarily manifested in a radical programme that questions the very fabric of liberal, bourgeois and capitalist society. Ideology, in this scheme, is the principal defining characteristic because "over the long term only parties based on ideology have succeeded in establishing themselves".[59] This assumption raises as many questions as it answers. At the general level, it is undoubtedly the case that ideology, by providing a broad set of precepts around which party members can cohere and with which its supporters can identify, does fulfil an important function. Ideology is a source of initial contact and of organisational cohesion for political activists who share a vision and some common preferences. But it may also, and quickly, become a source of contention. A discourse that explains and puts into historical context the party's internal development, as well as locating its 'proper' place in the broader spectrum of national politics, may just as easily encourage discord and disputation over its political direction. The significance of this for Green party development was quite apparent in the national profiles. On the one hand, deep factional rifts within many Green parties - especially during the early years of party formation and development - did little to improve either their effectiveness as radical challengers to the established political order, or to enhance their electoral appeal. In some notable cases - for instance, Denmark and the Netherlands - the distractions and the energy expended on ideological infighting, caused the Greens to lose political ground to other radical parties - a démarche from which they have so far not managed to recover.

What, then, are we to make of the ideological dimension? Clearly, all radical parties endure severe handicaps inasmuch as they present a challenging, even uncomfortable, vision of society and its ills. This would limit their political opportunities, even without any other obstacles to negotiate. The fact, however, that many Green parties have compounded their own difficulties by devoting scarce resources and limited energies to factionalism - a case of negative resource mobilisation if you like - does underline that we cannot take for granted that we are dealing here with a politically coherent movement. How then should we characterise the Green parties? Are they similar but different entities, or do they share, for all of their ideological petulance, a core belief system that distinguishes them from other radical party movements? Is there, after all - and putting these squabbles over doctrine into perspective - a generic 'green political identity' as von Beyme asserts, that separates this motley of 'radicals' from other assorted leftists? There are no straightforward answers to these questions, not even from those political scientists who have studied the Greens at closer quarters than von Beyme. Moreover, these academic disputes are far from incidental to the critical task of uncovering the meaning of Green party politics. These problematics go to the heart of the debate about whether the Greens do actually represent a 'new' politics. On one side of this discourse are those analysts who maintain that the Greens are indeed an entirely new type of party - and that, as such, they are defined by a novel ideology, the participatory and anti-elitist practice of politics, and they are supported by a 'new' type of voter.[60]

Poguntke has endorsed these propositions by playing down the significance of the ideological schism that has divided some Green parties into two apparently discrete party types. As he sees it "this distinction refers merely to varying degrees of radicalism. It does not appear to point to a fundamental difference that would justify speaking of two distinct types of parties. Both groups of parties have similar social bases, with 'fundamentalist' parties being characterised by a more pronounced new politics profile".[61] Muller-Rommel makes rather more of these distinctions, although they are, depending on which of his several commentaries on Green politics one chooses to read, seen by him more as differences of degree than of type. In his earlier work Muller-Rommel tends to emphasise these differences, although to be sure he never exaggerates them.[62] He points out that Green parties are ideological composites, containing both radical leftist and even conservative tendencies. Muller - Rommel is aware of the divergent roots of political ecology and delineates three categories of Green party in Europe: those red-green parties that emerged from radical leftist roots (as in the case of the Netherlands); a conservative route to ecologism, usually coming from agrarian parties (the case in Sweden and Finland); and the dominant trend by far, those new politics parties of various ideological mixes, with a post-materialist ethos - almost everywhere else.[63] Whatever their particular origins, Muller Rommel shares Poguntke's 'new politics' perspective; that both the red-green and pure green tendencies endorse 'new' and frequently post-materialist values including ecologism, but in various national cases extending beyond it to embrace other radical social and political causes. This means that Green parties cannot be neatly pigeonholed on the conventional left-right spectrum, and Muller-Rommel prefers to locate them on the old-new continuum.[64] In so far as the Greens address a new genre of issues, and appeal to new social groups alienated from the established parties,[65] he identifies the Greens as a 'new politics' phenomenon.[66]

In his later work Muller-Rommel further subdivides the generic 'new politics' phenomenon into two distinct ideological strands. Green parties, irrespective of their ideological roots, are subsumed into a discrete category defined by the prominence they give to ecologism per se in their ideological discourses and electoral programmes. These parties were preceded into the political fray by a small group of leftist, libertarian and radical parties founded, by and large, in the mid 1960s, supported for the most part by the youthful products of the student and new social movements,[67] and pursuing a new politics agenda with a distinctly leftist orientation. These radical parties were principally defined by their rejection of the bureaucratic, hierarchical and conformist tendencies of the establish 'old' left parties - deemed by critics cast in this mould to have abandoned their radical ethos.[68] While they shared many of the ideological predilictions of the Greens, including environmental concerns, these new radical parties have remained separate entities and, in some polities, are their main rivals for the same 'new politics' vote. These new left radical parties, compared with most Green parties, were primarily motivated by their distaste for the same authoritarian and elitist 'iniquities' of modern political systems, but were rather more focused on the 'exploitative' dimension of liberal capitalist societies than on their polluting or resource squandering consequences. Accordingly, their party programmes called for the public control of political decisions and economic policy; for industrial 'stakeholding' - a sharing in the profits of enterprises and at the workplace; a demand for radical social policies, a quantitative expansion of public welfare and its extension to new policy areas; a commitment to world peace and international disarmament - in opposition to the entrenched power of the 'military-industrial' complex; and a decommissioning of domestic nuclear energy installations and the abandonment of such programmes of energy production. Many of these radical parties likewise acknowledged a commitment to environmental protection as a logical extension of their pursuit of an improved quality of life over pure profit - but not as the central tenet of their belief system or political raison d'être. This revised and comprehensive classification permits Muller-Rommel to categorise all Green parties as variations on a common ideological theme - similar to yet distinct from their radical rivals.

Although Muller-Rommel was well aware that Green parties were formed some time after these new left parties - during the 1970s and 1980s - and remained 'different' inasmuch as they put ecologism at the very centre of their programmatic appeal, he argues that even these differences are more a matter of emphasis than of real substance. After all, both party types are exponents of a wholly new politics that shared a broad opposition to an 'old' and 'failed' politics. Poguntke and Muller-Rommel acknowledged that these complementary values, similar political dispositions and policy preferences between the various Green parties - who they refer to in a joint study as "the unharmonious family"[69] - and many of the other new politics parties, were more important than their nominal differences. All of these parties champion a distinctive, if varied, 'new politics' agenda. They promote similar, even overlapping policies; and they share an iconoclastic style of politics which prefers grassroots spontaneity and participation to disciplined procedures and political professionalism. In this account of radical new politics parties, both Green and new left and alternativist parties share a common political disposition. All of these 'new' parties embody, too, the three elemental characteristic of the 'new politics' ethos:-

(a) regardless of differences of emphasis, they adhere to a radical credo that employs, for the most part, a distinctive ideological lexicon compared with that of the 'old' left - a political discourse that addresses entirely different, essentially post-materialist, concerns to those which are the usual political currency of the left-right spectrum. [70] As such, these 'new' parties emphasise participation and equal rights rather than the productionist interests of labour and social democratic parties. The essential political currency here is a strong egalitarianism and a commitment to alternative lifestyles that appealed to some amongst the new middle class.[71] Although this schema recognises that there are indeed some differences of political orientation between the Greens and these new leftists, with the latter adapting rather more readily to a disciplined and formal party structure, these remain for all that largely cosmetic.

(b) All of these parties, to some degree, prefer direct to representative democracy. They practise participatory politics in their party structures, discount hierarchy and leadership, and recommend the virtues of individual self determination in the face of the authoritarian and bureaucratic state. [72] Both party 'types' practise politics in much the same way for, in Muller-Rommel's view, "despite some diversity in organisational structure and in programme demands.... the New Politics parties have a very similar network to citizen initiative groups at local, regional and national levels of the political system. Further, in many cases we can detect Alliances between New Politics parties and new political movements. In this respect, the New Politics parties differ substantially from the established parties".[73]

(c) The 'new politics' parties likewise appeal to a broadly similar electorate - to those younger, better educated members of a new or post-materialist middle-class. [74] The critical defining characteristic of this electorate, according to this model, is its radical outlook. A number of analysts have identified a distinctive new leftist orientation across the new politics spectrum that suggests a close ideological affinity between the Greens and the new left. For Muller-Rommel all variants of the new politics movement essentially identify with the same underlying values and draw support from those groups to whom such values are most conducive. To this extent, they display a "left wing post materialist profile (and thus) we refer to this group of voters as the 'New Left'.[75] Poguntke is drawn to a similar conclusion; that "the new politics conflict is not independent of the left right continuum... ecologism inspired by the new politics can be seen as part of a wider phenomenon which implies a new design of society". While he acknowledges that a conservative ecologism does exist, this is an almost eccentric and a far from usual expression of green ideas. The principal momentum for political ecology has come instead from radical new politics ideas that share much in common with new leftism. To this extent, the differences between Green parties "may be explained by different patterns of party formation or developmental stages, but it does not contradict our argument that those parties belong to the same family; the main criteria for the classification of parties are not only similarity or even identity, but also sufficient distance from all other parties".[76]

(ii)   The Greens as left libertarians

An alternative explanation for the rise of Green parties plays down the significance of this post-materialist or new politics thesis. Or at least, puts it into a less critical perspective. Those theorists who argue thus suggest that the claim to the distinctiveness of a 'new politics' paradigm is exaggerated. Instead, the impetus behind the formation of Green parties in this account is rooted, not in the exclusiveness of a 'new politics' phenomenon, but rather in the interaction or symbiosis of the 'old' politics with the 'new'. Kitschelt, for example, was less than impressed by what he called "the bland, informative label of 'new politics'", and without ignoring the existence of a new agenda, he based his account of the rise of Green parties "on the linkage between 'old' questions of economic (re)distribution and the 'new' politics of autonomy and democracy (for) the evidence supports the conclusion that the two cleavage dimensions are not entirely independent, but that the notions of 'left' and 'right' in citizens' self placement and their perceptions of the political field encompass both new and old politics".[77] Kitschelt saw political process as determining agency, rather than the reverse; that there was no rupture with the past, but rather a continuous process of development in which long established political trends and cultural preferences continue to impact on, and work through, contemporaneous issues. Contemporary radicalism, in this account, is the expression, in modern guise, of a deepseated radical tradition. It embodies a yearning for progress and improvement in the social order that draws its inspiration from over two centuries of radical discourse and practice.

Under present conditions, this radical instinct has found its expression in all manner of new politics causes - from ecology to feminism, as well as libertarian and civil rights issues.[78] On this basis, Kitschelt subsumes the Greens under the generic label of 'left-libertarian' parties.[79] The Greens, in this formulation, are seen as a political response to the routine issues left over from the socio-economic and political development of advanced societies, as much as they are a new force representing an entirely novel agenda. The Greens here are neither an element in an entirely new politics cleavage (pace Muller-Rommel, Poguntke, and Inglehart), let alone a unique political cleavage in their own right as Rudig and others have intimated. Instead, they must be located within a 'left libertarian versus a right wing authoritarian cleavage'.[80] Of course, Kitschelt acknowledges the relevance to left libertarianism of new cultural experiences identified in Inglehart's 'post-materialist' phenomenon.[81] But at the same time, the purported uniqueness of these radical instincts is, in his view, misplaced or at least exaggerated. Not that he understates the potential for the Greens, or any other variant of left-libertarian party, for reshaping society. The very fact that they are a contemporary expression of the deepseated anxieties - over resource allocation, power distribution, citizen autonomy versus the overbearing state, and so on - that have dogged the development of advanced capitalist society, per se, ensures their survival in the calculus of modern politics. At the same time, Kitschelt is by no means sanguine let alone deterministic about their chances, and stipulates some particular, even demanding, conditions that must be met if they are to survive let alone prosper. They must, for instance, reach out to embrace and strike political bargains with those adjacent radical parties with whom they have ideological programmatic affinities: for "Green parties must see themselves not as a single issue parties but in terms of the broader competitive space in which the most promising position is one that combines support for ecology with left libertarian social and economic policies in order to attract significant shares of the electorate".[82] Kitschelt believes that ecologism under certain competitive conditions, has to settle for accommodating to these other radicalisms - for Green parties are viable only in countries where they do not face an already established left libertarian party with a left socialist label, and as long as conventional left parties do not fully embrace their agenda or attempt to steal their ideological thunder. The problems faced by the Green parties in Denmark, Norway, Sweden, the Netherlands, Portugal, Italy, Spain and France, underline the importance of these tactical and strategic observations, whether or not we countenance the starkness of Kitschelt's patterning of the principal cleavages of contemporary European politics.

(iii)   Green today, gone tomorrow; ecologism as relative deprivation

All of the accounts of the rise of both Green and ideologically adjacent parties reviewed so far share a perspective that identifies the ecology phenomenon as a political reflection of deepseated ideological and social crises. The Greens in this paradigm are a response to structural shifts in the fabric of modern societies. In differing degrees, these accounts of the greening of European politics regard such parties as either a permanent fixture on the political landscape in their own right, as long as they obey the usual rules of the political game; or otherwise view ecologism as a radical addendum grafted onto the agenda of other types of leftist party.

Some commentators, however, take entirely the opposite view. They choose to see the Greens as ephemeral, or at least as the outcome of contingent events that will preclude them in the long run from consolidating a clear space in the electoral and party political landscape: more a case of a radical itch easily gratified, than a radical instinct working to unravel the political fabric. These are the least persuasive accounts of the Green parties because they deny much of the evidence for the persistence of 'new' politics and the contribution to it of the ecology movement, even if this does not always find its most persistent or effective expression in the party political format. That a 'new' politics now exists alongside as it were, the 'old' politics, challenging its continuing dominance of contemporary political discourse, its exclusive control of policy agendas, and its near monopoly of political competition, party systems and electoral politics, is no longer seriously disputed by those social scientists who study political change. What does remain, however, as an issue of serious academic contention, is the long term significance and impact of this development on the style and practice of democratic politics, and on the dynamics of party competition. The critical questions that political scientists have greater difficulty resolving are those about the nature and consequence of such broad changes for the conduct and future condition of the political order.

At the centre of this academic discourse are questions about the reach, scope and durability of the 'new' politics. One school of thought remains much less convinced about the electoral viability of Europe's Green parties, and indeed about whether they can sustain their political challenge in what are some of the world's most materially advanced, individualistic and prosperous societies. After all, the Greens are the proponents - in all of their forms - of a universal ethic that puts collective notions of welfare before individualism. Ecologism

446

identifies with ideas about self sacrifice in pursuit of the common purpose, places a higher ethical priority on the public goods than on self indulgence or material gratification, and prefers a long term rather than a short term outlook on social development. These are all difficult commitments to sustain let alone to deliver in what are, after all, some of the most hedonistic societies in the world. What is at issue here is the staying power of these harbingers of post-material politics - the extent to which they are capable of shifting the balance of politics away from the prevailing bourgeois political culture, thereby to consolidate the new politics in the shape of a durable party presence. Several commentators remain unconvinced that the Greens can overcome the considerable odds stacked against them in this regard. Jens Alber, for instance, regards the Green challenge as an ephemeral one rooted, by and large, in a reactive protest waged by those economically disadvantaged and politically inchoate 'counter elites', drawn from amongst the victims of the structural shifts and economic crisis that enveloped European societies from the late 1970s onwards. Alber's analysis of the new politics phenomenon has focused on the structural disparity between the exponential supply of better educated, socially aware and intellectually critical graduates, and a marked decline in suitable employment opportunities vis a vis their perceived status and expectations. A further cause of social flux and political uncertainty here was identified as a general partisan dealignment, a loosening of political identity, and a discernible mood of disaffection - not least amongst the young - with authority in general and political elites and their failed policies in particular. In Alber's estimation, this potent mix by no means leads inevitably to a permanent rupture in the fabric of European politics. It amounts, instead,much less to a shift in political fault lines than to a temporary irritation, a brief interlude in the normal sequence of political development - and above all a hiatus easily overcome by effective elite performance, managed by artful steering and good governance, in order to correct the drift and restore what passes for political normality in liberal democratic polities.[83]

A similar line of argument has been adopted by Burklin,[84] who remained similarly unimpressed by the long term impact of the 'green wave' on western European politics. Burklin, too, endorsed the cyclical thesis and identified, not so much a major political disjunction underway, as a contingent response by a disaffected and minority interest to the vagaries of socio-economic change in advanced capitalist societies. Burklin focused on the disaffection of a specific group - the absence of social integration amongst the younger and better educated cohorts. Alienation in these terms is, however, in this account neither a fixed nor a permanent condition. For as these marginalised elements mature, they are more likely to acquire, in Burklin's estimation, new levels of social responsibility with careers to pursue and families to support. This, in turn, makes for greater conformity and eventually induces the pursuit of materialism to satisfy immediate wants. Accordingly, as these 'rebels' cease to be 'detached' and become more attuned to the conventional rhythms of society and its economic mores, they are likely to become assimilated into the political mainstream with its instrumental mores and short term outlook.[85]

This particular account of the 'greening' of politics has an obvious appeal for those committed, for whatever reason, to the 'nil' or minimal change hypothesis. Apart from its complacency, however, the model is seriously flawed in other directions. Burklin's basic premise - that of the fickle quality of a Green vote rooted in the situational dissatisfactions of youth - failed to account for certain facts that challenged head-on its fundamental assumption of an electorate principally motivated by insecurity. In fact, Green voters are over-represented amongst those sectors who enjoy higher than average levels of job security. There is also a problem of logical consistency in this account of 'greening'. In short, it fails to adequately explain why what is clearly a materialistic perception of grievances should point its 'victims' towards a movement essentially dedicated to non-materialist goals. Kitschelt has presented some damning empirical evidence to challenge this relative deprivation model. He points out that many left-libertarians who form radical attachments, are more motivated by ideals than self interest, and by optimism rather than narrowly focused short-termism. Many Greens are actually successful in making good careers in the public sector, the arts and education, and are likely in spite of or indeed because of this, to retain their values and political commitments.[86] Moreover, as these post-materialists 'mature', they are more likely than not to add to the stock of experience, common sense and realism available to the Green parties. This may well be why many of these parties have begun to resolve their internal factional debates over both organisation and strategy, in favour of a more practical outlook, and to make the necessary adjustments required to strike political bargains with other parties. On the positive side, Burklin's account does serve to remind us that there is a capricious quality about most political movements. It underlines, too, the role of material self interest as well as idealism behind much social and political protest. Another variant of this milieu approach identified the Greens as sectarian defenders of narrowly conceived niche values - and, as such, lacking in any real incentive to broaden their electoral appeal, or to construct pragmatic coalitions with other even ideologically adjacent parties. Such insular propensities likewise enhance the Green parties' tendency to factionalism.[87] This account, too, is overly skewed towards a narrow perception of the Green political mind. While obsessive ideologism and a utopian disposition may have been part of their political armoury at the outset, the Greens have proved rather more adaptive to the political game than their critics in this sceptical vein have given them credit for. They have begun to address their own organisational limitations, to make important strategic adjustments precisely to improve their electoral position, and as such, to increase their bargaining power within established polities.

The critique of this milieu approach can be developed further. We might point out here that the direction of economic development, and with that social change, is also more likely to consolidate the Greens than it is to bring about their political demise; that the actual location in the contemporary job market of an expanded and strategically important sector of functionaries, who maintain their cognitive distance from the productionist sectors of the economy, is bound to consolidate post-material preferences, and even to raise its political profile. Something akin to a spatial logic is at work here, gradually rather than spectacularly refashioning the political fabric. The structural shifts in the balance of economic power and in the nature of economic organisation, as classical capitalism is replaced by expanding post-industrial (tertiary and service) sectors delivering public goods or new types of private goods, are more rather than less likely to consolidate a 'new politics' constituency in contemporary politics. There is certainly no convincing evidence on the basis of the case studies, to indicate that the Greens are an obsolete force in politics, even if they are by no means a dominant one. In spite of a deteriorating economic climate that has been less than favourable to a post-materialist agenda, the Greens have consolidated their place in European party politics - in some countries, it has to be said, rather more convincingly than in others. Chandler and Siaroff, for example, whilst acknowledging that the fate of the German Greens does hinge as much on economic futures as the prospects for any other party, and thereby regard the downturn in the economic cycle as particularly damaging to their immediate political prospects, nevertheless remain sanguine about the Greens' capacity to survive. They argue that the "growing awareness of new policy dilemmas and redefinitions of issue priorities suggests that the Greens should not be viewed as a short term manifestation of cyclical protest but rather as an indicator of an ending social and political transformation".[88] While the omens might be more favourable for their survival in Germany than anywhere else, nowhere have Green parties entirely disappeared from the political scene. Moreover, they continue to attract not only their archetypical younger voters, but have also managed to hold onto many of those ageing radicals with post-material preferences who were originally attracted to the movement at the outset. Green parties that have acquired a degree of electoral loyalty - the valuable resource of partisanship - have been assisted in this task by resolving some of their own internal doubts about playing the conventional political game. As we have seen above, those Green parties that developed a coherent party structure - and were assisted in this organisational task by favourable opportunity structures (proportional electoral rules, relatively low access thresholds to legislatures, favourable party funding arrangements and so on) - have fared better in the survival stakes. Nor does the evidence support the argument that the Greens are incapable of overcoming their obsession with factionalism. Some Green parties performed better in this regard than others. But where these deep ideological divisions and organisational dilemmas are confronted - as they have been to some extent in most European Green parties - the foundations of workable and lasting political arrangements have been laid. Far from disappearing from the scene, the Greens have staked out their own, albeit modest, electoral territory, begun to develop successful working alliances with other parties, and in some cases become transformed - indeed reinvented - into a different type of party from the inchoate and ambivalent parties that first tentatively embarked on the electoral route in western Europe.

(iv)   **Ecologism sui generis - from positivism to middle range theory**

Some analysts contend that both the new politics model and Kitschelt's left libertarian cleavage, in their search for highly generalised categories of analysis, subsume too many of the differences within and between Green parties into what is a crude and thereby unhelpful typology. Rudig, for example, endorses the idea of ecologism sui generis - of a distinct 'Green' cleavage that owes little to conventional leftist ideas; one that appeals to a Green rather than post-materialist or new politics constituency. [89] While it shares some issues with this radical demeanour, for instance feminism and pacifism, it does so largely because these issues have an ecological as well as a leftist gloss. Above all, the evidence of a persistent even militant ecological faction in most Green parties, and in rather more of them than not the prevalence of pure green over red-green preferences - for instance, in the Green parties of France, Sweden, Switzerland, the UK, Ireland and in the Mediterranean parties - does suggest that the new politics or left-libertarian models are too exclusive and narrowly focused. These models are based on the prevalence of a new politics cleavage. Although there is some evidence from the national party profiles to support this view, we are left with the awkward fact that ecologism does not always identify with what are obviously post-material or left libertarian agendas. Rudig and Lowe were less than convinced by the notion of a catch-all 'post-materialism' as providing a sufficient explanation for the greening of European party politics. Without discounting the significance of these new issues in contemporary politics, they did point to critical variations in both the extent and the pace of the appeal of post-materialism amongst Europe's electorates. They properly insisted on a more focused and comparative study of the phenomenon - a model that weights the contribution of contingencies (issues and events), the national structural milieux that facilitate and mediate these issues, the precise circumstances of party formation, and those national opportunity structures that determine the development and prospects of all political parties and especially of new ones.[90] This is a plausible model. It does not preclude a major shift in the political values of western European societies in a radical or post-material direction. But neither does it take such a seachange for granted.

There are other equally credible models cast in the same conditional mould. Jahn's account, too, is measured in its analysis of the prospects for Green politics. It avoids any temptation to substitute grand theory or a single independent variable for sober and systematic analysis. Instead, Jahn concentrates his theoretical endeavours on building researchable hypotheses located in the middle range, and based on the comparable and altogether different experiences of the German and Swedish Green parties. He identifies several critical intermediate variables that could be applied just as well to the study of Green party formation elsewhere; the socio-economic environment, the prevailing issue agenda, and especially the cognitive opportunity structure - "the available cognitive and ideological resources for Green Politics".[91] Some political and social environments are, in effect, more favourable to the formation and survival of a distinctive Green party politics than others, as evidenced by the differential successes of the German and Swedish Green parties. In other words, structures, strategies and opportunities make all the difference to political and electoral outcomes. The structural elements that every new party must confront and negotiate have been identified above. They consist of the relative openness of national power structures and the receptiveness or otherwise of political and policy elites to influence from 'outsiders' over the policy agenda and through electoral impact over he structure of party competition itself; as well as other situational variables, not least, the electoral rules that determine such outcomes - what Kitschelt has defined as "opportunity structures".

As Kitschelt defines this crucial variable, "political opportunity structures are comprised of specific configurations of resources, institutional arrangements and historical precedents for social mobilisation", all of which facilitate - or hinder - the development of radical social movements. The scope of these movements to prosecute their cause and effect change "was shaped in certain pre-established ways by the channels and opportunities that political regimes offered to opponents to disseminate their message and disrupt established policies".[92] The very same 'logics' apply to the formation and development of radical political parties. Jahn, for instance, has extended the 'opportunities' variable to include ideological resources that might have a similarly facilitating or constraining effect on those parties dedicated to system change.[93] In this account, cultural resources available to new and/or radical parties, as well as the receptiveness of the native political culture to alternative ideas, along with the impact of contingent events, all contribute to either helping or hindering the cause of the new politics.

There does seem to be more theoretical mileage in conflating Kitschelt's institutional focus with Jahn's structural application, in order to devise a composite and altogether more flexible model of the resources that facilitate political change. Both writers avoid crude determinism or narrow didacticism. What these respective accounts do reveal is that the strategies available to radical parties depend to some extent on how they chart and steer their chosen political course. As we have already seen, every Green party is confronted by, and has to make, difficult political choices in this regard- whether or not to accommodate competing factors within party structures; how to conduct itself in the wider political environment; how far to compromise its preferences for loose party discipline and informal procedures; whether to build bridges to other parties in the parliamentary arena, and so on. Kitschelt has argued that, other things being equal, these strategic choices can make all the difference to the fate of Green parties, and may even stand between their political success or oblivion. Jahn's application of the opportunity variables to cultural resources improves on Kitschelt's narrow focus and expands the possibilities for a balanced explanation of the relative political fortunes of Green parties. For even the most disciplined, well organised and competently managed radical party is certain to struggle to consolidate itself in a political culture where the prevailing ideology, and what we might call the residual 'cognitive legacies', remain less than favourably disposed to that party's basic preferences. By expanding on Kitschelt's organisational focus, Jahn provides a somewhat clearer insight into the dynamics of party adaptation to the broader political environment. Jahn's detailed scrutiny of the 'real politics' of two Green parties illustrates these particular points and confirms the view that the prospects for Green parties everywhere are neither guaranteed to meet with success (the crude post-materialist thesis), nor doomed to obsolescence (the relative deprivation prognosis). Rather, they are dependent on how this configuration of mutual and institutional variables actually works out on the ground.

It is difficult to demur from Jahn's conclusion that "in spite of different programmes, organisational structures and political influence, most Green parties have similar backgrounds. Most began as networks of citizen initiatives and grass roots movements. Most were formed around single social and above all environmental issues which had to a large extent been neglected or mishandled by established political actors. However, there are important national differences in the character and strategies of new social movements, offering different resources to Green parties in each country".[94] Even a cursory comparison of the political culture and "the cognitive and ideological resources" of the two societies reviewed in Jahn's account - apparently quite similar in many ways - shows how bold generalisations such as the post-materialism thesis, or the 'new politics' cleavage, are wide of the mark when it comes to identifying the particular dynamics of any particular polity. Bennulf, for instance, has questioned "whether there really exists a new cleavage (or perhaps two new cleavages) in western party systems. Are we dealing with a new cleavage based on changing values ('post-materialism') or another phenomenon more broadly or more narrowly defined?"[95] This is indeed an appropriate question to raise. Or rather, it is an open minded, intellectually honest way to approach the patterning of contemporary politics.[96] And Jahn's multifarious and flexible model and its prudent methodology, is far more likely to yield measured answers to these critical questions than those models that start with the a priori assumption that something remarkable is under way in the European body politic. The evidence on this score is equivocal rather than conclusive. The 'old' and the 'new' politics continue to interact, and in all manner of permutations. In so far as post-materialism and new politics values are political currency in contemporary western Europe, they remain both contested in, and mediated through, the structural and cognitive legacies that predate them and continue to shape their political opportunities and to pattern their development.

(v) Synopsis

It is apparent from the commentary above that no single theoretical account offers a satisfactory explanation of the rise, development and prospects for Europe's Green parties. We have reviewed an array of models, each one of which has contributed some useful insights into what is an intricate and variable process. There is considerable evidence on the ground to endorse the view that a new politics cleavage is emergent and is contributing to the refocusing of the contemporary political agenda and - altogether more modestly - to the realignment of party politics. But this shift is by no means as far-reaching, as clearcut, or as politically destabilising for the old order it challenges as Inglehart, and those post-material theorists who took their intellectual cue from him, would have us believe. The 'logics' of Green party formation on the ground - the empirical touchstone by which any theoretical endeavour stands or falls - reveals both persistence and change at the heart of contemporary affairs. Old values, habits and anxieties continue to stand alongside new uncertainties and preferences. The political fabric retains both a degree of stability as well as its mutable quality. To this extent modern party politics has a paradoxical as much as an unequivocally progressive character. What the evidence does show is that the future of the Greens is not so much determined by narrow factors or singular variables such as values or fluctuating socio-economic cycles, but rather by those deeplaid structural circumstances that shape the sociology and politics of every advanced society. In short, the greening of European politics is neither a universal force sweeping all before it, nor an ephemeral one destined, sooner rather than later, to oblivion. The Green party phenomenon, is, on this reading, almost certainly here to stay. It is the outcome of situational, organisational, and even contingent circumstances, whose particular national configurations lead to variable outcomes. But outcomes, nevertheless, that share a persistent rather than an evanescent quality. For as Poguntke sees this situation, "the fundamental change in the social structure in advanced industrial societies adds to the plausibility of the hypothesis that new politics is more than a temporary phenomenon. The growth of the service industries and the public sector means that a substantial portion of the population is relatively well protected from the vagaries of the performance of the economy. This means that these individuals are psychologically less constrained to give priority to economic considerations. Manifestly, this development represents a persistent potential of support for new politics demands".[97]

The political potential released by these structural changes represents, at both the level of individual experience and group expectations, a challenge (whether latent or manifest) to the established political order. The mismatch between the preferences of new social groups and interests and those represented by the conventional parties is grist to the mill of radical politics. And while this is by no means always or directly translated into radical political behaviour, let alone steady support for new parties, the potential for political change becomes that much more feasible. The Green parties across western Europe presently occupy this intermediate status as emergent or chrysalis parties - evolving at different speeds depending on their habitat, but not quite yet fully fledged, with the notable exception of the German party, Die Grunen, as a significant force on the political landscape. A 'new' politics potential thus exists to some degree in every advanced society. We have identified a range of issues capable of activating this potential across the continent. The Green challenge in its various guises has been the most visible and persistent theme of this challenge to the status quo. The movement represents the continuing concern with nuclear safety as well as with road and other infrastructural incursions into the natural habitat. The Greens voice hostile reactions to the application of new technologies with their impact on health and lifestyles. They exhibit an awareness that tourism might be as much a pestilence as a panacea. They express concern, too, with animal welfare, the impact of climate change, the frailty of the food chain, and over the rapacious reach of the modern version of globalised capitalism, with its inbuilt structural unemployment, and endemic product and technology obsolescence. They likewise condemn the culture of excessive and individualistic materialism. We might add to this list the expansion of the radical agenda to encompass the accompanying pressures on welfare and other collective goods in the over-riding drive for competitiveness, and the insidious impact of new technologies as a form of social control undermining liberal freedoms. The list of current concerns is diverse and almost endless, and the Greens have something relevant to say on every one of these matters. For the scope of ecologism is as wide as those complex and multiple linkages that determine the social and economic structure of every developed polity.

The Green parties, in contrast to the single issue movements which continue to plough a distinct but narrow agenda, have risen to political prominence on the back of these new agendas. In order to survive, most of them have broadened their political appeal and established a visible if not yet a secure electoral presence. Whether this is a durable political base remains to be seen. But for the time being the Greens look, in almost every western European democracy, to have consolidated their political presence - an achievement that challenges head on the pessimistic predictions of their fate offered by Burklin and Alber. Even if this is a modest achievement, not least compared with their own political ambitions to revolutionise contemporary politics, it is one that suggests that they are capable of at least, political survival - and, with a fair wind, perhaps of something better. The Green parties are certainly not likely to disappear from the European political scene as its advanced and increasingly interdependent political economy throws up new crises and raises novel issues that the conventional political parties seem either disinclined or incompetent to address; or just as significant for the future of the new politics, incapable of doing so without revising their own agendas and fundamentally shifting their ideological preferences. There are other signs, too, of the Greens' impact on contemporary politics. The established parties have been rather more exercised by the Green parties than most of them would care to acknowledge. For they are not shielded from the wider socio-economic changes and cultural shifts that gave rise to Green parties in the first place. This is hardly surprising, for modern political parties are one of the principal "intermediaries between social change and political decision making in government structures".[98] As such, they have been obliged to confront, if reluctantly, the very same concerns that gave rise to the new politics. Amongst the most insistent of these dilemmas is the paradoxical quality of modern life. On the one hand the inordinate freedoms now enjoyed, and in no small measure due to levels of material prosperity unimaginable only a few generations ago. Yet, at the same time, these benefices have to be weighed against the costs of such improvements - their consequences for the quality of life, for the continuing amenity value of the natural and built environment, the social tensions and psychological stress caused by 'progress', the cultural impact of rapid socio-economic change, and so on. The traditional left, and indeed many of the 'old' parties in the centre ground of European politics, have been obliged by the sheer pace and reach of this transformation, to take stock of its cumulative consequences, whether socio-economic or political.

Contemporary political discourse is still obsessed with the idea of material progress. At the same time, the mood of confidence that pervaded the middle years of this century has, of late, been tempered by a rising sense of ambivalence and even doubt - a rebuttal of the positivism that once suffused the politics of materialism. In so far as these mainstream parties - and especially those on both the old and new left - have caught this mood and engaged in revisionism, they have reinforced this climate of doubt. To this extent the new and the old politics are far from being mutually exclusive. They are not yet engaged in a meaningful dialogue, but their practitioners now have more to say to each other across the generational and ideological divides that seemed, barely a decade ago, to represent a chasm of mutual incomprehension and antagonism. The Greens have played their part - and surely have yet more to contribute - in defining the new progressive dynamic that is stirring in the western European body politic. Green parties are amongst the leading harbingers of change. That fact alone establishes their claim to be considered as one of the principal agencies of contemporary political realignment. The Greens have contributed as much to the tenor of change by their impact on progressive parties in the political mainstream as they have on their own account. The established 'left' were defeated less by the rapid changes that overwhelmed Europe's advanced societies during the 1970s and beyond, than they were challenged by them. And in ways that called for a major revision of their traditional mores and shibboleths. The impetus given to this revisionism by the rise and impact of the new politics cannot be discounted in the radical equation. One outcome here has been what some recent commentators favourable to this project, choose to call the 'reinvention' of the left.[99] We might well, on the available evidence, widen the scope of this political enterprise and include the Greens in what amounts to a politics of renewal. It is altogether easier, of course, to conjure images of grand projects in manifestos than it is to carry them out in the real world of politics. The evidence from the case studies of a major transformation in the discourse let alone the practice of politics is more tendentious than it is transparent. Yet the Green parties have certainly played their part in these changes. They have everywhere begun to adjust to the limitations, as well as to the opportunities, on the continent's 'changing' political landscape. To this extent the Green parties and their project to bring about a challenge to what they see as a failed political order do represent an important element in the changing fabric of European politics. We cannot, of course, take this ambitious claim at face value. To merely state the case for change would be hyperbole. The existence everywhere in that political landscape, of parties committed to a new politics, is only part of the picture and in some ways the least significant. To acknowledge the significance of the 'party variable' requires more than an acceptance of what these parties represent - the fact of their commitment to a new politics, their ideological and programmatic repertoire, or of how they actually organise their affairs and practise politics. Although these are yardsticks of political change, as such they provide only a partial view of both the project and its wider implications. The 'party variable' also requires that we test the impact of these radical parties, not only according to their own lights - which might give a misleading, a partisan or at best a partial view - but against the background of the party systems that gave rise to them, and whose pattern of electoral competition and the arrangements for governance that are its principal outcome, provides the only objective measure of political change.

To acknowledge the importance of the party system per se on the functioning, behaviour and prospects of those individual parties that compete within it raises as many questions as it answers. Political scientists have long disputed which of many systemic properties is the most critical in determining party political outcomes. Duverger in his classic study of political parties identified the number and size of parties as the most important topographical features of any party system.[100] Other commentators prefer to emphasise the impact of the formal rules of inter-party competition - not least, electoral laws - as the primary determinants of the shape of any national party system.[101] Sartori, on the other hand, adopted a multidimensional perspective of party competition, which included amongst its categories the interactions between the respective parties.[102] The emphasis here on qualitative rather than on quantitative data reflects a rising sophistication in the study of party systems - an emphasis not so much on the numbers or size of parties, as on the contours of the inter-party game; on the width of the national ideological spectrum; the ideological space between the various party competitors; and thus, on the system's degree of fragmentation and conflict, rather than on its cohesion and consensus. In a recent analysis Pedersen, for instance, identifies the spatial quality, measured by the degree of ideological polarisation, as a critical factor that may contribute most to the degree of political volatility within any given party system.[103] Of course, any attempt at a systemic modelling of the contours of political change presents an immensely challenging prospect. It is obviously much easier to identify the structures of any one party than it is to attempt to account for the dynamic qualities of a given multiparty system. Nevertheless, the prize is well worth the effort needed to realise it.

The notion of placing discrete political parties in their broader environment, and focusing much less on intrinsic matters than on interactive ones, leads on to another important element in the equation of political change. Amongst the constraints that bear down on all parties - or for that matter, open up new opportunities for exerting influence in any given polity - is the precise format of intra-party competition. Party structure and behaviour, or indeed their ideological preferences, cannot be properly understood in isolation from the particular rules of the party system which shape political competition - that "totality of relationships of the parties one with another" - in which 'system' the idea of 'party interaction' provides a key element of momentum and a potential at least for change.[104] What is at stake here is a model of party politics that focuses on interaction - and that, even at this rarefied level of generalisation and abstraction, enables us to uncover some useful insights into the broad direction of political change in Europe's advanced liberal democracies. Of course, to acknowledge 'interaction' in party politics is hardly a novel observation. What is critical here, however, is the pace, extent and significance of these exchanges. Gordon Smith's discussion of this dynamic quality is a useful starting point for clearing the methodological ground. He identifies a pattern of interaction - what he calls the 'systemic properties'[105] of party political competition - which requires that we take note of the form of the interaction. Most notably, whether intra-party relationships are friendly or antagonistic; the extent to which these relations are shaped by the institutional framework in which they take place; the number and relative size of the parties involved in the party system, and the ideological space between them; the nature of the electoral contest and the degree to which this encourages partisan dealignment and a measure of electoral volatility; the social bases of the parties' support and the degree of exclusivity or overlap of the social cleavages to which political parties give expression. This systemic or exogenous perspective, rather than the functional or endogenous one we reviewed above in section 3(iii), is altogether more suitable for the measurement of the propensity for, and the extent of, change underway in respective national polities - from modest shifts to major transformations - and for which political parties remain the principal political vehicle. If we could not uncover a singular model of the Green party politics, how much less likely is it that we can expect to alight on a straightforward model of those party systems that contain them?

There are, in short, no simple models to be found here, even in similar societies and comparable political systems. Some party systems are more amenable to change than others, as the case studies above suggest. What we can say with greater certainty, is that the Green parties everywhere have fulfilled the adaptive function Smith ascribes to all effective or alert parties. They have given impetus to the change from the old to the new politics, and coped along the way with what we have identified as the 'radical predicament', albeit with different emphases and variable degrees of success.[106] To this extent, it is the party system rather than the respective parties per se that is the dependent variable here. In this systemic account parties are seen as neither closed nor rigid organisations. They are, instead, a transmission belt that reflects those deeper shifts underway in the socio-economic (structural) fabric of society. They provide a vehicle for expressing, for both party activists and electors, the changing expectations, rising fears and aspirations that filter inexorably into the political process and pattern its major ideological discourses. Smith has appropriately focused on the fluid rather than the static quality of the 'party variable'. He identifies it as an interactive process. Parties thus provide a feedback loop between society and governance, and although as he says, "electoral change appears as only one factor in the whole process it is the most fundamental. .... the electorate itself does not act autonomously, since voters are directly affected by the implementation of party processes, by the mobilising efforts of the parties, and by the more general impact of parties in society".[107] To this extent, parties and the systemic interactions, transactions and bargains that are the meat of party politics, provide important clues to the deeper changes underway in society. As such, they merit the special attention of political scientists concerned to unravel and chart the problematic of political change. For as Smith sees it, "parties have to be regarded as independent forces in two significant respects. They are, firstly, strategic actors. The special position they occupy in the political system enables them to initiate change as well as to alter its direction to their own advantage. Secondly, from another perspective, parties are reactive, that is 'adaptive actors'. Ultimately, parties have to be able to adapt if they are to cope with changing circumstances".[108] The case studies in this book support this general premise. Some of the theoretical implications that follow from this fundamental assumption are discussed in the concluding chapter.

Notes

1. See Max Weber, "Politics as a Vocation", in H.H. Gerth and C.W. Mills (eds), "From Max Weber" (London, 1968).
2. Thomas Poguntke, "New Politics and Party Systems: The Emergence of a 'New Type of Party"? West European Politics, 10 (1) 1987, at p.86.
3. Herbert Kitschelt, "The Green Phenomenon in Western Party Systems", in Sheldon Kamieniecki (ed) "Environmental Politics in the International Arena. Movements, Parties, Organisations and Policy" (Albany, N.Y. 1993)
4. G. Smith, op.cit (1989), at p.357.
5. Ibid (1989), at p.362.
6. A. Heath, R. Jowell, J. Curtice and G. Evans, "The rise of the new political agenda", European Sociological Review, Vol.6 (1) May 1990, pp.31-48.
7. For the most influential accounts of this debate, see C. Offe, "Konkurrenzpartei und Kollektive politisch Identital", in R. Roth (ed), "Parliamentarisches Ritual und politische Alternativen" (Frankfurt/Main, 1980) at pp.26-42; F. Muller-Rommel, "Partien neun Typs in Westeurope: Eine Vergleschende Analyse", Zeitschrift fur Parlamentsfragen 13 1982, at pp.369-90; ibid, "The Greens in the 1980s: Short term cyclical protest or indicator of transformation?" Political Studies 37 1989, at pp.114-22; F. Muller-Rommel, "New political movements and 'New Politics' parties in Western Europe", in R.J. Dalton and M. Kuechler (eds), "Challenging the Political Order; New Social and Political Movements in Western Democracies" (New York, 1990), at pp.209-31, alters the analytical focus from a new party type per se, to a new politics party; for a similar treatment, see T. Poguntke, "New Politics and party systems. The emergence of a new type of party?" West European Politics 10, 1987, at pp.368-92; and ibid, "The new politics dimension in European Green Parties", in F. Muller-Rommel (ed), "New politics in Western Europe" (London, 1989), at pp.175-194; see also O. Niedermayer, "Die Europawahlen 1989: Eine International verleichende Analyse", Zeitgeist fur Parlamentsfragen 20, at pp.467-68, where he

identifies what he regards as an increasingly successful new European party family which includes a spectrum of Green and left-liberation parties. M. Kuechler and R.J. Dalton, on the other hand, in "New Social Movements and the Political Order: Inducing Change for Long-term Stability", in "Challenging the Political Order" (1990), at pp.277-300, and T. Poguntke, "Grun-alternative Parteien: Eine neue farbe in weslichen parteien systemen", Zeitschrift fur parliaments gragen 18 1987, at pp.368-82, regard these new political forces as hybrid and movement parties. As does J. Raschke, "Krise der Grunen: Bilanz und Neubiginn" (Marburg, 1991). For a discussion of the behavioural aspects of the new politics, see S. H. Barnes, M. Kaase et al, "Political Action: Mass Participation in Five Western Democracies" (Beverley Hills, 1979); K. Hildebrandt and R.J. Dalton, "Political change or sunshine politics?" in M. Kaase and K. von Beyme (eds), "Elections and parties: German Political Studies" Vol.3 (London, 1978); and J. Raschke, "Politik und Westwandel in westlichen Demokratien", Aus Politik und Zeirgeschichte 36 1985, at pp.22-39.

8.   See P. Bachrach and M.S. Baratz, "The Two Faces of Power", American Political Science Review 57 (1963), at pp.632-42; R.A. Dahl, "Polyarchy: Participation and Opposition" (New Haven, Conn, 1971).

9.   F. Fukuyama, "The End of History", The National Interest (16) 1989, pp.3-18.

10.   D. Bell, "The End of Ideology: On the Exhaustion of Political Ideas in the Fifties" (Glencoe, 1960).

11.   For a discussion of this 'agenda', see R.J. Dalton, S.C. Flanagan, P.A. Beck (eds), "Electoral Change in Advanced Industrial Democracies: Realignment or Dealignment" (Princeton, 1984); R.J. Dalton, "Citizen Politics in Western Democracies: Public Opinion in the United States, Great Britain, West Germany and France" (Chatham NJ, 1988); and R. Inglehart and J.R. Rabier, "Political realignment in advanced industrial society: from class-based politics to quality-of-life politics", Government and Opposition 21 (1986), at pp.456-79.

12.   See R. Dalton, M. Kuechler and W. Burklin, "The challenge of new movements", in R. Dalton and M. Kuechler (eds), "Challenging the Political Order" (Oxford, 1990), at pp.3-23.

13.   R.J. Dalton, op.cit (1988), at pp.81-82; see also K. Hildebrandt and R.J. Dalton, "The New Politics: Political Change and Sunshine Politics?" in M. Kaase and K. von Beyme (eds), op.cit (1978); K.L. Baker (et al), "Germany Transformed. Political Culture and the New Politics" (Cambridge, Mass, 1981).

14.   Amongst his most influential work are R. Inglehart, "The Silent Revolution: Changing Values and Political Styles among Western Publics" (Princeton, 1977); ibid, "Political Action: The Impact of Values, Cognitive Level and Social Background", in Samuel Barnes, Max Kaase et al, op.cit (1979); ibid, "Post-Materialism in an Environment of Insecurity", American Political Science Review 75 (1981), at pp.880-900; ibid, "The Changing Structure of Political Cleavages in Western Society", in R.J. Dalton et al (eds), "Electoral Change in Advanced Industrial Democracies" (Princeton, NJ, 1984); ibid, "Value Change in Industrial Societies", American Political Science Review 81 (1987), at pp.1289-1303; and ibid, "Culture Shift in Advanced Industrial Societies" (Princeton, NJ, 1990).

15.   R. Inglehart, op.cit (1990), at p.76.

16.   William M. Chandler and Alan Siaroff, "Post Industrial Politics in Germany and the Origins of the Greens", Comparative Politics 18 1986, at p.304.

17. W.M. Chandler and A. Siaroff, op.cit (1986), at p.322.

18. Ibid (1986), at p.322.

19. A. Heath, R. Jowell, J. Curtice and G. Evans, op.cit (1990), at p.32; see also H. Kriesi, "New social movements and the new class in the Netherlands", American Journal of Sociology 94 (1989), at pp.1078-1116.

20. R. Inglehart and J.R. Rabier, op.cit (1986), at p.467.

21. Ibid at p.467.

22. See for instance, F. Boltgen and W. Jagodzinski, "In an Environment of Insecurity: Postmaterialism in the European Community, 1970 to 1980", Comparative Political Studies Vol.17(4) 1985; and W.P. Burklin, "Grune Politik. Ideologische Zyklen, Wahlen und Parteiensystem" (Opladen: Westdeutscher Verlag, 1984, at pp.216-20.

23. R. Eckersley, "Green Politics and the New Class: Selfishness or Virtue?" Political Studies 37 1989, at p.218.

24. E. Gene Frankland and Donald Schoonmaker, op.cit (1992), at p.55.

25. M. Kreuzer, op.cit (1990), at p.12.

26. R. Inglehart, op.cit (1990), at p.82.

27. William Tucker, "Environmentalism: The Newest Toryism", Policy Review Vol.14 1980 at pp.144-145.

28. James Savage, "Postmaterialism of the Left and Right. Political Conflict in Post Industrial Society", Comparative Political Studies, Vol.17 1985, at p.248.

29. For a stimulating and incisive account of the flaws of this model, see Brian Barry, "Sociologists, Economists and Democracy" (London, 1970), at chapters 3, 4 and 8.

30. C. Offe, "Challenging the Boundaries of Institutional Politics: Social Movements since the Sixties", in Charles S. Maier (ed), "Changing Boundaries of the Political" (Cambridge, 1987), at p.84. Why, for instance, did the sixties 'beatnik' and the eighties 'new age' movements show a greater receptiveness to ecologism than the 'hippies' of the seventies?

31. E. Gene Frankland and D. Schoonmaker, op.cit (1992), at pp.56-57.

32. W. M. Chandler and A. Siaroff, op.cit (1986), at p.303, maintain that there is no methodological contradiction between a values (sociological) and a structural approach to the problem of change - that this is largely a matter of emphasis. While it is the case that the two models can be reconciled, the classic contributors to the debate reviewed in this section do not encourage such eclecticism and pursue largely exclusive methodologies.

33. L. Zucker,"Institutional theories of organisation", Annual Review of Sociology 13 1987 at pp.443-464; D. Jahn, op.cit (1993); M.N. Zald and J. McCarthy (eds), "Social Movements in an Organisational Society: Collected Essays" (Oxford, 1987); P.B. Klandermans, "Linking the 'Old' and 'New' Movement Networks in the Netherlands", in R. Dalton and M. Kuechler (eds), op.cit (1990).

34. M. Kuechler and R.J. Dalton, "New Social Movements and the Political Order: Inducing Change for Long-term Stability?", in R.J. Dalton and M. Kuechler, op.cit (1990), at p.279.

35. H. Kitschelt, "Left-Libertarian Parties: Explaining Innovations in Competitive Party Systems", World Politics, 40 1988, at p.225.

36. E. Gene Frankland and D. Schoonmaker, op.cit (1992), at p.57.

37. See Herbert Kitschelt,"Political Opportunity Structures and Political Protest: Anti-Nuclear Movements in Four Democracies", British Journal of Political Science 16

(1986), pp.57-85.

38. Anthony Affigne, "Environmental Crisis, Green party power: Chernobyl and the Swedish Greens", in W. Rudig (ed), "Green Politics One" (Edinburgh, 1990), pp.115-32.

39. Julie Smith, "How European are European elections?", in John Gaffney (ed), op.cit (1996), pp.275-290.

40. H. Kitschelt, op.cit (1993), in S. Kamieniecki, op.cit (1993), at p.99.

41. N. Poulantzas, "Classes in Contemporary Capitalism" (London, 1975); E.O. Wright, "Class, Crisis and the State" (London, 1978); S. Mallet, "Essays on the New Working Class" (1987); A. Giddens, "The Class Structure of the Advanced Societies" (2nd ed, London, 1981).

42. C. Murphy and R. Tooze (eds), "The New International Political Economy" (Boulder, Col, 1991).

43. A. Gamble and A. Payne, (eds), "Regionalism and World Order" (Basingstoke, 1996).

44. J. Gershung, "After Industrial Society: The Emerging Self Service Economy" (London, 1978); A. Touraine, "The Post Industrial Society" (Paris, 1969).

45. T. Poguntke, op.cit (1987), at p.77.

46. H. Kitschelt, "Left-Libertarian Parties: Explaining Innovation in Competitive Party Systems", World Politics 40 1988, pp.194-234.

47. See Gunnar Sjöblan, "Political Change and Political Accountability: A Propositional Inventory of Cause and Effects", in Hans Daalder and Peter Mair, (eds), "Western Europe Party Systems" (London, 1983), pp.113-32; and Louis Maisel and Paul Sacks (eds), "The Future of Political Parties" (Beverley Hills, CA, 1975).

48. H. Kitschelt, "The Green Phenomenon in Western Party Systems", in Sheldon Kamieniecki (ed), "Environmental Politics in the International Arena. Movements, Parties, Organisations and Policy" (Albany NY, 1993), at p.94.

49. E. Gene Frankland and D. Schoonmaker, op.cit (1992), at p.57.

50. J. Raschke, "Political Parties in Western Democracies", European Journal of Political Research 11, (1983) at p.110.

51. R. Raschke, op.cit (1983), at p.113.

52. M. Kuechler and R.J. Dalton, "New Social Movements and the Political Order: Inducing Change for Long-term Stability?" in R.J. Dalton and M. Kuechler, "Challenging the Political Order: New Social and Political Movements in Western Democracies" (Cambridge, 1990), at p.290.

53. H. Kitschelt, op.cit (1988), and op.cit (1993).

54. See F. Muller-Rommel, op.cit (1982); op.cit (1989) and op.cit (1990); also T. Poguntke, op.cit (1987); op.cit (1989); and O. Niedermayer, op.cit (1989).

55. See M. Newman, "The west European left today: crisis, decline or renewal?" Contemporary Politics, Vol.1(3) 1995.

56. F. Muller-Rommel in R.J. Dalton and M. Kuechler, op.cit (1990) at p.225.

57. Ibid at p.225.

58. Klaus von Beyme "Political Parties in Western Democracies" (Aldershot, 1985) at p.3.

59. Ibid at p.29.

60. T. Poguntke, "New Politics and Party Systems", West European Politics 10 1987 pp.76 - 88, ibid, "The Organisation of a Participatory Party. The German Greens", European Journal of Political Research, 15 1987 pp.609-33.

61. T. Poguntke op cit (1987) at pp.86-87.

62.   F. Muller - Rommel, "Ecology Parties in Western Europe", West European Politics 5 (1) 1982 at pp.68-74 and ibid, "The Greens in Western Europe Similar but Different", International Political Science Review; vol 6 (4) 1985.

63.   F. Muller Rommel, op.cit (1982).

64.   F. Muller-Rommel in Dalton and Kuechler, op.cit (1990), at p.229.

65.   Werner Hulsberg, "The German Greens: A Social and Political Profile" (London, 1988), at p.10.

66.   F. Muller-Rommel, "Social Movements and the Greens : New Internal Politics in Germany "European Journal of Political Research (13) 1985 at pp.53-87.

67.   F. Muller-Rommel, "New Social Movements and Smaller Parties. A Comparative perspective", West European Politics, 8 (1985) at pp.41-54.

68.   F. Muller-Rommel in Dalton and Kuechler, op.cit (1990) at p.212.

69.   F. Muller-Rommel and T. Poguntke "The Unharmonious Family: Green Parties in Western Europe", in Eva Kolinsky, (ed) "The Greens in West Germany: Organisation and Policy Making" (Oxford, 1989).

70.   R. J. Dalton, "Citizen Politics in Western Democracies" (Chatham, NJ 1988).

71.   K. Baker, R. Dalton and K. Hildebrandt, "Germany Transformed" (1981), at p.152.

72.   F. Muller-Rommel, op.cit (1989), p.218.

73.   F. Muller-Rommel, in Dalton and Kuechler, op.cit (1990), at p.218.

74.   F. Muller-Rommel and T. Poguntke in E. Kolinsky (ed), op.cit (1989), at pp.21-22.

75.   F. Muller-Rommel, op.cit (1990), at p.218.

76.   T. Poguntke "New Politics and Party Systems: The Emergence of a New Type of Party?" West European Politics 10 1987, at p.87.

77.   H. Kitschelt, "The Green Phenomenon in Western Party Systems" in Sheldon Kamienieki (ed) "Environmental Politics in the International Arena. Movements, Parties, Organisations and Policy" (Albany NY, 1993) at p.95.

78.   H. Kitschelt, "The life expectancy of left-libertarian parties; does structural transformation or economic decline explain party innovation? A response to Wilhelm Burklin", European Sociological Review (65) 1988 pp.155-60.

79.   H. Kitschelt "Left Libertarian Parties : Explaining Innovation in Competitive Party Systems", World Politics, 40 1988 pp.194-234; see also ibid, "The Logics of Party Formation : Structure and Strategy of Belgian and West German Ecology Parties" (Ithaca, NY 1989).

80.   H. Kitschelt, op. cit (1993), at p.107.

81.   H. Kitschelt, op. cit (1988), at p. 97.

82.   H. Kitschelt, op.cit (1993), at p.107.

83.   See J. Alber, "Modernisierung, neue Spannungslinien und die politishchen Chancen der Grunen", in Politische Vierteljahresschrift, Vol.26 No.3 (1985), at pp. 211-26; and J. Alber, "Modernization, cleavage structures and the Rise of Green parties and Lists in Europe", in F. Muller-Rommel (ed), "New politics in Western Europe: The Rise and Success of Green Parties and Alternative Lists" (London, 1989).

84.   W. P. Burklin, "Grune Politik, Ideologische Zyken, Wahler und Partiensystem" (Opladen:West deutscher Verlag, 1984) at pp.216-20.

85.   See W. P. Burklin, "Governing Left Parties Frustrating the Radical Non Established Left: The Rise and Inevitable Decline of the Greens", European Sociological Review 3(2) 1987, pp.109-26; ibid, "The German Greens: The post-industrial non-established and the party system", International Political Science Review 6, 1985, at pp.463-81;

ibid, "Why study Political Cycles?" European Journal of Political Research 15 (1987), pp.131-46; and "A politico-economic model instead of sour grapes logics: A rejoinder to Herbert Kitschelt's critique", European Sociological Review 4 1988, at pp.161-66; for a similar theoretical approach, see also Hines, "Green voters in the Federal Republic of Germany and France: A Comparative Analysis" (Hovedoppgave, Institute for Comparative Politics, University of Bergen, 1989).

86. H. Kitschelt, op.cit (1988), at pp.155-60; and Burklin's rejoinder in W. P. Burklin, op.cit (1988).

87. Hans-Joachim Veen, "The Greens as a Milieu Party", in E. Kolinsky (ed), "The Greens in West Germany" (Oxford, 1989) at pp.31-59.

88. W.M. Chandler and A. Siaroff, op.cit (1986), p.323.

89. W. Rudig, "The Greens in Europe; Ecological parties and the European elections of 1984", Parliamentary Affairs 38 (1) 1985 at pp.56-72; ibid, "Green Party Politics Around the World", Environment 33 (8) 1991, pp.7-32; W. Rudig and M. Franklin, "Green Prospects: The Future of Green Parties in Britain, France and Germany" in W. Rudig (ed), "Green Politics Two" (Edinburgh, 1992) pp.37-58.

90. W. Rudig and P. Lowe "The Withered 'Greening' of British Politics; A Study of the Ecology Party" Political Studies (34) 1986 at pp.262-84.

91. D. Jahn, "The Rise and Decline of New Politics and the Greens in Sweden and Germany", European Journal of Political Research (24) 1993, pp.177-194, ibid, "Nuclear power, energy policy and the new politics in Sweden and Germany", Environmental Politics 1 (3) 1992, pp.383-417.

92. H. Kitschelt, "Political Opportunity Structures and Political Protest: Anti-Nuclear Movements in Four Democracies", British Journal of Political Science, 16 (1986) at p.58 and p.84.

93. D. Jahn, op.cit (1993).

94. Ibid (1993) at p.180.

95. M. Bennulf, op.cit (1995), at p.139.

96. See on this issue, P. Gunderlach "Recent Value Changes in Western Europe", Futures (24) at pp.301-319.

97. T. Poguntke, op.cit (1987) at p.77.

98. J. E. Lane and S. O. Errson, "Politics and Society in Western Europe" (2nd edition, 1991) at p.102.

99. For a useful overview of this debate, see M. Newman, op.cit (1995), at pp.134-145.

100. M. Duverger, "Political Parties" (London, 1954), at p.203; see also J. Blondel, "Party Systems and patterns of government in Western democracies", Canadian Journal of Political Science (2) 1968, at pp. 180-203.

101. See for instance, D. W. Rae, "The Political Consequences of Electoral Laws" (New Haven, 1971), at p.47.

102. G. Sartori, "Parties and Party Systems: A Framework for Analysis" (Cambridge, 1976), at p.44.

103. M. Pedersen, "The dynamics of European party systems: changing patterns of electoral volatility", European Journal of Political Research 7 1979, p.3.

104. Gordon Smith, "A System Perspective on Party System Change", Journal of Theoretical Politics 1 (3) 1989, at p.349; see the analysis by G. Sartori, op.cit, (1976), at p.44, where he refers to the context in which inter-party competition takes place.

105. G. Smith, ibid (1989), at p.350.

106.   See J. Rosenau, "The Study of Political Adaptation" (London, 1981).
107.   G. Smith, op.cit (1989), at p.355.
108.   Ibid (1989), at p.356.

12 Party systems in western Europe: persistence, adaptation or radical change?[1]

1.   The political boundaries of change and the changing boundaries of politics

The boundaries of contemporary politics are indeed changing as alternative values and rising expectations impinge on individual political consciousness, erode old certainties and alter those patterns of collective behaviour that fashion politics. There are many signs of such shifts in the currency of modern European politics, not least the emergence in every national polity of new social movements and political parties embodying radical aspirations that challenge the established political order and compete with those parties that reflect entrenched political traditions and the deeprooted social cleavages these organisations represent. The battle between the old and new politics - in which the Green parties almost everywhere are the principal, most persistent, political expression - shows no sign of abating, and indeed continues to gather momentum. This is not to suggest that the outright victory of the new over the old is assured, or that any particular outcome is guaranteed. For the prospects of 'change' and its shape or form remain constrained by accumulated legacies. The political landscape is molded by what Poguntke identifies as those "systemic boundaries that determine the maximum variation in the outlook of various parties in one system", even though "within those boundaries, however, new politics parties should be clearly identifiable as a product of this conflict over the dominant political paradigm and political style".[1]

The existence of new parties in any particular polity is only one measure - and an unreliable one at that - of the extent or prospect for real rather than cosmetic change. New parties may be little more than temporary eruptions of discontent, or no more than peripheral elements in the political landscape. Some commentators, as Peter Mair has observed, too readily confuse superficial changes - whether of organisation or ideology - with the altogether more complex matter of measuring the structural change in party systems;[2] and that "strictly speaking, we can speak of change only when we first can define what it is that has changed. Unfortunately, if inevitably, parties are rarely discussed in such terms. Rather, we tend to frame our discussion of a party *tout court* in terms of certain aspects or characteristics of that party - whether it is the electoral base, the policy profile, the governing role or whatever".[3] Even when this important distinction is acknowledged, residual difficulties remain in identifying the necessary and sufficient conditions of change at the structural level of any particular national party system. Of whether, for instance, we should regard electoral volatility, as between parties, as the principal gauge of change, of how to accurately measure the extent of such volatility, and over what timescale - for instance, whether between two consecutive elections or over a longer sequence. There is also the methodological problem, of measuring and identifying the extent to which any putative 'evidence' of electoral change can be construed as providing a clear challenge to the classical 'frozen cleavage' paradigm, and whether mere quantitative data or some other qualitative indicators ought to be accounted.

These are daunting problems but we can make some tentative suggestions as to how such an audit of change might proceed. The most reliable gauge of change, embracing the meaning and impact of new parties in any polity, is to examine their role in changing the shape of the party system that contains them - the extent to which the traditional mainstays of national party systems persist in the face of such new ideological and social challenges; or otherwise adapt to them in ways that alter the party system's fundamental configurations in some degree, in order to encompass the challenge. In short, it is the systemic properties of party systems, as Errson and Lane observe, rather than the emergence or decline in the electoral fortunes of particular parties, that determine the degree of 'real' change in any national polity.[4] Changes in the electoral prospects of singular parties are mere snapshots. As such they tell us little about the overall picture or the dynamics of any political system. Instead, Lane and Errson suggest a template of pattern variables as a suitable indicator for charting the interactions of the multiple elements of party system change.[5] The number and aggregate electoral strength of parties in a given system provides better clues to the underlying continuity or shift in the party political format over time. This variable, too, provides some measure too, of the system's coalitional potential, and of the nuisance value of 'extreme' or 'outsider' parties in a crowded parliamentary situation. Coalitional arrangements likewise provide an insight into the underlying patterns of partisan dealignment, and the prospective realignment of any given party system. Similarly, the variable ideological distance between parties in different party systems is more than a dimension of party competition. It reflects, too, the long term trends and shifts in the social fabric and in the patterning of social cleavages - as between left and right, the territorial axis, the post-material dimension and so on - which are translated into the partisan alignments that underpin party politics, and provide the crucial dynamic of electoral and party competition.[6]

These dynamic variables are a critical measure of the degree of flux in any system of national politics. But they impact on different parties in very different ways, rather than as a general force that touches each of them to the same degree.[7] It is the systemic quality of the interactions between parties that provides the most reliable clues as to the state of the political order and of the direction of change - for a party system is, in Ersson and Lane's estimation, "a set of objects with relationships between the objects and between their attributes and not simply an unordered set of political parties". It follows from this premise that the "vital (research) problem (is) to identify the systems' properties",[8] rather than merely to separate out any one party from its party system, and to seek to understand it in isolation from this national context. The analysis of the distinctive endogenous features of any party - its internal party machinery, policy procedures, ideological preferences - although important for what they tell us about that party's organisational modus operandi and ideological raison d'être, are not sufficient in themselves to explain its likely impact on its political milieu. What is needed instead is an exogenous perspective - one that takes proper account of the 'systemic properties' of the national party political environment. The case of Europe's Green parties indicates a mixed picture with regard to the prospects for political change across the continent. The circumstances of these new parties illustrates, on the one hand, a remarkable degree of durability by the mainstream party organisations, even if many of them have had to alter their own organisational arrangements and procedures to accommodate contemporary political preferences and expectations. The overall picture shows, too, how difficult it is for political newcomers to break onto the scene, and to successfully challenge the established political order. We should never underestimate the degree of persistence of any political system, even as we acknowledge its prospects for change. On the other hand, a sense of flux is also palpable on the contemporary political scene. New uncertainties, alternative values and radical agendas conspire to undermine routine patterns of partisanship. Moreover, these rising discontents with the supposed complacency of ruling elites, all vie to challenge the shibboleths and cosy nostrums of the old order. They find their behavioural expression in an increasing electoral volatility, and their organisational vehicle in the new movements and parties which have become a constant feature of the contemporary political landscape.

The assumption that 'change' is not only under way, but that it is a normal condition of the contemporary political scene is some considerable way from identifying why these shifts occur, and how far they have gone - let alone their long term significance for the political order. It does, however, at least mark a distinct break with the rather complacent outlook that once prevailed in the study of western European party politics and shaped its dominant theoretical paradigm. The study that established this paradigm of 'stable' western politics was Lipset and Rokkan's influential thesis, that the social cleavages established as these societies underwent the twin industrial and nation building revolutions during the nineteenth and early twentieth centuries had become the basis for a system of party competition that lasted the course, and continued thereafter an unbroken pattern of national politics.[9] The two earliest cleavages were derived from the era of national revolutions, when central or metropolitan nation building cultures confronted both residual peripheral cultures and the entrenched and privileged corporate elements of church or aristocracy. The industrial revolutions that either accompanied or followed on from these political changes also gave rise to a deep political antagonism - between, on the one hand, established landed interests and a new industrial class; and on the other between these new capitalists and an emergent working class. Both of these conflicts had a significant effect on the patterns of mass party politics that resulted from the democratisation ensuing from these socio-economic transformations. In short, these historic developments shaped Europe's developing party systems and - in Lipset and Rokkan's view - 'froze' them as the extension of the franchise and the emergence of party organisations around these cleavages, had the effect of narrowing the support market in a way that closed the electoral milieu to 'new politics'. This analysis was taken up as an orthodoxy by many commentators on party systems. Rose and Urwin endorsed the 'nil change' hypothesis when they likewise maintained that, "whatever index of change is used - a measure of trends or any of several measures of fluctuations - the picture is the same: the electoral strength of most parties in western nations since the war had changed very little from election to election, from decade to decade or within the lifetime of a generation. In short, the first priority of social scientists concerned with the development of parties and party systems since 1945 is to explain the absence of change in a far from static period of political history".[10]

This steady state perspective no longer prevails. The emphasis of recent research focuses less on frozen cleavages and more on the emergence of new cleavages.[11] The tendency now is to acknowledge political volatility rather than political persistence. As such, this academic revisionism presents a more fluid picture of emergent new parties, and of the adaptation or decline of traditional parties. Political shifts are now viewed, not merely as

465

haphazard developments; they reflect instead underlying social and value changes. Electoral change denotes movement in the traditional pattern of social cleavages, and this leads in turn to changes in party systems, resulting in an immensely complicated political map. This map includes the reconfiguration of class relations (the decline of the traditional working class and the rise of the new middle class); new economic patterns (the changing industrial structure, the decline of primary industrialism, and the growth of the service and tertiary sectors); a secularised culture; changing spatial patterns (the expansion of suburbia and the demise of ruralism, and with that the decline of agrarian parties, along with the consequences of this for family life). Dalton and Flanagan are amongst a legion of analysts who now place considerable weight on the political consequences of what they regard as a decline in the dominant social class cleavage at the root of electoral partisanship. As they see it, "throughout the postwar period the dominant partisan cleavage in most western democracies distinguished between working class and bourgeois parties. Recently, however, there have been increasing signs that the dominant class cleavage may also be moving into eclipse .... the traditional middle class - working class cleavage is weakening".[12] With that shift there are now some clear signs that a new emergent post-materialist cleavage is challenging its supremacy, and altering the battle lines of party competition in the process.[13] These developments, in turn, have modified the degree of polarisation in many European party systems - for instance, the steady demise of Communist parties across western Europe even before the implosion of the Soviet Union, and the changes, too, in both the ideological content and in the support base of the social democratic left and labour parties - without in any sense deradicalising European party politics. As part of this broad culture shift, new issues have been superimposed onto those established policy agendas that demarcated the 'old' politics - including the politicisation of the gender and civil rights issues, an increased prioritisation of quality of life concerns and the growth of single issue politics - beyond the conventional articulation and aggregation functions performed by the party system.

All of these indices of change have provided incentives for political realignment, inasmuch as they offer what Mair regards as "a more meaningful and flexible outlet for the demands of younger generations than can be afforded by the relatively moribund parties of the past. Thus, the traditional political alternatives qua organisations are more vulnerable; affective attachments have declined, and patterns of political representation are in flux".[14] In short, major changes are underway in the continent's political fabric involving transformations "in a pattern of political alignments which has more or less persisted since the beginning of mass democratic politics in western Europe. We are not just talking here about marginal change. Something much more fundamental is at stake. The problem is understanding what it actually means".[15] One element of this complex equation is undoubtedly the weakening of partisanship. Numerous commentators have observed that "electoral alignments are weakening and party systems are experiencing increased fragmentation and electoral volatility. Moreover, the evidence suggests that the changes in all of these nations reflect more than short term oscillations in party fortunes. This decomposition of electoral alignments can be traced to shifts in the long term bases of partisan support, party identification and social cleavages. Virtually everywhere among the industrial democracies, the old order is changing".[16] Flanagan and Dalton depict, too, a major shift in the methodological focus of political science to reflect what is under way on the ground. Thus, "within a single decade the major research question has changed from explaining the persistence of party systems to explaining their instability and volatility".[17] This theoretical shift, although clearly important, is by no means the whole picture. It would be misleading to suggest that this increasing volatility is an inexorable force sweeping all before it. Even those academics who endorse the idea of endemic change remain wary about making predictions beyond those 'the facts' will sustain, and they wisely avoid any overly simplistic notion of change. Dalton (et al), for instance, concede that, whatever their potential for thawing once-frozen cleavages and thereby changing the face of politics, "any of the new social cleavages ....must cross many hurdles before becoming integrated into the political process".[18] To that extent, the pattern of change exhibits a variable rather than a uniform quality.

Moreover, the time sequence under review here is, almost certainly, too attenuated to support any firm forecasts. The degree of electoral and other expressions of political change have fluctuated over time within and between individual countries. With high levels of flux apparent almost everywhere in the cathartic aftermath of world war two, following in the wake of the ideological and social upheavals that ensued then, the pace of change generally slowed as voter alignments settled down during the fifties. To be followed by a resurgence of electoral volatility on the back of quite rapid social changes thereafter. As Lane and Errson point out, "the level of volatility in all systems is anything but stable; the extent of net electoral change in the electoral strength of the political parties hovers considerably over time".[19] What is clear from the debate on political change is the difficulty in measuring its extent, even assuming that there is a consensus over the key variables.[20] In order to clinch the idea that long term change is indeed under way in the system, Mair adopts a more extended time scale than electoral analysts, who mostly begin their sequential analysis in 1945, usually employ. From this perspective he inclines to the view, not so much that the frozen hypothesis stands disproved over the postwar period but on the contrary that it was never much of a hypothesis in the first place![21] The evidence of a general flux in the social and political fabric may not amount to fundamental change in the fabric of the party system. Mair remains particularly cautious about the precise meaning and significance of the available aggregate data, and circumspect about the degree of rigour employed in surveys that apparently identify such clear trends for change. For as he sees it, while such "trends may be apparent, they can be traced back only through a limited period of time, and the situation which now pertains can be contrasted only with that which prevailed at most fifteen or twenty years ago... To be sure, trends over the longer period can be imputed through contrasts between different age cohorts; but at best, these remain estimates, and we lack genuinely equivalent data from earlier generations. In short, there is a severe problem of perspective".[22]

Few analysts now doubt that the old cleavage pattern is at least undergoing a degree of thaw.[23] Pedersen is especially disdainful of the complacent view that nothing fundamental is under way in the fabric of western European politics. Rather, contemporary developments "seem to indicate that, even if party systems may still reflect the traditional cleavage structure in society, the significant exceptions that Rokkan and Lipset were talking about are no longer few, but constitute a larger and growing part of all European party systems".[24] The critical question remains, however, not *whether* electoral volatility denotes changes beneath the surface of European party politics, but rather, at *what precise point* these developments become significant, and thereby indicate that meaningful changes are proceeding in any particular national party system. Something more than changes in ideological content, party rhetoric, or even periodic landslide defeats or victories for mainstream parties, or occasional 'breakthroughs' by outsider parties in single elections, are required in order to reasonably stake this particular claim. Moreover, these changes would have to be replicated over a longer political sequence than that between two elections, when contingent factors - a particular crisis, a perceived failure of governance or whatever - might easily generate a singular mood of discontent, encourage a resounding protest vote, or reflect adversely on the short term popularity of governing or mainstream opposition parties in ways that distort the 'usual' political picture. In the case of the Greens, evidence of this seachange might be seen, less in the emergence of these parties per se, or even their persistence as a marginal force over a period of time, than in their consolidation in 'normal' and especially parliamentary politics, their impact on the national political discourse, and some palpable signs of their influence on the programmes and strategies of the other (especially the mainstream) parties. And, not least, from evidence that these 'new' parties have begun to change the nature of national party competition, and with that the normal patterns of inter-party alignments.

2.   Conditions for new party development

Clearly, new political parties do not emerge spontaneously, but are an expression of deeper sociological forces. Changes in the shape or focus of party competition amount to something more far-reaching than the nominal shifts that occur in the polemical or programmatic content of established parties. Mair's calculus of party system change suggests that the outcome of ideological, strategic or electoral shifts indicates a degree of transformation, in both the shape and direction of party competition, as well as in the political order. According to this maximalist formula, if the degree of change merely amounts to a realignment of the usual social base of party support, or to the rise of a new set of issue concerns that leave untouched the underlying pattern of party competition, then this situation falls short of the elemental conditions of party system change. These are certainly rigorous criteria - as they should be in support of such such a crucial hypothesis - and we could hardly expect new parties under ordinary circumstances to easily fulfil all of them over the short term. But there should at least be some signs that things are beginning to shift if we are to take new parties seriously. While the Greens have clearly not taken any west European party system by storm, they are now at least entrenched in many countries. To this extent the Green challenge does begin to meet some of these significant criteria for political change, albeit more surely in some party systems - Germany for instance, where they have replaced the FDP as the third party, and almost certainly dented the SPD's chances of forming a government without at least acknowledging their existence - than in others. The Greens do also retain, almost everywhere, the potential for further consolidation on the back of a discernible new politics constituency and an emergent post-materialist cleavage. At the same time, future success is likely to depend on a combination of favourable circumstances - a series of eco-crises, rising public concern and, not least, the Green parties' own preparedness and aptitude to seize these opportunities by exhibiting a willingness to make the organisational compromises that, as we discussed in Chapter One, are indispensable for any serious political party to play the political game to maximum advantage.

In an early study of party change, Hauss and Rayside listed those critical variables that facilitate or otherwise hinder party development, and determine whether or not parties are likely to consolidate in the national political landscape or disappear as mere 'flash' parties. Although this study by no means claimed to offer a fully fledged theory of party development, it did identify a useful checklist of variables that are indispensable for guiding empirical research, and thus for building the testable hypothesis on which such mature theories must be based.[25] New parties are usually a response to a perceived sense of crisis, deep anxiety or discontent amongst certain elements of the electorate - although the sense that there is 'something wrong' with the state or its politics "need not entail anything as sweeping as divisions resulting from the industrial revolution or the Reformation. More fleeting issues or 'strains' have been shown to lie behind the development of some new parties".[26] What is essential for any viable research here, and ultimately for the value of any theoretical perspective yielded by it, is to identify those catalysts of discontent that facilitate political change via the medium of new party formations. Issues clearly play their part in igniting latent unrest, especially if there is a widespread perception that these concerns are not adequately expressed or represented by the established parties. At the same time issues per se, however radical their content or disruptive of elite complacency, are an insufficient cause of political rupture. They must also be politicised if the electorate, in any degree that matters for significant political change, can be persuaded to turn to new parties and abandon old partisanship loyalties.[27] It seems reasonable to claim here that, regardless of the abiding prospects for 'change', the established political order still retains considerable advantages and, not least, can depend on the deepseated partisan loyalties that sustain it. If the established parties keep their political antennae well tuned to the concerns of the electorate at large, it should prove difficult although by no means impossible for new parties to occupy part of their electoral ground. For "new parties develop when there is something wrong, that is, when a substantial number of people are concerned about a serious issue. New parties develop only when existing parties will not or cannot appeal to these discontented voters. In every sense in which a new party has done well, even only as a flash party, we can see that existing parties were unable to make their appeals".[28]

Change may well be endemic then in contemporary politics, but we should not underestimate the durability of entrenched partisan loyalties. Hauss and Rayside's study of party development concluded that most of the new parties in Europe that have prospered in the postwar period have emerged from situations in which they have not had to cope with intense ideological rivalry from other 'adjacent' parties. Or to compete for support amongst sections of the electorate already committed to other parties. In short, the problematic of party change exhibits a paradoxical quality. The more the prospect of political change presents itself, the greater the attendant risks operating to deter the prospective voters of alternative parties, without whose endorsement nothing much can happen. And so, as these authors see it - and the evidence of the case studies above endorses their conclusion - "to a great extent (new parties) are not masters of their own destiny. They cannot do well if there is no divisive issue to crystallise public opinion. They cannot do well, either, if the existing parties respond to the new discontented voters or if ties to these parties are strong enough to overcome that discontent. And they cannot do well if voters are convinced that support for a new party is tactically dangerous".[29]

The development of Europe's Green parties does much to confirm these working assumptions. Wherever the post-materialist niche was vacant and the Greens colonised it and largely made it their own, they tended to corner the new politics market. On the other hand, where that political space was already occupied by new left or libertarian parties or Green reticence allowed other radical parties to prosper - as was the case in the Netherlands, Denmark and, to an extent, in Portugal - the Greens have struggled to carve out a clear national political identity, and to secure a viable electoral niche in which to consolidate it. This is by no means the same thing as saying that any new party type will automatically develop - let alone thrive - where there is an unoccupied political space available to it. The key to electoral success lies instead in the capacity of any party, if it is to stay the course and entrench, to foster a strong and enduring sense of partisan attachment amongst its core or target electorate. This is a difficult task for any new party to accomplish, given the degree of political competition it is bound, as a potential 'usurper', to face. The outcome of this formidable challenge depends, not on the presence of one variable, but on a composite equation of several facilitating factors. Instrumental factors are no less important for determining outcomes here than sociological or cultural conditions. The most critical variable determining the opportunities for new, small parties with a modest electoral following, is obviously the particular rules of the electoral game. Majoritarian systems are distinctly hostile to new party development, even when the course of national events gives rise to the unusual levels of discontent that are most conducive to them. Proportional systems, on the other hand, tend to be more favourable to party innovation, if other preconditions are also in place.[30] This does not mean of course, ipso facto, that proportional electoral systems ensure, nor that plurality or majoritarian systems proscribe, small party development. Rather, these electoral arrangements may act either as a brake or as an accelerator of party political change, generated by the structural dynamics and accompanying the value shifts that are under way in every advanced society. These complementary factors notwithstanding, however, proportional systems do offer new parties such as the Greens a much better prospect of breaking into the political scene.[31] Moreover, this success is, in turn, likely to affect these parties' behaviour, and especially the way they orientate or adjust to the political system.

The broad constitutional make up of a polity may also play a key role in shaping the prospects and influencing the responses of new parties. Unitary or highly centralised states (the United Kingdom and France are western Europe's archetypal examples here) offer few opportunities (or levels) for meaningful political participation in, or for direct experience of governance, compared with the majority of European states that allow a degree of formal devolution, or boast fully federal constitutional arrangements. Several commentators have observed that the Presidentialism of the French 5th Republic, with its coalitional and centrifugal impact on the party system is far from encouraging to the survival of the sort of small radical parties which dominated that country's previous postwar regime.[32] Nevertheless, federal systems per se do not necessarily help small parties - other than those with a strong regional base - to become established. In Belgium, for instance, the new federal system has helped radical regional parties such as Vlaams Blok and the Front National more than it has the two 'regional' Green parties. Indeed, the very tenuousness of national identity here that required such constitutional accommodations in the first place has put much greater onus on the mainstream parties across the linguistic divide to adopt a form of consociationalism that buttresses the centre and, in the process, excludes, or rather, bypasses the Greens. In Germany, on the other hand, a federal system operating in a stable polity, where the axis of party competition is rooted in a conventional left-right adversarialism unmitigated by consociational considerations, has at least enabled the Greens to use Laender politics as a base, both for cooperation with the SPD and as a proving ground for their competence in government. Similar opportunities, albeit under the unique conditions of cantonal democracy, have enabled the Swiss Greens to establish a similarly strong base in community politics. In countries where the deconcentration of power provides small parties with a distinct local or regional presence and the prospect of power sharing (especially where this is encouraged by a proportional electoral system), these parties can only benefit - by way of shedding the 'wasted vote' reputation that dogs minor parties in the more discriminatory and arithmetically distortive plurality systems. These favourable opportunity structures, likewise, legitimise their political role vis a vis their target electorate, by giving them a relevance in the eyes of voters through a parliamentary presence, direct access to policy making elites, and even some influence over government. These attributes, in turn, furnish party activists with an incentive for improving and even professionalising their party structures and organisation. This may, in the case of some radical newcomers, help to modulate their ideological remoteness from mainstream politics. Or at least induce them to behave with less overt antipathy to its procedures and exigencies.

Electoral rules certainly play a significant part in determining the political prospects of such minor parties. It would, nevertheless, be simplistic to settle for a straight contrast between majoritarian and proportional systems. While it is the case that majoritarian systems - as in Britain, or in its modified form in France, where a second run off ballot by and large favours the established and catch-all parties of the mainstream right and left - unduly discriminate against minor parties, the reverse case - the clear advantages of proportionality systems for such parties - is less than clearcut. The fact of proportionality per se is not the critical factor here, but rather *how* proportionality operates; and, not least, the particular rules about electoral thresholds which may influence the pattern and outcome of the sort of tactical voting that spells electoral life or death for small parties. A survey of electoral data conducted by the Forschungsgruppe Wahlen (Mannheim) uncovered convincing evidence of negative tactical voting over a series of German land and federal elections. Many prospective Green votes were lost to the SPD, precisely because of doubts about a 'wasted' vote in view of the 5 per cent electoral hurdle. Other commentators, however, invert this argument, and maintain that such relatively modest thresholds, combined with proportionality, present no insuperable barrier to minor parties.[33] The same might be said about the rules on the state supplementing party finance. In some polities these rules are prohibitive to small, new parties without a mass membership, a steady source of supplementary income from individual activists or corporate sources - those factors necessary to sustain a vote sufficient to attract state funding. In Germany the rules on funding - which require no constituency deposits for candidates, and ensure that any party securing a minimum 0.5 per cent qualifies for campaign reimbursements from public funds - has actually helped rather than hindered the Greens. The party took advantage from the outset, securing some 4.5 million deutschmarks on the basis of its vote in the 1979 Euro-elections - a factor which persuaded the Greens there in 1980 to consolidate as a national party.[34]

To a large extent, the fate of new parties is determined by forces beyond their immediate control. But by no means exclusively so. The leadership function is a critical consideration here. How prominent party members in strategic roles 'read' the wider situation, respond to 'crises', cope with pressures, 'adapt' the organisation to these demands and so on, is a critical determinant of Green party performance, as indeed it is for any other party. The significance of the organisational response by party notables is acknowledged in the discussion throughout this study. Leadership qualities per se cannot make parties whose 'time' has not arrived, succeed. But the absence of an effective organisational response - including capable leadership - will certainly cause those parties with some prospects for success to squander their chances. For, as Hauss and Rayside see this situation, "a party can do well without a charismatic leader. It does need, however, at least a unified core of leaders committed to the idea of developing a new party which include most of those politicising the issue that made the party possible in the first place".[35] Finally, cultural factors contribute to the overall political prospectus in all sorts of ways - as preferences for, or expectations of, stable governance, notions of an 'appropriate' political culture may in some polities deter voters from 'gambling' with the vagaries of political change, even if the alternative on offer appeals, at one level, to a deep sense of discontent or disappointment with the 'fabric' or outputs of established politics. The straight choice between a known 'devil' and an unfamiliar one may present a dilemma that many voters will resolve pragmatically, by opting for the prosaic over the untried. The preference, for instance, for a two party or a stable and tested multiparty system, with only limited coalitional permutations from amongst familiar partners, may in these circumstances triumph over the rank uncertainty, or the unedifying prospect of political chaos presented by new and inexperienced parties.

In short, there are no certainties about the prospects for new parties, but rather opportunities whose outcomes depend on a combination of contingencies, circumstances, and institutional factors. Not least, the response of both established and newcomer parties alike to the particular national milieux in which they must operate.[36] The rise and development of new parties needs more than a sociological or cultural climate conducive to a 'new' politics. The prospects for political change remain uncertain and Hauss and Rayside's conditional analysis of new party development is right to underline the altogether problematic nature of the enterprise - an experience that is amply illustrated by the Green party experience throughout western Europe. The observation - that "there is a great deal of unpredictability in the link between the existence of a deep social and political division and the development of new parties, (that) this unpredictability exists largely because of factors we have called political facilitators (and) the politisation of a cleavage into a new political party depends on the stability of voter attachments to existing parties, to respond even symbolically to the discontented groups' grievances"[37] - is particularly apt. In so far as the Green parties have absorbed these important political lessons, and as made these critical connections, they have made their presence felt on the European political scene. The Greens have moved from their initial role as an uncertain movement to a full party status in almost every country we have reviewed. They have mobilised entirely new social groups into conventional politics, even to the point of representing - as we have seen in several of the case studies - a wholly new social cleavage. They have even changed in some measure the usual discourse of mainstream party politics, by causing the 'old' politics to acknowledge some of the issues raised by the 'new', as well as broadening the ideological cleavages that framed European politics, in order to encompass an entirely new political dimension. Of course, glib generalisations have no useful place in this analysis of political change. Each national case must be examined on its merits.

3.   'New' parties but persistent?

The Green parties have not been around all that long on the western European political scene, yet they have undoubtedly impacted on the contemporary ideological discourse, influenced the policy agenda and played a role in electoral politics at every level from the local community to the European Union. The Greens are clearly not going to disappear as an element in the national political equation in any of the western European countries reviewed in this study. The evidence from a sequence of elections across the continent suggests that there is a radical potential in the European electorate at large, even if it remains volatile and its outcome unpredictable. A useful comparison can be made here with a previous phase of emergent radicalism on Europe's political landscape. When the continent's socialist parties first arrived on the scene a century or so previously, their core support was small and unreliable. Few contemporary commentators in the 1880s, as Kitschelt has observed, could have predicted "the complex interaction of factors that would shape the trajectory of socialist parties",[38] and that eventually led to their political breakthrough. Part of the explanation for the new radical appeal is as a consequence of the rising uncertainty that infuses modern politics. The political outcomes of endemic social change are by no means as predictable as

472

commentators with a positivist inclination would prefer them to be. Nevertheless, the remorseless tide of change - cultural, structural, technological, economic - that has swept over the continent from every direction in recent decades has raised alike new aspirations and fears. Discontent and anxiety resides in the European body politic alongside expectation and optimism. In short, fear and hope coexist - an apparent contradiction that furnishes much of the continent's contemporary political dynamic. It is a dynamic that gives rise to new social groups and those political actors who represent them, and who exhibit non-deferential patterns of political behaviour that, despite the odds stacked against them, have begun to challenge the existing political order and confront the shibboleths that have guided it over recent decades. There are no assured outcomes here, but a radical potential, latent as much as overt, is nevertheless apparent.

The second overarching theme that shapes the prospect of political change is the signal shift in the contemporary European issue agenda. The prognosis here is equally uncertain but by no means hopeless for the Greens, or any other expression of the new politics for that matter. If the Greens, who have been the most politically persistent and electorally successful of the new wave parties, can accommodate the vagaries of an unhelpful issue agenda which has recently shifted against them during the recession of the 1990s - and if they can adjust to the unpalatable compromises necessary to consolidate and stay the course - they have both time, and indeed events, on their side. For the modern world is hardly going to become a more benign environment, either for nature per se or as a milieu conducive to nurturing humanity's deeper, non-material interests. As things currently stand, there are few encouraging signs for those who put a higher value on ecological than on material values, or who measure progress against yardsticks other than shallow materialism. Nothing, certainly, to suggest any resistance to a remorseless demography that will make the world a less densely populated place. Or to control its predatory industries and persuade a still largely unreflective population to use up fewer scarce resources, to manufacture less pollution, or to prevent those perennial accidents and disasters brought about by experimental technologies. One does not have to subscribe to an unmitigated 'doom sayer' credo to see that the very issues and concerns that have allowed the Greens to consolidate their distinctive political niche will not disappear. Or indeed to see that the prospects for a healthy ecosphere will worsen as eco-disasters, epidemics, climatic change, nuclear crises, habitat destruction and resource depletion exponentially unfold in the biosphere, and impact on individual lifestyles, alter group expectations, influence policy options, shape political agendas, mould economic futures, and change the ideological discourse that tries to rationalise and make sense of the conduct of modern life. Denominated thus, the world is an altogether less comfortable, more dangerous place. These circumstances suggest that the Greens will continue to play a part - albeit a variable one depending on the national setting - by giving political expression to these concerns and representing those very issues that gave rise to ecology parties in the first place.

Of course, the particular salience of these ecological and related new politics issues cannot be generalised. Their relevance and political purchase rises and falls with circumstances, rather than occupying a uniform status at the heart of the contemporary political discourse. Moreover, the appeal of ecologism will continue to fluctuate in accordance with the complex rhythms of political life and the competition from rival issues. Anthony Downs presciently predicted the vagaries of the ecological issue in these terms when it was barely alive on the political agenda.[39] The ecological predicament may be a permanent, even worsening, one, but it has to compete for attention with any number of other influential interests and causes. Perceptions of what *matters* are what really set the agenda of everyday politics. Ecological issues have undoubtedly slipped down that agenda in recent years as recession, the end of the Cold War and its consequences for international security, and concern with global shifts in economic power, have reinforced the primacy of 'old' politics concerns.[40] Nevertheless, this recent priority slippage has by no means relegated green issues to complete obscurity. Even with the relative discounting of ecological concerns in the face of an assertive materialism, an underlying sense of urgency remains about the very issues of sustainability and economic futures on which the Green parties have based their case and made their political appeal. In these circumstances it is easy to concur with Bennulf's assessment that, periodic fluctuations notwithstanding, "in all likelihood, environmental problems will be with us for the foreseeable future, meaning that ecology is not an issue that will disappear. It might go down but not away on the agenda. Thus, most likely, ecology will continue as a politicised issue in most countries. The environment, like taxes and defence cuts, will become an ingrained fixture of politics. Viewed in this way, the green breakthrough of the 1980s will be permanent. Ecological issues will be part of the politics of the future".[41]

4.	Organising for radical change - some strategic considerations

Green parties are by no means the only way of advancing the cause of ecology. An impressive array of green pressure groups exist at every level - from the transnational milieu to the local context - which offer an altogether more focused and direct way of accessing the polical process by campaigning for specific policy changes.[42] Pressure groups not only have their own distinctive style, but they also possess clear advantages vis a vis party political activity. Not least, they can concentrate their resources and direct their energies towards single issue causes.[43] As such, they attract a wider audience because they are able to assemble alliances across conventional party lines, including the mainstream parties, who may feel less compromised and be brought to see advantages in dealing with what are, for the most part, moderate groups compared with a convenient perception of Green parties as extreme, unduly idealistic, or inflexible.[44] But there are also constraints on the single issue or lobbyist approach. Even the 'big' and broadly based Green lobby groups tend to devote much of their energy to specific and localised causes, which fragments their impact and dilutes the Green message. As Boggs has observed, "if local movements reveal the shrinking capacity of normal politics, they nonetheless remain parochial, diffuse and ideologically unfocused. Loosely organised grassroots networks can win adherents and lay the foundations of community, but they lack the strategic direction and flexibility required for political effectiveness"[45] which is, after all, the principal raison d'être of the party agency.

	Moreover, the autonomy and spontaneity that in some circumstances is a useful resource for single issue groups, may also serve to mislead and induce in them a naive belief that the world can be fundamentally changed by a series of disjointed, uncoordinated incremental if radical endeavours. Nothing could be further from the truth in the complex, pluralistic politics of advanced societies. Local or grassroots energy is indispensable to any radical strategy for change. But the process is complicated, and fraught with both unavoidable compromises and certain disappointments. In order to be effective any radical initiative requires a considered strategy - and an organised political agency to foment and facilitate it. As Claus Offe has pointed out, "in their demands, new movements do not anticipate a lengthy process of transformation, gradual reform, or slow improvement, but an immediate and sudden change".[46] Whereas a cohesive political strategy can lend this endeavour an indispensable long term perspective, and help to deliver it more surely than an inchoate and frequently competing medlay of pressure group campaigns. Political parties, again, provide the most suitable agency for aggregating such diverse movements into an effective, cogent strategy. Not that this collective function is an easy one to facilitate, as the evidence of persistent factional strife in Green parties well illustrates. It may be difficult, but it is indispensable if the greening of European politics is not be abdicated to the mainstream parties who, at best, manifest only a cosmetic, instrumental, or short term interest in the project. The attendant problems here are evident in those Green parties which have found themselves representing the very same issues as the green lobby. The sense of rivalry is sharpened by a disparity of objectives - a situation that is made more difficult when diverse Green groups are obliged by circumstances to cooperate in order to maximise their political impact. As Boggs assesses this dilemma, "this merger process is fraught with ambiguity, insecurity and imminent road blocks. If grassroots struggles are diffuse and consumed with identity objectives, parties by definition are committed to winning power, to pursuing workable strategies and tactics. Movements jealously protect their own territories and identities against hierarchical and instrumental incursions of parties, however those parties may be ideologically defined. It follows that radical movements in particular will often resist the logic of electoral competition and interest group representation that is the hallmark of pluralist democratic politics. Such movements will prefer direct action over state governance, issue specificity over coalition building, and social protest over policy formation".[47] The tension between movement orientation and party status is undoubtedly a persistent one, and has been faced by every Green party to some degree. But it must be resolved if green radicalism is to persist as an effective force for change. In truth, any radical movement, under the conditions that prevail in the politics of contemporary advanced societies, can no longer afford the self indulgence of untrammelled iconoclasm and ill-disciplined protest that tends to be the political hallmark of new social movements. Political survival is at least as much a matter of discipline and sound organisation as it is of principled passion or radical energy. Blake's dictum about the the need for radical endeavour to avoid mayhem is as relevant as ever it was.

There are other limitations, too, even on those ecological campaign and single issue groups that - absorbing the lessons of experience - are content to become involved in normal politics and to put pragmatism before outright withdrawal from, as they see it, a 'tainted' politics. Some of the pragmatists who dominate the green lobby can be altogether too cautious or sensible in this regard. The management style of Europe's green lobby - especially organisations such as Greenpeace and Friends of the Earth - means that they tend to put a narrow organisational rationality and specific or focused goal achievement before the sort of broader ideological concerns on which most Green parties have expended considerable effort. What is required for political success over the duration is a more balanced perspective, of the sort that is best provided by the party format. For all of the achievements that have accrued from the green lobby, a specialised role nevertheless remains for Green parties in advancing the cause of ecology in its fullest, most enduring sense. Green parties have a distinctive role to play. They continue to stand alongside, and indeed to supplement, the work of the green lobby. At one level they give ideological issues a more constant and permanent political profile than they would enjoy if their sole political expression was left to single issue campaigns, or to the vagaries of disparate or pressure group activity. Political parties are thus uniquely placed to put the environment question per se - in all of its expressions - before the electorate. To keep it to the forefront of political debate, and thereby in the minds of key political elites and policy makers alike. Parties by their very nature aggregate environmental issues, prioritise them as circumstances and the state of public opinion demands, and make important connections between these issues and those other adjacent policy matters that shape the national, and increasingly, the international agenda. To this extent, the party agency strengthens the prevailing sense that the environment is a central policy concern, rather than a series of narrowly conceived issues of marginal relevance to public policy. They do so in a way that gives the 'green dimension' an overarching coherence in the policy making universe.

In order to maximise these opportunities, the Greens do have to help themselves - to develop their political instincts beyond a naive trust in fate or a nebulous sense of political destiny of the sort that has driven many other radical movements on the fringes of the political mainstream. At the strategic level, too, the Greens have to acknowledge their present limitations. They cannot expect to become a significant force in European national politics as things currently stand. The 'catch-all' strategy recommended to mass parties is beyond their capabilities and certainly contrary to their own predilictions. The Greens are content to be niche parties but, at the same time, they must adopt an effective strategy appropriate to that preferred status. Not least, they must strive to mark out and court an altogether more distinctive electoral territory than the mass electorate available to more conventional parties. The Greens have to tread a fine line here between on the one hand cultivating a distinctive ideological appeal and consolidating an electoral niche based on post-material and new politics concerns; and on the other, the need to reach beyond this inclusive ideological ghetto of the Green faithful and, by making the sort of organisational adjustments that confront all modern parties engaged in the complex calculus of pluralistic parliamentary politics, to consolidate a rather broader electoral base that will enhance their leverage in national politics. This delicate calculus necessarily requires a degree of pragmatism and a caution that sits uneasily with the Greens' radical ethos. Much of the prospective support the Greens must attract if they are to consolidate their place in the parliamentary scene is singularly unimpressed by mere posture politics, or grand but futile gestures. This is a politically astute constituency, by and large, who guard their votes jealously and expect to see them translated into a degree of influence, rather than wasted in a vain protest. The discrepancy between the potential Green electorate, illustrated by the sheer scale of membership of green interest groups and support for ecological causes, and a much smaller turnout for Green parties at the polls, reveals the extent of this predicament. In the circumstances, the various Green parties cannot afford to be detached from, or avoid engagement within, their national political milieux. If they are to effectively engage in real politics, they must needs follow some basic precepts. These are, inter alia:

a)   To carve out a distinctive political market for their principal issue agenda. But in a way that connects it as far as possible with the logistics of the party system in which they must operate to achieve these objectives. We will develop this argument further in section (5) below.

b)   It follows from the logic of engagement here, that Green parties - or any other minor niche party for that matter - must constantly take the political temperature, be alert to changing electoral prospects and to the possibilities for radical initiatives, in so far as these exist in a volatile political climate. And where possible, they must seek to build alliances with those other parties prepared, for whatever reason - whether from ideological empathy or for altogether narrower strategic calculations such as an appetite for political influence or the lure of office - to engage them. Furthermore, as the Green parties embark on this strategy, they would do well to take stock of their own limitations. A degree of cautious humility is never misplaced in the practice of modern party politics. The omens are by no means unfavourable to them, but nor are they redolent with the promise of a Green breakthrough. The post-material issues that favour the Greens are certainly increasing their political salience, but they have by no means displaced the material or productionist issues that continue to figure in the concerns of a large swathe of public opinion, and which persist in shaping the policy outlook of the mainstream parties. As far as the Green parties' most likely allies on the left are concerned, a narrow materialist focus - rather than the universal biosphere - remains the principal focus of progressive politics, even if this essentially class-based and productionist discourse is itself changing in response to sociological shifts in social structures and the cultural norms that reflect them. If the Greens are intent on participating in an effective alliance for change, they must assimilate this critical fact and incorporate it into their political strategies. For as things presently stand, the Greens need to engage the left more than the left depends on them. In the real world of politics, circumstances rather than a priori preferences are what dictate strategy. The Greens may prefer a discourse that is rooted in universal precepts rather than narrow political sectarianism, but in order to engage effectively in politics requires that they make some serious adjustments to the world as it is. In so far as the Greens are a movement with radical preferences this means, to an extent, assimilating into their own distinctive socio-economic critique, elements of both the old and new left's class/exploitative analysis of the elemental dynamics of contemporary society.[48]

There is as much a practical imperative behind such an intellectual accommodation as an ideological one. A new ideological consensus is a necessary precursor if the Greens are to engage the left in a meaningful dialogue, rather than merely antagonise it. Boggs is undoubtedly correct in his critique of the futility of the Greens' attempts - or for that matter those of any other new social movement - to persuade the progressive mainstream of European politics to make an irrevocable 'break' with the modernity paradigm that is as deeply rooted in the common cultural fabric of advanced societies as it is in the individual mindsets of their citizens. It is an altogether more likely outcome of the present political flux that the only viable agents of real change in contemporary societies will be broadly based radical coalitions that represent new issues which complement and incorporate those perennial leftist concerns with social justice, an equitable redistribution of social goods, civil rights, effective control of private and public corporatism, and so on. This does not mean, of course, that the Greens must be passive supplicants to a hegemonic socialist tradition that has already been found wanting in all of its forms - whether as Marxism, Eurocommunism or social democracy - as a critique of modern capitalism the world over.[49] The left, too, has begun to question its own narrow assumptions about the sources and direction of progressive change and has embarked as much out of necessity as conviction on a major enterprise of reinvention. As one perceptive commentator sees this project, "the very aim of a unified socialist world view, or politics, may be hopeless in a post modern age where the reproduction of dispersed social interests, agencies, identities, and meanings holds sway on a global level. The historical vision of 'socialism' as a teleological end may well have lost its once powerful theoretical and political attraction never to be revived again by efforts to reconstitute organisational forms, leadership, strategies and tactics".[50] This may well be true, but it does not mean that the socialist critique has entirely lost its popular appeal,[51] let alone its intellectual perspicacity, or that a new post-material paradigm which challenges many of the a priori assumptions on which that critique rests, is capable of replacing it. At least not yet. What is needed instead is an ideological synthesis and a political accommodation between two complementary, if by no means identical, radical traditions that, as projects premised on a far-reaching revision of socio-economic organisation underpinned by a broad humanism, are both driven by a transformative rather than a conservative ethic.

To this extent, ecologism and socialism share something important in common, and have a great deal to say to one another even across persistent barriers of mutual suspicion. In essence, the old and the new politics agendas are by no means as mutually exclusive as the ideological extremists in both camps maintain.[52] Both the Greens and the conventional left parties share a mutual concern with the impact of globalism on the socio-economic order. In particular, globalism has increased in spades the acute difficulties of controlling those massive, exploitative and potentially destructive forces (both social and ecological) unleashed by the multinational production, distribution and fiscal networks of contemporary capitalism.[53] At the same time, it has pushed them even further beyond political control than in the days when the traditional mode of capitalist production was contained by national boundaries, and subject - at least in principle - to forms of national political management. All progressive politicians have a common interest in addressing those multiple, mutually reinforcing disempowerments that lie at the heart of the contemporary crisis of politics, and which continue to fuel the moral anxieties and inflate the material discontents of many ordinary citizens. Some of these vexations find political expression as xenophobia, racism or other atavistic tendencies. But for many more 'citizens' they undermine a formerly deeprooted faith in the civic virtues of conventional politics and call into question the abilities of its practitioners to address their base concerns and calm their elemental fears.[54] It is this residual loss of faith in the established order to resolve the perennial problems of economic security, ecological balance and social justice, that presents the progressive side of politics in all of its expressions with its best political opportunity. The Greens can play their part in this radical project - if they can bring themselves to compromise their ideological preferences and make the necessary adjustments to their political strategy. The prospect beckons. Whether the Green parties will rise to the occasion and seize their chance, is more a matter of a contingency than of certainty.

c)   The Greens must be fully aware, too, of the attendant risks and limits of such political cohabitations. Not least, that these more established parties of the left may not be won over by mere short term cooperation - that they may prefer to remain distinct rivals of the Greens over the longer term. And that the Greens might, as weaker members of any broad based radical coalitions find themselves compromised or even electorally squeezed by such a political embrace. For such dalliances, ill thought out or weakly negotiated, might well legitimise the claim of these 'allies' from the political mainstream to have 'greened' sufficiently and to be altogether better representatives of the Green constituency. We have suggested evidence above to illustrate that all of these 'rules' continue to be very much part of the strategic plan of Green party politics in western Europe - albeit more surely implemented by some parties than others. Moreover, the old left entertain as many reservations about embracing new politics issues as the Greens continue to have about striking a Faustian bargain with parties motivated as much by opportunism as by any genuine conversion to post-materialism. The main disincentive for the left - or at least for those 'productionists' who remain influential in most of Europe's socialist and social democratic parties - is the short term political costs of ideological realignment. Both the elites and the ordinary grassroots members of these leftist parties remain, for the most part, divided into two distinct groups; a traditional productionist tendency rooted in 'old' agendas, and those modernisers and new leftists - by no means a cohesive group - who are amenable to a revisionism which takes the form, either of an updated, sanitised materialist agenda, or otherwise of a more radical alternativist approach to new politics issues. This latter group are, of course, keen rivals of the Greens because they appeal to the same post-materialist and progressive constituency. The productionist left in its *ouvrièrist* or modernising guise, remains as uncomprehending of 'quality of life' issues as they ever were and continue - at a time of widespread deindustrialisation - to put jobs before ecological sensibilities. At the same time, they remain receptive to many of the social issues and civil rights causes that have become the currency of all new left movements and of many Green parties.

Nevertheless, in the shifting sands that are contemporary leftist politics, and as socialist parties engage in what has become a febrile search for a relevant and reconditioned political message, there is scope, too, for real political cooperation and manageable if sub-optimal trade offs. Not that these bargains will be easily struck. Many real obstacles and difficult choices remain to be overcome. Pessimists, or new politics optimists depending on their normative outlook, prefer to see stark incompatibilities between the old left and the practitioners of the new politics. As Muller-Rommel sees their predicament, "the socialists are, therefore, trapped between two cultures, although only a minority of the electorate is on the New Politics side. The majority in most west European democracies stands in the center (sic) of the political spectrum. Whatever the socialist parties might be able to gain from the New left, they risk losing from among the Old Left voters. Consequently, the only viable strategy for the socialists is to attempt some reconciliation of old politics (in order to integrate the majority of the Socialist parties votes) and a moderate revision of New Politics (in order to attract New Politics parties' voters)".[55] This is clearly a risky political strategy whichever side engages it. It is easy to see why pessimism might prevail as to its likely outcomes and why, too, Muller-Rommel has concluded that "a radical realisation of the 'New Politics' issues is beyond the reach of the Socialist parties".[56] This realignment may well be a distant prospect as things currently stand. But this is, even so, an unduly gloomy conclusion. There are, indeed, some positive signs that a tentative reappraisal of available options is under way on both sides - green and red - as the practice and development of radical politics in many of Europe's national polities reviewed in Part Two reveals.

The prospects for the Greens will be immeasurably improved in these circumstances, if they can consolidate their electoral bridgehead by winning support beyond their usual core constituency in the new middle class. This may seem a tall order on their present showing, but not one that is entirely beyond them. The more palpable the sense of an ecological crisis, the more receptive even the productionist constituency is likely to become to the Green message. The evidence of the national profiles from Ireland to Sweden suggests a modest incursion into electoral constituencies previously aligned to the mainstream parties, confirming Rohrschneider's prognosis that "mass publics probably continue to be sympathetic to New Politics cues and resist any attempt by established elites to marginalise ecological issues".[57] The picture is, however, a far from uniform one and we might, on the evidence, be more readily persuaded by Kitschelt's historical perspective on the problem of party development and political change - that circumstances as much as the *idées fixes* of ideology are what determine political outcomes. Political parties are not static; their fate, as Panebianco reminds us, is determined by the interplay of current resources and strategic calculations as much as it is by any rigid or unreflective adherence to inherited ideas.[58] If they are to survive, let alone prosper, political parties must respond to their immediate environment and adapt to them - to engage in 'social learning' and to utilise the political resources available to it.[59] This process of adjustment is more a matter of redefining reality than it is of abandoning idealism altogether. As Zucker succinctly puts it, "interpretations of reality are seen as being socially created and institutionalised (i.e. in political practice and the party's format, procedures and programmes), functioning as objective rules and determining the interpretation of new situations. These institutionalised interpretations define what is possible and alternative interpretations appear to be meaningless".[60] While the cultural legacies of the past and institutional stasis do place constraints on the potential for change, the determined *rélance* of the socialist idea, as 'old' left parties everywhere have been confronted by declining support - not least amongst their core constituency - and massive shifts in the political economy of modern capitalism, suggests a real opportunity for the left to engage the new politics and to strike bargains with adjacent radical movements that would have seemed unthinkable, because they were electorally unnecessary, only a decade or so ago.

5. The constraints of party systems on political change

This process of adjustment holds out as many pitfalls for the Greens as it does for the left. Whatever the national logistics of each particular case, it is obvious, too, from the available evidence, that the Green parties are much more likely to confront these dilemmas and to be tempted to engage in these political manoeuvres where multiparty systems, encouraged by favourable proportional electoral systems, are in place. But even these procedural rules are only an outline facilitating factor. Difficult choices still have to be made 'on the ground' by the leadership cadres and activists who exert disproportionate influence over these parties' political arrangements. As we have seen, the very same predicaments that confront Green parties everywhere are resolved - or not as the case might be - in different ways and over variable periods of time, from one country to another. This is not to suggest that the available choices are infinite, or that the existing procedures and rules of multiparty politics in any given system does not have its own operating logic that constrains or influences these choices. Political scientists have begun to address this question of the Green parties' place in the operations of multiparty systems as these parties have recently become more stable actors, and have been drawn more surely in some places into the calculus that determines who forms the government or opposition, which is the principal rationale of every democratic party system. Kitschelt has identified what he takes to be an implicit 'logic' at work here. In essence, the behaviour of parties is principally affected by the shape of the national party system - by the ideological distance and thereby the competitive space between them, and how this plays with each party's potential electorate. Kitschelt notes that "in multiparty systems with at least four serious competitors, vote maximising parties have incentives to spread out over the competitive space. Thus, the greater the number of parties located on the main competitive dimension, the more likely the left-libertarian parties will have to confine themselves to a market share at the extreme end of the left-libertarian continuum".[61] In this calculus Kitschelt identifies a clear correlation between the number of likely competitors and the pursuit of a defined electoral niche or market. We have certainly seen examples of a similar logic at work in the national case studies. But a variety of motives are responsible for such behaviour. For this outcome is by no means necessarily an insular expression of narrow utopianism - although it might on occasion take that form. In its most rational expression, nurturing a narrow constituency is merely a case of making the best of a crowded and highly competitive party political landscape, rather than a blind retreat into utopianism. Moreover, building from a narrow but secure electoral base makes sense in these circumstances. For it at least secures sufficient votes - depending on the precise electoral rules - to win seats and thus a visible place in national politics. And on the strength of that, perhaps a place, too, in the elaborate rituals and complex calculations that lead to the formation of governments in most of western Europe's democratic polities. Whether as direct participants (as in Italy and Finland); or by providing parliamentary support and an endorsement of a potentially sympathetic, or at least a responsive government coalition - the background to much recent discussion of the SPD's political prospects and the role of the Greens in any future left of centre coalition that has surrounded recent national elections in Germany; as well as in Sweden, France, Belgium and Greece, after uncertain electoral outcomes.

Of course, there is no 'iron law' or immutable logic of change under way, even in these unsettled times. It may well be the case that those Green parties which successfully expand their electoral base and broaden their ideological foundations beyond the narrow dependence on a single issue which leaves them vulnerable to political asset stripping are much more likely to consolidate and thereby survive the rigours of competitive party politics. It may equally be the case that the Greens' political survival is an altogether surer prospect in a less crowded ideological landscape - one where the electoral competition is less intense. But as we also know from practical experience, sound political strategy and effective leadership can improve a party's prospects, even in otherwise difficult situations. Compare in these terms the fortunes of the French Greens with those of their British counterparts, or those of the two Belgian Green parties with the electoral tribulations of their Dutch neighbours. By the same token, indecisive leadership can worsen an otherwise promising situation, as illustrated by the case of the Swedish Greens in the late 1980s. Political outcomes are, then, by no means predetermined but reflect instead the circumstantial or contingent factors, and those structural parameters - not least, the constraints imposed by the arrangements of national party systems - which affect the way political choices are exercised and limit the options available to party activists, without entirely dictating them in every detail. To this extent, Green parties - indeed political parties per se - have to walk a tightrope between the pitfalls and payoffs of accommodating to the conventional rules of national party competition. Clearly, even within the usual constraints imposed on new parties by the weight of established procedures, by conventions and by the weight of expectations, deliberative political action - the exercise, in so far as this is ever possible, of 'choices' - by the determinant actors in the Green parties themselves can help to shape the inter-party bargains that stand in most European polities between relative political success and continued marginality. It is this pragmatic outlook that facilitates those political trade offs, that contribute so much to the effective electoral outcomes which, over time, refashion every national party system. Without in any sense exaggerating the prospects for such small, and still for the most part marginalised, parties, the effective exercise of such deliberative choices may, at the very least, alter the political odds, however modestly, in their favour - a shift that might in the long run make all the difference between survival and obsolescence.

Compromise in these terms does not mean, however, that radical parties must of necessity, abandon their ideological credentials. Rather, they must shape these to the last of practical politics which remains, as ever in liberal democratic systems, 'the art of the possible'. Accentuating or underlining the clear differences (of ideology, values, political preferences and programmatic content) between Green parties and those other national party competitors, while at the same time looking for mutual trade offs and points of contact, requires political skill of a high order. For one thing, neither public opinion nor the political market place is particularly receptive to parties that began life as anti-system parties, and in their earliest days deliberately flouted most of the rules of the political game. The Greens' rivals, even amongst the mainstream parties of the left, are little more favourably disposed to them than are the conservative parties. By and large the political establishment choose to see these radical activists, measured against the narrow electoral calculus that dominates strategic thinking in most mainstream parties, as merely an electoral nuisance - and one that offers little more than a convenient protest vehicle, especially but not exclusively to disgruntled leftist voters. In these circumstances their initial response tends to be defensive - to seek to outbid them for the 'concerned environment' and even the post-material vote. The Greens, for their part, do not possess suitable resources for intense or prolonged ideological trench warfare - an all-out contest to win over a sizeable proportion of an increasingly fluid leftist vote. Instead, they are now rather better placed - national and local circumstances permitting - to avoid the sort of insular or exclusivist politics that prevailed in most Green parties when they first emerged on the European political scene a decade or so ago. There is altogether more mileage for them in these circumstances, in building political bridges to their potential allies in the radical mainstream. There is convincing evidence of such a strategic shift in the national studies discussed above. There has been a discernible tendency for accommodation in the strategy of most European Green parties. An inclination if not yet an appetite for maximising their opportunities within the milieu of 'normal politics'. A two stage process appears to be under way here. As we have witnessed in the case studies, Green party strategists have, time and again, mitigated the negative costs and adverse consequences of such a competitive crowding of the new left territory that is opening up amongst the expansive new politics constituencies of the postwar generations, by playing up their distinctive ecological appeal with a target electoral clientele - most notably, amongst the younger, better educated or post-material middle class cohorts who are a growing presence on the contemporary electoral landscape. Once established, and with a foothold in national politics, the parliamentary cadres, and what passes for the national organisations who manage these parties' affairs, tend to be drawn - although with important differences of pace and tractability - into an altogether shrewder game of adjustment and compromise. Many of these Green parties have sought, in some measure and when the dust of the electoral battle has settled, to cash whatever modest influence over policy this electoral dividend accords them. Either by cooperating with other radical parties - the role of the Italian Greens in the centre-left Olive Tree Coalition provides a recent example here; or otherwise working with mainstream parties across the political spectrum in some form of parliamentary, consociational or even governmental arrangement, in order to exert a degree of influence in the policy process - as in the recent decision of the Finnish Greens to participate in a coalition government faced with some awkward short and medium term decisions.

An aptitude for playing politics, and the decision to embark on that particular route, are only part of what is undeniably a difficult and politically taxing scenario. For the usual problems that accompany such electoral and political calculations are compounded here by the fact that the Greens are by no means the only parties engaged in this radical calculus. Democratic politics everywhere is an elaborate minuet not a virtuoso performance. The Greens' principal rivals - both their radical niche 'neighbours' as well as their more vigorous competitors on the mainstream left who compete for the 'progressive' vote - are bound to engage in a vote maximisation strategy of their own. In so far as these other parties behave rationally in electoral terms, they too are as likely to respond with their own stratagems in a 'crowded' political market place where new politics issues have acquired an increasingly important resonance, by trying to move onto the same political territory as the Greens. Most of these established parties are suffering a noticeable decline in the partisan loyalties of their once secure support base. Old fashioned partisanship and voter fidelity are at a discount today. Politics is increasingly a volatile enterprise with all parties on the lookout for salient issues and marketable agendas that will bring them new sources of support. Yet the mainstream parties are long enough established to have developed both a taste and an acute instinct for political survival - a preparedness to change in order to conserve and to hold onto the political space and electoral territory that is their surest route to political power. The parties of the broad left in particular are by now sufficiently well aware of the dealignment phenomenon - of the consequences of political change over the duration, of the generational and value shifts, the changes in cultural norms, and the emergence of new fears and expectations amongst the electorate at large - all of which makes them acutely alert to those very issues that are most likely to keep them in political contention. These shifts have made them nervous and much less likely than their predecessors in the sixties - when this seachange first began to register - to dismiss altogether the 'new politics' as ephemeral, self indulgent or merely 'trendy'. One response has been to rise to the radical challenge by attempting - albeit with varying degrees of alacrity - to move onto the same political territory the Greens and other new politics parties had initially tried to claim as their own. This embrace of the new issues has helped, in turn, to legitimise them - to bring them onto the mainstream political agenda. To this extent, the 'greening' of politics presents the Green parties with an opportunity as much as a threat. On the one hand it may make for a kind of trench warfare between the Greens and the left. But it may also encourage - in the face of the rising uncertainties associated with altogether new forms of global capitalism that threaten both the eco-system and the social balance of advanced societies - electoral alliances and even parliamentary accommodations. The consequences of these political shifts are far from obvious or uniform. In some circumstances they might lead to the absorption of the Greens into a broad radical alliance - although there are no signs anywhere that Green party obsolescence is imminent or even likely. A more likely outcome is that political cohabitation will sharpen their national profile and secure for them a more favourable public image and greater electoral support than they currently enjoy. There are, however, no certain outcomes from any of these possible responses to the Greens' role in national politics, let alone any unequivocal guarantees that these parties can survive or prosper in a political and sociological landscape as full of uncertainties, hard choices and traps for the unwary, as there are opportunities for political progress.

Somewhat less pressing but still difficult choices, face those national Green parties that occupy a less crowded party system. Where there is clearer political distance and more ideological space between these systems' various parties - either because there are fewer of them and therefore a lower coefficient of competition, and thus a chance to occupy a distinctive ideological niche, or because the ideological terrain is less densely mapped and/or the new politics agenda enjoys less overt support, as in the case of the new Mediterranean democracies until quite recently, Ireland and, for altogether different sociological and historical reasons compounded by these countries' majoritarian electoral systems, the United Kingdom and France - there may be less immediate pressure on the Greens to resist or otherwise accommodate their most pressing rivals. Nevertheless, the option of practising an exclusive forum of radical politics may yield little by way of political influence, and continues to raise the very same awkward choices that confront Green parties in more formally competitive systems. If the Greens wish to exert a degree of real influence, rather than to merely practise the politics of oppositionalism for its own sake, they have little choice anywhere but to treat with parties who currently regard them as unworthy or unreliable allies, and even as rivals for the visible if volatile radical constituency. Once this nettle is seized, as it has been by many national Green parties, the prospects for a Green breakthrough still remain fraught with difficulties. For one thing, these parties possess fewer resources than they would wish for in order to maximise their limited political clout. In either situation, the immediate prospects for an effective strategy of accommodation capable of exerting real influence - as many of the European Green parties that have already embraced it have discovered - are by no means redolent with instant let alone easy success. The Greens, in any type of party system, may well find that it is an altogether more daunting task to convince the mainstream centre-left parties, whatever their own immediate political difficulties or need for allies, that the consolidation of their electoral positions, or in some cases the altogether more serious matter of the revival of their declining political fortunes, may well depend on them abandoning their own prejudices and entering the uncharted territory of political pacts or other cooperative arrangements with the smaller niche parties of the new or post-material left. In politics as in everything, old habits and comforting illusions die hard.

We should, of course, preface these observations about vote maximisation strategies and their contribution to party survival with the usual caveat. Mainstream, and especially 'catch-all', parties are more likely - almost by definition - to be driven by this narrowly instrumental electoral imperative, but not exclusively so. Clearly, political man does not live by bread alone, or any other commodity for that matter. Ideological preferences - the entire gamut of normative, ethical and other affective considerations - continue to play their part in shaping the outcomes of 'normal' party politics. Even if these are more potent considerations amongst the non-professional 'politicians' at the grassroots level than they are in the parliamentary or leadership tiers of any party. This means that there will be intra-party battles within the radical mainstream parties, too, not only over the electoral costs-benefits calculus of working with new politics parties, but also over the meaning of such cooperation in ideological terms and, by extension, its programmatic content. The fact that most of Europe's mainstream left remains wedded - albeit less surely now than previously - to a productionist, growth oriented, and class-based agenda, suggests that there will be as much friction as consensus surrounding any such accommodations. The situation as it stands is fraught with ambiguity. What this means for the future shape and direction of radical politics in western Europe remains more problematical than certain. On the one hand, the instrumental considerations concerning vote maximisation that no serious party with even half an eye to survival can afford to ignore, demand a degree of moderation, of cross party accommodations, and those mutual understandings which most of these new parties have found unappealing even if unavoidable. A degree of success here in striking such bargains has merely accentuated this predicament. The more entrenched the Greens have become over time as a parliamentary group, and by consolidating a distinct electoral niche, the more pressing has been the need to confront and resolve these dilemmas. This predicament has exercised Europe's Green parties more than any other single issue. It has, as the case studies well illustrate, made heavy demands on their political energies and occupied much of their ideological imagination over the duration. The picture here is a complex one, nevertheless, with many national variations. At the same time some general trends are apparent. Not least, the broad inclination of the dominant factions in most European Green parties to conflate instrumental vote maximisation (as a precondition for political survival) with a principled notion that their political raison d'être is about changing the world through action and involvement, rather than basking in the ethereal idealism of moral detachment - a Green version if you like of the pragmatic Leninist injunction to break ideological eggs if the political menu promises omelettes!

We might reasonably expect the European Green parties to continue to pursue this 'politics of radical accommodation', and in the process to gauge its impact, both on Europe's other radical and especially leftist parties, as well as on the dynamics and shape of the continent's national party systems per se. This process of political adjustment has only recently begun. Understandably enough, with so much residual suspicion to overcome on both sides, this is at best a tentative strategy of accommodation between the Greens and other radical parties, apparent in some but by no means all of western Europe's party systems. To this extent the Greens are contributing to the process of political change in two distinct but related areas. In so far as they represent new politics issues and give voice to a new, non-class interest, they have caused the mainstream left parties to re-examine their own fundamental credos, if not yet to abandon them. Moreover, the role of Green parties in regular national party competition has drawn attention to the emergence of a new post-material cleavage that underlines the deep shifts in the sociological foundations on which western European party politics are based. By extension, this presages a prospective change in the pattern of national party systems across the continent. Where the Greens have managed to strike bargains with mainstream parties, the likelihood is that these alliances of political convenience - which is all they amount to at this stage, whatever their long term implications for the future direction of party politics - will not lead, as many Green fundamentalists feared when the 'realists' first embarked on such political accommodations, to political asset stripping as a preface to certain oblivion. There is no evidence from any of the case studies reviewed above to suggest that the moderate Greens, by playing 'normal politics', are courting disaster by precipitating their own demise. The attendant risks or political opportunity costs of flirting with the establishment 'devil' are more than offset by the positive political pay offs - the acknowledgement of the Greens' role as legitimate national parties; the sense that these parties can effect policy changes; and the fact, as a consequence, that a Green vote, at least in electoral systems based on proportionality, is not a 'wasted' vote. This optimistic appraisal by no means implies a misplaced teleological vision of inevitable success for the Greens. Clearly, some Green parties are better placed and indeed hold better cards than others as they embark on this hazardous game. What is equally clear, however, is that most Green parties are now managed by cadres or factions who have begun to assimilate the critical lesson that sooner or later confronts all radical parties embarked on the parliamentary route: namely, that withdrawal from normal politics presents even greater threats to their chances of survival than engagement with the bourgeois polity and its temptations.

The relentless oppositionalism preferred by the fundamentalists has been replaced, for the most part, by a cautious engagement within the system. Nor are these pragmatists under any illusions about the inherent weakness of their current position. In the circumstances that currently prevail, it is more a case of making the best of things, rather than of any inflated expectation that a radical seachange is imminent in the trajectory of European party politics. A repositioning of radical politics may well be under way, but the strongest political hand still belongs to those parties of the mainstream left, even though these parties, too, face new uncertainties in a world where all the established landmarks - of class, the nation state, an old fashioned and adversarial industrialism, and all the once dependable axioms and ideological shibboleths associated with this social structuration - are in flux. The old left also faces hard choices and may feel it has too much invested in the past to easily contemplate engaging the new politics of radical 'futures'. By the same token these leftist parties have much to lose by bestowing legitimation on their prospective radical challengers, with their insistent claim to better represent the progressive wing of European politics. The political dangers of conceding too much political or ideological ground to such radical 'upstarts' calls to mind the apt metaphor of pandora's box! In short, there are attendant political risks for both sides of forging a new radical consensus. These risks will need to be fully accounted in situations where bargains between them might possibly be brokered. As Kitschelt has perceptively observed, "the political costs of such (cooperative) strategies are too high in terms of diminishing the overall electoral strength of the left and reducing the parties' chances to participate in government office to expect them to become the standard operating procedure of the conventional left. Thus, the Green and other left-libertarian parties may thrive in an environment of increasing 'product differentiation' among political parties in parliamentary democracies. On a speculative note, we may conclude that such parties are driving forces precipitating the end of the age of large 'catch-all' parties".[62]

The reticence on the left - or in some cases its studied hostility - about treating with those parties embodying new politics preferences is entirely understandable. As it is, too, amongst those Green parties engaged in brokering political pacts with the 'old' radicalism they have set out to challenge. Politics is competitive and, above all, a 'rough trade'. This caution may be a short term phenomenon, but for the time being, it presents a significant blockage in the way of the realignment of progressive politics in Europe. In some ways we could hardly anticipate at this early stage, a more positive response. After all, the 'old' left remains locked into a political outlook fashioned in very different circumstances to those which prevail today. All major parties carry heavy ideological baggage acquired in their formative stages which they find it hard to jettison. The left parties, as we have seen, have all gone through their own distinctive national variant of the generic crisis that has visited the European left during recent years. Few if any of them are well enough equipped to show the capacity for effective strategic thinking that comes from that rare combination, in any party driven by short term electoral rationality, and afflicted by ideological stasis, of a clear sighted historical vision, or the tactical flexibility necessary for steering a prudent course through the rapidly changing political and socio-economic terrain that is contemporary Europe. At the same time, this constant flux has taken its toll and impinged heavily, even on those conservative institutions that are established political parties. The left in particular over recent years has faced a monumental crisis of political identity, a failure of ideological nerve, and a steady loss of support - more damaging in some national settings than in others - which has obliged them to revisit their fundamental beliefs with an unprecedented degree of humility. This crisis has, at the very least, caused them to give serious thought to the meaning and purpose of radical politics a century or more after the emergence of the industrial order and the rise of the classic capitalist society that first called them into existence. If the Greens have begun to revise some of their earlier preconceptions of the political game, so too have their prospective allies on the old left begun to look, and with a less ideologically jaundiced eye, at these new parties. And even to consider how they might usefully cooperate with them to bring about an appropriate, modernised radical response to the unparalleled problems generated by late capitalism.

What is clear from the Green side of this emergent progressive equation, is that something akin to a political accommodation - we can put it no more surely than that - is discernible in the strategic orientations and ideological deliberations of many of western Europe's Green parties. Not that every Green party has approached this organisational task with quite the same degree of verve or effectiveness. Some of them are clearly more favourably disposed, less burdened by ideological constraints, or simply better organised and led, to make such pragmatic adjustments. But to some extent, all Green parties are impelled by the very circumstances in which they choose to operate to confront these predicaments and the challenges they present, and sooner rather than later. Social movements and even single issue lobbyists are more likely to remain impervious to the politics of compromise than are those radical political parties engaged in the parliamentary game. The principal advantage of Green parties over ecology pressure groups in this regard follows on from the central rationale of party politics per se; that they seek, whatever their enduring ambivalence about 'normal' politics, to play a part in governance - whether at the local, national, or what passes for government at the level of the EU, in so far as this organisation has acquired considerable influence over Europe wide environmental standards. We must not, however, overstate the case. The likelihood is that the Green parties will, for the time being, continue to occupy a place on the political margins. As they gain in experience, however, and learn from the experience of engaging in 'real' politics rather than merely indulging in polemics, and as they begin, too, to resolve the deep dilemmas that plague all new and especially radical parties, they will become altogether better equipped to exploit those political opportunities that present themselves. We have already seen enough evidence of this tactical shrewdness - in France, Finland, Sweden, Italy and so on - to suggest that there is a future for Green party politics across western Europe's multiparty systems. It is also the case that the Greens will be less likely to effectively participate in the political game if they refuse to constructively engage these other parties. This consideration was uppermost in the recent collective deliberations of the Green party that faces the most hostile opportunity structure and unreceptive political culture anywhere in western Europe and was, thus, less inclined to adapt to the conventional party political game. An attempt latterly, to abandon the electoral route and renege on party politics was defeated in the British Green Party's autumn 1996 conference. The mood of implicit realism here was captured by the argument of a leading party activist, that "this party has a duty to speak loud and clear .... regardless of the amount of votes we receive".[63] To this extent, fomenting political change is less about engaging in a straightforward conflict between the old and the new forms of politics, than it is about participating in an altogether more complex, ambivalent, even confused series of compromises between that part of the political establishment most receptive to new agendas, and its radical challengers - with each one of these bargains constructed according to variable national circumstances. The critical dynamic in such 'historic compromises' - amounting in effect to interfaces between two entirely different, frequently competing sets of political impulses and agendas - will principally (although by no means exclusively) be the engagement of the Greens with the various forces of the established left.

The Greens may have to bide their time until particular national circumstances strengthen their political hand. But in an age of increasing dealignment, shifting (and looser) partisanship, and rising political volatility, they look to be well placed to play their part in a new radical politics. The important changes that confront the traditional left parties as they engage, for a host of reasons - from the decline of the bluecollar workforce to the spectacular implosion of Communism - in the difficult task of ideological reinvention and political renewal are likely to open up novel opportunities for various forms of cooperation and prospective radical coalitions.[64] The political ferment on the radical side of western European politics has thrown up, as we saw in the case studies, many examples across the continent of an incipient reorientation in radical politics in which a red-green exchange has played a telling part. Some of these accommodations have been more purposive and successful than others. Most of them, certainly, have been tentative and fraught with difficulties for the reasons we have already discussed. There is no singular formula for ensuring success here. Much depends on circumstances, personalities and the accumulated legacies of past traditions - all of which may facilitate or hinder the current project for radical renewal. Any number of motives might be attributed to this project, including personal aggrandisement and other equally cynical ploys to shore up the ailing fortunes of the mainstream parties. Michel Rocard's attempts to re-radicalise the PSF and to spark its political renewal by tapping into the source of radical energy generated by France's vibrant new social movements, or the German SPD's tentative flirtation with the idea of a red-green coalition at the national level to mirror similar Laender arrangements, both seem to fit this category.[65] On a more positive note, the renewal of the Italian left after the demise of the PCI and the disgrace visited upon the Socialist party as the old regime crumbled in the face of political corruption and bureaucratic entropy, released a new sense of radical purpose that subsumed the Greens in the sort of political dialogue that has occurred elsewhere on the continent, from Finland down to Greece.[66] There are no definite payoffs from these political realignments. They present as many pitfalls as they do opportunities for those Green parties who engage in them. Indeed, ironically enough, the successful greening of European politics has damaged Green party prospects as much as it has enhanced them. One of the most notable but double edged achievements of Green parties over the duration, has been the extent to which they have helped to 'green' the mainstream agenda. The increased salience of ecological concerns amongst Europe's publics has persuaded many otherwise materialist parties to try to 'steal' the Greens' ideological clothes. Imitation may, in some circumstances, be the sincerest form of flattery, but this political larceny was more opportunistic than earnest, even as it was facilitated in some measure by the Greens' own difficulties in coming to terms with their awkward predicament, of adjusting to a role in 'normal' politics.

The dilemmas, hard choices and compromises faced by these anti-system parties as they reluctantly accommodated to the rules of the conventional political game, caused them to invest scarce resources - time, energy and finance - in fighting internal ideological battles that weakened their resolve and distracted them from facing their political enemies without. Meanwhile, their mainstream rivals were able to assimilate those nominal aspects of the green cause that suited their short term political purposes. There was nothing sinister in this tactical ploy. All parties, regardless of their preferences and principles are in the political market to win votes and to extend their electoral constituency. This instrumental and pragmatic incentive is especially sharpened when electoral volatility, and the levels of partisan dealignment that usually accompany it, leave small niche parties vulnerable to the more predatory instincts that drive the large 'catch-all' parties seeking to build viable governing coalitions. The Greens have, to an extent, been vulnerable to these depradations. There are distinct dangers here for the Greens, and more than a suggestion that they must remain on their guard, even as they treat with these other parties at the parliamentary and other levels of governance. The most likely formula for success in these circumstances suggests a mixture of compromise and caution - a need, on the one hand, to be pro-active. To reach out to other parties, to be energetic participants in the reinvention or repositioning of radical politics in western Europe that will be one of the major projects for the new millennium, rather than to remain aloof from the fray and invite ideological asset stripping by other parties in search of relevant agendas. In order to play their part in this radical project to the best effect, the Greens must develop a secure and effective party format as a means of consolidating what they have so far contributed to the contemporary discourse and practice of politics. Unless the Greens actively engage in this exercise of radical renewal - and are prepared in the process to become fully involved in the practicalities of coalitional politics - they are unlikely to advance their cause, and risk other, better placed, parties distorting their novel message. At the same time, they need to be aware of the intrinsic dangers to their radical credentials of such a strategy of inclusivism. There are as many hazards here as rewards. For as Bennulf has rightly identified these potential perils, "it might seem paradoxical, but if the Greens are too successful in promoting and politicizing the environmental question they may find themselves out-competed - on their own ground by other parties. Increased attention on environmental issues means higher electoral stakes for everybody, forcing all parties who want to stay alive to stake out their own green claim".[67]

6.   Aperçu: the radical predicament revisited but resolved?

Change is a problematical rather than a positivist phenomenon. It may occur suddenly and take on dramatic form, but it is no less significant for the ultimate shape of things if it slowly unfolds in incremental stages. The fact of political change in western Europe is undeniable, even if the matter of its pace and direction remains open to question. Change continues to alter the continent's political landscape and the Green parties have entrenched and retained, sometimes against considerable odds, their place in that prospect. The future may not quite be 'green' in the sense preferred by the more radical exponents of ecologism, or anticipated by some of the academic commentators who reflect their excessively optimistic predictions. But the future does remain open to a steady, almost inexorable influence of green ideas and policy preferences, as Green parties consolidate - unspectacularly if surely - their distinctive electoral niche, develop their party organisations, proselytise their ideas, and thereby impact firmly on the continent's current issue agenda. The Green parties have undoubtedly come a long way politically in a relatively short time. Most of them, after a tentative start when they had to face serious predicaments over ideology and political disposition, and come to terms with a persistent ambivalence about playing inside the political system, have taken their opportunities and become the harbingers of a new radicalism, rather than merely a 'flash' phenomenon of limited political duration. To this extent the Green parties throughout western Europe are a persistent if hardly a leading force in national party politics. They are, however, sufficiently well placed, and have resolved many of those earlier ideological anxieties and organisational predicaments that distracted them from the business of playing 'normal' party politics, to enable them to respond effectively enough to the rising anxieties and concerns that will undoubtedly dominate the politics of the new millennium.

Political forecasting is always a hazardous business but there are some clear signs from this overview of Green parties that contemporary social conditions and economic circumstances in advanced European societies are likely to entrench rather than uproot the Greens in the political landscape. As two close observers of the Green phenomenon over the first full decade of its operation have concluded: "as long as ever-expanding bureaucracies impinge on individual self-determination, as long as the menace of nuclear annihilation is not banned, and as long as one environmental catastrophe is only upstaged by yet another - frequently worse - disaster, it seems likely that Green parties of various kinds are here to stay".[68] In some ways, however, this somewhat bland, even deterministic analysis ignores many of the situational factors which will determine the relative political success or failure of Europe's Green parties. The mere existence of salient issues capable of mobilising public opinion in favour of environmental reforms, is hardly sufficient of itself to guarantee the survival let alone the political success, of Green parties per se. These unpropitious circumstances have prompted some commentators to regard the Greens as merely 'flash' parties without the effective means of political survival. Burklin, for instance, was confident in his prediction that even Die Grunen, with apparently firmer roots than most Green parties, amounted to little more than a "transient protest vote, basically by the new educated classes"

489

yet to be fully integrated into German society. He further predicted that "the Greens will decline drastically as soon as unemployment eases and the Social Democratic Party has redefined its role as spokesman of the less integrated political left".[69] This assertion, on the evidence adduced above, may prove to be premature, but it does serve to remind that the Greens, even in their strongest locations, are far from guaranteed a secure place in the political firmament. The Greens certainly continue to face considerable handicaps.[70] As we have seen, these parties tend to be inexperienced, fractious, and incapable of circumventing the entrenched established parties, and what are often discriminatory or otherwise unfavourable opportunity structures. For Kitschelt, "they symbolise basic problems of advanced industrial nations which have long been neglected by the political forces in power - and for which there are no easy solutions. Regardless of actual support in terms of mass mobilisation, favourable ratings in public opinion polls, or votes for movement parties, the new movements represent widespread, if not universal concerns".[71]

The Greens have mounted a challenge to the contemporary political order. They have left their mark on contemporary politics and contributed to the reformulation of its issue agenda.[72] In so doing, however, they have been obliged to adapt to the exigencies and constraints of practical politics. Some close observers of this phenomenon have detected in the 'logics' of new party development, an irresistible process of 'institutionalisation' beyond merely the formal adoption of party status. This recurrent phenomenon was evident in each one of the case studies. The dilemmas confronting a purposive radicalism that seeks to engage the political order, rather than to indulge in vacuous polemics, imply that those political activists who would seriously pursue the goal of socio-economic change, must adjust to the system they find themselves operating within as much as they challenge it. The party agency has been the key to resolving this radical predicament, and it is not difficult to see why this is so. The process of 'party government' is the central organising principle of the liberal democratic politics that prevails throughout western Europe. It is at this level, as much as in the discourse of politics or on the streets, that serious radicalism must make its pitch for change. In Kuechler and Dalton's prognosis, "the form of party government is the dominant common trait of western European democracies. Parties are at the heart of the political process, and any significant change in the political order will affect the composition of the party system and/or the role and function of parties in general. The most direct challenge to the political order by the new movements, then, lies in the entry of movement parties into electoral competition".[73] The prevalence of the party phenomenon in the political order explains why it was that Green parties were formed in the first place - to access the policy system and to concentrate political influence where it is most effective. The fact that political parties in democracies exist in a competitive party milieu, and that this systemic quality requires that parties must orientate to one another rather than disengage, also explains why it is that even radical parties seeking to change things cannot afford to indulge in political detachment. They must engage instead and treat with their rivals, in ways that inevitably compromise their highest ideals and blunt their radical cutting edge. All political parties are constrained by their involvement in real politics, but radical parties are compromised more than most; for as these commentators identify the radical predicament, "the price for short term success in the political agenda, for being efficient and reliable in the eye of the larger public, is the alienation of significant parts of the movement".[74] This is indeed a serious predicament and one that, as we have seen has preoccupied, sooner or later, all of Europe's Green parties in some measure. Some of these parties have resisted this fate more readily than others, but all of them have, eventually, been obliged to take their fate in their own hands, to embrace the system, to build bridges to other parties, however tentatively, and thereby to connect with the political system as the first and essential stage in representing an alternative agenda. It is this mutable patterning of inter-party relations, more than the incremental shifts in intra-party arrangements, that provides the significant clues to the direction of political dealignment and realignment in any national polity.

The Green parties have begun to make these adjustments, but they have not yet been rewarded with the levels of support that might quieten those activists who remain wary of such compromises. This does not mean that the political payoff to date has been negligible. The European electorate is now more aware of environmental issues than barely a decade ago, even if it remains preoccupied in what has so far been a decade of economic and political crisis, with the same materialist concerns that have shaped its political preferences for most of the present century. The Greens have assisted in the gradual greening of politics, too, by encouraging other parties to incorporate an environmental dimension and a green rhetoric into their own priorities. The overall picture remains a mixed one. So far, there are few convincing signs of any imminent political breakthrough for the west European Green parties. They have helped to shift the balance of the current political discourse, without decisively replacing the old politics with the new. In the light of this altogether conditional appraisal of the circumstances which help or hinder the success of new movement parties, Rudig's balanced analysis of the fate of the Green parties is surely a more realistic one than either the outright pessimism or unguarded optimism apparent at the extremes of this debate. Undoubtedly, as Rudig points out, "new, urgent environmental issues will come up again, but the roller coaster of ecological issues is difficult for Green parties to manage and it makes them dependent on outside forces beyond their control".[75] This is an equivocal verdict, however, rather than a negative one as far as Green party futures are concerned. Those unfavourable institutional or cultural constraints which do so much to circumscribe the scope for effective ecological politics in otherwise stable systems, by no means, however, preclude a determined response by well organised and politically astute Greens, to overcome these structural disadvantages or minimise their negative impact. The potential impact of ecological issues on the public imagination should never, as Chernobyl or a catalogue of less serious disasters illustrate, be underestimated. On a more positive note, there are clear signs that, in spite of recent setbacks, environmentalism has risen up the agenda of the global political economy. The 118 nation states who participated in the latest Uruguay Round agreement of the GATT accepted that trade policy should be linked inextricably to Green issues.[76] The World Bank has paid similar attention to the insistent arguments of the environmental lobby.[77]

The current evidence of climatic change, and other serious imbalances between the ecosphere and the technosphere, suggest that the environment issue is here to stay. It may well be, that over the short or even the medium term, the most palpable consequence of the emergence of Green parties has been to offer a timely reminder to the old politics parties to improve their act. And that, as a direct consequence of this, as two close observers of these events have noted, "no drastic changes in the political order appear imminent in the immediate future, but (rather) a slow evolutionary process of adaptation has been induced, producing stability by way of change".[78] Over the longer term, however, a combination of the rising awareness of environmental crises amongst the public at large, and the presence of parties that can speak to these anxieties more coherently and persuasively than their party political rivals, and represent them at the heart of the political process, suggests rather better prospects. Nor are the Greens passive victims of political circumstances entirely beyond their own scope to influence and alter to their own electoral advantage.[79] Rudig's analysis of the critical questions of adaptation and political competence is at least as relevant as his insights into the institutional and cultural obstacles to a widespread Green party breakthrough in European politics. Unfavourable circumstances only explain so much. The fate of these parties still remains in their own hands, if they are to take full advantage of the favourable issues at their disposal. The refusal to be pragmatic, to face and resolve organisational dilemmas, or else to abandon political and ideological ghettoes as much of their own making as anything, will continue to condemn them to political failure at worst. Or at best, will ensure only occasional electoral success based on periodic protest voting. Without facing political realities head on, treading as it were Weber's 'hard boards' of real politics, and embracing both compromise and change, Green parties will continue to do little more than scratch the surface of their electoral potential. As Rudig has presciently observed: "To survive, Green parties have to build a stable electorate that identifies with the party and votes for it on a regular basis. The influence of salient environmental issues is particularly acute and unsettling if the Green electorate is volatile and does not identify more closely with the party.... Green party success and failure can be explained, to a large extent, by comparing the combination of environmental issues and conflicts with the resources available for Green parties. But Green parties also need to maintain organisational continuity".[80]

This is propitious advice indeed. These are the stark choices that continue to confront Europe's Green parties. In order to survive, let alone to prosper politically, they need to solve a radical conundrum that predates them. Indeed, one that challenged an earlier generation of new and radical parties on the left. On the one hand, to cope with the critical requirements of effective organisation, the imperative of the disciplined practice of politics, and the need to make the compromises required for broadening their electoral base beyond the Green cognoscenti, as a preface to an effective national presence by playing within the party political system. Alongside these challenges there remains the other compulsion of these parties, to retain a genuinely radical profile and to avoid blurring the 'seagreen incorruptibility' and that pristine vision that demarcates radical politics in all of its expressions from its soggy imitations. The evidence from this study of Europe's Green parties over the past two decades or so suggests that this radical predicament is certainly being confronted. In ways that depend on national circumstances, the aptitude for facing up to and resolving such hard choices is helping to ensconce these parties in national party systems almost everywhere. This process is more likely to continue into the next century than it is to fall into abeyance. The Greens are here to stay and, as with the socialist parties that were responsible for the last great historic realignment of European politics a century or more ago, it is to the long term that we should look for their lasting influence on both the continent's changing policy agendas and on its evolving patterns of party politics.

Notes

1. T. Poguntke, "New Politics and Party Systems: The Emergence of a New Type of Party?" West European Politics (10) 1987 at p.81.
2. Peter Mair, "The Problem of Party System Change", Journal of Theoretical Politics, 1(3) 1989, at pp.251-76; see also ibid, "Myths of Electoral Change and the Survival of Traditional Parties", European Journal of Political Research 24(2) 1993, at pp.121-133.
3. P. Mair, op.cit (1989), at p.255.

4. S. Errson and J.E. Lane, "Democratic Party Systems in Europe: Dimensions, Change and Stability", Scandinavian Political Studies, Vol.5(1) 1982.

5. Ibid; for a similar patterning model, see M. Pedersen, "On Measuring Party System Change: A Methodological Critique and a Suggestion", Comparative Political Studies, Vol.12(4) 1980, pp.387-403.

6. See also, G. B. Powell, "Voting turnout in thirty elections; partisan, legal and socio-economic influences", in R. Rose (ed), "Electoral Participation: A Comparative Analysis" (1980), at p.13; and H. Daalder, "Party elites and political development in Western Europe", in J. LaPalombara and M. Weiner (eds), "Political Parties and Political Development" (Princeton, 1966), at pp. 43-71.

7. M. Pedersen, "The dynamics of European party systems: changing patterns of electoral volatility", European Journal of Political Research 7 1979, especially at p.4.

8. S. Errson and J.E. Lane, op.cit (1982), at p.67.

9. S.M. Lipset and S. Rokkan, "Cleavage structures, party systems and voter alignment: an introduction", in S.M. Lipset and S. Rokkan (eds), "Party Systems and Voter Alignments" (New York, 1967), at p.67.

10. R. Rose and D. Urwin, "Persistence and Change in Western Party Systems since 1945", Political Studies 18 1970, at pp.287-313.

11. R.J. Dalton et al in R.J. Dalton, S.C. Flanagan and P.A. Beck (eds), "Electoral Change in Advanced Industrial Democracies: Realignment or Dealignment?" (Princeton, 1984); see also S.C. Flanagan and R.J. Dalton, "Parties Under Stress: Realignment or Dealignment in Advanced Industrial Societies", West European Politics 7 (1) 1984, pp.7-23.

12. S.C. Flanagan and R.J. Dalton, ibid (1984), at p.10.

13. R.J. Dalton, S.C. Flanagan and P. Beck, "Political Forces and Partisan Change" in ibid (eds) "Electoral Change in Advanced Industrial Democracies: Realignment or Dealignment?" (Princeton, 1984), at pp.455-57.

14. P. Mair, op.cit (1989), at p.253.

15. Ibid (1989), at p.254.

16. R.J. Dalton, S.C. Flanagan and P.A. Beck, in ibid (eds), (1984), at p.451.

17. S.C. Flanagan and R.J. Dalton, op.cit (1984) at p.8.

18. R.J. Dalton, S.C. Flanagan and P.A. Beck, op.cit (1984), at p.457 and p.460.

19. S. Lane and J.E. Errson, op.cit (1982), at p.90.

20. M. Pedersen, op.cit (1979), at p.24; see also O. Borre, "Electoral instability in four Nordic countries 1950-1977", Comparative Political Studies 13 (1989) especially at pp.62-63.

21. P. Mair, op.cit (1989), at p.264-65; for a complementary study that draws broadly similar conclusions, see M. Shamur, "Are Western European Party Systems 'Frozen'" Comparative Political Studies 17 (1) 1984, pp.35-79.

22. P. Mair, op.cit at p.262.

23. See S. Wolinetz, "The Transformation of the Western European Party System Revisited", West European Politics 2 (1) 1979, pp.4-28; see also M. Pedersen, "Changing Pattern of Electoral Volatility: Explorations in Explanation", in H. Daalder and P. Mair (eds), "Western European Party Systems: Continuity and Change" (London, 1983); and M.A. Maguire, "Is there Still Persistence? Electoral Change in

Western Europe, 1948-1979", in H. Daalder and P. Mair (eds), op.cit (1983), at pp.67-94.

24. M. Pedersen, op.cit (1983), at pp.34-35.

25. C. Hauss and D. Rayside, "The Development of New Parties in Western Democracies Since 1945", in L. Maisel and J. Cooper (eds), "Political Parties: Development and decay" (London, 1978).

26. C. Hauss and D. Rayside, ibid (1978), at p.36.

27. See C. Boggs, op.cit (1995), at chapters 4-6, on why Europe's established socialist parties, with all of their advantages, have found difficulty in harnessing the contemporary radical potential - a fact which puts the considerable task facing new parties looking to make an electoral breakthrough in its proper perspective.

28. C. Hauss and D. Rayside, op.cit (1978) at p.46.

29. C. Hauss and D. Rayside, op.cit (1978), at pp.50-51.

30. See D. Rae, "The Political Consequences of Electoral Laws" (New Haven, Conn, 1971).

31. C. Hauss and D. Rayside, op.cit (1978), at pp.43-44.

32. H. Kitschelt, op.cit (1990); F.L. Wilson, "When Parties Refuse to Fail: The Case of France", in K. Lawson and P. Merkl (eds), "When Parties Fail: Emerging Alternative Organisations" (Princeton, 1988), at p.526.

33. See E. Gene Frankland, "Germany. The rise, fall and recovery of Die Grunnen", in D. Richardson and D. Rootes, op.cit (London, 1995).

34. Ibid at p.26.

35. C. Hauss and D. Rayside, op.cit (1978), p.51.

36. C. Hauss and D. Rayside, op.cit (1978) at pp.47-48.

37. C. Hauss and D. Rayside, ibid (1978), at p.54.

38. H. Kitschelt, "New Social Movements and the Decline of Party Organisation", in R. J. Dalton and M. Keuchler (eds), "Challenging the Political Order: New Social and Political Movements in Western Democracies" (Oxford, 1990) at p.203.

39. A. Downs, "Up and down with Ecology: The Issue Attention-Cycle", Public Interest (28) 1972, pp.38-50.

40. J. Hofrichter and K. Reif, "Evolution of Environmental Attitudes in Western Europe", Scandinavian Political Studies 13, (1990), at pp.119-146.

41. M. Bennulf, "Sweden - The rise and fall of Miljopartiet de grona", in D. Richardson and C. Rootes, op.cit (1994), at p.181.

42. See the account by Hein-Anton van der Heijden, Ruud Koopmans, Marco G. Guigui in Research in Social Movements, Conflict and Change, Supplement 2 Part two, 1992, pp.1-40.

43. See D. Rucht, "Environmental movement organisations in West Germany and France: Structure and inter-organisational relations", in P.G. Klandermans (ed), "Organizing for change: Social movement organisations in Europe and the US" (Greenwich CT, 1989); W. Rudig, "Peace and Ecology Movements in Western Europe", West European Politics 3(1) 1988, at pp.29-30; A. Jamieson, R. Eyerman and J. Cramer, "The Making of the New Environmental Consciousness: A Comparative Study of the Environmental Movements in Sweden, Denmark and the Netherlands" (Edinburgh, 1991); and M. Finger and P. Sciarini, "Integrating new Politics into Old Politics: The

Swiss Political Elite", West European Politics, 14 (1) 1991, pp.98-112.

44. See R. W. Cobb, J. K. Ross and M. H. Ross, "Agenda Building as a Comparative Political Process", American Political Science Review 70 1976, pp.126-138; P. Leroy and A. de Geest, "Environmental movement and environmental policy", (Antwerp/Amsterdam, 1985).

45. C. Boggs, op.cit (1995), at p.235.

46. C. Offe, "Reflections on the Institutional Self-Transformation of Movement Politics: A Tentative Stage Model", in R.J. Dalton and M. Keuchler, op.cit (1990), p.238.

47. C. Boggs, op.cit (1995), at p.239.

48. See for instance, R. Miliband, "Divided Societies" (Oxford, 1991), at p.110.

49. See M. Harrington, "Socialism: Past and Future" (New York, 1990).

50. C. Boggs, op.cit (1995), at p.182.

51. Ibid at p.217.

52. C. Boggs, op.cit (1995), at p.213.

53. See Winifred Ruigrok and Rob van Tulder, "The logic of International Restructuring" (London, 1995), especially at chapters 6-8.

54. See U. Beck, "Risk Society" (London, 1992), especially at chapters one and two.

55. F. Muller-Rommel, "New Political Movements and 'New Politics' Parties in Western Europe", in R.J. Dalton and M. Kuechler, op.cit (1990), at pp.229-230.

56. Ibid at p.230.

57. Robert Rohrschneider, "Environmental Belief Systems in Western Europe. A Hierarchical Model of Constraint", Comparative Political Studies 26(1) 1993, at p.24.

58. Angelo Panebianco, "Political Parties: Organisation and Power" (Cambridge, 1988).

59. This is a critical issue that John Dunn has raised in the context of the global environment. See John Dunn, "Western Political Theory in the Face of the Future" (1993 edition), at Conclusion (1992), especially at pp.134-137.

60. L. Zucker, "The role of institutionalization in cultural persistence", American Sociological Review 42(4), at p.728.

61. H. Kitschelt, "The Green Phenomenon in Western Party Systems", in S. Kamienieki (ed), "Environmental Politics in the International Arena. Movements, Parties, Organisations and Policy" (New York, 1993), at pp.103-104.

62. H. Kitschelt, op.cit (1993), at pp.107-108.

63. The Guardian, 21.9.96.

64. See Jonas Pontusson, "At the End of the Third Road: Social Democracy in Crisis", Politics and Society No.2 (1990).

65. For a discussion of some of these issues, see A.S. Markovitz and P.S. Gorki, "The German Left: Red, Green and Beyond" (Oxford, 1993).

66. See the discussion in Michael Harrington, op.cit (1990).

67. M. Bennulf, op.cit (1994), at p.181.

68. F. Muller-Rommel and T. Poguntke, "The Unharmonious Family: Green Parties in Western Europe", in E. Kolinsky (ed), op.cit (New York, 1989), at p.28.

69. Wilhelm Burklin, "Governing Left Parties Frustrating the Radical Non-Established Left: The Rise and Inevitable Decline of the Greens", European Sociological Review 2 (September, 1987).

70.   L. Elliot, "The Green time bomb that won't be defused", The Guardian, 6.9.93.

71.   M. Kuechler and R.J. Dalton, "New Social Movements and the Political Order: Inducing Change for Long-term Stability?", in R.J. Dalton and M. Kuechler, op.cit (1990), at p.296.

72.   C. Offe, "Challenging the Boundaries of Institutional Politics: Social Movements since the Sixties", in C.S. Maier (ed), "Changing Boundaries of the Political" (Cambridge, 1987).

73.   M. Keuchler and R.J. Dalton, op.cit (1990), at p.297.

74.   Ibid at p.295.

75.   W. Rudig, op.cit October 1991, at p.30.

76.   "Greening the Gatt", Financial Times, 23.2.94.

77.   "Word Bank bows to Green lobby", The Guardian, 27.9.93.

78.   M. Kuechler and R.J. Dalton, op.cit (1990), at p.298.

79.   For a discussion of the relationship between continuity and institutionalisation, see M. and J. Charlot, "Les Groupes politiques dans leur environment", in J. Lecca and M. Grawitz (eds), "Traite de science politique" iii (Paris, 1985).

80.   W. Rudig, op.cit (October, 1991), at pp.30-31.

References

B. Aardal, Green Politics: A Norwegian Experience, *Scandinavian Political Studies* 13 (1990).

B. Aardal, *Energy and Environment: A Study of Voter attitudes and party profiles 1977-1985* (1991).

A. Adonis, Great Britain, *Electoral Studies* 8 (1989).

A. Affigne, Environmental Crises, Green Party Power: Chernobyl and the Swedish Greens in W Rudig (ed), *Green Politics One* (1990).

S. Aguilar - Fernandez, The Greens in the 1993 Spanish General Election: A Chronicle of a Defeat Foretold, *Environmental Politics* 3 (1994).

J. Alber, Modernisierung, neue Spannungslinien und die politischen Chancen der Grunen, in *Politsche Vierteljahresschrift*, 26 (1985).

J. Alber, Continuities and Changes in the Idea of the Welfare State, *Politics and Society* 16 (1988).

J. Alber, Modernisation, cleavage structure and the Rise of the Green Parties and Lists in Europe, in F Muller - Rommel (ed), op cit (1989).

D. Alexander, Pollution policies and politics: the Italian environment, in .F Sebetti and R. Catanzaro (eds), *Italian Politics: A Review* 5 (1991).

J. Amodia, Personalities and Slogans: The Spanish Election of October 1989, *West European Politics* 13 (1990).

P. Anderson, Components of the national culture, in A. Cochrane and R. Blackburn (eds), *Student Power* (1969).

J. O. Andersson, The Economic Policy Strategies of the Nordic Countries, in H. Keman, H. Paloheimo and P. F. Whiteley (eds), *Coping with the Economic Crisis* (1987).

E. Anners, Conservatism in Sweden, in D. Hancock and G. Sjoberg (eds), *Politics in the post welfare state* (1972).

T. J. Anton, *Administered Politics: Elite Political Culture in Sweden* (1980).

J. Araujo, *La Muerte Silenciosa Espana haciel desastre ecologico* (1990).

R. Bahro, *Building the Green Movement* (1986).

K. L. Baker et al, *Germany Transformed Political Culture and the New Politics* (1981).

S. Barnes and M. Kaase (et al), *Political Action; Mass Participation in Five Western Democracies* (1979).

S. Barnes, P. McDonough and A. Lopez Pina, The Development of Partisanship in New Democracies: The Case of Spain, *American Journal of Political Science* 29 (1985).

B. Barry, *Sociologists, Economists and Democracy* (1970).

S. Bartolino, The Membership of Mass Parties: The Social Democratic Experience 1889-1978, in H. Daalder and P. Mair (eds), *Western European Party Systems. Stability and Change* (1983).

S. Bartolino and P. Mair, *Ideology, competition and electoral availability: The stabilisation of European electorates 1885 - 1985* (1990).

M. Bax, *Harpstrings and Confessions: An Anthropological Study of Politics in Rural Ireland* (1976).

U. Beck, *Risk Society* (1992).

E. Bedung, The Environmentalist Party and the Swedish Five Party Syndrome, in K. Lawson and P. Merkl, *Why Parties Fail* (1989).

D. Bell, *The End of Ideology:On the Exhaustion of Political Ideas in the Fifties* (1996).

D. Bell, *The Coming of Post - Industrial Society* (1973).

D. Bell, *The French Socialist Party. The Emergence of a Party of Government* (2nd ed 1988).

D. Bell (ed), *Western European Communists and the Collapse of Communism* (1993).

J. L. Bennahmias and A Roche, *Des Verts de toutes les couleurs:histoire et sociologie du movement ecolo* (1992).

M. Bennulf, The rise and Fall of Miljopartiet de grona, in D. Richardson and C. Rootes (eds) op cit (1995).

M. Bennulf and S. Holmberg, The Green Breakthrough in Sweden, *Scandinavian Political Studies* 13 (1990).

S. Berglund, The Finnish General Election of 1987, *Electoral Studies* 6 (1987).

S. Berglund, The Finnish Parliamentary Election of 1991, *Electoral Studies* 10 (1991).

S. Berglund and U. Lindstrom, *The Scandinavian Party Systems:A Comparative Study* (1978).

H. Bergstrom, Sweden's Politics and Party Systems at the Crossroads, *West European Politics* 14 (1991).

H. Berrington, New Parties in Britain: Why some live and most die, *International Political Science Review* 6 (1985).

H. G. Betz, Strange Love? How the Greens began to love NATO, *German Studies Review*, 12 (1989).

P. Bew, E. Hazelkorn and H. Patterson, *The Dynamics of Irish Politics* (1989).

K. von Beyme, *Political Parties in Western Democracies* (1985).

K. von Beyme, The Role of Deputies in West Germany, in E. Suleiman (ed), *Parliaments and Parliamentarians in Democratic Politics* (1986).

J. Bigas, Paginos Verdes, *Guia de Recursos Ambientales* (Barcelona 1991).

J. Bigas, Ecologism in Spain: Commentary on the Spanish Case, in Maria - Pillar et al (eds) op.cit (1992).

L. Bille, Denmark:-The Oscillating Party System, *West European Politics* 12 (1989).

R. Biorcio, L'elettorato verde in R.Biorcio and G.Lodi (eds), *La sfida verde: il movimento ecologista in Italia* (1988).

R. Biorcio and G. Lodi (eds), *La sfida verde: il movimento ecologista in Italia* (1988).

A. H. Birch, *The Concepts and Theories of Modern Democracy* (1993).

T. Bjorklund and O. Hellvik, Green Issues in Norwegian Politics, *Politica* 4 (Arhuus 1989).

J. Blondel, Party Systems and patterns of government in Western democracies, *Canadian Journal of Political Science* 2 (1968).

A. Blowers, Transition or Transformation? Environmental Policy under Thatcher, *Public Administration* 65 (1987).

V. Bogdanor and D. Butler (eds), *Democracy and Elections: Electoral Systems and their Consequences* (1983).

C. Boggs, *Social Movements and Political Power* (1986).

C. Boggs, *The Socialist Tradition: from Crisis to Decline* (1995).

B. Boll and T. Poguntke, The 1990 All-German Election Campaign, in D. Farrell and S.Bowler (eds), *Electoral Strategies and Political Marketing* (1992).

F. Boltgen and W. Jagodzinski, In an Environment of Insecurity: Postmaterialism in the European Community, 1970 to 1980, *Comparative Political Studies* 17 (1985).

M. Bookchin, *Post Scarcity Anarchism* (1971).

O. Borre, Recent Trends in Danish Voting Behaviour in a Multi-party System, *Scandinavian Political Studies* 8 (1973).

O. Borre, The Social Bases of Danish Electoral Behaviour, in R.Rose (ed), *Electoral Participation: A Comparative Analysis* (1980).

O. Borre, Critical Electoral Change in Scandinavian, in R. J. Dalton et al (eds), op cit (1984).

O. Borre, Denmark, in I. Crewe and D. Denver (eds), op cit (1985).

O. Borre, The Danish General Election of 1987, *Electoral Studies* 7 (1988).

O. Borre, Electoral instability in Four Nordic Countries, 1950-77, *Comparative Political Studies* 13 (1989).

O. Borre, The Danish General Election of 1990, *Electoral Studies* 10 (1991).

D. Boy, Le Vote Ecologiste en 1978, *Revue Francaise de Science Politique* 31 (1981).

G. Boyle, *Nuclear Power: The Windscale Controversy* (1978).

R. G. Braungart, Family status, socialisation and student politics: a multivariate analysis, *American Journal of Sociology* 77, (1971).

G. Braunthal, *The West German Social Democrats: 1969 - 1982, Profile of a Party in Power* (1983).

J. Bridgeford, The Ecological Movement and the French General Election of 1978, *Parliamentary Affairs* 31 (1978).

S. Brint, 'New Class' and Cumulative Trend Explanations of the Liberal Political Attitudes of Professionals, *American Journal of Sociology* 90 (1984).

E. Browne and J. Dreijmanis (eds), *Government Coalitions in Western Democracies* (1982).

I. Budge and H. Keman, *Parties and Democracy, Coalition Formation and Government Functioning in Twenty States* (1990).

I. Budge, D. Robertson and D. Hearl, *Ideologies, Strategy, and Party Change. Spatial Analysis of Post-War Elections. Programmes in 19 Democracies,* (1987).

W. P. Burklin, *Grune Politik Ideologische Zyklen, Wahlen und Parteiensystem* (1984).

W. P. Burklin, The Split between the Established and Non Established Left in Germany, *European Journal of Political Research* 13 (1985).

W. P. Burklin, The German Greens: The Post Industrial Non Established and the Party System, *International Political Science Research* 6 (1985).

W. P. Burklin, Governing Left Parties Frustrating the Radical Non Established Left. The Rise and Inevitable Decline of the Greens, *European Sociological Review* 3 (1987).

W. P. Burklin, A politico-economic model instead of sour grapes logics: A rejoinder to Herbert Kitshelt's critique, *European Sociological Review* 4 (1988).

F. H. Buttel, The Environment movement: historical roots and current trends, in C. R. Humphrey and F. H. Buttel (eds,) *Environment, Energy and Society* (1980).

P. Byrd, Great Britain. Parties in a changing Party System, in A. Ware (ed), *Political Parties. Electoral Change and Structural Response* (1987).

P. Byrne, *The Campaign for Nuclear Disarmament* (1988).

P. Byrne, Great Britain: The 'Green Party', in F. Muller - Rommel (ed), op cit (1989).

P. Byrne, and J. Lovenduski, Two New Protest Groups: The Peace and Women's Movements, in H. Drucker et al (eds), *Developments in British Politics* (1983).

F. Capra and C. Spretnak, *Green Politics* (1985).

N. Carter, Whatever Happened to the Environment? The British General Election of 1992, *Environmental Politics* 1 (1992).

N. Carter, The 'Greening' of Labour, in M. J. Smith and J. Spear (eds), *The Changing Labour Party* (1992).

R. K. Carty, *Party and Parish Pump: Electoral Politics in Ireland* (1981).

R. K. Carty, Ireland: From Predominance to Competition, in S. Wolinetz (ed), *Parties and Party Systems in Liberal Democracies* (1988).

F. Castles, *The Social Democratic Image of Society* (1978).

F. Castles, (ed) *The Impact of Parties. Politics and Policies in Democratic Capitalist States* (1982).

R. Cayrol, The Electoral Campaign and the Decision Makings Process of French Voters, in H. Penniman (ed), *France at the Polls 1988 and 1986* (1988).

A. Cederna, *The Destruction of Nature in Italy* (1975).

P. Ceri, The Nuclear Power Issue: A New Political Cleavage Within Italian Society? in R. Nannetti, R. Leonardo and P. Corbetta (eds), *Italian Politics: A Review* 2 (1988).

T. Chafer, The Anti-Nuclear Movement and the Rise of Political Ecology, in P. Cerny (ed), *Social Movements and Protests in Contemporary France* (1982).

T. Chafer, The Greens in the Municipal Elections, *Newsletter for the Study of Modern and Contemporary France 11-16* (1983).

T. Chafer, The Greens in France: An Emerging Social Movement, *Journal of Area Studies* 10 (1984).

W. M. Chandler and A. Siaroff, Post Industrial Politics in Germany and the Origins of the Greens, *Comparative Politics* (1986).

M. and J. Charlet, Les Groupes politiques dans leur environment, in J. Lecca and M. Grawitz (eds), *Traite de science politique* 3 (1985).

B. Chubb, *The Government and Politics of Ireland* (2nd ed 1992).

C. H. Church, Swiss History and Politics since 1945, in *Western Europe: A Handbook* (1988).

C. H. Church, Behind the Consociational Screen: Politics in Contemporary Switzerland, *West European Politics* 12, (1989).

C. H. Church, The development of the Swiss Green party, *Environmental Politics* 1 (1992).

R. Clogg (ed), *Greece in the 1980s* (1983).

R. Clogg, *Parties and Elections in Greece* (1987).

R. W. Cobb, J. K. Ross and M. H. Ross, Agenda Building as a Comparative Political Process, *American Political Science Review* 70 (1976).

A. Cole, *French Political Parties in Transition* (1990).

A. Cole & B. Doherty, France. Pas comme les autres - the French Greens at the crossroads, in D. Richardson and C. Rootes (eds), op cit (1995).

P. Commins, Ireland: A Sociological Profile, in P. Clancy et al (eds), *Ireland: A Sociological Profile* (1986).

D. Conradt and R. Dalton, The West German Electorate and the Party System: Continuity and Change in the 1980s, *Review of Politics* 50 (1988).

S. Cosgrove and A. Duff, Environmentalism, Middle Class Radicalism and Politics,

Sociological Review 2 (1990).

G. Cox, Centripetal and Centrifugal Incentives in Electoral Systems, *American Journal of Political Science* 34 (1990).

I. Crewe and D. Denver (eds), *Electoral Change in Western Democracies: Patterns and Sources of Electoral Volatility* (1985).

J. Curren (ed), *The Future of the Left* (1984).

J. Curtice, The 1989 European Election: Protest or Green tide? *Electoral Studies* 8 (1989).

H. Daalder, Opposition in a Segmented Society, in R. A. Dahl (ed), *Political Oppositions in Western Democracies* (1966).

H. Daalder, Party elites and political development in Western Europe, in J. LaPalombara and M. Weiner (eds), *Political Parties and Political Development* (1966).

H. Daalder, Extreme Proportional Representation: The Dutch Experience, in S. E. Finer (ed), *Adversary Politics and Electoral Reform* (1975).

H. Daalder, The Netherlands, in S. Henig (ed), *Political Parties in the European Community*. (1979).

H. Daalder, Changing Procedures and Changing Strategies in Coalition Building, *Legislative Studies Quarterly* 11 (1986).

H. Daalder (ed), *Party Systems in Denmark, Austria, Switzerland, the Netherlands and Belgium* (1987).

H. Daalder, The Dutch Party System. From Segmentation to Polarization - and Then? in H. Daalder (ed), *Party Systems in Denmark, Austria, Switzerland, the Netherlands and Belgium* (1987).

H. Daalder and P. Mair (eds), *Western European Party Systems: Continuity and Change* (1983).

H. Dachs, Citizen Lists and Green - Alternative Parties in Austria, in A. Pelinka and F. Plasser (eds), *The Austrian Party System* (1989).

R. J. Dalton, The West German Party System between Two Ages, in R. J. Dalton et al (eds), op cit (1984).

R. J. Dalton, Cognitive Mobilisation and Partisan Dealignment in Advanced Industrial Democracies, *Journal of Politics* 46 (1984).

R. J. Dalton, Political Parties and Political Representation. Party Supporters and Party Elites in Nine Nations, *Comparative Political Studies*, 18 (1985).

R. J. Dalton, *Citizen Politics in Western Democracies* (1988).

R. J. Dalton, S. C. Flanagan and P. A . Beck (eds), *Electoral change in Advanced Industrial Democracies: Realignment or Dealignment.* (1984).

R. J. Dalton and M. Kuechler (eds), *Challenging the Political Order: New Social and Political Movements in Western Democracies* (1990).

J. J. Damborenea (ed), *Desarollo y Destruccian: una introduccion a los Problemas Ecologico de Espana* (Madrid 1990).

S. Del Campo, I. F. Tezanos and W. Santin, The Spanish Political Elite: Permanence and Change, in M. Czudowski (ed), *International yearbook of elite studies* (1983).

N. Demertzis, Greece: Greens at the periphery, in D. Richardson and C. Rootes (eds), op cit (1995).

K. Deschouwer and P. Stouthysen, *The Electorate of AGALEV* (1982).

K. Deschouwer, Belgium: The 'Ecologists' and 'AGALEV', in F. Muller-Rommel (ed), *New Politics in Western Europe: The Rise and Success of Green Parties and Alternative Lists* (1989).

K. Deschouwer, Patterns of Participation and Competition in Belgium, *West European Politics* 12 (1989).

A. De Swaan, The Netherlands: Coalitions in a Segmented Polity, in E. C. Browne and J. Dreijmanis (eds), *Government Coalitions in Western Democracies* (1982).

W. Dewachter, Changes in a Partiocratie: The Belgian Party System from 1944 to 1986, in H. Daalder (ed), op cit (1987).

L. De Winter, Belgium; Democracy or Oligarchy? in M. Gallagher & M. Marsh (eds), *Candidate Selection in Comparative Perspective* (1988).

P. Diamandouros, Transition to and Consolidation of, Democratic Politics in Greece, 1974-83: A Tentative Assessment, *West European Politics* 4 (1984).

M. Diani Italy: The Liste Verdi in F. Muller-Rommel (ed), *New Politics in Western Europe* (1989).

G. Di Palma, *Antipathy and Participation: Mass Politics in Western Societies* (1970).

G. Di Palma, *Surviving without Governing: The Italian Parties in Parliament* (1977).

J. Ditfurth, *Lebewild und gefahrlich Radikalogische Perspectiven* (1991).

A. Dobson, *Green Political Thought* (1990).

B. Doherty, The Fundi Realo Controversy: An analysis of four European Green Parties, *Environmental Politics* 1 (1992).

C. Donob, Social Change and Transformation of the State in Italy, in R. Scase (ed), *The State in Western Europe* (1980).

M. Donovan, Party Strategy and Centre Domination in Italy, *West European Politics* 12 (1989).

C. Duchen, *Feminism in France: From May '68 to Mitterrand* (1986).

J. Dunn, *Western Political Theory in the face of the future* (1993 edition).

M. Duverger, *Political Parties* (1954).

R. Eckersley, Green Politics and the New Class: Selfishness or Virtue? *Political Studies* 37 (1989).

K. Eder, The New Social Movements and the Decline of Party Organization, in R. J. Dalton and M. Kuechler (ed), op.cit (1990).

L. Edinger, *West German Politics* (1986).

G. Eley, Reviewing the Socialist Tradition, in C. Lemke and G. Marks (eds), *The Crisis of Socialism in Europe* (1991).

S. Errson and J. E. Lane, Democratic Party Systems in Europe: Dimensions, Change and Stability, *Scandinavian Political Studies* 5 (1982).

G. Esping - Andersen, *Politics against Markets. The Social Democratic Road to Power* (1985).

G. Esping - Andersen, Post-industrial cleavage structures: A Comparison of Social Stratification in Germany, Sweden and the United States, in F. F. Piven (ed) op cit (1991).

R. Eyerman and A. Jamison, *Social Movements. A Cognitive Approach* (1991)

P. Farneti, *The Italian Party System 1945 - 1980* (1985).

K. Featherstone and D. Katsoudas, *Political Change in Greece: Before and After the Generals* (1987).

K. Featherstone, The 'Party State' in Greece and the Fall of Papandreou, *West European Politics* 13 (1990).

K. Featherstone, Political Parties and Democratic Consolidation in Greece, in G. Pridham (ed), *Securing Democracy. Political Parties and Democratic Consolidation* (1990).

J. Fitzmaurice, *Politics in Denmark* (1981).

J. Fitzmaurice, *Austrian Politics and Society Today* (1991).

J. Fitzmaurice, The Extreme Right in Belgium: Recent Developments, *Parliamentary Affairs* 45 (1992).

J. Fitzmaurice, *The Politics of Belgium: A Unique Federalism* (1996).

J. Fitzmaurice and G. Van den Berghe, The Belgian General Election of 1985, *Electoral Studies* 5 (1986).

R. Flacks, The revolt of the young intelligentsia: revolutionary class consciousness in post - scarcity America, in R. Aya and N. Miller (eds), *The New American Revolution* (1971).

H. Flam (with A. Jamison), The Swedish Confrontation over Nuclear Energy - A Case of a Timid Anti-Nuclear Movement, in H Flam (ed), *States and Anti-Nuclear Movements* (1992).

S. C. Flanagan and R. J. Dalton, Parties under stress: Realignment of Dealignment in Advanced Industrial Societies, *West European Politics* 7 (1984).

P. Flora and J. Alber, Modernization, Democratization, and the Development of Welfare States in Western Europe, in P. Flora & A. Heidenheimer (eds), *The Development of Welfare States in Europe and America* (1981).

D. Foss and R. Larkin, *Beyond Revolution: A New Theory of Social Movements* (1986).

E. Gene Frankland, The Role of the Greens in West German Parliamentary Politics, *Review of Politics,* 50 (1988).

E. Gene Frankland, Green Politics and Alternative Economics, *German Studies Review,* 11 (1988).

E. Gene Frankland, Does Green Politics have a future in Britain? in W. Rudig (ed), *Green Politics One* (1990).

E. Gene Frankland and D. Schoonmaker, *Between Protest and Power: The Green Party in Germany* (1992).

E. Gene Frankland, Germany: The rise, fall and recovery of Die Grunen, in D. Richardson and C. Rootes op.cit (1995).

E. Gene Frankland, The Austrian Greens: From Electoral Alliance to Political Party, in W. Rudig (ed), *Green Politics Three* (1996).

E. Gene Frankland, The Greens' Comeback in 1994: The Third Party of Germany, in R. J. Dalton (ed), *Germans Divided* (1996).

M. Franklin, *The Decline of class voting in Britain. Changes in the Bases of Electoral Choice, 1964 - 83* (1985).

M. Franklin, T. Mackie, H. Valen (et al), *Electoral Change Responses to Evolving Social and Attitudional Structures in Western Countries* (1992).

J. Frears, *France in the Giscard Presidency* (1981).

J. Frears, The French Presidential Election, *Government and Opposition* 23 (1988).

J. Freeman, A Model for Analyzing the Strategic Options of Social Movement Organizations, in J. Freeman (ed), *Social Movements of the Sixties and Seventies* (1975).

J. W. Friend, *Seven Years in France: Francois Mitterrand and the Unintended Revolution* (1989).

A-P. Frognier, *Le Vote ecologiste et d'extreme-droit en Wallonie* (1992).

D. Fuchs and D. Rucht, Support for New Social Movements in Five Western European Countries, in C. Rootes and H. Davis (eds), *A New Europe? Social Change and Political Transformation* (1994).

F. Fukuyama, The end of History, *The National Interest* 16 (1989).

J. Gaffney (ed), *The French Presidential Elections of 1988. Ideology and Leadership in Contemporary France* (1988).

503

J. Gaffney, *The French Left and the Fifth Republic. The Discourse of Communism and Socialism in Contemporary France* (1989).

J. Gaffney (ed), *Political Parties and the European Union* (1996).

P. Gaiter, *The Swedish Green Party. Responses to the Parliamentary Challenge, 1988 - 90* (1991).

M. Gallagher, Disproportionality in a Proportional Representation System: The Irish Experience, *Political Studies* 23 (1975).

M. Gallagher, *The Irish Labour Party in Transition, 1957-1982* (1982).

M. Gallagher, *Political Parties in the Republic of Ireland* (1985).

M. Gallagher and R. Sinnott (eds), *How Ireland Voted, 1989* (1990).

M. Gallagher, M. Laver and P. Mair, *Representative Government in Modern Europe* (2nd ed 1995).

T. Gallagher and A. M. Williams (eds), *Southern European Socialism* (1989).

T. Gallagher, The Portuguese Socialist Party: The Pitfalls of Being First, in T. Gallagher and A. M. Williams (eds), *Southern European Socialism* (1989).

G. Galli, *Il Bipartismo imperfetto: Communisti e Democristiani in Italia* (1996).

A. Gamble and A. Payne (eds), *Regionalism and World Order* (1996).

X. Garcia, J. Reixach and S. Vilanova, *El Combat Ecologista a Catalunya* (1979).

G. Garrett and P. Lange, Performance in a Hostile World: Economic Growth in Captitalist Democracies, *World Politics* 38 (1986).

G. Garrett and P. Lange, Political Response to Interdependence: What's 'Left' of the Left?, *International Organization* 45 (1991).

J. Gelb, *Feminism and Politics. A Comparative Perspective* (1989).

P. Gerlich, E. Grande and W. C. Muller, Corporatism in crisis. Stability and change of social partnership in Austria, *Political Studies* 36 (1988).

J. Gibbons (ed), *Contemporary Political Culture in a Post Modern Age* (1989).

A. Giddens, *The Class Structure of the Advanced Societies* (2nd ed 1981).

R. Gillespie, *The Spanish Socialist Party. A History of Factionalism* (1989).

R. Gillespie and T. Gallagher, Democracy and Authority in the Socialist Parties of Southern Europe, in T. Gallagher and A. M. Williams (eds), op.cit (1989).

K. Gladdish, Opposition in the Netherlands, in E. Kolinsky (ed), *Opposition in Western Europe,* (1987).

K. Gladdish, The Centre Holds. The 1986 Netherlands Election, *West European Politics* 10 (1987).

J. Goul-Andersen, Decline of Class Voting or Change in Class voting? Social Classes and Party Choice in Denmark in the 1970's, *European Journal of Political Research* 12 (1984).

J. Goul-Andersen, Denmark, Environmental Conflict and the 'Greening' of the Labour Movement, *Scandinavian Political Studies* 13 (1990).

J. Goul-Andersen, 'Environmentalism', New Politics and Industrialism: Some Theoretical Perspectives, *Scandinavian Political Studies* 13 (1990).

D. Granberg and S. Holmberg, *The Political System Matters: Social Psychology and Voting Behaviour in Sweden and The United States* (1988).

S. Gronmo, Conflict Lines in Party Politics, 1969-1973: Some Effects of the EC Struggle, *Tidsskrift for Samfum Forskning* 2 (1975).

P. Gunderlach, Recent Value Changes in Western Europe, *Futures* 24 (1992).

R. Gunther, Electoral Laws, Party Systems and Elites: The Case of Spain, *American Political Science Review* 83 (1989).

A. Gunther, G. Sani and G. Shabad, *Spain after Franco. The Making of a Competitive Party System* (1988).

C. Haerpfer, Austria, in I. Crewe and D. Denver (eds), op.cit (1985).

C. Haerpfer, Austria: The 'United Greens' and the 'Alternative List/Green Alternative', in F. Muller-Rommel (ed), *New Politics in Western Europe* (1989).

P. Hainsworth, Breaking the Mould: The Greens in the French Party System, in A. Cole (ed), op.cit (1990).

D. Hamilton, *After the Revolution; The New Political Landscape in East Germany* (1990).

M. Hamilton, *Democratic Socialism in Britain and Sweden* (1989).

M. Donald Hancock and J. Logue, Sweden: The Quest for Economic Democracy, *Polity* (Autumn/Winter 1984).

G. Hansen, Civil Disobedience: A threat to Representative Democracy? in B. Hagtvedt (ed), *The Difficult Disobedience* (1981).

R. Harmel and K. Janda, *Parties and Their Environments. Limits to Reform?* (1982).

M. Harrington, *Socialism: Past and Future* (1990).

C. Hauss, *The New Left in France. The Unified Socialist Party* (1978).

C. Hauss and D. Rayside, The Development of New Parties in Western Democracies Since 1945, in L. Maisel and J. Cooper (eds), *Political Parties: Development and Decay* (1978).

P. R. Hay and M. G. Hayward, Comparative Green Politics: Beyond the European Context? *Political Studies* 36 (1988).

J. Hayward, Ideological Change: The Exhaustion of the Revolutionary Impetus, in P.A. Hall, J. Hayward and H. Machin, *Developments in French Politics* (1990).

S. Hazareesingh, *Political Traditions in Modern France* (1994).

A. Heath, R. Jowell, J. Curtice and G. Evans, The Rise of the New Political Agenda? *European Sociological Review* 6 (1990).

H. Heclo and H. Madsen, *Policy and Politics in Sweden: Principled Pragmatism* (1987).

R. Helenius, The Finnish Social Democrats, in W. Paterson and A. H. Thomas, *Social Democratic Parties* (1988).

J. H. Helm, Citizen Lobbies in West Germany, in P. H. Merkl (ed), *Western European Party Systems* (1980).

W. Herenberg, *Die Grunen; Regierungs partner von morgen?* (1992).

K. Hildebrand and R. J. Dalton, Political Change or sunshine politics? in M. Kaase and K. von Beyme (eds), Elections and parties; *German Political Studies* Vol.3 (1978).

K. Hill, Political Change in a Segmented Society, in R. Rose (ed), *Electoral Behaviour: A Comparative Handbook* (1974).

D. Hine, Leaders and Followers. Democracy and Manageability in the Social Democratic Parties of Western Europe, in W. E. Paterson and A. H. Thomas (eds), *The Future of Social Democracy* (1986).

D. Hine, The Italian Socialist Party, in T. Gallagher and A. M. Williams (eds), op.cit (1989).

D. Hine, *Governing Italy: The Politics of Bargained Pluralism.* (1993).

D. Hine, Federalism, Regionalism and the Unitary State: Contemporary Regional Pressures in Historical Perspective, in C. Levy (ed), *Italian Regionalism: History, Identity and Politics* (1996).

M. Hirsch, The 1984 Luxembourg Election, *West European Politics* 8 (1985).

E. Hobsbawm, The crisis of today's ideologies, *New Left Review* 192 (1992).

J. Hofrichter and K. Reif, Evolution of Environmental Attitudes in Western Europe, *Scandinavian Political Studies* 13 (1990).

S. Hug and M. Finger, Green Politics in Switzerland, *European Journal of Political Research* 21 (1992).

C. Hughes, Cantonalism: Federation and Confederacy in the Golden Epoch of Switzerland, in M. Burgess and A-G. Gagnon, *Comparative Federalism and Federation* (1993).

W. Hulsberg, The Greens at the Crossroads, *New Left Review* 152 (1985).

W. Hulsberg, *The German Greens: A Social and Political Profile* (1988).

R. Inglehart, The Silent Revolution in Europe: Intergenerational Change in Post Industrial Societies, *American Political Science Review* 65 (1971).

R. Inglehart, *The Silent Revolution, Changing Values and Political Styles among Western publics* (1977).

R. Inglehart, Political Action: The Impact of Values, Cognitive Level and Social Background, in S. Barnes, M. Kaase (et al), op cit (1979).

R. Inglehart, Post Materialism in an Environment of Insecurity, *American Political Science Review* 75 (1981).

R. Inglehart, Changing Paradigms in Comparative Political Behaviour, in A. Finifter (ed), *Political Science: The State of the Discipline* (1983).

R. Inglehart, The Changing Structure of Political Cleavages in Western Societies, in R. J. Dalton, S. C. Flanagan et al (eds), op.cit (1984).

R. Inglehart, Value Change in Industrial Society, *American Political Science Review* 81 (1987).

R. Inglehart, *Culture Shift* (1990).

R. Inglehart and P. R. Abramson, Generational Replacement and Value Change in Eight West European Societies, *British Journal of Political Science* 22 (1992).

R. Inglehart and I. R. Rabier, Political realignment in advanced industrial society: from class-based politics to quality-of-life politics, *Government and Opposition* 21 (1986).

G. A. Irwin, The Netherlands, in P. H. Merkl (ed), *Western European Party Systems* (1980).

G. Irwin and K. Dittrich, And the Walls came Tumbling Down: Party Realignment in the Netherlands, in R. J. Dalton, S. C. Flanagan and P. A. Beck (eds), op.cit (1984).

R. A. Isaak, *International Political Economy: Managing World Economic Change* (1991).

J. Jaffe, The French Electorate in March 1978, in H. R. Penniman (ed), *The French National Assembly Elections of 1978* (1980).

D. Jahn, Nuclear Power, Energy Policy and New Politics in Sweden and Germany, *Environmental Politics* 3 (1992).

D. Jahn, The rise and decline of new politics and the Greens in Sweden and Germany, *European Journal of Political Research* 24 (1993).

D. Jahn, Changing Political Opportunities in Germany: The Prospects of the German Greens in a Unified Germany, *Current Politics and Economics of Europe* 14 (1994).

D. Jahn, Ecological Discourse in Decline? The Political Agenda in Sweden and Germany between the 1970s and 1990s, *unpublished paper* (1996).

A. Jamison, R. Eyerman, R. Cramer and J. Laessoe, *The Making of the New Environmental Consciousness Movements in Sweden, Denmark and the Netherlands* (1990).

T. Jarvikoviski, Alternative Movements in Finland. The case of Koijarvi, *Acta Sociologica* 24 (1981).

A. Jenssen and O. Lishaug, Post-materialism and Elections in Norway, *Norsk Statsvitenskapelig Tidsskrift* 2 (1988).

W. Kaltfleiter, A. Legitimacy Crisis of the German Party System? in P. H. Merkl, op.cit

(1980).

G. Katsiaficas, *The Imagination of the New Left: A Global Analysis of 1968* (1987).

D. Kavanagh, *British Politics: Continuities and Change* (1985).

K. A. Kennedy (ed), *Ireland in Transition: Economic and Social Change since 1960* (1986).

R. O. Keohane and J. S. Nye (eds), *Transnational Relations and World Politics* (1972).

H. Kerr, The Swiss Party System, in H. Daalder (ed), *Party Systems in Denmark, Austria, Switzerland, the Netherlands and Belgium* (1987).

H. Kitschelt, Political Opportunity Structures and Political Protest: Anti-Nuclear Movements in Four Democracies, *British Journal of Political Science* 16 (1986).

H. Kitschelt, Organization and Strategy in Belgian and West German Ecology Parties, *Comparative Politics* 20 (1988).

H. Kitschelt, Left Libertarian Parties: Explaining Innovation in Competitive Systems, *World Politics* 40 (1988).

H. Kitschelt, The life expectancy of left-libertarian parties: does structural transformation or economic decline explain party innovation? A response to Wilhelm Burklin, *European Sociological Review* 65 (1988).

H. Kitschelt, *The Logics of Party Formation: Structure and Strategy of Belgian and West German Ecology Parties* (1989).

H. Kitschelt, New Social Movements and the Decline of Party Organisation, in R. J. Dalton and M. Kuechler (eds), op.cit (1990).

H. Kitschelt, The Medium is the Message: Democracy and Oligarchy in Belgian Ecology Parties, in W. Rudig (ed), *Green Politics One* (1990).

H. Kitschelt, La gauche libertaire et les ecologistes Francais, *Revue Francaise de Science Politique* 40 (1990).

H. Kitschelt, The 1990 German Federal Election and the National Unification, *West European Politics* 14 (1991).

H. Kitschelt, The Socialist Discourse and Party Strategy in West European Democracies, in C. Lemke and G. Marks (eds), op cit (1991).

H. Kitschelt, The Green Phenomenon in Western Party Systems in S. Kamieniecki (ed), *Environmental Politics in the International Arena. Movements, Parties, Organizations and Policy* (1993).

H. Kitschelt, *The Transformation of European Social Democracy* (1994).

H. Kitschelt, Austrian and Swedish Social Democrats in Crisis. Party Strategy and Organization in Corporatist Regimes, *Comparative Political Studies* 27 (1994).

H. Kitschelt and S. Hellemans, The Left-Right Semantics and the New Politics Cleavage, *Comparative Political Studies*, 23 (1990).

H. Kitschelt and S. Hellemans, *Beyond the European Left: Ideology and Political Action in the Belgian Ecology Parties* (1990).

P. B. Klandermans (ed), *Organizing for Change Social Movement Organization Across Cultures* (1989).

P. B. Klandermans, Linking the 'Old' and 'New' Movement Networks in the Netherlands, in R. J. Dalton and M. Kuechler (eds), op.cit (1990).

O. Klinberg, M. Zavalloni, C. Louis - Guerin and J. Ben-Brika, *Students, Values and Politics: A Cross Cultural Comparison* (1979).

A. Knapp, Proportional but Bipolar: France's Electoral System in 1986, *West European Politics* 10 (1987).

O. Knutsen, The Priorities of Materialist and Post Materialist Values in the Nordic Countries - A Five Nation Comparison, *Scandinavian Political Studies* 12 (1989).

O. Knutsen, Cleavage Dimensions in Ten West European Countries. A Comparative Empirical Analysis, *Comparative Political Studies* 22 (1989).

O. Knutsen, Materialist and Post-materialist Values and Social Structure in the Nordic Countries, *Comparative Politics* 23 (1990).

O. Knutsen, The Materialist/Post-Materialist Value Dimensions as a Party Cleavage in the Nordic Countries, *West European Politics* 13 (1990).

T. Koelbe, *The Left Unravelled. The Impact of the New Left on the British Labour Party and the West German Social Democratic Party, 1968-1988* (1991).

A. Kofler, Between old symbolic worlds and New Challenges. A Glance at the Internal Life of the Parties, in A. Pelinka and F. Plasser (eds), *The Austrian Party System* (1989).

N. Kogan, *A Political History of Italy: The Post War Years* (1983).

E. Kolinsky, *The Greens in West Germany: Organisation and Policy Making* (1984).

E. Kolinsky, The Green Party: A New Factor in the West German Political Landscape, in E. Kolinsky (ed,) *Parties, Opposition and Society in West Germany* (1984).

E. Kolinsky, Women in the Green Party in E. Kolinsky (ed), *The Greens in West Germany: A Social and Political Profile* (1988).

M. Kreuzer, New Politics: Just Post-Materialist? The Case of the Austrian and Swiss Greens, *West European Politics* 13 (1990).

H. Kriesi, New Social Movements and the New Class in the Netherlands, *American Journal of Sociology* 94 (1989).

H. Kriesi, R. Koopmans J. W. Duyvendak and M. G. Clugni, New Social Movements and Political Opportunities in Western Europe, *European Journal of Political Research* 22 (1992).

M. Kuechler and R. J. Dalton, New Social Movements and the Political Order: Inducing Change for long-term stability, in R. J. Dalton and M. Kuechler (eds), op cit (1990).

M. Laakso and R. Taagepera, Proportional Representation in Scandinavia: Implications for Finland, *Scandinavian Political Studies* 1 (1978).

A. Ladner, Switzerland, in F. Muller-Rommel (ed), op.cit (1989).

R. Ladrech, Social Movements and Party Systems: The French Socialist Party and New Social Movements, *West European Politics* 12 (1989).

W. M. Lafferty, The Political Transformation of a Social Democratic State: As the world moves in, Norway moves right, *West European Politics* 13 (1990).

W. Lafferty, and O. Knutsen, Postmaterialism in a Social Democratic State, *Comparative Political Studies* 17 (1985).

J. Lambert, Origins, Praxis and Prospective - The British Environmental Movement, *International Journal of Sociology and Social Policy* 12 (1992).

T. Lancaster and M. S. Lewis-Beck, The Spanish Voter Tradition, Economics, Ideology, *Journal of Politics* 48 (1986).

J. E. Lane and S. O. Errson, *Politics and Society in Western Europe* (2nd ed 1991).

J. E. Lane and S. O. Errson, *European Politics, An Introduction* (1996).

P. Lange and S. Tarrow, *Italy in Transition: Conflict and Consensus* (1980).

G. Langguth, *The Green Factor in German Politics* (1986).

J. LaPalombara, *Democracy Italian Style* (1986).

M. Laver (et al), Patterns of Support, in M. Laver, P. Mair and R. Sinnott (eds), *How Ireland Voted* (1987).

M. Laver, Party Competition and Party System Change. The Interaction of Coalition Bargaining and Electoral Competition, *Journal of Theoretical Politics* 1 (1989).

M. Laver, Party Policy and Cabinet Portfolios in Ireland 1992 - 93: Results from an Expert Survey, *Irish Political Studies* 9 (1994).

M. Laver and N. Schofield, *Multi party government* (1990).

M. Laver and K. A. Shepsle, Coalitions and Intraparty Politics, *British Journal of Political Science* 20 (1990).

K. Lawson and P. Merkl, *Why Parties Fail* (1988).

C. Lemke and G. Marks (eds), *The Crisis of Socialism in Europe* (1992).

D. Leonard, Benelux, in V. Bogdanor and D. Butler (eds), op.cit (1983).

D. Leonard, The Belgian General Election of December 13, 1987, *Electoral Studies* 8 (1989).

R. Leonardi and D. A. Wertman, *Italian Christian Democracy: The Politics of Dominance* (1989).

U. Leone, *Polluted Italy* (1970).

P. Leroy and A. de Geest, *Environmental movement and environmental policy* (1985).

C. Levy (ed), *Italian Regionalism: History, Identity and Politics* (1996).

S. Lewis and S. Sferza, French Socialists between State and Society, in G. Ross, S. Hoffmann and S. Malzacher (eds), *The Mitterrand Experiment* (1987).

M. Lewis-Beck, France: The Stalled Electorate, in R. J. Dalton, S. C. Flanagan and P. A. Beck (eds), op.cit (1984).

M. Lewis-Beck and H. Eulau, Economic Conditions and Electoral Behaviour in Transnational Perspective, in M. Lewis-Beck & H. Eulau (eds), op.cit (1985).

J. D. Liefferink, P. D. Lowe and A. P. J. Mol (eds), European Integration and Environmental Policy (1993).

A. Lijphart, *The Politics of Accommodation: Pluralism and Democracy in the Netherlands* (2nd ed 1975).

A. Lijphart, The Dutch Electoral System in Comparative Perspective, *Netherlands Journal of Sociology*, (1978).

A. Lijphart and R. W. Gibbard, Thresholds and Payoffs in List Systems of Proportional Representation, *European Journal of Political Research* 5 (1977).

A. Lijphart (et al), A Mediterranean Model of Democracy? The Southern European Democracies in Comparative Perspective, *West European Politics* 11 (1988).

H. Lippelt and O. Lindstrom, The Swedish Elections of 1985, *Electoral Studies* 5 (1986).

H. Lippelt, Green Politics in Progress: Germany, in M. P. Garcia - Guadilla and J. Blauert (eds), Environmental Social Movements in Latin America and Europe, *International Journal of Sociology and Social Perspectives* (1967).

S. M. Lipset and S. Rokkan, Cleavage Structures, Party Systems, and Voter Alignments. An Introduction in S. M. Lipset and S. Rokkan (eds), *Party Systems and Voter Alignments Cross-National Perspectives* (1967).

O. Listhaug, The Norwegian Parliamentary Elections of 1985, *Electoral Studies* 5 (1986).

G. Lodi, L'azione ecologista in Italia:dal protezionisma storica alle Liste Verdi, in R. Biorcia and G. Lodi (eds), *La sfida verde : il movimento ecologista in Italia* (1988).

H. Lohneis, The Swiss Election. A Glacier on the move? *West European Politics* 7 (1984).

P. Lowe and A. Flynn, Environmental Politics and Policy in Britain in the the 1980s, in J. Mohan (ed), *The Political Geography of Contemporary Britain* (1989).

P. Lowe and J. Goyder, *Environmental Groups in Politics* (1983).

A. P. Lucardie, *The New Left in the Netherlands 1960-1977; A Critical Study of New Political Ideas and Groups on the Left in the Netherlands with Comparative References to France and Germany* (1980).

P. Lucardie, J. Van der Knoop, W. Van Schuur and G. Voerman, Greening the Reds or Redding the Greens? The Case of the Green Left in the Netherlands, in W. Rudig (ed), *Green Politics Three* (1996).

K. R. Luther, Austria's Future and Waldheim's Past: The Significance of the 1986 Elections, *West European Politics* 10 (1987).

C. Lyrintzis, Political Parties in Post Junta Greece: A case of 'Bureaucratic Clientelism'? in G. Pridham (ed), op.cit (1984).

C. Lyrintzis, PASOK in Power: The loss of the 'Third Road to Socialism', in T. Gallagher and A. M. Williams (eds), op.cit (1989).

X. Mabille and V. R. Lorwin, Belgium, in S. Henig (ed), *Political Parties in the European Community* (1979).

H. Machin, Stages and Dynamics in the Evolution of the French Party System, *West European Politics* 12 (1989).

M. A. Maguire, Is there still Persistence? Electoral Change in Western Europe, 1948 - 1979, in H. Daalder and P. Mair (eds), op.cit (1983).

C. S. Maier (ed), *Changing Boundaries of the Political* (1987).

J. Maier, *The Green Parties in Western Europe* (1990).

P. Mair, The Problem of Party System Change, *Journal of Theoretical Politics* 1 (1989).

P. Mair, Myths of Electoral Change and the Survival of Traditional Parties, *European Journal of Political Research* 24 (1993).

P. Mair and M. Laver, Proportionality, PR and STV in Ireland, *Political Studies* 23 (1975).

L. Maisel and P. Sacks (eds), *The Future of Political Parties* (1975).

L. Maisel and J. Cooper (eds), *Political Parties: Development and decay* (1978).

M. Manor, The 1990 Danish Election. An Unnecessary Contest? *West European Politics* 14 (1991).

J. M. Maraval, The Socialist Alternative: The Policies and Electorate of the PSOE, in H. R. Penniman and E. M. Muhal-Leon (eds), *Spain at the Polls, 1977, 1979 and 1982* (1985).

B. Marin, Austria - the Paradigm Case of Liberal Corporatism? in W. Grant (ed), *The Political Economy of Corporatism* (1985).

B. Marin, From Consociationalism to Technocorporatism: The Austrian Case as a Model Generator? in I. Scholten (ed), *Political Stability and Neo-Corporatism: Corporatist Integration and Societal Cleavages in Western Europe* (1987).

S. Marklund, Welfare State Policies in the Tripolar Class Model of Scandinavia, *Politics and Society* 16 (1988).

A. S. Markovits and P. S. Gorski, *The German Left: Red, Green and Beyond* (1993).

A. Marradi, Italy: From Centrism to Crisis of the Centre Left Coalitions, in E. Browne and J. Dreijmanis (eds), *Government Coalitions in Western Democracies*, (1982).

G. Mavrogordatos, The Emerging Party System, in R Clogg (ed), *Greece in the 1980s* (1983).

G. Mavrogordatos, The Greek Party System: A Case of Limited but Polarized Pluralism? *West European Politics* 4 (1984).

J. McCormick, *British Politics and the Environment* (1991).

J. McCormick, Environmental Politics, in P. Dunleavy, A. Gamble et al (eds), *Developments in British Politics* 4 (1993).

A. McCulloch, The Green Party in England and Wales: Structure and Development: The Early Years, *Environmental Politics* 1 (1992).

A. McCulloch, The Green Party in England and Wales: Branch Organization and Activity, *Environmental Politics* 2 (1993).

P. McDonough, A. Lopez-Pina and S. H. Barnes, The Spanish public in political transition, *British Journal of Political Science* 11 (1981).

P. McDonough and A. Lopez-Pina, Continuity and Change in Spanish Politics, in R. J. Dalton et al (eds), *Electoral Change in Advanced Industrial Democracies* (1984).

A. Melucci, The New Social Movements: A Theoretical Approach, *Social Science Information* 18 (1980).

P. H. Merkl (ed), *Western European Party Systems* (1980).

D. Meth - Cohn and W. Muller, Leaders Count: The Austrian election of October 1990, *West European Politics* 14 (1991).

R. Michels, *Political Parties: A Solciological Study of the Oligarchical Tendencies of Modern Democracy* (1962 edition).

M. Micheletti, The Swedish Election of 1988, *Electoral Studies* 8 (1989).

M. Micheletti, Swedish Corporatism at a Crossroads: The Impact of New Politics and New Social Movements, *West European Politics* 14 (1991).

D. Miliband (ed), *Reinventing the Left* (1994).

L. Mjoset, Nordic Economic Policies in the 1970s and 1980s, *International Organization* 41 (1987).

J. Modeley, Norway's 1989 Election: The Paths to Polarized Pluralism? *West European Politics* 13 (1990).

N. Mouzelis, *Modern Greece: Facets of Underdevelopment* (1978).

E. Moxon-Browne, *Political Change in Spain* (1989).

W. Muller, Privatising in a Corporatist Economy. The Politics of Privatization in Austria, *West European Politics* 11 (1988).

W. Muller, Party Patronage in Austria, in F. Plasser and A. Pelinka (eds), op.cit (1989).

F. Muller-Rommel, Ecology Parties in Western Europe, *West European Politics* 5 (1982).

F. Muller-Rommel, Social Movements and the Greens: New Internal Politics in Germany, *European Journal of Political Research 13* (1985).

F. Muller-Rommel, New Social Movements and Smaller Parties: A Comparative Analysis, *West European Politics* 8 (1985).

F. Muller-Rommel, The Greens in Western Europe: Similar but Different, *International Political Science Review* 6 (1985).

F. Muller-Rommel, The Greens in the 1980s :Short term cyclical protest or indicator of transformation? *Political Studies* 37 (1989).

F. Muller Rommel (ed), *New Politics in Western Europe: The Rise and Success of Green Parties and Alternative Lists* (1989).

F. Muller-Rommel, New political movements and 'New Politics' parties in Western Europe, in R. J. Dalton and M. Kuechler (eds), op.cit (1990).

F. Muller-Rommel and T. Poguntke, The Unharmonious Family: Green Parties in Western Europe, in E. Kolinsky (ed), *The Greens in West Germany* (1989).

F. Muller-Rommel and T. Poguntke, Die Grunen, in A. Mintzel and H. Oberreuter (eds), *Parteien in der Bundesrepublik* (1992).

F. Muller-Rommel and G. Pridham (eds), *Small Parties in Western Europe* (1989).

F. Muller-Rommel and H. Wilke, Socialstrucktur und "postmaterialistische"

Wertorientierungen von Okologisten, Eine empirische Analyse am Beispiel Frankreichs, *Politische Vierteljahresschrift* 22 (1981).

C. Murphy and R. Tooze (eds), *The New International Political Economy* (1991).

D. Murphy and R. Roth, In Many Directions at the Same Time? The Greens - An Artifact of the 5 Per Cent Clause? in R. Roth and D. Rucht (eds), *Neue Soziale Bewegungen in der Bundersrepublik Deutschland* (1987).

J. Mushaben, "The Struggle Within", in B. Klandermans (ed), *Organizing for Change* (1989).

R. Nannetti, R. Leonardo and P. Corbetta (eds), *Italian Politics: A Review* 2 (1988).

B. Nedelmann, New Political Movements and Changes in Processes of Intermediation, *Social Sciences Information*, 23 (1984).

D. Nelkin and M. Pollak, The Politics of Participation and the Nuclear Debate in Sweden, The Netherlands and Austria, *Public Policy* XXV (1977).

D. Nelkin and M. Pollak, *The Atom Beseiged: Extra Parliamentary dissent in France and Germany* (1981).

M. Newman, The west European left today: crisis, decline or renewal? *Contemporary Politics*, 1 (1995).

P. Nikiforos Diamandouros, Greek Political Culture in Transition: Historical Origins, Evolution, Current Trends, in R. Clogg (ed), *Greece in the 1980s* (1983).

C. Offe, New Social Movements: Challenging the Boundaries of Institutional Politics: Social Movements Since the Sixties, in C. S. Maier (ed), *Changing Boundaries of the Political* (1987).

C. Offe, Reflections on the Institutional Self-Transformation of Movement Politics: A Tentative Stage Model, in R. J. Dalton and M. Kuechler (eds), op.cit (1990).

M. O'Neill, Of Watermelons and cucumbers: Europe's green parties - an exercise in ideological mapping, *Contemporary Politics*, 1 (1995).

M. O'Neill, Oil on the Troubled Waters of Greenpeace, *European Brief* 2 (1995).

M. O'Neill, The Pursuit of a Grand Illusion, *European Brief* 3 (1995).

M. O'Neill, New Politics, Old Predicaments: The Case of the European Greens, *Political Quarterly* 68 (1997).

J. Paastelo, Finland: The Vihreat, in F. Muller-Rommel (ed), op.cit (1989).

A. Panebianco, *Political Parties: Organization and Power* (1988).

A. Panebianco, The Italian Radicals: New Wine in an Old Bottle, in K. Lawson and P. H. Merkl (eds), op.cit (1988).

E. Papadakis, The Green Party in Contemporary West German Politics, *Political Quarterly* 54 (1983).

E. Papadakis, *The Green Movement in West Germany* (1984).

Y. Papadopoulos, The Swiss election of 1987: A 'silent revolution' behind stability, *West European Politics* 11 (1988).

Y. Papadopoulos, Parties, the State and Society in Greece: Continuity within Change, *West European Politics* 12 (1989).

Y. Papadopoulos, Quel role pour les petits partis dans la democratique direct, *Schweizerisches Jahrbuch fur Politische Wissenschaft* 31 (1991).

A. Pappalardo, The Conditions for Consociational Democracy: A Logical and Empirical Critique, *European Journal of Political Research* 9 (1971).

F. Pappi, The West German System, *West European Politics* 7 (1984).

A. Parisi and G. Pasquino, Changes in Italian Electoral Behaviour: The Relationship between Parties and Voters, in P. Lange and S. Tarrow, *Italy in Transition: Conflict and Consensus* (1980).

F. Parkin, *Middle Class Radicalism: The Social Bases of the British Campaign for Nuclear Disarmament* (1968).

S. Parkin, *Green Parties: An International Guide* (1989).

W. Paterson and G. Smith (eds), *The West German Model: Perspectives on a Stable State* (1981).

M. Pedersen, The dynamics of European party systems: changing patterns of electoral volatility, *European Journal of Political Research* 7 (1979).

M. Pedersen, On Measuring Party System Change: A Methodological Critique and a Suggestion, *Comparative Political Studies* 12 (1980).

M. Pedersen, Towards a New Typology of Party Lifespans and Minor Parties, *Scandinavian Political Studies* 5 (1982).

M. Pedersen, Changing Patterns of Electoral Volatility: Explorations in Explanation, in H. Daalder and P. Mair (eds), op.cit (1983).

M. Pedersen, The Birth and Life and the Death of Small Parties in Danish Politics, in F. Muller-Rommel and G. Pridham (eds), *Small Parties in Western Europe* (1989).

H. Peillon, *Contemporary Irish Society: An Introduction* (1982).

A. Pelinka, The Nuclear Power Referendum in Austria, *Electoral Studies* 2 (1983).

A. Pelinka and F. Plasser (eds), *The Austrian Party System* (1982).

O. Petersson, The 1976 election: New Trends in the Swedish Electorate, *Scandinavian Political Studies* 1 (1978).

O. Petersson, Democracy and Power in Sweden, *Scandinavian Political Studies* 14 (1991).

O. Petersson and H. Valen, Political Cleavages in Sweden and Norway, *Scandinavian Political Studies* 2 (1979).

B. Pijnenburg, Political Parties and Coalition Behaviour in Belgium. The Perspective of Local Politics, *European Journal of Political Research* 15 (1987).

O. Piulats, Una Historia Reciente del Movimiento Verde, *Integral* (Barcelona, 1989).

F. F. Piven (eds), "*Labour Parties in Postindustrial Societies*" (1991).

F. Plasser, The Austrian Party System between Erosion and Innovation, in A. Pelinka and F. Plasser (eds), op.cit (1989).

F. Plasser and P. Ulram, Major Parties on the Defensive. The Austrian Party and Electoral Landscape after the 1986 National Council Election, in A. Pelinka and F. Plasser (eds), op.cit (1989).

T. Poguntke, The Organisation of a Participatory Party. The German Greens, *European Journal of Political Research* 15 (1987).

T. Poguntke, New Politics and Party Systems: The Emergence of a New Type of Party? *West European Politics* 10 (1987).

T. Poguntke, *Alternative Politics: The Green Party* (1993).

T. Poguntke, Goodbye to Movement Politics? Organizational Adaptation of the German Green Party, *Environmental Politics* 1 (1992).

T. Poguntke with B. Bull, Germany, in R. Katz and P. Mair (eds), *Party Organizations: A Data Handbook* (1992).

J. Pontusson, At the End of the Third Road: Social Democracy, in *Crisis, Politics and Society* 2 (1990).

J. Porritt and N. Winner, *The Coming of the Greens* (1988).

G. B. Powell, Voting turnout in thirty elections: partisan, legal and socio-economic influences, in R. Rose (ed), *Electoral Participation: A Comparative Analysis* (1980).

R. Premfors, 'The Swedish Model' and Public Sector Reform, *West European Politics* 14 (1991).

B. Prendiville, France: Les Verts, in F. Muller-Rommel (ed), op.cit (1989).

B. Prendiville, The Return of the Elusive Social Movement? Le Printemps de Decembre, *Modern and Contemporary France* 29 (1989).

B. Prendiville and T. Chafer, Activists and Ideas in the Green Movement in France, in W. Rudig (ed), op.cit (1990).

G. Pridham (ed), *The New Mediterranean Democracies: Regime Transition in Spain, Greece and Portugal* (1984).

G. Pridham, *Political Parties and Coalition Behaviour in Italy* (1988).

G. Pridham, Italian Small Parties in Comparative Perspective, in F. Muller-Rommel and G. Pridham (eds), *Small Parties in Western Europe: Contemporary and National Perspectives* (1991).

G. Pridham and S. Verney, The Coalitions of 1988-90 in Greece: Inter-party Relations and Democratic Consolidation, *West European Politics* 14 (1991).

R. Pronier and V. J. le Seigneur, *Generation Verte: les ecologistes en politique* (1992).

J. Puig, *L'Ecologisme* (1991).

G. Rabinowitz, S. E. MacDonald and O. Lishaug, New Players in an Old Game, Party Strategy in Multi-party Systems, *Comparative Political Studies* 24 (1991).

D. Rae, *The Political Consequences of Electoral Laws* (1971).

J. Raschke, Political Parties in Western Democracies, *European Journal of Political Research* 11 (1983).

J. Raschke, *Krise der Grunen: Bilanz und Neubeginn* (1991).

J. Raschke, *Die Grunen: wie sie wurden was sie sind* (1993).

L. Rebeaud, *La Suisse Verte* (1987).

A. Recio, The Ecologist Movement in Spain - Boomerang of the Development Model, in Maria-Pillar Garcia-Guadilla and Jitta Blauert (eds), special edition on social movements and development of the *International Journal of Sociology and Social Policy* Vol.12 (1992).

Gosta Rehn, The Wages of Success, *Daedalus*, (Spring 1984).

K. Reif, National Electoral Cycles and European Elections 1979 and 1984, *Electoral Studies* 3 (1984).

K. Reif and H. Schmitt, Nine Second Order National Elections: A Conceptual Framework for the Analysis of European Election Results, *European Journal of Political Research* 8 (1980).

M. Rhodes, Piazza or Palazzo? The Italian Greens and the 1992 Elections, *Environmental Politics* 1 (1992).

M. Rhodes, Italy: Greens in an overcrowded political system, in D. Richardson and C. Rootes (eds), op.cit (1995).

D. Richardson and C. Rootes (eds), *The Green Challenge: the development of Green parties in Europe* (1995).

J. Ridgeway, *The Politics of Ecology* (1970).

B. Rihoux, Belgium: Greens in a divided society, in D. Richardson and C. Rootes (eds), op.cit (1995).

M. Robinson, *The Greening of British Party Politics* (1992).

T. Rochan, *Mobilizing for Peace: Anti-nuclear Movements in Western Europe* (1989).

J. Rohr, *La Democratie en Suisse* (1987).

R. Rohrschneider, The Roots of Public Opinion Towards New Social Movements: An Empirical Test of Competing Explanations, *American Journal of Political Science* 34 (1990).

R. Rohrschneider, Environmental Belief Systems in Western Europe. A Hierarchical Model of Constraint, *Comparative Political Studies* 26 (1993).

S. Rokkan and H. Valen, The Mobilization of the Periphery, in S. Rokkan (ed), *Approaches to the Study of Political Participation* (1962).

P. Van Roosendahl, Centre Parties and Coalition Cabinet Formations. A Game Theoretic Approach, *European Journal of Political Research* 18 (1990).

C. Rootes, Student radicalism: politics of moral protest and legitimation problems of the modern capitalist state, *Theory and Society* 9 (1980).

C. Rootes, Student Radicalism in France: 1968 and after, in P. Cerny (ed), *Social Movements and Protest in France* (1982).

C. Rootes, The Greening of British Politics? *International Journal of Urban and Regional Research* 15 (1991).

C. Rootes, Political System, The Green Party and the Environment Movement in Britain, *International Journal of Sociology and Social Policy* 12 (1992).

C. Rootes, The new politics of the new social movements. Accounting for British exceptionalism, *European Journal of Political Research* 22 (1992).

C. Rootes, Britain. Greens in a cold climate, in D. Richardson and C. Rootes (eds), op.cit (1995).

R. Rose (ed), *Electoral Change: A Comparative Handbook* (1974).

R. Rose and J. McAlister, *Voters Begin to Choose* (1980).

R. Rose and D. Urwin, Persistence and Change in Western Party Systems since 1945, *Political Studies* 18 (1970).

J. Rosenau, *The Study of Political Adaptation* (1981).

G. Ross and J. Jenson, French Rainbows: Towards a New Left in France? *Socialist Review* 18 (1988).

J. F. Ross, *The Irish Electoral System: What It Is and How It Works* (1989).

D. Rucht, Environmental movement organisations in West Germany and France: Structure and inter-organisational relations, in P. G. Klandermans (ed), *Organising for change: Social movement organisations in Europe and the US* (1989).

W. Rudig, Peace and ecology movements in western Europe, *West European Politics* (11) 1988.

W. Rudig, Green parties and the European Union, in J Gaffney (ed), *Political Parties and the European Union* (1996).

W. Rudig, Peace and Ecology Movements in Western Europe, *West European Politics* 3 (1988).

W. Rudig, The Greens in Europe: Ecological Parties and the European Elections of 1984, *Parliamentary Affairs* 38 (1985).

W. Rudig (ed), *Green Politics One* (1990).

W. Rudig, The Greening of Germany, *The Ecologist* 13 (1983).

W. Rudig, Green party politics around the world, *Environment* 33 (1991).

W. Rudig (ed), *Green Politics Two* (1992).

W. Rudig (ed), *Green Politics Three* (1996).

W. Rudig and M. N. Franklin, Green Prospects: The future of Green parties in Britain, France and Germany, in W. Rudig (ed), *Green Politics Two* (1992).

W. Rudig and P. Lowe, The Withered 'Greening' of British Politics: A Study of the Ecology

Party, *Political Studies* 34 (1986).

W. Ruigrok and R. van Tulder, *The Logic of International Restructuring* (1995).

B. Saarlvik, Sweden: The social base of the parties in a developmental perspective, in R. Rose (ed), op.cit (1974).

B. Saarlvik, Scandinavia, in V. Bogdanor and D. Butler (eds), op.cit (1983).

B. Saarlvik and I. Crewe, *Decade of Dealignment* (1983).

W. Saffran, France, in M. D. Hancock et al (eds), *Politics in Western Europe* (1993).

R. C. Sahr, *The Politics of Energy Policy Change in Sweden* (1985).

D. Sainsbury, The 1985 Swedish Election. The Conservative Upsurge is Checked, *West European Politics* 9 (1986).

D. Sainsbury, The 1988 Swedish Election. The Breakthrough of the Greens, *West European Politics* 12 (1989).

D. Sainsbury, Swedish Social Democracy in Transition. The Party's Record in the 1980s and the Challenge of the 1990s, *West European Politics* 14 (1991).

D. Sainsbury, The 1991 Swedish Election. Protest, Fragmentation and a Shift to the Right, *West European Politics* 15 (1992).

G. Sainteny, Les Dirigeants Ecologistes et le Champ Politique, *Revue Francaise de Science Politique* 37 (1987).

G. Sainteny, Le vote ecologiste aux elections regionales, *Revue Politique et Parliamentaire* (1987).

G. Sainteny, Les Verts: Limites et interpretation d'un success electoral, *Revue politique et Parliamentaire* (1989).

G. Sani, The Political Culture of Italy: Continuity and Change, in G. Almond and S. Verba (eds), *The Political Culture Revisited* (1980).

G. Sani and G. Sartori, Polarization, Fragmentation and Competition in Western Democracies, in H. Daalder and P. Mair (eds), *Western European Party Systems* (1983).

G. Sartori, European Political Parties: The Case of Polarised Pluralism, in J. LaPalombara and M. Weiner (eds), *Political Parties and Political Development* (1966).

G. Sartori, *Parties and Party Systems* (1976).

D. Sassoon, The 1987 elections and the PCI, in R. Leonardi and P. Corbetta, *Italian Politics: A Review* (1989).

J. Savage, Post-materialism of the Left and Right. Political Conflict in Post Industrial Society, *Comparative Political Studies* 17 (1985).

T. Scharf, Red-Green Coalitions at Local Level in Hesse, in E. Kolinsky (ed), op.cit (1989).

T. Scharf, *The German Greens* (1994).

F. Scharpf, *Crisis and Choice in European Social Democracy* (1991).

B. Schiller, The Swedish Model Reconsidered, in M. D. Hancock, J. Logue and B. Schiller (eds), *Managing Modern Capitalism: Industrial Renewal and Workplace: Reform in the United States and Western Europe* (1985).

I. Scholten (ed), *Political Stability and Neo-Corporatism: Corporatist Integration and Societal Cleavages in Western Europe* (1987).

W. Schonfield, Political Parties, the Functional Approach and the Structural Alternative, *Comparative Politics* 15 (1985).

S. Schuttemeyer, Denmark: De Grunne, in F. Muller-Rommel (ed), *New Politics in Western Europe* (1989).

A. Scott, The Austrian General Election of 1986, *Electoral Studies* 6 (1987).

M. Shamur, Are Western European Party Systems 'Frozen'? *Comparative Political Studies*

17 (1984).

D. Share, Dilemmas of Social Democracy in the 1980s. The Spanish Socialist Workers Party in Comparative Perspective, *Comparative Political Studies* 21 (1988).

D. Sidjanski, The Swiss and their Politics, *Government and Opposition* 11 (1976).

D. Singer, *Is Socialism Doomed? The Meaning of Mitterrand* (1988).

J. Sinnott, Party Politics in Spatial Representation: The Irish Case, *British Journal of Political Science* 16 (1986).

R. Sinnott, *Irish Voters Decide: Voting Behaviour in Elections and Referendums, 1918-1994* (1994).

G. Sjoblan, Political Change and Political Accountability: A Propositional Inventory of Cause and Effects, in H. Daalder and P. Mair (eds), op.cit (1983).

G. Smith, The German Volkspartei and the Career of the Catch-All Concept, in H. Doring and G. Smith (eds), *Party Government and Political Culture in West Germany* (1982).

G. Smith, A System of Perspective on Party System Change, *Journal of Theoretical Politics* 1 (1989).

G. Smith, *Politics in Western Europe* (1990).

G. Smith, Stages of European Development: Electoral Change and System Adaptation, in D. Urwin and W. Paterson (eds), *Politics in Western Europe* (1990).

J. Smith, How European are European elections? in J. Gaffney (ed), op.cit (1996).

M. P. Smith-Jespersen, A Danish Dilemma. The Election of May 1988, *West European Politics* 12 (1989).

M. Spourdalakis, *The Rise of the Greek Socialist Party* (1988).

B. Steel and T. Tsurutani, From Consensus to Dissensus. A Note on Post-industrial Political Parties, *Comparative Politics* 18 (1986).

J. Steiner, *European Democracies* (2nd ed 1991).

S. Steinmo, Social Democracy vs Socialism: Good Adaptation in Social Democratic Sweden, *Politics and Society* 16 (1988).

M. A. Sully, *A Contemporary History of Austria* (1990).

L. Svasaland and U. Lindstrom, Scandinavian political parties and the European Union, in J. Gaffney (ed), op.cit (1996).

S. Tarrow, The Phantom at the Opera: Political Parties and Social Movements of the 1960s and 1970s in Italy, in R. J. Dalton and M. Kuechler (eds), op.cit (1990).

R. Taylor, Green Politics and the Peace Movement, in B. Coates, G. Johnson and R. Bush (eds), *A Socialist Anatomy of Britain* (1985).

A. Thomas, 1945-197 *Parliamentary Parties in Denmark 1945-1972* (University of Strathclyde Occasional Papers 13 1973).

J. Thomassen and J. van Deth, How New is Dutch Politics? *West European Politics* 12 (1989).

G. Thorborn, Swedish Social Democracy and the Transition from Industrial to Post-industrial Politics, in F. F. Piven (ed), op.cit (1992).

D. Thurer, Switzerland: The Model in Need of Adaptation?, in J. J. Hesse and V. Wright (eds), *Federalising Europe?* (1996).

C. Tilly, European Violence and Collective Action Since 1700, *Social Research* 52 (1985).

S. Tindale, Sustaining Social Democracy: The Politics of the Environment, in D. Miliband (ed), op.cit (1994).

L. Togeby, Political Radicalism in the Working Class and the Middle Class, *European Journal of Political Research* 18 (1990).

A. Touraine, *The Post Industrial Society* (1971).

B. Tromp, Party Strategies and System Change in the Netherlands, *West European Politics* 12 (1989).

W. Tucker, Environmentalism: The Newest Toryism, *Policy Review* 14 (1980).

P. V. Uleri, The 1987 referendum, in R. Leonardi and P. Corbetta, *Italian Politics: A Review* 3 (1989).

P. Ulram, Changing Issues in the Austrian Party System, in A. Pelinka and F. Plasser (eds), op.cit (1989).

D. Urwin and W. Paterson (eds), *Politics in Western Europe* (1990).

L. Uusitalo, Are Environmental Attitudes and Behaviour Inconsistent? Findings from a Finnish Study, *Scandinavian Political Studies* 13 (1990).

C. M. Vadrot, *Historique des Mouvements ecologistes* (1980).

H. Valen and S. Rokkan, Norway: Conflict Structure and Mass Politics in a European Periphery, in R. Rose (ed), *Electoral Behaviour: A Comparative Handbook* (1974).

H. Valen, *Elections and Politics - A Changing Society* (1981).

C. van der Eijk, G. Irwin and K. Niemoller, The Dutch Parliamentary Elections of May 1986, *Electoral Studies* 5 (1986).

C. van der Eijk and K. Niemoller, Electoral Alignments in the Netherlands, *Electoral Studies* 6 (1989).

E. Veding, The Environmentalist Party and the Swedish Five Party Syndrome, in K. Lawson and P. Merkl (ed), op.cit (1988).

H. J. Veen, The Greens as a Milieu Party, in E. Kolinsky (ed), *The Greens in West Germany* (1989).

H. J. Veen and J. Hoffmann, *Die Grunen zu Beginn der neunzinger Jahre* (1992).

S. Verney, Between Coalition and One-Party Government: The Greek Elections of November 1989 and April 1990, *West European Politics* 13 (1990).

G. Voerman, A Drama in Three Acts: Communism and Social Democracy in the Netherlands since 1945, in M. Waller, S. Courtois and M. Lazar (eds), *Comrades and Brothers. Communism and Trade Unions in Europe* (1991).

G. Voerman, The Netherlands' Green Paradoxes, *Capital, Nature, Socialism* 3 (1992).

G. Voerman, Premature Perestroika: The Dutch Communist Party and Gorbachev, in D. Bell (ed), *Western European Communists and the Collapse of Communism* (1993).

G. Voerman, The Netherlands: Losing colours, turning green, in D. Richardson and C. Rootes (eds), op.cit (1995).

A. Vollmer, W. Templin and Werner Schulz, *Grune und Bundnis 90* (1992).

M. Waller, The Radical Sources of the Crisis in West European Communist Parties, *Political Studies* 37 (1988).

M. Waller, S. Courtois and M. Lazar (eds), *Comrades and Brothers. Communism and Trade Unions in Europe* (1991).

M. Waller and M. Fennema (eds), *Communist Parties in Western Europe* (1988).

F. Walter, *Les Suisses et l'environment* (1990).

A. Ware, *Political Parties and Party Systems* (1996).

K. Werner Brand, Cyclical Aspects of New Social Movements: Waves of Cultural Criticism and Mobilization Cycles of New and Middle Class Radicalism, in R J. Dalton and M. Kuechler (eds), op.cit (1990).

J. Whalen and R. Flacks, *After the Barricades: The New Left Grows Up* (1989).

J. Whyte, Ireland: Politics Without Social Bases, in R. Rose (ed), *Electoral Behaviour: A*

Comparative Handbook (1974).

B. Wicha, Party Funding in Austria in A. Pelinka and F. Plasser (eds), op.cit (1989).

L. Wilde, *Modern European Socialism* (1994).

F. Wilson, When Parties Refuse to Fail: The Case of France, in K. Lawson and P. Merkl (eds), op.cit (1988).

F. Witte, Belgian Federalism: Towards Complexity and Asymmetry, *West European Politics* 15 (1992).

S. B. Wolinetz, The Transformation of the Western European Party system Revisited, *West European Politics* 2 (1979).

S. B. Wolinetz, *Parties and Party Systems in Liberal Democracies* (1988).

I. Worlund, The Election to the Swedish Riksdag 1988, *Scandinavian Political Studies* 12 (1989).

B. Wynn, Windscale: A Case Study in the Political Art of Muddling Through, in T. O'Riordan and R. Turner (eds), *Progress in Resource Management and Environmental Planning* 3 (1980).

M. N. Zald and J. McCarthy (eds), *Social Movements in an Organizational Society: Collected Essays* (1987).

R. Zarinski, *Italy: The Politics of Uneven Development* (1972).

L. Zucker, Institutional Theories of Organization, *Annual Review of Sociology* 13 (1987).

Index